Sports in American History

From Colonization to Globalization

Second Edition

Gerald R. Gems, PhD
North Central College

Linda J. Borish, PhD
Western Michigan University

Gertrud Pfister, PhD
University of Copenhagen

HUMAN KINETICS

Library of Congress Cataloging-in-Publication Data

Names: Gems, Gerald R., author. | Borish, Linda J., 1961- author. | Pfister, Gertrud, 1945- author.
Title: Sports in American history: from colonization to globalization /
Gerald R. Gems, PhD, North Central College, Linda J. Borish, PhD, Western
Michigan University, Gertrud Pfister, PhD.
Description: Second edition. | Champaign, IL: Human Kinetics, [2017] |
Includes bibliographical references and index.
Identifiers: LCCN 2016025301| ISBN 9781492526520 (print) | ISBN 9781492546443
(ebook)
Subjects: LCSH: Sports--United States--History. | Sports—Social aspects--United States--History.
Classification: LCC GV583 .G46 2017 | DDC 796.0973--dc23 LC record available at https://lccn.loc.gov/2016025301

ISBN: 978-1-4925-2652-0 (print)

The web addresses cited in this text were current as of October 2016, unless otherwise noted.

Senior Acquisitions Editor: Myles Schrag; **Developmental Editor:** Judy Park; **Managing Editor:** Stephanie M. Ebersohl; **Copyeditor:** Patricia L. MacDonald; **Indexer:** Nancy Ball; **Permissions Manager:** Dalene Reeder; **Graphic Designer:** Denise Lowry; **Cover Designer:** Keith Blomberg; **Photograph (cover):** © AP Photo; **Photographs (interior):** © Human Kinetics, unless otherwise noted; **Photo Asset Manager:** Laura Fitch; **Photo Production Manager:** Jason Allen; **Senior Art Manager:** Kelly Hendren; **Printer:** Sheridan Books

Printed in the United States of America   10 9 8 7 6 5 4 3 2 1

Human Kinetics
Website: www.HumanKinetics.com

United States: Human Kinetics
P.O. Box 5076
Champaign, IL 61825-5076
800-747-4457
e-mail: info@hkusa.com

Canada: Human Kinetics
475 Devonshire Road Unit 100
Windsor, ON N8Y 2L5
800-465-7301 (in Canada only)
e-mail: info@hkcanada.com

Europe: Human Kinetics
107 Bradford Road
Stanningley
Leeds LS28 6AT, United Kingdom
+44 (0) 113 255 5665
e-mail: hk@hkeurope.com

E6758

Contents

Preface   vii

Acknowledgments   xi

Foreword   xiii

Chapter 1   **Sporting Experiences in Colonial America, 1400–1750**   1

Native American Pastimes and Sports   3

Influence of Religion on English Colonists   10

Sport in American Colonies   13

Summary   30

Chapter 2   **Sport and Pastimes in the American Revolutionary Era and Early National Period, 1750–1820**   33

The Great Awakening and the Place of Sport   35

Consumerism and Changing Patterns of Colonial Life   40

The Enlightenment in America and Ideas of Sport and the Body   42

Frontier and Backcountry Sport   44

Women's Active Recreation in the Revolutionary Era
  and Early National Period   47

Native American Sport   48

Sporting Practices During the American Revolutionary War   48

Turn of the Nineteenth Century and Societal Patterns   54

Summary   54

Chapter 3   **Antebellum Health Reforms and Sporting Forms, 1820–1860**   57

Overview of the Antebellum Period   59

Health Reformers   62

Muscular Christianity   63

Women and Physical Activity   66

Rural Sporting Practices   72

Rise of Agricultural and Sporting Journalism   77

Sporting Practices of the Middle and Upper Classes   79

Public Spaces for Health and Sport   81

Sporting Pastimes of African Americans and Native Americans   83

Immigrants and Sporting Cultures   87

Summary   91

Chapter 4   Rise of Rationalized and Modern Sport, 1850–1870   93

Concept of Modern Sport   95

Subcommunities and the Growth of Modern Sport   99

Sporting Fraternity   105

Growth of Sports Clubs and Advancing Rational Recreation   110

Growth of American Team Sport and Competition   113

Rise of Intercollegiate Sport   119

The Civil War and Sporting Experiences   122

Summary   122

Chapter 5   New Identities and Expanding Modes of Sport in the Gilded Age, 1870–1890   125

Sport and Social Stratification   127

Maintaining Ethnic Forms of Leisure   131

Development of an Intercollegiate Sporting Culture   136

Male Sporting Culture   140

Business of Sport   142

Gendered Sport, Class, and Social Roles   150

Regulation of Sport: Amateurism Versus Professionalism   155

Summary   156

Chapter 6   American Sport and Social Change During the Early Progressive Era, 1890–1900   157

Social Reformers of the Progressive Era   158

Play and Games in American Ideology   160

Recreational Spaces   167

Back-to-Nature Movement   173

Ethnic Groups   175

Body Culture   178

Sport and Technology   179

Modern Olympic Games   180
Summary   186

Chapter 7   **Sport as Symbol: Acculturation and Imperialism, 1900–1920**   **187**

Sport, Ethnicity, and the Quest for Social Mobility   188
Assimilation of Disparate Groups in American Society   195
Challenging Gender Boundaries   202
Resistance to Social Reform   207
Sport and Colonialism   210
Sport During World War I   215
Summary   217

Chapter 8   **Sport, Heroic Athletes, and Popular Culture, 1920–1950**   **219**

War, Depression, and the Shaping of America   222
Social Change and the Spread of Sport   224
Heroes in the Golden Age   246
Media and the Commercialization of Sport   253
Summary   258

Chapter 9   **Sport as TV Spectacle, Big Business, and Political Site, 1950–1980**   **261**

Sport in the Cold War   263
Evolution of the Sport–Media Relationship   265
Coverage of Alternative Heroes   275
Professional Sport and Labor Relations   276
Sport and the Civil Rights Movement   279
Sport, Narcissism, and the Existential Search for Self   289
Scientific Advancements and the Growth of Sport   290
Summary   292

Chapter 10   **Globalized Sport, 1980–2000**   **295**

Corporate Sporting Culture   298
Drawing Fans to Baseball   305
Michael Jordan and the Growth of Professional Basketball   307
Intercollegiate Sport and the NCAA   309

Women and Sport   310
Drug and Body Abuse Among Athletes   315
Violence in Sport   317
Discrimination at the End of the Twentieth Century   320
Individuality and Sport Icons   321
Alternative Sports   323
Summary   325

Chapter 11   Sport in the Early Twenty-First Century, 2000–2015   327

Business of Professional Sports Teams   328
Intercollegiate Sport and Conference Changes   333
Title IX and Sport Leadership   336
Women's Professional Teams and Endorsements   337
Modern Olympic Challenges and Stars   338
Sporting Crises   339
Traumatic Brain Injury   343
X Games and Alternative Sports   344
Sports Across the Populace   345
Rise of the Runner   346
The Future of Sport   347
Summary   349

Afterword   351
Bibliography   355
Index   373
About the Authors   385

Preface

The intense media coverage of sport in American culture in the twenty-first century, highlighting issues such as professional players' salaries, amateurism, gender equity, scandals, and nationalism, has developed out of the rich and complex history of sport since early America. The study of American sport history provides a critical context for understanding how sporting activities have changed and how various factors have shaped them. The investigation of topics such as sport in Native American cultures, the growth of modern sport, gender perspectives on sport, and religious influences on sport shows the importance of sport in society. *Sports in American History: From Colonization to Globalization* provides a comprehensive, new approach to examining underexplored issues and groups in American sport history.

This text resulted from friendships involving diverse circumstances. To some degree, two of the authors experienced and have studied the historical ethnic, religious, gender, and social-class factors that affected the assimilation of immigrant groups and the nature of sport for more mainstream groups. The third author, a non-American with expertise in the study of international sport history, has been able to cast a critical eye on American society from the perspective of an international scholar affected by the globalization of American culture. Their education in related fields (although with PhDs in different academic programs) and their interdisciplinary scholarly endeavors involving mutual interests have brought them together in a common quest to increase understanding of the ways in which sport shapes American history, and in turn how the context of American history shapes sporting practices. This book explores the process of Americanization and resistance by some newcomers to America through the eyes of those who have often been forgotten, or whose stories have been considered unimportant, or in some instances whose stories have been invisible in American sport history. It is the sport history of those diverse Americans as well as the stories of the authors as they have experienced it in academic and athletic contexts. The collaborative process of developing and writing this book began in conversations at a sport history conference in 2003, and it required knowledge from all of the authors' areas of expertise and the respect and cooperation needed to produce such a comprehensive book.

Audience and Scope

This book is a core text for undergraduate courses in American sport history, American studies, and sport studies, but it will also be useful for graduate students and scholars in sport history and sport studies. The book not only provides a narrative history of sport in the United States but also challenges and enables students to address difficult and controversial issues as they study sport and history in their diverse contexts in culture. For students in the fields of American history, sport history, American studies, gender studies, and other areas of study, this book provides a framework for understanding how and why sport intersects with many facets of American society. To that end, evidence-based insights and primary sources are provided in order to explain the role of sport in the social construction of American culture over time. Sport is not just a reflection of the larger society; therefore sport is examined as an agent of change. Even the term *sport* changes in meaning over time and particular events, and its uses are traced by the various peoples in the regions that came to make up the United States.

This text draws attention especially to women, minorities, and the multitude of ethnic and religious groups that have composed American society—and to their historical role in the construction of sport culture. Whereas most American sport history texts are written by men and about men—especially white men—this book is more inclusive of women and nonwhites because they, too, have shaped the meaning of sport in the United States. Various peoples in the past have influenced concepts of sport as played by white men in the integration of gender, ethnicity, race, and religion of diverse groups. Therefore, this historical study delineates that the designation of whiteness has itself been a contested issue not only for African Americans but also for Asian Americans, Native Americans, and Hispanic Americans, as well as some European migrants who may now take their whiteness for granted. Such insights will allow students to develop new and alternative perspectives, examine sport as a social and cultural phenomenon, generate better understandings of current sport practices, reflect on future developments, and engage in lively discussions.

Throughout much of the text, the authors illuminate the struggles that resulted in the ongoing construction of American culture and the central place of sport in that culture. Any society will involve the norms, values, and behaviors of one dominant group that subordinate or alternative groups may challenge. In sport history, sport becomes part of this contested terrain of a dominant group seeking to establish the norms, values, and standards for the community. That is, immigrants and ethnic groups, as well as white Protestant mainstream Americans, influence sport in American history. Women, too, influence sport in American society through their struggle to gain access to sport and values associated with sport, typically the prerogative of white men. Diverse primary sources about sport are featured in this text, beginning with the colonization of American society and continuing through recent times with the globalization of sport. Showing how individuals of ordinary and extraordinary circumstances played, promoted, criticized, capitalized on, or fought for human rights and equality in sport and society, this text offers a more complete rendering of sport in the experiences of American peoples.

The book also provides context about certain historical years and eras in which particular conditions affected the course of events involving sport. For example, the reform movements in pre–Civil War years played a key role in the expansion of sport and changing attitudes about sport for men and even some women. Certain conditions in the aftermath of World War I enabled Adolf Hitler to assume leadership of Germany, and that influenced political and sporting events in the United States and in the Olympic Games. Hitler's ascent to power would be impossible—even unthinkable—in Germany today, but sports still involve politics on a local, regional, national, and international scale as discussed in the concluding chapter. The authors carefully note the conditions and contexts of each era in order to inform readers about the factors that spurred or impeded change over time. For example, the concept of quantification—and the compilation of records and statistics that so fascinate American sports fans—were unnecessary and virtually unheard of before the advent of technological advances and industrialized urban centers.

Likewise, the invention of the bicycle during the nineteenth century elicited wholesale reforms not only in women's dress but also in courtship patterns and in a quest for greater independence. The athletic successes of female and black athletes fostered scientific investigations of evolutionary theories and the social stratification that divided and continues to divide American society. Such contextualization encourages students to question gender roles as well as racial and ethnic stereotypes, consider cause-and-effect relationships, and examine the role of sport in social processes and social change in American society.

How This Book Is Organized

The book is divided into sections based on historical periods, providing context for each era, from the indigenous tribes of premodern America through colonial societies to the global dominance of modern American popular culture. A handy time line is provided for ready reference. Chapters are arranged both chronologically (by eras) and topically (by issues or concepts). The ebb and flow of history and the ways in which people participate in sport and society at times mean an overlap in critical time periods in American sport history; factors that influence social history and sport history persist in some chapters so that discussion of issues may refer to events that occurred before the chronological span covered in a chapter. Readers might trace the influence of the Puritans in colonial America and later other majority white religious groups who exercised power and, in turn, ascertain their lasting influence on American culture. Students also learn about the challenges to that power that resulted in a more heterogeneous, pluralistic society and grasp this connection to sport. Thus particular attention is drawn to the factors of race, religion, ethnicity, gender, social class, the economy, and politics in the social developments in American culture.

Special Features in the Second Edition

Each chapter includes objectives, an introduction, a summary of points covered, and discussion questions to aid students and instructors in class preparation. Unique features include the use of primary documents from each era, including photographs, posters, and quotations. Students will notice that many of the historical quotations derived from primary sources retain their original spellings, which may look like misspellings to modern readers. For example, "ʃ" indicates a long s, so "ʃo" is pronounced "so." Other sections of the text retain the original vocabulary and grammar used in a particular period, such as the reference to "woman's rights" in the nineteenth century. The text also contains two types of sidebars. People and Places sidebars offer glimpses into the lives of those people who as individuals or as part of institutions affected, or were affected by, sport during a historical period. International Perspective sidebars, written by European scholar Gertrud Pfister, offer innovative comparisons at a time when Americans seemingly lack knowledge of other cultures and globalization issues. The features might prompt discussions about how sport may be viewed from national perspectives and from international perspectives, or how some groups within a society perpetuate their power and status by invoking sport, as in the current construction of sport stadiums and museums as sites of remembrance, nostalgia, and enactment of particular views about a sport hero or event in a nation's history.

Updates to the Second Edition

The revised second edition includes new sidebars and new historical images, as well as additional material in two new chapters. Information has been updated and enhanced relative to racial and ethnic groups, early football, the bachelor subculture, and the sport programs of American missionaries in Asia and the Caribbean in chapter 7. Chapter 9 includes greater attention to ice hockey and basketball, particularly to the participation of African American athletes; and the new chapter 11 covers more recent events after the turn of the twenty-first century. New material covers women's greater involvement in sport; greater commercialization and the role of media; new adventure and extreme sports coverage; and issues, controversies, and scandals relative to sexuality, performance-enhancing drugs, concussions and brain-injury debates, and labor issues. Prognostications on the future of sports provide fodder for class discussions.

eBook
available at
your campus bookstore
or HumanKinetics.com

Instructor Resources

In addition to the thoroughly updated content, this edition also offers several instructor resources to aid in teaching a class with this textbook:

- **Instructor guide.** Includes a sample syllabus, descriptions of key philosophical and religious systems and terms, suggested readings and films, and a set of cumulative exam questions that span eras and help students make thematic connections from the semester.
- **Test package.** Includes 170 questions including true-or-false, multiple-choice, short-answer, and essay questions.
- **Presentation package.** Includes more than 175 PowerPoint slides that present the textbook material in a lecture-friendly format.

You can access all of the ancillaries at **www.HumanKinetics.com/SportsInAmericanHistory**.

Closing Remarks

Of course, no book can provide all the answers—or all the questions. This book is a starting point and entry into the fascinating field of sport history for furthering students' journeys on their own path to inquiry, reflection, contemplation, and research. The authors incorporate the latest scholarship to facilitate students' understanding of sport and history. This book contains an extensive bibliography of sources and primary documents and a determined focus on and broad coverage of the less-known or untold stories of sport—those of the nonwhite, the middle and lower ranks, the less powerful, the working class, and the various "others" whose histories are no less important to the ongoing construction of sport in American culture.

This book is the result of a cooperative venture over several years. The authors have developed a stronger spirit of friendship and scholarly inquiry rather than a competitive spirit that at times has dominated sport in American history. As intellectual teammates, the authors offer an innovative, lively, and inclusive book on sports in American history.

Acknowledgments

The second edition of this work was again greatly assisted by Myles Schrag, who promoted and supported the project and brought it to fruition, with the collaboration of Judy Park, Stephanie M. Ebersohl, Patricia L. MacDonald, Nancy Ball, Dalene Reeder, Denise Lowry, Keith Blomberg, Laura Fitch, Jason Allen, and Kelly Hendren of Human Kinetics, Inc. They are a pleasure to work with! We thank our sport history colleague David Wiggins for his expertise and the friendship he shared during our work on the book.

The coauthors each acknowledge the valuable help provided to them in their individual work on this project.

This book emanated from discussions about a new and comprehensive study in American sport history and what such a book might look like when Amy Tocco of Human Kinetics approached Linda Borish and Gerald Gems at a sport history conference. These fruitful discussions yielded an exchange of ideas, and Amy spearheaded our book proposal through the initial review process at Human Kinetics, after which we began working with other dedicated colleagues in developing our book; we are grateful to Amy for her assistance, enthusiasm, and guidance. In supporting the development and completion of this collaborative book project, we are indebted to the excellent editors at Human Kinetics. We wish to deeply thank Myles Schrag and Amanda Ewing for their diligence, tact, patience, and expertise. They offered terrific assistance in providing insights and answering our queries, making this a wonderful academic experience. We also acknowledge the contributions of these Human Kinetics colleagues who assisted us in the phases of our work: Dalene Reeder, Laura Fitch, Jillian Evans, Patrick Sandberg, Nancy Rasmus, and Bridget Walczak. Despite the geographic distances among the coauthors while writing the book (being in different U.S. and international locales posed a challenge at times), the ongoing efforts of the editors spurred us to work together in a truly joint endeavor. We acknowledge the critical comments offered by the anonymous reviewers, whose own expertise and suggestions have made our book a better product; their knowledge aided us in our efforts to create a new American sport history book, and we are grateful for the time they devoted to the review process.

Our colleagues in the North American Society for Sport History, the International Society for the History of Physical Education and Sport, and others in American studies organizations have shared their vast knowledge with us over the years, and they encouraged us to develop a book on American sport history that integrated the experiences of many diverse Americans. In formal sessions at conferences or in informal gatherings, many of our colleagues aided us in creating a more complete book, and we deeply thank them. The research pursued for this endeavor could not have occurred without the outstanding assistance of numerous archivists and librarians in various locales who, as caretakers of the past, make our work possible. For the written and visual evidence in our book, we are indebted to the many people who helped us acquire the historical materials that appear throughout our work.

I would like to acknowledge Kim Butler, archivist, and the librarians of Oesterle Library at North Central College for their research assistance and the provision of photos.

—Jerry Gems

I wish to acknowledge the valuable contribution of the Burnham-Macmillan History Endowment Grants I received at Western Michigan University, which allowed me to travel to national and international conferences and to share research with colleagues. I would like to acknowledge the importance of a sabbatical leave taken during the 2005–2006 academic year at Western Michigan University in order to devote necessary time for research, writing, and acquiring images and primary sources for this book. I thank Marion Gray, professor and chair of history, and Thomas Kent, dean of the College of Arts and Sciences, for their support in providing a sabbatical award. Thanks, too, to my colleagues in the Department of History who have viewed American sport history as a valuable part of our curriculum and encouraged my research in the field. In addition, I thank the Hadassah-Brandeis Institute, Brandeis University, for granting me a research associate position to continue my ongoing research on gender issues, sport history, and American Jewish women. Thanks to my parents, Hope and Philip Borish, whose love and encouragement in this and other intellectual endeavors, and previous sporting ones, provide guidance. And thanks to my identical twin, Anne, during all those years of playing doubles together, for helping me learn about cooperation, not solely competition, as a necessary component in completing significant work with good colleagues. During the work on the second edition of this volume I thank History Department chair José A. Brandão for his support of my work in sport history and for useful discussions.

—Linda J. Borish

I would like to acknowledge Henriette Arnoldus, librarian at the Department for Exercise and Sport Sciences at the University of Copenhagen, for research assistance.

—Gertrud Pfister

Foreword

I assume I am like everyone else in the discipline of sport history in that I have always depended a great deal on survey texts. If properly done, they provide essential context on how sport has changed over time, important information on those people and events that have contributed to the development of sport, and insights into the relationships among sport and other societal institutions. They are also inclusive, careful to impart details as to how people of different races, ethnicities, gender identities, socioeconomic statuses, political affiliations, and religious backgrounds have both influenced and been affected by their participation in sport at all levels of competition. If done properly, moreover, they are clearly written, pay close attention to organization and structure of the narrative, and are accessible to students and sport specialists as well as a more popular audience.

With these characteristics in mind, I am pleased to say that *Sports in American History: From Colonization to Globalization* has been properly done and should be read by everyone who has an interest in acquiring a deeper understanding of the history of American sport. I am impressed, among other things, by the depth and breadth of the text as it covers in fresh detail the evolution of sport in America from 1400 to the present day. I am impressed by the listing of objectives, summary of points covered, and discussion questions included in each chapter of the text. I am also very impressed by the effective utilization of primary documents and wonderful images used throughout the text. From my experiences in the classroom over some 38 years in higher education, I know how much students at both the undergraduate and graduate levels of instruction benefit from being introduced to original material and how effective

that material is in bringing to life the joy and excitement and poignant nature of sports.

I am not the least bit surprised by the quality of this book, as I am very familiar with the academic backgrounds and many scholarly contributions of the three people who came together to craft it. Jerry Gems has added immeasurably to our understanding of sport through his many publications on everything from sport and American imperialism to sport among Italian Americans. His work is always of the highest quality, characterized by solid research, careful analysis, and historically accurate interpretations. Linda Borish has provided, through a plethora of scholarly publications, greater insight into American sport history, especially as it pertains to women and Jewish involvement in sport and physical activity. Her scholarship has always been based on original archival materials and very thorough in regard to historical analysis and interpretations. Gertrud Pfister has published widely and often in sport history, adding a great deal to our understanding of the development of sport on a national and international basis. Her scholarship has been excellent in every respect, notable for cogent analysis and very smart interpretations.

Collectively, Gems, Borish, and Pfister have written a terrific book. They should be applauded, as they have put together a survey text that will certainly be widely used and referenced. It is a book in which essential primary and secondary sources have been brought together in an effort to chronicle the development of sport in America as it moved from a more informal, unorganized activity to a highly structured and organized phenomenon. It should be essential reading for those interested in one of America's most influential and important cultural institutions.

David K. Wiggins
George Mason University

Chapter 1

Sporting Experiences in Colonial America
1400–1750

CHAPTER OBJECTIVES

After reading this chapter, you will have learned about the following:

- The foundations of sport in colonial America emerging from the peoples of various cultures

- The significance of sporting practices and recreation for diverse groups of Native Americans

- The attitudes of various European colonists about sport and physical exercise and how these attitudes shaped sporting patterns in American colonies

- The influence of religion on sport throughout the American colonies

- The importance of social class, race, and gender in the growth of sport in colonial America

- The types of sports played in colonial America, as well as regional variations in sport

In the 1500s, the Aztecs played tlachtli, a Native American ball game. Such sporting activities drew the attention of white settlers and missionaries, who viewed Native American sports based on their own conception of sport from their white European heritage. In describing the game, Spanish missionary Fray Bernardino de Sahagún noted distinctive features of the game's players, equipment, and victory prizes:

> They [the rulers] played ball. There were his ball-catchers, and his ball-players. They wagered [in this game] all [manner of] costly goods—golden necklaces, green stone, fine turquoise, slaves, precious capes, valuable breech cloths, cultivated fields, houses, leather leg bands, gold bracelets, arm bands of quetzal feathers, duck feather capes, bales of cacao—[these] were wagered there in the game called tlachtli.

> On the two sides, on either hand, it was limited by walls, very well made, in that the walls and floor were smoothed. And there, in the very corner of the ball court, was a line, drawn upon the ground. And on the walls were two stone, ball court rings. He who played caused [the ball] to enter there; he caused it to go in. Then he won all the costly goods, and he won something from all who watched there in the ball court. His equipment was the rubber ball, the catcher gloves, girdles, and leather hip guards.

Sahagún 449–450

Three groups of people shaped the sporting heritage in colonial America: Native Americans (the original inhabitants of North America), Africans (forced against their will to come to the New World as laborers and slaves), and white Europeans (especially those from Great Britain). All played a role in the patterns of sport that developed in colonial America, and the cultural worlds of Native Americans and Africans collided with those of European peoples colonizing North America in the 1500s and 1600s. The religious patterns, social-class structures, race, gender roles, ethnicity, and regional environments of these three peoples all contributed to colonial America's sporting traditions.

Before Christopher Columbus reached the New World in 1492, several million Native Americans lived in North America, and they maintained cultural worlds distinct from the European cultures, including Native American ball games and ceremonies related to their sporting activities. Thus, European colonists did not, as some have maintained, discover a "virgin wilderness," lacking settlements and peoples. Rather, Europeans encountered cultures, environments, and societies quite different from what they left behind in such countries as England, Spain, France, and Portugal.

Historian Carl Guarneri has explained that early encounters between Europeans and Native Americans "illustrated features that would characterize the collision between European and North American peoples of the next two centuries: the quest for riches, the exchange of goods, the power of legends about the New World, clashes of religious worldviews, the impact of disease, technological gaps in warfare and food production, and the violence of exploitation, enslavement, and resistance" (29). In this period of early contact between Native Americans and Europeans, various societies of Native Americans existed in the New World. Despite the European perception (which would become a stereotype) that "typical" American Indians all shared certain characteristics, the fact is that "native societies of North America were enormously varied. Their practices ranged from hunting and gathering to farming and craft production, and their languages and religions were more varied than those of Europeans" (32). Indeed, the inhabitants that Europeans desired to colonize and conquer in the sixteenth and seventeenth centuries were not undiscovered—they were merely new to the Europeans, and the Native Americans embraced their own religious, economic, political, and social beliefs.

On the eve of the European colonization, the North American continent featured varying tribes in the North, the Midwest, and the Southwest. Guarneri has identified six broad groups of native peoples, indicating the diverse nature of Native American societies: the Anasazis, peoples of the Great Plains, the Mississippians, the Eastern Woodland peoples, the Hunter-Gatherers of the North and Northwest, and other variations of Native American societies demonstrating varying patterns and links with other tribes.

The Ancestral Puebloans, or Anasazis, resided in the dry American Southwest and used complex sys-

Pre-1492	1492	1492	1517
▪ Native American games played	▪ Christopher Columbus lands in America	▪ Spanish expel Jews and Moors (Muslims) from Spain	▪ Martin Luther begins Protestant Reformation and attacks Catholicism

tems of irrigation to grow corn, beans, and squash. Later, because of drought, they resettled in areas now known as Arizona and New Mexico, and they developed the Acoma, Hopi, and Zuni pueblos. These Native Americans were later encountered by Spanish conquistador Francisco Vásquez de Coronado, who termed them the Pueblo Indians (Guarneri 30–31). Other indigenous peoples lived in the Great Plains and pursued buffalo as a main source of their way of life. These seminomadic tribes included the Cheyenne, Arapaho, Pawnee, and Sioux, and their people exhibited warrior skills and hunted on the Plains (Guarneri 29, 31). Another group of native inhabitants, known as Mississippians, lived in the Mississippi and Ohio River Valleys. They established societies in the American Midwest and Southeast, cultivating crucial foods such as corn, beans, and squash. The Cahokia mound builders developed a large society of more than thirty thousand people near present-day St. Louis, with temple mounds, orderly cornfields, and structures (Guarneri 31; Rader, *American Ways* 4).

Other tribal societies included the Eastern Woodland peoples, who inhabited the Atlantic seacoast in parts of what is now the United States, as well as parts of what is now southeastern Canada. Tribes in this region pursued hunting, fishing, and agriculture at various times, with farming and fishing in the summer, and moving in smaller bands for hunting in the winter. This group included the Iroquois nation, a league of six tribes covering the areas now known as northern New York and Pennsylvania. Iroquois culture included participation in physical activities and sport. Furthermore, "because of their unity and physical prowess, and because their territory was between French and English zones of settlement, the Iroquois would figure primarily in colonial wars" (Guarneri 32). As discussed later in this chapter, such collisions between Europeans and Native Americans would influence the nature of sport in early America. Another of the tribal societies was the Hunter-Gatherer group of the North and Northwest. These tribes engaged in hunting and gathering and in fishing in the waterways of California and the Pacific Northwest. Inhabitants remained in their small villages, away from colonizing European settlers, until the late

eighteenth century. According to Guarneri, the sixth group of Native American peoples consisted of "Variations and Connections." This refers to the diversity of native peoples. The native groups of North America had widely varying practices, languages, and religions (Guarneri 32).

These diverse peoples and landscapes of North America influenced the nature of sport in the early decades of the New World and—along with the varying attitudes about sport (both those that favored and those that were critical of certain types of games and pastimes)—formed the basis of early sporting experiences. Experienced by a range of men and women in diverse Native American, slave, and colonial communities, sport thus became part of colonial society, with different meanings for different peoples amid the debates and challenges of settling the New World.

Native American Pastimes and Sports

Long before Europeans colonized the New World, Native Americans led physically active lives in pursuits necessary to their sustenance and religious beliefs. They used their fishing and hunting prowess, as well as their expert knowledge of the land and water, for field sports. Colonists in the various regions might adapt these sporting practices in their own outdoor excursions in hunting, fishing, and fowling. Indigenous peoples in their native societies swam and canoed along waterways as a means of passage, and children learned to swim at an early age. Fishing, as well as hunting with a bow and arrow, provided food, and hunting also served military purposes in times of war. The practice of archery also involved training games and competitions.

Other games, such as hoop-and-pole contests, provided additional training, as well as opportunities for wagering. In such contests, played throughout the North American continent by all tribes, males rolled a hoop along a flat field, and individuals or teams attempted to pierce the hoop with spears, darts, or arrows (King 18; Koppedrayer 21–22; Dyson 148–149). Indeed, indigenous peoples

1530s	1558	1565
■ John Calvin launches religious reform	■ Elizabeth I crowned Queen of England	■ St. Augustine, Florida, founded by the Spanish (first permanent European settlement in the New World)

in America played a wide variety of games, including marbles and shinny, a game similar to hockey. The latter could be played on the ice during the winter and was enjoyed by men, women, and children. Tribes of the Northwest and Southwest played shuttlecock, a game similar to badminton, in which an object (sometimes a corn husk with feathers) was kept aloft with paddles or hands. For the Zunis of the New Mexico region, it also held deeper religious meanings, signifying spiritual power or favor and often involving wagers (Meneses 280–281).

Archery

For Native Americans, archery was a utilitarian necessity. Among the Sioux tribes of the Western plains, boys shot arrows through rolling hoops that approximated the moving targets presented by animals. In the Mandan tribe of the Dakotas, men practiced a form of speed shooting in which they competed to see who could keep the most arrows aloft at one time. In the Southeast, Cherokees held contests—for men, women, and children—in which cornstalks served as targets.

Early accounts by white European travelers reported the athletic skills of the indigenous peoples in archery. James Rosier, a British explorer, noted (ca. 1605) the archery equipment of Native Americans in New England: "When we went on to shore to trade with them, in one of their Canoes I saw their bowes and arrows, which I tooke up and drew an arrow in one of them, which I found to be of strength able to carry an arrow five or six score stronglie" (Rosier, qtd. in Altherr, Part 1 38). The proficiency of Native American archers was also noted by British clergyman Charles Wooley,

Archery was an important aspect of many Native American cultures, as George Catlin, noted researcher and painter of Native Americans, shows in his painting *Archery of the Mandans*.

Reprinted from Rare Book Division, The New York Public Library. (1845). Archery of the Mandans. Retrieved from http://digitalcollections.nypl.org/items/510d47da-dc0a-a3d9-e040-e00a18064a99.

1585	1586–1588	1588	1607
■ First English settlement founded on Roanoke Island off North Carolina coast	■ English settlers founded other settlements on Roanoke Island	■ Defeat of the Spanish Armada by the English	■ Jamestown Colony founded in Virginia (first permanent English settlement in North America)

who traveled in colonial New York in about 1678 and wrote about the indigenous peoples in the New York area: "Before the Christians especially the Dutch came amongst them they were very dexterous Artists at their bows, insomuch I have heard it affirm'd that a Boy of seven years old would shot a Bird flying" (Wooley, qtd. in Altherr, Part 1 39).

Running

Running also served utilitarian purposes, as when messengers needed to search for food, deliver goods, or carry news of war or other important events between tribes. Iroquois runners in the Northeast could cover 240 miles (385 kilometers) of their tribal network over a three-day period. In the Southwest, Native American tribes integrated running into cultural practices. The Aztec relay runners of Mexico brought news of conquistador Hernán Cortés' arrival to King Montezuma in 1519 by rushing 260 miles (420 kilometers) in only 24 hours. In 1680, the Pueblo tribes of New Mexico organized a successful revolt against their Spanish overlords by means of a system of running messengers that coordinated their attacks. Running also held particular religious significance for the tribes of the Southwest. Religious rituals, rites of passage in puberty, fertility ceremonies, and competitive contests all involved running activities, some of which required phenomenal displays of endurance. Both males and females engaged in kickball races that required the continuous propulsion of a ball over a long course in a contest of skill and stamina. Sometimes sticks were substituted for the balls, and stick races, serving as fertility rites, covered distances as long as 25 miles (40 kilometers). Not unlike the artifacts and memorabilia of modern sports halls of fame, favorite sticks, believed to possess magic, were treasured by runners for many years (O'Fearghail 29–30; Meneses 168; Collier 262–266).

Horse Riding

Humans' need to deliver messages on foot diminished when European explorers introduced the horse to North America in the Columbian Exchange. (The Columbian Exchange was when Europeans and Native Americans interacted in a mutual transfer of animals, plants, and diseases. Since this transfer of products and diseases continued long after 1492 for centuries, Guarneri suggests it is more accurate to call it "the Post-Columbian Exchange.") In fact, "first brought to America by Columbus, horses helped the Spanish conquistadors to overpower native peoples"; however, with the use of horses spreading "through Spanish outposts, Native Americans acquired them by trading, raiding, or rounding up runaways" (Guarneri 56, 65). Native Americans considered the horse to be a sacred animal and treasured it accordingly as a prized possession. Members of tribes of the Western plains became skilled equestrians, and both men and women engaged in horse races within their own tribes and against other clans. Races often covered 3 or 4 miles (about 4.5 to 6.5 kilometers), and winning riders gained considerable prestige and material goods. In 1806, Nez Perce riders even challenged members of the Lewis and Clark Expedition to a horse race as they explored the northwestern territory of the newly acquired Louisiana Purchase, which doubled the size of the young United States (Johnson 105–106).

The Shoshone Indians of northern Utah participated in horse races as part of their sporting heritage, having worked along with Eastern Shoshone Indians to develop their herds of horses for hundreds of years. For the Shoshone people of the Washakie colony in northern Utah, breeding horses provided a step "to developing a horse racing tradition." Horse teams of the Washakie farmers were skilled at breaking horses, as "[t]heir ancestors had raced horses for pleasure as well as for purse by wagering on outcomes, and the Washakie residents of the early twentieth century rekindled the earlier flame by competing with their white neighbors at horse racing" (Kreitzer 237). Thus, the rich tradition of horse racing for the Shoshone Indians persisted over the centuries as recalled by ancestors as they raced horses against nonnative peoples. The enthusiasm for horse racing also took hold among Shoshone peoples in other areas, such as Owyhee, Nevada; Fort Washakie, Wyoming; Fort Hall, Idaho; and Skull Valley, Utah. In each of these areas, tribes

1609	1618	1619	1620
■ Santa Fe, New Mexico, founded by the Spanish	■ King James I proclaims the *Book of Sports* in England	■ First slaves imported to Virginia from Africa	■ Pilgrims founded Plymouth Colony

held "horse races that coincided with other holiday celebrations such as the Fourth of July and county fairs. These races were well organized, right down to the monitoring of track sizes, specific distances to run and other regulations" (Kreitzer 237). Clearly, then, the horse influenced the sporting traditions of diverse Native American tribes.

Lacrosse

The most prominent competition in Native American culture was lacrosse. Played throughout the North American continent, lacrosse went beyond Native American everyday life as a magical, religious, ritualistic activity—and as a pragmatic one, providing training for war. Funerals and memorial ceremonies included lacrosse games. Top lacrosse players won esteem, and upon death some were even buried with their lacrosse sticks. North American Indian cultures played versions of lacrosse in various regions, and "in playing lacrosse, the name given by the French to a stick-and-ball game, groups of both men and women engaged in a far more vigorous sport" than games of chance (Rader, *American Ways* 8). Lacrosse required teamwork yet allowed for individual brilliance on the playing

George Catlin painted this horse-racing scene of the Minatarees in the mid- to late 1860s.

George Catlin, *Horse Racing—Minatarrees,* Paul Mellon Collection. Image courtesy of the Board of Trustees, National Gallery of Art, Washington.

1630	1632	1636	1664
■ Massachusetts Bay Colony founded by Governor John Winthrop and the Puritans	■ George Calvert (Lord Baltimore) develops Maryland with grant of land	■ Harvard College founded	■ English capture New Netherlands from the Dutch, renaming it New York

field. The popular game had flexible rules. There were no out-of-bounds lines, fields were irregularly constructed, and games were played with varying numbers of players (sometimes in the hundreds). Players wore no protective equipment and sometimes competed in the nude, like ancient Greek Olympians. The Choctaw tribes of the Southeast even allowed players to use two sticks. Goals were set at great distances, depending on the number of players; in fact, in one game played in 1721 by the Miami Indians of the Midwest, a European spectator judged the goals to be as far as 2 miles (3.2 kilometers) apart (Vennum 237). Lacrosse games tended to be a communal activity, with participants encouraged by drummers and chanting women (Twombly 35–36). Gambling on games involved substantial wagers. In 1794, the Seneca and Mohawk tribes (members of the Iroquois Confederacy) settled a land dispute by means of a lacrosse game. A 1797 rematch featured 500 players per side, with 60 from each tribe engaged in the game at one time. In the Huron tribe of the Northeast, players bet not only their material goods but also their own wives, children, and personal freedom. Losers might also forfeit their hair or even their little finger. Not surprisingly, such conditions led to furious and sometimes deadly contests. The Algonquians considered the game to be sacred; the Cherokees of the Southeast blamed the outcome of lost games on powerful medicine men who influenced tribal fortunes. Players cleansed their bodies by means of fasting and laxative use before games, as well as sexual abstinence. Southeastern tribes conditioned their players for the rigors of the game by performing painful scarification rites to enhance their powers of endurance (Vennum 28).

The Choctaw Indians' playing of lacrosse also drew interest from Europeans. George Catlin, noted researcher and painter of Native Americans, described a Choctaw lacrosse match: "Each party had their goal made with two upright posts, about 25 feet [7.6 meters] apart, set firm in the ground, with a pole across at the top. These goals were about forty or fifty rods [220 to 275 yards, or 200 to 250 meters] apart," and at "a point just half way between, was another small stake, driven down,

where the ball was to be thrown up at the firing of a gun, to be struggled for by the players. . . . The sticks with which this tribe play, are bent into an oblong hoop at the end, with a sort of slight web of small thongs tied across, to prevent the ball from passing through." The ball players held the stick in one hand and leaped in the air to catch the ball in the webbing of the stick or to throw it to a fellow player. The players did not wear moccasins or, for that matter, any clothing except the breechcloth around the waist, along with "a beautiful bead belt, and a 'tail,' made of white horsehair or quills, and a '*mane*' on the neck, of horsehair dyed of various colours." A score was made when "the ball was passed between the stakes of either party, or was counted for their game, and a halt of about one minute; when it was again started by the judges of the play, and a similar struggle ensued; and so on until the successful party arrived to 100, which was the limit of the game, and accomplished at an hour's sun, when they took the stakes," as the sunlight ended. At the end of the ball game, the players, "by a previous agreement, produced a number of jugs of whiskey, which gave all a wholesome drink, and sent them all off merry and in good humour, but not drunk" (Catlin, qtd. in Riess, *Major Problems* 27–30). Catlin's writings and paintings provide a European American view of this Native American sport. Catlin described the ball playing of the Choctaws as "most beautiful sport," and his paintings of it outnumbered all of his other paintings of the Choctaw tribe (Goodyear 139). This team game of lacrosse played by Native Americans in colonial America changed over time as other peoples adopted it as part of American society.

European travelers in colonial America were often fascinated by lacrosse, and they provided numerous descriptions of the game, although, as in the following account by Baron de Lahontan, a French traveler in the Northeastern region in about 1703, they sometimes used derogatory language for the players, representing their white European perceptions of the ball play of Indian tribes:

The Savages, who commonly play at it in large companies of three or four Hundred at a time, fix two Sticks at five or six Hundreds Paces diſtance from

1665	1692–1693	1676	1681
▪ Horse racing appears in New York Colony	▪ Salem Witch Trials conducted	▪ Bacon's Rebellion in Virginia	▪ William Penn establishes Pennsylvania with grant of land

Ball Playing Among the Sioux Indians by Seth Eastman.
Photo courtesy of Library of Congress, LC-USZC4-4810 DLC.

each other; They divide into two equal Parties, and tofs up the ball about half way between the two Sticks. Each Party endeavour to tofs the Ball to their side; fome run to the Ball, and the reft keep at a little diftance on both fides to affift on all Quarters. . . . [T] his Game is fo violent that they tear their Skins, and break their legs very often in ftriving to raife the Ball. All thefe Games are made only for Feafts or other trifling Entertainments; for 'tis to be obferv'd, that as they hate Money, fo they never put it in the Balance, and one may fay, *Intereft is never the occafion for Debates among them.*

Baron de Lahontan, qtd. in Altherr, Part 1 439
(italics in original)

Such curiosity doomed the British soldiers of Fort Michilimackinac in 1763, when the Ojibwa and Sauk tribes of the Midwest used lacrosse as a subterfuge for retaliation. They initiated a lacrosse game outside the walls of the fort and even threw the ball inside on occasion to test the garrison's response. When soldiers opened the gates and

ventured outside to become spectators, the Native American bystanders, who harbored weapons under their cloaks, attacked to avenge their people and lands lost at the hands of the white invaders. Those in the fort who survived the carnage faced slavery at the hands of the Native Americans (Vennum 88–103).

Later, in other parts of the continent, white spectators traveled to watch the games without serious repercussion. In 1765, a game between Cherokee women drew great interest, and Ojibwa games featured both boys and girls. The Dakota people even played men against women, though the latter enjoyed numerical superiority, with five women for every male opponent (Vennum 184). The incursion of whites into native lands, and their consequent appropriation of land, had inevitable repercussions. Differing moral attitudes and the imposition of white standards led to bans on gambling, the required wearing of Western-style clothing, and harassment by Christian missionaries of native tribes who played lacrosse on Sundays rather than attend church services (Vennum 104–117).

Shinny and Double Ball

Shinny—a sort of field hockey using decorated, curved sticks to propel a ball—was played throughout the continent, mainly by women in some tribes (such as the Crees), but only by men in others (such as the tribes of northern California).

1690s	1732
■ Shift in labor practices from white indentured servitude to black slave labor in the Chesapeake region	■ Schuylkill Fishing Co. established in Philadelphia

The Crows even had mixed teams. Double ball, on the other hand, was played almost exclusively by women. Similar to lacrosse, the game involved two balls strapped together and thrown using sticks, and it served as a test of endurance—a decidedly different quality than those expected of white women. As with men's games, women gambled on double ball, marking another big difference between native women and colonial Anglo women (Keith 101–102). As Oxendine has pointed out, the important role played by women in American Indian societies was reflected in sporting activities: "North American Indian women participated in ball games as active, agile players and as avid, ardent spectators" (22). He wrote that women played all known games, albeit often with different rules.

Toli and Other Forms of Stickball

In the Mississippi region of North America, the Choctaws played a traditional native game called toli (more commonly known as stickball), which derived from roots in pre-Columbian times and eventually developed into lacrosse. Many variations of toli were played by Native American tribes (Stepp 285). An early account of the Choctaws playing stickball was provided by a Jesuit priest around 1729, but the game had likely been played by the tribe even earlier. It exhibited aspects of warfare and was used to settle disputes. A single game might "last for days with almost no boundary on where it [the game] was played and teams could number in the hundreds" (Stepp 287). A description of the toli game played among the Choctaws in the pre-Columbian period conveys the physical nature of the sport:

> The rules of the game were minimal. . . . Defensive tactics were varied and often brutal. Preventing opponents from scoring often meant tripping, tackling, or striking the head or body of a foe with the hand or an unyielding hickory racket. As a result, injuries were frequent, and some games were actually terminated before a winner was determined owing to casualties that decimated one or both ranks.
>
> Stepp 287

International Perspective
Traditional European Games and Festivals

In the Middle Ages and early modern times, numerous traditional sporting activities were common in Europe as components of fairs and festivals (Eichberg).

In many countries, such as Denmark, Flanders, England, and Italy, football games were popular and took place at religious festivals. Huge crowds of participants gathered and tried to move a ball to a certain point such as a river. The game was rough; many participants were injured and others totally exhausted. The fields were trampled underfoot, fences destroyed, and dams ruined. The winning group was rewarded with beer.

Horseback riding, sack races, shooting, and foot races were also conducted as folk games and as part of festivities that featured similar procedures and elements. The *place* where the festival was held was a familiar location in everyday life that acquired a special significance (sometimes even a sacred character) only through the festival. The streets and squares of a town, the meadows and fields between villages, and sometimes the church or the graveyard could be transformed into a location for games and festivities.

Traditional games mirror preindustrial attitudes toward *time*. Time was not experienced and used as a linear, quantitative, and abstract structure. It was not measured, and in races it was not the time that counted but simply the victory over one's opponents. Games in a preindustrial context were also not part of people's leisure time (which did not exist in a modern sense) but were embedded in the social and cultural context.

The festive atmosphere was an important characteristic of preindustrial games. Festivals were accompanied by exuberant and sometimes tumultuous amusements in which eating and drinking and music and dance often played a central role. Physical activities such as bucket contests (i.e., filling a fountain with buckets of water or dumping a bucket of ice water over someone's head), fighting for balance, and tug-of-war were all accompanied by fun and laughter.

A further characteristic of traditional games was that the participants were not trained, specialized athletes but often came together by accident. Sometimes teams were formed from certain groups: the married against the single men, people living in one part of town against the population of another area, or even men against women. Often these festive games had their roots in mythical or magical beliefs and rituals.

One such event, the running of the bulls in Pamplona, Spain, dates to a twelfth-century religious rite made famous by Ernest Hemingway in his novel *The Sun Also Rises*. Today it is a major tourism event that draws tens of thousands of participants from around the world.

Betting on the outcome of a toli game played by the Mississippi Choctaws by non–Native Americans became commonplace with increased white and Native American interactions in the late nineteenth century. Yet some white settlers wanted to curb the violence of the game, as deaths occurred in high-stakes matches, and in 1889 the Mississippi legislature banned gambling at stickball games (Stepp 287).

Varied stick-and-ball games drew the interest of other Native Americans in the Mississippi region, with some being played by both men and women. In 1700, a Jesuit missionary, Father Paul du Ru, witnessed a type of stickball played among the Muskogees; he noted that they gambled on the outcome, and he described differences between the men's and women's versions:

> We walked to the village where there were games and a great dance. The men play in pairs; one of them has a ball in the hand and throws it ahead. Both of them run as fast as they can, throwing a big stick after this ball, and as well as I could make out, the one whose stick is closest to the ball wins the play. Then the one who wins throws the ball next time. This is a rather strenuous game; nevertheless it is played by both old and young. . . .
>
> [The women] separate into two parties between two large posts in the square. Somebody throws a little ball in the center, and the one who seizes it first tries her best to run around the post on her side three times, but she is prevented by the women of the opposite party who seize her if they can. When she can no longer resist them, she throws the ball to her people who make a similar effort to run around their posts. Sometimes the ball falls into the hands of the other side which then tries the same manoeuvre. The games are very long and ordinarily when they are over the women plunge into the water to refresh themselves. Sometimes the men play this game also.
>
> du Ru 455

White settlers also wrote journal accounts of other sporting activities pursued by Native Americans. Englishman William Wood described Native American sports in New England in his *New England Prospect* in 1634, noting that the indigenous inhabitants played soccer (or football, as he termed it), along with other active sports:

> For their ſport activitie they have commonly but three or foure; as footeball, ſhooting, running and ſwimming: when they play country againſt country there are rich Goales, all behung with Wampompeage [shells], Mowhackies, Beaver skins, and blacke Otter skinnes. . . . Their Goales be a mile [1.6 kilometers] long placed on the ſands, which are as even as a board; their ball is no bigger than a hand-ball, which ſometimes they mount in the Aire with their naked feete . . . ſometimes alſo it is two dayes before they get a Goale, then they marke the ground they winne, and beginne there the next day. Before they come to this ſport, they paint themſelves, even as when they go to warre. (qtd. in Altherr, Part 1 160–161)

Although Wood appreciated the vigorous soccer played by the indigenous peoples in Massachusetts, he claimed that English people were superior: "[O]ne English . . . [is] able to beate ten *Indians* at footeball" (161).

As with other sports and pastimes, Native American peoples often bet on these games, and, as sport historian George Eisen has commented, "We must remember that gambling in Indian cultures was both a pastime in itself and an activity that accompanied all sport events" ("Early" 10). For example, the Iroquois and Seneca Indians played a ball game and "the teams were composed of phraties, a unit established partly for social and partly for religious purposes." At the game played at tribal councils the "ball was made of stuffed deerskin, about the size of a soccer ball. Before the game started, members of each phraty placed bets, consisting usually of articles of personal property, thus adding to the general excitement of the contest" (Dewey 736). The attitudes of white settlers viewing Native American sports, however, often reflected the religious perspectives of Europeans about sport and society as they embarked on settling North America.

Influence of Religion on English Colonists

In Europe, on the eve of cultural contact with the New World, the ongoing clash between Catholics and Protestants continued. Spain was unified under the Catholic monarchy of Ferdinand and Isabella, which resulted in the Inquisition against Jews, Muslims, and false converts, and the Spanish conquest of Granada in 1492 ended the Muslim presence in southern Spain. In coming to America, Columbus and other Spanish conquerors "believed that the new lands had been opened to them by God as a reward for their religious zeal and a challenge to expand Christianity's domain." Other European colonists in the New World, such as French Jesuit missionaries and English Puritans, "shared the desire to establish godly realms [there]. . . . In their case, religious expansionism received an additional push from the Protestant Reformation, which after the

1520s produced an all-out contest between Protestants and Catholics for minds, hearts, and territory in the Christian and 'heathen' worlds" (Guarneri 38).

These religious tensions influenced European colonists' views of the appropriateness of physical exercise and sport. Europeans came to the New World both for religious reasons and in a quest for wealth, and both religious and profit motives influenced the types of physical activity and sport that they accepted or prohibited in establishing colonies in North America. Several colonists desired to perpetuate their own cultural and economic ways, and this influenced their descriptive accounts of Native American sport. The colonists' "approach toward Indian culture and recreation, biased as it was, indicated their general attitude toward man, God, and society. . . . [T]hese early Pilgrims in some ways predetermined modern American attitudes toward sports and specifically ethnic sports" (Eisen, "Early" 15).

Calvinism

In the 1530s, John Calvin called for religious reform in Europe. "Reform" Protestants, as Calvinists were often known, spread their religious beliefs throughout the sixteenth century to England, Scotland, France (French Protestants), and the English colonies. Calvinists preached a doctrine of predestination—that one's fate was known by God and that only a select few would be chosen by God for salvation, while all other souls would be damned. In Calvinism, society was theocratic, and God was sovereign. The struggle to be a good Christian, to believe one would be one of the "saints" rather than one of the "sinners," permeated all aspects of life. Calvinist authorities "insisted upon personal austerity, public fasting, evening curfews, and intensive religious instruction. They prohibited dancing, card playing, heavy drinking, and fashionable dressing" (Rader, *American Ways* 32). Calvin made little distinction between body and soul in seeking salvation; both needed to be free of sin. In fact, "of all the leaders of the Protestant Reformation who held, at best, an ambivalent attitude toward amusement and games, John Calvin was the most important." He promoted a strict doctrine, and, in Geneva, Switzerland, from 1541 to 1564, "he attempted to construct a 'theocracy,' a reign of godliness. Amusements and games took a beating" (Baker 74). The most ardent followers of Calvinism, the English Puritans, would bring this scrutiny of pastimes and sport—in their view, physical exercises and amusements lacking positive attributes for health and well-being—to the English colonies. During the late sixteenth and early seventeenth centuries, Puritans railed against various "devilish pastimes," and this outlook influenced the nature of sport and physical activities when Puritans immigrated to the New World. As Baker has stated, "In North America, as well as in England, the age of Puritan prohibitions is an important chapter in the history of sports" (72).

Church of England

During the Protestant Reformation, King Henry VIII of England divorced Catherine of Aragon without Pope Clement VII's consent and created and proclaimed himself head of the Church of England (also known as the Anglican Church) in 1534, thus ending the ancient ties between England and Rome. In doing so, Henry "inadvertently opened the door to centuries of religious strife" (Rader, *American Ways* 32). Henry died in 1553, and religious affiliations of the crown crossed from Protestantism to Roman Catholicism during the reign of Queen Mary (daughter of Henry and Catherine of Aragon), who adopted her mother's religion. Protestants persecuted during Mary's reign desired to escape to places adhering to Calvinism. Upon Mary's death in 1558, the state religion shifted back to Protestantism with the accession of Queen Elizabeth I (Henry VIII's daughter) to the throne.

The rule of Queen Elizabeth I influenced religious viewpoints about sport in the new colonies. King Henry's support of horse racing, for example, was endorsed by Elizabeth, and, while jousting contests declined for young gentlemen, horse racing appealed to the court of ladies and nobility: "Despite the demise of the armored knight the horse remained essential not only for mobility on the field of battle but also for transportation, the pleasures of hunting, and competitive sports" (Baker 62). Tennis also became popular among the royal ranks. Henry VIII had owned seven rackets, had built a tennis court at Hampton Court (now purportedly "the oldest in the world still in use"), and had constructed two indoor and two outdoor courts at the Palace of Westminster. He had even played a doubles match with the Emperor, the Prince of Orange, and the Margrave of Brandenburgh in 1522 (Baker 62; Gillmeister 79). Queen Elizabeth continued this support for tennis; she "refrained from playing tennis but loved to watch matches involving the leading nobles of the realm" (Baker 66).

In 1588, England defeated the Spanish Armada in a battle on the high seas, and Protestant England triumphed over Catholic Spain, freeing itself from

Spanish expansion. English colonists then pursued their expansion overseas with "westward fever," looking to the New World to carry their religion and values around the world, which of course included converting Native American peoples to their faith. Protestant attitudes of English men and women in the upper ranks of society extended into the world of play and sport in English colonization efforts. Sports for the royals of England, however, did not transfer to different social ranks that emerged over time in early colonial America as colonists in the early settlements faced the quest for survival in the New World.

Puritanism

During the Protestant Reformation, the strict religious doctrine upheld by the English Puritans prohibited sports and games that they saw as immoral or failing to serve any useful purpose. Yet when Puritans immigrated to the New World, various communities and religions that developed over time incorporated some sporting practices. The banished activities included improper dancing, drinking, prostitution, violent sports, games, and wild festivals. Puritans believed that such physical exercises and sport detracted from their devotion to God and from community building. In fact, most Protestants frowned upon amusements as "idle" use of time, rather than useful activity to improve physical and moral health. Yet for instruction of youth, Calvin believed that certain recreations were acceptable, including archery, swimming, walking, fishing, and hunting.

The English men and women who followed the rigid tenets of Calvinism, with its intent to do away with the rituals and hierarchy of the Church of England, desired to reform Protestantism in the late sixteenth and early seventeenth centuries, and they became known as Puritans. They wanted to "purify" Protestantism during the reign of King James I, who led the kingdom upon Elizabeth's death. The king's dislike for the Puritans was reciprocated by them (Rader, *American Ways* 34). English Puritans wanted to curtail popular recreations and maintain Sabbatarianism, or the keeping of the Sabbath (Sunday) as the Lord's day of prayer. They disapproved of the sporting activities of the English aristocracy, who often engaged not in productive hard work but in games and popular amusements that, to the Puritans, represented idleness. Sunday was a "realm where holy day and holiday vied for power" (McCrossen 9).

The Puritans objected to the supremacy of the wealthy class in England and to their way of

King James I and the Puritans differed greatly in their views of recreation on the Sabbath.

Reprinted from The Miriam and Ira D. Wallach Division of Art, Prints and Photographs: Print Collection, The New York Public Library. James I, King of Great Britain, France and Ireland, Defender of the Faith. Retrieved from http://digitalcollections.nypl.org/items/510d-47da-25d2-a3d9-e040-e00a18064a99.

life, which included playing such sports as tennis, fencing, bowling, and quoits (a kind of ring toss). In condemning such pursuits, English Puritan Philip Stubbes, critic of popular pastimes, wrote in 1581 in *The Anatomy of Abuses,* "Any exercise which withdraws us from godliness, either upon the Sabbath or any other day, is wicked, and to be forbidden." Stubbes also railed against the popular sport of football, or soccer, as did other critics who viewed this game as a violent sport of peasants that was connected with gambling. Stubbes deemed football as "a friendly kind of fight [rather] than play or recreation, a bloody and murdering practice [rather] than a fellowly sport or pastime" (qtd. in Baker 75). Thus both religious and class conflict emerged over Sabbatarianism.

English Puritans also attacked the popular recreations of the lower ranks. They considered gambling on sports and games by either class to be a sin and a squandering of resources. The Puritans also attacked the activities of the English masses that they linked to Catholic festivals and pagan rituals as occasions to engage in frivolous contests and to gamble on "blood sports," such as bullbaiting, bearbaiting, cockfighting, and ratting. These violent sports, where animals mauled one another until one was victorious, would be a target of Puritans both in England and in the American colonies. In sum, the Puritans criticized those who spent their days in gambling, drinking, merriment, blood sports, pastimes, and games for living an immoral and undisciplined way of life rather than serving the Lord in the Church of England.

The battle between Puritans and non-Puritans (of various classes and moral persuasions) over "time to play" and "time to pray" was addressed in an important declaration by King James I in the *Book of Sports*, issued as a royal proclamation in 1618. It stated that sport embodied social purposes, such as military and political uses, and, predictably, this stance taken by the king and his Anglican majority generated conflict with the Puritan minority. In part, it read as follows:

> We heard the general complaint of Our people, that they were debarred from all lawful Recreation, and exercise upon the Sundayes afternoone, after the ending of all Divine Service, which cannot but produce two evils: The one, the hindering of the conversion of many, whom their Priests will take occasion hereby to vexe, persuading that no honest mirth or recreation is lawful or tolerable in Our Religion, which cannot but breed a great discontentment in Our people's hearts. . . . The other inconvenience is, that the prohibition barreth the common and meaner sort of people from using such exercises as may make their bodies more able for warre, when Wee, or our Successors, shall occasion to use them. And, in place thereof, sets up filthy tiplings and drunkennesse, and breeds a number of idle and discontented speeches in their Ale houses, For when shall the common people have leave to exercise, if not upon the Sunday and holy daies, seeing they must apply their labour, and win their living in all working daies?

> qtd. in Riess, *Major* 22–23

The king declared that certain sports promoting health were acceptable:

> Our pleasure likewise is, Our good people be not disturbed . . . or discouraged from any lawfull recreation. Such as dancing, . . . Archery, . . . leaping, vaulting, or any other such harmlesse Recreation,

nor from having of May Games, Whitson Ales, and Morrisdances, and the setting up of Maypoles, and those sports therewith used so as the same be had in due and convenient time, without impediment or neglect of Divine Service. . . . But withall we doe here account still as prohibited all unlawfull games to bee used upon Sundayes only, as Beare and Bullbaitings, Interludes, and at all times, in the meaner sort of people, by Law prohibited, bowling.

> qtd. in Riess 23

This declaration by King James I challenged the devout Puritans seeking to uphold their religious codes. The king ordered his proclamation to be published throughout the country, and the asserting of such political positions about sport, labor, religion, and social class prompted some devout Puritans to seek a new location where they could worship and enforce their religious tenets as they saw fit. In 1633, the Declaration on Sports was reissued by King Charles I—again casting traditional sport as beneficial to the well-being and military readiness of the people. The Puritans who viewed sport as a profane undermining of religion "gritted their teeth about such a prospect and whenever possible tried to undercut the proclamation in England and New England" (Altherr, Part 1 1). In the American colonies, then, the settlers developed a sporting heritage drawing on their attitudes from Europe.

Sport in American Colonies

The changing cultural, religious, and economic landscape in England during the authority of King James I prompted English Puritan leaders, as well as leaders of what was known as the Virginia Company of London, and the English men and women forced to labor in the New World as indentured servants, to colonize North American regions. The cultural traditions these colonizers brought with them—and their interactions with the indigenous peoples and Africans in North America—shaped the development of active recreation, physical exercise, games, and sport in colonial American society. Immigrants' reasons for coming to the colonies varied by region, and a range of physical activities and sporting pursuits emerged in the various colonies. The rest of this chapter explores how peoples, places, and beliefs shaped colonial sports in the South, the North, and the Middle Colonies.

Jamestown, Virginia

Differences between traditional British culture and that of the American colonies became apparent in

International Perspective

Sport and Religions: Contested Relations?

Religions and physical cultures (including modern sports) are linked in numerous ways depending on the principles and practices of both the religion and the sport. Physical activities, such as running and dancing, can be religious rituals; and religious ceremonies can be used to support success in sport competitions. Followers of a particular religion will evaluate the various physical cultures differently from those who are nonbelievers.

The link between worldview and physical culture can clearly be observed in the rise of modern sport, which from the end of the nineteenth century spread all over the world, without meeting with the same measure of acceptance in all societies, however. This is revealed, for example, by an analysis of sporting success at the Olympic Games. The countries with the highest numbers of participants and victories are countries in which a "Protestant ethic" and a large degree of secularization go hand in hand with a high level of industrialization (Overman 2011).

Since religions invariably prescribe codes of conduct, including rules on the use of the body, sport has always been explicitly or implicitly a matter of concern for religions—and vice versa. Numerous examples may be cited to illustrate that body ideals and movement cultures correlate with religious convictions. The Olympic Games of Greek antiquity and the Greeks' belief in their gods, for example, are grounded in the same basic philosophy.

This is equally true of modern sport and modern societies. Religions, which regard the body as the servant of the soul, reject the cult of the body which is demanded by sport. By contrast, the ascetic ideals and deferred gratification patterns inherent in many religions (in which rewards are deferred until an existence after death) are of advantage in meeting the demands made on the body in training and contests. Apart from religion, however, traditions, conditions of life, political and social circumstances, and numerous other factors influence the diffusion as well as the forms and the level of sport in a society.

Societies, religions, and sports use age and gender as central categories for the distribution of rights and duties. Many religions assume a polarity of men's and women's "natures" and prescribe different ideals, norms, and behavioural patterns for both genders. Since the female body is considered to be seductive, weak, and in need of protection, it is often covered by taboos. This is true for many religions, not only in Christianity but also in Islam. There are numerous debates about Muslim athletes, e.g., about their sport clothing. In 2008, an independent group of scholars drafted the declaration "Accept and Respect" which focused on the rights of women to live (and play sports) according to their Muslim faith. Neither religious leaders nor sport federations should have the right to decide about a dress code which is not acceptable for the athletes. Religious issues play a major role in American sport as, for example, the practice of team prayers illustrates. In Europe, athletes may pray, but if they do it, they do it privately. Team prayers have become an issue to sport policies in the United States as they have been judged illegal. Another issue is clothing, as female athletes in particular cover their bodies and their hair because of religious prescriptions.

the first settlement at Jamestown, Virginia, founded in 1607. Jamestown became the first permanent English settlement in the New World. Rather than a colony governed as a political unit of England, Jamestown was founded as a business enterprise, owned by the Virginia Company of London, answering to King James I. The primary purpose of the Virginia Company from the beginning was to make a profit for shareholders, merchants, and political officials investing in their colony in the New World, with King James as head of the enterprise. While initially the king granted a charter to the Virginia Company with a desire to Christianize the Native Americans, the greater goal was a quest for profit by the king and his supporters in England.

Captain John Smith, the military commander of the settlement, arrived in Jamestown to find a harsh environment and climate in the early years. Colonists faced death and hardship, and Smith had to enforce strict laws requiring that all contribute to the colony's welfare. Yet the uneasy combination of gentlemen seeking wealth and gold in the venture and lower-ranked unskilled servants (some with criminal backgrounds) needing to perform manual labor, instead of men like farmers and blacksmiths, represented a challenge to the intense work required to sustain Jamestown in the initial years. Lack of supplies, conflict between men of the upper rank and those of the lower rank over labor with young men resisting hard physical tasks, while some of the English settlers engaged in hunting and fishing for their sustenance, resulted in disease and malnutrition. All of this led to a struggle to survive, known as a "starving time" in Jamestown. Between 1607 and 1609, only about 60 of the approximately 900 settlers sent to Jamestown survived. John Smith, the first strong leader of the Virginia colony, stated that unskilled servants "never did know what a day's work was" (qtd. in Nash et al., Brief 5th ed. 52).

The settlement did, of course, survive, and tobacco became the cash crop of Jamestown and of other settlements in Virginia and Maryland. Strong demand for "the jovial weed" back in England motivated English planters to seek cheap labor to grow this work-intensive crop, and initially most of the labor was done by lower-ranked and unemployed immigrants who became indentured servants, selling their labor for four to seven years in return for passage across the Atlantic Ocean to the American colonies. English colonists did try to enslave American Indians and force them to do the hard work of planting crops. The Powhatan Confederacy of the Chesapeake region, led by Opechancanough, resisted the English planters' incursion into their lands, but a war in 1622 failed to halt the growth (Nash et al., Brief 5th ed. 56–57). In 1619, the first Africans were forced to come to the British colonies in North America when 20 blacks arrived in Jamestown as captives of Dutch privateers. This unfortunate group marked the beginning of the shift to slavery that would transform the labor force in the colonial South by the end of the seventeenth century. Through much of

the 1600s, however, Southern gentry depended primarily on indentured servants, who made up 75 to 80 percent of Chesapeake laborers during this period.

This changing population in the Virginia colony during the 1600s would shape an ethic of leisure for wealthy Chesapeake planters bent on finding other persons to perform grueling physical labor in the fields while they themselves enjoyed pastimes and sport. Southern gentry—young, white noblemen who would acquire large tracts of lands and were averse to manual labor—frittered away their time at bowling, cards, horseback riding, and gambling, while forcing physical labor first by new immigrants and servants, then by black slaves. This powerful Southern gentry would display its cultural values and social status in the sporting practices of the Chesapeake region.

Southern Colonies

The colonies in the Chesapeake region of Virginia and Maryland, as well as the colony of South Carolina, developed with different motives and populations than the American colonies in other regions. These Southern colonies played a pivotal role in the sporting traditions and pastimes in the early decades of colonial America. The wealthy white Southern gentry, the indentured servants (men and women) who worked for years under harsh labor contracts, the black slaves, the single male laborers, and the Native Americans all shaped the work and sport patterns in these colonies. Key factors included social class, race, gender, and religion in the diverse mix of peoples in the region. At times, sport divided groups, serving as a site of conflict between slave owners and slaves, or between lower-class laborers and plantation owners; at other times sport united peoples of the same race or class in maintaining their power and status over other groups in colonial American society.

On plantations, masters used horses to traverse their land holdings, to oversee their slaves and crops, to travel to other locales, and to engage in sporting contests. Horse racing, card playing, and gambling went hand in hand with the status of a wealthy planter in the Southern colonies. In 1724, a Virginia writer remarked, "The common planters, leading easy lives, don't much admire labor or any manly exercise except horse-racing, nor diversion except cock-fighting." The Virginia legislature ruled cockfighting illegal by 1740, but the law had little influence on residents' sporting habits. The Southern colonists even imported

Jamestown in the 1630s, as illustrated by Keith Rocco.
Courtesy of the National Park Service.

fighting cocks from England and Ireland (qtd. in Guttmann, *Sports: The First Five Millennia* 120).

Many wealthy Southern planters used sport as a way of asserting and enjoying their socioeconomic status, and the development of horse racing and cockfighting was in turn intertwined with socioeconomic developments. One of the biggest changes, of course, was the shift to black slaves as the dominant force of labor in the South. The major shift to black slaves occurred first in Virginia, the leader both in slavery and in Southern sporting traditions, and after 1660 the slave population increased. As the supply of indentured servants from the surplus of unemployed lower-class young white men, the poor, and "the undesirables" from England decreased, the English entered the African slave trade in the colonies—in New England and in the South. Southern planters justified their forcing of Africans into chattel slavery by means of their ethnocentric belief in white superiority and in the Englishman's superior culture. In short, the planter elite wanted slaves in order to maintain their wealth and power in the South, and they increasingly codified the racist structure of slavery in the form of laws that defined slaves as legal property bound to a life of enforced labor.

The planters' perceived need to enforce the slavery of Africans intensified after class conflicts in Virginia pitted wealthy white planters against lower-ranked white farmers seeking to advance in their mobility. In 1676, farmer Nathaniel Bacon desired more land to increase his social status and, along with other white farmers, demanded that Native Americans be driven off or killed in order to free the land they coveted. They fought not only against native tribes but also against Governor William Berkeley's militia and the gentry in the government. This violence of white farmers against white militia and upper-rank colonists led to a civil war of class and race conflict in Virginia, and, although Bacon's Rebellion dissipated quickly upon his death from dysentery, the Southern gentry moved forcefully to reestablish the unity of white Southerners of different social classes. Wanting to quell the growth of a rabble-rousing class of poor whites, they embraced slavery in order to solidify the lower and upper white ranks to dominate over black slaves. In this way, whites of various social classes could join in controlling blacks in a hierarchy of power dependent upon the notion of a superior white race. In this social structure, even poor white farmers might aspire to own slaves, and while many could not afford to do so, they could still believe in their racial superiority over blacks. Thus "a racial consensus, uniting whites of different ranks in the common pursuit of a prosperous slave-based economy, began to take shape" (Nash et al., Brief 5th ed. 59–60), and the introduction of slavery into agricultural life in the Southern American colonies would have an impact on race, society, and sport—especially on the increasing popularity of horse racing.

Horse Racing and Gambling in Southern Gentry Culture

Horse racing prospered throughout the colonies, especially in the Southern region. Rationalizing it as a necessity for the improvement of breeding, colonists built horse-racing tracks in areas that were home to plantations and horse owners in Virginia, Maryland, and South Carolina in the 1660s. As historian Timothy Breen has explained, "The great planters' passion for gambling, especially on quarter-horse racing, coincided with a period of far-reaching social changes in Virginia," and, "by 1700, the ruling gentry . . . [were] united as they had never been before" (31).

The horse racing and gambling highly identified with these influential Southern gentry consisted of contests on the racetrack as well as between only those planters with enough money for the high-stakes wager on the horse race. Tobacco plantation owners embraced the values of materialism, individualism, and competition in sport and everyday life, and their practice of horse racing and high-stakes gambling visibly displayed their unity and power over the women in the family (who were typically spectators rather than competitors), the lower-ranked white farmers and workers, and of course the black slaves in colonial American society. The quarter-horse races of Virginia "were intense contests involving personal honor, elaborate rules, heavy betting, and wide community interest," and this "deep play" exclusive to the Southern gentry demonstrated that a "horse was an extension of his owner; indeed, a man was only as good as his horse" (Breen 32, 34). The power of the male gentry, along with the deference they garnered from the less powerful members of society, was apparent at horse-racing events. Only those planters of great means could afford the privilege of gambling for large sums at these public spectacles. One such was William Byrd II (1674–1744), owner of one of the earliest Virginia plantations, Westover plantation in Charles City. The Byrd family participated in the gentry culture as enthusiastic horse racers and breeders. By the 1720s and 1730s, for planters like William Byrd and

Horsemanship: Haute École and "Horse Ballet"

In many epochs and cultures, horse riding has been a means to an end: Horses have been put to use for transportation, for hunting, and in war. In the European Middle Ages, riders in armor on horses were the most powerful and frightening contestants on the battlefield. These elite warriors formed a new order of nobility, the order of knighthood, which lost its importance in the thirteenth century with the introduction of new weapons and new methods and tactics of warfare. During the Renaissance, horse riding grew into an amusement of the aristocracy and served thenceforth as an element of noble presentation in courtly festivities. The art of horse riding for its own sake—horsemanship—reached its apex in the Baroque Period (1600 to 1750).

Gentlemen members of court were well acquainted with poetry, art, and music, and they were proficient in mathematics, dancing, horse riding, and fencing. In accordance with the refined habits and tastes of the court, the ideal of education was that of the "cavalier," who stood out on account of his extravagant dress, noble manners, and strict adherence to the code of conduct of the courtly society. On horseback he was an artist, molding the horse into a work of art and accentuating the aesthetic dimensions of riding. The object was to master the skills of the "high school" (haute école) of horsemanship, that is, the highest level of dressage, which aimed not to tame but to train the animal systematically and progressively over many years. In the haute école, the natural gait of the horse is altered—for example in the piaffe, in which the horse trots without moving forward, and in the capriole, in which the horse jumps in the air and lands again on the same spot.

During the Renaissance, this new form of horsemanship spread from Italy to France and later to England and Germany. An important role in this process was played by textbooks and manuals, which appeared in numerous editions and were translated into various languages. Italian and French riding academies served as the centers of horsemanship, where young aristocrats from all over Europe were trained in the art of the "high school."

The great role played by horsemanship at European royal courts is revealed in sources relating to life at the court of Louis XIV, the Sun King, who kept about six hundred riding horses at Versailles. Louis himself was out on his riding courses every day with his courtiers, accompanied by orchestral music and devoting his time to the art of riding.

A royal birth or wedding prompted extravagant festivities which lasted for several days and involved music, dancing, and theatrical plays, as well as horse carrousels and horse ballets. The term *horse carrousel* covered a variety of performances, including a kind of polonaise (dance) on horseback and exhibitions of groups of riders (quadrilles) in splendid costumes who enacted a set subject. It also included forms of tilting, in which the galloping rider had to insert his lance through a small ring or knock a helmet off a wooden stand. In 1662, for example, a carrousel with five hundred noblemen on horseback was performed at the Louvre for the French royal court on the occasion of the birth of one of Louis' sons.

Even more artistic than the carrousel was the "horse ballet," a dance on horseback in which a group of riders executed figures to music. The largest known horse ballet was performed at the wedding of Leopold I the Holy Roman Emperor, with the Spanish Infanta, Margarita Teresa, in 1667. A total of 1,700 riders rehearsed for an entire year before the event, with the emperor himself executing the most complex of figures to the music of 100 instrumentalists.

Thus, knights' tournaments in the sixteenth to eighteenth centuries were no longer contests but shows, in which, with regard to decoration and costumes, no limits were set on either fantasy or wealth. The monarch's prestige rested on the success of such extravaganzas. Social changes in the eighteenth century—above all the French Revolution and the ensuing wars—marked the end of the "high school" of horsemanship. The ostentatious royal courts vanished, and along with them the studs and stables, the riding academies, and the cavaliers and the ladies of court who had admired the skills of horse riding.

A reminder of this bygone age can be seen in the Spanish Riding School in Vienna (founded in 1572), which preserves and cultivates the haute école of horsemanship. It is the best-known home of classical equitation and a magnet for tourists who flock to see the exhibitions performed by magnificent Lippizaner stallions.

Information from Spanish Court Riding School. <http://www.wien-vienna.com/hofreitschule.php>; Horsemanship. 2008. Encyclopædia Britannica Online. <http://search.eb.com.ep.fjernadgang.kb.dk/eb/article-9106288>; Sports. 2008. Encyclopædia Britannica Online. <http://search.eb.com.ep.fjernadgang.kb.dk/eb/article-253555>.

Robert "King" Carter, quarter-mile (0.4-kilometer) racing was "*the* sport in Chesapeake" (Struna, *People* 98). Byrd, writing in his diary, documented horse races in the summer and fall of 1740:

> 1 May 1740 After dinner we walked to the race but were soon forced to retire for the rain.
>
> 8 May 1740 About 12 the company went to the race and so did my family and I gave them all money and sent a pistole myself by Mr. Hall who brought back two about 4 o'clock.
>
> 7 August 1740 My son was gone to the race. . . .
>
> 30 October 1740 After dinner we had a race which I went not to but won 20 shillings.
>
> qtd. in Altherr, Part 1 249

The horse racing of the Southern elite planters enabled these powerful men to display their status and authority, while the lower sorts in colonial society—women, poorer planters, servants, and slaves—stood at a distance, watching the races rather than participating, thus reinforcing the prominence of the male gentry in both sport and society. After the race, the tavern, or ordinary, as it was called, provided a venue for sports, drinking, and gambling by common planters who lacked the wealth and status of the gentry.

The races also involved legal contracts in Virginia courts and maintained that gentlemen and their horses raced and gambled only against their social peers. An order from the York County Court on September 10, 1674, proclaimed that

> James Bullocke, a Taylor, haveing made a race for his mare to runn w'th a horse belonging to Mr. Mathew Slader for twoe thousand pounds [907 kilograms] of tobacco and caske, it being contrary to Law for a Labourer to make a race, being a sport only for Gentlemen, is fined for the same one hundred pounds [45 kilograms] of tobacco and caske.
>
> Whereas Mr. Mathew Slader & James Bullocke, by condition under the hand and seale of the said Slader, [agreed] that his horse should run out of the way that Bullocke's mare might win, w'ch is an apparent cheate, is ord'ed to be putt in the stocks & there sitt the space for one houre.
>
> qtd. in Altherr, Part 1 242

Records from Henrico County in the late 1600s show the importance of gentlemen appearing as witnesses in cases about horse races and wagers:

> William Randolph, aged about 38 years, Deposeth: That about Saturday last was a fortnight this depon't

> [deponent] was at a race at Mawvern hills [Malvern Hill] at w'ch time Mr. Wm. Epes and Mr. Stephen Cocke came to this depon't and desired him to take notice of ye agreem't: w'ch was That ye horse of ye s'd Epes and the horse of Mr. Wm. Sutton was to run that Race for ten Shillings on each side, and each horse was to keep his path.
>
> qtd. in Stanard 296

Thus, the races at the numerous courses in the Chesapeake region held cultural, monetary, and legal significance. Wagers served as badges of honor for the gentlemen planters who owned the horses and needed to uphold their social status by putting large stakes on the races. No race could be cancelled under the rules of the competition unless one of the horses died between the date of the wager and the time set for the contest (Carson, *Colonial* 51).

Public notices of upcoming horse races appeared in town newspapers and gazettes. One Joseph Butler advertised his willingness to race in this announcement on September 10, 1744, in the *South Carolina Gazette*:

> Joseph Butler of Charles Town will run his Gelding CHESTNUT, from the Quarter Houſe to Charles Town, with any Horſe, Mare, or Gelding that can be brought againſt him by the firſt Day of *December* next, for 500 or 1000 *l.* Inch Weight, the loweſt Horſe carrying 13 Stone. Enquire of the Printer, w[h]o will inform you of one in Charles Town that will enter into the Articles, upon the above Terms, in the Subscriber's behalf. Joseph Butler
>
> qtd. in Altherr, Part 1 238

Another advertisement in the *South Carolina Gazette* publicized a race to be run in April 1747 by "any Horſe, Mare or Gelding" at the house of Isaac Peronneau, with the winner garnering the prizes of "a handſome quilted Buck-ſkin ſeat ſaddle, Bridle and Houſing, Value 30 *l.* Alſo a handſome ſilver Watch and ſeveral other Things To be raffled for" (qtd. in Altherr, Part 1 239).

The sport of horse racing persisted as a favorite recreation of Southerners. Gentry and plantation owners continued to race in contests in Maryland and Virginia and in Charleston, South Carolina, as well as in less formal contests. Near Charleston, wealthy South Carolinians constructed a horse-racing track as early as 1665. The state's diverse population of white Christians, Jews, free blacks, and slaves may well have prompted a range of people to watch the races at the course. Jews settling in Carolina, along with Huguenots (French Protestants), desired freedom of worship and rights to trade in Charles Town (later, Charleston): "Gentiles and Jews raised their voices in protest" against England, and, in "aspiring to higher status, Jewish men and women sought the same marks of social standing that gentiles were seeking" (Rosengarten and Rosengarten 75, 88). As a symbol of gentility, horse-racing contests drew Southerners of distinction, and Massachusetts lawyer Josiah Quincy Jr., visiting Charleston in 1773, noted the popularity of the races:

> March 16th. Spent the morning ever since five o'clock, in perusing public records of the province; . . . am now going to the famous races.
>
> The races were well performed—but Flimnap beat Little David (who had won the last sixteen races) out and out. The last heat the former distanced the latter. The first four mile [6.4-kilometer] heat was performed in eight minutes and seventeen seconds, being four miles. Two thousand pounds sterling were won and lost at this race, and Flimnap sold at public venue the same day for 300L sterling! . . .
>
> At the races I saw a fine collection of excellent, though very high-priced horses, and was let a little into the singular art and mystery of the turf!
>
> qtd. in Altherr, Part 1 240–241

Other Southern Outdoor Pursuits

The planters of both the wealthier and the poorer ranks hunted birds, squirrels, and other animals using various hunting equipment such as pistols and bows and arrows. Fishing was a popular pastime on the waterways in the South, as in colonies throughout British North America. The sports that Southern planters and their children participated in often took place at their plantations, meaning that only those of the upper rank had the opportunity to do so. In 1721, at the Westover home of Virginia planter William Byrd II, located on the James River, Byrd set to constructing a bowling green, noting progress in diary entries. On March 16, he "began to turf the bowling green." On March 24, he "walked about the garden" to see his "people lay the turf." And by May 10, the green appeared ready for use in a game with the Reverend Peter Fontaine. Guests of the Byrd family at Westover continued to bowl on pleasant summer afternoons 20 years later. In another volume of Byrd's diary, he recorded 10 games in August 1739, when he played with neighbors, business agents, and his 11-year-old son, William. His interest in bowling persisted during the following summer, when he

noted 32 pleasant evenings when guests bowled with him, and in the last summer of the diary, 1741, Byrd played a bowling game almost every July afternoon. He and his friends also played cricket at Westover in the early 1700s (qtd. in Carson, *Colonial* 77, 81).

Although faced with a shorter winter season than their Northern counterparts, Southern colonists also engaged in ice skating on ponds. Men and women might skate for fresh outdoor air, and even ice skating could involve wagering for Southern sportsmen. Byrd's companions at Westover enjoyed skating when the weather permitted. On a cold December day in 1709, after having skated with friends the previous day, Byrd took again to the ice and "slid on skates, notwithstanding there was a thaw." That same evening, Byrd and his friends "gave Mr. Isham Randolph two bits to venture on the ice. He ventured and the ice broke with him and took him up to the mid-leg" (qtd. in Carson, *Colonial* 86). Other Southern colonists skated, walked, hunted, fished, rode horses, had cockfights, and gambled away from plantations over time. Indeed, "[f]or gentleman, slaves, and all in between, cockfights, horse races, and even fox hunts had become regional passions" (Gorn and Goldstein 27). Still, access to sports by mainly the white, wealthy, landowning gentry persisted, and they exercised their prerogative in playing sports and displaying their control over landholdings, slaves, and public competitions.

Those Southern colonists who wanted to uphold religious propriety with Sabbath Day observance supported statutes prohibiting sport on the day of rest. In the territory of colonial Carolina, set up by the English King Charles II, the promise of religious freedom and the lure of free land attracted people seeking to establish a settlement for the upper classes to maintain hold over the land and colonial government. In 1701, North Carolina and South Carolina became separate colonies, with South Carolina relying heavily on slave labor for the grueling work of cultivating rice on plantations, while North Carolina practiced slavery but also developed other economic industries. A North Carolina provincial law circa 1741 urged colonists to maintain the Sabbath as a day of religious reflection: "*An Act, for the better Observation and keeping of the Lord's Day, commonly called Sunday, and for the more effectual Suppression of Vice and Immorality.*" This law called for people on Sunday to "carefully apply themselves to the Duties of Religion and Piety; and that . . . no Person whatsoever, shall upon the Land or Water, do or exercise any Labour, Business or Work, of ordinary Callings . . . nor employ themselves either in hunting, fishing or fowling, or use any Game, Sport or Play, on the Lord's Day." Anyone fourteen years of age or older in North Carolina caught violating this prohibition on sport or pastimes "shall forfeit and pay the Sum of Ten Shillings, Proclamation Money" (qtd. in Altherr, Part 1 9).

The promise of religious tolerance in Carolina's Fundamental Constitutions of 1669 brought Christian dissenters and Jews from England to the Carolinas, and in the new British settlement of Charles Town religious dissenters conducted business and practiced their religions (Rosengarten and Rosengarten 60). The prohibition on sport and recreation on the Sunday Sabbath remained the custom in colonial South Carolina, and a provincial law enacted in about 1712 sustained observation of "the Lord's Day, commonly called Sunday" and listed prohibited activities: "No public sports or pastimes, as bear-baiting, bull-baiting, foot-ball playing, horse-racing, interludes or common plays, or other unlawful games, exercises, sports or pastimes whatsoever shall be used on the Lord's-Day" (qtd. in Altherr, Part 1 7). Violators were subject to a monetary fine. Despite such efforts, the impulse to play even on a day of rest persisted, although legal efforts of colonial governments strived to curtail sporting activities. Laws passed by colonial governments suggest that some colonists wanted to play sports on their day off from regular labor.

On other days the residents of South Carolina of upper social status might play sports such as tennis, and other South Carolinians might participate in foot races as well as sporting practices such as ball playing, horse racing, and pastimes. Eliza Lucas Pinckney, on her Charleston plantation, refers to the sport of tennis in her letter book in 1742, offering insight into the game in her own writing. In one passage, she made an intriguing reference to another socially charged activity, that of diving: "But if the diver should pretend each of these perls as Big as a Tennis ball . . ." (qtd. in Altherr, Part 1 108). In fact, on plantations in South Carolina and the Chesapeake region, swimming and diving in deep waterways for such treasures as pearls marked physical and racial divisions between white slave owners and their enslaved swimmers, as explored in the next section.

Slaves and Plantation Realities of Play

When plantation slaves were not toiling in the fields from sunup to sundown, they enjoyed some free time to indulge their pleasures or engage in sporting activities that provided sustenance. Plantation masters dominated slaves in forcing them to perform hard physical labor, but when slaves were in their own quarters, away from the master, in the evenings or on the Sabbath or holidays, they wanted diversions from their work. As Wiggins notes, "Regardless of how cruel the plantation became for slaves, their struggle for survival never became so severe that it destroyed their creative instincts or prevented them from establishing their own way of life" (*Glory* 3). Slaves engaged in their recreation in the confines of their physical environment. Fishing supplemented their diets, but only the most trusted slaves were allowed guns for hunting. Slaves maintained elements of African cultures in their dances and music, and in such performances they might also play the role of the trickster, mimicking or mocking their white owners in the form of pretentious caricatures unknown to the masters. Moreover, "[a]lthough slave labor in fields, foundries, and workshops was normally suspended on Sundays, it is impossible to call Sunday a day of rest for enslaved Americans. Most slaves used their day in hunting, fishing, and gardening" (McCrossen 12–13). Generally on Sundays, "when there was little work, . . . the slaves both young and old would dress up in hand-me-down finery to do a high-kicking, prancing walk-around. They did a take-off on the high manners of the white folks in the 'big house,' but their masters, who gathered around to watch the fun, missed the point" (Wiggins, "Sport and Popular Pastimes" 74). At times, slaves also had to entertain their masters as jockeys in horse races, and they sometimes worked as horse trainers or as boxers or wrestlers in rough physical contests wagered upon by their owners. Slaves themselves gambled at bowling, cards, and dice games, although Southern legislatures tried to ban such activities by the 1830s (Wiggins, "Sport and Popular Pastimes" 74).

With their lives inevitably rooted in physicality, slaves took pride in their physical prowess. They competed in horse and boat races, foot races, and jumping contests; utilitarian sports such as swimming also proved useful. Since many plantations and fields were located near waterways, African slaves used swimming skills learned in their native homelands. As historian Kevin Dawson has explained, "From the age of discovery up through the nineteenth century, the swimming and underwater diving abilities of people of African descent often surpassed those of Europeans and their descendants. Indeed, most whites, including sailors, probably could not swim" (1327). According to Dawson, from the medieval period through the late nineteenth century, most whites could not swim, and in the Middle Ages, "numerous factors caused a devaluing and discarding of swimming," including religious reasons; concerns by doctors about the effect of immersion in water; and beliefs about the dangers of bodies of water, uncertain elements, and creatures contained within bodies of water (Dawson 1333). Whites' reluctance to swim compared with the skills in swimming exhibited by blacks persisted; in the "late nineteenth century, westerners were evidently averse to the freestyle because it generated more splashing than the breaststroke," although "blacks, Asians, and Native Americans had demonstrated its speed and strength to them for centuries" (Dawson 1334). Slaves used their swimming ability in the rivers and ponds on or near plantations for both competitive and practical purposes. On one South Carolina plantation,

> John Clinkscales contended that in the antebellum years one of his father's slaves . . . named Essex was "by odds the best swimmer on [his] father's place" and possibly even the county, suggesting his reputation was perhaps earned in interplantation contests. In the seventeenth century Richard Ligon observed a planter-organized contest in which Barbadian slaves had to catch a duck placed in a large pond. The captor was awarded the duck, presumably to eat or sell it. The proprietor of these Sunday "recreations," Colonel Drax, "calling for some of his best swimming *Negroes*, commanded them to swim and take this Duck; but forbad them to dive, for if they were not bar'd that play, they would rise up under the Duck, and take her as she swome, or meet her in her diving, and so the sport would have too quick an end."
>
> Dawson 1341

Many slave women on Southern plantations had also learned to swim in their African cultures, and they used that physical ability in antebellum slave life. "Whether organized by slaves themselves or by slaveholders, contests probably offered the winners prestige in the slave quarters. They indicated that bondwomen could beat their male counterparts. In addition to providing enslaved participants and observers with merriment, the communal nature of such contests, as of other recreations and sports, probably enhanced slaves' sense of community" (Dawson 1341).

The physical prowess that slaves displayed in their swimming feats stood in contrast to the reluctance of white colonial men and women to engage in swimming activities. Furthermore, "West-

ern women probably refrained from swimming because most people swam nude, and western standards of modesty did not tolerate public disrobing by white women" (Dawson 1341). In a 1696 treatise on swimming, the author stated that "it is most certain that the Indians, and the Negroes, excel all others in the Arts of Swimming and Diving. It is to them the Ladies are obliged for their Ornaments of Pearl; they are the Divers who fish for them; they are also very useful for recovering Anchors and Merchandizes that have been cast away" (qtd. in Dawson 1333).

Moreover, in a physical test of vigor and swimming agility, slaves also encountered creatures of the sea in "blood sports" differing from those engaged in by white Southerners in animal contests on land. Slaves engaged in these physical activities while the master often kept a watchful eye on their swimming pursuits. Slaves "fused swimming to blood sport when they fought sharks, alligators, and manta rays to amuse themselves and to demonstrate their skill and strength—and perhaps their manhood" (Dawson 1341). In one instance in the Carolinas in 1700, a slave adeptly wrestled with a shark, and John Lawson reported that "some [Negroes], and others, that can swim and dive well, go naked into the Water, with a Knife in their Hand, and fight the Shark, and very commonly kill him, or wound him so, that he turns Tail, and runs away'" (qtd. in Dawson 1342). While such displays of bravery in the water—along with diving for pearls, an arduous and dangerous task—challenged the health and physical strength of the slaves, such pursuits also enabled them at times to display prowess and work away from the harsh labors and strict supervision of the fields. In diving for pearls, especially, slaves might earn material rewards, although slave masters demanded most of the finds; divers were frequently forced to sell them to their owners (Dawson 1348, 1349).

Yet the competitions of slaves in some sporting activities revealed the realities of their harsh lives of bondage. Drawing on their parents' experiences, slave children often played games that emphasized the need to cooperate with, rather than eliminate, one another. Accordingly, "[e]ven the various dodge ball and tagging games played by the children contained designed stratagems within the rule structure that prevented the removal of any participants." The devastating loss of a father, mother, brother, uncle, grandparent, or other family member sold by a plantation master meant that the pastimes of children emphasized loyalty and solidarity in slave quarters (Wiggins, *Glory*

11). The time that children and parents might spend together in pastimes proved precious, and it became a valuable reprieve from the cruel institution of slavery.

New England Colonies

Sport in colonial America was also shaped, of course, by those English colonists who immigrated to New England—a much different environment—with their own particular ideas about family and religion. New England colonists initially strived to maintain their devout religious outlook in their everyday lives, and this stance shaped attitudes about sport and, in turn, the patterns of sport pursued in these colonies. The sports that New Englanders deemed most valuable offered practical and healthful benefits in accordance with the colonists' views on mind, body, and soul.

Pilgrims in Plymouth

In 1620, William Bradford founded Plymouth Colony in Massachusetts. A discontented Englishman, Bradford wanted to practice religion as a Separatist, that is, separate from the Church of England. He and his Pilgrim followers wanted to determine the religion, laws, and social customs of their new colony. The rigors of survival efforts—building houses, clearing land, making clothes, planting crops, and preparing food—left little time for play, and Bradford and his followers held an attitude toward diligence that was duly summarized in the phrase "in detestation of idleness." Thus, when Bradford, on Christmas Day of 1621, witnessed a group of newly arrived immigrants at play in the streets of Plymouth, their decision to engage in pastimes rather than work (on a day not supported as a holiday of the Pilgrims) generated tension between the immigrant laborers and Bradford, who was intent on implementing his religious codes. Bradford wrote about the incident in his account of Plymouth Plantation:

> On the day called Christmas day, the Governor called them out to worke, . . . but the most of this new company excused them selves and said it was against their consciences to work on that day. So the Governor tould them that if they made it a matter of conscience, he would spare them till they were better informed. So he led-away the rest and left them; but when they came home at noone from their worke, he found them in the street at play, openly; some pitching the barr, & some at stoole-ball, and shuch like sports. So he went to them, and tooke away their implements, and tould them that was against his conscience, that they should play

> & others worke. If they made the keeping of it a mater of devotion, let them kepe their houses, but ther should be no gaming or revelling in the streets.
>
> Bradford 82–83

Thus, Bradford viewed the pastimes as idleness and attacked such amusements as counter to the religious observances of the colonists in Plymouth.

Similar tensions were stirred in a 1627 incident wherein Thomas Morton wanted to celebrate the naming of the colony by erecting an 80-foot (24-meter) Maypole at Merry Mount, similar to one he had seen in England. Bradford was not pleased to see youth dancing at the Maypole and participating in what he considered immoral behavior. He claimed that Morton and his fellow merrymakers were engaged in "drinking and dancing aboute it many days together, inviting Indean women for their consorts, dancing and frisking together . . . and worse practices." Bradford deemed these actions to be pagan celebrations, like "the feasts of the Roman Goddes Flora, or the beastly practices of the madd Bacchinalians." To halt such revelry, Bradford sent Morton to England and made "that May-polle to be cut down," ending these celebrations in the colony (Bradford 141–142).

Puritans in New England

Although the Pilgrims wanted to separate themselves from nonbelievers in their Plymouth Colony, Puritans in England at the time fervently wanted to establish a godly community and practice their religious tenets free of opposition, and so they began immigrating to New England, where they soon outnumbered the Pilgrims. During this Great Migration, more than twenty thousand Puritans came to the United States between 1629 and 1640 (Rader, *American Ways* 34). As a part of this wave, John Winthrop led a group of Puritan immigrants to the Massachusetts Bay Colony in 1630. Winthrop, a devout religious leader, desired to found a new religious colony in contrast to what he saw as lax religious laws in England. Winthrop and his followers of men and women in families sailed to the New World to found a utopian community, "a City upon a Hill," as a model for the world to imitate in reforming society. Indeed, Winthrop believed that the Puritans had made a covenant with God and that God would watch over them if they strictly followed His laws. Winthrop emphasized the need for conformity in order to fulfill the utopian mission of church, family, and state linked together in a Puritan community of religious codes, and this covenant or contract with God shaped the

People & Places

Cotton Mather

Cotton Mather of Boston, Massachusetts, was the leading Puritan minister in New England in the late seventeenth century and early eighteenth century—a third-generation Puritan clergyman. He expressed firm attitudes about the type of sports he deemed healthful and beneficial to Puritans, as well as those he deemed sinful and to be prohibited. Mather pronounced that the observance of the Sabbath meant to serve the Lord and pray, rather than to play sports, as in this 1703 statement from *The Day Which the Lord Hath Made*: "Sports on the Lords Day! Never did any thing ſound more ſorrowfully or more odiouſy, since the day that the World was firſt bleſs'd with ſuch a day" (qtd. in Altherr, Part 1 7). Mather also preached against mixed dancing, drinking, violent sport, and other physical exercises he viewed as harmful to the body and soul. He

especially identified youth as straying from the Puritan codes in engaging in sporting pursuits: "Some of our Rising Generation have been given up to the most abominable Impieties of Uncleaness, Drunkenness, and a Lewd, Rude, Extravagant sort of Behavior. There are the Children of Belial among them, and Prodigies of Wickedness" (qtd. in Dulles 1965, 20).

At the same time, he declared that outdoor physical exercise—such as walking, hunting, fishing, boating, and other diversions he termed innocent—could fortify the mind and body for work. Mather chronicled his own experience with such healthful sport, although acknowledging an accident in his 1716 fishing excursion:

> This Day a singular Thing befel me. My God, Help me to understand the Meaning of it! I was prevailed withal, to do a Thing, which I very rarely do, (not once in Years) I rode abroad with some Gentlemen, and Gentlewomen, to take the country Air, and to divert ourselves, at a famous Fish-pond. In the Canoe, on the Pond, my Foot slipt, and I fell overboard into the Pond. Had the Vessel been a little further from the Shore, I must have been drown'd. But I soon recovered the Shore, and going speedily into a warm Bed, I received no sensible HARM (qtd. in Altherr, Part 1 201).

Photo courtesy of Library of Congress, LC-USZ62-92308.

Puritan perspective on sport and the body during the initial period of the Great Migration.

The Puritan beliefs upheld and enforced by Winthrop, who served as both the Puritan head of the church and the governor of Massachusetts Bay, dictated the religious creed of the colony, the basis of all activities in the Puritan community. Puritans believed in predestination, with no free will for persons—only God knew which souls were to be predestined for heaven or hell—and in the Covenant of Grace, which held that only by God's grace can one be saved or become one of the elect, one of the "visible saints" of the community. Puritan

religion challenged what they termed the Covenant of Work, which was the belief that one's own hard work, or human ability, conveyed a sign of God's choosing those who were saved. Nonetheless, the Puritan work ethic meant that all persons needed to contribute to the community for its service to the Lord. In Massachusetts Bay Colony, every person was to pursue a "calling" to serve God and work for the well-being of the community, rather than for individual achievement and glory. In keeping with this tenet, Puritan attitudes espoused by the leaders on sport and recreation emphasized that sport as a lawful activity must serve a useful purpose for one's health, whether physical or moral, in the community. Winthrop even wrote in his diary of the need for replenishment of mind and body to offset the labors of physical and spiritual pursuits in building the New England colony: "I examined my heart, and findinge it needfull to recreate my minde with some outward recreation, I yielded unto it, and by a moderate exercise herein was much refreshed" (qtd. in Gorn and Goldstein 32). Thus, Puritans in colonial America, with their emphasis on spiritual vigor, may be viewed perhaps as "the moral athlete of yesteryear" (Lucas and Smith 113).

Puritan restraints on sport, games, and popular amusements stemmed from moral and religious convictions that also shaped their political, social, and economic considerations in colonial life. Rigid rules of conduct prohibiting sports (e.g., laws in Massachusetts, Rhode Island, and Connecticut) banned activities including dice, card games, quoits (a ring-toss game somewhat similar to horseshoes), bowls, ninepins, and other games. Puritans viewed gambling as evil and frivolous, and it also ran counter to their focus on productive activity that was necessary for the colony to survive and maintain the social and economic basis of communal activities. The Puritan belief in lack of free will to change one's situation in society meant that if one experienced a change in status, it was the result of religious conversion, not human ability to change one's economic standing. Sabbatarianism remained important for the Puritans. They protected Sunday, a day of prayer and rest, with their "blue laws" that restricted popular recreations, sports, games, and pastimes, and Puritan officials punished violators. Sunday laws, "known as 'blue laws' because of the supposed color of paper on which they were published in colonial Connecticut, emerged out of widely shared respect for Sunday. Both law and custom set the day apart from the rest of the week" (McCrossen 10). In a 1630 incident in Massachusetts Bay, when one John Baker failed to uphold the Sabbath, court officials ordered that he "be whipped for shooteing att fowle on the Sabbath day" (qtd. in Guttmann, *Sports: The First Five Millennia* 118).

Puritan leaders did allow sports such as fishing, fowling, archery, and hunting, which they viewed as useful since they provided food and wholesome bodily recreation for church authorities and residents in the community. However, to uphold the Sabbath and curtail blood sports, some colonial New England newspapers published announcements intended to stop such behaviors. The *New England Weekly Journal,* for example, printed an article on September 25, 1732, addressing cruelty to animals:

> A Sportſman's Dog or Horſe are his Boſom Friends; he is fonder of them than his Wife, would ſerve them ſooner than his Brother, had rather feed them than the Poor, and is more ſolicitious for their Education and preſerving the Breed, than for the Heir of his Family and Fortune; But when grown old or diſabled, they are both neglected and treated with Cruelty and Contempt.
>
> . . . Horſes, in particular, frequently die under the Tyranny of their Drivers, and the Hardſhip of their Toil, and we even make a Sport of their Miſeries.
>
> Throwing at *Cocks* is an annual Inhumanity. *Bull-baiting* is a ſtanding Diverſion, and the Pain of the Creature at the Stake, and the Wounds of his Enemies the Dogs, is ſometimes Sport to the Great and Polite, as well as the Butcher and Carman. *Duck-hunting* is another of the ſame Kind, and an *Owl* is often joyn'd to double the Cruelty and Entertainment together. *Cock-fighting* and *Horſe-racing* are Barbarities in the higheſt Vogue, and Ladies are now as fond of the laſt, as the moſt ſavage amongſt us.
>
> But who or what are they which we treat in this inhuman Manner? Why Part of the Works of the Deity we worſhip, Creatures made like our ſelves, as fond of Pleaſure and as ſenſible of Pain; only rang'd in a lower Rank in Life, perhaps to try how we ſhould deſerve more Happineſs, by being ſtudious to preſerve theirs.

"Cruelty to Animals" 1

The only organized spectator sport in New England in the eighteenth century was horse racing. Notably, "[m]ore formal horse racing began in two areas of Rhode Island: Newport and an area called the Narragansett country." In the 1720s, "both of these towns began to provide horse racing not only to local residents but also to other New Englanders willing to travel to see organized, high-quality racing." By the 1730s, racing promoters hired professional riders, advertised horse matches weeks in advance, and held dozens of races in a single day (Daniels, *Puritans* 173). Horse racing also began to expand in Massachusetts. Boston newspapers carried advertisements for horse races as early as 1715, and in the 1720s advertisements announced races held a few miles outside the city. A typical notice in May 1721 offered a punch bowl valued at 10 British pounds as prize for a 3-mile (4.8-kilometer) race on Cambridge Heath. Interested parties could enter any horse not higher than 14 hands and carrying a jockey of nine stone (about 125 pounds or 57 kilograms) after paying the entry fee of 20 shillings (Altherr, Part 1 287). By the 1760s, horse races were staged frequently at several sites in eastern Massachusetts, close to Boston and near some of the urban regions of Connecticut (Daniels, *Puritans* 173).

Yet the Puritan utopian vision encountered challenges as new immigrants brought their own ideas about labor, leisure, sporting activities, and religion to the New World. Many newcomers rejected the rigid Puritanism, and change during the second generation of Puritans weakened the hold of religion on the New England way of life. A decline in church membership reflected New Englanders' need to address how to maintain adherence to Puritan beliefs, and the Halfway Covenant of the mid-seventeenth century diluted the religious experience necessary for becoming a Puritan. The Puritan leaders—that is, the New England Congregational clergy—adopted the Halfway Covenant that "allowed for children of church members, if they adhered to 'forms of godliness' to join the church even if they could not demonstrate that they had undergone a conversion experience" (Nash et al., Brief 5th ed. 115–116). In addition, mid-seventeenth-century colonists in New England often rejected the stricture against sport and games and felt an interest in achievement in their work and social roles. Yet, despite some challenges, ordinances to preserve the traditional religious outlook and limit recreation and sport persisted, such as one that a clerk in Boston proclaimed in the *Boston Weekly Newsletter* in August 1736:

> *Whereas there are ſeveral good and wholſome Laws of this Province made to prevent the Prophanation of the Lord's-Day, forbidding the Exerciſe of any Labour, Work, or Buſineſs, or the uſe of any Game, Sport or Recreation, Swimming in the Water, uneceſſary Walking or Riding in the Streets, Lanes, Highways, Common-Fields or Wharves on ſaid Day, the Evening preceeding, or Evening following: Notwithſtanding which many Perſons do tranſgreſs in the above Particulars;*
>
> *Reſolved,* That for the future more effectual Care be taken for the puniſhing thoſe who ſhall offend againſt any of the aforementioned Laws; alſo that

A typical city tavern was a place for both rest and relaxation.

Photo courtesy of Library of Congress, LC-USZC2-1370.

the Diſorders and Breaches of the Laws reſpecting Licenſed Houſes be duly Proſecuted. And the Clerk of the ſaid Court is herby directed to publiſh this Order in the publick Prints. Atteſt. Byfield Lyde, Cler.

Lyde 2 (italics in original)

As religious adherence waned and New Englanders of the next generation in the seventeenth century increasingly wanted to obtain economic improvement and enjoy amusements, games, drinking, and gathering in places for social and leisure pursuits in the community, the places for public meeting expanded beyond the traditional church as the center of the Puritan community.

As the number of taverns in colonial America increased, they became a locus for amusements and sporting pursuits popular among colonists of various social classes. Some wealthier men gambled on sport, while others came as spectators, and some lower-rank colonists brought their skills for a contest in cards or the blood sport of animal baiting or cockfighting. In the growing cities of the Northeast, such as Boston, New York, and Philadelphia, taverns became widespread as places for colonists and travelers to meet for respite from travel, to enjoy food and beverage, to participate in sport and games, and to communicate with each other; indeed, taverns became nodes in a network of venues for the exchange of information. In Massachusetts, some moral codes remained in force, so that tavern keepers were to prohibit shuffleboard, bowling, and dancing, which the authorities believed led to gambling, illicit sexual activities, and lack of productivity. In tavern culture, card and dice games were commonly played, and many taverns also provided space for ninepins alleys or bowling greens (Struna, *People* 70). Rather than adhering to the preaching of Puritan ministers, some colonists recognized taverns as a site of profit making and demonstrated their human ability by competing at sport and gambling in order to gain money in their own version of the work ethic. From about 1700 to 1749, the Black Horse Tavern in Old Saybrook, Middlesex County, Connecticut, regularly featured tavern sports, card games, drinking, and gambling, particularly for the rowdy young men who worked in the town's maritime and shipbuilding industries. This tavern also served as an inn, where travelers coming to New England might stay and partake of food, beverage, and sport as a diversion from their tiring travels and tasks. The tavern welcomed travelers and townspeople with the sign "Entertainment," clearly marking a shift away from the strict earlier codes constraining sport and amusement in New England society.

Public gatherings—not only in taverns but also in the public square and common grounds in New England towns—brought colonists together in militia drills, training exercises, and amusements. Young men engaging in militia training gained wide acceptance, and New England officials allowed men to wrestle (Daniels, *Puritans* 168). Sometimes entire troops "took part in sham battles and shooting contests," displaying their skills for spectators gathered specifically to watch the event (Struna, *People* 79).

Middle Colonies

In 1681, King Charles II of England conferred on William Penn, a reformer and ardent Quaker, the proprietorship of Pennsylvania in the middle region of colonial America. Penn received the land in lieu of payment for large debts that the King owed him, and, like other Protestant reformers in colonial New England, he put forward his religious views as the basis of the new colony. He wanted to provide Quakers with a colony where they could practice religious freedom and establish a model community in the New World. He wanted to base

People & Places

Harvard College

Young men from prominent New England families who attended Harvard College (founded in 1636 in Cambridge) faced Sabbath laws in their time away from classes. Puritan minister Thomas Shepard Jr. wrote a letter to his son at Harvard to give his opinion on his son's use of time, telling him to pursue serious study and to "recreate your Self a little, and so to your work afresh; let your recreation be such as it may stir the Body chiefly, yet not violent." He also urged him to let the recreation "be never more than may Serve to make your Spirit the more free and lively in your Studies" (ca. 1670, qtd. in Altherr, Part 1 14). The effort to curtail drinking, gambling, and rowdy activities fit with the religious orientation of the college; according to historian Bruce Daniels, "Even at places like Harvard, even during the militia gatherings that offered the greatest opportunities for young men to indulge in disreputable behavior, one does not find accounts of ball games occurring." Sports deemed more appropriate for young men in the outdoors offered benefits to refresh the mind and body. Fishing was perhaps the most popular and accepted colonial sport, and the Harvard administration officially approved of "fishing and fowling" for Harvard students (Daniels, *Puritans* 167, 169).

Reprinted from The Miriam and Ira D. Wallach Division of Art, Prints and Photographs: Print Collection, The New York Public Library. (1743). *A prospect of the colleges in Cambridge in New England.* Retrieved from http://digitalcollections.nypl.org/items/510d47d9-7abc-a3d9-e040-e00a18064a99.

this "Holy Experiment" on the teachings of radical seventeenth-century preacher George Fox. As a follower of Fox, Penn belonged to a particular religious sect in England in the 1640s and 1650s known as the Society of Friends, or Quakers. Fox's theology—based on a belief in the Holy Spirit or "Inner Light"—shaped Penn's leadership in instituting codes about religion, recreation, the Sabbath, and interactions with American Indians in the colonies. His passionate focus on the Quaker faith allowed little tolerance for sport in the middle colony of Pennsylvania. William Penn established an earlier colony in North America in 1674, "West New Jersey that sputtered at first," but then it waned; for the Quakers, therefore, when Penn received the royal charter for Pennsylvania in 1681, they reestablished their place in colonial North America (Nash et al., Brief 5th ed. 76–77).

Sporting Pastimes in Colonial Pennsylvania

In the Pennsylvania colony, William Penn and the Quakers promoted a religious outlook dissimilar to that of the Puritan men and women who settled in the 1600s in British North America. Quakers trusted direct inspiration, a special communication with God, rather than the rigid institutional church and the strict power of men as ministers and heads of the colony. Quakers believed that by intensive searching and discussion with ordinary laypeople, known as "Public Friends," they could understand the Inner Light. In their distinctive beliefs in creating the colony as a refuge from persecution and open to different religious backgrounds, the Quakers accorded colonial women in the community extraordinary equality at a time when other colonists upheld patriarchal domination in family and society. According to Fox, the Inner Light could be communicated to females as well as males, and Penn established his colony in Pennsylvania in accord with this religious principle and the attending views of men's and women's roles in public activities.

Not surprisingly, Penn's Quaker beliefs influenced the nature of sport and recreation in the new colony. Quakers believed in simplicity and virtue as the path to God, marking quite a contrast with the conspicuous consumption of Southern gentlemen and planters, with their horses, plantations, slaves, sporting equipment for billiards and other pursuits, and games of chance such as dice. Such diversions and recreations—and the ornamentation and materialism pertaining to them—drew criticism from the colony's officials as potentially interfering with Quaker worship. Their focus was firmly

on the spiritual well-being of individual men and women, rather than on building wealth and social status in order to garner respect and gain control in the hierarchical structure over common and lower-rank farmers, women, servants, and slaves, as was characteristic both of colonial Southern sportsmen and of the wealthy men and merchants of colonial New England. Quakers refused to tip their hats to their social betters in deference or wear fancy clothing as a display of social status. Of significance for the place of sport in Pennsylvania, the Quakers also refused to bear arms or fight in military campaigns, as their colony was known as a "Peaceable Kingdom." As a result, they did not engage in public sporting displays of manly prowess on muster days or in military training as was done in Massachusetts, or hold shooting matches as other colonies did. Physical, violent sports linked with guns—as well as competitions in boxing, bullbaiting, and revelry—held no cultural significance for Quaker men and women in colonial Pennsylvania and New Jersey.

Penn and his Quaker followers addressed the issue of sport and recreation explicitly. While their laws generally promoted religious freedom, some laws mandated strict adherence to the Sabbath, thus limiting sport and recreation. Quaker leaders declared Sunday a day of religious meetings and

William Penn.
Photo courtesy of Library of Congress, LC-USZ62-106735.

rest from daily work, and blue laws prohibited card games, cockfights, bearbaiting, gambling, drinking, carousing, and other amusements deemed offensive. Friends did allow participation in sports recognized as wholesome and in innocent pastimes for health benefits and practical recreation. Colonists in Pennsylvania and New Jersey could enjoy ice skating, sleighing, walking, swimming, fishing, and hunting. And, as in other colonies in American society, horse racing took place in Pennsylvania because of the importance of horses in colonial American transportation and agriculture. Gambling on races, however, was prohibited.

Sporting Interests and Challenges to the Quakers

Quaker ministers and authorities faced a challenge in trying to enforce regulations that barred illegal amusements. As the population of Pennsylvania increased, many non-Quakers came to the colony in the early eighteenth century with their own values and motives for settling in the area, and from 1715 through 1740 Pennsylvania underwent political, social, and economic changes. Quakers' control over laws and social customs weakened. New immigrants, including Germans, Scots-Irish, and nonbelievers from England settled into the colony and challenged the stern moral codes and blue laws that restricted sport and recreation. Some of the newcomers formed lower classes of laborers and enjoyed tavern sports, drinking, gambling, and boisterous social gatherings. Other new Anglicans who did not share Quaker religious ideals—such as merchants who possessed wealth and power—desired to partake of sports and display their social status. Philadelphia became a hub of political, business, and social activity, with some residents engaging in increased recreation and sporting pursuits that included physical exercise in horse racing, bowling, and skating, as well as the pastimes of billiards and card playing and the drinking and gambling that often accompanied them. Even blood sports such as cockfighting and bullbaiting grew more popular.

Eventually, organized elite sports clubs were founded, although Quakers heard their leaders instruct them to stay away from the sports, diversions, and amusements available in such associations. Upper-class gentlemen and politicians established the social and sports organizations to foster their interests in common pursuits and sporting endeavors—for example, "the Colony in Schuylkill, founded in 1732, for its fishing, hunting, and dining pleasures" (Jable, "Pennsylvania's"

119), and the Philadelphia Jockey Club, organized in 1766 to provide a venue for horse racing. Thus, the Quaker faith gave way to other leisure and consumer interests of colonists. While William Penn's Holy Experiment faltered with the diversity of the Pennsylvania population and the rise of secular institutions such as the tavern, the early blue laws "revealed the existence of sports and pastimes in a society where the dominant political and social force shunned these activities." It turned out that "many early Pennsylvanians had a strong need to play, and sports and amusements fulfilled that need" (Jable, "Pennsylvania's" 119, 121).

New York Colony

Dutch settlers came to New Netherlands in the New World in 1624, where in New Amsterdam (later named New York City) a trading post drew newcomers to the colony. The Dutch people brought sport and pastimes to the new colony as part of their culture and social customs. In the Dutch settlements along the Hudson River, taverns served as the principal site of recreation. There, both men and women played a game similar to handball. The Dutch also introduced a game called kolf, which bore some similarity to both golf and ice hockey in using a ball and a club to project the ball. Stray balls that hit persons or property proved harmful in the colony, and in order to regulate game play, an ordinance was put in place in 1656 at Fort Orange and Beverwyck. It stated that magistrates, "having heard divers complaints from the burghers of this place against the practice of playing golf along the streets, which causes great damage to the windows of the houses and also exposes people to the danger of being injured," thus determined that this "is contrary to the freedom of the public streets." Therefore, "their honors . . . hereby forbid all persons to play golf in the streets, under penalty of forfeiture of fl.25 for each person who shall be found doing so" (qtd. in Altherr, Part 1 158).

More popular was the game of skittles, a form of bowling. Patrons also found laughter in scaring cats caged in a barrel. The cats were released by throwing the bowling pins at the cage, which was broken open. Geese suffered a more drastic fate, as they were hung from ropes or trees, and the rider who could pull off the greased neck won the animal for dinner. The popular "gander-pulling" contest could also be played with the greased live goose suspended on a wire stretched between two poles, as an adventurous, active person attempted to pull down the geese while riding on horseback or moving through rapid water in a boat.

Rather than catering to a rigid religious vision that tended to constrain colonists' sporting activities and diversions, the New Netherlands settlement harbored various religious and ethnic groups. The heterogeneity of New York City included a range of religious and ethnic customs, along with diverse sporting practices. In 1654, the first Jewish settlers came to America when 23 Jews, including women and children, emigrated from Brazil to New Amsterdam. This marked the beginning of Jewish life in America, and, like other immigrants, they came for the promise of freedom of religion in the New World. The lack of rigid Sabbatarianism in New Amsterdam made it a logical starting place for such immigrants. Still, as in other colonies, strict observance of the Sabbath on Sunday remained a pronouncement of New Amsterdam's public officials. To uphold observance of the Sabbath, the Governor, Peter Stuyvesant, banned sporting and other physical activities deemed counter to the spirit of the Lord's Day. In January 1656, Stuyvesant proclaimed the rules for adherence to the Sabbath, announcing that Sunday was a day of "fasting and prayer for God's blessing[,] protection[,] and prosperity in trade and agriculture but principally for a righteous and thankful use of his blessing and benefits." The language of his order, however, shows very well what people actually did on Sundays! "We interdict and forbid, on the aforesaid day of Fasting and Prayer during Divine Services, all labour, Tennis-playing, Ball-playing, Hunting, Fishing, Travelling, Ploughing, Sowing, Mowing and other unlawful games as Gambling and Drunkenness, on pain of arbitrary correction and punishment already enacted against the same" (qtd. in Altherr, Part 1 5). Dutch officials enforced the Sabbatarian law once again during the following year, when records of a court case stated, "The officer, plaintiff, against Claes Hendericksen Meeuwes Hoogenboom defendants Gusbert van Loenen. The plaintiff says that Jan Daniel, the under-sheriff, reported to

him on the 7th of March, being the day of prayer ordered by the honorable director general of New Netherlands and proclaimed here, the defendants played hockey on the ice, demanding therefore that said defendants be condemned to pay the fine indicated in the ordinance." The defendants, however, gave a different view of events. "The defendants, appearing, maintain that they did not play hockey and promise to prove it. The parties having been heard, the court orders the defendants to produce their evidence on the next court day" (qtd. in Altherr, Part 1 462). When the British captured New Amsterdam in 1664, they renamed it New York. The Dutch pastimes, however, continued.

The colony's outdoor environs provided venues for men and women to participate in winter sports on the snow and ice, such as skating, sleigh riding, and hockey. British clergyman Charles Wooley observed the skating in New York City and noted it in his journal in about 1678. He commented on the lively skating: "And upon the Ice its admirable to see Men and Women as it were flying upon their Skates from place to place, with markets on their Heads and Backs" (qtd. in Altherr, Part 1 462–463). As late as 1748, a British subject claimed

Gander-pulling, a Dutch pastime, was a contest that involved pulling a greased goose from its hanging place.

Reprinted from J.A. Lucas and R.A. Smith, 1978, *Saga of American sport* (New York: HarperCollins), 546.

that "[t]he Dutch are a most unusual breed. They construct sleighs in the most fanciful fashion, some of them in the shape of swans and other water birds. They race them on the frozen ponds and they pretend that winter is not a season of cold and death. They also erect booths on the ice and spend endless hours skating and quaffing warm liquid out of pewter cups. Their penchant for racing on even the most fragile ice quickens the blood. They fly with great swiftness, mindless of the dangers to themselves and their horses" (qtd. in Twombly 22). The Dutch enthusiasm for ice skating, experienced by both women and men, would later appear evident in the success of female Dutch ice skaters in the modern Olympic Games, and in this middle colony the Dutch demonstrated great love of sport and amusements for men, women, and children.

Horse racing was established in America in 1665 when Governor Richard Nicholls founded the Long Island Course in New York.

© Bettmann/Contributor/Getty Images

Men and women of the New York colony also took part in bowling, ninepins, a variety of ball games using stakes or rackets, marksmanship, fishing, hunting, and archery. Thus, like other groups of colonists in British North America, the Dutch colonists made sport part of their experience. In more favorable climates in New York, horse racing gained popularity, as it did throughout colonial America. In 1665, Governor Richard Nicholls announced a horse race to occur near Hempstead, New York. While the race was mainly for improving the breed of horses, rather than amusement, it proved popular, and the swiftest horse was rewarded with a silver cup. More generally, horse racing gained popularity in various regions of the country. As it persisted in locales such as Philadelphia (with its Philadelphia Jockey Club), men of gentility and high social status patronized clubs for horse racing throughout the Northeast. By the nineteenth century, racing became widespread in American culture, and in both "North and South, there were racecourses on the outskirts of most large towns and many in smaller communities" (Larkin 283). The practice of Sunday observance as a day of rest, although common, faced challenges in the New York colony and elsewhere. "Virginians raced and gambled on horses, the enslaved in North and South tended their own plots and went to market in nearby towns, and fishermen in Marblehead, Massachusetts, repaired to taverns rather than church" (McCrossen 12).

Summary

People of diverse backgrounds—Native Americans, Europeans, and Africans—inhabited settlements in the New World and engaged in sporting forms and pastimes during the colonial years. The presence of peoples of various religious, economic, social, and political perspectives, with their diverse racial, ethnic, and gender identities, meant that colonists participated in a range of recreations and amusements in their patterns of work and play. Sporting activity was often engaged in informally, but for colonists of higher status and wealth, sporting pursuits also took place in more formal incarnations.

DISCUSSION QUESTIONS

1. How do the concepts of sport in the precolonization period and the period of American colonial development differ from current or more recent concepts of sport?

2. What are some of the characteristics of Native American sport?

3. In what ways did religion affect the growth of sport in the early American colonies?

4. Explain some of the similarities and differences between the sports played in various colonies.

5. What were the sporting experiences of African Americans in early colonial America?

6. Explain the ways in which men and women of various groups of colonial Americans participated in sport and how sporting practices illustrated gender differences.

Chapter 2

Sport and Pastimes in the American Revolutionary Era and Early National Period

1750–1820

CHAPTER OBJECTIVES

After reading this chapter, you will have learned about the following:

- How some traditional sports served practical purposes and persisted from the earlier colonial American period

- The Great Awakening's role in shaping attitudes about sport in various parts of colonial American society

- The importance of Enlightenment ideas in American sport, physical exercise, and care of the body

- The meanings of sport in frontier society

- How economics, consumer changes, and social rank shaped access to sport for Americans of diverse backgrounds

- The place of sport in the American Revolutionary era

- The role of sport and active recreation for women in the New Republic

- The nature of ongoing interest in the various uses of horses and horse racing

Revolutionary leader, diplomat, and inventor Benjamin Franklin (1706–1790) of Philadelphia embodied the characteristics of a self-made man. He stressed virtue and self-help—as well as physical and mental vigor—as American values. In both his thinking and his sporting pursuits, Franklin displayed colonists' increasing emphasis on individualism and on the practical education of mind and body through mental and physical exercise. He wrote in his autobiography about his belief in the importance of "Bodily Exercise":

> [As a young boy] living near the Water, I was much in and about it, learned early to swim well, & to manage Boats.... [I]n a Boat or Canoe with other Boys I was commonly allow'd to govern, especially any case of Difficulty.... [U]pon other Occasions I was generally a Leader among the Boys. (9–10)

During a sojourn in England, Franklin recollected his impressive swimming ability:

> I stripped & leaped into the River, & swam from near Chelsea to Blackfriars, performing on the Way many Feats of Activity both upon & under Water, that supris'd and pleas'd those to whom they were Novelties. I had from a Child been ever delighted with this Exercise, had studied & practis'd all Thevenot's Motions & Positions [in *The Art of Swimming*], added some of my own, aiming at the graceful & easy, as well as the Useful. All these I took the Occasion of exhibiting to the Company, & was much flatter'd by their Admiration." (53–54)

His triumphant swimming display prompted a British noble to ask Franklin to teach his two sons to swim. Sir William Wyndham "wish'd to have them first taught Swimming; and propos'd to gratify me handsomely if I would teach them. . . . [I]f I might remain in England and open a Swimming School, I might get a good deal of Money" (Franklin 55). He declined and returned to the American colonies but continued to pursue his interest in swimming, developing a wet suit for skin diving, and, at age 25, writing a book on swimming and the buoyancy of water (Twombly 39).

In a shift from earlier colonial culture, an increasing number of colonists in the eighteenth century stressed proper care of the body to uphold physical and moral health by using their own abilities rather than succumbing passively to God's will. In developing American society during a time of growing challenges to the bonds of the British Empire, some colonists asserted the place of human and individual agency rather than the view of God as all-powerful as asserted by earlier colonists. Franklin proved to be perhaps the most famous swimmer in American colonial history, and his experiences as a printer, statesman, reformer, civic-minded leader, and American revolutionary figure offered a shift from Puritanism by expressing confidence in human ability in endeavors ranging from physical activity to politics. These changed beliefs about the human body were joined by new attitudes toward the use of science and intellectual inquiry, all of which fed into new views of

Benjamin Franklin, colonial American printer, became a leading statesman and gained fame as an inventor, scientist, and promoter of moral virtues, as well as an advocate of physical ability.

Photo courtesy of Library of Congress, LC-D416-29337.

1730s–1750s	1750s	1756–1763	1764
■ First Great Awakening of religious revivals in American colonies	■ The Enlightenment in American colonies shapes new ideas about reason, the body, and science	■ Seven Years' War fought (also known as French and Indian War); ends with the signing of the Treaty of Paris	■ Sugar and Currency tax acts imposed by England

physical health and sport in colonial American culture.

In the 1700s, a growing quest for economic and political opportunity, and a desire to have a voice in colonial affairs in pursuit of democracy, brought about a change in the outlook of colonists on the eve of the colonies' fight for independence from England. Many colonial North Americans of varying social rank began shaping an American identity based on their experiences of religion, politics, sport, economics, and work. With many colonists focused increasingly on the quest for material wealth and status—catalyzed by growing individualism and faith in human ability—diverse views of sport and physical activity arose among the heterogeneous groups of colonists. Religious leaders, however, expressed deep concern about many colonists' pursuit of economic status and desire for material rather than spiritual wealth, and they worried that the rising values of freedom, self-improvement, and upward mobility threatened the fabric of American society. Thus, debate over the place of sport in this period of tremendous economic and population growth pitted certain colonists against others; the assorted viewpoints on sport and physical activities also played a part in the growing tension between individualism and maintenance of a rigid sense of community in American life during the revolutionary era.

Stated more generally, changes in colonial American life in the middle decades of the eighteenth century prompted a clash between "old" and "new" cultural values. Growing emphasis on science and reason, for example, conflicted with the Northeastern Puritans' emphasis on religion and Biblical codes. Some colonists purported their belief in deism, the notion of God as a sort of clockmaker, the original supreme creator of the universe who set events in motion and then stepped away. These cultural and religious changes in colonial American life, along with colonists' experiences during the American Revolutionary Period, altered ideas and activities related to sport in these decades when colonists shaped a new American society.

The Great Awakening and the Place of Sport

Amid the tensions between old and new values in the middle period of the eighteenth century, religious revivalism swept the colonies. This movement, known as the Great Awakening, involved not only religious inspiration but also a general ferment of new ideas about colonial American society, power, equality, and individualism. It produced a widespread experience—with religious revivals in all colonies touching all classes, ages, and races—and as the first intercolonial event the Great Awakening bound the colonies together in one step of a process that would culminate in the American Revolution. From 1730 to 1760, throughout the American colonies, "this quest for spiritual renewal challenged old sources of authority and produced patterns of thought and behavior that helped fuel a revolutionary movement in the next generation" (Nash et al., Brief 3rd ed. 101). The consequences of the Great Awakening in colonial America reached far beyond the religious sphere, and colonists' changing cultural values also affected sport. The call to colonists to awaken from their religious slumber came together with the clergy's powerful mid-eighteenth-century message that people should engage in moral pastimes and sport instead of vulgar and frivolous activity. Popular revivalism thus carried social and political implications that were reflected, among other things, in viewpoints on sport and the use of leisure time.

New England Colonial Awakening, Faith, and Pastimes

Religious and civic leaders in New England worried about the decline in Calvinist thinking and adherence to religious principles. The Puritan elite were alarmed by the increasing emphasis placed on good works and human reason by Benjamin Franklin, Thomas Jefferson, Dr. Benjamin Rush, and other colonial leaders who employed new scientific and intellectual approaches to understanding their world. In his famous 1741 sermon

1765	1766	1770	1773
■ Stamp Act and other taxation acts; colonists resist Stamp Act	■ Jockey Club founded in Philadelphia	■ Boston Massacre occurs	■ Boston Tea Party occurs

"Sinners in the Hands of an Angry God," Jonathan Edwards, of Northampton, Massachusetts, used a fire-and-brimstone approach to urge young people to seek salvation only through God's grace, rather than through the notions of human ability and good works. Edwards' forceful urging to those people straying from congregations and ignoring God's power, justice, and fury at sin awakened listeners and spread to other locations throughout New England; clergy members intensified their calls to curtail boisterous pastimes and unwholesome sports. George Whitefield preached to large audiences as an English believer of the Methodist branch of the Anglican Church, and he proclaimed a "new life" for colonial Americans in his tour of the colonies in 1739 and 1740. His emotional appeals in open-air revivals reached thousands of colonists, and he stressed that all souls—no matter one's status, race, gender, or age—could achieve conversion. This kind of public preaching to large audiences expressed democratic rather than traditional messages of faith, with the emphasis on devoting time to the soul rather than to amusement and sport. The clergy frowned upon horse racing, whether with white or black jockeys, as they did with other forms of frivolity. One itinerant Methodist minister in Virginia in 1772 complained to another about horse racing and black jockeys: "[A]s there was to be a horse-race that afternoon, I began to speak freely of the absurdity of it, and shewed [sic] how rediculus [sic] it is for gentlemen of sense to ride many miles to see two or three horses run about a field with Negroes on their backs" (qtd. in Altherr, Part 1 281).

Indeed, zealous clergymen such as Jonathan Edwards generally viewed sport and recreation, tavern activities (gaming, gambling, drinking), and animal sport as sins. Their admonition to colonists to uphold the Protestant work ethic, rather than waste time in such frivolous pursuits, spread throughout town and countryside. In passionate sermons appealing to the congregants to seek moral salvation, Edwards exclaimed, "Are there not some here who have debased themselves below the dignity of human nature by wallowing in sensual filthiness, as swine in the mire?" (Nash et al.,

Brief 3rd ed. 102). This intense call to conversion entailed spending time on church-going rather than tavern-going, and even elite New Englanders and leading citizens of the Northeastern cities needed to heed the religious message of the Great Awakening if they "awakened" to the societal changes after hearing such sermons.

The moral campaign of the Great Awakening also included efforts to enforce Sabbath codes and close taverns on Sundays. A Boston law specifically ordered that "[t]he Lord's Day not be prophaned [sic] by boys, or idle persons swimming or skating thereon, &c." Likewise, a Vermont statute of 1787 stated that no one "shall upon land or water, do any labour, business or work . . . of any kind whatever . . . nor use any game, sport, play or recreation, on the first day of the week or Lord's day." Such offenses were punishable by a fine of 10 shillings. In 1797, in Maine, one of the itinerant missionaries, Paul Coffin, a Congregationalist, assessed the residents as follows: "The people here are much reformed. Formerly, they lived in strife, excess in drinking, shooting on the Lord's day, &c. These vile practices are now forsaken" (qtd. in Altherr, Part 2 2–3). Traditional utilitarian sports touted as appropriate for health and exercise—such as fishing, hunting, and horseback riding—were still accepted.

Southern Colonies, Critics of Sport, and Social Elites

By the Revolutionary Era, the distinct development of regional cultures was clearly in evidence in the South, in New England, and in the Middle Colonies. The climate, soil, landscape, and slave labor that supported profitable tobacco and sugar crops in the South differed from those of the North, with its greater diversity of agricultural and industrial development (Cobb, *Away* 9–10). In 1785, Thomas Jefferson remarked upon what he saw as the differing demeanors of the newly independent residents of the United States: "In the North they are cool, sober, laborious, independent, jealous of their own liberties, and just to those of others, interested, chicaning, superstitious and hypocritical in their

1774	1775	1776	1776–1783
■ First Continental Congress held in Philadelphia	■ Second Continental Congress convenes ■ Battles of Lexington and Concord	■ Declaration of Independence signed	■ American Revolutionary War fought

Dr. Benjamin Rush

Dr. Benjamin Rush, Philadelphia physician and writer of medical and health books in the mid-1700s, and a signer of the Declaration of Independence, commented on sport and physical health based on his medical knowledge of the body. Using Enlightenment thinking, he combined scientific, medical, and moral stances in advocating practices to support a healthy mind and body. Rush urged Americans to pursue forms of exercise and sport that he deemed healthful, and his numerous sermons and books gave recommendations for physical education for students.

In 1772, Rush wrote *Sermons to Gentlemen Upon Temperance and Exercise,* in which he encouraged young men to pursue horseback riding, noting the significance of such sporting activity for the well-being of the gentlemen:

> RIDING ON HORSEBACK is the moſt manly and uſeful ſpecies of exerciſe for gentlemen. Biſhop Burnet expreſſes his surprise at the lawyers of his own time, being ſo much more long-lived . . . than other people, conſidering how much thoſe of them who become eminent in their profeſſion, are obliged to devote themſelves to conſtant and intenſe study. He attributes it entirely to their RIDING the circuits so frequently, to attend the different courts in every part of the kingdom. . . .

> But we ſhall hereafter mention another cauſe which concurs with this, to protract their lives. It may be varied according to our ſtrength, or nature of our diſorder, by walking-pacing-trotting- or cantering our horſe. . . . In riding, to preſerve health, eight or ten miles a day are ſufficient to anſwer all the purpoſes we would wiſh for. (qtd. in Altherr, Part 1 15–16)

Rush also joined fellow Philadelphian Benjamin Franklin in recommending that Americans of various ages engage in swimming:

> Too much cannot be ſade in praise of SWIMMING, or as the poet of Avon expreſſes it—"buffeting the waves with lofty sinews." Beſides exercising the limbs, it ſerves to wash away the duſt, which is apt to mix itself with the ſweat of our bodies in warm weather. . . . I would strongly recommend the practiſe of bathing, and ſwimming, frequently in the ſummer ſeaſon. (qtd. in Altherr, Part 1 29)

Rush commented on swimming for students in an essay he presented at a Methodist academy on August 2, 1790. He noted that because the Methodists banished every "ſpecies of play from their college . . . the healthy and pleasurable exerciſe of swimming, is not permitted to their scholars, except in the preſence of one of their maſters" (qtd. in Altherr, Part 2 22). He proposed what he viewed as appropriate physical activities for male youth in his 1790

Benjamin Rush.
Photo courtesy of Library of Congress, LC-USZ62-97104.

essay "On the Amusements and Punishments Proper for Schools." Lamenting that many youth had sedentary habits, he urged that "the amusements of our youth shall consist of such exercises as will be most subservient to their future employments in life," in particular supporting outdoor exercise and agricultural pursuits (qtd. in Hartwell 24). Rush's 1772 sermons gave a list of other sporting activities he also deemed healthful for males: "To all theſe ſpecies of exerciſe which we have mentioned, I would add, SKEATING, JUMPING, alſo, the active play of TENNIS, BOWLES, QUOITS, GOLF, and the like" (qtd. in Altherr, Part 1 224–225). Rush also encouraged appropriate education of women at the Young Ladies' Academy of Philadelphia. He suggested that "dancing might be pursued as a form of healthful activity" (Park, "'Embodied Selves'" 71). Other health and physical education writers offered advice about appropriate physical activities for women, which is discussed below.

Rush also advocated temperance and proper diet as part of his health reform program informed by the Enlightenment. In 1784, in his *Inquiry into the Spirituous Effects of Liquor on the Human Body and Mind,* he addressed the potentially horrible impact of hard liquor on physical and mental health. He said that beer, wine, and cider may be used for medicinal purposes but distilled spirits prove harmful to one's physical well-being. He urged Americans to alter their diets and to exercise to improve their physical health. The pamphlet "was a masterpiece. Its rational arguments, logic, and incisive examples made it both the century's most effective short piece and also a model for later temperance publications." In fact, by 1850 "more than 170,000 copies had been circulated" (Rorabaugh 40–41). Rush's widespread influence on eighteenth-century attitudes about physical exercise, sport, and care of the body persisted into the following decades.

religion. In the South they are fiery, voluptuary, indolent, unsteady, jealous for their own liberties, but trampling on those of others, generous, candid, without attachment or pretensions to any religion but that of the heart" (qtd. in Cobb, *Away* 10).

In the Southern colonies and rural areas, traveling or itinerant preachers rode on horses to bring their message of religious conversion to the varied population throughout the region. Such circuit riders appealed to diverse open-air crowds of Southerners, exclaiming that no social distinctions existed in the eyes of God and that all people—white and black, rich and poor, women and men—needed to engage in the religious experience. New denominations of Baptists and Methodists gained converts, and a growing number of colonists heard the message of equality and individualism in the circuit riders' sermons. By 1860, approximately 75 percent of Southern churchgoers adhered to the Baptist or Methodist traditions (Cobb, *Away* 48).

These "New Lights" preachers challenged traditional authorities and their mandated sporting patterns, and, foreshadowing ideas of the Revolution, focused on individualism rather than deference to the Southern elite. When these calls to resist the authority of one's "betters" were heard at revival meetings by ordinary white men and women, free and enslaved blacks, and lower-rank farmers, they accepted and applied them to the sports, gambling activities, and other trappings of leisure practiced by plantation owners and other Southern elites. Benjamin Latrobe, an architect who traveled throughout the new country, remarked upon his experience of a gentry gathering at a Virginia horse race on April 21, 1796: "Everybody here is so engaged in talking of Lamplighter, the Shark mare, the Carolina horse, etc., that I am as much at a loss for conversation as if I were among the Hottentots. . . . The concourse upon the race ground was very great indeed—perhaps fifteen hundred person. It cannot be of much interest to know that Lamplighter, the favorite of the field, upon which all the odds were laid, was beaten two successive heats, and came in only third. . . . I have now got into Mr. Shore's house for the day, and feel a little more at home than in the buzz of betting on the

course" (qtd. in Altherr, Part 2 303). Supporters of the Great Awakening desired to severely decrease just this kind of intense enthusiasm for sport and gambling expressed by Southern genteel society and upper-rank sportsmen in the region.

Thus the ministers and followers of the evangelical religious movement challenged the Southern gentry's control of the lower-rank colonists and slaves with their message of people of diverse backgrounds joining their crusade, as well as their displays of public prowess and shows of wealth in the form of sports and recreations. The religious leaders criticized the sporting activities and public recreations typically involving drinking and frivolity, such as horse racing, gambling, court day, cockpits, the muster field, and election day. The New Lights challenged both these social and sporting practices of Southern gentry and the traditional hierarchy they controlled: "Against the system in which proud men were joined in rivalry and convivial excess was set a reproachful model of an order in which God-humbled men would seek a deep sharing of emotion while repudiating indulgence of the flesh" (Isaac 168). Thus the rigid deference previously accorded to the Southern elite demonstrated at the race track, or in watching these gentleman planters as they engaged in field sports, gave way to newer values of equality and the fellowship of believers. By seeking to include lower-rank whites as well as slaves among their brothers and sisters, then, religious dissenters challenged not only the conspicuous display of sport and recreation exhibited by the Southern gentry but also the very order of traditional Virginia itself. As Isaac has stressed, "The social world of the Baptists seems so striking a negative image of gentry-dominated milieus that it must be considered to have been shaped to a large extent in reaction to the dominant culture" (163–164).

Elkanah Watson, an agriculturist and advocate of improved farming who promoted the benefits of practical competitions for American farmers (as discussed in chapter 3), criticized the behavior he witnessed at a bloody cockfight during a trip to Virginia with a prominent planter. He noted that "the moment the birds were dropped bets ran high,"

1783	1787	1788	1789
■ Peace treaty signed with England in Paris	■ Constitutional Convention held ■ Northwest Ordinance begins; expansion of land in the old Northwest	■ Constitution ratified ■ Messenger (top racehorse) imported from England	■ First U.S. Congress; George Washington elected president

and he commented on the vicious battle between the birds and the animated responses of the crowd:

> The little heroes appeared trained to the business, and not the least disconcerted by the crowd or shouting.... [A]dvancing nearer and nearer, they flew upon each other at the same instant with a rude shock, the cruel and fatals gafts being driven into their bodies, and at times, directly through their heads. Frequently one, or both were struck dead at the first blow, . . . and in the agonies of death would often make abortive effort to raise their heads and strike their antagonists. I soon sickened at this barbarous sport, and retired under the shade of a wide-spread willow, where I was much better entertained in witnessing a voluntary fight between a wasp and spider.

> qtd. in Riess, *Major* 27

Watson was not only alarmed by the deadly fight between the birds but also found his moral character jarred by the crowd of both genteel people and lower-rank spectators of the blood sport. He was "deeply astonished to find men of character and intelligence giving their countenance to an amusement so frivolous and scandalous, so abhorrent to every feeling of humanity, and so injurious in its moral influence," and he loathed the accompanying habits of "gambling and drinking, in the waste of time, and often in the issues of fighting and duelling" (qtd. in Riess, *Major* 27).

Despite moral criticisms, however, animal blood sport continued, as did unusual forms of hunting animals for sport rather than for food and healthful exercise, and accounts of such activity appeared in newspapers. Consider an article titled "Country Sport," reprinted in several newspapers (among

them the *Commercial Advertiser,* the *Hampden Federalist,* and the *Columbian Centinel*), which described a sporting event for men in Canton, Ohio, that took place on December 26, 1816:

> About the 1st inst. according to previous notice, a company of about 700 Men collected from different parts of Worthington, Ohio, where they organized themselves: had their hunting ground particularly marked out in a hollow square of an oblong from 5 miles wide by 8 long [8 by 13 kilometers]. In the centre of which was a mile [1.6 kilometers] square—They formed round the oblong and commenced their march toward the centre square about sunrise; and astonishing as it is not the less true, the result was in killed—2 Wolves, 3 Bears, 33 Deer, and 117 Turkeys.

> "Country Sport" 3

Thus traditional sports and social gatherings for men continued even as some Americans questioned the value of such activity in the new society.

Cockfighting drew spectators who gambled and enjoyed rowdy behavior at the matches.

Photo courtesy of Library of Congress, LC-USZ62-120656.

1791	1793	1800	1802	1803
▪ Bill of Rights ratified	▪ Eli Whitney invents the cotton gin	▪ Washington, D.C., becomes U.S. capital city	▪ National Race Course opens near Washington, D.C.	▪ Louisiana Purchase made

Consumerism and Changing Patterns of Colonial Life

In the 1760s, colonial Americans increasingly realized that their cultural world seemed to be differing from that of England, and they would soon seek to break away decisively from the English monarchy and English identity. Before that, however, as historian Carl Guarneri has discussed, the Atlantic system of trade "transmitted religious ideas as well as material goods" to the American colonies. The trends of the Great Awakening and increasing production of consumer goods traveled across the ocean together as American colonists began to acquire materials and goods beyond those needed for survival: "Without intending to, the Great Awakening aligned religion with the consumer revolution." It was only in 1763—and "[o]nly after Britain began reorganizing imperial relations" (Guarneri 86–87)—that Great Britain and the North American colonies moved toward armed conflict. The end of the Seven Years' War with the Treaty of Paris signed in 1763 initiated the taxation on the American colonies imposed by Great Britain to raise money for its war debts, and these economic restraints and severe political acts of taxation by England limited the colonists' economic and political freedom in American society.

At the time of the Great Awakening, the prominent role played by the British in the colonies and in Atlantic trade spurred changes in colonial American economic and cultural life. These shifts originated in Britain, where "the combined forces of urbanization, rapid population growth, and increased workshop production sparked a 'consumer revolution' that made more and more goods available to families above the poverty line. The Atlantic trade exported this consumer revolution by showcasing an 'empire of goods' to colonists" (Guarneri 85–86). Thus, in this period preceding the growth of tensions between the British Empire and the American colonists in the Revolutionary Era, an Anglo-American culture arose based in part on newly developing British practices and customs adopted by colonials aspiring to middle-rank status. The combination of rising incomes among colonial American families and decreasing prices of British manufactured goods meant that more material objects now found their way into American life. Items such as English teapots, cups, silverware, furniture, and clothing marked the new consumerism of middle-class American colonists. "Social occasions such as tea drinking and card playing became consumption rituals as well as opportunities to use special accessories or show off new possessions" (Guarneri 86). During economic hard times, this consumerist seeking of British goods would decrease and be manifest in strained relations between the colonists and the British Empire.

While some lower-rank colonists strived via the consumer revolution to obtain the trappings associated with the wealthier colonists, cultural and sporting trends were defined in no small part through the specification of certain places for given social classes to perform their sport and leisure activities. Historian Richard Bushman has suggested that those classed as ladies and gentlemen required appropriate environments for asserting their gentility and pursuing their pastimes: "Gentility did not suggest new activities for people; it elevated old ones. Singing, cardplaying, eating and drinking, conversing went on in every tavern. All that distinguished genteel drawing rooms was the manner of the people and the style of the objects that surrounded them" (xviii).

Taverns for refined men conducting business, politics, and social activities served different purposes than did the taverns for ordinary laborers, sailors, travelers, and other men seeking gaming, drinking, and sporting pastimes. Many taverns—sites of consumerism where patrons enjoyed food, beverages, hospitality, games, and sport—catered to colonists in the lower and lower-middle ranks of colonial America. They were frequently associated with men engaging in rowdiness, drunkenness, blood sport, and gambling. Such taverns became a target of reform and refinement by middle- and upper-class colonial officials. Massachusetts politician and patriot John Adams expressed deep concern about the rise of taverns, pronounc-

1804–1806	1806	1807	1810
■ Lewis and Clark Expedition conducted	■ American trotter Yankey runs a mile (1.6 kilometers) in 2:59	■ First agricultural fair (Berkshire, Massachusetts) founded by Elkanah Watson, with horse races and contests of physical skills and rural skills such as plowing	■ Tom Molineaux, a freed black man, loses English championship boxing match to Tom Cribb

ing them "the eternal Haunt of loose, disorderly People." Adams described the colonists who frequented taverns thusly: "Young People are tempted to waste their Time and Money and to acquire habits of Intemperance and Idleness that we often see reduces many of them to Beggary, and Vice" (qtd. in Bushman 161). In contrast, the City Tavern of Philadelphia, which opened in 1773, appealed to refined gentlemen such as Adams and other leaders of the Revolutionary Era. Adams met there with other delegates for the First Continental Congress in 1774, and it provided a place to honor patriotic leaders including George Washington at the end of the Constitutional Convention in September 1787. Other taverns, however, continued to attract a less refined sort of patron, and the boisterous crowd's drinking, gaming, and

The Man Full of Trouble Tavern in historic Philadelphia is the only surviving tavern building from pre-Revolutionary Philadelphia.

Photo courtesy of Library of Congress, HABS PA, 51-PHILA, 276-5.

gambling formed the heart of tavern culture. In this light, perhaps another colonial Philadelphia establishment, the Man Full of Trouble Tavern, was aptly named.

In urban areas with many taverns, some supporters of wholesome recreation urged curtailment of the drinking and amusements typical in taverns and encouraged steps to honor the Sabbath with worship rather than the sport of boys or youth pursuing outdoor physical recreation. On May 13, 1789, in Philadelphia, one correspondent begged

leave, through the channel of the *Federal Gazette,* to recommend to the *Corporation,* to LESSEN the number of taverns, huckſters, and dogs, in the city of Philadelphia and to paſs laws, to PREVENT the following evils. . . .

1. The noiſe of carriages from diſturbing places of public worſhip on Sundays.

2. The ſports of boys on Sundays every where, and of every kind, eſpecially ſuch of them as are carried on near places of worſhip. Swimming and ſkeating on Sundays, are improper. They corrupt our youth, and expoſe our city to the contempt of ſober foreigners.

3. The practice in ſome taverns of entertaining citizens on Sundays, eſpecially in the evenings.

4. Drunkeneſs, and profane ſwearing, by punishing both in the moſt exemplary manner.

5. Galloping horſes, through our ſtreets, whereby many children have been killed, or had their bones broken.

6. *Firing out the old year,* as it is called, whereby much miſchief has been done, and ſick people greatly diſturbed and injured.

"Philadelphia" May 13, 1789, n. pag.

In the rural areas of the Midwest, with population increasing in lands acquired via the Northwest

1812	**1815**	**1816**	**1819**
■ War of 1812 fight against Great Britain	■ Battle of New Orleans fought	■ First American yacht, *Cleopatra's Barge,* built in Salem, Massachusetts	■ *American Farmer* magazine founded by John Stuart Skinner to cover outdoor sport and rural health

Ordinance under President Thomas Jefferson, laws enacted to address gambling and sport in tavern culture cast such practices as immoral. An Ohio law of February 1, 1805, pronounced in one section

> [t]hat if any perſon licenſed to keep a tavern, or any retailer of wine, ſpiritous liquors or ſtrong drink, ſhall knowingly permit or allow of any ſporting or rioting in ſuch houſe, or on the premiſes, on the ſabbath, or at any time knowingly allow or permit any kind of betting or gaming for money or an other value, either at cards, dice, billiards, bowls, hovel-board, fives, or an other game of hazard or chance . . . , every ſuch tavern-keeper or retailer, on being thereof legally convicted before any court having cognizance thereof, ſhall, for every ſuch offence, be fined in any ſum not exceeding twenty dollars, at the discretion of the court, with coſts.
>
> qtd. in Altherr, Part 2 19

While many in the elite class forwent tavern visits in favor of their own leisure outings, they did not necessarily give up the sporting pursuits typically associated with these venues. As Bushman has explained, "Tavern life seemed degrading to the elite, yet they played cards and drank in their own parlors. Elegant tables, finely finished chairs, and the attire and posture of the players transformed the meanings of these activities" (53). In contrast to rural farmers and lower-rank people, colonial elites believed their amusements to be appropriate in their genteel culture as markers of their consumerism and leisure apart from ordinary folks.

The Enlightenment in America and Ideas of Sport and the Body

The Enlightenment drew on the seventeenth-century scientific investigations by thinkers who emphasized belief in human reason and the scientific method. Two such men were John Locke, who developed influential theories of the human mind and of political philosophy, and Isaac Newton, whose work on the laws of nature advanced the scientific revolution. The intellectual movement forged an age of reason and pursuit of progress and scientific discovery. In America, the gentry and well-educated colonists began to focus on rationalism and science rather than on Calvinist doctrines of faith. The Enlightenment also influ-

enced thoughts about sport and how the human body functioned.

In this vein, Benjamin Franklin hailed the advantages of turning to strategy and reasoning, rather than divine influence, in one's pastimes. In his 1779 essay "The Morals of Chess," Franklin wrote, "For life is a kind of chess, in which we have often points to gain, and competitors or adversaries to contend with. . . . [I]ts effects on the mind, be not merely innocent, but advantageous, to the vanquished as well as the victor" (Franklin 233). Thus adherents of the American Enlightenment combined intellectual and physical culture in order to delineate a rational mode of inquiry to investigate the world and human beings.

In 1810, a children's advice book titled *Youthful Recreations* stated that "it must be confessed, that youth is the time to obtain a stock of health, and that is best promoted by moderate exercise." The text continued:

> For he who ſits by the fire all day,
>
> And Never goes abroad to play
>
> May keep himself from being cold,
>
> But may not live till he is old.

The author of *Youthful Recreations* also promoted other advice and sporting activities:

> To prevent *bodily weakness and infirmity*, exercise is necessary. . . . To play with *battledore* [bat or racket] and *shuttlecock* or with a *trap and ball,* is good exercise." Furthermore, good physical health was not the domain only of wealthy children: "Children of the affluent, but even such of the poor who are impelled by necessity to pick cotton, card wool, to sit and spin or reel all day, should have at least one hour, morning and evening, for some youthful recreation. . . . [T]hey should at least play *Hop-Scotch.*
>
> qtd. in Altherr, Part 2 17

Physical education became part of the effort to train white Protestant American boys and young men of the upper class to fulfill their prescribed gender roles in the mid-eighteenth century. These boys, sons of better-educated fathers and members of genteel families, learned about health of mind and body as part of the Enlightenment mind-set. Because of their privileged way of life, many of these males did not perform physical labor in agriculture or other manual tasks to exercise their bodies. Supporters of physical education in the

Shuttlecock as illustrated in the book *Youthful recreations*, printed about 1810, which is in the Rosenbach Collection of Early American Children's Books in the Free Library of Philadelphia.

Reprinted from J. Johnson, 1816, Youthful Recreations. Accessed from HathiTrust Digital Library. https://babel.hathitrust.org/cgi/pt?id=mdp.39015065528781;view=1up;seq=20;size=75.

private schools for boys included Noah Webster and Dr. Benjamin Rush, both of whom were "decidedly favorable to bodily exercise of certain kinds." Webster, author of a hugely influential American dictionary, gave a speech on physical training for young men in Hartford, Connecticut, in 1790. In his "Address to Young Gentlemen," Webster stated that it "should be the business of young persons to assist nature, and strengthen the growing frame by athletic exercises." He urged that when "it is not the lot of a young person to labor, in agriculture or mechanic arts, some laborious amusement should constantly and daily be pursued as a substitute, and none is preferable to fencing. A fencing skool iz [sic], perhaps, as necessary an institution in a college as a professor of mathematics." Webster recommended, too, that these well-to-do young gentlemen partake of such sports as running, football (soccer), quoits, and dancing to offset their lack of physical training (qtd. in Hartwell 23–24).

Young white men of privilege in the United States received their training for political and business careers at institutions of higher education such as Harvard, Yale, Princeton, Brown, King's College (now known as Columbia University), William and Mary, and Thomas Jefferson's University of Virginia. These institutions were created to develop an educated male citizenship for demo-cratic and public positions. Their curricula included proper care of the body, mind, and soul, and they integrated physical activities into academic life to help students maintain a wholesome mind and body. The athletic pursuits, however, lacked the organizational and competitive structure of modern sports. At Yale, for example, a school law enacted by the college president and fellows on October 6, 1795, restricted sporting activity near the campus: "If any Scholar ſhall go a-fiſhing or ſailing, or more than two miles [3.2 kilometers] from the College, upon any occaſion, without leave from the Preſident, a Profeſſor, or a Tutor, shall undreſs himſelf for ſwimming in any place, expoſed to public view, he may be fined not exceeding thirty four cents." Princeton student James Garnett wrote about the sports he played in March 1813: "With respect to our amusements we have had a great many since the good weather commenced; in the vacant hours we exercise ourselves by running, jumping, throwing quoits and pitching." Timothy Dwight, Yale president, noted the sports played on campus by students in the early 1800s as part of his observances about learning and morals in New England: "Boys and men play at football, cricket, quoits, and at many other sports of an athletic cast; and in the winter are peculiarly fond of skating. Riding in a sleigh, or sledge, is also a favorite diversion in New England" (qtd. in Altherr, Part 2 25, 103).

The expansion of sport for male students at colleges would not occur until the early decades of the nineteenth century. In 1826, Harvard would become the first American college to start a gymnasium, and organized competitive sports would follow even later (as is explored in subsequent chapters). For now, the select young men in these academic and social contexts might heed the advice given on sport and culture by John Adams to his son John Quincy Adams: "I would advise you, my Son, in Skating, Dancing, and Riding, to be always attentive to this Grace," to perform such activities as skating not just with vigor but with "an Elegance of Motion" (qtd. in Bushman, 200–201). In the new nation, for the sons of republican men to achieve manly vigor, "economy, industry, and hardihood" must go together with grace and refinement (Bushman 201). As part of the cultural matrix in which these elite young men assumed their gender and socioeconomic privilege, then, certain kinds of sporting activity signified civility versus vulgarity and helped mark one's place in the new democracy.

International Perspective

GutsMuths and the Beginning of Physical Education

Johann Christoph Friedrich GutsMuths (1759–1839) has exerted a great and enduring influence on the development of physical exercise throughout the world. People from many countries have visited Schnepfenthal, Germany, where he lived and worked, and his writings have been translated into many languages. In 1802, an American edition of his *Gymnastik für die Jugend* (*Gymnastics for Youth*) was published in Boston but wrongly attributed to Christian Gotthilf Salzmann. The curious spelling of GutsMuths' name, incidentally, was his own invention.

After GutsMuths' studies, it was chance that brought him in 1785 to Salzmann's Philanthropinum in Schnepfenthal (Thuringia, Germany), a school which was to become the center of GutsMuths' activities for 50 years. The philanthropists—literally, "friends of mankind"—were committed to the ideas of the Enlightenment and conceived a revolutionary pedagogy based on the responsibility of individuals for themselves, their potential for development, and their striving for perfection. Their (utopian) aim was to create a new kind of human being: an enlightened citizen guided by reason. A further revolutionary idea was that of a holistic education to improve the body as well as the mind. The philanthropists were of the opinion that reason could develop only through practical experience and cognition—that is, through the senses—and consequently that physical education and bodily exercise were indispensable. The Philanthropinen were boarding schools in which these ideas were put into practice.

In Schnepfenthal, GutsMuths developed the first systematic form of physical education based on the new pedagogy and named it after the gymnastics of Greek antiquity. In his most important work, *Gymnastik für die Jugend* (1793), GutsMuths expounded on the significance of physical exercise in an education founded on reason and intended for practical use. At the Philanthropinen, the (male) pupils were taught a wide variety of physical exercises ranging from running, lifting, and carrying to balancing and climbing. The program of the pupils' physical activities included not only games but also gardening and hiking. Nearby lakes provided opportunities for swimming in the summer and skating in the winter. Assuming that one's surroundings could be taken in only through the senses, the philanthropists schooled their pupils' faculties of seeing, hearing, and feeling. The philanthropists' ideas of respecting childhood, self-fulfillment, and the importance of play and games were based on notions of utility: From their perspective, play meant "work under the mantle of youthful joy" (GutsMuths, "Gymnastik" 209).

After the turn of the century, GutsMuths was increasingly influenced by nationalistic political ideas. In his last book on gymnastics, a manual for the "sons of the fatherland" appearing in 1817, he tried to achieve a synthesis of his gymnastics system and that of Friedrich Ludwig Jahn's Turnen, which aimed at the liberation of Prussia from the French occupation and the unification of Germany as a nation-state (Pfister, "Cultural").

Frontier and Backcountry Sport

In contrast to citizens of the growing cities and rural communities witnessing the resurgence of religion and morality—as well as the urban centers disseminating new scientific ideas, inventions, and views of health and the body—those living in the less populated frontier or backcountry areas, with their harsher landscapes, faced a different set of physical demands in daily life and in sporting activity. House or barn raisings brought frontier settlers together in a communal purpose and provided opportunities for sport. An Illinois resident in the first decade of the nineteenth century asserted that "The whole neighborhood assembled and split rails, cleared land, plowed up the field, and the like. In the evenings of these meetings, the sports of throwing the mall, pitching quaits [quoits], jumping and the like, generally closed the happy day" (qtd. in Altherr, Part 2 20).

Historian Elliott Gorn has analyzed this rough-and-tumble way of life for frontiersmen and the physical, brutal sports these men embraced as a demonstration of their honor in rural areas. No-holds-barred fighting held an important place in the culture of the Southern backcountry. Gorn has explained that contestants began their brawl in an outdoor space that the spectators surrounded, and "fighters battled each other until one called enough or was unable to continue. Combatants boasted, howled and cursed" (Gorn, "Gouge and Bite" 36–37). The pummeling, gouging, and pulling of the opposing fighter's eyes, hair, or other body parts demonstrated the physicality of the fighter who withstood the violent battle to claim victory. These fierce fights were viewed as a way for rough-and-tumble fighters to defend their honor and physical skills in rural Maryland, Virginia, Georgia, and in frontier regions of Kentucky, Alabama, and the Carolinas, where the harsh environment forced inhabitants to struggle for existence through hunting and subsistence farming. Thus, rather than the work ethic, temperance, and moral and religious values touted by government officials and clergy in colonial towns and settled communities, the backwoods culture of frontiersmen and their families exalted other values and skills. As Gorn has remarked, "eye-gouging matches were focal events in the culture of lower-class males who still relished the wild ways of old"; whereas the upper-class or educated "gentleman's code of honor insisted on cool restraint, eye gougers gloried in unvarnished brutality" (Gorn, "Gouge and Bite" 39, 49).

Numerous accounts of the violent sport described the bloody and brutal fights witnessed by spectators in the backcountry. Travelers from other countries were astonished by these sporting brawls, and their recordings of what they witnessed in their journeys through the American backcountry vividly expressed their wonder at such fights. A French traveler to Virginia in 1791 detailed the frontier style of fighting: "The manners of the poor people of that region are rude and violent. They swear, get drunk, gamble and fight often. They have a way of fighting which is not in use among the Americans in the East. The fighters use their fists, feet, and teeth. They are of one mind to gouge each other's eyes out." He also noted that the spectacle took place "amid applause from the ferocious circle urging them on." A traveler in Virginia in 1796 claimed that "[i]t is by no means uncommon to meet those who have lost an eye in combat, and there are men who pride themselves upon the dexterity with which they can scoop one out. But what is worse than all, these wretches in their combat endeavour to their utmost to tear out each other's testicles. Four or five instances came within my own observation, as I passed through Maryland and Virginia . . . [and] in the Carolinas and Georgia . . . the people are still more depraved in this respect than in Virginia." He concluded "that in some particular parts of these states, every third

33

Rough fighting in the Southern backcountry enabled men to show their physical skill and pride by incurring and inflicting bodily injury in these brutal sporting contests.

Photo courtesy of Lilly Library, Indiana University, Bloomington, Indiana.

or fourth man appears with one eye" (qtd. in Altherr, Part 2 135–137).

In recounting what they saw during travels in the backcountry, some critics noted gender-related and socioeconomic aspects of these rituals in which rural men fought against other men to degrade each other's honor and body. Men exhibited their physical courage and pride in these sporting brawls and defended their own honor and the honor of family members in their violent clashes. One 1798 account claimed that

[t]he citizens of North Carolina, who are not better employed, spend their time in drinking, or gaming at cards and dice, in cock fighting or horse-racing. Many of the interludes are filled up with a boxing match; and these matches frequently become memorable by feats of gouging. . . . The victor for his expertness, receives shouts of applause from the sporting throng, while his poor, eyeless antagonist is laughed at for his misfortune. . . . [T]his more than barbarous custom is prevalent in both the Carolinas, and in Georgia, among the lower class of people.

qtd. in Altherr, Part 2 135

The practice of gouging spread throughout the backwoods areas of the frontier. Some Easterners believed that half of the residents of Kentucky no longer had eyes by 1793 and that, a decade later, nearly a third of the Pennsylvania Germans had only one eye. A Connecticut resident traveling through the Pennsylvania area wrote that he "saw one day a horse with one eye, carrying on his back the husband, wife and child, each with only one eye" (qtd. in Altherr, Part 2 138). A few years later, in Ohio, a traveler tried to comfort a man whose nose had been bitten off in a fight, but the victim replied, "'Don't pity me, pity that fellow over there,' pointing with one hand to another who had lost an eye, and showing the eye which he held triumphantly in the other" (Altherr, Part 2 141).

Despite laws against maiming or gouging in New York, New Hampshire, Pennsylvania, Kentucky, Illinois, Indiana, Louisiana, Tennessee, Georgia, and Missouri, the practice persisted. In the frontier areas, and especially in the South, rough-and-tumble fighting held cultural significance; men expressed their honor and physicality in their efforts to be the victorious combatant. A South Carolina backcountry judge aptly summarized the sporting practice of gouging and fighting in the American backcountry in this declaration: "Before God . . . I never saw such a thing in the world before. There is a plaintiff with an eye out! A juror with an eye out! And two witnesses with an eye out!" (qtd. in Rader, *American Ways* 77).

Though this fighting without rules between fellow frontiersmen of equal or similar status was commonplace, other types of fights were staged at times to highlight social class and race differences. Southern sportsmen who owned plenty of land and slaves and thus assumed elite status in their patriarchal, hierarchical culture would sometimes stage boxing matches that pitted slaves against one another, and this ritual carried its own meanings, as explored in the next chapter.

International Perspective

Boxing and the Civilization Process

Norbert Elias (1897–1990) was one of the most distinguished sociologists of the twentieth century. In his major two-volume work *The Civilizing Process*, he emphasizes the links between social conditions and the human psyche, taking as his example the changes in both rules and behavior in post–Middle Age Europe. The growth of towns and the establishment of royal courts and aristocracies led to increased "chains of interdependence," which led to the concentration of power in the sovereign state and to the internalization of control in individual subjects.

Elias is one of the few eminent sociologists to have dealt with sport in his writings. In "The Genesis of Sport as a Sociological Problem," he applied the basic principle of his civilization theory to sport, demonstrating that the norms and rules of physical activities, along with their structures and patterns of interpretation, are dependent on the particular level reached in the civilization process. Elias constructed a link between the brutality of the sport of pankration (similar to ultimate fighting) in Greek antiquity and the idealization of the warrior, and the dependence on nature and the inability to plan ahead and the way that war and violence were taken for granted in this period of history.

Pankration was reportedly invented by the heroes Hercules and Theseus, who fought using a combination of wrestling and boxing. In antiquity, pankration was part of the Olympic contests and was also used in training soldiers. Many different forms of combat were involved, and everything was allowed with the exception of biting and gouging out the opponent's eyes. The match ended when one of the contestants conceded defeat, was knocked unconscious, or was dead, and deaths were a regular occurrence. If the match had not been decided by sunset, the contestants struck each other alternately with their fists until one of them gave in.

According to Elias, contact sports with rules governing the way they are carried out reflect the "standards of civilized behaviour" in modern societies. In wrestling, and especially in boxing, rules were successively introduced to reduce the dangers to life and limb and then later to prevent injuries altogether. Numerous rules and regulations—addressing, for example, which areas of the body one is allowed to hit, as well as weight classes, ring dimensions, number and length of rounds, rest breaks, gloves, mouthpieces, head protection (in amateur boxing), and, last but not least, the role of a referee, who can end an unequal match—transformed boxing from a fight to the death into a sport which meets the standards of civilized conduct in industrial nation-states. Whether the various subcultural "ultimate" combat sports with "no holds barred" signify a regressive step in civilization is a point of discussion, not the least because civilization processes are not linear but occur in long-term surges and waves (Elias and Dunning).

Women's Active Recreation in the Revolutionary Era and Early National Period

Gender prescriptions defining white women's roles remained in force in the early eighteenth century. Whereas upper-class white males might participate in some sport and physical exercise at the new colleges, such as Harvard and Princeton, young women were barred from attending such institutions. Indeed, women at this time in colonial American society faced restrictions imposed by a patriarchal culture and religion, including gender expectations assigning them to roles in the domestic realm as wives, mothers, daughters, sisters, and upholders of moral values that they were expected to share with the family at home and in places of worship, rather than attending facilities of education that seemed suited only for men and boys. During this time, women possessed no legal, political, or economic rights, although many were keenly aware of the rights, privileges, and legal standing of their husbands and brothers of the middle and upper classes, who garnered social and political positions and public deference. During the Enlightenment in America, a few eighteenth-century writers posited that, "[s]ince the limbs and organs of both sexes are basically the same," there "must be one best diet, regimen and type and amount of exercise to develop the human body regardless of the sex of the individual" (Park, "'Embodied Selves'" 71–72). But such viewpoints remained far from the mainstream commitment to separate educational, social, and sporting behaviors for women and men. Women's domestic responsibilities, along with society's prohibition of travel by morally upright women without chaperones or families, limited their chances of partaking in the popular recreations of Southern gentry or Northern gentleman in billiard halls, cardrooms, and taverns.

The noncompetitive physical activities of walking, gardening, bathing, and even horseback riding—practical, active recreations deemed healthful for the female constitution and for supporting the domestic care of children—might be pursued by some women, depending on their age and status and the urban or agricultural setting in which they lived. As distinguished historian Allen Guttmann has written, "None of the contests that we commonly classify as sports was thought suitable for women"; in fact, in early America, women's sports "were limited to husking bees, quilting contests, and other competitions directly related to women's domestic labor" (Guttmann, *Sports: The First Five Millennia* 119). Women who attended public sporting displays might contribute their domestic skills in providing food, but their status apart from the male participants in the active recreations reaffirmed the gender differences enforced at the time. The social interchange at public gatherings such as shooting matches, muster days, court days, and the like did at least offer some relief from women's mundane daily tasks. Women of lower rank might support their husbands or brothers embattled in the rough and brutal fighting on the frontier by joining spectators who witnessed the public contest. In the early national period, observer Daniel Drake noted that these civil affairs typically gave way "to a heterogeneous drama of foot races, pony races, wrestling, fighting, and general uproar" (qtd. in Larkin 274).

In society's genteel ranks, the rowdy and gambling crowds of young men, male laborers, and travelers seeking respite from the road at taverns were deemed inappropriate company for women of religious faith and middle- and upper-rank social status. Thus, while taverns might accommodate women as travelers in appropriate quarters, "their barroom clienteles were almost exclusively male" (Larkin 282). Those places setting themselves apart from the slew of typical taverns in early American cities—"a tiny handful that polite society called their own"—hosted dinners and balls for the leading political figures and the social elite. Taverns for genteel entertainment contrasted with those catering to the "lower-class vices—cursing, fighting, lewdness, and drunkenness" (Bushman 161, 164). In these finer taverns, no bearbaiting, gambling, or vulgar behavior greeted the women, who instead enjoyed refined social events. So, too, card games played by young women in the refined environments of their private homes contrasted with such games played in the public gathering spots. Bushman has described differences in the pastimes of the higher and lower socioeconomic classes in early American culture: "Cards played on a mahogany table by the light of candles in silver holders, the genteel must have believed, was different than cards in the greasy hands of a day laborer in a dark tavern with a mug of beer at his elbow." Elite women, like their male counterparts, could enjoy their leisure activities in a beautiful environment that in their view "helped to change ordinary forms of vulgar entertainment into cultivated expressions of enlightenment and civilization" (Bushman 52).

The daily lives of children were similar during the 1700s, before they learned tasks to perform along gender lines. Young girls might enjoy some of the same recreations and pastimes near their home environs that young boys engaged in. For example, girls and boys both enjoyed playing games such as hide-and-seek and tag, and they pursued outdoor sporting activities such as sledding and skating. The physical activities of "both sexes mixed competition with collaboration but the boys placed a stronger emphasis on their rivalries and the girls stressed their cooperation more heavily" (Rotundo 34). As girls got older, their play diminished, while boys pursued more physically rigorous sports and games, and at that point gender identity in sport manifested the separate gender roles in American society. Some American women and men, however, probed the physical capabilities of women to participate in sport and active recreation, and in the early decades of the nineteenth century some women began to engage in more physical activities and sport. Even in the last decades of the eighteenth century, "an increasing number of American men and women argued that women were far more capable, stronger, healthier—and even wiser—than they were customarily pictured to be; or at least they could become so if their development were not arrested by social customs and false and limiting conceptions of their abilities" (Park, "Embodied Selves'" 91). The social activism of women and men seeking to expand sporting and physical activities for women is addressed in following chapters.

Native American Sport

While the white male citizens of the new republic struggled with the meanings of democracy and the quest for social mobility, and females, too, sought to identify their place in the new republic, the indigenous tribes contended with the usurpation of their lands, the imposition of an alien culture, and pressure to assimilate to the white world. By 1791, a French nobleman who observed Native Americans in the Northeast claimed, "The games of their children are those of ours; they have ball and tennis, racing and shooting with the bow, for youth" (qtd. in Altherr, Part 2 66). By the turn of the nineteenth century, the Oneida tribe of western New York had adopted quoits while continuing the sport of archery. Fur trader Daniel Williams Harmon observed the Assiniboine archers of the Northern American (Canadian) plains in the early 1800s and remarked, "Their youth, from the age of four or five to that of eighteen or twenty years, pass nearly half of their time in shooting arrows at a mark; and to render the employment more

interesting, they always have something at stake, which is generally nothing more than an arrow, or something of small value." He judged the archers to be "the best marksmen, perhaps, in the world. Many of them, at the distance of eight or ten rods [44 to 55 yards, or 40 to 50 meters], will throw an arrow with such precision, as twice out of three times, to hit a mark of the size of a dollar" (qtd. in Altherr, Part 2 66). But not all tribes assimilated willingly or peacefully. On the Western frontier, the Apaches of Arizona resisted white incursions throughout the nineteenth century, and as early as 1807 U.S. soldiers feared their bowmen. Writing in about 1807, Lieutenant Zebulon Pike stated that their arrows were more than a yard (or meter) long: "With this weapon they shoot with such force as to go through the body of a man at a distance of 100 yards [91 meters], and an officer told me that in an engagement with them, one of their arrows struck his shield and dismounted him in an instant" (qtd. in Altherr, Part 2 66).

The most popular indigenous sport continued to be lacrosse. Throughout the 1780s and 1790s, white observers wrote accounts of games they witnessed among the Iroquois Confederacy in New York, the Shawnees of Kentucky, the Creeks of Alabama, the Cherokees of Tennessee, and the Chickasaws of the Mississippi Valley, as well as the Ottawas of the Lake Superior region. The Corps of Discovery, sent by President Thomas Jefferson to explore the lands of the Louisiana Purchase from 1804 to 1806, witnessed a game among the Mandans of the Dakota region. Zebulon Pike, who explored the Great Plains and the Rocky Mountains, also wrote of seeing a lacrosse game: "[T]his afternoon they had a great game of cross on the prairie, between the Sioux on the one side, and the Puants (Winnebagoes) and Reynards (Fox) on the other." The wagers reached sums up to the amount of some thousand dollars at that time, Pike reported, and the game featured 200 to 300 participants. Pike stated that "the Sioux were victorious—more I believe, from the superiority of their skill in throwing the ball, than by their swiftness, for I thought the Puants and the Reynards the swiftest runners" (Altherr, Part 2 422–427, 427–428 [quote]).

Sporting Practices During the American Revolutionary War

The changing cultural, social, political, religious, and economic landscape in the American colonies was marked by a series of moves and countermoves leading to the heightened tensions of the 1760s and 1770s, when the colonies sought independence from the English crown. The fight for freedom and democratic principles of equality, however, did not extend to blacks, indigenous peoples, women, or poor whites. During the American Revolutionary Period, ideas about tempering sport and leisure pursuits revealed the serious nature of the impending political, social, economic, and military challenges in the young nation. The shift in the colonies toward challenging the social and political power of the elites who controlled resources and property—and the joining together of colonists to battle England in the Revolutionary War—generated a cautious view of sport during the war and in the new nation at the end of the eighteenth century.

As the American Revolution approached amid increasing tensions with England—linked to the monarchy's decision to impose harsh taxes and curtail political freedom and assemblies in the colonies—the moral and political rhetoric of colonial patriots allowed little room for gaiety, popular recreations, and sport in forging an independent American nation. The work ethic, rather than a play ethic, pervaded the colonial struggle for independence in the 1770s and 1780s. In struggling to implement the possibilities of democracy, individualism, liberty, and political freedom to dissolve the ties of empire with England, colonial advocates of independence called for diligence, morality, and hard work. Political and religious leaders gave little opportunity for the luxuries of leisure and sport, instead urging the American people to unite in the arduous struggle for freedom from England and establish a republican form of government in the new nation. The patriotic leaders and political thinkers in the new republic believed the inhabitants of the nation needed to pursue virtue and self-improvement in moral activities rather than indulge in offensive and wasteful pastimes.

The American colonists convened the First Continental Congress in 1774 in Philadelphia to respond to increasing hostilities with Britain, and in this step toward establishing a democratic governing body the place of pastimes and sport became part of the deliberations. A resolution passed that the colonies "discountenance and discourage every species of extravagance and dissipation, especially all horse-racing, and all kinds of gaming, cock-fighting, exhibition of shows, plays, and other expensive diversions and amusements" (qtd. in Rader, *American Sports* [2004] 16). In these tumultuous years leading to the colonists' rebellion, the focus on the national crisis curtailed the time and

means for engaging in sport. When the Congress ratified the Declaration of Independence of the 13 colonies on July 4, 1776, however, the grand celebration did allow for sport and amusement. Indeed, on July 3, in Philadelphia, patriot John Adams had written to his wife Abigail in Massachusetts about the momentous occasion: "I am apt to believe that it will be celebrated by succeeding Generations, as the great anniversary Festival. . . . It ought to be solemnized with Pomp and Parade, with Shews [sic], Games, Sports, Guns, Bells, Bonfires and Illuminations from one End of this Continent to the other from this Time forward forever more" (Adams 115). Of course, this tradition of celebrating American independence with games and sport persisted, and in 1816, the *New Hampshire Patriot* published an article describing events that took place on the 40th anniversary of the nation's founding: "Salutes of artillery were fired at sunset, and sports, festivity, and fire-works, closed the evening. . . . Independence was proclaimed on every hill and reverberated on every valley. It

George Washington helped foster the idea of physical fitness and military might as exhibited in his physical stature and prowess on horseback.

Photo courtesy of Library of Congress, LC-USZ62-72497.

was as if all had sworn a confirmation of freedom before gods and men" ("Fortieth Anniversary" 2). American celebrations of Independence Day would include different activities as new sports were developed in the early nineteenth century.

In the newly formed republic, politicians and other authorities continued to mark out a place for moderate and useful sport, the value of which had been manifested in the sporting skills and physical vigor displayed by many soldiers and generals during the American Revolution. Virginia planter George Washington, a key Revolutionary War general whose considerable physical ability had served as a model for his men in the Continental Army, later did the same for all citizens as president of the United States. Washington "set an example for his men by taking part in sports when he could find time in his busy schedule." He played ball games and wicket, a form of cricket. Moreover, Washington's physical health and commanding public presence, exhibited in his magnificent patriotic leadership, also popularized his favored pursuits of horseback riding and foxhunting. Other soldiers played "fives," a variation on handball, as well as the bowling game of ninepins, familiar to many colonists (Ledbetter 30–32), and of course the physical abilities displayed in horsemanship and swimming proved useful in various wartime situations. Washington promoted sports in correspondence in 1777 in Norristown, Pennsylvania: "Games of Exercise for amusem't, may not only be permitted but encouraged" (qtd. in Altherr, Part 1 16). In his diaries, he recounted foxhunting outings in Virginia in several entries:

19 March 1773: "Went a hunting. Found a Fox by Muddy hole Plantation and killd it after a chase of two hours 3 Quarters."

5 October 1773: "Went a hunting in the Neck with Mr. Custis & Lund Washington. Found a Fox & after runng. it two hours & half lost it."

5 December 1785: "It being a good scenting morning I went out with the Hound. . . . Run at different two foxes but caught neither. My French Hounds performed better today; and have afforded hopes of their performing well, when they come to be a little more used to Hunting and understand more fully the kind of game they are intended to run."

10 January 1786: "Rid to my Plantation in the Neck, and took the hounds with me. About 11 Oclock found a fox in the Pocoson at Sheridens point and after running it very indifferently and treeing it once caught it about one Oclock."

Altherr, Part 1 378, 387; Part 2 354–355

Washington also helped publicize the specific need for physical fitness for military might: "Bodily accomplishments have ever been assigned a prominent place in the codes of the soldier and the gentleman; and every outburst of military ardor in our history has led to attempts to engraft certain kinds of technical training upon the general training of the rising generation" (qtd. in Hartwell 24). Both the Revolutionary War and nineteenth-century wars in the United States followed this pattern.

Use of Horses

The practicality and popularity of the horse in American life persisted after the Revolutionary War. Thomas Benger of Pennsylvania took steps to improve the breeding stock of American horses by importing a famous British racehorse, Messenger, to Philadelphia. Derived from Arabian thoroughbreds, Messenger produced a line of great champions that included American Eclipse, Whirlaway, Man o' War, Swaps, and Secretariat (Twombly 29). An American breed known as the Morgan horse also emerged in the post-Revolutionary era in Vermont. The breed originated with a small horse, owned by Justin Morgan, that "had the strength of a beer-wagon brute and the style and speed of a thoroughbred." The horse worked the field during the week, reputedly hauling loads greater than his own weight, while winning races in Vermont and western Massachusetts on weekends. With such remarkable qualities, the horse was prized as a stud, and he fathered a line of horses that dominated harness racing throughout the nineteenth century (Twombly 33–34).

Various forms of horse racing spread throughout the United States, and early U.S. presidents demonstrated their horsemanship. In particular, "George Washington and Thomas Jefferson took immense pride in their horses and bred them to improve the bloodlines of saddle, work, carriage and racehorses." Washington helped organize races in Alexandria, Virginia, and was recognized as an excellent horseman himself. While Jefferson was president, he frequently rode horses for exercise, and he "rarely missed the meets at the National Race Course in Washington, D.C., which opened just outside the city boundary two miles [3.2 kilometers] north of the White House in 1802" (White House Historical Association n. pag.).

Racecourses also appeared elsewhere in the new nation and drew keen interest. In 1806, the American trotter Yankey covered a mile (1.6 kilometers) in just under 3 minutes. Organized horse racing in the South was centered in New Orleans, where a racetrack was constructed on the nearby Hampton plantation by 1815. That venue was supplanted by the Metairie track in 1837, as New Orleans became the hub of modern sport in the region (Guttmann, *Sports: The First Five Millennia* 121). The following advertisement from the *City Gazette* in Charleston, South Carolina, on February 26, 1816, gave racegoers the list of horses for the day:

> *Sports of the Turf.*—This day, at 12 o'clock, will be run for, over the Washington Race Course, the Proprietor's Purse of *One Thousand Dollars*. For this race, which, it is supposed, will be the best contest during the week, the following horses have been entered:
>
> Mr. Winn's r. h. Ringleader, 5 years old, 95 wt. pink dress.
>
> Col. Richardson's s. m. Miss Fortune, 6 years old, 95 wt. blue and red.
>
> Mr. Singleton's s. g. Little John, 5 years old, 95 wt. black and red.
>
> Commodore Dent's Rattler.
>
> *Sports of the Turf,* n. pag.

Horse racing would continue as a popular sport, and new forms began to develop, as explored in subsequent chapters.

Sport for Exercise

Political officials in the new republic urged people to engage in sport for physical well-being and invigorating exercise, rather than for wagers or profit seeking. As John Adams engaged in his patriotic duties in the American Revolutionary Era, he offered the following thought to his learned, independent-minded wife Abigail on raising their children in their Massachusetts home: "[M]ake your children *hardy, active* and *industrious*"—qualities viewed as virtues for this next generation of Americans in the early Republic (qtd. in Bushman 199). Those sports deemed valuable for moral and physical health gained the approval of republican leaders, even as they criticized what they saw as the idle amusements, sports, and vices current in European powers. Toward the goal of promoting healthful exercise, "what may well have been New England's first sports association, the Shad and Salmon Club of Hartford, [was] organized in the 1780s to promote outings and a series of fishing contests" (Daniels, *New England* 170). For yeoman farmers, gentlemen, and patriots, these outdoor sports invigorated the body and engaged one in

nature rather than in violent activity, and, while they had been popular for some time, they now featured an organized format in which upstanding male New Englanders could partake of outdoor excursions enabling appropriate exercise in their communities.

The growth of outdoor sports for white middle- and upper-rank men continued in the Philadelphia area with the establishment of organizations for sport and physical recreation. One of the long-standing and influential fishing clubs of the United States, the Schuylkill Fishing Company, was founded in 1732 and expanded in the latter decades of the eighteenth century. In promoting exercise, sport, and sociability, the "Schuylkill Fishing Company of the State in Schuylkill," known also as "The Colony of Schuylkill," was founded by followers of Philadelphia Quaker William Penn. The club linked its fishing privileges to Native American inhabitants (the Quaker faith called for peaceful relations with the Indians) who lived along the Schuylkill River by paying homage to Tammany or Tamamend, "a band chief of the Delaware or Lenni-Lenape Indians," whose name meant "the affable" or "the worthy one" (MacGregor 393). To honor Tammany as its patron and saint, the sportsmen of the Schuylkill Fishing Company "established a saint's day for the Indian chief—the first of May, the day that marked the official opening of their fishing season"—a ritual that "was celebrated to assure a successful season of fishing" (MacGregor 393–394). Members of this club enjoyed catching fish and partaking of other recreations on the water, as well as hunting in the woods. After the American Revolution, the company became known as the State in Schuylkill.

Records of the Schuylkill Fishing Company reveal the sports that its members enthusiastically pursued in the Philadelphia area through the nineteenth century. Earning membership in the club was "by no means easy," as no gentleman was "placed on the roll of probation until eight members signif[ied] approval." After then serving an apprenticeship for at least six months, the candidate had to be supported by a majority of club members in order to gain admission and join other members in pursuing "on the banks of the river the fishing, fowling, and feasting." Each member of the club was "provided with his own bateau, tackle and bait, apron, hat, etc." In the eighteenth century, the club's officers met regularly in the building known as the Castle near the Schuylkill River (Watson 291, 293–294, 296–297). Members wrote about their sporting experiences, as in this

A print of men and women trout fishing, published by John Walsh & Co. in the nineteenth century.
Photo courtesy of Library of Congress, LC-DIG-pga-03304.

communication from William Parsons to Thomas Stretch, governor of the Schuylkill Fishing Company, regarding fishing by the club on May 7, 1775: "And as to what relates to the Fishery of the several Waters within the limitts of their Embaſsy they have been very aſsiduous not only in searching for and catching but in dreſsing and eating of Fish" (qtd. in Altherr, Part 1 214). In addition, the group's records indicate the types of fish these sportsmen encountered in their outings. In *A History of the Schuylkill Fishing Company of the State in Schuylkill, 1732–1888* a member chronicled the following:

> Circa 1789: "That Mr. Benjamin Scull, the *Prince of Fishermen*, produced a Trout, which he this day took in Schuylkill that measured *fifteen inches*" [0.4 meter].
>
> 15 September 1791: "Be it remembered that on the fifteenth day of September last, a *Sturgeon* of four feet [1.2 meters] in length, leaped on board one of the vessels belonging to the fleet, opposite to the Castle, of which the company then present, made a delicious repast."
>
> qtd. in Altherr, Part 2 233

The men in this club also enjoyed engaging in other upper-class sports with leading citizens of Philadelphia. Several members also held membership in the elite Gloucester Fox Hunting Club—for example, Samuel Nicholas, admitted to the Schuylkill Fishing Company as member No. 102 on May 1, 1760, who was among the 27 founders of the Gloucester club in 1766, as well as First Officer of the American Marines in 1775. Gloucester members marked their covenant this way: "We the subscribers, being about to provide and keep a kennel of Fox Hounds, do mutually agree with each other in the manner following," with further text outlining the amount to be paid as well as rules and regulations that members would follow. Members of both the Schuylkill Fishing Company and the Gloucester Fox Hunting Club included leading Philadelphians such as John Dickinson, Levi Hollingsworth, Thomas Mifflin, Robert Morris, and Samuel Morris Jr. (Fagan 3, 9, 11–14).

Republican Motherhood

For white American women of the new republic, the Revolution's promise of freedom failed to include them, and the gender-based constraints they faced in many areas of life extended to sporting endeavors and pastimes. Abigail Adams, wife of Revolutionary patriot John Adams, urged her husband in her correspondence in 1776: "In your new code of Laws, I pray you remember the Ladies." Moreover, she remarked pointedly on the authority of men in the patriarchal system: "Do not put such unlimited power in the hands of the Husbands. Remember all Men would be tyrants if they could" (qtd. in Kerber 12, 23). During the Revolutionary War, women participated in political acts such as staging boycotts, signing petitions, and aiding husbands and sons in managing businesses, but they did not gain suffrage or other rights in the new republic, as the Revolution fell short of extending equality and freedom to women. Instead, a new ideology developed regarding women's relation to the political sphere, with a particular focus on the prescribed roles for the female gender. In this young democracy, the notion of women's roles in the republic emerged to praise the value of mothers as educators, nurturers, and child bearers who raise sons to be virtuous, active citizens in a democratic society. Their Revolutionary War experiences prompted some women to consider the male, public, political sphere as not solely isolated from their domestic sphere, since, as "Republican Mothers" (Kerber 146–147), they could be involved in the republican society by utilizing their domestic skills as guardians of the home, thus imparting virtue and morals to their children for participation in democracy.

To fulfill these gender-specific domestic roles in helping to shape public affairs in the new nation, some women argued for access to education in female academies, since better knowledge and skills in reading, writing, and caring for the health of family members could prepare women to be better mothers. This would expand white women's influence beyond the home, but such influence stemmed from their gender-based domestic role—women's sway in the public would be derived from domestic power rather than equality in the American republic. The education in female academies emphasized female attributes in training young women to became mothers and wives. In the idea of Republican Motherhood, supporters "at least recognized the importance of health as the state in which women must exist to fulfill that ideal." At this time in the early republic, however, "they had not . . . moved concertedly to link physical performance and sport and health" (women would do this in the early nineteenth century). Women in various regions continued to engage in walk-

Abigail Adams of Massachusetts wrote about women's experiences in the American Revolutionary Era, supported women's expanded opportunities, and reminded her husband, patriot John Adams, to consider the role of women in the new nation.
Photo courtesy of Library of Congress, LC-USZ62-112534.

ing, riding, and gardening; after 1790, therefore, "the everyday sporting life of 'republican mothers' changed little" (Struna, "'Good Wives'" 247, 249). At the end of the eighteenth century, gender lines remained in force in American society in sporting practices and political customs.

White women of the middle and upper classes might participate in some of the acceptable sports for health and outdoor exercise. In the Northeast, winter sports included sledding, with women and men sometimes participating together. In 1794, British traveler William Priest described sledding in Philadelphia:

> The chief amusement of the country girls in winter is sleighing, of which they are passionately fond, as indeed are the whole sex in this country. I never heard a woman speak of this diversion but with rapture. . . . The tavern and innkeepers are up all night; and the whole country is in motion. When the snow begins to fall, our planter's daughters provide hot sand, which at night they place in bags at the bottom of the sleigh. Their sweethearts attend with a couple of horses and away they glide with astonishing velocity; visiting their friends for many miles round the country.

qtd. in Altherr, Part 2 441

Abigail Adams expressed her viewpoint on hunting, a typically male sport, in a letter to Thomas Brand-Hollis on September 6, 1790:

> A lovely variety of birds serenades me morning and evening, rejoicing in their liberty and security; for I have as much as possible, prohibited the grounds from invasion, and sometimes almost wished for game laws, when orders have not been sufficiently regarded. The partridge, the woodcock, and the pigeon are too great temptations to the sportsman to withstand.
>
> qtd. in Altherr, Part 2 330

A woman in Philadelphia who recorded her own experiences with sleighing in wintertime expressed her displeasure at the amusements that took place in taverns after a sleighing excursion for outdoor exercise. Ann Warder, wife of a British merchant, wrote in her diary on December 7, 1786:

> After dinner Jerry Parker took Sally, Lydia, and myself and son, out sleighing, which I found much more agreeable than expected. We met several parties starting out as we returned. This pastime is abused; large parties collect and riotly go together to taverns where they sup and return at all hours of the night.
>
> qtd. in Altherr, Part 2 440

For Republican Mothers, the public sphere of taverns and rowdy sport went against the moral and gender codes of the late eighteenth century.

The manly worlds of politics, sport, and public institutions remained generally off limits for women in the gendered structure of early American life. The opening of early educational academies to middle- and upper-status women, however, would be part of a long path toward defining women's roles in American society and sport in the next century. The emphasis on the heroism and physical skills demonstrated by men in the Revolutionary War—and on the strength and courage possessed by male leaders of the government—indicated in negative fashion the limitations on freedom and equality for women in American society generally and in sporting experiences particularly. As historian Linda Kerber has explained about the Revolutionary Era and the early republic, "Men took pride in qualities that distinguished them from women." For men such as George Washington, John Adams, and Thomas Jefferson, "who remodeled the American polity after the war remodeled it in their own image. . . . Women's weakness became a rhetorical foil for republican manliness" (11).

Turn of the Nineteenth Century and Societal Patterns

The passion for sport demonstrated by some citizens in both the urban and rural areas of American society in the eighteenth century may have been tempered by the realities of the Revolutionary War and the ensuing need for the American people to focus on building the new nation. In the early decades of the nineteenth century, however, changing economic, social, political, and cultural contexts in both city and country life shaped new forms of sport and physical activity, examined next in chapter 3.

The War of 1812, known as the Second War for American Independence, again called on the military and physical strength of American soldiers to defeat the British. The use of the horse by such military heroes as Andrew Jackson, a future president of the United States and a skilled horseman, added to a spirit of optimism and growth in the nation. The final victory at the Battle of New Orleans by the United States ushered in rapid economic, social, cultural, technological, and population changes in the first half of the nineteenth century. Such changes influenced viewpoints on sport and transformed the types and organization of sport experienced by men and women in American culture.

Summary

As the colonial society matured into a new republican nation, breaking its bonds with England, the physical activity evident in American life involved traditional sports that were often organized locally in informal contests. Yet several sports came under fire from religious proponents of the Great Awakening and from genteel political leaders who challenged them as immoral and impractical in the expansion of a new American society. On the frontier, at the horse track, and in the tavern, competitive forms of sport were often accompanied by gambling and consumerism that contrasted with the moral and religious pursuits encouraged by preachers. In addition, amid intellectual trends of the Enlightenment, economic trends of the consumer revolution, and the vicissitudes of the American Revolutionary Era, sport in the early national period was also shaped by the realities of social class, race, gender, and locale, with white men being the main partakers of sport and public culture.

DISCUSSION QUESTIONS

1. Why does sport have a place in American culture during times of economic, political, or military conflict, as occurred during the American Revolutionary Era?

2. On what basis did religious critics and preachers of the Great Awakening argue the need for American colonists to abstain from certain sports and activities?

3. Why was the Enlightenment important in promoting sport and physical education in the young nation, and who were some of the leaders in this promotion of sport for exercise?

4. Explain differences in men's and women's sport and leisure activities during this period. How were these differences influenced by traditional gender roles?

5. What sporting activities seemed important in forging the new republic, and why?

Chapter 3

Antebellum Health Reforms and Sporting Forms
1820–1860

CHAPTER OBJECTIVES

After reading this chapter, you will have learned about the following:

- The importance of antebellum health reformers in promoting a positive attitude about exercise and sport

- The role of both women and men in advocating sport and physical education for women

- Views of rural health and sport for women and men in the Antebellum Era

- The development of sporting journalism and its influence on antebellum American culture

In his widely acclaimed article "Saints, and Their Bodies" (first published in *Atlantic Monthly* in March 1858), Thomas Wentworth Higginson, health reformer and advocate of vigorous sporting activity, proclaimed the moral and physical benefits of sport for Americans in the vibrant period of change in antebellum American culture. Higginson linked morality and muscles, especially for men, as key preparation for filling their roles in a democratic nation: "There is in the community an impression that physical vigor and spiritual sanctity are incompatible" (583). To counter that prevailing attitude, Higginson urged a new outlook on sport for a strong nation of sturdy men and moral vitality:

> Physical health is a necessary condition of all permanent success. To the American people it has a stupendous importance, because it is the only attribute of power in which they are losing ground. Guarantee us against physical degeneracy, and we can risk all other perils. . . .
>
> We love to encounter in the contests of manhood those whom we first met at football, and to follow the thoughts of those who always dived deeper, even in the river, than our efforts could attain. . . . [W]e may hope for a reaction in favor of bodily exercises. And when we once begin the competition, there seems no reason why any other nation should surpass us. . . .
>
> But even among American men, how few carry athletic habits into manhood! . . . Full grown men are, of course, intended to take not only as much, but far more active exercise than boys. . . .
>
> Passing now to out-door sports (and no one should confine himself to in-door ones,) we . . . rank water first. A square mile even of pond water is worth a year's schooling to any intelligent boy. A boat is a kingdom. . . .
>
> [M]eet Nature on the cricket ground or at the regatta; swim with her, ride with her, run with her, and she gladly takes you back once more within the horizon of her magic, and your heart of manhood is born again. . . .
>
> "Saints" 585–586, 589, 591, 592–593, 595

Higginson and other like-minded antebellum reformers campaigned for causes including education reform, abolitionism, woman's rights, and temperance. These reformers expressed nationalism in seeking to establish a populace made up of strong, vital, and moral citizens—after the War of 1812 and especially during the antebellum years—in order to advance the young democratic nation. To counter criticism that the United States was a nation of weak, puny, nonathletic citizens when compared with those of England and other countries, activists such as Higginson touted health reform and strove to promote gender-based physical training for men and women. Higginson, especially, posited that these reform movements must rest on the sound moral and physical health of individual citizens, and, in this time of rapid change, a large portion of the white middle class in urban and rural settings placed increasing emphasis on physical exercise: "A restlessness and a slowly growing desire for physical freedom and expression seemed near. The apostle for this new awareness was Thomas Wentworth Higginson" (Lucas, "A Prelude" 54).

Thomas Wentworth Higginson, health reformer and advocate of physical activity.

Image courtesy of Library of Congress, LC-USZ62-73367.

1819–1830	1820	1820–1860
■ *American Farmer* edited by John Stuart Skinner	■ Missouri Compromise passes	■ Antebellum reform movements: health reform, physical exercise, publications on sport and health for men and women, critics' attacks on sporting activities deemed immoral

Overview of the Antebellum Period

The process of transformation in the first half of the nineteenth century in the United States involved social, economic, geographic, technological, and religious changes, and, in turn, these changes shaped the health and sport movement of antebellum America. The United States strove to define itself as a separate nation, with its own customs and culture, and sport became a part of this cultural expression. Although the English language was retained, many British customs and practices, as well as forms of governmental organization and democracy, took on a very different cast. The nature of the American people and society was also brought into question by the continuing development of differing regional lifestyles within the expanding country. The regulation of the physical and spiritual body emerged as central concerns in the largely white, Protestant, slaveholding republic, which of course was also populated by Native Americans, free and captive African Americans, Hispanics, an increasing number of newer European immigrant groups, and groups of Asian immigrants coming to the western United States. The transformation of a traditional, rural, agricultural society into a modern, urban, industrial one in the North—through the application of science and technology from the early 1800s to the eve of the Civil War—shaped the twin movements to pursue physical health and sporting forms for diverse groups of people in the young nation. In this chaotic period, rural–urban interactions and inevitable tensions between rural and urban values came to light in ideas put forward about sport by many voices (both male and female) for reform.

In other facets of culture, citizens of the new republic strove to carve out a clear sense of what it meant to be an American. U.S. authors created literature with a specific focus on distinctly American stories, such as "Rip Van Winkle," *The Last of the Mohicans*, and *Moby-Dick*. Some women, including Harriet Beecher Stowe, author of *Uncle Tom's Cabin*, questioned the patriarchal nature of American society, with its ongoing practice of slavery and the domination of political and economic life by white men. A small group of particularly articulate woman's rights supporters called for equal rights and suffrage in their "Declaration of Sentiments," modeled after the Declaration of Independence, at the 1848 woman's rights convention held in Seneca Falls, New York, marking the beginning of the woman's rights movement in the United States. Noteworthy American women Elizabeth Cady Stanton and Susan B. Anthony led this effort in the antebellum years. During these decades of active social reform and social change, groups of ethnic and religious immigrants also sought to establish their place in the American polity and society.

In the Antebellum Period, the United States expanded both in population and in territory, and this growth influenced sport in various parts of the nation and for sundry groups of Americans. After 1820, a growing number of immigrants made the hard journey to America. German, Irish, Jewish, and English immigrants, as well as some Asian immigrants to the West Coast, swelled the population and typically migrated to the burgeoning cities. In the 1830s, about six hundred thousand immigrants came to the United States, and during the 1830s through the 1850s, five to six million people had immigrated to America (Walters). In 1815, 18 states existed in the Union, and Louisiana was the westernmost of them. By 1860, the nation included 33 states, including California and Oregon on the Pacific coast. This expansion of land and people was marked by growing belief in Manifest Destiny by white, middle-class Americans. This ideology held that westward expansion revealed the destiny of Americans to succeed and fulfill God's plan for the American nation, which gave them a divine right to conquer the land and its native inhabitants. Manifest Destiny provided a moral mission for expansion from the East to the West and encouraged land-hungry settlers to move ever westward, creating a frontier society even as urbanization took hold in the Northeast. Many American families in the Midwest left places like Missouri to seek a better life and acquire farm land in the West, and some went west to a region they thought might improve the health of family

1821	1823	
▪ First public high school opens in Massachusetts	▪ Catharine Beecher founds Hartford Female Seminary, offering physical and domestic education for females ▪ Monroe Doctrine proclaimed	▪ Round Hill School founded (Massachusetts) and includes physical education as an integral part of the curriculum ▪ North–South horse races staged: American Eclipse defeats Sir Henry

members. They crossed the Overland Trail in the 1840s in an arduous journey to new lands.

Manifest Destiny led American settlers into Texas, at the time still a territory of Mexico, in the early nineteenth century. There, white settlers mixed with Mexicans in another frontier society, and their labor and leisure intertwined as Mexican vaqueros' work skills of riding and roping evolved into the sport of rodeo. Hunting and fishing provided both sport and sustenance, and gambling at cards, billiards, and horse racing consumed hours for many men. At least three horse tracks existed in Texas by the early 1830s (Dyreson, "Sporting" 278). For women, quilting remained both a pastime and a necessity, and community dances sometimes lasted through the night. Despite such pleasures, frontier life proved difficult and violent. Both white and Tejano (denoting a Texan of Mexican descent) settlers in Texas revolted against their government in 1835, producing the independent republic of Texas, which was annexed by the United States in 1845. Continued conflict with Mexico erupted into the Mexican-American War from 1846 to 1848, which resulted in the U.S. acquisition of California and the Southwest.

The Gold Rush of 1848 brought fortune seekers, most of them single men, to California from around the world (including China), creating a polyglot society of immigrants of different backgrounds and faiths, such as Jews, Protestants, and Catholics. Among the varied recreational pastimes introduced were bull-and-bear fights and snow skiing. The latter proved practical for mail delivery during the winter. Downhill skiing was popular in the mountainous regions of the western United States, and, as farm families began emigrating from the Midwest to the western frontier along the Overland Trail in search of better land and economic opportunities, women joined in this sport as well.

During the Antebellum Era, reform campaigns were fueled by the Second Great Awakening, a spiritual fervor spread in revival settings in which many Americans experienced a zeal for religion. In this religious movement, antebellum health reformers usually linked physical health with moral and spiritual health. One's spiritual well-being went

BULL AND BEAR FIGHT. California

Bull-and-bear fights in the early nineteenth century proved a popular pastime in frontier communities.

Art and Picture Collection, The New York Public Library. *Bull and Bear Fight.* New York Public Library Digital Collections. Accessed September 21, 2016. http://digitalcollections.nypl.org/items/510d47e1-42eb-a3d9-e040-e00a18064a99.

hand in hand with one's physical well-being in the tenets of the Awakening's millennialism; that is, belief in a thousand-year reign of peace and prosperity starting with Christ's return to earth required citizens to possess good moral and physical health. During the Awakening, Baptists and Methodists made particularly strong gains in the South, and by 1860 almost 75 percent of Southern Christians adhered to one of the two denominations (Cobb, *Away* 48). Despite such religiosity, however, different regions of the country continued to disagree over the issue of slavery.

Views of human variety were affected by efforts throughout the nineteenth century to establish the nascent field of anthropology's scientific credentials by means of racial studies and analyses of ethnic, socioeconomic, and gender groups. White American scholars studied Native American tribes and noted physical, social, and cultural differences. They generally deemed Native Americans to be heathens or, at best, "noble savages." Ventures into pseudoscience in the early decades of the nineteenth century, at a time when doctors and medical professionals had not yet articulated

1825	1828–1836	1830s–1840s	1831
■ Erie Canal opens ■ First trotting track opens (Long Island, New York)	■ Andrew Jackson serves as U.S. president	■ Second Great Awakening occurs	■ *A Course of Calisthenics for Young Ladies* published ■ *Spirit of the Times,* founded by William T. Porter, publishes sports results

professional standards, also included those who claimed to determine one's interior makeup from physical characteristics. Phrenologists studied the structure of and bumps on human skulls in order to judge mental faculties, and physiognomists examined facial features in order to judge character. The mid-nineteenth-century scientific revolution set in motion by the works of Charles Darwin provided greater impetus to the focus on differences and classifications. Scientists generally debated the number and types of races but labeled the various cultural groups as savage, barbarian, or civilized. Theories of evolutionary progress put forward by Anglo-Saxon scientists typically placed Anglo-Saxon Protestant groups at the apex of a proposed racial hierarchy. The stereotypes associated with such rankings became rationalized, justified, and entrenched, as the general public assumed the legitimacy of this purportedly scientific research. Belief in the survival-of-the-fittest paradigm was used to rationalize the continual westward expansion of the country and the related taking of Native American land and Mexican territory. With backing from the government, U.S. settlers considered it their God-given right, and their country's Manifest Destiny, to spread their particular form of civilization to supposedly less-advanced peoples. While the skin color with which one was born served as a major determinant of social acceptability, other qualities—middle-class social values and aspirations, standards of decorum, and a specific brand of morality—required diligence.

Some scholars have used the term *whiteness* to describe this standard of acceptability in the new American society. Whiteness afforded particular rights and privileges in American society, which generated a quest for it that persisted into the twentieth century. But whiteness in this sense meant more than skin color. Poor or working-class whites also lacked social capital, and Catholics, Jews, and other non-Protestants failed the test due to their religious convictions. The southern and eastern European immigrant groups that followed the Irish to the United States faced similar strident discrimination: One New York commentator stated, "[i]t is no uncommon thing to see at noon some swarthy Italian . . . resting and dining from his tin kettle, while his brown-skinned wife is by his side" (Jacobson, *Whiteness* 56). Slavs worked the blast furnaces in factories, "which were too damn dirty and too damn hot for a white man" (Arnesen 18). Some Americans described Jews as lecherous peddlers with high-bridged noses, thick lips, and bulging eyes, and regular newspaper cartoons reinforced such stereotypes in the form of caricatures (Diner).

This myriad of changes in the United States altered culture, landscape, and sport and pastimes. While Americans overwhelmingly worked the land on their own farmsteads or as farm laborers in rural areas, an increasing number of people flooded into urban areas of the North to pursue new forms of labor in an industrial context. Thus even as the rural agricultural society persisted in some regions of the country, people in the growing Northeastern cities developed new modes of manufacturing products and new ways of making a living, and these changes provided the context for new sporting forms and consumption of information about sporting activity.

Amid massive changes in population, land expansion, immigration, and new forms of transportation, such as turnpikes and the first railroad (the Baltimore and Ohio in 1828), white middle-class Americans often looked around and saw problems to solve in order to ensure the growth of American society. Reformers, those men and women who sought to improve society by working both with individuals and with social structures, contemplated new ways to shape American society. Reform movements—such as the antislavery crusade, temperance campaign, the woman's rights movement, education and health reform, and sport campaigns—held some characteristics in common. Antebellum reformers believed in the new beginnings of their democratic society, and no problem was so great that it overwhelmed their optimism. The evil of slavery could be abolished; women could win the right to own property, vote, and earn a living wage; the sin of drunkenness could be eradicated; education for the young could be provided in public schools to develop an educated

1832	1833	1835	1836
▪ Black Hawk War fought	▪ Oberlin College founded (first coeducational college)	▪ The Great Foot Race (international pedestrian race) is sponsored by John Cox Stevens and held at Long Island's Union Course	▪ Battle of the Alamo fought

citizenry for democracy; and physical weakness and bad diet could be mended through appropriate health practices, sport, and exercise.

Health Reformers

As reform activists sought to improve the physical constitution of antebellum Americans, the historical context of the health and sport movement was shaped by gender, socioeconomic, and rural-versus-urban distinctions. In their critique of the social, physical, and moral condition of American citizens, reformers such as Catharine Esther Beecher, Thomas Wentworth Higginson, Sylvester Graham, Dr. William Andrus Alcott, and Mary Gove Nichols—along with other white, middle-class activists—envisioned an ideal society in which robust individual and collective health would serve as the basis of American culture. These reformers found plenty of problems to address in the changing cultural conditions of the urban environment.

In their campaign to save American society by resolving the ill health of its citizenry and providing suitable sporting activities, antebellum health reformers advocated a plan for self-help. Thomas Wentworth Higginson, a soldier and minister who graduated from Harvard Divinity School, supported athletics, favored abolition and woman's rights, and promoted the value of robust health and the benefits of sport in articles published in popular magazines and books. He stated in 1859: "Health is the central luminary of which all the stars that spangle the proud flag of our common country are but proud satellites" (Higginson, "The Murder of the Innocents" 355). Like-minded reformers of health and physical well-being presented good hygiene as a moral obligation and bad hygiene and disease as evil; whether the obligation was to God, the race, the nation, or oneself, failure to fulfill the laws of health constituted immorality. The gospel of health exemplified the religious zeal of antebellum reform activism (Borish, "The Robust Woman"; Cayleff; Whorton).

Dr. William A. Alcott (1798–1859) wrote numerous books and manuals urging both men and women to reform their ways in order to achieve bodily health and pursue sports that he deemed morally appropriate. His popular works—including *The Young Man's Guide* (published in 1833 and in many later editions), *The Young Woman's Guide*, the *Library of Health*, and *The Laws of Health: Or, Sequel to The House I Live In*—addressed health, hygiene, sport, and recreation. In these self-help manuals, Alcott proclaimed his view that for Americans "healthy bodies meant healthy spirits" (Park, "'Embodied Selves'" 88). In *The Young Man's Guide*, Alcott denounced gambling as immoral and clearly identified the sporting activities he viewed as useful: "Gaming is an evil. . . . Let me warn you, then, my young readers,—nay, more, let me *urge* you never to enter this dreadful road." Alcott further asserted that gaming led to a horrible alliance: "I mean gambling, intemperance, and debauchery." Instead of these unwholesome practices, Alcott recommended selected recreation and sporting activities for young men: "Recreations they must have; active recreation, too, in the open air. . . . Some of the most appropriate are playing ball, quoits, ninepins, and other athletic exercises; but in no case for money." He also listed skating as a good outdoor sport (qtd. in Menna 15–17, 19). He also wrote manuals about physical health addressed to young women, which are discussed later in this chapter.

Other health reformers in middle-class antebellum culture urged urbanites to partake of wholesome exercise and pay attention to their stomachs in seeking a healthy diet. Sylvester Graham postulated a more radical idea known as the vital force theory. Graham believed that particular foods excited the nervous system, leading it to possible temptation. He thus linked food and nutrition to morality and declared that people ought to abstain from alcohol, coffee, tea, spices, meat, and other foods that might excite the stomach and harm digestion. To combat the perceived effects of such unhealthy foods, he invented a bland substance known as the Graham cracker. Another reformer interested in improving the body, Mary Gove Nichols, promoted hydropathy, or the water cure, as a means to vigorous health and care of women's health ailments. She described hydropathy in her *Experience in Water-Cure* (1850),

1837	1837–1838	1841
■ Mount Holyoke (all-female school) requires student exercise ■ Financial panic of 1837 occurs	■ "Trail of Tears" (forced relocation of Cherokee tribe) occurs	■ Catharine Beecher publishes *A Treatise on Domestic Economy, for the Use of Young Ladies at Home, and at School*; best seller on women's domestic activities and need for physical health

asserting that immersing the body in water baths and using cold water to clean the body provided refreshment, and that appropriate exercise and loose-fitting clothing enabled a woman to pursue better health (Cayleff 36).

Proponents of the health and sport movement concluded that the poor habits of urban men and women—be they horrible eating practices that led to dyspepsia, or a failure to practice invigorating outdoor exercise—led to their lack of physical vigor. Instead, activists argued, city folks should pursue the kind of activity that (so the reformers believed) farm folks of the past had engaged in. Higginson had the following to say about his middle-class contemporaries who exhibited frail health: "Dolly the Dairy-Maid is becoming to our children as purely ideal a being as Cinderella" (qtd. in Borish, "Benevolent America: Rural Women" 949). Recurring images appeared during the nineteenth century of the healthy farm family partaking of fresh air and wholesome physical activity; in contrast, urban health reformers decried the physical weakness of contemporary Americans in cities. Higginson concurred with Catharine Beecher's findings in assessing the serious problem of female ill health, but he focused primarily on males in diagnosing the poor health of Americans in the Antebellum Era. Yet it was not just urbanites and males alone who succumbed to dyspepsia. A farm journalist in *The Plow: A Monthly Journal of Rural Affairs* in 1852, queried, "Who Has Got The Dyspepsia?" and berated, "Don't all speak at once. We know most of you have got it" (qtd. in Borish, "Benevolent America" 321).

Muscular Christianity

In his famous 1858 article "Saints, and Their Bodies," Thomas W. Higginson argued that energetic health went hand in hand with men's productive activities and religious beliefs. A sound mind

People & Places

Almira Phelps

Almira Hart Lincoln Phelps (1793–1884) promoted female education and advocated physical education in her curriculum. Phelps wrote several textbooks and essays that were influential during the nineteenth century, beginning with *Familiar Lectures on Botany* (1829). One of her most significant books, *The Female Student, or Lectures to Young Ladies on Female Education,* first published in 1833, emphasized the importance of physical exercise in addition to academic exercises in the classroom for white middle-class students. Like her counterparts (male and female) in the health reform movement, Phelps included gymnastics for women in her recommended program (Chisholm 738). The following excerpt from *The Female Student,* titled "Health [and] Neatness," suggests Phelps' view of physical education and female gymnastics:

> The term physical education is used in reference to the improvement which can be effected in the human frame and the senses, by a proper system of discipline. . . . The body is an instrument which the mind directs; and as in this state of existence they must dwell together, it becomes of great importance that they should mutually promote the welfare of each other. . . .
>
> Calisthenics [from two Greek words, signifying grace and strength], or female gymnastics is very properly becoming a branch of education. I have, however, seen with regret, that many of you appear to engage in physical exercise with reluctance, as if every moment taken from your studies were time lost. With the view already given of the intimate connection between the mind and body you must be convinced that the latter cannot with impunity be neglected. (qtd. in Menna 20, 21–22)

1840s	1843	1844	1845
▪ Immigrants moving westward on Overland Trail	▪ First collegiate rowing club forms at Yale	▪ Telegraph invented by Samuel Morse; enables rapid communication of news and sporting results ▪ New York Yacht Club founded	▪ Texas annexed

and body would enable white, urban, middle- and upper-class men to pursue important opportunities in business and politics. Physically and morally fit men could support their families with economic gains and achieve respected positions in a young democracy. In lauding the benefits of wholesome sport for young men, Higginson drew on English sporting traditions. Furthermore, "[t]his powerful and pervasive English love of athletics, first noted in the exclusive public schools, was intensified and gained international fame by the publication of the phenomenally popular *Tom Brown's Schooldays*" (Lucas 51–52). Written by Thomas Hughes, this 1857 work featured young men being instructed in classics for the mind, religion for the spirit, and athletics for the body, based on the positive role assigned to athletics at Rugby School by headmaster Thomas Arnold. Hughes' book "became an instant success on both sides of the Atlantic," and American reformers embraced in this "idealized picture of vigorous boy-life" the benefits of competitive sport, marking a shift in outlook on the body and religion in antebellum American society. The concept of the "noble, idealized Christian athlete" became part of the reform message of those Americans urging sport and physical activity as acceptable and healthful for youth in American culture (Lucas 52). Therefore, white men in positions of political and religious leadership ought to make physical culture part of their own training, according to this outlook on health, sport, and antebellum American life.

For Higginson and like-minded reformers, men ought to be "Muscular Christians," engaging in certain behaviors deemed appropriate for their gender. Muscular Christianity referred to the belief that the body was the temple of God and that cultivating one's body for the glory of God developed morals and built character. The Muscular Christian embodied the best of physical culture and moral virtue in a trilogy of mind, body, and spirit. Higginson's concept, like Beecher's "cult of domesticity" (which prescribed virtue for women, as discussed later in this chapter), revealed the workings of gender ideology. Muscular Christianity embraced muscles, morality, and manliness in athletics. In spreading the gospel of health, Higginson

Tom Brown's school days, the popular book written in 1857 by English author Thomas Hughes, influenced antebellum American reformers to promote wholesome sport along with spiritual and academic training for young men.

From T. Hughes, 1857, *Tom Brown's Schooldays* (Adamant Media Corporation).

emphasized the need for men to be physically fit in order to pursue their proper roles, and the movement constituted a considerable part of the health reform crusade, in which cultivating the body for a strong constitution and cultivating the mind for knowledge went together. Higginson himself was "America's version of the [M]uscular Christian," reaching a wide audience with his writings and lectures. Indeed, Higginson was a model of the antebellum social-reform outlook. Influenced by "the optimism of the period," he became "a symbol and a champion of the newer and better day and an especial apostle of the new crusade for health and happiness" (Lucas 55).

1846–1848	1848	1849
▪ U.S. fights war with Mexico	▪ Seneca Falls Woman's Rights Convention held in New York; right to vote for women first proposed ▪ German American immigrants found the first Turner society in the United States ▪ California Gold Rush occurs	▪ Tom Hyer fights Yankee Sullivan in barefisted boxing match

Higginson posited alarming consequences for men if they ignored the laws of health, and he detailed how sports could resolve this problem. In particular, he criticized the terrible eating and sedentary habits of middle-class urban men, whom he believed were suffering from dyspepsia. Higginson's letters in the 1850s to an archetypal urban businessman, "Dolorosus" (sad one), elaborated the drastic consequences of this dreaded malady on men's careers. Based on his gendered perspective, Higginson linked Dolorosus' dyspeptic plight to his having to give up his business at age 35 due to ill health. Puny, sickly men, Higginson believed, could not fulfill their roles in the world, and, in place of such supposedly effeminate businessmen, he articulated a vision of hearty men pursuing their career interests. Whether a man was a businessman, politician, or conqueror of the West, success depended on male physical health, and sport promoted the necessary vigor and vitality (Borish, "The Robust Woman").

Proponents of Muscular Christianity touted sport as essential for building character, leadership, competitiveness, courage, teamwork, and discipline. Thus they emphasized sport as a kind of positive training for manhood, one that helped men develop physical and moral fitness they could transfer into their appropriate pursuits in American society. Reformers such as Higginson, Oliver Wendell Holmes, and Henry David Thoreau (who lived in a small hut at Walden Pond, near Concord, Massachusetts, and authored *Walden*) believed that outdoor sport for boys promoted physical strength and prepared them for manhood (Gems and Borish, "Sports, Colonial Era" 637–643). Holmes encouraged men to engage in sport into their older age. He commented on physical activities in his 1858 series of articles titled "The Autocrat at the Breakfast Table" in the *Atlantic Monthly*. In the following excerpt, Holmes described specific sports that he believed were invigorating for American men and acknowledged the positive view of sport expressed by "a young friend" who had recently written "an admirable article in one of the journals"—a direct reference to Higginson's "Saints, and Their Bodies." Holmes described how

sport could play a vital role in a man's life, and he identified his own love for

> one particular form of active exercise and amusement, namely *boating*. For the past nine years, I have rowed about, during a good part of the summer, on fresh or salt water. My present fleet on the river Charles consists of three rowboats. . . .
>
> When I have established a pair of well-pronounced feathering-calluses on my thumbs, when I am training so that I can do my fifteen miles [24 kilometers] at a stretch without coming to grief in any way, when I can perform my mile [1.6 kilometers] in eight minutes or a little less, then I feel as if I had old Time's head in chancery, and could give it to him in my leisure. . . .
>
> I do not deny the attraction of walking. . . . Walking is an immeasurably-fine invention, of which old age ought constantly to avail itself.
>
> Saddle-leather is in some respects even preferable to sole-leather. . . . Riding is good. . . .
>
> Boxing is rough play, but not too rough for a hearty young fellow. . . . I dropped into a gentleman's sparring exhibition only last evening. . . .
>
> But boxing you and I are too old for, I am afraid. I was for a moment tempted, by the contagion of muscular electricity last evening, to try the gloves.
>
> qtd. in Kirsch, *Sports* [Vol. 3] 22, 23–24, 26, 27

Reformers generally viewed the outdoor sports of rowing, swimming, and vigorous horseback riding as properly manly pursuits for males of various ages. Higginson went so far as to say, "Without a boat one is so much the less a man," and, knowing that owning a boat might pose an economic challenge, he also said, "To own the poorest boat is better than hiring the best" ("Saints" 593). Team sports, including baseball, cricket, and football—"contests of manhood"—were also deemed beneficial to men ("Saints" 594).

Thus Muscular Christianity combined manly athleticism with the quest for fulfillment in the world. Sport became both a training ground for men and, thanks to the reform movement, a more widely accepted form of leisure activity. This program, spearheaded by white, middle-class reformers,

1851	1854	1858
■ Young Men's Christian Association appears in United States	■ Young Men's Hebrew Association founded in Baltimore ■ Gadsden Purchase made	■ Muscular Christianity movement in the United States emerges with Thomas W. Higginson writing famous article, "Saints, and Their Bodies," promoting moral and physical health

stressed physical vigor, moral courage, and religion, and it provided advice to male youth on the healthfulness of sport as an antidote to urban temptations and sedentary ways. Institutions were formed in the burgeoning cities of the Northeast—including the Young Men's Christian Association (YMCA), which appeared in the United States in 1851—to combine muscles and morals in building physical and spiritual health based on Muscular Christianity. The concept of bringing youth under the arm of a religious organization also took hold among Jewish men, who founded the first Young Men's Hebrew Association in the United States in 1854. These influential organizations, and women's roles in them, are given attention in the next chapter, which addresses the expansion of organized sport and the new cultural and physical spaces developed to foster it.

Women and Physical Activity

Everywhere they looked in the burgeoning Northeastern cities (in contrast to the countryside), white, middle-class, Protestant social reformers witnessed an alarming degeneration of female health. As a result, women were failing to fulfill the gender-based urban ideal of "the cult of domesticity" or "the cult of true womanhood" (discussed later in detail). Women's primary role in urban antebellum culture was a multifaceted one as wife, mother, moral guardian, and nurturer, and to fulfill this biological and social reproductive role they needed vigorous health. How could a mother make her home a loving haven and train her children to live in an active democracy if she were a perpetual invalid? Female sickness was antithetical to domestic tranquility and child rearing. It took a robust woman to properly inhabit her assigned arena—the domestic sphere—and fulfill her roles in the cult of true womanhood.

Catharine Beecher, a white, middle-class reformer who wrote widely on women's issues in antebellum society, lamented in 1856 that city women were pursuing a path of physical and mental destruction that resulted in "a race of *sickly and deformed pigmies*" ("Health" 400), whereas country women sustained their hardy well-being through domestic labor. Beecher wrote many of her important works during this time—including *A Treatise on Domestic Economy, for the Use of Young Ladies at Home, and at School* (1841), *Letters to the People on Health and Happiness* (1855), and *Calisthenic Exercises for Schools, Families, and Health Establishments* (1856)—and founded the

Hartford Female Seminary in 1823 as a forum for disseminating her ideas on domestic and physical education. Beecher set the tone for discussion of the debilitating effect of city life on women's health. Although she saw the urban environment as detrimental to the health of both men and women, in her comments on city life she particularly perceived women's health as "precarious" and demonstrated "the ubiquity of the image that linked women with infirmity in the middle decades of the nineteenth century" (Sklar 205). Thus, a sense of urgency pervaded the gospel of health as preached by antebellum American health reformers.

In rhetoric infused with religious fervor and a perfectionist creed, Beecher and other urban reformers urged Americans to heed "the laws of health and happiness." Beecher's deep concern about female health registers in the following pronouncement:

> You, my female friends, may I enter your nursery, your parlor or your kitchen? I have matters of interest to present in which everyone of you have a close personal concern. . . .
>
> [I]f a plan for *destroying female health* in all the ways in which it could most effectively be done were drawn up it would be exactly the course which is now pursued by a large portion of this nation. . . .
>
> The *standard of health* among American women is so low that few have a correct idea of *what a healthy woman is*.
>
> *Letters* 7–8, 122

Health reformers such as Beecher and Dr. William Alcott, who wrote self-help books on health and contributed articles to antebellum periodicals on health and exercise, paid particular attention to social class as a factor in the poor health of city women. In Beecher's ideology, health was a problem both for wealthy, leisured women and for poor, working women. The urban environment of both groups threatened their well-being.

In Beecher's view, upper-class ladies rejected productive housework as a means of sustaining physical vigor, choosing instead to employ domestic servants, and as a result they were afflicted with sickly constitutions due to a lack of physical activity. Beecher tried to dispel the prejudice, rooted in social-class mores, against middle- and upper-class women performing their own housework. She advocated domestic work as one possible cure for female maladies. What better way to strengthen the muscles and invigorate one's body than through active domestic exercise? Daughters gained physical fitness in the employments of "sweeping, dusting, care of furniture and beds . . . and nice cooking." According to Beecher, a young lady who "will spend two hours a day at the wash-tub, or with a broom, is far more likely to have rosy cheeks, a finely-moulded form, and a delicate skin, than one who lolls all day in her parlor or chamber, or only leaves girt in tight dresses to make fashionable calls." In sum, Beecher praised "the gentle exercise and *amusement* of housekeeping" (qtd. in Borish, "The Robust Woman" 143). Beecher gathered anecdotal evidence to support her case. She asked married ladies she met in her travels to list the names of women in their community who were healthy. The sad picture that emerged showed few if any healthy women. Yet her findings were based on upper-class, urban women, who devoted little time to physical exercise. Moreover, some women may not have volunteered information about their own health. For some upper-rank women, so-called fashionable diseases of ill health may have served at times as a way to escape domestic duties.

Catharine Beecher promoted health reform and physical education at her female schools, emphasizing women's proper gender role in antebellum American culture.

Harriet Beecher Stowe Center, Hartford, CT.

Working-class women, on the other hand, endured horrible conditions detrimental to their well-being. Their bodies were debilitated by long hours spent working in noisy, unventilated rooms. Indeed, factory life proved disastrous for female fitness. Thus, Beecher's message was that all ranks of women in the city seemingly faced health complaints and needed healthful physical activity to improve their physical well-being. In her view, urban female physical weakness required a female solution—a gender-based program of sport and physical exercise.

In contrast, health champions Beecher and Higginson idealized the health of farm men and women. Farm women, in particular, embodied perfect health, according to these reformers who envisioned farm life as bucolic and health-promoting for females, especially when compared with the lives of sickly urban women. Hence, a rural–urban dichotomy emerged in the beliefs of these reform-minded advice givers who lamented the perceived passing of a golden age in America's agricultural past. They posited a clear difference—in terms of health and happiness—between the active, outdoor life of rural farm families and the sedentary life of urban folks in their own generation.

Not all, however, believed that farm life was ideal. In their urban boosterism touting the technological, commercial, and sporting advantages of the city, some journalists criticized farm life as inferior to modern city life. Farm journalists vigorously responded by expressing their disdain for the corruptions and wealthy trappings of the city that enticed farm youth and jeopardized their moral and physical health. The farm press constructed positive images of rural women's health, such as an 1868 description in the *Massachusetts Ploughman* of a farmer's daughter with "the glow of health upon her cheek" ("The Farmer's Daughter" n. pag.).

The home-leaving of farm boys and girls alarmed reporters of New England agriculture, and the farm press emphasized the well-being of daughters as a factor in rural depopulation. Many rural daughters welcomed the chance to leave the farm, with its fatiguing domestic work, seeking instead to gain access to middle-class urban cultural experiences. The agricultural press featured common farmers who defended their agricultural way of life and wanted young women to remain on the homestead, but many young women wanted to escape the countryside. Rural women who gave advice in farm journals tended to side with farm girls who portrayed the health-depleting tasks of their life on the farm. This view of farm life stood in stark contrast to the idealized myth of farm life filled with health-giving physical exercise, as envisioned by urban health reformers such as Beecher and Alcott, and in contrast to the image of farm daughters' vim and vigor endorsed by farm men. Writing in 1846 for the *American Agriculturist,* a female correspondent advocated that these girls "need reforming mentally and physically" (Borish, "Benevolent America" 950). Yet in the debate on the physical condition of farm daughters, farmers wanted to maintain the status quo. While more progressive farm men and journal editors promoted improved farming methods to enhance farm life, they criticized the rising expectations of farm girls who sought cultural options, as well as better physical health and physical recreation, away from their domestic labors. Some farm girls did leave the countryside to work in the newly established textile mills such as those in Lowell, Massachusetts, to earn some money for their families or themselves and gain some freedom from the rigors and restraints

they faced as farm daughters in everyday rural life. Historian Thomas Dublin noted that between 1830 and 1860, "tens of thousands of young, single women . . . left their hill country farms in northern New England and sought employment in the expanding factory towns" (3). Some New England farm daughters worked in the mills for only a few years until marriage, and others left the mills to find better employment opportunities in the city. For young farm women, the mills "offered individual self-support, enabled women to enjoy urban amenities not available in their rural communities, and gave them a measure of economic and social independence from their families" (Dublin 23–24). Farm women who stayed behind in the countryside were often aware of the tensions between the rural and the urban worlds as written about in letters by their female kin and friends who worked in the mill towns, as well as in the rural and urban periodicals addressing the physical condition of women in antebellum American culture.

Beecher's *Calisthenic Exercises for the Schools, Families, and Health Establishments* featured many descriptions and illustrations of exercises appropriate for women.

Reprinted from C. Beecher, 1856, *Physiology and calisthenics for schools and families* (New York: Harper & Brothers).

Physical Education

Physical education became an integral component of the curriculum at Catharine Beecher's schools for young women. The prescribed gender roles for young middle-class women and girls contoured the remedy of sporting activities and physical exercise promoted by Beecher and her fellow female education reformers. In 1831 a treatise titled *Course of Calisthenics for Young Ladies,* "purported to have been written by an American mother, was published in Hartford, Connecticut" with the author "designated only by the letter 'M'" (Park, "Embodied Selves'" 77). Some chroniclers of physical education have attributed this volume to Catharine Beecher; in the book, she urged young women to participate in "free and light gymnastics and musical drill" (qtd. in Hartwell 29).

Beecher introduced calisthenics at her first institute, Hartford Female Seminary, in 1823, and

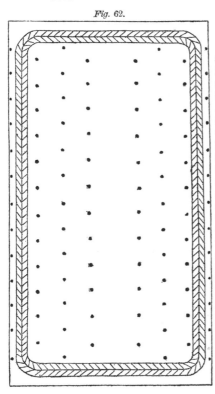

SECOND COURSE—HALL EXERCISES.

CONSTRUCTION OF A CALISTHENIC HALL.

Fig. 62.

Fig. 62 represents a Calisthenic Hall on the scale of twenty feet to an inch. Around the outer portion is a walking-path. The dots represent *stations* for the pupils while exercising. They are to be made of bits of black walnut four inches square, inlaid. They are to be five feet distant, and arranged as in the drawing. Every pupil is to have her appointed station, so as to have no confusion in arranging for exercises.

Design of a calisthenics hall in Beecher's *Calisthenic exercises for the schools, families, and health establishments.*

Reprinted from C. Beecher, 1856, *Physiology and Calisthenics for Schools and Families* (New York: Harper & Brothers).

girls at her schools generally performed calisthenics for improving physical health. Taught by a female physical education instructor, such exercises were often designed with a therapeutic orientation to strengthen specific parts of a woman's body. Beecher assured critics that this regimented form of activity would not injure women's health, and she also faced ideological hurdles in promoting calisthenics and sport for women. Contemporary definitions of femininity included a lack of robustness and physical vigor, which limited female participation in sport and public activities. To put it another way, the kind of physical strength needed in order to achieve total health and autonomy in the public world was viewed as an unnatural condition for women and one incompatible with femininity (Verbrugge; Vertinsky, *The Eternally Wounded Woman*). Beecher's program of activity went in tandem with acceptable gender views of women's physical well-being for white, middle-class, urban Protestant females. As part of reform in the Antebellum Age, such physical activities for women as those endorsed by Beecher did not challenge gender prescriptions of woman's sphere. Later women's schools would build on Beecher's model of sport and physical education in advocating appropriate gymnastic training and calisthenics as suitable for the female gender, such as the early sport programs at Smith College, Mt. Holyoke, Vassar, and other educational institutions for women.

Outdoor Sports

Health advisors proclaimed that outdoor sporting forms offered important benefits to women who were supposedly lolling in their urban households. They praised walking and horseback riding, for example, for their power to invigorate women in the fresh open air. So, too, gardening provided health and aesthetic dividends for the woman and her family. Catharine Beecher advised women to maintain their physical vigor as well as to engage in sporting forms fitting for the female gender. Beecher urged women to exercise outdoors in what she termed a "Temple of Health," with "a variety of pleasant walks, and shades, and flowers, to attract and please in the summer months, and other arrangements provided for outdoor sports and exercises in winter" (*Letters* 169). Ice skating in public parks and private ponds proved a popular sport and an invigorating pastime for women and girls (as explored later in this chapter).

At times, those of middle- and upper-rank status enjoyed games of croquet, which offered

Women's Physical Education
in Early Nineteenth-Century Europe

The European "grandfathers" of gymnastics (among them Johann Christoph Friedrich GutsMuths, Friedrich Ludwig Jahn, and Per Henrik Ling) focused exclusively on physical exercises for the male sex, but women and girls were increasingly being discovered as target groups for physical education from the 1820s onward. Amid the political and social changes that followed the French Revolution—including the growing gender-based division of labor (ascribing to women the role of housewife and mother and to men the role of breadwinner employed outside the home)—the health of the supposedly "weaker sex" began to attract the interest of male doctors and educators. Since women were barred from higher education and academic professions, however, they took virtually no part whatsoever in professional discussions about education and physical exercise for the female sex.

Among the first to champion physical exercise for girls was Phokion Heinrich Clias (1782–1854), who trained Swiss troops, worked for three years as a captain in the British Army, and became superintendent of physical training at the royal military and naval schools. In 1841, he was invited to France to work with schools and the military in Paris. Clias conducted numerous courses of physical training, including courses for girls and women. His book *Kalisthenie* (1829), in which he wrote about his experiences in London, was a landmark in the history of women's physical education. Its influence can be attributed in large part to the emphasis Clias placed on gentle exercises to enhance female grace and beauty.

Clias' successor in London was Gustavus Hamilton, who had already published his "Elements of Gymnastics for Boys and Calisthenics for Young Ladies" in 1827. That year also saw the publication of G.P. Voarino's "A Treatise on Calisthenic Exercises, Arranged for the Private Tuition of Young Ladies," which may well be the first book exclusively devoted to women's physical exercise. Like other educators, the author emphasized that gymnastics could improve the shape of the body as well as prevent and even cure "bodily infirmities" and deformities (Todd 11).

J.A. Beaujeu prescribed for his female pupils much more complex and strenuous exercises than Clias and Voarino. His motto was "Head up, legs down," and exercises such as "the flying course" required considerable strength and effort. In his "Treatise on Gymnastic Exercises, Or Calisthenics for the Use of Young Ladies," published in 1828, he described exercises that had been introduced at the Seminary for the Education of Young Ladies in Dublin in 1824. Besides his work at the Royal Hibernian School, where the sons and daughters of military personnel were educated (and where the curriculum included physical education), Beaujeu and his wife ran a "female gymnasium" (Todd 11). Madame Beaujeu also took calisthenics to the United States, where she opened a school in Boston in 1841.

In the 1830s, additional works appeared (including that of Johann Adolf Ludwig Werner in Germany) that stressed grace and graceful exercise. By contrast, the French doctor Antoine Bureaud-Riofrey laid emphasis on strength and stamina. In his "Physical Education Especially Adapted to Young Ladies" (published in Paris in 1835, in a German edition in 1837, and in English in 1838), he recommended 10 hours of daily exercise for 7-year-old girls and 5 hours daily for 14-year-old girls. Exercises included walking, dancing, and swimming, as well as free exercises, weight training, and activities with batons or dumbbells or on the horizontal bar.

European literature on girls' and women's physical exercise and education was also read with interest in America, with calisthenics finding especial favor. The more vigorous physical activities, however, such as those recommended by Beaujeu and Bureaud-Riofrey, were suited to neither the ideals of femininity nor the notions of propriety and decorum to be found in the New World.

Information from Todd, Jan. "The Classical Ideal and Its Impact on the Search for Suitable Exercise: 1774–1830." *Iron Game History* 2.4: 6–16.

healthy and social interactions in a coeducational setting. By the 1860s, in fact, croquet had become a fashionable recreational craze, but rampant cheating by women who moved or concealed the ball with their hoop skirts apparently diminished the pleasure for male players who played to win (Sterngass). The middle-class press wrote about croquet and noted the appeal of the sport for women, as in the following humorous poem published in *Harper's Weekly* in 1867:

> Given—the smoothest of lawns,
> With the turf closely cut and elastic;
> Given—the fairest of girls,
> With spirits enthusiastic;
> Given—a number of swells,
> Of the type most delightful and pleasing;
> Given—sides made up of these,
> With the usual chaffing and teasing;
> Given—the hoops duly placed,
> And the mallets and balls all selected;
> Given—the game has commenced,
> Then this to find out you're expected:
> What length of time will it be—
> Allowing for feints and pretenses—

> Ere, in the course of the game,
> "Spooning" in earnest commences?

> "A Croquet Problem" 583

For the most part, however, reformers put forward noncompetitive individual sports as the favored therapy to correct the health problems of women and girls. For many women linked to the domestic arena, sporting activities such as walking and gardening could be enjoyed within the domestic context—a crucial factor in antebellum American culture, with its gender ideology holding that women should not participate in the public, male world of competition and spectators.

Bloomer Costume

Whether in urban or rural life, some women asserted their right to wear the new "bloomers" sporting costume to improve their health and participate in outdoor exercise for increased mobility and health. Elizabeth Smith Miller introduced the costume in the spring of 1851 for comfort while gardening. She wrote that "Turkish trousers to the ankle with a skirt reaching some four inches below the knee, were substituted for the heavy, untidy and exasperating old garment" (i.e., her long skirt).

A game of croquet, a popular sporting pastime and social outing for middle-class Americans.
Photo courtesy of *Harper's Weekly*, Sept. 8, 1866.

After adopting this costume, Miller went to Seneca Falls, New York, to visit her cousin Elizabeth Cady Stanton, a woman's rights activist. Stanton "had so long deplored with me our common misery in the toils of this crippling fashion that this means of escape was hailed with joy and she at once joined me in wearing the new costume" (qtd. in McClymer 47).

Also joining in was Stanton's friend and neighbor, Amelia Jenks Bloomer, editor of the reform newspaper *The Lily*, who advocated the costume in her paper, after which, as Smith recalled, "the dress was christened with her name." However, while wearing the bloomer costume, Elizabeth Smith Miller and Mrs. Stanton endured ridicule, as Smith Miller recounted: "We endured, in various places much gaping curiosity and the harmless jeering of street boys." She asserted, moreover, "All hail the day when we shall have a reasonable and beautiful dress that shall encourage exercises on the road and in the field—that shall leave us the free use of our limbs" (qtd. in McClymer 47–48). Thus bloomers became a key issue in the movements for woman's rights and dress and health reform. Amelia Bloomer wore the new costume and published an image of herself wearing it in 1851. It avoided the risks of tight-laced fashions (such as corsets that restricted waistlines to a mere 17 inches) that injured women's bodily health, as well as the typical skirts sweeping the ground. Appropriate shoes—rather than fashionable, painful ones—also formed part of the looser-fitting costume, which became increasingly popular. An item published in the *Granite Farmer* in 1851 informed readers that "[t]he Bloomer style of ladies' dresses, which consists of a short frock and Turkish trousers, seems to be gaining ground fast in all directions" (qtd. in Borish, "Benevolent America" 954).

The bloomer costume spurred heated discussion about the appropriateness of antebellum women wearing a male garment (trousers) in public view, and, more broadly, about women's health, physical emancipation, and power in farm life. Several farm women offered an endorsement of bloomers, joining their urban sisters in wearing this new kind of clothing that challenged male authority. Wearing the new outfit, farm women conveyed their desire to engage in physical activity with suitable attire for sturdy health and greater mobility.

Rural Sporting Practices

Sport and physical recreation for rural men and women went hand in hand with physical health within a gendered context. Some physical amusements on the farm proved practical for both men and women, such as swimming, walking, and horseback riding. In other sporting forms, farm men and women might participate in gender-separate recreation, such as fishing and the winter sports of skating and sledding. Yet leisure time to pursue such physical activities often belonged more to the farm men, who, unlike farm women, were not tied to the domestic labors of the farm (indoors and out), including child-care responsibilities and household tasks that often lasted late into the evening. Farm men typically spent their day outdoors working at hard, dirty, physical tasks, but they were at least outside in the fresh air and away from the domestic work spaces that were often sloppy, odorous, and full of kitchen refuse. Farm women, on the other hand, spent long hours at indoor tasks, shut up in the farmhouse, which restricted their opportunity to partake of the same pure outdoor air. A farm woman contributing to the agricultural press acknowledged that many

Woman in the bloomer costume, designed to promote freedom of mobility in physical activity for women.
Photo courtesy of Library of Congress, LC-USZC2-1978.

farm women typically remained tied to indoor and smelly domestic chores. She commented on the gender-related dimensions of the fresh-air question, asserting in 1845 that "it was the height of folly for a farmer's wife to think of rambling in the woods for flowers, and that it was perfectly useless to inhale the air . . . unless she ran out in a great hurry to see what was the matter with the chickens, or to look up eggs for some purpose of cookery" (qtd. in E.M.C. 287–288).

Rural health reformers in antebellum New England argued that farm dwellers needed certain kinds of physical exercise in the open air, not health-depleting labors, to better their physical vigor. One journalist, writing in the 1852 *New England Farmer,* declared, "It is quite a mistake to consider the labor of the day as equivalent to exercise." He believed that "[a]thletic sports and out of door exercises, of every description, are no less conducive to the morals, and happiness, than they are necessary to the perfect health of the young of both sexes" ("Physical Recreation" 483–484). In fact, health reform that valued healthful physical exercise and sporting activity became part of the larger reform activism in both rural and urban areas as several health proponents participated in other reforms of the Antebellum Era.

In some areas, baseball bridged the gap between urban and rural life because of its being played in the open air, on green pastures, with no industrial clock to determine the length of the game. Canadians in the Ontario region recorded baseball games as early as 1838, and by the 1840s baseball clubs proliferated throughout the eastern United States, competing against each other despite a variety of rules and field configurations. The growth of baseball, explored in the next chapter, would accelerate by 1858, when clubs formed the National Association of Base Ball Players and adopted the New York version of the rules.

Agricultural Fairs

In the early 1800s, in order to prepare themselves as future farmers, boys in rural areas competed in contests at agricultural fairs by demonstrating their farming skills. The first agricultural fair was held in 1810 in Pittsfield, Massachusetts, and others soon followed. New England agricultural societies initially sponsored local fairs, originated by gentleman farmer Elkanah Watson, "father of the agricultural fair," who wanted to spread agricultural improvement to ordinary farmers of Massachusetts. In 1807, after Watson exhibited two merino sheep, he recalled that "[m]any farmers, and even women, were excited by curiosity to attend this first novel, and humble exhibition." By 1811, the Berkshire Agricultural Society incorporated in order to foster the interests of common farmers (Neely 21, 61; Borish, "'A Fair'").

The public spectacle of the agricultural fair—a special leisure event on the farm family's calendar—featured men and boys, and women and girls, engaging in certain recreations compatible with gender-based expectations in field events—plowing and mechanical arts—and domestic arts, respectively, although at times women bucked conventions in their sporting behavior. Farm women and men, as well as agricultural reformers and male promoters, all participated in agricultural fairs, which provided a venue for leisure, sporting events, and celebration of agricultural pride. Thus, these annual fall exhibitions, lasting three or four days, served as social, educational, and recreational events for the farming community as part of the agricultural reform movement in the early and middle nineteenth century. Fairgoers enjoyed the break from their laborious routines and the chance to display their physical skills. By the middle decades of the century, country fairs flourished at the county, state, and regional levels in what constituted a "golden age of the agricultural fair" (Butterfield 289–297). Male and female participation in New England agricultural fairs changed over time—from the inception of the fair in the early nineteenth century as a practical event for the farming community to a more complex leisure- and profit-oriented event in the century's middle years—along with shifts in the workings of gender in rural society.

In the context of the fair, farm women participated as both spectators and competitors in public leisure activities that were usually the prerogative of men in the gendered conventions of farm life. In the pattern of activities at the fair, women's integrated work and leisure experiences persisted when they displayed their domestic products. Farm men, however, claimed power as judges at the fair, conferring awards of excellence to farm women who displayed their cultural power in bread and butter making, home manufactures, and fine arts. Some women challenged male authority at the fair and competed in nontraditional contests, such as female equestrianism, thus extending their interest in competition to the horse track. Such contests placed women in forms of competition that contrasted with the socially constructed images of feminine sporting behaviors; women's physical recreations deemed controversial at the agricultural fair clashed with the kinds of physical activities deemed appropriate for them in rural health-reform campaigns. Juxtaposing domestic arts competitions with the physical display of the female body in horse racing generated controversy about gendered recreational practices in rural New England. Rural improvers wanted women to compete publicly for prizes only through the display of domestic skills. Such competitions integrated work and recreation yet extended farm women's proficiency in the domestic sphere to the public sphere, where they could gain social prestige and recognition. One rural New England booster encouraged farm women in this way: "[F]air ones of the dairy, and all ye tidy housewives, that give honor and reputation to Yankeedom, the time draws near for you to show *your* prowess; yes, to exhibit to the world how important to the farmer is the farmer's wife" (Thomas n. pag.). In contrast, women who raced horses around the track, as men did, were criticized by agricultural traditionalists.

More generally, the agricultural press exhibited divided opinion on the "Horse Question" at the fair. Some farmers worried that farm men and women attending the horse track were faced with temptations that should be challenged in the age of antebellum reform, such as gambling, drinking, and other immoral behaviors. Agriculturists preaching improvement in exhibitions of farm life clashed with profit-seeking fair promoters who wished to capitalize on the popularity of horse races, which lured large crowds, often at the expense of more mundane exhibitions of large pumpkins, plump cattle, and horticultural splendors (Borish, "'A Fair'"). The addition of women's horse races increased the number of patrons at the fairgrounds and fanned the controversy for some farm progressives who believed it was not a woman's right or place to ride horses for prizes.

One critic who joined the chorus condemning the appearance of women on the racecourse put it this way: "Horse-jockeys, horse-fanciers, fast horses and 'fast women' have been the most

Agricultural fairs in the nineteenth century provided a place for agricultural contests and festivities for farm families.

Image courtesy of Library of Congress, LC-DIG-pga-00607.

conspicuous objects on most of the 'fair grounds,' the present season." He went on to compare the parade of female equestrians to the parade of domestic animals:

> Our daughters as well as our horses, girls of tender age, girls of larger growth, and even wives, as well as fillies, pacers and breeding mares, are brought on to the course for exhibitions, and gazed at, and criticized by thousands, and praised and flattered, and caressed, for the same reasons as the animals which they drive, beauty of skin, and form and limb, and grace of action.
>
> "Cattle Shows" 14–15.

One racing opponent put it this way: "Will not these females soon answer the description of a 'fast woman'?" Such advice givers deemed horseback riding beneficial to women's health and acceptable within their gender conventions but clearly drew the line at seeing women ride competitively for premiums ("Female Jockeys" 142). Female horse racers at the agricultural fair paraded their bodies in sport, which in many advisors' minds pushed too hard against the usual gender dimensions of women's contests in rural society.

Despite these concerns, women persisted in taking part in such public contests. In California, women displayed their equestrian skills in races and exhibitions, even flouting convention by riding in the straddle position common to males, rather than sidesaddle as expected of women. By 1858, a national equestrian convention for women was held at Union Course on Long Island, and four thousand spectators attended. Substantial prizes included a $500 piano for the winner of one race (Kirsch, *Sports* [Vol. 3] 187–191). Thus, horse racing not only questioned gender roles but also highlighted regional differences as discussed in the next section.

Horse Racing and Harness Racing

Southerners bred their horses for speed, while Northerners favored endurance, but the two regions disagreed, of course, on far more than horse breeding, as abolitionism and industrialization threatened the plantation lifestyle of the South. Such differences played out in the sporting world in 1823, when Northern industrialist Cornelius Van Ranst, owner of the racehorse American Eclipse, accepted a challenge from North Carolinian William Ransom Johnson, owner of Sir Henry, to pit the two horses against each other in a best-of-three match over a 4-mile (6.4-kilometer) course

for a purse of $20,000. A betting frenzy ensued, as supporters of each horse wagered astronomical sums. One Virginia plantation owner bet five years of cotton production on the Southern champion, while a Northern cotton mill owner countered with three years of his profits on American Eclipse. Congressman John Randolph wagered $10,000 and his entire wardrobe on the Northern horse (Twombly 40). The contest took place at the Union racetrack on Long Island before a reported sixty thousand spectators, with the horses splitting the first two heats before American Eclipse emerged as the winner. In the following years, such intersectional horse races intensified, as did the North–South regional conflict.

Harness racing also emerged as a significant sport in antebellum American culture. Historian Melvin Adelman judged harness racing to be the first modern sport in America because of its organization and commercialization, which began in the New York metropolitan area: "Sportsmen began racing their 'roadsters' (as street trotters came to be called) because it provided them with an amusement which was convenient, participatory and relatively inexpensive. Third Avenue quickly emerged as New York's major trotting area. . . . Early nineteenth century trotting consisted almost exclusively of . . . impromptu contests, [but] permanent structures began to emerge" ("The First" 8). Horse racing became so popular that newspapers, such as William T. Porter's *Spirit of the Times,* began reporting the results in 1831, and race results and statistics from the harness track became a key component of modern sport during the Antebellum Period.

The interest in trotting races intensified with the formation of the New York Trotting Club in 1824 and 1825 on Long Island as the first organized trotting club in America. The press reported on techniques used by the club to improve the breed, efforts to promote the sport, the construction of a course for harness racing sponsored by the club, and racing matches between the New York club and groups from other Northeastern locales (Adelman, "The First" 9). The trotting club also disseminated sports information (modern sport characteristics are discussed in chapter 4). In a trotting race on November 17, 1847, Black Hawk faced Jenny Lind in a match involving $500 per mile (1.6-kilometer) heats at the Union Course. Trotting races in the Northeast generated interest among horsemen and race fans alike, and, in a distinct departure from thoroughbred racing, which was steeped in the wealth of the elite men and

Advertisements for harness-racing matches informed spectators of upcoming races and purses for the winning horse.

Photo courtesy of Library of Congress, Portfolio 64, Folder 39.

families who owned thoroughbreds in the United States, "[m]ost of the owners of trotting horse and the proprietors of trotting tracks, however, appear to have been middle class in origin. The different social origins affected the entire tone of the two turf sports . . . [, and] harness racing enticed a broader segment of the populace" (Adelman, "The First" 13).

The middle-class status and decorum of the gentlemen who owned the trotters increased the visibility of harness racing, and spectators enjoyed watching the trotters race at the tracks. Thoroughbred horse racing faced hard times during the economic depression that began in 1837, and harness racing tended to generate new sporting interests in American horses. Adelman has stated, "As thoroughbred racing collapsed throughout the North in the decade following the Depression of 1837, the sporting press took increasing note of the activities of the trotting horse. . . . In contrast to the aristocratic and foreign thoroughbred, the trotter was perceived as the democratic, utilitarian, and, by logical extension, the American horse" ("The First" 10). Owning trotters for the harness track symbolized a middle-rank businessman's respectability and social standing in the community. In Bridgeport, Connecticut, Nathaniel Wheeler, who gained his middle-class position as an industrialist in the sewing machine industry, owned trotting horses and underscored the importance of the sport for gentlemen.

People & Places

Nathaniel Wheeler

Nathaniel Wheeler cofounded the Wheeler and Wilson Manufacturing Company and served as company president. Wheeler was a self-made man in the nineteenth century, using technological know-how from his work as a carriage manufacturer in Watertown, Connecticut, to build a very successful business in the sewing machine industry. Wheeler and inventor Allen B. Wilson established their company in Watertown with patents for a sewing machine, and in 1856 the company moved to Bridgeport and expanded its sewing machine production.

Wheeler lived in his spacious home with his wife, Mary Crissy Wheeler, and their children. In her domestic activities and philanthropic work, Mary Wheeler exemplified "the cult of domesticity" in antebellum American life for middle- and upper-class women, while Nathaniel Wheeler embodied the sporting gentleman displaying his wealth in business and leisure. Nathaniel Wheeler owned several trotters in his stable at the Bridgeport home and also possessed carriages. As Wheeler and Wilson Manufacturing Company continued to make profits, Wheeler could enjoy various leisure activities, such as harness racing and sleigh and carriage racing (*Communities*). Thus Wheeler and Wilson Manufacturing Company (later taken over by the Singer Company) provides an example both of the prosperity that the owners and managers of new technology possessed in the nineteenth century and of the display of status through sporting activity.

The race between trotting horses Black Hawk and Jenny Lind, 1847.

Image courtesy of Library of Congress, LC-USZ62-7745.

The growth of harness racing after the economic depression increased the popularity of sport in the middle of the nineteenth century. Observers of the races included rural and urban sport enthusiasts. As Adelman has explained, "Harness racing surged to the forefront of not only the turf world, but modern sport in general, because more than any other sport of the day it captured the flow of the American experience. In common with other forms of popular entertainment, the emergence of trotting as a spectator sport was a product of the two dynamic forces—urbanization and economic expansion—transforming and modernizing American life" ("The First" 14).

Rise of Agricultural and Sporting Journalism

The United States was a mostly agricultural nation in the Antebellum Period, and the focus on betterment of farming spurred development of the agricultural press, with attention to the health of farm families and improved techniques for farming. One such publication, the *American Farmer,* was founded in 1819 in Baltimore, Maryland, by John

Stuart Skinner, "the pioneer and father of American farm journalism" (Demaree 23). Devoted to improving agriculture, the journal covered numerous aspects of agriculture and rural economy. Of particular note, Skinner developed two special departments in the *American Farmer:* a sporting section and a women's section. Skinner regularly included articles and advice on sport, recreation, and physical health for farm men and women, and his propensity for exercise, recreation, and sporting pursuits—along with his own belief that such activities were essential to the well-rounded American—led him to increase the coverage of sport in the *American Farmer* between 1819 and 1824, and eventually (in 1825) to launch a section titled "Sporting Olio"—that is, sporting miscellany (Berryman). The column proved popular, and, in a representative sentiment, Skinner opined in 1825, "How much better to repair to the fields, the woods or the neighbouring streams, at the close of a week of hard study or sedentary labour, and there spend the afternoon in gunning, fishing, swimming, bowling at ninepins, pitching quoits, etc., according to one's fancy and the season, than to abuse whole days in *militia mustering!* frequenting gaming-houses, whiskey drinking, etc."

(qtd. in Demaree 33). In "Sporting Olio," Skinner shared his love of outdoor sport, covered horse racing, and gave information on breeds of animals of interest to agriculturalists.

Skinner also established the "Ladies' Department" in the *American Farmer* as a place to deliver articles and practical material for rural women—farm mothers and farm daughters—in order to make his journal of interest to the whole farm family. In this department, Skinner wanted to present "subjects for the rational amusement and instruction" of feminine readers (qtd. in Demaree 33). Skinner printed articles on rural women's health, recipes and food preparation for the family, outdoor exercise, and recreation. The *American Farmer also* published articles on reform issues "and the rise in popularity of outdoor sports" (Berryman and Brislin 60). Later in the Antebellum Period, other farm journals followed his lead by introducing their own columns of advice on the physical health and exercise of farm women as well as men. Thus Skinner provided an important forum for rural Americans and others who paid attention to the condition of farming in antebellum American society and integrated information about good health and good farming for rural readers in the pages of his magazine.

Skinner eventually sold *American Farmer* but continued to capitalize on his sporting and horse-racing interests by creating *American Turf Register and Sporting Magazine* in 1829. This sports journal became the first of its type in the United States. In fact, Skinner's magazine "was more influential than any other factor of its day in improving the breed of American horses" (Demaree 36).

The editors of the *Homestead* agricultural journal in Connecticut sought to address the needs of rural, middle-class supporters of what they called "improved farming." As agricultural historian Sally McMurry has explained, progressive farm men and women of the rural middle class read agricultural journals for "book farming," to gain the advice of agricultural reformers promoting scientific and profit-oriented farming. These rural journals "aimed for an audience of practical farmers" (McMurry 1–2). In this vein, *Homestead* proprietor Mason C. Weld and his fellow editors wanted to dispel prejudice against book farming and communicate information to genuine farm men and women. The magazine aimed to help farmers "put the farm in trim and the cattle in good case, and [make] the door yard bloom with flowers and the garden laugh with vegetables" ("To Our Friends" 787).

Practical farming information was accompanied by material on physical health and sporting activity, as well as advertisements of products intended for use in work and play. Advertisements (pitching items such as horse-keeping gear) and horse-racing results appeared alongside entries with titles such as "On the Preservation of Health," "Bathing or Washing in Winter," and "Recreation." Another topic was the well-known Sylvester Graham diet of brown bread, debated by both rural and urban folks. One reader of the *Yankee Farmer* declared his distaste for the touted Graham diet: "Where are the *Grahamites*? frozen, starved or grown so lean that they have been blown away" ("Where Are the *Grahamites*?" 2–3). In short, some viewed it as anything but a useful diet for sport and physical activity.

Thus, the printing press made it possible for sports journalism to reach both city residents and those in outlying rural regions. Agricultural journals provided a forum for discussing sport and physical education, and their editors wished to promote American nationalism by boosting the well-being of the nation's citizens, many of them residing in rural areas. In addition to *American Farmer* and *American Turf Register,* information about healthful sports was spread by such publications as *Spirit of the Times*, *American Agriculturist*, and regional periodicals including the *New England Farmer* and the *Boston Cultivator*. These publications formed the beginning of what sport historian Stephen Hardy has described as "an industry of providers, even though the production of sporting goods appears to have lagged behind the production of formal ideology." As part of larger commercial trends in sport and leisure in the early decades of the nineteenth century, these periodicals were important in promoting the practice of sporting pursuits and the associated economic activity: "Consumers who could *read about* sports in specialty publications tended to *play* sports with goods furnished through homecrafting, merchant importers, or local artisans" (Hardy, "Adopted" 134).

As Americans moved increasingly to urban regions, so did the providers of sports information in an expanding market and a culture ripe for communications about sport and sport-related products. Immigrants to the city continued to read magazines, including newer urban ones. Numerous city newspapers provided coverage (listing statistics and records and recounting noteworthy feats) of horse racing, harness racing, ball games, pugilism matches, and other sporting pastimes. Such publications in the early and middle decades of the nineteenth century included the *New York Herald* and the *New York Times*. During this period, "The editors of the major sports journals wielded enormous power over the antebellum sporting scene. William T. Porter, editor of the *Spirit of the Times,* and John Stuart Skinner, editor of *American Turf Register and Sporting Magazine,* influenced the nature and direction of sport reporting and writing, cultivated a sporting audience, and shaped the development and appeal of sport prior to the Civil War" (Menna 35).

Sports journalism of the early and mid-nineteenth century included articles that advocated development of a more robust American citizenry through exercise and sport. This attitude went hand in hand with the growth of modern sport, as discussed in chapter 4. For example, here is an excerpt from an article in the *American Turf Register and Sporting Magazine* titled "On Exercise" (November 1838):

> Exercise prevents disease, or rather perhaps fortifies the body against it. If good health were a commodity that could be brought like a box of "Morrison's pills" or other health-conferring nostrums, who is there that would not hurry to the mart and purchase eagerly, even though they were obliged to swallow that box as well as its contents at one unsavory mouthful? . . . [T]ake exercise at least once a day, so as to excite the natural heat, and other functions of the body; take that exercise which has the most general effect upon the system, and which induces you to be in the open air; *be regular* in taking exercise. . . . [W]hen you do eat you may be assured that exercise adds more relish to your food than "the King of Oude's Sauce" or any other condiment of that diction that ever was invented.
>
> qtd. in Menna 33–34

Magazines such as *Atlantic Monthly, Harper's Weekly*, and *Frank Leslie's Illustrated Newspaper* also published articles on the benefits of good health and physical exercise and sport.

Sporting Practices of the Middle and Upper Classes

While the antebellum agricultural and sporting press promoted benefits of physical exercise and of certain sports, some middle- and upper-class urbanites, along with men seeking to expand their business activities in growing rural towns and cities, pursued sports affiliated with higher socioeconomic status. In the South, still rural in many areas and generally less urbanized than the North, certain sporting practices persisted from the early nineteenth century. In places where new technology was more readily available, middle- and upper-class men often integrated it into sporting contests to promote their visibility as higher-ranked sportsmen and businessmen.

Dueling

The more sophisticated gentlemen of the South settled their disputes of honor by means of dueling, usually with swords or pistols. Used in Europe for centuries, the practice had migrated to America with the colonists. A duel could be staged when the honor of a white upper-rank male was challenged by another man in the form of an insult to his character, honesty, wife, or even mistress. The loss of one's honor from not defending oneself might affect family pride, status, and social esteem for years. Even prominent Americans engaged in the practice. Stephen Decatur, an American naval hero in the War of 1812, fell mortally wounded in an 1820 duel. Before becoming president in 1828, Andrew Jackson fought numerous duels, allegedly killing several men in the process. South Carolina even had a dueling club, and such confrontations occurred on a regular basis at a selected site in New Orleans. Although Virginia outlawed dueling in 1809 and other states followed (including New York in 1828), duels continued legally in Washington, D.C., for another decade. The U.S. Navy permitted dueling as late as 1862, and as late as 1870 residents of Savannah, Georgia, dueled over the results of a sailboat race (Holland 142, 149, 272). Practice of this ultimate form of competition perplexed religious reformers, and itinerant ministers traveled the backcountry on moral crusades to preach against such uncivilized transgressions against the human body. Such developments signaled the imposition of a middle-class culture and standards of decorum in American life.

Steamboat Races

Along the waterways, steamboat races were thrilling passengers and onlookers by the 1830s. These events were dangerous, as overheated boilers sometimes exploded with fatal consequences, but such risks failed to quell the activity. Steamboats transported spectators to sporting events, carried passengers to clandestine boxing matches or steamboat races, and, in the absence of or before the invention of the telegraph, communicated news of the results of contests. In particular, steamboats competed in the 1830s on the Mississippi and Hudson rivers, showing off the new steam technology of the Antebellum Era (Menna 87). By the 1850s, steamboats were also racing on the Great Lakes and on the Sacramento River in California. The following description from the *Spirit of the Times* conveys the excitement of an 1832 race along the Hudson River between the steamboats *Erie* and *North America*:

At the hour of starting, our wharves were crowded by multitudes of interested spectators, all eagerly watching the busy preparations for the coming contest. The North America shot away from the dock first, but being compelled to sweep around a vessel laying in her course, she gave the Erie an opportunity to come along side and thus it is said, they left the city neck and neck. Now came the tug of war, and none could witness the contest between these two perfections of art, without emotions of awe and sublimity.

The tide was favorable and they scud away with almost terrific rapidity—now one and now the other ahead; but at no time was the distance between them sufficient to give alarm or hope to either. . . .

A few short hours decided this closely contested race. The North America arrived at the foot of State street dock eight minutes ahead of the Erie, making the passage from New York to Albany in the extraordinary short time of nine hours and thirty minutes.

qtd. in Menna 88

The most famous steamboat race was the exciting contest between the *Robert E. Lee* and the *Natchez VI* in July 1870, spanning 1,278 river miles (2,056 kilometers) from New Orleans to St. Louis and finally won by the *Robert E. Lee* after three days of action.

Yachting

In New England, wealthy Boston merchant George Crowninshield built a yacht for the then-princely sum of more than $50,000. Dubbed *Cleopatra's Barge* and launched in 1816, Crowninshield's vessel embarked on a European voyage in 1817. He raced and defeated continental yachtsmen and intended to return in 1818 to challenge sailors of the Baltic countries but suffered a fatal heart attack in the interim. The magnificent yacht was sold for a pittance and turned into a trading ship in Hawaii. It took three more decades before those of similar interests founded the New York Yacht Club (in 1844), and the first America's Cup yacht race was staged in 1851, as discussed in the next chapter.

The Great Mississippi Steamboat Race, **Currier & Ives**, July, 1870.
Image courtesy of Library of Congress, LC-USZ62-5315.

Public Spaces for Health and Sport

For New Yorkers of various social classes, ethnicities, and races, the creation of Central Park (the first landscaped public park in the United States) in the 1850s provided a place to play sports and enjoy fresh air in natural environs within a major city. With the increased pace of urbanization in the Antebellum Era, sports played in city streets came under criticism as a potential threat to persons moving about in the walking cities, as they were known, including businessmen, clerks, and the residents and visitors attending stores and buildings. In the early decades of the nineteenth century, New York city officials had wanted to keep sport out of the parks in busy areas where working-class men and youth playing games sent errant balls—or ran—into busy streets, thus perhaps endangering city folks who were passing by. For example, in 1816, the *New York Courier* addressed the passing of a park-related law which legislated

> that no person or persons shall play at ball, quoits, or any other sports of play whatsoever in the public ground, commonly called the Park, in the third and sixth wards, of the said city, nor in the Bowling Green, nor on the Battery, in the first ward of the said city, nor throw stones, nor run foot races, in, over or upon either the said Park, Bowling Green or Battery; under the penalty of five dollars for every offence.

> A fit and proper person shall be appointed to be called the keeper of the Park, whose duty it shall be to see the provisions of this ordinance are observed, and also to prevent all riots and noise, in or adjacent to the said Park, Battery and Bowling Green, and to report all offenders to the Attorney of the Board.

> "A Law" 3

The appeal of city parks as potential sporting areas for working-class and young people was reflected in a statement by one J. Morton, the Clerk of the Common Council: "[I]f any offence shall be committed against this ordinance, by any minor, apprentice, servant or slave [many slaves were still held in the antebellum North], the penalty in such case be paid by the parent, guardian, master, or owner (as the case may be) of the person so offending" ("A Law" 3).

Providing appropriate grounds for sport and play in growing urban areas thus became a key issue for civic-minded public officials. Eminent white, middle-class New Yorkers, as well as reformers such as writer Walt Whitman, educator Horace Mann, and journalist Sarah Josepha Hale, championed the need for a public park in New York City. Mayor Ambrose Kingsland's 1851 proposal of a 160-acre (65 hectare) space started the necessary political process for establishing Central Park. Built to promote the moral and physical health of urban residents in a wholesome natural setting—and to promote political power, urban boosterism, and real estate, among other motives—Central Park provided the framework for creation of other public parks in the United States. The park's famous designer, Frederick Law Olmsted, and his codesigner Calvert Vaux, allotted space for sporting activities in the open air to serve the youth of the city, but the park became a contested space, as various public groups expressed claims to it, often clashing over whether park grounds should be used for active sports and ball games or reserved for less boisterous recreations such as enjoying nature through walks and rambles. Sporting events usually attracted rowdy crowds, as well as gambling and fast horses and carriages, whereas city officials believed that park grounds were best used for calmer recreations, more fitting for elite groups strolling in the park (Rosenzweig and Blackmar). Rules instituted by park supervisors initially restricted sporting activity in the park and instead encouraged visitors to partake of the fresh air and scenery through more peaceful kinds of recreation.

Olmsted and Vaux's vision of Central Park relied on their "Greensward Plan" for controlling the types of activity and movement in the park. "In an effort to keep out sporting men and trotting matches, the Greensward plan had omitted long, straight drives; some newspapers worried that Central Park might turn into an 'aldermanic commons for fast driving'" (Rosenzweig and Blackmar 244), and, given the growing popularity of harness racing, such concerns seemed realistic. Park commissioners determined speed limits for carriages and horses, although debate usually ensued. The speed limits and absence of straight roads failed, however, to keep out those wanting to race, and arrests for speeding initially occurred as part of the "ban on fast driving" that park officials "intended to ensure not only safety but gentlemanly refinement." Class-based tensions in the park persisted, as park and city officials wished to maintain the park as a place of beauty and quiet recreation and to keep out those visitors deemed undesirable to gentlemen (Rosenzweig and Blackmar 245–246).

Early on in the history of Central Park, lower-rank groups wanting to play sports and ball games prompted the park board to at least consider their interests, or, perhaps more accurately, consider how to prevent them from being realized. Central Park historians Rosenzweig and Blackmar have researched park visitors' use of the grounds, as well as the class bias displayed by the refined gentlemen of the park board. Even before the park opened to the public, some of the early baseball clubs in New York (baseball is discussed further in chapter 4) asked the board to provide ball grounds for their use. Clubs for baseball, cricket, and other sports followed with their own petitions to park commissioners. As Rosenzweig and Blackmar have written, "The ball clubs saw the new park as the answer to their dreams, but Olmsted and the board began to wonder whether their presence might prove instead to be a nightmare" (249). Ball games, with their large teams and crowds and boisterous activities, worried park commissioners and like-minded park visitors from the upper class, who envisioned the park as a place of more refined recreation.

In an annual report about Central Park, the class issue surfaced in the restrictions that board members wanted to enforce on the behavior of people playing sports. It would not be possible "to satisfy the requirements of the numerous cricket, ball, and other adult clubs within the area of the Park, and at the same time preserve in the grounds an appearance that would be satisfactory to the much more numerous class that frequent the Park for the enjoyment of the refined and attractive features of its natural attractions to those that visit it merely as a picture." Park commissioners believed that sport and other vigorous physical activity that threatened the "picture" portrayed by natural scenery in the park needed to be curtailed. The officials supervising Central Park in the 1850s and 1860s believed that excluding ball games was an effective means to prevent "match games and the objectionable features that have been the frequent attendant of these games" (qtd. in Rosenzweig and Blackmar 249). Similar concerns surfaced about the use of public space at the playgrounds and rural scenery in the park—and about the type of sporting behavior exhibited by schoolboys. To limit activity by working-class youth, park authorities required boys to show a certificate from a teacher confirming their good attendance and character, but many working-class boys during this period did not attend school beyond their early years. Schoolgirls, too, gained access to the fields for certain sporting games such as croquet. Notably, "[t]he park would be open to women's recreation, but only to those genteel and restrained forms of exercise that the park's male

manager deemed appropriate" (Rosenzweig and Blackmar 249, 251).

One of the most popular sports pursued by women in Central Park was ice skating, which gave them an outdoor pastime on the frozen waterways to promote health and enjoyment. Whether skating with other women or girls or in a mixed-gender skating party, women turned increasingly to ice skating during the Antebellum Period. Writing about the rage for skating in Central Park, a *Harper's Weekly* journalist noted that park commissioners had provided good ice for the skaters, who had "turned their ponds and swamps for good use, by flooding them every cold night, and inviting skaters to try them every morning. The idea has been a hit." The winter sport attracted "thousands of persons of both sexes" at Central Park, and, "[t]hroughout the North and East, skating . . . [had] long been a favorite amusement with ladies as well as men" ("Skating" 101). Skating drew not only both sexes but also young and old alike, and young children just learning joined more experienced skaters in having their share of slips. One humorous illustration of the day showed a youngster observing the skating mishap of a policeman.

In warmer weather, women and young girls turned to swimming for healthful exercise. Women learning to safely care for and avoid the drowning of their children near waterways might swim in the public baths of Central Park. Swimming provided a means for women to achieve physical health and to prevent horrible drowning of family members, frequently reported in urban and rural newspapers of the day. While private baths were enjoyed by women of higher social status and means, public baths with a swimming pool provided a place where city women of modest means could learn to swim. A *New York Times* account of a bathhouse swim school in Central Park Garden indicated that visitors "would not only have witnessed feats of skill and endurance performed by women and girls. . . [b]ut by atoms of humanity not more than 4 to 5 years old" (qtd. in Johns and Farrell-Beck 55).

Tensions also arose in other cities, such as Boston and Chicago, over the number and types of participants engaging in sport in public spaces. As early as 1851 in Chicago, an ordinance was enacted to prohibit ball playing in parks. City fathers reasoned that such a law might dispel the image of the rapidly growing city as a frontier community. Then, as now, public amenities attracted the middle class and businesses to the city. By that time in burgeoning Midwest cities where urban men and

Women ice skating on the ladies' pond in Central Park, displaying their skills beside the other skaters.

Image from *Harper's Weekly*, 1860, Skating on The Ladies' Skating Pond.

women might partake of sports, games, and the beauty of park grounds, Chicago vied with St. Louis, Cincinnati, and Milwaukee for commercial dominance in the West.

Sporting Pastimes of African Americans and Native Americans

While middle- and upper-class white Americans touted the benefits of sport and exercise for health and desired to engage in new sporting experiences, the white Protestant majority held sway over the minority groups of African Americans and Native Americans. African Americans in Northern urban areas faced severe restrictions on their sporting experiences because of discrimination in public parks and facilities, and enslaved African Americans in the South confronted the shackles of bondage enforced by owners as they sought to create their own sporting and recreational activ-

ities within the slave community. Both free and enslaved African Americans sought the rejuvenation and toughness they might gain through sport and exercise to withstand both Southern white masters and powerful Northern whites who held economic, political, and social power. As a result, separate African American sporting organizations began to develop in the North, as free blacks continued to pursue their sporting heritage. Native Americans, on the other hand, were increasingly forced off of their lands in the East and moved to the West because of political ideologies (i.e., Manifest Destiny) in order for white families and land seekers to gain new and better land for settlement. Native Americans tried to maintain their cultural and sporting practices, such as lacrosse, but the forced western migration altered some of their sporting experiences.

African Americans

The white South's increasing dependence on slave labor to grow the tobacco, rice, and cotton that supported its agricultural way of life led to a growing population of slaves. Inside the slave community, from sundown to sunup, away from the harsh rigors of grueling labor and the master's watchful eye, slaves created their own world of culture and recreation to survive the brutalities of slave life. Slaves desired to gain some autonomy over their own lives in the time away from the fields and houses where they were subjected to the daily regimen of hard labor. In addition to singing, making music, and dancing, they used their physical skills in various sporting forms.

In the Southern plantations of the gentry, an informal boxing match between slaves was a common occurrence, and wealthy planters would also "frequently organize formal boxing contests and pit their slave champion against other slave champions from different plantations of the community." Historian David Wiggins has remarked that slave owners often won more on their wagers during these fights than on horse races. According to some accounts, once extremely good "boxer-slaves" earned fortunes "in bets for their masters, [they] were given their freedom and moved away from the South so they could ply their fistic trade to better financial advantage for themselves" (Wiggins, "Good" 273).

To meet that goal, the earliest black athletic stars had to travel abroad. One who did was Tom Molineaux, and it is not clear whether he was born to freedom or secured his liberty through his athletic skills. In any case, he embarked in 1809 for England, where he met another American-born black fighter, Bill Richmond. The latter became his trainer, and a year later Molineaux fought Tom Cribb for the championship of England before a hostile crowd. Molineaux disputed his loss to the champion but suffered the same fate in a rematch. He later turned to wrestling and died in Ireland in 1818.

Slaves enjoyed horse racing and often staged spontaneous and very informal races on the plantation. They would also accompany their masters to other plantations, and when the master rode, the slaves might do so as well, perhaps sharing in some of the excitement. Often they went simply as spectators, but frequently they were trainers or jockeys as well, and they did participate in racing contests, wherein skilled black jockeys earned pride in their horsemanship. A slave named William Greene was a jockey for several years on Edward Hamilton's plantation. "I remained with him [Hamilton] from nine years old until I was twenty," explains Greene. "He then took me to be a race rider. He kept a number of fine noble

Tom Molineaux (pictured) lost to Tom Cribb in a championship boxing match in England.

From B. Spears and R. Swanson, 1988, *History of sport and physical education in the United States* (Dubuque, IA: Wm. C. Brown), 153.

horses, with a number of race horses; and being of the right size for a rider he took me to ride races." Similarly, Jacob Stroyer, who lived on a South Carolina plantation, was first employed as a trainer of racehorses and then became a jockey (Wiggins, "Good" 273–274). Given the importance of horse racing in the nineteenth century, slaves became a key part of this sport. "From the beginning of American racing, some of the nation's most prominent turfmen were Southerners, and at the track they practiced sophisticated and complex forms of human bondage and believed that they demonstrated how integral slavery was for building a powerful and prosperous United States, how richly they deserved Northern deference for their economic imperatives and customs" (Mooney 6). Austin Jones, the enslaved black man who was the jockey for North Carolina planter Willie Jones, served as a groom and later as a trainer and stable supervisor. For Southerners, "the racetrack was not just a stage on which white men acted out the world they wanted to make. It was a place run on the labor and skill of black men" (Mooney 1, 6).

The Futurity Race at Sheepshead Bay by **Currier & Ives** shows black jockeys racing.
Image courtesy of Library of Congress, LC-USZ62-14022.

African Americans in the North, who generally worked manual-labor and low-paying jobs because of racial discrimination, might participate in horse-racing activities, although sometimes it took a bit of cleverness to pull off. The following account from the black press revealed how one black servant outwitted his master and displayed athletic prowess in his riding skills despite Sabbath restrictions on sport. In "An Unexpected Race," a story published in the 1855 *Provincial Freeman*, in a large town in Worcester County, Massachusetts, a clergyman named Ridewell owned a cherished horse. Of Baptist sentiment, Ridewell was "very rigid in his ideas of moral propriety. He had in his employ an old negro, named Pompey, and if this latter individual was not so strict in his morals as his master, he was . . . very cunning. . . . Pomp was a useful servant, and the old clergyman never hesitated to trust him with the most important business." Yet in this town, several individuals feared not what Mr. Ridewell preached, and instead of attending Sabbath church service they would gather on Sunday evenings upon a piece of land "in the outskirts of the town, and there race horses." This place, hidden from view by woods, allowed the participants to hold horse races without the

knowledge of officers or others who might have stopped them. Here, the African American servant manifested his cleverness. Pompey's knowledge of horses came into play, as "the good old clergyman owned one of the best horses in the country. This horse was of the old Morgan stock, with the mixture of the Arabian blood in his veins, and it was generally known that few beasts could pass him on the road." Mr. Ridewell, as a preacher, took no worldly pride in his horse, and in fact "stoutly declared that the fleetness of his horse never afforded him any gratification." Pompey knew that this valued horse remained in the pasture, because the clergyman lived close to the church and thus always walked to meeting. Pompey discovered that the horse races were on tap and decided to enter his master's horse on his own,

for he felt sure that old Morgan could beat anything in the shape of horseflesh that could be produced in that quarter.

So on the very next Sunday evening, he hid the bridle under his jacket went out into the pasture and caught the horse, and then off to the spot where the wicked ones had congregated. Here he found some dozen horses assembled, and the races were about to commence. Pomp mounted his beast, and at the signal, old Morgan entered into the spirit of the thing, and came out two rods [11 yards, or 10 meters] ahead of everything. So Pomp, won quite a pile, and before dark he was well initiated in horse-racing. . . . He did so again, and again he won . . . [and so] for two months, [could be seen] making his appearance upon the racing ground every Sunday afternoon . . . . And during this time Pompey was not the only one who had learned to love the racing. No, for old Morgan himself had come to love the excitement of the thing, too, and his every motion when upon the track showed how zealously he entered into the spirit of the game.

Cobb, "An Unexpected Race" n. pag.

Yet the racing by Pompey and his cohorts did not remain secret to a deacon viewing it from a distance, and developments eventually led to an "unexpected race" involving the minister. Reverend Ridewell, morally outraged at such Sabbath races, thought he, fellow deacons, and others shocked at the races might catch them in the act by going to the spot. On the following Sabbath evening, he ordered Pomp to bring up Morgan and put him in the stable. When the clergyman and his horse then came upon the race scene, "The horses of the wicked men were just drawing up for a start as the minister approached, and some of the riders who at once recognized 'old Morgan' did not recognize the reverend individual who rode him." One of the jockeys asked the minister if he was there for the first race, and the stunned clergyman responded, "Wicked men!" Just at that moment, the race leader shouted, "And off it is!" and Reverend Ridewell was drawn into the race: "Old Morgan knew that word too well, for no sooner did it fall upon his ears than he struck out his nose, and with one wild snort he started, and the rest of the racers, twelve in number, kept him company." The minister's efforts to halt the fast-racing Morgan were futile, and those present admired what appeared to be his riding skill. One approached him afterward and said, "'[Y]ou ride well. . . . We had not looked for this honor'" (hence the name "Ridewell"!). The matter was then resolved, as Pompey informed his master that "[s]ome of those wicked men had been in the habit of stealing old Morgan from the pasture, and racing him on Sabbath afternoons. Pomp found out this much—but he could not find out who did it." The whole incident was resolved such that Reverend Ridewell was cleared, with no immoral actions on his part, and he could finally "laugh with right good will when he spoke of his unexpected race. Be sure there was no more Sab-

bath racing in town," by Pompey or others (Cobb, "An Unexpected Race" n. pag.).

In the South, slaves' swimming skills, utilized by masters for work on the waterways near plantations, could also be displayed in informal swimming pastimes. Bill Crump, a slave in antebellum North Carolina, remarked that he worked in the fields from sunup to sundown (as quoted in Dawson with the dialect spoken): "[W]e had a couple of hours at dinner time tar swim or lay on de banks uv de little crick an' sleep. . . . 'bout sundown master let us go swim ag'in iff' ne we anted to do it" (qtd. in Dawson 1340).

At other times, plantation masters organized formal swimming contests. As with similar owner-organized competitions in boxing, wrestling, and racing on horseback or on foot, swimming races gave slaves a chance to display physical prowess and gain self-esteem. These contests pitted the best swimmers of one planter against those of another planter (as discussed in chapter 1), and, as with other staged slave sports, plantation owners often wagered on the outcome. Victory in such a contest likely provided slaves with prestige among their fellows in the slave quarters.

Some enslaved swimmers also participated in blood sport in the water. Slaves who showcased their stamina and swimming skills in battling sharks, alligators, and other dangerous sea creatures might find masters wagering on their athletic exploits. Whether the slaves who defeated such sea animals were allowed to keep them for their own use as food, as was sometimes the case when slaves went fishing or hunting, may not be knowable. In either case, such displays of fierce aquatic skills may have enabled slaves to express some strength and pride within the slave institution that was designed to fully crush their humanity and independence. Indeed, "bondmen may have used aquatic blood sports to display and affirm their masculinity" (Dawson 1341).

Throughout the South, African Americans faced strict segregation, and the vast majority remained slaves throughout the Antebellum Period. Although some slaves were forced to become boxers, wrestlers, or jockeys for their owners' amusement, many slaves created and enjoyed their own diversions, such as singing and dancing at parties, hunting, and fishing. Josiah Hanson, a slave who later became a minister, remarked that "[t]he sternest and most covetous master cannot frighten or whip the fun out of us" (Wiggins, "Sport and Popular Pastimes" 62).

Even in areas of the country where slavery was not practiced, rigid racial segregation in rural and urban locales in early nineteenth-century America still made it unlikely for free blacks to integrate into sporting facilities. Still, free black men and boys were united in lively activities such as boxing, track-and-field events, hunting, and fishing. In antebellum cities such as Boston, free blacks formed their own churches because of their exclusion from white churches and their desire to have black preachers leading their important meeting and spiritual space. Free blacks also desired to have their recreational space safe from racial discrimination.

Native Americans

Native American inhabitants battling white encroachment in the Midwest and Southeast were often forced to move westward to lands less populated by white settlers. In their still-unconquered western lands, Native Americans continued to practice their rapidly vanishing pastoral and, for some such as the Plains Indians, nomadic lifestyle of following the buffalo herds. In addition to hunting, they engaged in dances and stickball games (especially lacrosse), and tribes of the Southwest practiced long-distance running rituals. Lacrosse seemed to be inherent in most Native American cultures, and the contest often involved masses of players. White missionaries, however, railed against the gambling and nudity that accompanied some games. An 1825 game in Georgia drew a crowd of three thousand people and bets of $3,500 total (Vennum 111, 277). By the 1830s, Eastern tribes who had more exposure to white society adopted more formal rules, enforced by referees, and whites became commonplace as spectators at games among the Iroquois Confederacy in New York. By 1848, the Cherokees of the Southeast adorned themselves in their best clothing for such matches.

The interplay of Anglo and Indian cultures inevitably produced a hybrid population and sporting culture. The nascent field of anthropology took great interest in physical differences, socially constructing the concept of race in the process. Within that context, footracing gained great favor in the 1830s, and professional runners competed for stakes and publicized their efforts with pseudonyms meant to draw attention, such as "the American Deer," "the Boston Buck," and "the Yankee Clipper." The racialization of bodies produced stereotypes, and it was widely believed that Native Americans were more powerful runners. Louis Bennett, the product of a mixed union between a Scotsman and a Seneca woman, capitalized on this notion by adopting the name "Deerfoot" and running in a loincloth and moccasins with a feather in his hair. He became a national sensation when he succeeded in breaking the record for a 10-mile (16-kilometer) run. In 1835, Henry Stannard, a Connecticut farmer, had been the first to run 10 miles in less than an hour (59:48). Deerfoot embarked on a tour of Great Britain in 1861, where he lowered the record to 51:26.

Immigrants and Sporting Cultures

Immigrants to the United States in the middle decades of the nineteenth century brought their cultural, linguistic, religious, culinary, and athletic practices to their new country. To maintain their ethnic identity and form a community with their fellow immigrants amid the larger white, Protestant, and often elite population, immigrant groups created their own cultural and physical spaces to experience sporting forms brought over from their homelands. In ethnic-minority athletic clubs, newly arrived immigrants organized leisure activities to promote their own language, values, and cultural traditions among their youth. Newcomers to American cities encountered a cultural and physical environment of people, surroundings, and behavior considerably different from those of their homelands, and sport became a way for men and women to foster a sense of fellowship with those of similar ethnicity, race, social class, or experience. Indeed, "[s]port clubs, as one type of voluntary association, became one of the basic means by which certain groups sought to establish subcommunities within the larger society." These subcommunities allowed members to participate in sport and maintain their cultural identity (Rader, "The Quest" 356–357). Ethnic sporting, social, and drinking practices—especially those of young men—sometimes clashed with the interests of white, educated, middle-class social reformers and their agenda of promoting physical activity and sport linked with good health, proper morals, and preferred gender and behavioral codes. Over time, however, ethnic sporting clubs would influence the sporting habits of native-born Americans (as discussed in the next chapter).

German American Turners

Germans were among the first immigrants to the new United States. Charles Beck, a member of the German Turner gymnastics movement, traveled to

Massachusetts in 1825. There he was employed at the Round Hill School, founded two years earlier in Northampton by Joseph Cogswell and George Bancroft. The school introduced physical education to its curriculum, and Beck instituted an outdoor gymnastics site. Charles Follen, another German Turner, was employed as an instructor at a Boston gymnasium and instructed students at Harvard University in gymnastics in 1826. Yet another Turner, Francis Lieber, arrived the following year to direct the Boston gym and operate its swimming pool.

Many Germans migrated to America in 1848 during a time of political revolution in Germany. These immigrants formed voluntary associations modeled on those in their native country, known as Turner societies. German immigrants founded the first Turner society in the United States in Cincinnati, Ohio, in 1848, followed by a Turner society located in New York, and then one in Philadelphia in 1849. In 1851, a group of German immigrant men in Indianapolis formed a new organization to foster athletic and cultural activities from their homeland and called it the Indianapolis Turngemeinde. This Turner society, referring to the German word *Turner,* meaning a tumbler or gymnast, was founded by August Hoffmeister, Jakob Metzger, Alexander Metzger, Clemens Vonnegut, John Ott, and Karl Hill (Stempfel 5). These German Turners in America endorsed gymnastics for attaining physical fitness as part of their educational emphasis, encapsulated in the motto "a sound mind in a sound body" (from the Latin "mens sana in corpore sana"). German immigrants of some of the Turner societies joined together to establish the national Turner organization in America in 1850 to nurture their cultural practices, language, and beliefs. They wished to promote the German gymnastic system, focused on a program of marching, free exercise, and gymnastics drills, as well as dancing for girls, and they promoted apparatus-based exercise using equipment such as the balance beam, rings, horse, parallel bars, and vault, as well as games and play. These early German American Turner societies drew on the philosophy of Friedrich Ludwig Jahn (1778–1852), known as the father of German gymnastics, and they merged athletic interests with ethnic interests in seeking fellowship with other German newcomers to American cities.

The same year the Indianapolis Germans founded their Turner society (1851), the German American sports event known as the National Turnfest took place in Philadelphia. Featuring gymnastics, disciplined physical exercises, and athletic endeavors such as running and jumping, the National Turnfest is the oldest ongoing amateur athletic contest in America. Thus, the German Americans who founded the first Turner society in 1848 became pioneers in physical education in the United States; additional Turner societies followed in Milwaukee, Chicago, Louisville, and other cities with large German immigrant populations. Until the mid-1850s, when there were established German populations in various cities, all of these Turner societies owed their organization and growth to the numerous German immigrants who came to the United States to escape the revolutionary uproar in Germany in 1848 and 1849 and to pursue their political views in freedom (Hofmann; Barney).

The Turners of Indianapolis included gymnastics from their earliest days, when they used founder John Ott's furniture factory. "The front yard was used for physical exercises. The gymnastics apparatus consisted of a horizontal bar; later money was raised among the members for a set of parallel bars" (Stempfel 5). The Indianapolis Turngemeinde, known as the Gymnastic Community, merged with the Indianapolis Socialistischer Turnverein, and the new organization became known as the Social Gymnastic Club. These German American Turners joined together to build their first Turnhalle, or Turner Hall, which remained a hub of German life for immigrants, offering the use of gymnastic apparatus, a library, lectures, and musical and theatrical performances. The start of the Civil War, during which many German Americans joined the Union Army, led to inactivity and the eventual closing of the Turnhalle.

The German Turners in Milwaukee also played an active role in gymnastics and competitive exercises in implementing the Turner philosophy of "a sound mind in a sound body." Business leaders in the German American community founded the Milwaukee Turners in July 1853. Led by George Brosius, known as the American Turnfather, the Milwaukee Turnverein emphasized the German gymnastic system of using apparatus and physical exercise drills. Brosius had come to Milwaukee in 1842 with his family, and he began teaching physical instruction at the Turnverein Milwaukee in 1854. Milwaukee Turners who were physical education instructors promoted the introduction of physical education and gymnastics in public schools in Wisconsin and the nation. German American Turners formed communities throughout the United States, from the East Coast to the West Coast, and spread their intellectual and sporting ideas to men and women.

International Perspective

Turnen: On Politics, Bodies, and Feminism

Among the "revolutionary events" of 1848 in Germany was the founding of a women's *Turner* club. In view of the situation of the "weaker sex" in the nineteenth century, women's gymnastics was indeed revolutionary. Women were deprived at that time of all political rights and barred from a university education as well as academic professions.

The first initiatives on girls' gymnastics were taken in the 1830s, as increasing numbers of doctors and teachers advocated gymnastics for girls so they could later serve as good mothers and diligent housewives. Thus, teachers of *Turnen* and the owners of private *Turnen* institutes offered gymnastics courses for girls with promises to improve their beauty, grace, and health. Several private schools for the daughters of wealthy families added gymnastics to their curricula in order to be able to compete on the education market by offering an attractive array of subjects. Although gymnastics was encouraged as part of girls' education, the question of whether adult women should take part in gymnastics was met with almost unanimous rejection.

Demands for women's emancipation had already been voiced in the eighteenth century as a consequence of the Enlightenment. These demands were taken up again in the liberal climate of the years preceding the March Revolution of 1848, when numerous women were filled with enthusiasm about the patriotic and liberal ideas of the bourgeoisie, and many of them joined democratically oriented associations and societies. Besides clubs and institutes for women's education and women's support, this era saw the founding of women's *Turner* clubs in many German towns.

In 1846, for example, a "female *Turner* club" was opened in Mannheim, whose members were "highly respectable ladies of the town" and which "set itself none other than the doubtless very agreeable task of encouraging *Turnen* among young school-aged females." Considerably more revolutionary was the women's *Turner* club in Frankfurt, founded in 1848 by eight "maidens" and three women aged between 18 and 50. The women pledged to "meet twice a week, 'untrussed', in linen *Turnen* dress. All physical constraints limiting free movement and impairing health should be rejected and cast off, outside the *Turnen* grounds as well." The dress of the female *Turner*, equally revolutionary, consisted of "trousers and usually short blouses." The purpose of the association, according to its members, was the fight against the "decay and degeneration" of the assumedly "weak sex" (Pfister 1981).

The female gymnasts stood up for "equality with men" and for a "future world revolution." Thus, they met not only to practice gymnastics but also for "a weekly gathering in addition to the *Turnen* sessions so that the intellectual purpose of our club is also kept alive." (Pfister 1981).

However, these modest beginnings of an independent women's *Turnen* movement did not survive the collapse of the 1848 revolution, and the clubs closed down in the early 1850s. When the revolution failed, many of the *Turner* who had taken an active part in the movement immigrated to the United States.

Information from Pfister, G. "1848 und die Andfänge des Mädchen—und Frauenturnens." *Deutsches turnen* (1981): 1, 8-10; 2, 29-30; 3, 47-49.

Pfister, Gertrud. "Physical Activity in the Name of the Fatherland: Turnen and the National Movement (1810-1820)." *Sporting Heritage* H.1 (1996): 14–36.

Scottish Caledonian Clubs

Scottish settlers perpetuated traditional Highland games in New York as early as 1836; they formed the first Caledonian club in Boston in 1853 and went on to form numerous Caledonian clubs in various areas during the 1850s. These Scottish newcomers to America wished to sustain their language, native costume, music, dance, foodways, games, and athletics in their new home. The many Caledonian clubs that followed typically limited their membership to those of Scottish lineage.

At their athletic meets, they competed in several events: long jump, high jump, running, sack races, blindfolded wheelbarrow races, vaulting, putting heavy stones, caber (pole) tossing, and tugs-of-war, as well as dancing Highland flings and a gambol with broadswords. In the late 1850s, the New York Caledonian Club began to commercialize and professionalize its annual games by charging admission fees and offering cash prizes to winning competitors. Widespread interest in the events drew as many as twenty thousand spectators at the games in New York City, and Caledonian

The Caledonian and Thistle clubs playing the Scottish national game of curling upon the frozen pond in Central Park, New York, as shown in Frank Leslie's illustrated newspaper.

Photo courtesy of Library of Congress, LC-USZ62-108125.

clubs eventually opened their competitions to non-Scottish athletes of various races or ethnicities (Rader, *American Sports* [2004] 69). Some of these Caledonian contests also drew the attention of American-born athletes and spectators, and the running, jumping, and weight-throwing contests were eventually adopted as modern track-and-field events by young, white, upper-class men.

Irish Americans

Antebellum Irish taverns and boxing clubs in the Northeast became popular sites for young, working-class Irish men to sharpen their pugilistic skills and enjoy beer, gambling, and camaraderie with each other. In the gender-divided social world of Irish men and women in the nineteenth century, the physical space of the tavern and the sporting behaviors associated with it were clearly marked as male terrain. Approximately 70 percent of prizefighters in the Antebellum Era were Irish or Irish American, and pugilism fostered a rising nationalism in the United States, as Irish newcomers, stridently opposed to the British overlords who

occupied their ancestral homeland, challenged English fighters (Riess, *Sport* 87). The adoption of British prizefighting rules, which forbade hitting below the belt or punching a downed fighter and provided for referees or umpires, signaled a further transition to regulated, middle-class standards of sporting decorum, in contrast with the no-holds-barred practices typical on the American frontier. Before the new rules took effect in the United States, a New York boxing match in 1842 had produced a fatality, as Thomas McCoy bled to death.

In 1849, Tom Hyer, backed by nativists, defeated Irish immigrant Yankee Sullivan in a bout that portrayed internecine social tensions between the native-born and newcomers. At the same time, John Morrissey (1831–1878), another Irish immigrant, exemplified the possibility of ascendance from street brawler to respectability. One of eight children born to a poor family in Ireland, Morrissey emigrated to Troy, New York, and then traveled to New York City to test his toughness. In 1853, he defeated Yankee Sullivan under British rules and claimed the American boxing championship. He successfully defended his title in 1858 against

American John C. Heenan in a fight held in Canada. Morrissey retired with fame and fortune as proprietor of a gambling establishment, as explored further in the next chapter.

Heenan, however, challenged Tom Sayers, the British champion, in 1860. The fight, staged in Great Britain, lasted 43 rounds over a period of 2 hours and 20 minutes but produced no decision, as both men claimed the championship. The fight carried great cultural significance, as the young United States was divesting itself of British influence in search of its own identity. Sport thus assumed the role of surrogate warfare, as the United States moved toward international prominence throughout the remainder of the century (Kirsch, *Sports* [Vol. 3] 142–147).

Meanwhile, the Irish presence in boxing remained prominent in the Antebellum Era. Morrissey's postretirement ventures as a gambling-hall proprietor included building a lavish parlor at Saratoga Springs, New York, and his political connections allowed him and his business associates to construct a racetrack there. More generally, the boxing bouts of the middle nineteenth century manifested the ethnic and cultural conflicts of the larger society, as Yankee (typically Protestant) fighters sparred against Irish Catholic fighters, thus highlighting anti-Irish sentiment and concern about the thousands of new immigrants entering many of the cities and organizations in the Northeast.

Asian Americans

Most immigrants to America in the early and middle nineteenth century came from European groups; however, after the discovery of gold in 1848 in Sutter's Mill, California, some Chinese immigrants began to appear. Asian immigration—that is, "meaningful Chinese immigration to the United States[,] begins roughly with the California gold rush of 1849. . . . Between the beginnings

of the Chinese migration in 1848 and the passage of the Chinese Exclusion Act in 1882, perhaps three hundred thousand Chinese entered the United States" (Daniels, *Coming* 239). During the Gold Rush, these were mostly single young men; the larger period of Chinese immigration to the western United States, mainly California, occurred after the Civil War. Most of the sporting organizations formed by Chinese people in California, in response to the racial discrimination they faced, arose in the latter part of the nineteenth century. Some Chinese Americans participated in sports by the 1890s in the San Francisco Bay Area, including "hundreds of contests ranging from boxing and cycling to Caledonian games, baseball, football, and more" (Park, "Sports" 446). Organizations designed to promote sport for Chinese American youth began to emerge in the early twentieth century.

Summary

The Antebellum Period marked a time of widespread change for Americans in rural and urban life—and for immigrants coming to America. From the 1820s through the 1850s, health reformers and advocates developed a positive outlook on the need for vigorous exercise and sport in order to advance a nation of sound American men and women. Yet not all inhabitants of the United States gained access to sporting opportunities or were included in the programs touted by reformers and sports journalists. Increased attention by people of diverse backgrounds to sport, along with the growth of industrialization, urbanization, and technological innovation—as well as the influence of social-class distinctions and gender and race lines that remained in the culture—provided the framework for modern competitive sport in the nineteenth century, as discussed in the following chapter.

DISCUSSION QUESTIONS

1. Compare the influence of sports journalism on attitudes about exercise and sport in the Antebellum Period and in the present period of the twenty-first century.

2. Why did exercise and sport form a focal point for many male and female antebellum health reformers during the decades of the 1820s through the 1850s? Identify some of these reformers and compare their recommendations.

(continued)

3. Explain the ways in which rural and urban tensions influenced health and sport movements in the Antebellum Period.

4. What factors affected the development of women's sport and physical education in antebellum American culture?

5. How did sport become part of the cultural experience of white Americans in the emerging middle class? Of immigrants? Of other minorities in antebellum American culture?

Chapter 4

Rise of Rationalized and Modern Sport
1850–1870

CHAPTER OBJECTIVES

After reading this chapter, you will have learned about the following:

- Factors shaping the rise of modern sport in the middle years of the nineteenth century in the United States
- Specific ways in which social class shaped the organization of sports clubs and associations
- The importance of the sporting fraternity to competitive sport and economic interests in sport
- The establishment of rationalized recreation and sport, as well as the ways in which this process was affected by issues related to gender, race, and ethnicity
- The effect of nationalistic beliefs on the emergence of American team sports
- Issues related to the development of the first intercollegiate contest in the United States
- The effect of the Civil War on sporting experiences in the United States

The basis of modern organized team sports emerged in the early days of American baseball, which gained popularity in the mid-nineteenth century, as described by Charles Peverelly in his *Book of American Pastimes* (1866):

> The game of Base Ball has now become beyond question the leading feature of the out-door sports of the United States, and to account for its present truly proud tradition, there are many and sufficient reasons. It is a game which is peculiarly suited to the American temperament and disposition; the nine innings are played in the brief space of two and one half hours, or less. From the moment the first striker takes his position, and poises his bat, it has an excitement and vim about it, until the last hand is put out in the ninth inning. . . .
>
> It is also, comparatively, an economical recreation; the uniform is not costly, the playing implements, colors, and furnishing of a neat club-room, need not occasion an extravagant outlay when divided, pro rata, by the members of the full club. . . . [T]he great mass . . . can participate in this healthgiving and noble pastime.
>
> The game stands today in a proud and fairly-won position—scarcely requiring eulogy from any source. Dating from the years when the Knickerbocker Club [1845], closely followed by the Gotham, Eagle, and Empire, gave their colors to the breeze as rallying points for the lovers of the game to muster at, it has grown with giant strides until its organizations are the pride of numberless villages, towns, and cities, all over the land. . . . Having no debasing attribute, and being worthy of the presence of the good and the refined, it has everywhere been countenanced and encouraged by our best citizens; and of the thousands who gather at important matches, we have always noted with sincere gratification that the ladies constituted an honored proportion.

qtd. in Levine, *American* 35–37

In the middle decades of the nineteenth century, the growth of sports such as baseball accelerated in American society, and a variety of perspectives were forwarded on the meanings of sport as an expanding form of cultural activity in the United States. Some advocates touted the benefits of American sports during this time period—one of

intellectual, technological, scientific, and social changes, as well as continued population growth. In the decades preceding the Civil War, sport grew rapidly; during the years of brutal fighting, sport was of course affected by the war but continued to be played at various times and places throughout the conflict.

The reasons for modern sport's rapid development during this period were various, and the growth was of course affected by larger issues of gender, race, and social class. The gendered aspect of baseball was noted by William Wood, physical education instructor and author of physical training and athletic manuals, who wrote in 1867 that "Base Ball [may be] truly called the American National Game. There is scarcely a city or town or village in the United States where this invigorating and manly exercise is not to some extent enjoyed" (*Manual* [Vol. 1] 14). Yet other commentators on American life expressed concern that giving too much time and emphasis to playing and promoting sport detracted from appropriate values of a work ethic, especially for those in the lower and middle classes. After traveling to communities in the northeastern United States, correspondent William Clift, authoring his columns using the name Timothy Bunker, wrote an essay titled "Base Ball Clubs," in which he countered the view of many antebellum health and sport reformers: "Base ball, as it is played now, is getting to be a great nuisance," because it "makes good ball players, but bad farmers and mechanics, bad husbands and fathers. I am not ready to have the plow beams whittled into ball clubs just yet" (Clift 304, 306).

This chapter examines the development of various sports and the wide attention generally paid to sports between 1850 and 1870, as the popularity of sports intensified and sporting journalism and commentaries on sporting activities continued from the ebb and flow of the antebellum years, examined in chapter 3. Sports that were either emerging or growing considerably during this period included early forms of baseball, horse racing, footracing, yachting, rowing and crew, boxing, gymnastics, and racket sports. These years also brought the country's first intercollegiate sporting action and, more generally, saw sport become a major part of

1840s	1845	1848
■ Southern expansion of slavery and antislavery movements continue (into the 1860s)	■ New York Knickerbocker Base Ball Club organized ■ Alexander Cartwright records baseball rules of the Knickerbocker Club	■ First Women's Rights Convention in Seneca Falls, N.Y.

popular culture for diverse peoples in the United States. The various rationales for organizing sports during this time period evoked an assortment of viewpoints on sports.

Concept of Modern Sport

From the 1840s until the eve of the Civil War, the number of American city dwellers increased because of immigration, industrialization, and the growth of new occupations. The stream of people—from overseas and from rural America—pouring into factories in increasingly cramped cities such as New York, Boston, and Chicago prompted concern about the need for urbanites to engage in physical exercise and sport in order to offset their otherwise sedentary routines. The development of sport in this urban American culture was also influenced by technological innovations in home and work life, along with changes in communication and transportation. As historian Steven Riess has explained, "The evolution of the city, more than any other single factor, influenced the development of organized sport and recreational athletic pastimes in America. Nearly all contemporary major sports evolved or were invented in the city" (Riess, *City* 1). The city served as the locale for key moments in the development of American sporting culture; it was the site of the first organized, rationalized (i.e., justified with beneficial reasons for playing sports in the eyes of supporters and played with rules), commercialized, and professional sports. In the process of urban cultural expansion, sporting culture also expanded because of changes in the city's physical environment and structures, increases in urban population, and the circulation of fresh perspectives on sport expressed by peoples of varied social class, race, gender, and ethnicity.

Indeed, the city became the focal point of modern sport. As discussed in chapter 3, health and sport reformers during this period called on citizens to engage in healthy activity as a way to provide the incipient nation with a population marked by sound moral and physical strength. These proponents saw modern American sport

and physical recreation as an antidote to the enervating effects of long hours of work, school study, and intellectual business pursuits for many white Americans of the middle class. Whether performing exercises with an "Indian club" (a bottle-shaped club of varying weight) for increased strength and vigor or participating in rowing, ball games, or gymnastics in newly formed athletic clubs, urban dwellers increasingly made sport a central part of urban American life in the middle decades of the nineteenth century.

This crucial period brought the development of new sporting forms, as well as the continuation

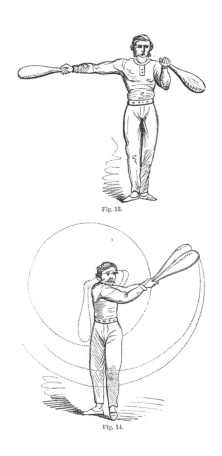

Fig. 13.

Fig. 14.

Indian club exercises were designed to develop a healthy body.

Reprinted from W. Wood, 1867, *Manual of physical exercises: comprising gymnastics, rowing, skating, fencing, cricket, calisthenics, sailing, swimming, sparring, baseball. Together with rules for training and sanitary suggestions* (New York: Harper Brothers).

1850	1851	1852	1854
■ Compromise of 1850 passes; deals with slavery issues and sectional conflicts ■ Fugitive Slave Act passes (part of Compromise of 1850)	■ First America's Cup yacht race staged	■ First intercollegiate athletic contest held (Yale vs. Harvard rowing)	■ Kansas–Nebraska Act passes

and growth of previously practiced physical recreations, all of which were part of a transition from premodern to modern sport in American culture. Sport historian Allen Guttmann has articulated key characteristics of the nature of modern sport: secularism, equality, rationalism, bureaucratic organizations, quantification, and the quest for records (*From Ritual to Record*). Drawing on this framework, other sports historians have examined how these modern forms of sport were characterized. As historian George Kirsch has explained it, "Democratization, rationalization, bureaucratization, specialization, regional, national, and international competition, extensive media coverage, and fascination with numbers all characterized the new style of athletics." In addition, as modern sport emerged in the mid-nineteenth century, "Sporting clubs and associations of organizations [voluntary associations] scheduled matches and legislated regulations to govern play on and off the field" (*Sports* [Vol. 3] xiv). The nature of urban life, in which work and leisure patterns were increasingly regulated by the clock and by social stratification, led to an increasing emphasis on outcomes of sporting contests and on recording performance statistics and breaking records. Other elements of modern sport include equality of opportunity for all players (in theory, as players in a given competition play by the rules, all have a fair chance to win), competition as a key factor in American culture at a time when many male leaders and politicians viewed competition as a means of achieving success and victory, and codification of rules. The emergence of these attitudes influenced the growth of sport in the middle of the nineteenth century. As Kirsch has said, "Professionalism and commercialism inevitably followed as the mania for sports spread throughout society. . . . Spectators paid to see their heroes in action; the telegraph and printing press kept millions abreast of the latest results" (*Sports* [Vol. 3] xiv). Similarly, historian Melvin Adelman has posited six main characteristics that differentiate modern sport from premodern sport: organization, rules, competition, role differentiation, public information, and statistics and records. Although the transition may not have occurred in one swift line of change, the rise of modern sport was marked by clear movement toward these characteristics ("The First" 6–7).

The modern sporting boom in America was initially a male-dominated movement, with men serving as the players, managers, and, in many sports, the spectators. Women did of course participate in this cultural development in their own ways, although as in earlier times (covered in preceding chapters), gendered ideology and customs meant that women's sports and other recreational physical activity developed in different ways from men's.

Influence of Transportation on the Development of Modern Sport

Major urban centers that served as hubs for railroad routes became key cities in the rise of sport in the mid-nineteenth century. Railroads such as the Baltimore and Ohio (begun in 1828) replaced transportation by boats and barges, moving goods and humans faster over long distances and playing a crucial role in bringing people together to play and watch urban sports in larger numbers. By 1840, 3,000 miles (4,828 kilometers) of track had been laid, mainly in the Northeast. By 1850, some 30,000 miles (48,280 kilometers) of track linked the Eastern and old Northwestern (lower Midwestern) sections of the country (Nash et al., Brief 5th ed. 283), and cities such as New York, Boston, Philadelphia, Chicago, Baltimore, and St. Louis became known for their rich sporting cultures for the upper, middle, and lower classes.

The railroad expanded the city from a local walking environment, with close proximity required in order to secure sites for sporting activity, to a larger setting where participants could travel to other destinations in order to watch or compete in sports. Some towns aided railroad companies in securing passengers when sports teams and their followers traveled to neutral destinations for competitions in locales served by a railroad line. In the summer of 1852, Harvard and Yale competed in the first intercollegiate athletic contest when a railroad company sponsored a race to promote its resort at Lake Winnipesaukee in New

1857	1858	1859
■ U.S. Supreme Court decides Dred Scott case regarding slavery and citizenship	■ Muscular Christianity movement emerges, with Thomas Wentworth Higginson writing "Saints, and Their Bodies," promoting moral and physical health ■ National Association of Base Ball Players founded	■ First intercollegiate baseball game played (Amherst over Williams 73-32) ■ U.S. championship regatta in Boston won by Joshua Ward

England as the Cradle of Modern Sport

Games and dances, physical activities, performances and movement cultures have always existed in all societies. On closer scrutiny, we detect that the multifaceted world of sport and games has culture-specific patterns, and from the nineteenth century onward a specific form of physical culture developed in England. This was modern sport, which is characterized by the (theoretical) equality of opportunity and an orientation toward performance and competition. The most important trait of modern sport is its orientation toward the setting and keeping of records. In this way, performances in running, for example, can be compared with each other even though they take place at different times and in different places, without the runners ever having met each other. As Guttmann has emphasized, the principle of competition and the pursuit of records have had numerous consequences, including quantification of performance, standardization of apparatus and facilities, bureaucratization, specialization, rationalization (i.e., a logical relationship between means and ends), and professionalization (*Games*). Thus it is not a specific movement or pattern of movements that makes a physical activity a sport but the principles and intentions underlying it. Even if abstract performances and records may have existed in other epochs and cultures, the combination of the principles just enumerated is typical of sport in industrialized Western countries.

In considering why England became the cradle of sport, a number of theories have been put forward, ascribing the origin of sport variously to Puritanism or the Enlightenment and the world views associated with these movements. In addition, aside from its social structure and relatively high level of industrialization, one must also take into account the country's protected position as an island, its political system of constitutional monarchy, its imperialist policies, and the power it derived from the British Empire at large.

According to Dunning and Sheard, rugby, cricket, pedestrian races, and especially boxing matches were organized before the Industrial Revolution. Boxing developed from fist fighting to a sport based on rules and regulations in which younger members of the aristocracy and gentry also participated in the middle of the eighteenth century. Besides boxing, the struggle for yards (meters) and against seconds also became fashionable and was enthusiastically taken up in rowing, running, and horse racing. Originally, members of the English upper class used their watermen or footmen in order to compete; later, gentlemen themselves competed against each other. Part of the attraction of these competitions lay in the betting that accompanied them; in turn, betting made regulations and standardization necessary to ensure that money changed hands only after a fair competition.

Dunning and Sheard explain the development of modern sport with England's distinct social configuration. The early dissolution of feudalism gave peasants the opportunity to play their rough games, and the relative independence of the aristocracy from the monarchy opened the way for a wide range of rural pastimes.

The emergence of modern sport is not only an outcome of the specific socioeconomic conditions in England but also a part of the modernization processes which took place in Europe during the transition from the eighteenth to the nineteenth century. There is undoubtedly a connection between the rise of sport and the adoption of the values, standards, and structures of industrialization—including rationality, technological progress, the abstract organization of time, and an economy aimed at the accumulation of capital.

Sport was initially restricted to the English upper class, then to the upper and middle classes, before it finally reached the workers. Moreover, the rise of sport was closely connected with the educational system. During the nineteenth century, sport gained new importance and a new meaning in English public schools (Mangan). Headmasters used games, especially football and cricket, as a form of social control in the belief that the wild folk football games had to be regulated and thus tamed in order to discipline the players. Between 1850 and 1890, sports and games became compulsory in the leading public schools. Competition also arose between schools and universities, the best example of which is perhaps the famous boat race between Oxford and Cambridge, held for the first time in 1829.

By the end of the nineteenth century, sport in England had developed into an established system, with national and international associations, well-defined rules, and enormous popularity.

Hampshire (as explored in some depth later in the chapter). Thus cities featuring railroad hubs gained economic and promotional advantages, since trains could both bring sports teams and spectators into the urban culture and transport them away from the city to other sports sites.

After the Civil War, the growth of sport was also influenced by completion of the transcontinental railroad, linking the East and the West, in 1869. The railroad provided a critical mode of transportation for moving people, both as sportsmen and sportswomen and as spectators, along with sporting goods and products. The transcontinental railroad would play a major role in the growth of travel by professional sports teams to California and other Western regions. It also enabled the staging of national sporting events that brought together sports journalists, promoters, urban boosters, and thousands of spectators to watch boxing matches, baseball games, and other contests.

Railroads thus provided new opportunities to city politicians, capitalists, civic leaders, and boosters. City builders developed and promoted commercial amusements and amenities, bringing new sporting structures and venues to the urban masses. The invention of the telegraph in 1832 by Samuel F.B. Morse, which was in operation by 1844, improved communications and made railroad travel more efficient thanks to its capacity to disseminate information about schedules. Thus, in the booming city life of the mid-nineteenth century, entrepreneurs and transportation managers who were increasingly aware of the expansion of sport could now cater to those men and women with sufficient wealth and leisure time to take part.

Influence of the Media on Modern Sport

As sport coverage grew in newspapers and sporting journals (as discussed in chapter 3), manuals and advice books also increased the dissemination of sport-related information. In cities and towns, men and women reading about sport at home and in educational institutions found new books touting positive effects of sport, describing rules, and introducing new sports equipment. Typical publications included *The Book of Sports* by Robin Carver (first published in Boston in 1834); *Athletic Sports for Boys: A Repository of Graceful Recreations for Youth* (1866), which described boxing, fishing, rowing, sailing, fencing, skating, gymnastics, and other sports; and Diocletian Lewis' book about his system of exercises in *New Gymnastics for Men, Women, and Children* (1862). In 1867, William Wood published his well-illustrated *Manual of Physical Exercises, Comprising Gymnastics, Calisthenics, Rowing, Sailing, Skating, Swimming, Fencing, Sparring, Cricket, Base Ball, Together*

Manuals written about sport and physical exercise popularized sport in American culture and informed the public about a range of sports such as cricket.

Reprinted from W. Wood, 1867, *Manual of physical exercises: comprising gymnastics, rowing, skating, fencing, cricket, calisthenics, sailing, swimming, sparring, baseball. Together with rules for training and sanitary suggestions* (New York: Harper Brothers).

The Cut.   The Drive.

1860	1861	1861–1865	1862
■ Abraham Lincoln elected as president ■ South Carolina secedes from the Union	■ Amherst College offers nation's first male physical education program ■ U.S. Civil War begins with shots fired at Fort Sumter, South Carolina	■ U.S. Civil War fought	■ Morrill Land Grant Act passes for development of public universities

with Rules for Training and Sanitary Suggestions. Wood later penned *The Law of Athletics, Showing How to Preserve and Improve Health and Beauty, and to Correct Personal Defects Caused by Want of Physical Exercise* (1880), which included material on sports he deemed health building.

Writings by health reformers and sports enthusiasts such as Thomas W. Higginson, Catharine E. Beecher, Almira Phelps, and Dr. William A. Alcott (discussed in chapter 3) offered rationales and positive creeds about exercise and sport for a nationalistic spirit, for religious reasons, for the sake of individual good health, and for provision of a citizenry fit to perform its roles in the young democratic society. In addition, as sport became more organized, rationalized, and popularized, advertisers fanned and tapped into Americans' enthusiasm for sport by promoting sports equipment, publicizing sport competitions, and selling fashions and products to an expanding market of consumers in the urban economy.

Other forms of communication were used to disseminate scores and circulate accounts of athletic performances. The telegraph provided a means for sports and newspaper journalists to report on the results of athletic contests for an increasingly sports-hungry urban public, which feasted on news of intercity competitions in cricket and baseball, as well as results from the horse track, the boxing ring, and, later, international competitions that tested American nationalism in the arena of sport.

Subcommunities and the Growth of Modern Sport

Subcommunities based on social class and status played a key role in the new forms of sport that emerged in antebellum America, as many middle- and upper-class white citizens wanted specifically to separate themselves from the immigrants and poor workers crowding into the cities. The elite sports played by the upper classes, and the sports clubs organized to help the wealthy play and socialize with each other, introduced new sporting contests to American culture. Historian Benjamin Rader has investigated the evolution of subcommunities and elite sport in the experiences of white, native-born Americans of the upper class. These groups "tried to cope with the new urban-industrial society by forming subcommunities based on status. The socially exclusive club became the main agency of status ascription" (Rader, "The Quest" 361). Membership in these clubs—which depended on wealth, gender, and race—served as a badge of exclusivity for the men who joined them for sport and leisure pursuits. These elites participated in aquatic sports such as yachting and some rowing events, as well as racket sports, in the latter part of the century.

Yachting

John Cox Stevens founded the New York Yacht Club in 1844, establishing himself as the premiere yachtsman in the country. As a prestigious, socially acceptable sport, yachting linked Stevens with New York City's elite citizens. To foster his passion for sport and American exceptionalism (i.e., his belief that the democratic principles and moral and physical vigor of American culture made it superior to all others), Stevens wanted to show the supremacy of American yachtsmen by taking on the mighty British yachtsmen of the 1850s. Specifically, he wished to build a yacht to dethrone the British, and his boat, the *America*, handily defeated 18 British rivals in 1851(a trophy was not awarded until 1857), thus earning him an onboard visit from Queen Victoria.

The exclusive nature of the New York Yacht Club required would-be members to possess money and social status; it was an elite group, and participating in it carried considerable prestige. Each member paid $40 in dues for the first year and $20 annually thereafter. Of course, members also owned high-priced yachts, and "the club prescribed expensive uniforms . . . and sponsored regular balls and social cruises to Newport, Rhode Island, Bar Harbor, Maine, and other nearby wealthy summer resorts" (Rader, "The Quest" 362). The 1857 *Constitution of the New-York Yacht*

1863	1865	1866	1868
■ President Abraham Lincoln issues Emancipation Proclamation	■ Lee surrenders at Appomattox ■ President Abraham Lincoln assassinated ■ Thirteenth Amendment passes by Congress, abolishing slavery	■ Ku Klux Klan forms ■ New York Athletic Club founded	■ Fourteenth Amendment ratified, providing citizenship to freedmen

Club, based on the original rules drafted in 1844, indicated the strict requirements for membership, as well as the money needed for owning a yacht suitable for the club:

> Each candidate for admission must be proposed and seconded in writing; the name and address of the candidate, with the names of the members proposing and seconding him, must be sent to the Secretary. Members shall be elected by ballot. A quorum to consist of representatives from five Yachts, and two black balls shall defeat an election. . . .
>
> All voting to be by representatives of Yachts; each Yacht to be entitled to one vote. . . . No yacht shall be presented unless she has been launched and a certificate signed by the Measurer, filed with the Secretary, specifying her tonnage and rig; and no representation shall be admitted upon any Yacht not now represented in the Club, smaller than twenty-five tons.

qtd. in Kirsch, *Sports* [Vol. 3] 60–61

Prompted by Stevens' success, other elite yachting clubs entered races in various cities and maintained their associations for elite urban men (Gorn and Goldstein 78). Northerners, such as James O. Nixon, who purchased the *New Orleans Crescent,* helped found the Southern Yacht Club in New Orleans in 1849 (Guttmann, *Sports: The First Five Millennia* 121). The organization owning Stevens' *America* boat (a syndicate he established) presented the trophy cup to the New York Yacht Club, stipulating that international yachtsmen should compete for it in future races, and the success of the America's Cup continues today.

People & Places

John Cox Stevens

The sporting career of John Cox Stevens (1785–1857) shows the critical place of sport in the 1840s through the 1870s for elite white men in America. Stevens initiated spectacles of sport to enhance his own status as a wealthy businessman and as a promoter of American cultural values in competition with international rivals. Stevens was a leading patron of sport in the Antebellum Era, using his wealth to support such sports as horse racing, yachting, and pedestrianism (walking or running for competition) and to secure fields for ball games. To maintain some social and moral distance from sportsmen of lower socioeconomic rank, he did not patronize boxing matches. In 1831, working with his brother, Stevens established the park of Elysian Fields in Hoboken, New Jersey, across the river from New York City. As historian Benjamin Rader has noted, "In establishing Elysian Fields, nurturing the turf, and sponsoring pedestrianism, John Cox Stevens displayed a typical range of interest for a wealthy antebellum sportsman" (*American Sports* [2004] 37). Stevens' participation in the elite sport of yachting, however, reinforced his lofty position in the incipient nation.

Courtesy of the Stevens Institute of Technology.

1869

- Transcontinental railroad completed
- First intercollegiate football game played (Rutgers vs. Princeton)
- Knights of Labor workers' union founded
- Cincinnati Red Stockings become first pro baseball team

Rowing and Regattas

As with other sports during the growth of organized, commercialized sport and rationalized recreation, boating and rowing were typically seen as male pursuits. The vigorous and physical nature of rowing drew praise from antebellum health reformers, sports boosters, sports journalists, advice givers, and city leaders. Thomas Higginson perhaps expressed this view most succinctly when he claimed that rowing a boat went together with developing manliness. Similarly, physical education instructor and sports advocate William Wood declared, "Rowing is popular because it is a manly and healthful sport and pastime. . . . There is perhaps no sport or exercise in the world which affords a fairer or better trial of the finest qualities of manhood" (*Manual* 92).

The nation's numerous waterways—harbors, rivers, and canals—made rowing available to many of the workers in the maritime trades and to the middle- and upper-income men in rowing clubs. In the mid-nineteenth century, both amateur and professional rowing matches and regattas were staged at city waterfronts in places such as New York City (as well as various localities in upstate New York), Boston, Philadelphia, and Washington, D.C. Sport historian Ronald Smith has determined that, aside from thoroughbred and harness racing, rowing gained more attention than any other sport in the 1830s (*Sports* 27). Men from the middle and upper classes established the earliest rowing clubs, amateur boat clubs established for the enjoyment of the sport, to provide opportunities for what they viewed as a recreational activity appropriate for their status:

> Many clubs were being organized in New York, such as the Wave, Gull, Cleopatra, Pearl, Halcyon, Ariel, Minerva, and Gondola, and they, in 1834, formed the Castle Garden Amateur Boat Club Association, with a boat-house at Castle Garden; this was the first association of the kind in the United States and it had as objects both rowing and recreation. Among the members were many of the fashionable young men of the time, and the barge parties from Castle Garden were recognized among the pleasures of New York. But they were famous racing clubs as well, and the *Wave* was known to all oarsmen. . . . The Rollins brothers were members of the *Wave* crew and had a considerable reputation as amateurs. The Gazelle and the Gull were other noted clubs, the beautiful blue *Gull* finishing second to the *Wave* in several regattas.
>
> Crowther and Ruhl 7–8

A regatta held by the New York Amateur Boat Club in September 1837 drew a throng of at least ten thousand people (Rader, *American Sports* [2004] 40), and rowing also gained interest in other cities, including Boston, where, on August 5, 1842, the first regatta took place over the Chelsea course. The next year, New York oarsmen came to row against fellows enthusiasts from Boston (Crowther and Ruhl 12–13). Two other prominent clubs were the Narragansett Boat Club (1838) of Providence, Rhode Island, and the Detroit Boat Club (1839). The Narragansett club, now the oldest boat club still existing in the United States, grew steadily: "As the 19th century matured, so did the Narragansett Boat Club. It became a premier social and athletic organization of Providence's East Side" (Crowther and Ruhl 10–11; Narragansett Boat Club n. pag.). The Detroit club, also one of the oldest continuous boat clubs in the United States, served as both a boating and a social club for men. In one of the early contests, the club brought a "four-oared clinker from New York, and in the next year bought a Crolius boat and got it around the Erie Canal. With these craft a two-mile (3.2-kilometer) race was pulled from Hog Island (now Belle Island) to the boat-house on May 24, 1843—the first race in Western waters." A fire in 1848 destroyed the boat house and all but one boat, but the club reorganized and built other clubhouses (Crowther and Ruhl 11).

In the decades preceding the Civil War, both society and sport confronted the issue of slavery, and rowing at times dealt with rising intersectional tensions in boating matches between Northern and Southern clubs. As rowing was developing into a more modern sport—with organized clubs, rules, competitions, and improved equipment and techniques—regional pride in winning a match on the water appealed to socially respected young men. In December 1837, an article in *Spirit of the Times* referred to slavery in discussing a proposed match between a New York City boat club and one from Georgia:

> The Aquatic Club of Georgia has not yet withdrawn its challenge to our New York cracks, to row a straight mile (1.6 kilometers), for $10,000 aside, $2,000 ft. The Georgia boat is named *The Lizard*, and it will be observed by the following from *The Advocate*, published at Brunswick, Ga., that our Clubs cannot take the exception raised last Fall on account of the color of the crew of the Georgia boat. . . .
>
> "THE AQUATIC CLUB OF GEORGIA.—The challenge which this club published to the New York boatmen has never been noticed in any official manner. A gentleman of this city met some of the Whitehallers during the summer, and learned from them that they

would not consent to row against black servants; but if the gentlemen of Georgia would row their boat, the case would be different. The challenge of the Georgia Club says nothing of the rowers, and the New Yorkers would have avoided the injury their reputation has suffered had they made inquires of the proper persons. We are authorized to say that the Lizard shall be manned by gentlemen, who, we warrant, shall, be the equals of Knickerbockers in bone and muscle, blood and sinew."

qtd. in Menna 107

It seems that the race never did occur, but of course the intense debate on slavery continued in various arenas in antebellum America.

In 1851, rowing expanded in Boston, and the Union Boat Club, "which has always contained men who stood for the best in the sport, was formed." At first, the club did not hold races, but in 1854 the city of Boston "decided to make the regatta part of the Fourth of July Celebration"—that is, part of the tradition (as we have seen in earlier time periods) of engaging in sport and other active pastimes on Independence Day. The Boston regattas "were open to both professional and amateur oarsmen," yet the line "was being drawn between amateurs and professionals, [although at this point] . . . it was still a very hazy one." Professional rowing would take off in the late 1850s and the 1860s, but it was in these earlier years that questions about amateurs and professionals competing in the same match (whether in rowing or other sports) began to be part of modern sport (later chapters address challenges to the amateur code). In 1857, the Union Boat Club became a key association in the formation of the Beacon Cup Regatta for amateur oarsmen, and they performed well in these rowing contests, wherein they competed against various other clubs organized in the 1850s (Crowther and Ruhl 22–23).

The rich history of rowing in nineteenth-century American sport involves another important rowing club, the Potomac Boat Club in Washington, D.C., which participated in many regattas on the Potomac River. Initially founded as the Potomac Barge Club in 1859, the club attracted male citizens of good social and economic standing to its membership ranks. Along with other Washington, D.C., area rowing clubs, the Potomac club formed the Potomac River Rowing Association. At the time, rowing enjoyed widespread popularity and drew huge crowds of spectators, and performances by professional rowers stimulated young males and older amateurs to form rowing clubs in locales with good

waterways. The Potomac Boat Club competed against other clubs and hosted athletic and social events for the middle- and upper-rank men of the club and their families; the clubhouse later hosted other sports, too, such as swimming and canoe races (Gems and Borish, "Sports, Colonial" 639). The club also hosted national regattas. In June 1859, the *Washington Star* hailed the rowing and athletic activities of the club: "We are glad to know that some of our prominent citizens have turned their attention to this pleasant and healthy exercise; for certainly there is no city in the Union where this exercise is more needed and can be so successfully prosecuted as in this, where there are so many engaged in sedentary pursuits and where we have such a magnificent stream as our broad Potomac" (qtd. in Proctor 8). Over the years, the club continued to draw elite Georgetown members to participate in rowing and social events. Professional rower Charles Courtney competed in matches on the Potomac River and later became coach of the Potomac Boat Club before going on to establish the rowing team at Cornell University. In fact, in the 1850s, amateur rowing—the first intercollegiate sport in the United States—continued to be part of the growth of modern sport in colleges and other institutions. Professional rowing, however, gained prominence beginning in the late 1850s, with the physical prowess of oarsmen generating matches for money and drawing numerous spectators.

The rapid spread of rowing clubs in the 1850s ground to a halt when the Civil War began in 1861. Until then, races to determine the champion sculler of the United States generated strong interest among spectators and gamblers. One such was the Championship Regatta held in Boston on October 24, 1859, featuring six scullers and won by Joshua "Josh" Ward of Newburgh, New York: "A few vigorous strokes to close with, and Joshua Ward, still the champion, made his boat fly rapidly along, and crossed the line first, amid ringing cheers!" Ward beat out Thomas Doyle of Boston by 10 seconds. "Ward is the best man, and this year, at all events, is not likely to deprive him of the laurel he has so worthily won," reported the *New York Clipper* (qtd. in Kirsch, *Sports* [Vol. 3] 48, 49).

Josh Ward continued his rowing success in professional matches in the early 1860s. He and his siblings, known together as the Ward Brothers, competed against the Biglin Brothers, with "the more important races . . . [being] those for money," according to rowing chronicler Samuel Crowther Jr.:

Josh Ward stands out as the old rugged type of oarsman,—big, muscular and possessed of remarkable power and endurance; he could row a race at any distance, but was especially good on the longer courses, and his time of one hour and twenty-three minutes in the ten-mile (16-kilometer) match . . . on the Hudson at Poughkeepsie, has never been equalled; in his prime he held the records for nearly every course. The Ward family was then coming into rowing, and as it is undoubtedly the most famous of all the old rowing families, a word should be said of them.

Crowther and Ruhl 148–149

The family lived at Cornwall on Hudson, and the brothers' father, a hotelkeeper and fisherman, brought the boys up on the water. Several of Josh's brothers also became outstanding oarsmen—John, Ellis, Gil, Charles, and Hank—and "Josh and Ellis had almost perfect sculling form." In August 1862, Josh Ward was challenged by James Hamill, a champion rower who won "sculling matches about Pittsburg"; Hamill surprised the country by defeating Ward on the Schuylkill River to win the national professional sculls title. Ward regained his title in a much-ballyhooed rematch at Poughkeepsie in 1863 (Crowther and Ruhl 148–149, 150). *Frank*

Leslie's Illustrated Newspaper reported on the race and declared Ward to be "The Champion Sculler of America":

The great race between Ward and Hamill, at Poughkeepsie, on the 23d of July, has restored to the brows of Ward the chaplet of Champion which he saw so suddenly and unexpectedly wrested from him last September by James Hamill, of Pennsylvania, when, over-confident of his superiority, he allowed his young antagonist to win the two successive races on the Schuylkill.

"Joshua Ward" 315

The rematch paid each rower $500 a side to row a 5-mile (8-kilometer) course on the Hudson beginning at Newburg. The competitors had trained intensely, and the spectators were eager for the race. Here is part of the account from *Frank Leslie's Illustrated*:

Poughkeepsie on the day of the race was crowded with strangers from Boston, New York, Philadelphia and Pittsburg, and betting on the result was quite animated and exciting. . . .

At every stroke his [Ward's] success became more a matter of certainty, and, without relaxing his

A professional rowing match for a championship between James Hamill and Walter Brown, with the racers vying for the $4,000 purse.

Image courtesy of Library of Congress, LC-USZ62-684.

exertions, he continued to pull as strong and regularly as he had done at the first, the firing of the signal gun of victory proclaiming him the winner of the race by 10 lengths, and restoring to him his forfeited title of Champion Oarsman of America.

"Joshua Ward" 315

The 1860s saw additional keenly fought rowing matches between professionals, and in 1867 James Hamill again competed for big money and a championship title, facing Walter Brown of Portland, Maine, with a $4,000 purse at stake for the 5-mile (8-kilometer) race on the Hudson River. More than fifty thousand spectators gathered on the banks to watch the evenly matched oarsmen, "and the betting was larger than on any previous race in this country" (Crowther and Ruhl 156). This heated contest was distinguished by the fact that each sculler had a barge with oarsmen behind him, and questionable tactics included the brandishing of pistols:

> In Hamill's [barge] was John Biglin, and Charlie Moore steered for Brown; Biglin and Moore flourished each a pistol, and every moment one or the other was threatening to shoot as the opposing barge happened to come too near the rival sculler. Amid such a volley of curses the two rowed on. Brown was a very fast starter, and he at once took a couple of hundred yards' [183 meters'] lead and attempted to give Hamill a wash, but Hamill, though slow at the start, came up, passed Brown, and reached the stake-boat four lengths ahead. At that time only one stake-boat was provided for a race, and the boat that first reached it had the right of way, and the other man must go around him. Hamill attempted to make a close turn, and the strong ebb-tide took him hard on the boat and he could not get loose. Brown was close behind him, and seeing the predicament, headed directly for Hamill, broke his boat and put Hamill, who could not swim, into the water to be picked up by his pilot. Then Brown went on down and claimed the race; Stephen Roberts, the veteran oarsman, was referee; Brown's people claimed that no foul had occurred, and, of course, Hamill's backers asserted their rights. . . . [T]o increase the excitement, the dock, on which the crowd stood, fell in, and about half of them went into the water. When all had been calmed, the referee gave the race to Hamill on the foul.

Crowther and Ruhl 156–157

These two outstanding rowers continued competing in races into the late 1860s.

Racket Sports

In addition to aquatic sports, wealthy men in metropolitan areas also used racket sports in reinforcing their elite status. Sports clubs offered indoor racket sports for elite and upper-class men seeking healthful exercise during the winter season. Racket (or *racquet,* as it was often spelled then) sports gained popularity in the mid-nineteenth century, especially in New York City, where wealthy gentlemen formed the Racket Court Club on Broadway in 1845. The club "soon became one of New York's most prominent social clubs . . . [and it] remained exclusive into the 1850s, when it banned tradesman from membership" to prohibit middle- and working-class men from becoming members, preserving membership only for the very rich men of the city (Kirsch, *Sports* [Vol. 3] 297, 298). *The Constitution and By-Laws of the Racket Court, Adapted 7th May, 1845* codified the club's intention of maintaining certain standards for members:

> [Club members wish] to keep a place where they and their friends can have the benefits of taking athletic exercise, and enjoying judicious recreation and relaxation of both body and mind, without being compelled to mix with uncongenial associates; and aware that the permanent existence of such an establishment can only be secured by a strict adherence to the restrictions upon gambling, and rules governing the admission of members, and strangers to be introduced by them . . .
>
> Besides the game of Racket, requiring a court of 40 by 120 feet [12.2 by 36.6 meters], and a Bowling Saloon in the rear, the premises on Broadway, covering a space of about 55 feet [16.8 meters] square, will contain a Reading Room well supplied with newspapers and periodicals, a Billiard Room, two Whist and Chess Rooms, a Refectory, and if approved of by the members, a Gymnasium.

qtd. in Kirsch, Sports [Vol. 3] 298–299

Indoor sport was also offered by a number of public racket clubs in the 1850s. As with many of today's public tennis courts, players had to sign up for a court, and rules sometimes depended on the size of the court. Following are excerpts from "Rules of the Game in a Close Court," printed in the *New York Clipper* on January 7, 1860:

> 1. Subscribers who agree to Play together must subscribe their names on a Slate placed near the Marker, they can then take the Court in the order their names are inscribed. . . .
>
> 3. To secure the Court for a Double Match, it is requisite that three of the persons who are to play should have their names inscribed; two for a single match. . . .
>
> 10. Person playing Matches of general interest, may play FIVE Games, whether there **are** two, *three, or four* players. . . .

4. In serving, the server must stand with one foot within the compartment allotted for the server, the out player into whose court the ball is to be served, may stand where he pleases; . . .

5. The ball must be served above and not touching the cut line on the front wall, and it must strike the ground (before it bounds) within, and not touching the line enclosing the Court opposite to where the server stands.

qtd. in Kirsch, *Sports* [Vol. 3] 304–305

These early forms of racket sport would evolve into indoor rackets and tennis in the latter years of the nineteenth century. The Racquet Court Club Building (New York City), built in 1875, served as an urban recreational and commercial building for wealthy businessmen. This athletic club was one of the first in New York City and housed one of the earliest indoor tennis courts.

Sporting Fraternity

Various groups, usually composed of men, influenced the rise of sport in urban America. The group referred to as "the sporting fraternity" engaged in sports of various moral and physical dimensions, often in marked contrast to the supposedly healthful and status-building (and more rationalized and organized) physical activities espoused by educated, middle-class, civic-minded Victorian men, who viewed wholesome sport as crucial to building the vigor and high moral character called for in citizens of the new urban culture and economy. Also known as "the fancy," the sporting fraternity consisted of an informal brotherhood of men sharing values and interests—a sort of solidarity, involving a passion for drinking, gambling, talking, fisticuffs, and social get-togethers associated with their preferred sports (Rader, *American Sports* [2004] 32). The so-called "rowdy bachelor culture" featured young unmarried men acting as pleasure seekers, gamblers, drinkers, and competitors, and shaping a sporting culture quite at odds with that favored by those who sought to create what they saw as an upstanding culture of physical activity. The sporting fraternity—which included working-class men, ethnic minorities, bachelors, saloon and tavern keepers seeking profit, city dandies, and members of the middle and elite classes desiring pleasure and profit for themselves in sporting enterprises—engaged in an array of antebellum urban sports, which linked these groups of men in expressions of masculinity. American studies scholar Simon J. Bronner has explored "manly traditions" and how highly gendered exhibitions of manliness occur in various ethnic and class contexts. He writes that "gender display is . . . a range of identities variously expressed and negotiated" (Bronner xii). In antebellum America, men's sporting behavior took place largely in locations separate from the daily living areas inhabited by both sexes together, and it involved symbols and activities intended to demonstrate participants' manliness. Young middle-class and wealthy men seeking adventure in the bachelor subculture of saloons found a place for the shared pursuit of hedonism, dissipation, and masculine prowess.

Notable in the sporting fraternity were Irish immigrant men, who brought their sporting and drinking traditions to America as part of the largest immigrant group in the mid-nineteenth century. Historian Steven Riess has noted that in the urban sporting fraternity, "all part of the male bachelor subculture, these sportsmen measured manliness by skill at wenching, drinking, gambling, and fighting" (*City Games* 15). The sporting fraternity's particular choice of sports left its imprint on the physical spaces and events of modern sport as it expanded in the middle decades of the century.

Boxing

The sporting fraternity relished the pugilism found in the taverns, gambling institutions, and other facilities of the Victorian underworld. In particular, bareknuckle fights (i.e., without gloves) at this time were frequently bloody confrontations between young urban males seeking money from the gamblers who bet on their physical prowess. A fighter's courage was challenged by the typically brutal fighting of his opponent, and, in sharp contrast to the relatively wholesome self-defense art of boxing or sparring, the prizefighting of this sporting fraternity emphasized not developing health and agility but gaining pride and victory through the gambling. In his manual on physical exercise and sport, William Wood illuminated the perceived difference between boxing or sparring as a respectable sport and the vicious bareknuckle boxing practiced by the working-class and ethnic-minority groups of tavern culture: "This manly exercise has no necessary connection with the brutal and disgusting exhibitions of the 'Prize Ring.' An accomplished sparrer is as such, no more a vulgar bruiser than an elegant penman is a forger or counterfeiter, or a clever gymnast, who can climb a ladder 'hand over hand,' is a burglar" (*Manual* 238).

As with billiard contests in this Victorian counterculture, bareknuckle boxing matches drew spectators from across the spectrum of society. The antiboxing legislation of the Antebellum Period meant these illegal boxing matches were staged in the secluded rooms of the sporting fraternity's saloons, in rural locations, or on seafaring vessels in order to escape the notice of legal authorities. Such settings highlighted the underworld aspect of these gatherings of bachelors and fancy men of Victorian culture, and the swearing and drinking, the gambling, the bloody violence, and the pleasure seeking all emphasized the supposed manliness of the world of boxing. Some boxers and saloon keepers achieved a kind of success in this world of physicality and illegal sport, rather than in the rationalized, middle-class, Protestant world of the work ethic promoted by many male Victorian leaders. As historian Benjamin Rader has observed, "The prizefighter, with his immense strength, muscular body, and swift, decisive answers, represented [for some] an appealing alternative to the effeminate self-effacing Victorian idea of manhood" (Rader, *American Sports* [2004] 44).

Taverns and Billiard Halls

The rapid growth of sports in antebellum urban cities took place in a variety of venues supported by the sporting fraternity. The saloons and taverns fostered competitive games, sports, and drinking, especially for working-class men, whose brand of billiards was marked as different from the billiards played in the homes of the wealthy, sober, and elite in Victorian America. Saloon billiards, taking place amid the usual gambling, drinking, and bantering of working-class men, often took the form of highly competitive contests. A description of the billiard table by James Hall in 1828 noted characteristics seemingly fitting for the sporting fraternity gathered in the saloon:

> The stained and dirty floor was strewed with fragments of segars [cigars], playbills, and nut shells, the walls blackened with smoke seemed to have witnessed the orgies of many a midnight revel. . . . A set of benches attached to the walls, and raised sufficiently high to overlook the table, accommodated the loungers, who were not engaged at play . . . [and who] sat or reclined solemnly puffing their segars, idly sipping their brandy and water, or industriously counting their chances of the game.
>
> qtd. in Riess, *Major*, 51–52

In the 1850s, with billiard halls accessible to working-class men in the cities where they worked

and lived, the sporting fraternity played billiards frequently. In 1858, Michael Phelan of New York defeated Ralph Benjamin of Philadelphia to win $1,000 in the first major billiard contest in the United States (Kirsch, *Sports* [Vol. 3] 283). Phelan, a major promoter of billiards, competed against John Seereiter in Detroit the following year for a large sum of money. The bets of their boosters also loomed large at the table. The billiards play engaged the audience of men and women from 7:30 one evening until 5:00 the next morning. Phelan emerged victorious and supposedly earned $15,000 for his effort. With the bachelor subculture supporting billiard halls and taverns that showcased the sport, a talented player might earn considerable money through gambling and plying his skills before spectators (Rader, *American Sports* [2004] 41; Riess, *City* 17).

To the delight of gamblers, billiard halls sometimes staged animal contests as well—cockfights and rat fights, for example. In response, sport and health promoters who were developing a positive philosophy about the value of sport and exercise offered their moral outrage, as captured in 1867 in a *Harper's Weekly* illustration with the title "*Cruelty to Animals*—'Which Are the Brutes?'"

Such criticism of animal cruelty did little to curtail the staging of animal blood sport in the nineteenth century.

The Miriam and Ira D. Wallach Division of Art, Prints and Photographs: Print Collection, The New York Public Library. H. Bergh, president of the Society for the Prevention of Cruelty to Animals: *Cruelty to Animals—Which Are the Brutes?* from *Harper's Weekly,* February 23, 1867. New York Public Library Digital Collections. Accessed September 12, 2016. http://digitalcollections.nypl.org/items/510d47dc-9074-a3d 9-e040-e00a18064a99

Pedestrianism

The spectators and gamblers affiliated with pedestrianism (professional footraces) in the mid-nineteenth century played a key part in the recreational culture of the sporting fraternity; in fact, only horse racing drew larger crowds than this test of individual physical achievement. In this period of early commercialized sport, pedestrianism was a sport with more modern characteristics than mere impromptu footraces, and it provided early opportunities for working-class athletes to earn an income with their physical prowess. For example, John Cox Stevens—famous sportsman and promoter of upper-rank Victorian sporting culture as a way to demonstrate American identity and nationalistic spirit against mighty British competitors—offered a $1,000 purse to the winner of an 1835 event heralded as "the Great Foot Race." The race intensified sporting fever for footracers and competitive race walkers and attracted spectators to watch these athletes perform. This "great trial of human capabilities," as described in the *American Turf Register and Sporting Magazine*, drew a field of international competitors vying for the cash prize offered by Stevens for the successful racer who completed the 10-mile (16-kilometer) course in less than an hour; he would add to the purse another $300 for the triumphant pedestrian who outraced all his competitors in the allotted time and thus earned all the prize money. The race was held at the Union Race Track in Long Island, where fans cheered the nine competitors. American farmer Henry Stannard of Killingsworth, Connecticut, won the race, finishing in 12 seconds less than an hour—among those he defeated were an Irishman and a Prussian who covered the 10 miles but took more than the hour allowed—and the American crowd lauded their countryman's victory. In "The Great Foot Race" the *American Turf Register and Sporting Magazine* provided the following coverage:

> Stannard, the winner, we understand, has been in good training for a month. He is a powerful stalwart young man, and did not seem at all fatigued at the termination of the race. He is greatly indebted to Mr. Stevens, for his success; Mr. S. rode round the course with him the whole distance, and kept cheering him on, and cautioning him against over-exertion in the early part of the race; at the end of the sixth mile [roughly the 10th kilometer], he made him stop and take a little brandy and water, after which his foot was on the mile [1.6-kilometer] mark just as the thirty-six minutes were expired; and as the trumpet sounded he jumped forward gracefully, and cheerfully exclaimed, 'Here am I to time;' and he was within the time every mile. . . . He was called up to the stand and his success (and the reward of $1,300) was announced to him, and he was invited to dine with the Club [New York Jockey Club]; to which he replied in a short speech thanking Mr. Stevens, and the gentlemen of the Club for the attention shewn to the runners generally throughout the task.

> qtd. in Riess, *Major* 52–54

The popularity of the Great Race of 1835 led to other pedestrian races at the Beacon Race Course in Hoboken, New Jersey, in the 1840s. These races, featuring professional American pedestrians competing against their British counterparts, drew spectators eager to see the quest for American supremacy played out in sport. In 1844, one of these international races attracted a crowd of thirty thousand, who saw racers from England, Ireland, and the United States, as well as a Native American competitor. However, such events—usually accompanied by betting, drinking, rowdiness of spectators, and suspicion of fixed races—did not gain the support of health and morality-conscious Victorian sportsmen, and the growth of other sports (including team sports) dampened enthusiasm for pedestrianism by the eve of the Civil War. Nevertheless, Edward Payson Weston gained acclaim in a failed attempt to walk from Boston to Washington in 10 days in 1861, and six years later he successfully finished a 26-day marathon from Maine to Chicago, for which he earned a $10,000 prize (Kirsch, *Sports* [Vol. 4] 335). Weston traveled to Europe for a series of international races for the Astley Belt, contested in six-day endurance races. Although Weston lost to Daniel O'Leary of Chicago, he continued to set records into his old age, walking across the continent from New York to San Francisco in 100 days in 1909 at the age of 70 (Reisler).

During pedestrianism's heyday, American champions often found competition in the international ranks. One such runner, George Seward, "the champion Sport runner of the world, better known as the American Wonder," left New York by boat to compete in England in 1843. William Wood provided the following account in his 1880 manual *The Law of Athletics*: "On September 30th, 1844, he [Seward] ran 100 yards [91.4 meters] in 9 1/4 seconds; this record has stood the test of time." Seward not only excelled "at this distance, but also in 'Hurdling,' from one hundred and twenty to three hundred yards [110 to 274 meters]; hurdles regulation height, three feet six inches [1.1 meters]" (Wood 36). Seward practiced a serious physical training routine as a champion runner:

Rise between 6 and 7 A.M.—Pass the sponge over the body and rub dry.

Exercise.—A brisk walk of from three to five miles [4.8 to 8 kilometers] according to the weather; wash, rub dry, and good hand friction.

Breakfast at 8 or 8.30 . . .

Exercise 10.30.—Starting on a slow walk, increase the pace, coming in on a sharp run; go a good distance if the condition and weather will permit.

Dinner at 1 P.M. . . .

Exercise 3.30.—Walking and running moderately with a light dumb bell in each hand; dropping the bells with a spurt of a hundred yards [about 91 meters] or so.

Supper at 7. . . .

Bed at 10.

Wood, *The Law* 36–37

International Perspective

Mensen Ernst's Incredible Walking Feats

Mensen Ernst (1795–1843) was a Norwegian adventurer and globetrotter who gave up his occupation as a merchant sailor in order to pursue a "sporting career" as a runner. His "Sea, Land and Fast Journeys on All Five Continents," which made him prosperous and well known throughout Europe, are described in detail in a biography published in 1839.

As in the United States, pedestrianism had also become fashionable in Europe, and runners, or race walkers as they were also called, competed for the favor, as well as the money, of the curious public. In contrast to modern sport, there was no standardization of distances, conditions, or styles of running. Consequently, it was impossible to compare performance or establish records. But that was of no great importance to the runners, whose aim it was to increase suspense among the spectators—and thus the entertainment value of their performance—by thinking up ever greater sensations. To supplement their earnings, the runners took jobs as couriers or footmen, whose task it was to clear the way for noblemen's coaches. Mensen Ernst, for example, was in the service of Prince Pückler-Muskau for a time.

Like other race walkers, Mensen Ernst organized his runs himself. He wagered that he would cover a certain distance in a certain time and encouraged spectators to place bets. He also competed against dogs, horses, and other runners, and in most cases he won. From 1820 onward he staged his "productions" in numerous cities all over the European continent, for example in Copenhagen, Rome, Venice, and Constantinople. His spectacular performances attracted great crowds everywhere.

An extraordinary aspect of his achievement is to be seen in his ultra-long distance walks, in which he crossed deserts, climbed mountains, swam rivers, and had to overcome all manner of dangerous encounters with people and wild animals. In 1828, for example, he walked from Egypt to Germany via the Balkans, and in 1832 he wagered that he would cover the 2,500 kilometers from Paris to Moscow in 15 days. He managed the journey in 14 days, thereby earning 4,000 francs in prize money.

Ernst's most amazing achievement was his walk from Constantinople to Calcutta, which took him 59 days. In order to appreciate this achievement, it must be remembered that in those days there was neither motor transport nor telecommunications such as the telegraph or telephone. Ernst was completely on his own, having to rely on inadequate mapping to find his bearings and having to communicate with the inhabitants of the countries he traveled through. Besides having incredible stamina, he was endowed with little need for either sleep or the pleasures and comforts of life.

His wish to reach the source of the Nile prompted Mensen Ernst's last walk. He set off from Muskau in Upper Lusatia (Prussia) and, via Constantinople and Cairo, arrived at Aswan, where he fell ill with dysentery and died.

Was Mensen Ernst the greatest pedestrian of all times? Or was he also endowed with sharp business acumen, ably marketing his talent for race walking by embellishing his memories and exaggerating his adventures? It is entirely possible that hyperbole was an integral part of the business. After all, it was about public performance rather than sporting contest. However, the numerous newspaper reports that have survived clearly illustrate that there was a core of truth in the legend of Mensen Ernst.

Information from Wolfert, Raimund. *Globetrotter and Kosmopolit: Schnelläufer Mensen Ernst (1795-1843).* www.fuerstpueckler.de/zeitungsartikel/laufer.htm.

Horse Racing

Horse racing expanded in the mid-nineteenth century as a sport popular with both owners and the spectators who gathered at the track, and the sporting fraternity patronized the races. Horse racing, as a favorite sport for the upper class—especially thoroughbred horse racing—involved the promoters of the sport seeking to engage the interest of the broader public. The supporters of horse racing, such as horse breeders and track managers, strived to diminish the religious and other objections to their racing. In addition, horse-racing enthusiasts needed to solve numerous practical and financial problems so that they might make their events both entertaining and profitable. Organizers of the horse races needed to offer substantial prize money to draw quality horses for lively contests, and they needed to find suitable space and construct amenable facilities for horse owners, trainers, attendants, horses, and spectators (Kirsch, *Sports* [Vol. 3] 180–181).

Horse racing engendered the systematic breeding of horses during this period. As noted in chapter 2, the importation of the British racehorse Messenger in the post-Revolutionary years produced a series of championship horses. Messenger sired numerous offspring, including Abdullah, who birthed Hambletonian, who in turn emerged as the harness-racing sensation of the 1850s, when interest in that form of racing swelled (see chapter 3). Hambletonian raced for eight years, then produced 1,331 foals as a stud, earning his owner a sizable fortune in fees and considerable fame (Twombly 31). Meanwhile, harness racing developed a good following at the track. Lady Suffolk (known as "the Old Grey Mare") raced 162 times, and in 1859 Flora Temple defeated Princess, a California horse, in an intersectional race between East and West (Kirsch, *Sports* [Vol. 3] 214, 217).

In the growth of organized sport forms such as horse racing, distinctions of social rank were clear between those men of wealth and means and those of the lower ranks. For example, John Cox Stevens, a leader in the antebellum turf network, served as president or vice president of the New York Jockey Club for more than 22 years. While spectators of all classes might enjoy watching horse racing, only the wealthy ran the sport and owned the expensive animals.

Highly publicized antebellum races covered by the general and turf press included an important series of intersectional contests between North and South to determine supremacy on the racetrack. From 1821 through 1845, five horse races, known as the North-South races, or "The Great Intersectional Races," took place at the Union Race Track, opened in 1821 on Long Island. These races drew large, lively crowds, and the increasingly distinct cultural and economic characters of the North and South spurred heated debates on issues such as slavery, agricultural tariffs, and temperance that formed bones of contention between Northerners and Southerners in the decades preceding the Civil War. Crowds included both elite and lower-rank spectators, many of whom took a train to the racetrack.

In 1823, much to the delight of Northerners, the Northern champion Eclipse defeated the Southern horse Sir Henry for a $20,000 prize, and the North rejoiced again in 1842, when Fashion defeated Boston, the Southern favorite. In 1845, the Southern horse Peytona, from Tennessee, and the Northern horse Fashion faced off before a grandstand crowd numbering thirty thousand, with another twenty thousand amassed in hopes of getting a glimpse. Much to the displeasure of the Northerners at the track, Peytona triumphed over Fashion to win a purse of $20,000. The *New York Herald* covered race day, noting not only that the huge crowd added to the excitement but also that "the sectional feeling and the strong rivalry of sportsmen, and in one sense partizans—the vast sums of money pending on the race, attached a degree of absorbing interest to the result, quite proportionate to the great demonstration that took place." And on the makeup of the large crowd: "We saw many distinguished sporting characters, politicians, editors, reporters, managers, actors, devils, &c.," all of whom cheered the horses to the finish when "Fashion appeared to have the lead, but on approaching the draw gate[,] . . . not withstanding the mob closing on the track, Peytona led a way clear length in advance in 7.45.1/4" (qtd. in Riess, *Major* 57–61).

The economic gains by some of the boosters of the horse races, such as horse trainers or track managers, waned as mainly economic investments of the affluent horsemen yielded dividends. The economic and status benefits in the horse-racing industry were secured by the elite owners in "the sport of kings." By the advent of the Civil War, thoroughbred horse racing declined in the North because of such factors as the high amount of money needed to maintain horses, poor track management at facilities, meager attendance at regular horse meets, and decline in the breeding industry in the North. For some Americans, horse racing had served as a surrogate form of warfare, perhaps dissipating interregional tensions between

The famous North-South horse race in 1845. Peytona, the Southern horse, triumphed over Fashion, the Northern horse.

Image courtesy of Library of Congress, LC-USZ62-14099.

the North and South until mid-century as debates intensified on slavery. In any case, the end of the contest for dominance on the track did not, of course, put a stop to the political, economic, and moral arguments that persisted about slavery and states' rights as the two regions moved toward war. Racing could not stem the tide of intersectional crisis in the United States, and instead of battling on the turf of the track for supremacy determined by the speed of a horse, the North and South moved inexorably toward fighting it out on the turf of the nation as a whole for supremacy determined by the bloodshed, victories, and losses of human soldiers in the Civil War.

Horse racing did, however, continue after the war. In 1866, affluent members of the American Jockey Club opened Jerome Park in the Bronx as a racetrack for thoroughbreds. Wealthy business-man Leonard W. Jerome and his capitalist friends August Belmont, William R. Travers, and James R. Hunter had founded the American Jockey Club as an exclusive club, and the track they built, situated on valuable land in Westchester County, was an impressive sporting venue for the elite sport of thoroughbred racing, with a luxurious clubhouse, amenities, facilities for other sports, and sleeping quarters. To foster the respectability of horse racing, and to counter the negative image given by the drinking, gambling, and vice associated with the turf course, Jerome instituted rules and regulations to uphold his sense of proper moral and social-class conduct. No alcoholic beverages were to be sold, gamblers were to be prohibited, and appropriate decorum was encouraged (Riess, *City* 25; Rader, *American Sports* [2004] 49). The *New York Clipper* wrote about the new park, noting its elite aspect: "The attendance was very large, it being estimated that thirty thousand spectators were present . . . as well as many ladies." To popularize horse racing, it reported, "the public should be permitted to enjoy the privileges of our race tracks at a small charge for admission, say fifty cents," rather than the $2 and $5 admission fees that were charged. The report concluded, "Very few except the wealthy classes can afford to indulge in the 'luxury of horse racing'" (qtd. in Riess, *Major* 143). Thus, for the ordinary masses wanting to attend sporting contests, other sports would have to satisfy their desires.

Growth of Sports Clubs and Advancing Rational Recreation

The rise of American sport in the nineteenth century was shaped considerably by the interest of citizens (especially men) of differing social, ethnic, racial, and religious groups. While some single and young men pursued the sports favored in the rough settings of the sporting fraternity, many other men of the middle class decried those pursuits as immoral and wasteful of time. As an antidote, they touted a different version of sport deemed appropriate for respectable, disciplined, and hard-working "Muscular Christians." These men, seeking to participate in sport to achieve muscular and spiritual rectitude, wished to form voluntary associations for organizing appropriate sporting activity and rational recreation—robust physical exercise with the purpose of securing the health of the mind and body—to integrate into their urban experiences. These voluntary associations—formed by men with similar backgrounds, occupations, social classes, or ethnicities—served athletic interests centered on a particular sport or social club. The rise of sport during the mid-nineteenth century (1840 to 1870) was apparent in the number of sporting clubs organized for men and boys and in the spectators they often attracted to their competitions.

Gymnastics and Active Bodies

The extensive material published during this period on improving health and maintaining a sturdy body through physical exercise posited gymnastics as a powerful way to offset the ill effects of sedentary urban life, and gymnastics became part of a physical education movement featuring various forms of physical exercise promoted by instructors. German gymnastics, introduced by the German American Turners and intended to invigorate the body, was pursued in gymnasiums and YMCAs built in urban areas and in the schools. Dr. Diocletian Lewis, a Harvard-educated teacher and medical practitioner, founded his New Gymnastics to appeal to men, women, and children and promoted his program through lectures, publications, and direct instruction. Lewis "borrowed lavishly from German sources so that his 'New Gymnastics' were in the main neither new nor his own," but he did help publicize the usefulness of light gymnastics and popularized gymnastics for schoolchildren (Hartwell 31). The system promoted by Lewis involved the use of hand apparatuses, such as wooden dumbbells, wands, beanbags, and small rings, with appropriate sizes and weights for men and women. The exercises were performed to music and arranged so that both sexes could participate, using lighter apparatus suitable for women.

In addition to ardently promoting his New Gymnastics in numerous publications, Lewis put his regimen into practice as founder and proprietor of the Normal Institute for Physical Education in Boston in July 1861. This influential school provided teacher training, introducing gymnastics to instructors who then promoted the sport in programs across the United States (Park, "'Embodied'" 89). Here is Lewis in his *New Gymnastics for Men, Women, and Children* (1862): "This book describes and illustrates a new system of physical training. Like air and food, its exercises are adapted to both sexes, and to persons of all ages." He asserted the positive outcomes for people doing his gymnastics. "This system of exercises will correct drooping or distorted shoulders, malposition of the head, and many other common defects." Lewis described numerous exercises with clubs and dumbbells that a person could undertake in specific positions to strengthen particular parts of the body, and he eagerly encouraged both adults and children to engage in the sport.

Lewis also supported Catharine Beecher's introduction of calisthenics and physical education for women at her female institutions, and he recommended a gymnastics costume for women resembling the bloomer costume that Amelia Bloomer endorsed in the interest of women's rights and physical mobility. Catharine Beecher had organized the Milwaukee Female College in 1851 as a venue for implementing her philosophy of women's physical and domestic education, and the institution offered sporting activities such as gymnastics and horseback riding early in its curriculum for women's physical well-being. Beecher wanted to improve the physical education department in the 1860s with the construction of a calisthenics hall. Gender ideology at the time constrained women from playing more vigorous sports or competing in sports. Beecher included some of Lewis' gymnastics exercises in the program as gender-appropriate sporting activity to build the health of the women at the college.

Harvard College continued its educational program for physical and mental well-being for young men in the collegiate setting; it offered gymnastics and physical training to its students, and in the North a few educated free blacks might gain access to noteworthy educational institutions. Aaron Molyneaux Hewlett became the first African American on the Harvard staff, serving as the first director of the Harvard College Gymnasium, built in 1859, and as an instructor in physical education and curator of gymnastics equipment at the gymnasium from 1859 until his death in 1871. Hewlett's physical education instruction included the use of exercise equipment and clubs to strengthen the body and improve the form of male students. Hewlett's position on the Harvard staff contrasted sharply with the status of enslaved blacks during the Antebellum Era and with that of Southern blacks during the Civil War. Hewlett was predecessor to Dr. Dudley Sargent, director of the Hemenway Gymnasium and later director of the School of Physical Training at Harvard.

Instructors and authors touted a less vigorous form of physical exercise for the young American women attending female educational seminaries or reading health and domestic advice manuals about gymnastics. At Vassar, Mt. Holyoke, and Elmira Female College, young women used light handheld clubs or beanbags in their gymnastics. In fact, Diocletian Lewis' "gymnastic regimen eventually found its way to female seminaries, to early women's colleges, as well as to a few early, private coeducational colleges." Lewis' nineteenth-century gymnastics for women usually included a greater percentage of calisthenic exercises for female

Aaron Molyneaux Hewlett served as the first director of the Harvard College Gymnasium.

HUP Hewlett, A. Molyneaux (3a), olvwork173667, Harvard University Archives.

students than gymnastics exercises appropriate for male students, as the gendered reference to the name calisthenics suggests, and he stressed the need for female students to better their health by developing sturdy bodies and a capacity for agile physical movement. Advice givers on sport and physical education for women generally approved of gender-specific activities for women, rather than the energetic sports pursued by men, and many nineteenth-century gymnastics regimens "directed U.S. women to self-consciously cultivate bodies comprising impeccable thoraxes and rounded chests buttressed by straightened spines" (Chisholm 738, 744, 751).

Young Men's Christian Association

For men in the cities, appropriate cultural environs in which to participate in sport began to be constructed specifically for their gender and dominant religious practices. The Young Men's Christian Association (YMCA), founded in England in 1844, developed in the United States in 1851. In the 1850s, especially in urban areas such as Boston, New York City, Washington, D.C., and other places teeming with young single men and working-class laborers, the YMCA promoted a particular Protestant brand of Christianity and later began offering gymnasium facilities as an inducement to attract patrons to its cause. Before the Civil War, "the original purpose of the YMCA had been to offer spiritual guidance and practical assistance to the young men who were flooding into the nineteenth-century cities" (Rader, *American Sports* [2004] 106). To offset the lure of urban amusements such as dance halls and billiard halls, and to provide a safe place away from crime, vice, drinking, and gambling, the YMCA became a site of moral and physical activity for young urban men. Thus, the gymnasium, appealing to the athletic interests of young men in search of leisure pursuits, became an arm of the church, as YMCA facilities meant that young men might learn about both Christianity and sport, engaging in reading, recreation, and fellowship in a moral and safe environment. During the period of 1851 to 1870, as one historian has explained, the YMCAs "were trying to find a pattern of physical education that would meet existing needs and suit the era: physical work, as it was called at first, was not always seen as a legitimate function of the association" (Johnson xiii–xiv). In later decades, and with the pioneering leadership of Dr. Luther Halsey Gulick Jr., sport was given a larger place in YMCA programs.

By the 1870s, several YMCAs were equipped with weight-lifting apparatus and offered some sports programs to induce the practice of Muscular Christianity, which signaled a transition in the relationship between the spiritual and secular worlds. Whereas clergy had previously shunned physical pursuits as a possible sinful temptation or a frivolous pastime, the new perception of the body as the housing for the soul required physical strength, maintenance, and well-being. Racial divisions, however, remained in force in the YMCAs in many cities. Washington, D.C., was home to the first YMCA branch organized for African Americans, providing a place where black men and boys could engage in social and recreational activities. The branch was founded in 1853 by Anthony Bowen, a former slave. Thus, the YMCA became a venue where the pursuit of sound health through exercise and sport was a wholesome form of recreation that bridged the sacred and the secular for whites and some blacks, albeit in separate facilities.

Young Men's Hebrew Association

In 1854, in Baltimore, Maryland, a group of Jews established the first Young Men's Hebrew Association (initially called the Young Men's Hebrew Literary Association), marking the beginning of the YMHA movement in America to promote literary, social, moral, and athletic activities for Jewish youth. Since Protestant social clubs often excluded them due to anti-Semitism, German Jews organized YMHAs in other areas as well. The YMHAs patterned themselves after the YMCA in offering facilities for reading and recreation and promoting spiritual values for Jewish youth. After this early phase, the YMHA movement expanded greatly following the Civil War, and YMHAs in late-nineteenth-century cities offered educational classes, athletics, lectures, and social programs in an effort to assimilate young, male Jewish immigrants into American life.

As YMCAs promoted "Muscular Christianity," YMHAs wanted to promote "Muscular Judaism," as termed by Max Nordau, who founded this movement for Jewish youth by integrating physical fitness with spiritual values; they encouraged athletics along with spiritual development in order to counter stereotypes of Jewish people as weak and scrawny. There was also the question of participating in sport on the Sabbath, which of course was

Sunday for the Christian community and Saturday for the Jewish community; playing sports on their respective Sabbath days was initially prohibited by both Christian and Jewish Ys. As the number of YMHAs increased, a national governing association emerged for the YMHAs and for arranging sport and cultural programs. Later, plans developed to merge Young Men's Hebrew Associations and Young Women's Hebrew Associations, creating the forerunner of the Jewish Community Center movement in the twentieth century.

YMHAs developed permanent facilities in cities including New York, Philadelphia, Louisville, and New Orleans in order to attract new members and advance the pursuit of athletics for young men. Many YMHAs expanded from rooms for libraries and social clubs to include gymnasiums, swimming pools, bowling alleys, billiard rooms, and other recreational facilities. The New York YMHA featured gymnasium equipment in 1875 and opened a full gymnasium in 1877 (Kirsch, "Young Men's"; Borish, "Young Men's").

Ladies Auxiliaries of Sporting and Religious Associations

For Protestant and Jewish women, membership opportunities in their respective Christian or Jewish Ys for spiritual and sporting activities remained limited. Initially, in the 1880s, women typically formed Ladies' Auxiliaries of the YMCA or YMHA, an arrangement that withheld full membership from them and thus denied them full access to the organization's buildings and physical education programs. When women formed their own Young Women's Christian Association (YWCA) in Boston, they offered calisthenic classes for women. As women's roles expanded in this association, and others formed their own YWCAs or YWHAs, women's involvement in various sports increased. Ethnically specific religious organizations such as the Young Men's and Young Women's Hebrew Associations paralleled the white, Anglo-Saxon, Protestant programs in serving their own needs. Thus, sport became a tool for conversion in the contest for souls and ethnic identity.

Growth of American Team Sport and Competition

The expansion of modern sport by the mid-nineteenth century, especially for men and boys, also took the form of a rise in team sports marked by emphasis on competition, rules, associations of clubs, interest in performance and the keeping of statistics and records, and the spread of information about sports and the players. Moreover, spectators crowded the playing fields to watch men play team sports, and boys, too, began to learn the rules of the games. In particular, the team sports of baseball and cricket thrilled sports enthusiasts, journalists, and health-minded advice givers who heralded the value of team sports for men and boys. Baseball, in fact, became an American pastime, and nationalism surfaced in the attitudes toward it, especially in comparison with the British favorite of cricket.

Emergence of Baseball

The tradition of bat-and-ball games played by young men and boys before the 1840s and 1850s evolved into the popular pastime of baseball, which emerged as the premier sport in the United States by the latter part of the nineteenth century. Alexander Cartwright, a bank clerk and secretary of the New York Knickerbockers baseball club, recorded the rules in 1845 and as a result has been accorded the title "Father of American Baseball." The pioneering role of the Knickerbocker Base Ball Club was chronicled by Charles Peverelly in *The Book of American Pastimes* (1866):

> During the years 1842 and '43, a number of gentlemen fond of the game, casually assembled on a plot of ground on Twenty-seventh street . . . bringing with them their bats, balls, etc. It was customary for two or three players, occasionally during the season, to go around in the forenoon of a pleasant day and muster up players enough to make a match. The march of improvement made a "change of base" necessary, and the following year they met at the next most convenient place, the north slope of Murray Hill, between the railroad cut, and Third avenue. Among the prominent players were Col. James Lee, Dr. [Franklin] Ransom, Abraham Tucker, James Fisher, and W. [William] Vail, the latter better known in later years of the Gotham Club as 'Stay-where-you-am Wail.' In the spring of 1845 Mr. Alex. J. Cartwright, who had become an enthusiast in the game, one day upon the field proposed a regular organization, promising to obtain several recruits. His proposal was accorded to, and Messrs. W. R. Wheaton, Cartwright, D. F. Curry, E. R. Dupignac Jr., and W. H. Tucker, formed themselves into a board of recruiting officers, and soon obtained names enough to make a respectable show. . . . [I]t was suggested that as it was apparent they would soon be driven from Murray Hill, some suitable place should be obtained in New Jersey, where their

> stay could be permanent; accordingly, a day or two afterwards, enough to make a game assembled. . . [and] marched up the road, prospecting for ground on each side, until they reached the Elysian Fields, where they "settled." Thus it occurred that a party of gentlemen formed an organization, combining together health, recreation, and social enjoyment, which was the nucleus of the now great American game of Base Ball, so popular in all parts of the United States, than which there is none more manly or more health-giving.

> qtd. in Levine, *American* 37

This "manly" game, as it came to be heralded by followers, was played by fellow clerks, tradesmen, and laborers, but not, at this time, by professional baseball players. The early rules of baseball, as codified by the Knickerbocker Base Ball Club, established in baseball a key element of modern sport, and some other teams adapted the club's rules. Cartwright put forward the field for baseball in the shape of a diamond and placed bases 90 feet (27.4 meters) apart at the corners. The full set of rules, adopted in 1845 and printed in *Spirit of the Times* in 1855, included the following:

1. The Bases shall be from 'Home' to second base 42 paces; and from first to third base 42 paces, equi-distant; and from 'Home' to pitcher not less than 15 paces; . . .

2. The game to consist of 21 counts or aces, but at the conclusion an equal number of hands must be played.

3. The ball must be pitched, not thrown for the bat.

4. A ball knocked outside the range of the first or third base is foul. . . .

5. Three balls being struck at and missed, and the last one caught, is a hand out; if not caught, is considered fair, and the striker bound to run. Tips and foul balls do not count.

6. A ball being struck or tipped, and caught either flying or on the first bound, is a hand out.

7. A player must make his first base after striking a fair ball, but should the ball be in the hands of an adversary on the first base before the runner reaches that base, it is a hand out; . . .

8. Players must make the bases in their order of striking, and when a fair ball is struck and striker not put out, the first base must be vacant, as well as the next base or bases, if similarly occupied. . . .

9. A player shall be out if at any time when off a base he shall be touched by the ball in the hands of an adversary. . . . [But] if the ball drops it is not a hand out. . . .

10. A player who shall intentionally prevent an adversary from catching or getting a ball is a hand out.

11. If two hands are already out a player running home at the time a ball is struck cannot make an ace if the striker is caught out.

12. Three hands out, all out.

13. Players must take their strike in regular rotation. . . .

14. No ace or base can be made on a foul strike.

15. A runner cannot be put out in making one base, when a balk is made by the pitcher.

16. But one base allowed if the ball, when struck, bounds out of the field.

17. The ball shall weigh from 5 1/2 to 6 ounces [156 to 170 grams], and be from 2 3/4 to 3 1/4 inches [7 to 8.25 centimeters] in diameter.

qtd. in Kirsch, *Sports* [Vol. 3] 73–74

Various versions of the baseball rules abounded, with the Knickerbocker Rules or others (such as the Massachusetts rules) being played in baseball games in sundry towns and cities, especially in the Northeast. Sport historian George Kirsch has determined that the "New York game" won out over other versions of baseball because "[w]herever New York businessmen and newspapers appeared, they carried with them their local sport," and with New York gaining prominence as "the largest and most powerful city in the United States, it was also exporting and promoting its native sport as the American national pastime. . . . The 'Massachusetts game' was not as attractive and could not compete with the game from Gotham" (Kirsch, *Sports* [Vol. 3] 71–72). Massachusetts rules games were played on an irregularly shaped square field, which meant different distances between the bases. By turning the field diagram to create a diamond shape, Cartwright created equal distances between all bases. In the Massachusetts version of baseball the batter stood midway between first and fourth—that is, home base—and tried to hit the ball. A batter, after hitting the ball, ran around the bases until safe at a base or was put out. The ball player was retired from the side "if the catcher caught three missed balls, or if a hit ball was caught on the fly, or if he was struck by a thrown ball while running the bases (called 'soaking' or 'burning' a runner)" (Kirsch, *Baseball and Cricket* 54–55). One out typically ended the inning, and the first team that scored an agreed-upon number of runs won the baseball game.

An image of Base Ball, illustrating this popular outdoor manly sport in the mid-nineteenth century.

Image courtesy of Library of Congress, LC-USZ62-640.

From the 1850s through the early 1860s, the New York rendition of baseball gained traction, and the codified rules circulated among ball players. Acceptance of the New York rules set the number of players at nine and fixed the design of the field, with a base positioned at each corner of a diamond-shaped infield. A batter still got nine pitches, delivered underhand and designated as above or below the waist by the batter himself into the 1870s. In 1858, 22 clubs in the New York area organized an affiliation grandiosely titled the National Association of Base Ball Players, which adhered to amateur guidelines. The association included the Knickerbocker, Gotham, Eagle, Empire, Baltic, Harlem, Independent, Metropolitan, Champion, St. Nicholas, Excelsior, Star, Enterprise, Union, Liberty, and other clubs. These class-based gentlemanly clubs gradually gave way in the face of recruitment and professionalism as rivalries (and wagering) between clubs, neighborhoods, towns, and various occupations fostered a greater attention to winning. In August 1860, *Wilke's Spirit of the Times* reported on the excitement about a championship game to be played between two rival teams:

The Grand Base Ball Match.

The "rubber" or third trial between the Atlantic and the Excelsior Base Ball Clubs, for the honor of the championcy, will, we learn, be played sometime in the first week of September, and will, without doubt, attract the most numerous assemblage which ever gathered to watch a baseball championship in the United States.

In regard to the grounds, we have heard several named, we know of but one which appears appropriate and suitable, and that is the East New York Parade Ground, adjoining the Howard House. There is here some beautiful field of thirty acres. The ground is as smooth as a floor, and upon it some twenty or thirty thousand spectators may enjoy an uninterrupted view of the entire contest. The facilities for reaching this locality are unsurpassed, there being three railroads . . . [which] will [be], for a trifling fee, depositing passengers directly upon the grounds. We will feel positive that the committees of the respective clubs can do no better than to immediately secure the Howard House grounds.

"Base Ball" 389

The formation of more and more baseball clubs—made up of clerks, artisans, shopkeepers, and laborers—in both urban and rural areas soon meant there were plenty of teams to compete against one another for laurels and team pride. The spread of baseball also kept the game in the public eye and attracted more spectators. And, as an alternative to the tough, bloody, and often immoral sports found in saloons and commercial amusement halls, and to offset the physical weakness of businessmen occupied in sedentary jobs and lacking exercise in the fresh air, health and sport advocates promoted baseball as especially useful in helping middle-class Victorian men and their sons become Muscular Christians. Thomas W. Higginson offered his own experience of baseball in the 1850s in an *Atlantic Monthly* article written for his accountant friend Dolorosus ("sad one"). Higginson believed that the outdoor competitive sport of baseball enhanced the physical fitness of businessmen, and he supported his case by citing a game between his friends of the Excelsior and Union baseball clubs: The players displayed "manly figures and handsome, eager faces," in contrast to Dolorosus, who featured a "meager form and wan countenance," thus prompting Higginson to announce, "I am satisfied that no description can do justice to your physical disintegration." Rather than criticizing baseball players as idly wasting time, Higginson and fellow sport advocates urged the physically weak man who overused his brain and shunned physical activity to go outdoors to a baseball field (Higginson, "A Letter" 467–468).

Baseball gained a hold on the sporting practices of Americans of different social ranks, races, and ethnicities. In short, as sport and baseball historians have emphasized, baseball "may well have been the most important sport in the antebellum era. Although some Victorian critics condemned the game for the usual offenses, it was much less raucous than the old sports of the bachelor subculture" (Gorn and Goldstein 79). By 1866, at the Tenth Annual Convention of the National Association of Base Ball Players, held in New York City, 212 baseball clubs, hailing from numerous states, were members (Wood, *Manual of Physical Exercises* [Vol. II] 191–192). Historian Ronald Story has explored the cultural appeal of baseball in early American society and found that it was viewed as "a superb outlet for boisterous young males in a way that languid pursuits—fishing or the saloon games or backyard games such as horseshoes or marbles—were not." Moreover, playing baseball could serve men and boys well, insofar as "a reputation for baseball excellence carried over in other areas, lending status to players in a brawling era that held physical prowess and 'grit' in high regard" (Story 123).

Baseball led an emphasis on American team sport for men and boys that continued throughout the nineteenth century. Even during the Civil War, when other major sports events were drastically slowed by the brutal conflict raging at myriad sites in the United States, the popularity of baseball increased among the soldiers in the military fields far from their native cities or farms. Military regiments from numerous states played baseball during the war, and both Northern troops and Southern troops (who learned the sport from Northern prisoners of war) found the game a most welcome respite from the horrors of war. After the war, these troops helped to spread baseball across the nation, and as an indication of the growth of the game, especially as promoted by Union veterans, representation of baseball clubs in the National Association of Base Ball Players increased from 62 clubs in 1860 to 91 clubs from 10 states at the end of the war in 1865 (Rader, *American Sports* [2004] 54).

Historian George Kirsch has studied the growth of baseball in the middle decades of the nineteenth century and commented on the strength of its fandom even in its early years: "The vicarious involvement of the spectators in the thrill of victory was as obvious in the 1850s and 1860s as it is today. Every team had its 'club followers,' who identified with their heroes and came to root them to victory." This keen "partisanship intensified after the Civil War, especially among the fans of the leading nines" (qtd. in Riess, *Major* 104). *Frank Leslie's Illustrated Newspaper* reported on the exciting scene at a championship game played just months after the war ended:

> The Elysian Fields in Hoboken, New Jersey, were crowded on the 3rd. inst. [of this month] to witness the grand contest of the United States, between the Mutual Club of New York and the Atlantic Club of Brooklyn. Never before was there a vast assemblage of people gathered together for a similar occasion, and never has there been known in the annals of our national sports, such a closely contested game of base-ball, as that which took place on Thursday.
>
> "Base-Ball Match for the Championship" 356

The Atlantics won by a score of 18-12, and baseball would continue its ascent to the status of national pastime. It still had to compete, however, with the widely popular British sport of cricket for the leisure time of young men, and cricket prevailed in cities such as Philadelphia during the mid-nineteenth century.

The Championship Nine of the Union Base-Ball Club of Morrisania, New York.
Photo courtesy of Library of Congress, LC-DIG-ppmsca-09310.

International Perspective

Why Baseball Had No Chance in Germany

After the end of the eighteenth century, several related games developed in Europe in which the ball had to be hit with a bat or club. Rounders and cricket were played in England, and *Schlagball* ("hit the ball") was played in Germany. Cricket and a similar "German ballgame" are described in the famous book *Games,* published by Johann GutsMuths in 1796. European emigrants took these games to North America, where they became the roots of baseball. American soldiers reimported baseball to Germany after World War II, but without any great success.

At the end of the nineteenth century in Germany, Schlagball was a game for youngsters, flourishing in the context of the German games movement, which influenced the playground movement in the United States. With the arrival of modern sport and its focus on performance and competition, Schlagball became "sportified," meaning that new rules made the game faster, more difficult, and more competitive.

The Prussian authorities and the German Gymnastic Association propagated the game for physical education in schools and clubs because it was looked upon as a German game which could counteract the growing popularity of soccer (which had English roots). From 1898 onward, Schlagball was played during the German Turner festivals, and the first German championships in Schlagball took place in 1913. Schlagball was even included in the program of the Olympic Games planned for 1916 in Berlin, but World War I prevented the holding of the Games and therefore also the Olympic blessing of this German game. Still, Schlagball became increasingly popular in the 1920s; besides being played in many clubs, it was also a popular and widely played school sport. Girls and women, too, played Schlagball and had their own competitions and championships.

After World War II, however, the number of players and teams decreased continuously, and the game nearly disappeared from the sporting landscape. Identifiable reasons for this decline include its numerous and difficult rules, as well as the permanent changes to them caused by the need to adapt them to the increasing skills of the players. This often led to unclear situations and controversies. Schlagball thus did not fascinate spectators. Additionally, in the 1920s the Germans had already opted for soccer as their national game, one which closely mirrors the principles of modern sport: it emphasizes the fight of player against player; it has a continuous flow of action; it has a single criterion for success; it is easy to understand; and the rules, as well as the state of the game, are transparent even for spectators who do not play the game.

Information from GutsMuths, Johann Christoph Friedrich. *Spiele zur Übung und Erholung des Körpers und Geistes* (Games for exercise and recreation of the body and the mind). Schnepfenthal, 1796; Pfister, Gertrud. "Sozial- und Kulturgeschichte der Sportspiele (Social and cultural history of games)." Eds. A. Hohmann, M. Kolb, and K. Roth. *Handbuch Sportspiel* (Handbook Sport Games). Schorndorf: Verlag Karl Hofmann, 2005. 31–46.

Cricket

For sport-minded British immigrant men in the United States, the English sport of cricket proved immensely popular as part of their sporting heritage. Cricket, in fact, preceded baseball as a team sport followed by spectators, and it provided for the English what baseball provided for a growing number of Americans—a "national pastime" (in a phrase coined in 1856 by the New York Mercury baseball team). Accordingly, "[b]efore 1860 (and to a limited extent afterwards), cricket enjoyed its own popularity in the U.S. and the question as to whether cricket or baseball would ultimately capture the American sporting heart was still unanswered" (Majumdar and Brown 142). In the 1850s, the rise in nationalistic spirit in the United States fueled the sport press covering baseball and cricket; the increased interest in American identity at this time spurred baseball to wider appeal, and baseball would surpass cricket as an expression of national strength in sport.

Cricket was considered the first major organized American team sport, and it saw an upsurge in players in the 1840s. The St. George Cricket Club, for example, was formed in Manhattan in 1839. Cricket teams consisted mainly of middle- and upper-class men, and as many as four hundred cricket clubs, with ten thousand members, were playing matches by 1860, sometimes in intercity matches as far west as Chicago and Milwaukee (Riess, *City* 33). International competition began as early as 1840, with a match between the United States and Canada, and an English all-star squad defeated the North Americans in 1859. Cricket differed from baseball in equipment (e.g., wickets, bails, stumps, and flat bats), field dimensions, and rules (e.g., 11 players per side). Before the Civil War, cricket clubs proved popular in several American cities. Philadelphia became a leading cricket center, with wealthy Victorian men playing the sport to reinforce their social class and privileged position. Such elites might join the Philadelphia Cricket Club or other groups, as the city was home to some of the oldest cricket clubs in the United States. Club members in the Victorian era favored the "widely-held belief that moral, social, and vocational values could be developed through cricket. As a consequence, certain Philadelphians steered their sons toward the game with the intent of socializing them to be productive and successful adults" (Jable, "Social" 205–206). In suburban areas such as Germantown, cricket clubs offered a rural outdoor setting comfortably removed from the chaotic city. The Germantown and Philadelphia Cricket clubs played important roles in the success of cricket in nineteenth-century America, and cricket clubs were the precursors of the prominent country clubs built by the turn of the century, when sports such as tennis and golf, played by both men and women, surpassed cricket among the elite.

For most Americans, however, baseball seemed more appealing than cricket, since men played baseball at a swifter pace, and it gained popularity both among young men seeking athletic activities and among their supporters who came out to watch. A *New York Herald* journalist in 1859 addressed the lack of interest in cricket as compared with the enthusiasm for the American game of baseball:

[Cricket] is too slow, intricate and plodding a game for our go-ahead people. . . . In cricket a very smooth ground is wanted on account of the bowling as the ball must strike the ground before it reaches the batman or strikes the wicket. . . . In base ball very smooth ground is not required, but a rather larger space is necessary for cricket. . . . It occupies on an average about two hours to play a game of base ball—two days to play a game of cricket.

qtd. in Riess, *Major* 90–92

As cricket's star faded, baseball's fortunes rose. Indeed, "[a]s American nationalism emerged and strengthened, baseball, continually forged and molded to suit the needs of Americans, began to assert a stronger hold on the American public, eventually pushing cricket forever into the margins of American sporting life" (Majumdar and Brown 143). Baseball, a faster, rougher sport that featured striking displays of men's physical skills, captured the attention of American men. Compared with cricket, baseball was "aggressively physical"; it was also "simple to learn and unlike . . . cricket, easy enough to play to accommodate a range of ages and skills." Moreover, baseball offered "endless bursts of action and limitless quick sprinting with very little dead time in between" (Story 122–123). By 1860, baseball had become the preferred team sport of the nation, and its dominance continued during and after the Civil War.

Rise of Intercollegiate Sport

By the mid-1840s and 1850s, the sport of rowing enjoyed considerable popularity. Rowing clubs were formed for middle- and upper-class men and their sons, and rowing matches began to play a

People & Places

Henry Chadwick

One of the most influential early sports journalists was Henry Chadwick, who began his career in 1843 and by the 1850s was the leading sportswriter on cricket for the *New York Times*. Increasingly, however, he promoted the American game of baseball. As a sportswriter, he incorporated the baseball box score, previously used for cricket matches, and initiated the statistical categories of batting average, hits, total bases, and home runs. In 1858, Chadwick became a member of the National Association of Base Ball Players Rules Committee, and as committee chair he engineered a number of rule changes that modernized the game: the requirement of catching the ball on the fly to achieve an out (first-bounce catches had previously counted as outs), the switch from underhand to overhand pitching, and the establishment of a fixed distance between the pitcher and batter. The National Baseball Hall of Fame elected Chadwick to membership in 1938 in recognition of his important contribution to baseball and to sports journalism.

significant role in athletic life for young white men at some of the elite Eastern universities. Sons of the wealthy organized a collegiate rowing club at Yale College in New Haven, Connecticut, in 1843: "William J. Weeks, '44, purchased a four-oared Whitehall boat in New York, and bringing it to New Haven formed with Henry W. Buel, John W. Dulles, John McLoud, Virgil M. D. Marcy, John P. Marshall, and William Smith the first boat club at Yale, and which was also the first rowing organization at any American college" (Crowther and Ruhl 14).

Spurred by Yale's club and by the Chelsea regattas of the 1840s, Harvard College followed suit by forming its own rowing club in 1844. The "Yale oarsmen had their eyes on" the progress of Harvard's club, which in time led to a challenge to Harvard "'to test the superiority of the oarsmen of the two colleges,' and a race was arranged for August 3, 1852" (Crowther and Ruhl 16, 17). This crew race marked the first intercollegiate sporting contest in the United States. A railroad company carried the athletes, supporters, and spectators to the regatta as a way to promote both its railroad line and a resort in New Hampshire. Railroad Superintendent James Elkins "offered to pay for the transportation and lodging of the Harvard and Yale crews if they would race at Center Harbor on Lake Winnipesaukee, New Hampshire. Forty-one students from the two colleges accepted

the proposal," and thus commercialism and sport meshed in this first intercollegiate sporting contest (Kirsch, *Sports* [Vol. 3] 40). Harvard, in the Oneida boat, defeated three Yale crews in the 2-mile (3.2-kilometer) race to win the first prize—silver-mounted, black walnut oars. The *New York Herald* described the race as follows:

> On the day of the regatta, the boats came crowded to overflowing with passengers, and these, together with the people from the villages around, lined the wharfs and shore for some distance. The scene was extremely fine, as the boats lay all abreast, waiting for the sound of the bugle. The beautiful lake . . . the unruffled smoothness of the water, and the perfect silence of the throng around—all added to the beauty of the scene. . . .
>
> The prize regatta came off at four in the afternoon. The boats were towed off to a starting point upon the lake, two miles [3.2 kilometers] distant from the shore, in order to row towards the shore. It was almost precisely a re-enaction of the scene of the morning, save, perhaps, that the oarsmen bent somewhat more lustily to their oars. The result was the same as in the first race, there being nearly the same space between the boats. A pair of fine black walnut oars were presented, as the prize, to the Oneida. . . . The crowds dispersed highly gratified with the performance, the performers meanwhile adjourned to a very welcome repast at the Senter House.

qtd. in Kirsch, *Sports* [Vol. 3] 40–42

The enthusiasm for this first collegiate regatta led to another rowing match, when Yale issued another challenge to Harvard in 1855. The race took place on the Connecticut River at Springfield, Massachusetts, and once again Harvard triumphed. In 1858, *Harvard Magazine* "suggested that an association of colleges should be formed to hold annual regattas, . . . and on May 26 delegates from Harvard, Yale, Brown, and Trinity met at New Haven and evolved the College Union Regatta" (Crowther and Ruhl 28–29). Members raced on Lake Quinsigamond near Worcester, Massachusetts, and again Harvard proved victorious in 1859 (the race was canceled in 1858 because a Yale oarsman drowned during an outing). Yale would beat Harvard in another regatta, but Harvard triumphed in the regatta last held before the Civil War. The advent of the Civil War in 1861, however, halted the regattas, and many of the young men went off to war. When intercollegiate regattas resumed in 1864, the increasing rivalry between Yale and Harvard, along with Yale's intense desire to win, brought about a shift in tactics, as Yale students

REGATTAS

ON

LAKE WINNIPISSIOGEE!

THE BOAT RACES BETWEEN THE CLUBS OF

Harvard and Yale Colleges!

Will take place as follows, in the morning and afternoon of each day.

At Centre Harbor, Tuesday, August 3d.
At Wolfboro', Thursday, August 5th.

The following boats will contend for the prizes:

ONEIDA, from Harvard University. Uniform Red, Blue and White.
UNDINE, from Yale College. Uniform White and Blue.
SHAWMUT, from Yale College. Uniform White and Red.
ATALANTA, from New-York, but manned by students of Yale College. Uniform Blue and White.

These Boats were built at a great expense, and their crews are disciplined in the most perfect manner. They carry eight oars in a boat, and are from 35 to 40 feet long. The Races will consist of several one mile heats, and the ground has been so selected that any number of spectators, however large, will obtain each an equally good view with the other.

PRIZES will be publicly presented to the winners.

MUSIC by the CONCORD MECHANICS' BRASS BAND.

Arrangements have been made with the Boston, Concord & Montreal Railroad, to run special trains between Concord and Warren and the Lake in the morning and afternoon of the days of the Regatta to accommodate persons going and returning on the same day.

Fare in the special Trains HALF PRICE. The regular trains run as usual, giving persons from connecting roads an opportunity to witness the Regatta in the afternoon of each day.

N. B. BAKER, for the Committee of Arrangements.

July 28, 1852.

This flyer promoted the race between Harvard and Yale in 1852.

From www.rowinghistory.net.

hired a professional coach. The Yale crew featured its six best oarsmen to date, and they came ready to compete despite Harvard's great confidence. In the event, "the championship was taken from Cambridge, [with] Yale taking the lead soon after the start, and keeping it during the whole race" (Crowther and Ruhl 32–33). Other elite colleges and schools then adopted the same strategy, and, although initiated and organized by students without institutional sponsorship, boat clubs assumed affiliation with their schools, and heated challenges spurred competition in intercollegiate rowing.

In addition to matching skills with oarsmen from other colleges, rowing teams vied with international teams as well. In 1869, a four-oared crew from Harvard competed in England against the Oxford University rowing team in the first of several intercollegiate competitions between American and English rowers. The scene was the Thames River in London, where, in a hard-fought race, Oxford, familiar with the river from their numerous runs on the Thames and cheered on by local spectators, emerged victorious. In covering the contest, the *New York Times* conveyed the keen attention increasingly being paid to such vigorous competitions between groups of young men: "The two greatest commercial nations of the world were engaged yesterday, not in the usual pursuit of gain,

but in watching an extraordinary trial of strength between eight young men." Although Harvard lost, the contest evoked enthusiasm in America both for the sport and for such international matches: "An international boat race between nations like the American and English cannot, therefore, be regarded as a trivial incident," the *New York Times* reported, and these competitions challenged "the world to admire physical pluck, endurance, hardiness, a sound constitution, and other gifts, which we were intended to cultivate and rejoice in no less than in the pretentious intellectual forces" ("The *New York Times* Reports" 113–114).

The first intercollegiate baseball game was played in Massachusetts in July 1859, with Amherst College defeating Williams College by a score of 73-32. Because the game was being played in Massachusetts, the teams decided to use Massachusetts baseball rules. High scores were commonplace at that time as batters could call for the pitch to their liking, above or below the waist. Williams and Amherst agreed on the rules, including that each team would use its own ball, "which could be batted in any direction as in cricket, and they decided that the team which garnered 65 runs would be a victor." An issue in baseball rules at this time centered on catching the ball—if the player caught the ball on the fly or the first bounce, a

Currier & Ives print of the 1869 Harvard versus Oxford international boat race.
Image courtesy of the Library of Congress, LC-USZ62-847.

batter was considered out. Catching the ball on the fly "was considered more 'mannish'" and the two "schools decided to do the masculine thing" (Smith, *Sports and Freedom* 54). College baseball, however, did not take off as fast as other collegiate sports, such as rowing and, later, football and track and field. College football (i.e., one version of the game as played before the rules became standardized and modernized) was first played in the United States in 1869 by Rutgers and Princeton. The origins of these intercollegiate sports, as well as associations and mechanisms designed to organize college sports, are explored in later chapters.

The Civil War and Sporting Experiences

As the chaos and carnage of the Civil War dominated Americans' lives between 1861 and 1865, the growth of American sport was of course greatly slowed. The Northern states, transformed by industrialization and urbanization and critical to the sporting boom in the mid-nineteenth century, now turned the full attention and capacity of their large populations toward providing the resources and products necessary to defeat the Confederacy. Sport did persist, however, and, in addition to baseball other sports were engaged in whenever a soldier secured a few moments for diversion. Thus, boxing, horse racing, wrestling, swimming, hunting, and fishing continued to be pursued to varying degrees during the war. Soldiers' desire to participate in sport, rather than just watch, meant that many men also wanted to play sports after their wartime days were done: "Both Johnny Reb and Billy Yank were by nurture and by inclination participants. . . . Watching with no prospect of joining was like being shot and having your name spelled wrong in the newspaper" (Fielding 156). As a result, sports clubs developed throughout the country, as former soldiers continued their interest in athletic activities, which, free of the horrors of the Civil War, offered a pleasant way to engage in competition against other men.

The Civil War also had another effect on American sport in the 1860s. The deaths of thousands of white soldiers as well as free and enslaved blacks—due to military battles as well as disease and infection on the battlefield—generated a desire for robust military officers and troops trained for war in order to preserve the United States. In response, military leaders and the federal government moved to provide support for agricultural, land-grant colleges to train physically sound and mentally prepared men for military and other forms of service crucial to the nation's growth and development. These colleges, established with support from the Morrill Act of 1862, provided students with education in agriculture, engineering and mechanics, and home economics (for women admitted to colleges). Over time, educational institutions such as Penn State University (originally founded in 1855 and part of the growth of land-grant institutions), the University of Michigan, the University of Maryland, and Ohio State University integrated athletics and academics for young men in various regions of the country. These institutions provided the community structures and resources necessary to develop major athletic programs in the nation and promote sport for training a sturdy, physically energetic, male student body.

Summary

For individual athletes and teams in American sport from 1850 to 1870, the values linked with sport continued to form a critical component of American identities. The growth of modern sport provided competitive, rationalized, organized, and publicly recognized contests, with sports information disseminated through the press. These early modern sports often utilized new forms of technology, both for playing the game and for transporting players and supporters to competition venues. As specialized skills emerged in athletic performances, and as victories and records gained prominence in defining the sporting experiences of participants, betting persisted in several sports, meshing easily with early commercialism. As part of the rise of modern sport, specific social classes often formed their own subcommunities, such as yachting and rowing clubs, in order to separate themselves from immigrants or persons of different races or backgrounds. The so-called sporting fraternity spurred the growth of certain sports, including boxing, billiards, pedestrianism (footracing), and horse racing, and infused betting into its sporting culture. Sport also registered gender ideology—that is, ideas of what it meant to be a man or a woman—and an emphasis on using one's body in rational recreation and sport in order to fulfill the ideal of a healthy and physically vigorous citizen of the United States. Rivalries—for example, between associated baseball teams or collegiate rowing clubs—quickened the quest for supremacy in American sport, and team sports such as baseball meshed with the increasing nationalistic spirit. At the local and national levels, sport became increasingly integrated into everyday life for participants, managers, and spectators. It also occasioned debates about codes of conduct for fair play, and in the following decades the continuing rise of modern sport would sometimes generate criticism, as issues of amateurism and professionalism surfaced more vividly in the playing and marketing of sport.

DISCUSSION QUESTIONS

1. How did modern sport change with advancements in athletic performance, competition, technology, and sporting organizations?

2. What factors were critical to the shift from premodern to modern sport during the middle decades of the nineteenth century?

3. Why did certain groups of men and women affiliate with, and support, specific types of sport?

4. What role did spectators play in the various forms of sport and in advancing the boom in sports during this period?

5. How did members of the sporting fraternity participate in sport, and in what ways did they challenge the moral and health-related rationales for sport in the mid-nineteenth century?

6. Why did some sports develop as amateur pursuits, while others involved professionals?

7. Why did baseball emerge in the mid-nineteenth century as an especially popular team sport in America?

8. How did the first intercollegiate sport develop, and why was rowing such a popular sport from 1850 to 1870?

Chapter 5

New Identities and Expanding Modes of Sport in the Gilded Age
1870–1890

CHAPTER OBJECTIVES

After reading this chapter, you will have learned about the following:

- The relationship between urbanization and sporting culture
- The development of sport forms specific to social class and ethnicity
- The development and growth of intercollegiate sport
- The development of commercialized and professional sports
- The role of sports entrepreneurs and the media in the promotion of sport
- The relationship of sport to the bachelor subculture and concepts of masculinity
- The burgeoning of sport as a liberating experience for women

In November of 1869 the Rutgers student newspaper reported that the second of the three games of Foot Ball between Princeton and Rutgers was won by the former at their ball-grounds, on Saturday, the 13th inst. [of this month]. Eight out of fifteen was the game, but as Princeton won the first eight the other innings were not played. The style of playing differs, materially, in the two Colleges. A fly, or first bound catch, entitles (sic) to a "free kick," a la Princeton. We bat with hands, feet, head, sideways, backwards, any way to get the ball along. We must say that we think our style much more exciting, and more as Foot Ball should be. After the regular game two innings were played after our fashion, and we won them. It is but fair to our twenty-five to say that they never have practiced the "free kick" system. At half-past six we sat down to a very fine supper, prepared for us by our hosts. Speeches and songs, accompanied, of course, by the study of practical gastronomy, passed the time pleasantly until the evening train bore us Brunswickwards. We hope soon to welcome Princeton to New Brunswick for the third game, and beat them. Their cheer, sounding as if they meant to explode, but for a fortunate escape of air, followed by a grateful yell at the deliverance of such a catastrophe, still sounds in our ears as we thank them for their hospitality. If we must be beaten we are glad to have such conquerors.

qtd. in Kirsch, *Sports* [Vol. 4] 234

So began the game that would overtake the national pastime of baseball on college campuses by the end of the nineteenth century. It more resembled the British game of soccer, but, with rule modifications and a greatly diminished spirit of cordial hospitality, it would come to define the American character in the ensuing years. Indeed, American sport would be distinguished from British practices by a win-at-all-costs attitude, intense competition, and a thwarting of amateur ideals prevalent at American colleges and high schools by the end of the century.

In the ensuing years, American sport forms and practices increasingly diverged from the British models. The regulation of sport emanated from urban processes as the United States experienced a social transformation throughout the nineteenth century. The gradual transition from rural, communal, and agricultural society occurred more abruptly in some localities. Chicago, for example, erupted from a frontier outpost to a city of more than a million inhabitants in one lifetime. The new urban environment housed various ethnic, religious, and racial groups, each with its own interests, values, and recreational practices. This sometimes volatile stew combined with industrialization to produce social inequalities; various tensions and conflicts between races, ethnicities, and classes; and political struggles. All of these developments influenced sport in various forms and American society in numerous ways. They produced class-based sport forms and associations that unified some ethnic, religious, or class-based factions while excluding others. In all groups, however—regardless of class, race, ethnicity, gender, or religious affiliation—sporting practices moved from premodern to modern status, characterized by greater organization, rationalization, quantification, commercialization, and professionalization. Although sport in some respects unified particular groups and divided others, sports such as baseball and football began to establish particular national cultural characteristics.

The evolving nature of American society presented cultural dilemmas in the years following the Civil War. The carnage that eventually resulted in the emancipation of the slaves seemingly resolved the greatest cleavage in the American polity and held promise for the realization of a classless democracy. During the Reconstruction period after the war, education became somewhat available to freedmen, and some African Americans even won election to Congress. Their ascendancy proved short-lived, however, as the political compromises of the Republican and Democratic parties eventually undermined black gains. The disputed presidential election of 1876 resulted in the victory of a Republican, Rutherford B. Hayes, on the condition that he restore white Democratic power in the South, thus negating the Reconstruction advances of African Americans. Although technically they were still free, the resolution doomed generations of blacks to poverty as sharecroppers in the agricultural economy of the South.

The Civil War had been more than a battle over slavery. It resolved the question of the economic

1869

- Fifteenth Amendment passed by Congress, prohibiting denial of the right to vote based on race
- National Woman Suffrage Association founded by Elizabeth

Cady Stanton and Susan B. Anthony for suffrage and other women's rights
- American Woman Suffrage Association founded to promote suffrage

1874

- Tennis introduced to United States

nature of the republic, which had lingered since its inception, and Thomas Jefferson's independent yeoman farmer gave way to Alexander Hamilton's capitalist entrepreneur in the era known as the Gilded Age. In the industrial North, the unbridled pursuit of wealth, combined with growing acceptance of the Social Darwinist tenet of survival of the fittest, rationalized the plight of the poor as inevitable because of their own character weaknesses. Large corporations and trusts dominated the economy, and individuals such as Andrew Carnegie, Cornelius Vanderbilt, J.P. Morgan, and John D. Rockefeller amassed enormous fortunes. Bribery and corruption ran rampant in business matters, and U.S. senators also became millionaires in a modern secular world that distanced itself from the moral prohibitions of earlier eras. Sport, too, moved away from its premodern traits to assume modern characteristics. As described by Allen Guttmann, the practice of sport became rationalized and more secular. Bureaucratic governing bodies emerged to regulate competitions, as winning assumed greater importance. Professional athletes enhanced the probability of success (e.g., a professional pitcher could easily make the difference between winning and losing), and performances became quantified in the form of records that might allow for scientific measurement of human progress. Clubs and business owners sponsored events and teams to promote their identity or products; thus sport acquired commercial aspects and generated profits (Guttmann, *From* 62, 73).

Sport and Social Stratification

The highly visible accumulation of wealth and privilege upset notions of the United States as a utopian democracy. Within this context, sport and leisure practices both reflected and confounded American social ambiguities. While some sporting practices and their attendant crowds transcended class lines to present an egalitarian image, other sport forms reinforced class distinctions. Despite working-class roots, the Biglin Brothers reached championship status as professional rowers, and both baseball players and their fans often came

from the lower and middle rungs of the social ladder. Thoroughbred and yacht owners, however, operated in distinctly different and separate circles, espousing a particular value system. Victorian decorum stressed the virtues of sobriety, dignity, self-control, and a white Protestant religiosity. Yet sporting ventures of wealthy and middle-class young men led some to seek adventure in a bachelor subculture centered in the saloons. In such environs, men shared in the pursuit of hedonism, dissipation, and masculine prowess. In such ways, sport both separated and united the distinct social groups in America.

Religion and Sport in the Gilded Age

Sabbatarian laws, evident in earlier periods of American sport history and discussed in previous chapters, continued to impede sporting developments in the South, and white middle- and upper-class Protestants still regulated Sunday contests well into the twentieth century in the Northeast. Heavy concentrations of Irish and German immigrants, however, fostered liberalization in the Midwest, especially in the urban areas. As early as 1855, Germans in Chicago erupted in the Lager Beer Riot when the nativist mayor attempted to prohibit consumption of their favorite beverage. A death, injuries, and the imposition of martial law resulted in a referendum that overturned the legislation.

The Young Men's Christian Association expanded in the 1870s and offered physical training and sport programs to induce (as examined in the preceding chapter) the practice of Muscular Christianity among young, single men in various cities. Railroad companies hired the YMCA to provide wholesome forms of leisure to their employees, and the recreational link between railway firms and the YMCA became more pronounced after the national strike of 1877, when employees crippled and even destroyed much of the system in a violent confrontation over wage cuts. That same year, the YWCA, the female counterpart of the male organization, offered calisthenic classes for women in Boston, where in 1884 the YWCA

1875	1876	
■ First Kentucky Derby held	■ Telephone invented by Alexander Graham Bell	■ Intercollegiate Association of Amateur Athletes of America founded
	■ National League (baseball) founded	■ Westchester (New York) Polo Club founded
	■ Battle of Little Big Horn fought	■ First national track-and-field champion-ship held (New York Athletic Club)

Aesthetic dancing at the Baltimore YWCA.

Photo courtesy of Library of Congress, LC-B2-3690-10.

even constructed a gymnasium for the women of the city.

Minority ethnic religious groups, such as the Young Men's Hebrew Association (discussed in chapter 4), also added new locations and increased sporting programs, countering the Protestant orientation of the YMCAs. The "Jewish Ys" initially (before the turn of the century) catered to the athletic interests of Jewish men, with women becoming auxiliary members rather than forming (as they would later) separate Young Women's Hebrew Associations. At the YMHA of Louisville, organized by well-established Jews primarily to assist Eastern European immigrants, Isaac W. Bernheim, a Kentucky distiller and philanthropist, completed the gymnasium in 1890. One year later, the Louisville YMHA conducted separate classes for women. In the late nineteenth century, at both Jewish and Christian Ys, sport became a tool in the contest for souls, and sport took on a larger significance.

American Protestantism espoused individualism, a concept alien to the communal lifestyles of many immigrant groups, and, as industrialization and urbanization transformed American society in the post–Civil War era, ethnic groups maintained their alternative customs and practices in urban enclaves, homogeneous rural communities, and church parishes dominated by Old World clergy. Sport provided one means of assimilation and acculturation, but the process proved uneven.

Urbanization and the Continuing Promotion of Sport

Cities fostered the growth of sport, and technology sped its pace. The inventions and technological innovations detailed in chapter 4 gave way to other types of mechanization in the latter decades of the nineteenth century, and these, too, altered sport in American society. Electricity replaced gaslights in urban establishments, and sports clubs and entrepreneurs offered more commercialized entertainment for members and the general public. The growing manufacturers of sporting goods used the faster process of mechanization to produce sports

1877	1879	1880
■ Great Railroad Strike staged	■ Carlisle Indian School founded	■ Thomas Edison patents electric light bulb
	■ National Archery Association tournament held	■ League of American Wheelmen founded
		■ Laws instituted to enforce the segregation and disenfranchisement of Southern blacks

equipment, making sporting products available for home consumption in rural and urban houses as well as for use in organized sporting associations. Mail-order businesses sent advertisements and sports manuals to people in large cities, small towns, and rural areas alike. In the 1880s, sporting goods manufacturers such as Spalding, Rawlings, Reach, Meacham, and McClean promoted their wares to the public, as documented by sports historian Stephen Hardy: "Wherever or however the consumer might purchase an article of sporting goods—through the mail or at a hardware store, general store, department store, or the sportsman's 'depot'—the manufacturer wanted him to buy a specific brand." In developing and standardizing sports products, "[t]he marketing efforts of sporting goods firms clearly expanded opportunities and interest in active play among a wide range of Americans" ("Adopted" 141, 146). Thus, sporting practices continued to become more organized, rationalized, and quantified, a process initiated in previous decades, and in the Gilded Age sport more markedly took on the characteristics of capitalist enterprise.

Capitalism bred an unequal distribution of wealth, however, and as the fortunes of working-class employees diverged from those of their bosses, workers took notice and began forming unions to gain rights and better working conditions. Wage labor dictated long hours and minimal leisure time for workers, but sport sometimes masked the growing development of distinct social classes. Particular sport forms, such as billiards, might be played both in the parlors of the wealthy and in working-class saloons, and boxing matches drew spectators from across the spectrum of society.

Sport for the Elite

More often, sport forms distinguished between the social classes. Although spectators of all classes might enjoy horse racing, only the wealthy could own the expensive animals. Affluent members of the American Jockey Club opened Jerome Park in New York as a racetrack for thoroughbreds in 1866. Monmouth Park was established in 1870, and the Brighton Beach course in Brooklyn followed in 1879. A coalition of Democratic Party politicians and rich socialites controlled the sport in New York state throughout the remainder of the nineteenth century. Outside the Northeast, Pimlico commenced operations in Baltimore in 1870, and Churchill Downs opened in Louisville, Kentucky, in

People & Places

Alfred J. Reach

Allegedly the first openly acknowledged professional baseball player, Alfred J. Reach first starred as a catcher for the Philadelphia Athletics in 1865. He continued to play as an infielder through 1875. Reach also opened a store in which he sold baseballs, bats, and other equipment, and as the business prospered he took on a partner in 1881, Ben Shibe, who later owned the Philadelphia franchise in the American League. Shibe's leather works began manufacturing baseballs and gloves, and the American Association (a National League rival from 1882 to 1891) adopted the Reach baseball as its official game ball in 1882. By 1883, Reach owned the Philadelphia Phillies of the National League, and the Reach ball and the Reach baseball guide became the official American League standards after the turn of the century. The Reach Company patented a cork-centered ball in 1909, which was subsequently adopted to replace the rubber-centered ball, fostering a livelier game. The company expanded to manufacture other sporting goods, including golf equipment, and was eventually bought by the rival Spalding Company.

Information from www.baseball-reference.com/bullpen/A.J._Reach_Company

1881	1882	1883
■ United States Lawn Tennis Association founded	■ Chinese Exclusion Act passed ■ Pullman industrial recreation program launched ■ First country club established (Brookline, Massachusetts) ■ John L. Sullivan defeats Paddy Ryan for heavyweight boxing title	■ New York Athletic Club holds first national swimming championship

1875, with the running of the First Kentucky Derby, which established the state as another racing hub.

Railroad magnate Cornelius Vanderbilt favored harness racing, and his support lent a measure of prestige to the sport. The National Trotting Association was formed in 1870, and a national breeders' association followed in 1876. Harness racing remained a staple at rural county fairs, and the running of such contests at city tracks somewhat bridged the growing urban–rural divide. Venues such as ball parks and horse tracks provided an open-air, pastoral setting within the bustling cities as the urbanization process began to transform the economy from agriculture to industry.

Horse racing was democratic at least in the sense that spectators represented all classes, but racetracks began to construct specialized clubhouses with amenities for wealthy clientele. In 1871, the Metairie Racetrack in New Orleans designated a segregated section for African American patrons. Similarly, although racetracks organized betting that welcomed all comers, some required a minimum bet of an amount that excluded those with less disposable income. Independent bookies who operated at the tracks did accept small bets, and, in the cities, illegal poolrooms and bookmakers catered to less savory customers and urban workers unable to attend the events at the track. Such operations, protected by underworld figures and their allied politicians, formed a criminal nexus in many American cities, and they remained a focus of crusaders over the next 25 years, as moral reformers and clergy attempted to banish gambling from American society.

While horse racing transcended class lines in some ways, yacht racing necessarily attracted only the wealthiest sportsmen. The Southern Yacht Club, founded in New Orleans in 1849, enrolled elites as members and conducted its regattas on Lake Pontchartrain and the Gulf of Mexico. The Civil War interrupted such excursions, but the club reorganized and resumed operations after the hostilities ceased. For the wealthy, sport and leisure practices transcended regional boundaries as they traveled to warmer climates. Northern elites traveled south in the winter and established yacht clubs. In the North,

James Gordon Bennett Jr. assumed leadership of the New York Yacht Club. His daring victory in 1866 in the first transatlantic race, during which six lives were lost, garnered increased media attention for the sport, and new yachting clubs soon appeared in New York, San Francisco, Chicago, and Detroit (the Great Lakes provided suitable basins for competition in the Midwest).

In 1875, Bennett traveled to England, where he watched British army officers engage in a game of polo. The next year he introduced the game to his wealthy friends in New York, who formed the Westchester Polo Club. During the summers, they retired to their palatial retreats in Newport, Rhode Island, but continued their equestrian interests. Wealthy adherents disseminated the game in their travels, and polo clubs emerged throughout the United States and its colonies, in such places as New Orleans, San Antonio, Colorado Springs, Los Angeles, and Hawaii. West Point taught the sport to its cavalry officers, who then practiced it at their diverse duty stations. Like yachting, polo became a marker of social distinction in the form of a sport unavailable to the masses.

Bennett, perhaps the first great sports promoter in the United States, engaged in several other sporting ventures during the period. He sponsored Daniel O'Leary, a professional pedestrian (footracer), who competed for prize money:

> Great preparations are in progress and nearly completed for O'Leary's grand test race, the 156 hours "go-as-you-please," in which men and horses are to compete on equal terms for a purse of $4,000 . . . . The inclosure, grand stand, and other buildings . . . will be in readiness . . . when the tournament will be inaugurated with a match race for $500, in which Daniel O'Leary himself is to ride thirty miles . . . against three runners who are to go ten miles each. The runners are James McLeavy, the Scotch champion; White Eagle, the fleetest of foot of the Caughnawaga tribe of Indians from Canada; and Charles Price, the champion ten-mile runner of England.
>
> "O'Leary's Tournament" 3

Bennett also supported the first intercollegiate track meet in 1871, promoted foxhunting in Vir-

1886	1887	1888	1889
■ American Federation of Labor organized ■ Haymarket Affair occurs in Chicago	■ First women's amateur golf tournament held	■ Amateur Athletic Union organized, with national championships in boxing, fencing, gymnastics, swimming, track and field	■ Hull House settlement opens in Chicago; offers sport and athletic programs for immigrants

ginia, and built the attractive Newport Casino in Rhode Island in 1880, commissioning the famed architectural firm of McKim, Mead, and White to build and design the Victorian club. The Newport Casino provided a playground for the wealthy in New England, with spaces reserved for billiards, dancing, dining, bowling, lawn bowling, horse shows, archery, and lawn tennis. By this time, the eccentric Bennett had left for exile in Paris, having been ostracized by the moneyed social set for his vulgar behavior in polite company. His crudeness had degraded his privileged status. Still, he managed to implement increased sports coverage as heir to the *New York Herald,* and he later awarded prestigious international trophies to winners of auto and airplane races.

Other wealthy young men formed the New York Athletic Club (NYAC) in 1866 to participate in physical activity with like-minded counterparts. Two years later, the club was incorporated and commenced track-and-field competition. Club members distinguished between their own amateur pastimes and the practices of the professional pedestrians who pursued the sport for remuneration. Following the lead of the NYAC, numerous other elite and middle-class organizations formed metropolitan clubs. Adopting the British amateur code, they restricted membership by excluding all who gained compensation from their physical abilities. The ruling was meant to ensure equal competition and fair play, but a broad interpretation even eliminated many craftsmen and laborers of the working class who earned their wages by physical labor. It was a controversial issue. Many clubs allowed only amateur competition. "Open" competition allowed anyone to compete, but some amateurs lost their amateur certification if they competed in such affairs. Some clubs that sought competitive advantages used alleged amateurs but paid them in cash or kind clandestinely.

The NYAC assumed leadership of the amateur movement over the next decade by building a cinder track, introducing the use of spiked track shoes, and offering the first amateur national track-and-field championship (in 1876). It sponsored a national swimming championship for amateurs a

year later, and both wrestling and boxing tournaments in 1878. By the end of the decade, amateur clubs had proliferated as far as the Midwest. As modeled in the sporting practices of the English aristocracy, amateurs were prohibited from competing against professionals or accepting compensation for their efforts, and the concept of amateurism permeated interscholastic and intercollegiate athletics thereafter. By the 1880s, the NYAC limited its membership, thus devoting greater attention to maintaining its elite social status than to its athletic endeavors, and other aspiring "athletic clubs" soon established restrictive covenants to assure the desired constituency. Such clubs, marked by social status and prohibitive membership fees, fostered a tight network of financial, commercial, social, and religious contacts that controlled the business economy of many American cities. Such practices and associations created social divisions within the society quite at odds with notions of equality and a classless democracy.

In Philadelphia, the wealthy emulated the British in their adoption of cricket. Featuring leisurely contests that sometimes took two days to complete, played in pristine white uniforms, and interrupted by breaks for tea, the British game carried distinct symbols of the aristocracy. English immigrants brought the game to the area in the 1840s, and young Americans adopted it as their own, even excluding foreign-born citizens from the best clubs. Five socially exclusive clubs emerged in Philadelphia as high-status communities, and after the Civil War each group built an extravagant clubhouse on lush grounds to distinguish itself from clubs of more moderate means. In 1874, a Philadelphian all-star team traveled to Halifax, Nova Scotia, where it defeated British and Canadian teams.

Maintaining Ethnic Forms of Leisure

As the upper classes established clubs and sporting practices that reinforced their elevated social status in American society, a number of ethnic groups sought to retain their European cultures. The

1889 *(continued)*		**1890**	
■ First All-American football team selected	introduces water polo to the United States	■ Wyoming grants women suffrage	■ Brotherhood League (baseball) founded
■ Boston Athletic Association	■ First U.S. speedskating championship held	■ Sherman Antitrust Act passed	■ National American Woman Suffrage Association is organized, combining the two women's rights groups of 1869
		■ Polo Association (later called the United States Polo Association) founded	

German Turner associations, described in chapter 3, were the most prominent, with 317 clubs and nearly forty thousand members by 1894 (Hofmann 22). Other groups emulated the well-organized Germans.

Czechs

The Czechs organized nationalistic clubs known as Sokols based on the German Turner model in Prague in 1862. Like the Germans, they emphasized patriotism and gymnastics training to develop sound bodies as a bulwark against the Austrian Habsburg empire that imposed itself on local cultures. By the middle of the nineteenth century, Czechs began immigrating to the United States, where many took up residence in the Midwest, and in 1865 they established a Sokol in St. Louis. Like the German associations, the Czech Sokols faced division over issues of religion, splitting into contentious freethinkers (the pseudonym used at the time to designate atheists) and their Catholic opponents. Still, both factions stressed adherence to Czech culture and gymnastics, and they often performed mass drills. Such ethnic clubs maintained their communal societies and resisted assimilation into the American mainstream.

Poles

The Polish Falcon clubs followed the models of the Germans and Czechs, establishing similar units in the United States by 1887. The number of clubs, known as nests, reached a dozen within seven years, most of them in Chicago, which became the favorite American city for Polish immigrants. Like the Germans and Czechs, they promoted gymnastics, as well as their own language and culture, but the assimilation of second- and third-generation Poles brought a greater emphasis on American sport forms, such as baseball and football, by the twentieth century (Kirsch et al. 368–370). Poles developed particular skill in bowling, producing many champions in later years.

African Americans

While European clubs fought inclusion, African Americans sought integration, only to be denied. In the South, African American boxers and pedestrians did compete in New Orleans before the Civil War. Others played a game called raquette, similar to lacrosse, which drew large, integrated crowds, and interracial gatherings also witnessed the horse races at the Metairie Track in that cosmopolitan city. Throughout the rest of the South, however, African Americans faced strict segregation, and during Reconstruction even the more liberal city of New Orleans began enforcing Jim Crow conditions by segregating beaches and refusing to admit blacks to white athletic clubs.

In the North, free blacks generally enjoyed greater freedom than blacks in Southern states, but in 1867 the amateur National Association of Base Ball Players voted to exclude black players and clubs from membership. By 1876, the National League of professional players banned African Americans as well, and after the 1884 season Moses Fleetwood Walker, a mixed-race (black and white) catcher for Toledo of the American Association, lost his job when management failed to renew his contract, allegedly because Cap Anson, player-manager of the Chicago White Stockings, had refused to play games with an African American. Other white racists sided with Anson, and by the 1890s black ball players faced exile from major league teams, a condition that would persist for the next half century. As a result, they resorted to playing in minor leagues and semipro circuits and joining barnstorming clubs. The Philadelphia Orions had already assumed the latter status as early as 1882.

In the longer run, black athletes responded to this racism by forming their own parallel organizations and institutions in pursuit of sport and recreation. Blacks founded their own YMCAs in Richmond, Virginia, and Nashville, Tennessee, in 1867. In that same year, African American women, despite their relatively powerless position in society, founded their own baseball team, known as the Dolly Vardens, in Philadelphia. In the South, blacks were segregated into separate institutions, forced to play sports only among themselves, and in 1892 the first football game between black colleges was played by Biddle University (now Johnson C. Smith University) of Charlotte, North Carolina, and Livingstone College of nearby Salisbury.

Two years later, the League of American Wheelmen banned black cyclists from its ranks in order to appease its Southern members. Because black athletes were largely neglected, sport had little assimilative value in terms of general social acceptance and economic opportunity for African Americans during most of the nineteenth century.

Boxing remained one of the few sports open to blacks, because white spectators enjoyed watching the brutalization of African Americans. Whites developed stereotypes of blacks as cowardly,

People & Places

Moses Fleetwood Walker

Born in Ohio in 1857 to a black father and white mother, Moses Fleetwood Walker attended Oberlin College and the University of Michigan before earning his fame as the first African American professional baseball player in a major league. In 1884, Walker played catcher for Toledo of the American Association, and his brother Weldy also played for the team during part of the season. Toledo released the Walkers after that season, and Moses Fleetwood Walker then played for minor league teams through the 1889 season. He later became a successful entrepreneur, newspaper editor, author, and inventor of an artillery shell as well as improvements for motion picture projectors. In his writings, he advocated emigration of black Americans to Africa, a radical reaction to racism later adopted by Marcus Garvey, a black activist.

Photo courtesy of National Baseball Hall of Fame Library.

lacking manly courage and toughness, unable to sustain punishment, and therefore unfit to meet the standards of whiteness. Whites claimed that blacks were particularly susceptible to blows to the stomach, and they questioned blacks' endurance at a time when bouts might endure for a hundred rounds or more. White male southerners corralled black boys (whom they sometimes blindfolded) and made them engage in battle royals for the whites' own amusement so that they might wager on the last one standing.

Billiards was another sporting activity of African American males during this time, as reported in *The Spirit of the Times*:

> Let it be known that our colored citizens are not without ambition in a billiardistic way, and the balls, propelled by cues in ebony hands, are wont to echo muchly in the purlieus of the Eighth Ward of this city. Evening following evening the two tables in the room kept by Major Pool, at 149 Wooster Street, are nightly invested by a small brigade of negroes, and the balls are kept in lively agitation. Parties awaiting their turns, too, are numerous, and, with feet elevated before the fire, and reclining at an angle of about fifteen degrees, remind one forcibly of certain positions which were said to be assumed by certain Congressmen during parliamentary discussions. The room presents the appearance of a colored paradise, and the *habitues* seem perfectly at their ease, and undoubtedly regard their present *otium cum dignitate* as a faint reflex of the good

time coming, and not far distant in the future. As we are of the humanitarian sort, we heartily wish them godspeed; but trust that their newly acquired importance may not be used as a means of inciting them to act of lawlessness and violence.

> During the fall of 1870 considerable feeling was manifested between certain of the colored citizens who had acquired some knowledge of the game, and for the purpose of settling the point Major Pool procured a handsome cue which he offered as a prize to be contended for by the players who were so inclined, and which was to be symbolical of the Colored Championship. The cue is valued at $50. There were seven entries, consisting of J. Vaughn, C. Marsh, R. Huclus, William Miller, J. Joseph, W. Jackson, and the proprietor of the room, Major Pool. During the tournament, W.S. Widgeon of this city acted as referee, and J. Sands of Savannah and W.T. Jones of Philadelphia as scorers. The games were of 1,000 points each, at American four-ball caroms, each carom to count 3. The first game was between Vaughn and Marsh, the former winning by 244 points; highest run, 63. In the second game Huclus beat Miller by 196; highest run 54. Jackson and Joseph contended in the third game and the former was vanquished by 199; highest run, 39. The fourth game produced a lively display between Pool and Joseph. Pool finally won by 135 points, his highest run being 39. The contestants in the fifth game were Huclus and Pool. Won by the former with a majority of 235, he having again scored 54 as his highest run. (Wouldn't that be a good number to play first in the

lottery?) The struggles finally narrowed down to a contest between Huclus and Vaughn. After a long contest of one hundred and ninety one innings, Huclus pulled out ahead, by a score of 1,000 to 963. His highest run was 36, as against 27 by his opponent. Huclus was then amid much excitement, proclaimed champion. But we are told that "uneasy lies the head that wears the crown," and it has been again verified in this instance; for on Tuesday last the Championship Committee were handed the appended document, which shows that Vaughn does not consider the results of the last game as a true index of the comparative abilities of himself and Huclus:

NEW YORK CITY, Feb. 14, 1871

To Messrs. Wm. T. Widgeon, Wm. T. Jones, and S. Ellis, Committee for Colored Amateur Championship—*Gentlemen:* This is to notify Mr. Robert H. Huclus, Amateur Champion of New York City, that I hereby challenge him to play a match-game of billiards for the Championship and Champion cue at the earliest possible time allowed by the regulations. As I desire to play the first game according to the conditions of the tournament, an early answer is solicited.

Yours sincerely, John H. Vaughn

qtd. in Kirsch, *Sports* [Vol. 4] 314

Irish

Irish immigrants during this period were considered to be among the lowest on the social scale. In the South, Irish laborers performed the most difficult tasks since slaves, who were property, were considered more valuable. By 1850, Irish women composed 75 percent of the house servants in New York City. In 1874, an African American doctor described the Irish as

remarkable for open, projecting mouths, prominent teeth, and exposed gums, their advancing cheekbones and depressed noses carry[ing] barbarism on their very front. . . . [D]egradation and hardship exhibit themselves in the whole physical condition of the people . . . giving such an example of human degradation as to make it revolting. They are only five feet two inches, upon an average, bow-legged, bandy shanked, abortively featured, the apparitions of Irish ugliness and Irish want.

qtd. in Roediger, *Black* 56–57

The Irish gained a measure of whiteness and entry to the mainstream culture as they proved their mettle in the boxing ring and on the baseball field. Their social capital also rose with their eventual domination of the Democratic party, and the linkage of sport and politics allowed some, particularly

Irish Americans at first, to earn a measure of social and economic mobility. Politicians often sponsored working-class sporting clubs, whose toughs supplied political muscle as shoulder-hitting intimidators at the polls on election days. Irish political bullies acted as enforcers or protectors in rivalries with other urban and ethnic gangs. Such activities provided a foundation for the Democratic Party political machines that ruled big cities, most notably the Tammany Hall group in New York. In such an environment, boxers earned respect and even prominence.

In Chicago, Tom Foley, a member of the city's professional baseball team and an expert pool player, earned enough money to finance a large billiard hall. His physical abilities enabled him to assume entrepreneurial and political opportunities (much as John Morrissey used his success in boxing, as discussed in chapter 3). Foley won a seat on the Chicago city council as a member of the Workingmen's Party. Such advances fueled perceptions of sport as a meritocracy and as a means to socioeconomic mobility for poor Americans and the ethnic immigrant groups who flooded American shores from 1880 to 1920.

Boxing did, in fact, produce numerous heroes in specific ethnic groups, including the biggest sports star of the nineteenth century in bareknuckle fighter John L. Sullivan. Born in 1858 to Irish immigrant parents, Sullivan, known as "the Boston Strong Boy," earned his initial notoriety by challenging saloon patrons, boasting that he could beat any man in the house. In 1882, Sullivan easily defeated then-champion Paddy Ryan at a clandestine spot in Mississippi. By 1885, he was popular enough to draw ten thousand spectators for a New York City bout, and his performances established his status as the world's toughest man. In 1889, in the last of the bareknuckle championship fights, Sullivan conquered Jake Kilrain in a contest that lasted 75 rounds. Sullivan toured the country in theatrical performances and boxing exhibitions, and pictures of this working-class hero adorned countless saloons. As champion from 1882 to 1892, Sullivan imposed a color ban, refusing to fight black boxers, thereby asserting the whiteness of the Irish and marking the symbolic prize as one for whites only. He lost his title to another Irish American, "Gentleman Jim" Corbett, in New Orleans in 1892 under the new Marquis of Queensberry rules. The new rules prohibited wrestling, required boxing gloves rather than bare knuckles, provided for timed 3-minute rounds, and declared a knockout after a 10-second count by the referee. Sullivan's career thus witnessed the transition from the bareknuckle brawl (similar to saloon or back-alley fights) to a regulated, more strictly governed competition. In the process, working-class toughness and physicality merged with middle-class order and bureaucracy to produce a sport amenable to different layers of the social strata (Gorn, *Manly*).

The most famous of the nineteenth-century Irish baseball players, Mike "King" Kelly, exemplified the merger of sport, working-class masculinity, and the perception of meritocracy and social mobility. Born to Irish immigrants on the last day of 1857 in Troy, New York, Kelly began a pro career with Cincinnati in 1878 but reached stardom with Chicago from 1880 to 1886. He led the league in batting during the 1884 and 1886 seasons and scored the most runs in each of those years. A fast runner, Kelly was an expert base stealer, and his prowess was hailed in a popular song titled "Slide, Kelly, Slide." Stories abound about his legendary trickery as well as his adherence to the lifestyle of the bachelor subculture. On one occasion, when the umpire's back was turned, he allegedly sprinted across the pitcher's mound from first to third base, and the distracted official assumed he had stolen two bases. Another time, too hungover to play, he rested on the bench until a pop fly traveled toward him. Realizing the fielders could not make a play, he jumped up and announced his substitution as catcher before snaring the ball. As an outfielder, he supposedly ended a close game in the dusk when he leaped into the dark fog to grab a long drive with the bases loaded. The umpire called the batter out, and his teammates heartily congratulated him on the amazing catch, whereupon he admitted that the ball had traveled well over his head but that he had a spare in his pocket.

Such antics endeared Kelly to his fans, and he engaged in theatrical tours, supposedly being the first to sign autographs for admirers. His ghostwritten autobiography, released in 1888, helped create the genre of sports autobiography, as many players

John L. Sullivan: King of the bareknuckle boxing champions and the first great American sports hero.
Photo courtesy of Library of Congress, LC-DIG-pga-05673.

Mike "King" Kelly in his Boston uniform after being traded by A.G. Spalding in 1886.
Photo courtesy of National Baseball Hall of Fame Library.

would follow his lead over the next century. By this time, Albert Spalding, head of the White Stockings team, had less enthusiasm for Kelly's off-field gambling and drinking. Spalding had a Pinkerton detective follow Kelly, and the spy reported that Kelly stayed out until 3 a.m. drinking lemonade and that his leadership, as it were, proved detrimental to younger players. When confronted with the charges, Kelly's only amendment was that he drank straight whisky, not lemonade; he did not want his masculinity questioned. Spalding soon sold Kelly to the Boston club for the then-astronomical sum of $10,000. When the players revolted over the reserve clause—which allowed a team to renew a player's contract at will, thus preventing players from moving freely from team to team—to form their own league in 1890, Spalding, as head of the National League, offered Kelly $10,000 and a guaranteed contract to return. But Kelly, loyal to his coconspirators, maintained solidarity by stating that he "could not go back on the boys" (Pearson 199). Kelly's steadfast adherence to the honor code and the norms of the bachelor subculture contrasted with the values of those in the upper classes who saw drinking and carousing as immoral, unwholesome, and unproductive.

Development of an Intercollegiate Sporting Culture

As African Americans struggled for opportunities and other ethnic minorities distanced themselves from the mainstream culture, the children of the upper classes established the early norms for intercollegiate sport. In 1869, Harvard's crew journeyed to England for a match with Oxford on the Thames River. Although Harvard lost, the adventure stimulated interest in rowing, and other colleges formed rowing associations in 1870. Sixteen schools competed in the regattas, and smaller colleges managed to triumph over prestigious institutions such as Harvard and Yale. In 1873, as the nature of fair competition became a greater issue, the association banned the employment of professional coaches. The regattas of 1874 and 1875 drew large crowds and national media attention at Saratoga Lake, New York. Crew members followed a strict training regimen in the quest for victory, as American competitive spirit and greater emphasis on winning began to be felt on college campuses. Such traits emerged in other competitions and soon marked the national character. The events of the mid-1870s represented the heyday of collegiate rowing, as other sports began to gain importance.

Rowing was for a time the most popular intercollegiate sport; in fact, intercollegiate track-and-field competition served as a sidelight to the 1873 regatta, when the *New York Herald* offered a trophy for a two-mile (3.2-kilometer) race. Five track-and-field events appeared on the program the following year, and in 1876 the Intercollegiate Association of Amateur Athletes of America (IC4A) assumed authority for the track-and-field races. The open competitions offered by the New York Athletic Club, however, soon attracted college athletes and surpassed the allure of the regatta games. Track-and-field competition eventually

This cartoon portrayed the negative image of baseball players in the late nineteenth century.
Image courtesy of Library of Congress, LC-USZ62-42416.

gained ascendance and popularity and no longer needed an attachment to the crew races.

Four schools formed the College Union Regatta Association in 1858, and the regatta of 1859 also featured an intercollegiate baseball contest, in which Amherst beat Williams 73-32. (The rules of the game at that time greatly favored the batters, and such high scores were not unusual.) Throughout the 1860s, Harvard fielded an exceptional baseball team, with an undefeated string that lasted for seven years, and by 1870 home games drew as many as ten thousand fans. That summer, the team embarked on a tour through the East and Midwest, playing against both amateur and professional teams. After the Civil War, baseball spread to Southern college campuses, but Northeastern schools first formed the American College Baseball Association in 1879. A loosely run league, it tried to enforce weak eligibility rules, which allowed part-time students and faculty members to play on school teams. In many cases, colleges even employed professional players to enhance their chances of winning. Such developments blurred the distinction between elite sports and gentle-

manly behavior, constituting a further departure from the traditional and aristocratic sporting practices of British schools.

Winning assumed its greatest importance in the sport of football, where victory carried great symbolic weight in the context of Social Darwinist notions of masculinity and physical prowess. With no war being fought during the Gilded Age other than frontier skirmishes with Native Americans, young white men had few venues in which to develop and display such courage, and football provided the physical contact and martial strategies not found in other team sports. The roots of the game lay in English peasant soccer games. By 1827, Harvard students engaged in a general melee at the start of the school year in order to brutalize freshmen as a rite of passage. Yale took up the harsh welcoming ritual in 1840 and continued it until school authorities banned it in 1860. Boston schoolboys continued the roughness, but by 1868, Princeton student William S. Gunmere had adapted the London Football Association's rules for games at the New Jersey college. The regulations allowed for 25 players per team in a

Rowing became a major collegiate sport in the latter nineteenth century and fostered modern training devices such as sliding practice seats, as shown in this Muybridge photo.

soccer-style contest, and on November 6, 1869, Princeton traveled to Rutgers for the first intercollegiate match, won by the home team 6-4. Columbia joined in a triangular fray (a series of matches between three schools playing each other) in 1870, as rules became negotiable. In 1872, Harvard adopted rugby rules that allowed running with the ball. Harvard, not wanting to defer leadership to Yale or Princeton and favoring its own rules, declined to attend a rules convention the next year in which American schools began to depart from the British version of the game (Gems, *For Pride* 12). By 1876, other schools adopted the rugby rules, changing the emphasis from kicking to running.

Early football games were compared with boxing matches, and serious injuries were rampant.

Reprinted from J.E. Gorn and W. Goldstein, 1993, A brief history of American sports (New York: Hill and Wang), 157.

In the Midwest, students at the University of Michigan took up the game and arranged a contest with Cornell to be played in Cleveland in 1873, but Michigan president Andrew White interceded, stating, "I will not permit 30 men to travel 400 miles [about 645 kilometers] merely to agitate a bag of wind" (Nelson 32). For the most part, however, school administrators exercised little control over student activities at the time; students arranged their own rules conventions, games, and training, and accounted for their own expenses. They held their first official intercollegiate football championship in 1876. Yale defeated Princeton in a wild game featuring 11 players per side, but Harvard disputed Yale's claim to the title, as it adhered to 15-man teams. The athletic rivalry exposed deeper sentiments harbored by the Boston Brahmins, who sent their sons to Harvard, and the nouveaux riches, who sent their offspring to Yale. Such social tensions would be played out on the gridiron thereafter at the risk of societal and institutional pride, resulting in greater involvement and support by alumni, trustees, and other benefactors.

The 1877 championship was marked by greater commercialization, as the New York Polo Club offered a trophy and its grounds for the game. The location, in the nation's media capital and largest city, heightened expectations for profit and publicity, as well as the perceived importance of win-

ning. During the 1877 season, the *Tufts Collegian* complained about Yale's tactics: "[T]he gentlemen who compose the Yale team have cultivated a habit of losing their tempers, and mauling their antagonists with doubled fists. . . . [L]ookers-on, mostly students . . . showed their magnanimity by facetiously pelting our men with pebbles and second-hand tobacco quids" (*Harvard Advocate* 49).

The team captains at Yale and Harvard still differed over the number of players allowed to participate in the game for each side. Yale agreed to use 15 in 1878 but wanted a $100 guarantee for a Thanksgiving game, indicating a greater sense of commercialization. That year, Princeton emerged as the champion by beating Yale before a crowd of two thousand at Hoboken, New Jersey. Woodrow Wilson, future president of the United States, served as secretary for the Princeton coaches' board. Walter Camp, a pioneer of American football as player, coach, and sports journalist, captained Yale and became secretary of the rules committee, a position he held until his death in 1925.

By the latter 1870s, Harvard, Yale, and Princeton had adopted durable canvas jackets and pants, which replaced the tights previously worn by players. Evolution of clothing and equipment provided not only greater protection but also competitive advantage. Players greased their pants to hinder would-be tacklers, but the ongoing brutality of the game proved evident in numerous accusations of throttling (choking), kicking, and slugging of opponents. Frederic Remington, a Yale player and later a famous artist, allegedly dipped his jacket in slaughter-house blood in order to make it more "businesslike" for the 1878 contest with Harvard.

The game further deviated from soccer in 1880, when Camp introduced the scrimmage line; as in warfare, the game was thus increasingly marked by specific maneuvers (plays), concerted strategy, and territoriality. Two Kentucky teams, Centre College and Transylvania, played the first intercollegiate game in the South, which readily took to football's militaristic features.

When the overemphasis on ball control produced boring (often scoreless) contests, Camp introduced (at the 1882 rules convention) the concept of downs and yardage to be gained. Attempts to limit eligibility often faced disregard, and scoring still emphasized kicking, with 5 points awarded for field goals and 4 points given for kicks after touchdowns. Still, players and fans were drawn to a game featuring relative carnage that asserted one's masculinity. The 1883 rules still allowed for hacking, throttling, butting, and tripping. One might punch an opponent three times before being ejected from the game. The heartiest young men were drawn to the bloodbath, and football grew rapidly into the Midwest. By 1886, it had reached California.

The organized violence drew increasing numbers of spectators, further commercializing the game. In 1885, an impartial referee replaced the alumni who had previously officiated the games. Another umpire was added in 1888 to deter brutality, but spectators continued to fill the competitive venues. The 1893 Princeton–Yale game, billed as the national championship, attracted forty thousand spectators, including New York residents, alums, and spectators from as far as Oregon and Texas. A 4-hour parade preceded the contest, despite a severe economic depression. Opponents characterized the intercollegiate frays as "the playful gamboling of twenty-two prizefighters" (Gems, *For Pride* 25–26), and faculty members at the elite institutions attempted to intercede, with little success.

By this time, football had assumed particular characteristics that many Amer-

icans perceived as defining the national character. Walter Camp claimed that "our players have strayed away from the original Rugby rules, but in so doing they have built up a game and rules of their own more suited to American needs." Another proponent extolled the activity that "embodies so many factors that are typically American . . . . [V]irile, intensive, aggressive energy that marks for progress is the root which upholds and feeds American supremacy and American football" (Gems, *For Pride* 20).

Throughout the 1880s, new rules sparked specialization on the football field that resembled its counterpart in industrial factories. Players assumed particular roles for greater efficiency, as linemen and backs were assigned distinctive positions with specific duties. Before the end of the decade, football had surpassed baseball in popularity on college campuses.

THE TWELFTH PLAYER IN EVERY FOOTBALL GAME.

A newspaper cartoon portrayed the figure of Death hovering over any football game as casualty rates escalated.

Image from *World*, November 14, 1897.

People & Places

Walter Camp

This athletic pioneer played five sports at Yale but earned his fame in football. After serving as both player and coach on the Yale football team, he took on a larger role as Yale's supervisor of athletics from 1888 to 1906, in which position he raised money, generated alumni support, recruited top athletes, and developed training systems that led Yale to dominance on the gridiron in the Gilded Age. Camp garnered the accolade "Father of American Football," however, for his work on the rules committee, a loose association of schools and coaches, on which he served from 1878 through 1925. Among the most drastic changes, Camp advocated the introduction of a line of scrimmage, a limit of 11 players per side, a system of downs and distances, scoring changes that reduced reliance on kicking, and the practice of tackling below the waist. Along with sportswriter Caspar Whitney, Camp also created the first All-American team in 1889.

Male Sporting Culture

The bachelor subculture of the nineteenth century maintained its male gender identity and transcended class lines during the Gilded Age. Men of the bachelor culture shared a sense of physical prowess, toughness, and physicality as marks of masculinity. As modernization and increasing industrialization diminished the need for independent craftsmen and farmers throughout the nineteenth century, men gradually lost the sense of self-esteem and the social identity previously tied to occupations and physical labor on farms. Nine of every ten men were self-employed before the Civil War, but fewer than one-third enjoyed such status in 1910 (Gems, *For Pride* 5). The shoemaker, for example, lost his independence in becoming a wage laborer in the shoe factory, tied to a particular capitalistic work ethic and time discipline. He could no longer hunt or fish according to his will or set his own work pace, or even his own schedule. Industrialization robbed him of his former sense of self and the discipline of the clock reigned.

To compensate, men turned to the homosocial environment of the sporting world. Immigration demographics were skewed toward men, and the early American republic was largely a male society. During the Antebellum Period, five million immigrants, mostly young males, journeyed to the United States (Foner and Garraty 534), and, with limited opportunities for marriage, many men remained bachelors. By the mid-nineteenth century, 40 percent of young men between the ages of 25 and 35 remained single, and many of them found a sense of inclusion and camaraderie in the company of like-minded males, often joined by married men who sought refuge from the domesticity of the home. On occasion, the wealthy, too, entered the sports netherworld, courting social ostracism to maintain their identification with the cult of masculinity. But for the most part, these "sports," or "the fancy," as they were known, included craftsmen, volunteer firemen, working-class laborers, gamblers, petty criminals, and Irish immigrants who did not subscribe to the moral, religious, and social tenets of decorum and respectability that held sway among middle-class whites.

These men congregated in billiard parlors, theaters, brothels, and urban saloons to tell stories, brag, drink, smoke cigars, gamble, and seek the carnal pleasures offered by prostitutes or "sporting ladies." The urban saloons offered the male fraternity a club-like atmosphere where they might indulge themselves in luxurious surroundings. In New York City, Kit Burns' Sportsman's Hall offered seating for four hundred, and Harry Hill's Dance Hall, another of New York's more popular establishments, featured multiple bars for hard spirits, beer, and wine. It also included a concert hall and a stage for boxing and wrestling matches. At the Prairie Queen in Chicago, the winner of the boxing match received a house prostitute as a prize.

Saloons often included a back room where illegal boxing matches were staged (which had also been a practice in some antebellum establishments). Proprietors skirted the law by staging "exhibitions," for which no decision was rendered. Patrons paid an entrance fee to become "members" in such "clubs," and betting on the participants provided a sense of adventure and risk in otherwise mundane lives. Harry Hill won national fame as a boxing referee and as a repository for large bets. Billy McGlory, a New York underworld figure, charged 15 cents for entry at his promotions. His Grand Scarlet Ball, held at Armory Hall in 1883, included a cakewalk by African Americans, boxing matches of men fighting women, a beauty contest, and a masquerade ball (Gilfoyle 115).

Until 1882, when the Marquis of Queensberry rules gained ascendance, bareknuckle prizefights (i.e., boxing without gloves) proved to be the most popular form of entertainment in the country. By the 1880s, good bareknuckle fighters could earn as much as $500 for a single bout—equivalent to a laborer's annual wage. Boxers became heroes, rivaled only by top billiard players, and spectators paid as much as a week's wage to view and gamble on championship matches. Even before the Civil War, New York billiard parlors averaged annual revenues surpassing $10,000 each, and in 1865 billiard tables in Chicago were rented at a rate of $4,000 per day. Pool hustling became a tenuous occupation for many who were unable or unwilling to submit to the dictates of the industrial workplace. In the Midwest, however, John Brunswick, a Swiss immigrant, found lucre in business as a manufacturer of billiard tables. After starting in Cincinnati in 1845, he opened a Chicago office in 1848 and by 1879 had merged with the Balke and Collender companies to promote tournaments and sell his products to saloons. The manufacture and sale of sporting goods became a booming business.

While the bachelor subculture and the sporting fancy continued to enjoy blood sports such as cockfights, dogfights, and rattings, which thrilled spectators and offered myriad options for gambling, white middle-class moralists and reformers remained adamant that these sporting practices were unacceptable in mainstream culture. In ratting contests, for instance, gamblers bet on the number of rats killed by a dog in a stipulated time or on the amount of time it would take for the canine hunter to accomplish the grisly task of extermination. At Kit Burns' establishment, onlookers even paid to watch a local human celebrity known as Jack the Rat bite off the heads of the rodents (Riess, *Sport* 17).

Professional pedestrian races, which had gained popularity in the Antebellum Era, continued to stimulate gambling by the sporting fancy. The walkers or runners competed in endurance races at indoor venues; some races, in which either individuals or teams attempted to outlast or outdistance their competition, lasted as long as six days. Both men and women vied for prizes, sometimes in mixed-gender (men vs. women) encounters. By 1870 in New York, female swimmers were competing for prizes that included jewelry. Five years later, British swimming champion J.B. Johnson defeated the local champion in a 13-mile (21-kilometer)

People & Places

Thomas Eakins

Thomas Eakins (1844–1916) is now recognized as one of America's great realist painters, although he was largely ignored during his lifetime because of his then-scandalous indiscretions. Eakins was fascinated by human anatomy and bodily movement. He worked with Eadweard Muybridge as a photographer of early motion studies, now so prominent in the analysis of athletic activities. As an art teacher he insisted that both his male and female students observe and work from nude models.

Sport subjects provided the focus of much of Eakins' work during his career. In the 1870s he produced 24 paintings of rowers, a sport in which he was an active participant. Rowing was extremely popular during that era, and Eakins' depiction of working-class professional athletes showed his mastery of geometric perspective and

Image courtesy of the Library of Congress, LC-USZ62-85536.

the use of light. A decade later, *The Swimming Hole* (1884–1885) captured male nudes in a bucolic pastime in a natural setting, but it drew the ire of observers. In the 1890s, Eakins turned his attention to wrestlers and boxers in the homosocial environment of the bachelor subculture in which men publicly demonstrated their masculinity. Such works proved essential to the period study of American sporting art.

race in Philadelphia for $1,000, as international competition drew increasing attention (Kirsch, *Sports* [Vol. 4] 46).

More often, the sporting fraternity's "cranks" (serious fans), as they were known, wagered on horse racing with offtrack bookies, who accepted small bettors. Larger cities also had established poolrooms where laborers and white-collar clerks might place bets. Telegraph reports of race results at such places allowed nonspectators to participate in the speculation. For those who were less advantaged but still had some recreational time, unregulated outlaw tracks outside the jurisdiction of local authorities attracted patrons with low entry fees and access to independent bookies, some of whom even extended credit. Middle-class Americans viewed such operations with disdain, but violent incidents in Chicago did little to encourage change. There, George Trussell, a professional gambler who owned a champion trotter, engaged in shootouts on city streets with his rival, Cap Hyman. The violent confrontations ended when Trussell's girlfriend, "Irish Mollie" Cosgriff, killed him, allegedly for spending more time with the horse than with her.

Rowing and pedestrianism also provided early opportunities for working-class athletes to earn an income with their physical prowess. Among rowers, the Ward Brothers and Biglin Brothers became household names, and the artist Thomas Eakins portrayed the latter in several paintings during the 1870s. By that time, however, baseball had emerged as the premier sport in the United States, outdistancing the popularity of regattas, although nostalgic paintings and serene images of rowers on the waterways continued to interest American artists.

Business of Sport

In 1858, 22 clubs in the New York area established an organization presumptuously titled the National Association of Base Ball Players, which adhered to amateur guidelines. The class-based gentlemanly clubs gradually gave way to recruiting and professionalism as club, neighborhood, town, and occupational rivalries spurred greater attention to winning. Various versions of baseball rules still abounded in the mid-nineteenth century, but the Civil War gave priority to the New York rendition (New York rules superseded Massachusetts rules in the military camps and were carried back to veterans' hometowns), which set the number of players at nine and established the diamond-shaped infield with four bases equally aligned at its corners. As commercialization and club sponsorship assumed greater prominence, clubs attracted paying spectators to finance their operations. For important games, which might involve gambling or just club pride, individual stars might be paid for their services. The Brooklyn Excelsiors recruited young James Creighton, a star pitcher, with such inducements in 1860, and he is generally acknowledged as the first professional player. Al Reach became an openly acknowledged pro in 1865.

Professional Baseball Teams

Civic pride and commercial rivalry led Cincinnati to form the first known fully professional team in 1869. Cincinnati businessmen competed with those in Chicago, St. Louis, and Milwaukee for the hinterland trade, and baseball provided a means to publicize the municipality. Cincinnati hired the best players from Eastern clubs and sent them on a national tour from coast to coast. Salaries ranged from $600 to $2,000, and the professional Red Stockings returned undefeated, winning 58 contests and tying once. Chicago countered the next year with a professional team of its own. Merchants raised $15,000 in a joint stock company to field the White Stockings, with city leaders serving as the primary stockholders. The squad embarked on a campaign against other commercial centers and quickly proved their mettle. A crowd of 100,000 welcomed them home after a 157-to-1 win over Memphis.

The National Association of Base Ball Players split over the issue of professionalism at the 1870 rules convention. As a result, the National Association of *Professional* Base Ball Players (emphasis added) was formed in 1871, and it survived until 1876 as a loosely organized federation. Teams did not always play scheduled games, and players repeatedly broke their contracts when another team offered a better salary. A town of any size might buy entry into the league for a mere $10.

In 1876, that unwieldy arrangement gave way to a much more tightly structured organization known as the National League. William Hulbert, a member of the Chicago Board of Trade and president of the Chicago White Stockings, wrested control of baseball from the Eastern establishment by proposing an association run by club administrators rather than players. Hulbert cajoled other owners to reorganize the league based on sound business principles in order to maximize their profits, as the following document shows:

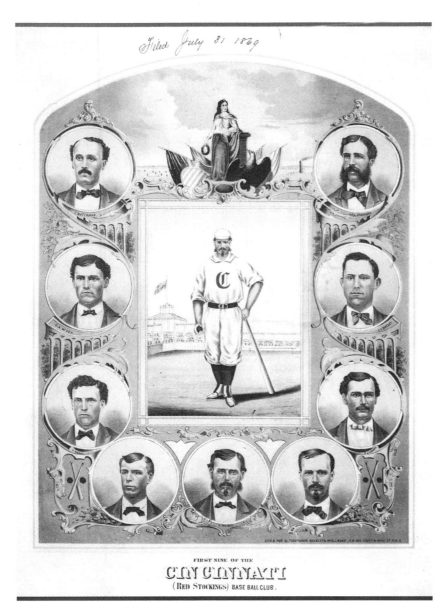

Filed July 31 1869

FIRST NINE OF THE
CINCINNATI
(RED STOCKINGS) BASE BALL CLUB.

The first professional baseball team hailed from Cincinnati.

Photo courtesy of Library of Congress, LC-USZC4 1291.

Chicago, Jan. 23, 1876

The undersigned have been appointed by the Chicago, Cincinnati, Louisville and St. Louis clubs a committee to confer with you on matters of interest to the game at large, with special reference to the reformation of existing abuses, and the formation of a new association, and we are clothed with full authority in writing from the above named clubs to bind them to any arrangement we make with you. We therefore invite your club to send a representative, clothed with like authority, to meet us at the Grand Central Hotel, in the city of New York, on Wednesday the 2d day of February next, at 12M (sic). After careful consideration of the needs of the professional clubs, the organizations we represent are of the firm belief that existing circumstances demand prompt and vigorous action by those who are the natural sponsors of the game. It is the earnest recommendation of our constituents that all past troubles and differences be ignored and forgotten, and that the conference we propose shall be a calm, friendly and deliberate discussion, looking solely to the general good of the clubs who are calculated to give character and permanency to the game. We are confident that the propositions we have to submit will meet with your approval and support, and we shall be pleased to meet you at the time and place above mentioned.

Yours respectfully,
W.A. HULBERT.
CHAS. A. FOWLE.

Kirsch, *Sports* [Vol. 4] 84

The thought was that if owners projected a more wholesome (and therefore more acceptable) white, middle-class, Protestant image that would appeal to like-minded middle-class citizens and families, they would also forbid gambling and Sunday games. They limited membership to assure a greater potential for profit. The initial membership consisted of larger cities: Boston, Chicago, Cincinnati, Louisville, Hartford, St. Louis, Philadelphia, and New York. The owners eventually regulated team schedules, ticket prices, and officiating, but labor problems persisted, as players known as "revolvers" jumped teams for better pay. Individual owners accommodated such moves when they placed their immediate self-interest and their desire to win above the interests of the league. In 1879, the owners agreed to a strategy designed to rectify this divisive issue—they employed a "reserve clause" in player contracts, which retained, or reserved, an athlete's service explicitly for one team only. Without constant bidding for players, owners held down their costs and increased their profits. Players lamented their lost freedom to negotiate their services but still enjoyed salaries that were three or four times higher than those of average working men. William Hulbert lorded over the league, enforcing his edicts in a dictatorial manner—including expulsions of New York, Philadelphia, and Cincinnati for violations of league policies—until his death in 1882. Thus, much like industrial magnates, baseball owners consolidated their resources in the face of rival leagues and maximized their profits at the expense of their employees.

> The following is the extraordinary rule adopted by the American Association at its schedule meeting: "And in case any player under reserve shall willfully hold off and refuse to sign a regular contract with the club that has him reserved, for the purpose of harassing the club, or compelling it to increase his salary, or who shall by any means, directly or indirectly, endeavor to attempt willful extortion from the club which has him reserved, he shall, on satisfactory evidence being furnished from the club so engaged, be placed upon the black list by the President and Secretary and notices issued to all clubs as provided by the constitution and the National agreement."
>
> *Chicago Tribune* 9

Employer–employee labor differences erupted in 1889, as labor relations in professional baseball reflected similar tensions in the industrial workforce throughout the United States. The players' revolt of 1889, led by John Montgomery Ward, the New York Giants' shortstop and a lawyer, started with the organization of the Brotherhood of Professional Base Ball Players in 1885. As with other early labor unions, the players banned together as workers in an attempt to win greater freedom and better salaries from their employers. The restrictive reserve clause allowed no opportunity to negotiate their contracts or seek better offers. When owners failed to address their concerns, players formed their own Brotherhood League (also called the Players' League) in 1890, competing for fans against both the National League franchises and the teams of the American Association (formed as a rival organization after the National League expelled Cincinnati in 1881). The American Association clubs, run mostly by brewery owners, used baseball as a means to sell their products but adhered to the same employment practices of the older National League.

The Players' League attracted most of the top players and found sponsorship from prospective owners who had been locked out of the National League oligarchy. The teams operated under a socialistic arrangement, whereby players and owners shared profits and club management, thus mounting a direct economic and philosophical challenge to the capitalist sport structure. They scheduled their teams in seven National League cities, forcing baseball fans to make a choice. Led by Albert Spalding, the National League retaliated by bribing star players to return, offering free tickets to its games, and providing franchise inducements to the players' sponsors. Both leagues absorbed financial losses in the cutthroat competition, but the established National League maintained greater resources. The Brotherhood League collapsed after a year, and the American Association lasted only until 1891. The National League then absorbed four of the American Association franchises and faced no further threats until the organization of the upstart American League in 1901.

Sport Entrepreneurs and the Making of Sporting Culture

Sport afforded entrepreneurial opportunities not only to players and owners but also to sports journalists. As discussed in chapter 4, Henry Chadwick, an English immigrant, found a career as a sportswriter, and in the 1860s he expanded his sports journalism by covering baseball for the *New York Herald*. He also served as editor of the *Beadle Base-Ball Player*, an early guide to the game, for more than 20 years. In 1867, Chadwick founded the *Chronicle*, a weekly paper that promoted baseball as a character-building influence on young men. Chadwick also established the box score and the batting average, an early means of quantification and analysis that heightened fans' interest in the game, and, as a member of the rules committee, he suggested a new rule requiring a batted ball to be caught on the fly, which was implemented after 1864 (Rader, *American Sports* [1983] 111).

Irish immigrant Richard Kyle Fox, another journalist who shaped modern American sport, assumed control of the *National Police Gazette* in 1877. Printed on pink paper, the *Gazette* offered salacious material that emphasized theatrical news, scandals, crimes, sports, and scantily clad women. The formula attracted a large working-class readership and could be found in all haunts of the bachelor subculture. Anthony Comstock and his Society for the Suppression of Vice campaigned to silence the publication but succeeded only in enhancing its notoriety. Fox promoted numerous pseudosports (such as ratting and clog dancing), as well as female weightlifting and cycling, but he proved most successful as a boxing promoter. He

The Soccer Craze in Europe and Beyond

Soccer was invented in England but soon became popular in Europe and South America. The soccer craze spread in two primary ways. First, it was exported to different countries by Englishmen who were not willing to forgo their leisure activities while living abroad, and second, it was imported to countries by travellers returning home from England, where they had seen and fallen in love with the game.

Ports such as Le Havre and Gothenburg were typically the places where English soccer enthusiasts first got together to play. English sailors took the game to Genoa and Naples in the 1880s, and British businessmen introduced it to Turin and Milan.

Teachers from various European countries such as Belgium and Switzerland were sent to England to familiarize themselves with the country's education system. Enthralled by the soccer craze they experienced there, they took it back with them and sparked the craze in the schools of their home countries.

In the Netherlands, sport was "the work of Englishmen resident in the Netherlands and of the Dutch who had been in England" (Guttmann 46). Here, however, sport met with strong resistance since physical education teachers rejected competition-oriented sport and favoured German *Turnen*.

One of the countries that promptly imported the game of soccer in its early years was Denmark, which had close economic ties with Great Britain. In 1889, the first national soccer association on the European mainland (the *Dansk Boldspil Union*) was founded there.

The British colony in Vienna "started the ball rolling" by forming the first soccer clubs in Austria in 1894, made up of factory and office workers of English firms. Soccer developed from a subculture of Vienna's English community into a cultural mass-market product capable of gratifying different groups of the population at the same time.

Thus, soccer had spread across the whole of Europe in the form of an association game even before the turn of the century.

At the start of the twentieth century, British soldiers and sailors, followed by British entrepreneurs, exported soccer, along with their culture, to other continents. Soccer thrived best in South America, where British capital and know-how dominated the markets and the British way of life served as a model for the upper classes. Britain's influence was especially strong in Argentina—most of all in the city of Buenos Aires, which had the largest British community outside of the Empire and subsequently developed into soccer's first stronghold in South America. In much the same way the sport also spread to Uruguay and Chile. In Brazil soccer was first played almost exclusively by British citizens of the middle and upper classes. After the turn of the century, the game rapidly became popular among all classes, including the black population. Generally, it can be said that "English commercial houses and colleges were the great propagandists for the sport that, in time, became the passion of the multitude" (Guttmann 61).

In contrast to its development in Europe or South America, sport spread to Africa under conditions of imperialism and colonization. The colonial powers took their values, norms, customs, and habits—along with their physical activities—to the regions they governed and controlled. In Kenya, for example, British officers and colonial government officials established a sport culture that was almost exclusively for the benefit of Europeans. Nevertheless, pupils at missionary schools also had physical education and sport lessons, which included soccer, and it was from these pupils that the "black elite" was recruited. In spite of this, soccer spread slowly in Africa, with a soccer association being founded in Kenya in 1922 but not until 1945 in Nigeria.

1904 saw the founding of the Fédération Internationale de Football Association (FIFA), which controls and guarantees international standards in soccer as well as its rules and its language. However, each country has its own history of soccer, and cultural differences can be observed, for instance, in the speed at which it spread, in the way it became anchored socially, in the extent and rate of its professionalization, in the styles in which it is played and, finally, in its myths. However, no studies have so far been undertaken to analyze and explain these differences against the backdrop of the social developments of each particular country.

Information from Guttmann, Allen. *Games & Empires: Modern Sports and Cultural Imperialism.* New York: Columbia University Press, 1994.

RIP ROARING FUN.

HOW THE MERCHANTS AND THE COWBOYS OF BUTTE CITY, MONTANA, RUN THE LOCAL CONCERT HALLS AFTER THEIR OWN FASHION.

The *National Police Gazette* attracted readers with sensationalized stories of crime, sport, and sex.
Image courtesy of Library of Congress, LC-USZC62-63903.

not only provided in-depth and sensationalized coverage of pugilistic events but also sponsored bouts of great interest. Fox created the system of weight classes and awarded bejeweled belts to the champions of each category. By the 1880s, his publication reached a weekly circulation of 150,000, nearly double that of the respectable middle-class *Harpers' Weekly.* The *Gazette* became the Bible of boxing, and by 1883 Fox's enterprise operated out of a $250,000 seven-story headquarters in New York City (Reel).

Another successful sporting entrepreneur was Albert Pope, who made his mark as a manufacturer of bicycles. Crude forms, propelled by riders who sat astride a framework over two wheels and walked, appeared early in the century. These velocipedes were replaced by the so-called English ordinary, introduced to the United States at the 1876 Centennial Exhibition held in Philadelphia and featuring the innovation of a large front wheel (four or five feet high) coupled with a small rear wheel. The rider perched on a small seat and steered with handlebars. Balancing atop the frame required considerable skill, but having mastered

it the cyclist might achieve considerable speed. Speeding cyclists, known as "scorchers," raced in parks and on city streets, posing a danger to pedestrians and those on horseback. The ordinary proved dangerous to riders as well, when the front wheel encountered rocks or holes, catapulting the rider over the front wheel—a fall known as a "header."

New cycles cost $100 each, and even a used one would bring $35. Pope's mass production lowered the costs, but the sport remained largely a middle-class pastime. Pope promoted the sport through magazines and cycling clubs, and he organized the first cycling club, in Boston, in 1878. The Chicago Cycling Club, founded a year later, became the largest of many in that city, and cycling organizations soon proliferated throughout the country. The activity proved especially attractive to young men and women who used cycles to elude their required chaperones in a break from the strict moral courtship regimen of the Victorian Era.

The large number of cycling clubs banded together in 1880 to form the League of American Wheelmen (LAW). With an extensive and

The bicycle offered new patterns of socialization and courtship as young men and women sought greater freedom from the restrictive etiquette of the Victorian Era.

Image courtesy of Library of Congress, LC-USZ62-28614.

growing membership, LAW gained considerable political clout. Candidates courted their votes, and officeholders catered to their demands, including requests for paved roads and parkways where enthusiasts might avoid the dreaded "header." Clubs provided road maps and organized "century rides" of 100 miles (161 kilometers). In turn, middle-class cyclists in cities such as Boston influenced the Better Roads Movement, and their desire for resting spots along the way during excursions outside the city helped promote middle-class tourism through the rise of new businesses offering places to eat, sleep, and repair bicycles en route. Bicyclists also formed a community of consumers purchasing products for their bicycles, as well as sportswear for their journey (Hardy, *How* 148, 160–163). Cyclists thus affected urban transportation networks and the early tourism industry even before the advent of the automobile.

Perhaps the most successful of the early sports moguls, Albert G. Spalding first earned fame as a player. Born the eldest of three children in a well-to-do Illinois family in 1850, Spalding found his boyhood abruptly changed by his father's death in 1858. The family soon moved to the town of Rockford, and by the age of 15 Spalding starred as the pitcher on the Forest City baseball club, Rockford's finest. At an 1867 baseball tournament in Chicago, Spalding garnered national attention when he pitched his club to victory over the Washington (D.C.) Nationals, considered the best team in the country.

The Chicago Excelsiors, another noteworthy team, promptly offered Spalding a spot on its roster and a job in Chicago with a substantial income. When his employer's business failed, he returned to Rockford and the Forest City team. The Rockford contingent's tour of the Midwest and East in 1870 included a victory over the Cincinnati Red Stockings. Harry Wright of the Boston Red Stockings, newly acquired as player-manager from Cincinnati, then offered Spalding $1,500 to join his club, and Spalding soon became the dominant pitcher in the newly formed professional baseball players association.

The following year, Spalding accepted an offer to play for the Chicago White Stockings, where he rose from player-manager to owner and then assumed leadership of the National League after the death of William Hulbert. In conjunction with the organization of the National League in 1876, Spalding and his brother had launched their own enterprise that same year. The Spalding Brothers sporting goods firm, headquartered in Chicago, soon reached national proportions with its marketing and manufacture of sports products and made him a millionaire.

In its first year, the Spalding firm produced the official league book and a baseball guide. By 1879, the business had acquired a bat factory in Hastings, Michigan, near a forest that supplied its materials

RHODE ISLAND.—FIRST NATIONAL MEET OF AMERICAN BICYCLISTS, AT NEWPORT, MAY 31st—THE PARADE OF THE CLUBS ON BELLEVUE AVENUE. FROM A SKETCH BY CHAS. UPHAM.—SEE PAGE 263.

Media images, such as this one of the first national cycle meet at Newport, helped to popularize the sport.

Image courtesy of Library of Congress, LC-USZ62-32016.

and thus minimized production costs. It was the first of many such plants that even employed workers in Scotland, Leeds, and London, and branch offices reached as far as Egypt. Its publications increased in the 1880s and produced Spalding's Library of American Sports. Spalding's sporting ventures eventually fostered a separate company that included 300 sports titles in Spalding's American Sports Publishing Company. These guides and books touted a range of sports and, of course, promoted Spalding sporting goods throughout the country (Hardy, "Adopted" 139, 146).

As Spalding further expanded his offerings, he sold products through mail-order catalogs to consumers across the nation. Product endorsements by professional athletes and company-sponsored "Spalding teams" enhanced belief in Spalding's wares as superior and "official" sports products. Spalding also enhanced the brand name by selling sports equipment supposedly used by big-league players and other successful athletes, and men, women, and children could be found using his sporting goods

for their own use and enjoyment. The Spalding line of goods included virtually all sports, as he bought out competitors and manufacturers of golf, tennis, football, basketball, and general exercise equipment, as well as uniforms. He produced gear for field sports, boats for outdoorsmen, and bicycles for urban cyclists. As his biographer Peter Levine has observed, his competitive drive eventually prompted him to seek a monopoly in the sporting goods market (*A.G. Spalding* 71–96).

By 1880, Spalding held the contract for the official league ball to be used in all games, and he declared other products produced by his firm to be "official" as well, regardless of whether they were actually so designated. In later years, he offered trophies to public school athletic leagues in big cities such as New York and Chicago, and even as far away as the U.S.-occupied Philippines, in order to gain players' and administrators' brand loyalty. In the 1888–1889 off-season, he organized a worldwide baseball tour intended to bring the American game and American ideals to other nations and, of course, expand his markets, but stops in Hawaii, Australia, Ceylon (now Sri Lanka), Egypt, Italy, France, England, Ireland, and Scotland produced only limited success and failed to supplant cricket within the British Empire. Nevertheless, Spalding gained an international presence, and the Spalding brand achieved wide visibility.

The presumptuous Spalding even attempted to rewrite history. Unwilling to accept the notion that his beloved game of baseball originated in Britain, he insisted that it evolved from American colonial practices. In 1905, he organized the Mills Commission, a group of former baseball administrators and associates, as well as two United States senators (but no historians) to determine the origin of the sport.

After a two-year study, the group determined that Abner Doubleday created the game at Coopers-town, New York, in 1839. At the time, few doubted the findings, although proof for such an allegation rested with a specious letter sent to Spalding. In 1911, Spalding produced his own history of base-ball, a year after he failed to gain a U.S. Senate seat from California, which reinforced the nationalistic myth of the American birth of the game. Although thoroughly refuted, the creation myth persists among many Americans (Block 16–17).

As entrepreneurs such as Spalding made their fortunes, other employers tried to maximize their profits by controlling their employees' leisure time through wholesome sport offerings. Employees who were hung over often didn't report to work on Mondays, or they were unproductive. Some of the employee teams (e.g., the Chicago Bears and Green Bay Packers) would eventually become fully professional.

Spalding's baseball tourists at the Sphinx, February 9, 1889. A.G. Spalding, wearing a pith hat, is in the middle of the picture.

Photo courtesy of the National Baseball Hall of Fame Library.

Industrial Recreation Programs

In the aftermath of the Great Railroad Strike of 1877, employers tried to gain greater control over largely immigrant and ethnic-minority workforces. Many employed the YMCA without success to initiate recreation programs and proselytize a particular brand of Protestant Christianity. In Chicago, George Pullman, builder of railroad sleeping cars, constructed an entire town south of the city to house his laborers and manufacturing plant. Pullman made sure his company town was far enough from the temptations of the big city, and his only saloon, in the company hotel, prohibited all but corporate officers. Pullman did, however, provide magnificent athletic facilities for track and field, rowing, soccer, cricket, tennis, baseball, football, ice skating, billiards, boating, and riflery. He reasoned that such amenities would provide wholesome leisure alternatives to the saloon and serve as a means of social control to produce reliable and efficient employees. The Pullman Athletic Association (PAA) was incorporated in 1882 as the first industrial recreation program in the United States.

The PAA produced several sport spectacles that brought fame and publicity to the company. The national rowing championship of 1883, held at Pullman, drew a crowd of 15,000 people, and newspapers provided extensive coverage of the annual road race for cyclists. Pullman hired professional coaches and top athletes, and some of the PAA's competitors earned national prominence. Pullman also offered a library, stores, and a total of 40 organizations to meet workers' needs, but the owner also served as landlord. Wages reverted back to the owner for rent, food purchases, and fees for use of the facilities. When the Depression of 1893 forced pay cuts, reduced working hours, and layoffs, the alienated workforce went out on strike, led by Eugene Debs, a prominent socialist. The threat of violence required U.S. Army troops to quell the confrontation.

Despite the hostility engendered by employer–employee confrontations, workers maintained their interest in sport. Labor unions began to organize their own baseball teams and provided billiard rooms and other facilities to enhance camaraderie. Companies, too, promoted similar programs for workers that became known as welfare capitalism. Extensive recreational programs were offered by, among others, the National Cash Register Company in Dayton, Ohio; the Pennsylvania Railroad; the Heinz Company of Pittsburgh; Hershey Chocolate Company; and United States Steel.

Gendered Sport, Class, and Social Roles

Men such as Spalding and Pullman established the forms and practices of modern American sporting culture with little regard for women's participation as workers at their companies in the years following the Civil War. However, in a gradual departure from the Antebellum Era, when their gender-prescribed role of sedentary urban living undermined their physical health, women did begin to assume a more active role in physical recreation and sport. For rural women, new forms of physical recreation might alter their physical condition in farming communities, while women who left the farmstead were introduced to new urban modes of sporting and leisure pursuits. White middle- and upper-class women with more leisure time and access to some educational institutions—in contrast with their working-class counterparts—

now found that some sporting practices seemed gender-appropriate within society's moral and social codes. And all women, in pursuing their physical and sporting activities, had to navigate relations with men within their class and ethnic contexts, even as challenges to constraints in women's dress (which typically limited physical mobility) and the desire to engage more actively in sport prompted several female reformers to more directly challenge the male hierarchy in American sport and culture by the late nineteenth century.

Pastimes for Working-Class Women

Working-class women competed as professional rowers as early as 1867, and in the 1870s they attracted attention as paid pedestrians and boxers. In 1871, five women competed in the regatta of the Empire City Rowing Club on a 2-mile (3.2-kilometer) course. Amelia Shean took the singles crown in a 17-foot (5.2-meter) workboat in a time of 18 minutes and 32 seconds. In 1876, Mary Marshall defeated a male opponent in a best-of-three walking race in New York City. Marshall competed against Bertha von Hillern, a German immigrant who became a celebrity as a pedestrian and who advocated exercise for women during 1876 and 1877. The following year, Ada Anderson arrived from England and drew thousands of spectators to her endurance walks. In 1878, she walked daily for a month and, on another occasion, covered 2,700 quarter miles (i.e., a total of 675 miles, or about 1,085 kilometers) in 2,700 quarter hours, sleeping on cots as needed (Kirsch, *Sports* [Vol. 4] 350). Her exploits prompted a surge of female pedestrians, with more than one hundred competing professionally by 1879 (Shaulis 39).

With such competition, some female walkers turned to other pursuits to earn a living. Louise Armaindo, May Stanley, and Elsa Von Blumen, for example, became endurance cyclists, while still others entered the harsh world of pugilism (Shaulis 43). Cycling enjoyed such popularity that it spawned early globalization efforts:

THE WHEEL.

MATTERS OF INTEREST TO DEVOTEES OF THE SILENT STEED.

A NEW COMBINATION.

PROFESSIONAL BICYCLING STARS GO ON A TRIP AROUND THE WORLD.

A combination of bicycle riders, to be known as "The League of Champions," was formed in Chicago week before last. Chicago's favorite, Mlle. Armaindo, the champion long-distance rider of America, heads the list. John S. Prince, short-distance champion; Henry W. Higham, long-distance champion of England; Fred S. Rollinson, ex-champion, and Thomas W. Eck, professional, comprise the party. All are under the management of Fred J. Engelhardt, the well-known manager of sporting celebrities. It is the intention of the "League" to give exhibitions and races in the leading cities throughout the West, thence to Australia and England. Armaindo, with a record of 843 miles in 72 hours, Price, with 486 miles to his credit at the end of 30 hours; Higham, with 1,040 miles in 72 hours; and Rollinson with 50 in 3 hours, is a sufficient guarantee of the strength of this organization. The "League" has entered into an agreement, a portion of which is decidedly novel. A pool is made of the earnings from which the expenses are paid. From what remains of any and all earnings of any member or the League collectively, 10 per cent shall be paid into a racing fund, which shall be used only for stake-money with outside challengers and for the expenses incident to a preparation for a race if no challenges are received from persons outside the League within a reasonable time, then the amount on hand will be put up to be contested by Armaindo, Higham and Prince in a six day race. Even then any outsider can by depositing a third of the amount on hand, enter and start in the race, the winner to take the entire stake. On the evening of Nov. 16th this combination left Chicago for Kansas City. At San Francisco Prince is to meet Charles Smith, champion of the Pacific slope, still a six days match will take place there for 10 percent of the gross receipts of the tour, which will be contested for by Prince, Higham, and Armaindo. They expect to sail for Australia on February 1, where Higham will try conclusions with Rolf, an Australian champion. Each one of the party takes two machines on the trip. The return home will be by way of England.

qtd. in Gems, *Sports* 155–156

Nell Saunders won a silver butter dish by beating Rose Harland in a boxing match. The middle class deemed such pastimes unseemly and unladylike. A Chicago reporter averred that "prize fights between

People & Places

Vaudeville and the Advent of Female Boxers in the Nineteenth Century

In the second half of the nineteenth century boxing was a fad in the U.S., and boxers such as John L. Sullivan and Jim Corbett were celebrities who earned not only immense sums of money, but they were also at the center of public attention. Typically, the most famous pugilists were men. However, at the same time, some women engaged in boxing and even gained a measure of fame. The first boxing bouts between women were organized in saloons, such as Harry Hill's Exchange in New York, and covered by the notorious National Police Gazette. But soon, women took on the sport and made a living from boxing.

Two of the most famous female pugilists of the time were Hattie Leslie and Hattie Stewart. Hattie Leslie was one of the participants in an early prize fight which took place in a barn on an island near Buffalo in 1888. Leslie won the fight, which was described as scandalous by the press. The male organizers of this event were condemned to several months in prison. Hattie Leslie, nicknamed the "female John L. Sullivan," gained a measure of fame, obtained the heavyweight championship, and drew audiences to her matches as well as to her performances in vaudeville shows. Her husband and manager adopted her name and became a successful businessman.

Although they never faced each other, Hattie Leslie and Hattie Stewart, the other famous heavyweight boxer of the time, were rivals. Stewart, too, was a champion, but even more successful on the vaudeville circuit, where she presented her boxing skills to large audiences. Her partners, Dick Stewart, and, after Stewart's death, Thomas Gillen, were also boxers and vaudevillians who supported Hattie's career until her retirement after the turn of the century.

The biographies of these women provide insight into extraordinary women, women who did not adopt the gender order of the time and who refuted the myth of the "weak" sex, not only via their bodily strength and their boxing skills, but also because they lived and acted in contradiction to traditional gender norms. As vaudeville was the main entertainment of the masses, the presentations of women boxers and other artists, such as female weightlifters, displaying "unwomanly" abilities may have had an impact on gender norms, or perhaps the transgressions of norms and rules were only possible because they occurred in a space which was clearly separated from the middle-class mainstream society.

men are beastly exhibitions, but there is an unutterable loathsomeness in the worse brutality of abandoned, wretched women beating each other almost to nudity, for the amusement of a group of blackguards, even lower in the scale of humanity than the women themselves" (Pierce, *A History* [Vol. 2] 468).

Middle-Class Sporting Pursuits

For middle-class white women, participating in pastimes that were more genteel allowed for a greater measure of acceptance. Women of the middle and upper classes played many sports, including croquet and tennis, that were deemed appropriate for their social position and gender. Women at the Staten Island Cricket and Baseball Club also engaged in archery and darts, and by 1880 archery clubs that accepted women could be found from coast to coast. In August 1879 in Chicago, 20 women competed in the first national archery tournament, with Mrs. Spalding Brown of Hastings, Michigan, crowned the champion. Women's fashions, however, greatly restricted their mobility and sporting opportunities, especially for middle-class and wealthy women who adhered strictly to the prescribed fashions of the age. Confined by corsets and bustles that accentuated gender differences, women competed mainly in relatively passive sports that did not infringe on masculine spheres or challenge displays of manly prowess. Women of this period who did engage in more active pastimes—on the tennis court, the golf links, or the water (rowing), or in collegiate sporting pursuits—paved the way for an increasing number of women to participate in more vigorous and competitive forms of sport in the decades to follow.

Croquet

Croquet became a fashionable recreation in America during the 1860s because, when played publicly on the front lawn of a family home, it allowed young, white, middle-class women to congregate with young men in a public group setting without the necessity of a chaperone. The croquet craze that began in the 1860s prompted women to play the game at home, as well as on their holidays at Gilded Age resorts that typically featured croquet lawns along with amenities for other sports such as swimming, tennis, and boating. Catharine Beecher played croquet with her sister Harriet Beecher Stowe on the lawn at Nook Farm, near Hartford, Connecticut, where Harriet lived. For middle-class women like those of the Beecher family, croquet

provided not only a pleasant outdoor sport but also a time for social gatherings of family and friends. A croquet rules book, *How to Play Field and Parlor Croquet* (1865), gave a sense of how to approach the game:

> While men and boys have had their healthy means of recreation in the open air, the women and girls have been restricted to the less exhilarating sports of indoor life. . . . Grace in holding and using the mallet, easy and pleasing attitudes in playing, promptness in taking your turn, and gentlemanly and ladylike manners throughout the game, are all points which it is unnecessary for us to enlarge on.
>
> qtd. in Dulles 191

The publication of rule books and the manufacture of croquet equipment by sporting goods companies helped generate enthusiasm for the game among women, as they purchased croquet equipment for family use.

Croquet held popular appeal for women during this period when middle-class Americans' lives were greatly affected by the gendered ideal of separate spheres of men's and women's endeavors. Generally, middle-class women pursued domestic and female-oriented activities, although at times women expanded their role in public sporting pastimes. Although viewed as a sport, croquet "was not [deemed] 'manly' like baseball; it did not demand physical strength and stamina; it was neither fast-paced nor highly competitive." As a family game, "[i]t was inclusive and sociable, gentle and genteel," and playing croquet "compensated for the stresses and strains of modern life by uniting all, young and old, male and female, on 'common ground'" (Lewis, "American" 373). On family lawns and resort grounds, women playing croquet partook of nature in a wholesome setting, and often in a mixed-gender context, but, it was thought, in such a way as to protect them and their families from rougher sporting scenes and activities deemed harmful, such as urban street life, saloons, gambling, drinking, and immoral and commercial amusements (Lewis, "American" 377).

During the croquet fad, women increased their participation in sport and sometimes tested traditional gender roles. Historian Jon Sterngass has investigated the nineteenth-century croquet craze in terms of gender roles and such behaviors as cheating: "Female grace and good manners may have been the ideal for the rule- and taste-makers, but on the croquet ground, a peculiar sort of gender reversal enabled women to temporarily jettison their passive role and dominate, if not humiliate, men. Women played the game seriously, enjoyed matching skills with men, and often emerged victorious." This image of women in croquet, of course, counters Victorian gender stereotypes, and thus the sport "challenged the superiority of males and undermined the concept of separate spheres" that was so prominent in nineteenth-century American culture (Sterngass 399, 405). Women might outwit men in a game of croquet, and they could use their long clothing to disguise shots by keeping the mallet hidden from the sight of other players or by using their hoop skirts to surreptitiously move the balls during the game. Some actions by women carried sexual connotations, such as when they lifted their long skirts, thus displaying their feet to male players. On some occasions, a male may have picked up a ball to set it in place for the croquet shot, showing his courtesy. A female player striking the ball with her mallet to direct it through the croquet hoop, demonstrating athletic skill, undermined the notion of separate spheres. Women hitting men's balls with a mallet, a symbolic reversal of gender power, presented a challenge to traditional roles while occurring in the mixed company of men and women. At times, women propelled their balls against those of male contestants, an act with implied sexual meanings. On croquet played in the nineteenth century, historian Jon Sterngass described how when a female croquet player had her ball next to her opponent's ball, "the tight croquet stroke could be interpreted as an act of symbolic castration. Men were 'forced' to look on helplessly as their female opponent lined up the two balls, lifted her skirt, placed her dainty foot on her own ball, and with a resounding thwack, hammered the other ball to parts unknown" (Sterngass 403). Such suggested sexual behaviors stirred up the moral and gender codes of the day.

Participants and observers commented on the cheating that seemed commonplace in croquet. In these situations, gender identity held no sway, as both middling women and men may have sometimes bent the rules to their own advantage. In his reminiscences about American summer resorts in the 1870s, William Dix noted that most Gilded Age resort hotels had croquet lawns, where "people wrangled and bickered and—let it be whispered—sometimes cheated over that effete game" (qtd. in Sterngass 402). Women also commented on their own cheating in the quest for victory at croquet. Katherine Rice, who attended Albany Female Seminary in New York and enjoyed playing croquet at the school, "complained in her diary in 1873 that in an unspecified game, 'Mattie cheated! cheated! cheated! cheated! cheated!!!!!! But no one seems to think that very unusual in her'" (qtd. in Sterngass 409; exclamations in original). The game itself involved competition, and as a result conventional gender roles could be contested as part of the action in the cultural space of the croquet lawn.

Lawn Tennis

In the spring of 1874, Mary Ewing Outerbridge introduced the game of lawn tennis to members of the Staten Island Cricket and Baseball Club after she had learned to play the popular English sport in Bermuda. She brought back a set of tennis equipment to show her brothers, who were also interested in sport: "Having gained the permission of her brother, A. Emilius Outerbridge, director of the [club] . . . she rigged up the net in a remote corner of the cricket ground without much ado. It was thus for the first time that lawn tennis was given the attention of a sports club and thus attracted public attention" (Gillmeister 209). One of Mary's brothers, Eugenius H. Outerbridge, suggested that the club hold a tennis tournament, and thus the first lawn tennis tournament in America took place on September 1, 1880, at the Staten Island Cricket and Baseball Club, in what reporters hailed as a national tournament. Doubles competitors included the team of Richard Dudley Sears and Dr. James Dwight, who later won five U.S. doubles championships as partners; Richard D. Sears later became seven-time U.S. singles champion (Gillmeister 208).

This tournament led to the organization of the United States National Lawn Tennis Association (USNLTA) in May 1881. The association wanted to provide standardized rules for scoring and equipment and sponsor a national championship. Delegates of the USNLTA decided that Rhode Island's newly constructed Newport Casino would serve as the championship site, and August 31, 1881, marked the first national lawn tennis championship. (Today, the Newport Casino Tennis Club hosts the International Tennis Hall of Fame and an annual men's tournament.) The early competitors in American tennis hailed from families of elite social and economic standing, and initially only men took part in the tournaments. Richard D. Sears recalled (in the 1930s) the inaugural years of tennis (in the 1880s) in the United States:

> A large number of the players wore Knickerbockers, with blazers, belts, cravats, and woolen stockings in their club colors. Their shoes were rubber-soled and generally of white canvas and buckskin. None of their sleeves were cut off, . . . while the large majority rolled them up. . . .

The second year the championship found all of the players serving overhand with more or less speed, mostly less, with everyone coming in to volley as soon as any good opening presented itself; but as both Dwight and I had taken up lobbing, a stroke, which, to be effective, requires a good deal of practice, a certain amount of discouragement appeared, and when these players also tried this stroke they generally lobbed much too short, giving us an easy kill.

qtd. in Gillmeister 212

Tennis grew increasingly popular among elite white men at country clubs and private tennis courts, and more tournaments were staged. As with earlier boat races, the playing of lawn tennis in the United States led to international competitions. In fact, according to tennis historian Heiner Gillmeister, "the greatest achievement of American tennis is the creation of the Davis Cup," in which competitors from various countries play singles and doubles matches for their national teams. A precursor to the first Davis Cup took place in 1883, when a team from England, then a world tennis power, defeated the American team (Gillmeister 213). In 1899, Dwight Davis commissioned the Davis Cup trophy, and in 1900 the first Davis Cup match was played, with the American team defeating the British Isles 3-0 in Boston. Members of the victorious team were Malcolm Whitman, Dwight Davis, and Holcombe Ward (Gillmeister 218), all of whom played for Harvard. Holcombe Ward was also an intercollegiate and national doubles champion that year.

Although competitive matches for women were only in their infancy at this time, tennis did gain popularity in the 1880s among white middle-class women who played at country clubs (especially those women with a father or brothers who held club membership), both as a social function and for healthy exercise. At one well-known club, the Germantown Cricket Club in Philadelphia, women played tennis and pursued some competitive opportunities. In 1887 and 1888, the club offered a women's tournament, which gained prominence and became the United States Tennis Championships for women in 1889.

Collegiate Activities

The white women of the upper and middle classes achieved greater freedom with the establishment of women's colleges. When his daughters were refused admission to existing colleges, Matthew Vassar opened his own namesake school for women's higher education in 1861. The institution included a gym for physical training, a horse stable, and opportunities for archery, croquet, and shuttlecock (badminton), and students also adopted ball games, boating, and gymnastics as healthful pursuits. By 1875, Vassar women fielded three baseball teams. Smith College followed suit in 1878, and Mount Holyoke organized a women's baseball team in 1884 (Guttmann, *Sports* [2004] 132–133).

The University of Wisconsin admitted women in 1873 and provided a gymnasium for their use. A year later, Henry Fowle Durant and Pauline Fowle Durant founded Wellesley College, with facilities including a gym and with students required to exercise. Students boated on the adjacent lake, where they skated during the winter; in warmer weather, they also practiced tennis. Wellesley women began adopting specific attire as

Depictions of new sport forms spread interest and fostered a more national and uniform sporting culture.

Image courtesy of Library of Congress, LC-USZC4-1180.

sportswear in the 1880s. Under the direction of Lucille Eaton Hill, who became director of physical training at the school, the women engaged in intramural but serious rowing competitions. The competitors learned from the men's crews at Harvard and Yale and even employed rowing machines for training purposes. By 1891, the best rowers composed an all-college crew. The next year, the women purchased modern shells with sliding seats for greater efficiency, and trousers soon replaced skirts (Warner, *When* 2006). At the Boston school later known as Radcliffe College, women imported Dr. Dudley Sargent from Harvard to teach gymnastics in 1881.

Even noncollege women increasingly engaged in physical activities. In addition to croquet, women gained a greater measure of exercise by ice skating; and the roller skating craze that swept the country during the 1870s provided evidence that females sought greater freedom in their lives.

During this post–Civil War period, active women of the Gilded Age continued their campaign for suffrage, divorce rights, temperance, and access to higher education. Such politically and physically active women upset the dominant patriarchal system, as they sought greater control over their lives and questioned the traditional expectations of the ideology of domesticity. As these women worked toward increasing their individual agency in American society, they used various recreational activities, such as croquet, skating, and later cycling, to enjoy a measure of new freedom unencumbered by Victorian prescriptions for feminine behavior.

Regulation of Sport: Amateurism Versus Professionalism

Class issues restricted freedom considerably for many male and female athletes during the later nineteenth century. The upper classes deemed those who played sport for money or other forms of remuneration to be undignified, unworthy, and highly questionable in their honor and motives. The elite assumed their social inferiors could be bought by gamblers, and their concept of amateurism rested upon the English aristocratic ideal of a man who engaged in sport for play or recreation rather than for compensation. The close association of professional boxers, pedestrians, and baseball players with gamblers and saloons of the bachelor subculture only reinforced such speculation and stereotyping.

The elite concept of amateurism conflicted, however, with perceived primary attributes of the American character—competitiveness and the need to win—and in the 1870s even elite Northeastern college students hired professional coaches to train them for regatta competitions. The regatta at the 1876 Centennial Exhibition in Philadelphia included both amateur and professional events, and by 1882 Harvard employed a professional coach for its track-and-field athletes. Yet men such as Albert Spalding and Henry Chadwick continued to extol the character-building qualities of sport and its promise as a means of social control for wayward youth. Thus, Americans wrestled with competing perceptions of the values of sport, and a plethora of sport-related governing bodies tried, with increasing difficulty, to regulate distinctions between amateurs and professionals. Among the first, the American Association of Amateur Oarsmen was organized in 1872, and the Intercollegiate Association of Amateur Athletes of America (IC4A) addressed similar issues for track-and-field competitions in 1876. Noncollegiate athletic clubs banded together in 1879 as the National Association of Amateur Athletes of America (N4A), offering national championships that were open to those it deemed nonprofessional.

Some athletes posed a dilemma for the governing body, and in the minds of status-seeking clubs the desire to win superseded class and eligibility issues. Lawrence "Lon" Myers represented such a problem for the Manhattan Athletic Club (MAC). As a slight and sickly youth, Myers took up baseball and track as a remedy. Although less than 5 feet 8 inches (176 centimeters) tall and a mere 115 pounds (52 kilograms), he became the world's greatest runner, with records from 50 yards (46 meters) to a mile (1.6 kilometers). The MAC, desirous of his services, willingly overlooked his Jewish ancestry and provided him with paid employment at the club. Like other "amateurs" of the era, Myers quickly pawned the medals and trophies he won for ready cash. In 1885, the MAC even organized a fundraiser that provided $4,000 to their champion. Myers accumulated such riches as an amateur for eight years before publicly declaring his professionalism in an 1886 stakes race with British champion Walter George. The runners split the gate receipts for the commercialized event, which drew six thousand spectators for the first race in a best-of-three series at varying distances. Myers won easily at 1,000 yards (about 914 meters) and again at three-quarters of a mile (1.2 kilometers) to pocket the $2,000 prize money, still representing the MAC. In 1888, fifteen prominent athletic clubs, upset with the N4A's reluctance to confront the sham, joined together in the Amateur Athletic Union (AAU), an organization that managed to supersede all others as the primary governing body and regulator of amateur sport in the United States. Notions of amateurism would be increasingly challenged with the growth of intercollegiate and interscholastic sports, particularly as larger numbers of working-class youth entered the educational institutions in the twentieth century.

The vast flow of immigrants to America after 1880 presented issues well beyond amateurism; yet sport held great value in addressing the myriad concerns. At the dawn of the Progressive Era, social reformers developed a particular ideology of socialization, education, assimilation, and acculturation associated with the practice of sport. They attempted to bring greater cohesion and homogeneity to American society based on a clearer identification of what it meant to be an American.

Summary

This chapter has examined the forces, conditions, and issues that promoted and affected sport in the late nineteenth century. The increasing urbanization of American society, the ongoing immigration of largely European ethnic groups, and the presence of divisions based on race, ethnicity, and social class all played major roles in the organization of American society and the practice of sport. Class differences were registered in the composition of athletic clubs, the governance of sport, and debate over amateurism and professionalism. Sports entrepreneurs adopted business practices to both commercialize and professionalize athletic contests.

Sporting practices also played a major part in gender relations and the definition of gender roles. Power sports, in particular, along with the bachelor subculture that followed their practice, marked one's masculinity, while women increasingly challenged their prescribed domestic roles and restrictive clothing through their participation in sporting activities. The Gilded Age thus proved to be a transitional era in the growth and meaning of sport in American culture.

DISCUSSION QUESTIONS

1. In what ways did sport unite Americans during the Gilded Age?

2. In what ways did sport cause divisions within the society?

3. How did gender play a role in sport in the Gilded Age?

4. How did the town of Pullman serve as a social experiment? Was it successful?

5. How did sport assume an expanded commercial role?

6. How did entrepreneurs shape a sporting culture?

7. What role did sporting practices play in perceptions of social mobility?

8. How and why did professional teams emerge?

Chapter 6

American Sport and Social Change During the Early Progressive Era
1890–1900

CHAPTER OBJECTIVES

After reading this chapter, you will have learned about the following:

- The Progressive reformers' vision of American society and the reactions of alternative groups

- The changes wrought in American culture by industrialization and the need for urban and suburban recreational spaces

- The rise of football as an athletic spectacle

- The role of physical education and interscholastic sports in the assimilation of immigrants

- The significance of technological advancements on sport during the era

- The transformation of the modern Olympic Games from a peace movement to a nationalistic enterprise

The intense rivalries that emerged in association with big-time intercollegiate football programs during the Progressive Era reflected changes occurring in American society as a whole. The use of paid professional coaches marked a greater emphasis on winning, which became a characteristic trait of American culture, as corporations and college teams alike sought to dominate their rivals. Noted Harvard football coach Bill Reid became immersed in the heated rivalry between Harvard and Yale. He wrote in his diary about the quest for victory, his prioritizing of winning above his players' other activities, and his expectation that players would attend practice even at the expense of academic work:

> Some of the men were a little late getting down to the field this afternoon and I got after them. Brill it seems came down fifteen minutes late having been attending a lecture which he said he was afraid to cut. Knowing as I do that the marks for November hour examinations will not be in until after the Yale game, I knew that he could not be put on probation and so I told him to cut whenever it was necessary in order to be on time for practice. I don't care how much of a student a fellow cares to be at other times—[but] four days before the Yale game . . . I don't see how a man can help feeling that hardly anything is more important than to beat Yale.

qtd. in Smith, *Big-Time* 291, 300–301

In sport, as in the larger American society, such attitudes about winning and gaining wealth, as well as corruption and other perceived problems in the excesses of the Gilded Age—together with the rapid transition from a rural agricultural economy to an urban industrial one—caused many to question the nature of the evolving American culture. Social critics known as Progressive reformers urged a variety of changes to address the problems, curb the excesses of the Gilded Age, and improve the lives of the burgeoning urban population. They often targeted the growing number of immigrant newcomers to America, and they often employed sport in a variety of programs to educate and assimilate immigrants and address perceived social ills.

This chapter examines how immigration, industrialization, urbanization, imperialism, and the assimilation of disparate groups changed the face of America.

Social Reformers of the Progressive Era

The Progressives, consisting of loosely organized or independent white, Anglo-Saxon, Protestant (WASP) men and women, led the way as social reformers. They proposed a wide variety of goals, remedies, and middle-class values to confront social ills such as corrupt government, unbridled wealth, exploitation of the masses, and unequal rights in a supposedly democratic republic. Their analyses and solutions derived from a distinct Protestant moral code known as the Social Gospel. Moral crusaders campaigned against pornography and prostitution and in favor of temperance. In 1919, the success of the latter effort resulted in the passage of the Eighteenth Amendment (commonly known as Prohibition), which prohibited the manufacture, sale, and transport of nonmedicinal alcohol and prohibited beer and liquor consumption, thus curtailing the favored leisure activity of many Americans, especially among ethnic minorities (Powers, *Faces* 82–83). Therefore, the measure imposed a particular morality based on ethnic, religious, and class differences.

Reformers also sought to enable fair competition within the capitalist economic system, as workers organized themselves into labor unions to achieve better wages and conditions. Most workers labored at least 10 hours a day, 6 days a week, for $9 per week (Blum et al. 467). Some labor leaders, such as Eugene Debs, advocated socialism; others favored anarchism, or, in the case of the Industrial Workers of the World (IWW), more radical or even violent means to achieve their ends of a more equitable society. In this environment, a series of conflicts between employers and their workers questioned the nature of American liberty, democracy, and opportunity. A national railroad strike in July 1877, for example, crippled the transportation network, and Chicago, the center of the anarchist movement, witnessed the Haymarket Massacre on May 4, 1886, when an altercation between workers

1891	1892		1893
■ James Naismith invents basketball	■ Senda Berenson becomes director of physical education at Smith College, Massachusetts	■ Corbett defeats Sullivan in first gloved bout for heavyweight championship	■ Economic depression occurs
	■ Pudge Heffelfinger becomes the first pro football player	■ First women's basketball game played at Smith College	■ First Stanley Cup awarded

Overcrowded tenements led to conditions ripe for propagation of contagious diseases. Children were commonly put to work as well, shown here putting strings on merchandise tags, with some as young as six stringing over a thousand a day.

Photo courtesy of Library of Congress, LC-USZ62-108765.

and police killed eight and wounded sixty. The police responded with indiscriminate gunfire that felled many more. Over the next eight years, Chicago suffered 528 strikes, at a cost of $9 million (Gems, *For Pride* 3–4).

Workers confronted employers throughout the 1890s, and an army of unemployed citizens even marched on Washington in 1892. By the early twentieth century, the federal government had incorporated some Progressive measures and moved to bust the large corporate trusts, dissolve commercial monopolies, and impose an income tax on the more affluent to address the exploitation of human and commercial resources. At the local level, workers in settlement houses (social agencies located within immigrant neighborhoods) and park supervisors worked to assimilate children and used sport as a means to distract them from the radical sympathies of their parents.

Investigative journalists known as "muckrakers" exposed the corrupt practices of politicians

and employers that fostered poverty among the multitudes that immigrated to America in search of betterment. During the 1870s, 2.5 million people arrived in the United States, followed by another 5 million in the 1880s; from 1865 to 1915, the number of immigrants reached 25 million. By 1890, 80 percent of New Yorkers were foreigners or children of immigrants (Garraty 444, 473, 477).

Urban ghettos housed millions of people, often in overcrowded tenements marked by abysmal conditions that spawned disease and crime, and city services neglected hygiene or even basic amenities for those who were impoverished. In 1882, 50 percent of the children in Chicago died before age five (Pierce, *A History* [Vol.3] 55). Social work, a new vocation, emerged as an antidote, and many of the social workers were educated women who found in the new occupation a parallel to the caretaking roles previously assigned to them in the domestic sphere. Some women also challenged social inequality in gender-based crusades such

1894		1895	
■ Pullman Strike staged	■ United States Golf Association (USGA) forms	■ William Morgan invents volleyball	■ First American auto race held
■ Coxey's Army marches on Washington	■ Temple Cup Series begins in baseball	■ American Bowling Congress forms	■ *Plessy v. Ferguson* Supreme Court decision allows segregation
		■ Big Ten Conference forms	
		■ USGA holds men's and women's national amateur golf championships	

as campaigning for suffrage, birth control, and general respect.

Progressive reformers devised a three-tiered procedure designed to assimilate the various ethnic and working-class groups residing within the national borders, and sporting activities factored into this process. The first step rested partly upon humanitarian concerns. Children worked long hours in factories, and because of fatigue they often fell victim to injury or even death. Horses trampled others who played or worked in the streets. Progressives campaigned for child labor laws that restricted full-time employment, but such measures met with opposition from parents. With no minimum wage requirements in effect and no retirement plans for workers, immigrant families relied on a full complement of household laborers to make ends meet and to care for the sick, the unemployed, and the elderly.

Unemployed children simply roamed the streets, joining gangs or engaging in petty crimes or mischief. Progressives then passed mandatory education laws (the second step) that required children to go to school. By 1918, every state had enacted such legislation (Clement and Reiner 476). Truancy officers enforced mandatory attendance, but a captive audience did not assure either learning or Americanization, as many ethnic-minority children did not speak English. In this regard, physical education proved a boon and soon became a requirement (the third step) in many public schools. Trained physical educators taught children to play competitive American sports such as baseball, football, and basketball, and these forms of competition ingrained the basic tenets of the capitalistic economic system; team sports also taught the rudiments of the cooperation and leadership necessary to a democracy. Moreover, supervised games taught deference to authority in the form of a coach, referee, or umpire—a lesson cherished by capitalistic employers facing radical or stridently unhappy workers. Employers' ardent belief in the transformative powers of sport prompted them to provide funding, which, along with state resources, could be used to support the increasing number of public schools charged with achieving the acculturation goals.

Play and Games in American Ideology

The overcrowding of cities called for a restructuring of urban landscapes and the creation of open space. At the 1893 World's Columbian Exposition in the host city of Chicago, historian Frederick Jackson Turner announced the closing of the American frontier and claimed that the frontier experience was integral in shaping the American character: without lands or American Indian tribes to conquer, and with the massive influx of European immigrant groups, the aggressive, militaristic, independent character of the American WASP culture faced decline, if not extinction. Psychologist G. Stanley Hall offered some hope for WASPs in his recapitulation theory, which asserted that societies, like individual human beings, passed through evolutionary stages evident in their styles of play. In this view, simple running and throwing activities reflected primitive stages that gave way to games of chase or tag resembling hunting experiences. Eventually, children learned more complex and cooperative games that required leadership, strategy, and the characteristics of civilized societies.

Hall's beliefs merged with the pragmatic educational philosophy of John Dewey, one of his former students, to provide a firm foundation for the play movement. In Dewey's scheme, one learned by experience—by participation in activities that might encompass leadership, teamwork, and self-sacrifice for the good of the whole. For example, baseball, the primary vehicle at the time for instilling such values in ethnic-minority youth, might mesh the seemingly incongruous values of ethnic communalism and American individualism, since all players worked together as a defensive team but gained individual honors with the bat. Through the ideas of Hall and Dewey, then, sport gained legitimacy, and by the end of the Progressive Era, historian Frederic Paxson declared sport to be the new frontier, in which Americans or immigrants might seek the social mobility no longer available in the West, as well as psychological release from urban stress.

1896	1897	1898	1898–1900
■ First modern Olympics held (Athens, Greece)	■ First Boston Marathon held ■ Cheyenne Frontier Days launches	■ Hawaii annexed ■ Spanish-American War fought	■ African American Major Taylor reigns as cycling champion

Within this context, playing sports and games assumed an essential role in the physical training and moral education of youth. Under the guidance of coaches and trained physical educators, it was hoped that boys in particular might learn to become loyal, disciplined, ethical, and patriotic Americans—rather than degenerate hoodlums—by engaging in games and physical activities, especially team sports such as baseball, football, and basketball that elicited the desired outcomes of cooperation and respect for authority. Authorities hoped that by learning to follow a leader and play together, students would learn the practical application of democratic principles. Accepting the judgment of referees or umpires instilled obedience, while the competitive nature of sport reinforced the basis of a capitalistic economy. Moreover, football promoted the martial qualities deemed necessary to keep the nation strong and defend the tenets of capitalism, democracy, and individual rights. Theodore Roosevelt claimed that

> in any republic, courage is a prime necessity for the average citizen if he is to be a good citizen; and he needs physical courage no less than moral courage, the courage that endures, the courage that will fight valiantly alike against the foe of the soul and the foes of the body. Athletics are good, especially in their rougher form, because they tend to develop such courage.
>
> qtd. in Gems, *For Pride* 77

Despite the death of one of his own players in 1909, University of Virginia president Edwin Alderman refused to ban football, stating that "in dealing with this game you are dealing with our national characteristics" (Gems, *For Pride* 83).

Boys had long initiated their own interscholastic contests in baseball and football. They scheduled games with a variety of opponents, arranged travel to playing sites, and covered their own expenses, resisting any attempts by school authorities to regulate their extracurricular activities. Thus, while educators and administrators debated the values of the gymnastics curriculum, male students continued the pursuit of competitive sport forms throughout the late nineteenth century.

Physical Education of Youth

At the college level, American educators adopted European gymnastics systems to improve the fitness levels of both male and female students. In 1885, Oberlin College in Ohio began training physical educators. The German Turners offered their own courses in Milwaukee and Boston, and graduates of the Turner system introduced German gymnastics to public high schools in Kansas City in 1885 and throughout the Midwest thereafter. In 1889, Mary Hemenway, a wealthy Bostonian, founded the Boston Normal School of Gymnastics, which favored the Swedish system that emphasized flexibility rather than strength. At Harvard, Dr. Dudley Sargent introduced weight-training machines and anthropometric measurements. The YMCA opened its own teacher-training center in Springfield, Massachusetts. These various competing philosophies and training methods became known as the Battle of the Systems, as colleges and public high schools deliberated on the best procedure for training students.

In the cities, the transition to rationalized, commodified sport continued. In 1888, students in Boston high schools formed a football league, and similar organizations soon appeared throughout the Midwest. In Chicago, the high school football league charged dues, which covered the cost of a championship banner. The second-place team received the remaining cash in the league treasury. Trophies, rewards, and media attention promoted school spirit, communal pride, and an intense desire to win. High school newspapers lionized school athletes, local merchants honored them, and students feted their warriors with banquets and adulation as well as financial support. Intense rivalries triggered the use of "ringers"—exceptional athletes who were only part-time students or who had no affiliation with the school at all. Lax eligibility regulations plagued contests at both the interscholastic and intercollegiate levels, and even faculty members played in some competitions. In 1891, the Manual Training High School in the Chicago league protested that it was the only league member actually using its own students. Such practices openly violated the amateur standards of the governing bodies and upset reformers who adhered to a belief in sport as a character-building mechanism.

In June 1893, the University of Illinois invited high schools to participate in its athletic meet, an event that drew more than two hundred athletes for track-and-field events, cycling races, a football kick, and a baseball throw. The University of Chicago, founded with John D. Rockefeller's money, opened in 1892 and began offering interscholastic tournaments in track and basketball. Its coach and athletic director, Amos Alonzo Stagg, played in the first-ever basketball game, a sport invented by James Naismith at the YMCA School in Springfield, Massachusetts, in 1891. On March 10, 1892, Stagg wrote the following letter to his sister, Pauline Stagg:

Despite its violent aspects, many educators valued the lessons inherent in football.

Image from *Harper's Weekly*, Oct. 31, 1891.

There is a great furor among the boys in the school over a new game which Naismith our center rusher invented, called basket foot ball. It is played indoors in the gymnasium or some good sized room. Any number of persons on a side. A basket with large enough opening to take the ball easily is hung at each end about eight feet from the floor. The object is for the ball to be thrown or pitched into these baskets. The ball cannot be run with, although no limitations are placed on any one when not having the ball. This of course places a premium on passing the ball to others and so work it down the field. Fouls are declared for running with the ball and for kicking it. Any one has a right to the ball at all times if he can get it. I think the game could be easily adapted to girls—the main point being to get a basket as big as a house. The faculty of the school play the best team composed of the Secretarial men tomorrow. We expect a great time.

qtd. In Gems, *Sports* 143

The game was intended to provide a winter activity that would occupy energetic young men during the interim period between football and baseball seasons, and it further allowed physical educators to gain greater control over unruly males throughout the entire year. The early rules, however, permitted a high number of players and the use of rough tactics akin to those of a wrestling match. A few months later, Senda Berenson, an instructor at Smith College in Massachusetts, devised alternative rules for women's play, and the game soon became a favorite of high school girls as well. Berenson organized the first women's game, in 1892, after reading about the new game of basketball at Springfield College. She modified the men's rules to make the game less rough, divided the basketball court into three zones, and thereby restricted strenuous play. Girls could not cross over the zones, which necessitated a cooperative strategy to score points. No physical contact between players was allowed, so that they could not "snatch" the ball or block players as in the men's game (Hult, *Century* 24–25). Basketball quickly became a popular sport for women and girls of diverse ethnic backgrounds at various social organizations and settlement houses. Josephine Wilkin, in a letter to her mother on March 6, 1892, related the first game played at Smith College:

Friday afternoon at the Gym, we played a game, instead of going through the ordinary performances. Two waste-paper baskets were hung, one on either side of the Gym about three feet above our heads. Two of the girls choose sides, + those on our side were distinguished from the other by handkerchiefs tied on their arms. Three girls from each side were sent over to the other and the game began. We had a football which was to be touched only with the hands, + the object was to get it into your opponent's basket + keep it out of your own. When it was sent over to our side, the girls on that side who had been sent from the other tried to get it and throw it into the basket while the rest tried to catch it + throw it back to their helpers on the other side. See? It was great fun, + very exciting, especially when we got knocked down, as frequently happened. The side I was on had the misfortune to be beaten, but we had the ball in their basket several times, including the first time.

qtd. in Gems, *Sports* 147–148

Some women, like their male counterparts, participated in sports for physical health and competition, but they did so in a disputed context, as physicians, psychologists, and educators debated the appropriateness of sport for women. Some of these authorities worried about the stress of competition, while others feared damage to reproductive capacities or the accumulation of aggressive male characteristics. Nevertheless, women found a variety of sporting opportunities in the schools, settlement houses, and industrial recreation programs.

In 1895, William Morgan, a graduate of the YMCA Training School, invented volleyball, another indoor sport, at nearby Holyoke, as adults increasingly sought to assume greater control over students' extracurricular activities. Thereafter, YMCA missionaries carried both games throughout the world, as sport provided one means of attracting young men in the quest for converts. As the new century approached, then, sport presented a battleground contested by various groups, as immigrants struggled with assimilation, youth rebuffed adult control in schools and play spaces, and professional athletes challenged the amateur ideal.

In 1898, faculty members at the Chicago high schools formed the Board of Control to govern student athletics. They standardized rules, established eligibility requirements, addressed unsporting

Senda Berenson initiated women's basketball at Smith College in 1892.
Image courtesy of Sophia Smith Collection, Smith College.

behavior, and prohibited money prizes. The Board of Control scheduled contests only at approved sites, such as school gyms, YMCAs, or settlement houses, where adults might oversee students' activities. The Board even enacted competitive divisions based on size and weight to equalize competition. Students, however, protested the loss of their freedom and the curtailment of their own initiatives. They even revolted, attempting to establish their own league outside the jurisdiction of school authorities. The venture failed when the superintendent of schools expelled the revolutionary students (Pruter, "Chicago High").

School rivalries extended well beyond the local scene. By the turn of the twentieth century, high school teams traveled throughout the country for regional and national competitions. Debates over contrasting styles of play resulted in a national football showdown. Eastern schools favored the plodding, mass plays (i.e., players closely bunched to produce mass force) and brute strength exhibited by the New England college teams, while Midwesterners favored speed, end runs, and reverses, sometimes running in excess of one hundred plays during a game (no huddles). For some time, challenges between the Eastern and Midwestern college powers went unheeded, but in 1902 Brooklyn's Polytechnic High School met Chicago's Hyde Park High School in a postseason confrontation in Chicago. The Midwestern style of play overwhelmed the New Yorkers, and Chicago won by a score of 105-0. Brooklyn claimed that Poly did not represent its best team, and Charles Ebbets, owner of its professional baseball team, guaranteed funding for a rematch in New York the next year. In the event, darkness forced a cessation, with Chicago's North Division High School in a commanding 75-0 lead over Brooklyn Boys' High.

New York fared better than other localities in its regulation and administration of local high school sports. Dr. Luther Gulick became director of physical training in the New York school system in 1903 and instituted a comprehensive athletic program that offered competition in baseball, basketball, soccer, swimming, tennis, track and field, crew, cross country, lacrosse, and riflery. Boys could earn distinctive badges for successful completion of physical fitness tests, and classes might win honors by surpassing average scores of other classes. School teams competed for district and city championships symbolized by trophies that were proudly displayed at schools. In 1907, a crowd of fifteen thousand witnessed the championship baseball game held at the Polo Grounds.

The organization of the Public Schools Athletic League (PSAL) in New York included even the elementary schools. In 1905, a girls division was created to offer folk dancing, but it limited athletic competition in other activities to intramural events. Numerous other cities adopted the New York model, as adults increasingly controlled students' leisure pursuits. As child labor laws directed considerable numbers of ethnic-minority and immigrant youths into the school system, adult educators employed sport in efforts to Americanize them. For others who remained outside the jurisdiction of school authorities, Progressive reformers employed similar strategies for supervised play instruction at parks, playgrounds, and settlement houses across America. When successful, such programs served as an effective social control device, curtailing juvenile delinquency and increasing adult guidance.

Emergence of Football

Football gained dominant status as the preeminent sport on college campuses during the Progressive Era. Thanksgiving championship games became urban spectacles by the 1880s, as fans paraded to games and alumni feted their warriors in sumptuous banquets held after the games, in which teams strove for regional prestige and national recognition. The parade before the 1893 Yale–Princeton game started four hours before kickoff. Richard Harding Davis described the lively scene in *Harper's Weekly*: "The city surrenders herself to the students and their game as she never welcomes any other event, except a Presidential election. . . . [E]very other young woman you meet, and every little boy, and elderly men even, begin to parade Broadway with bows of blue stuck on their persons, or long strips of orange and black ribbon . . . which proclaim their allegiance and their hopes" (qtd. in Riess, *Major* 117). Forty thousand fans attended and paid as much as $150 each for box seats. Some came from as far as Oregon and Texas, and a hotel bartender was entrusted with $50,000 in wagers from complete strangers.

The cult of the athletic hero was reinforced when football pioneer Walter Camp and sportswriter Caspar Whitney began naming an All-American team in 1889 to signify individual and specialized excellence. Between 1865 (when the Civil War was ended) and 1898 (when the Spanish-American War was fought), young men had found no war in which to prove their courage and masculinity, and football sufficed as a worthy alternative, given the injuries and deaths produced by its mass play

Harvard and Princeton football game.

Photo courtesy of Library of Congress, LC-USZ62-78261.

and brutal tactics. Nearly one hundred colleges were fielding teams by 1892, and football assumed distinct military purposes. As Senator Henry Cabot Lodge put it, "the injuries incurred . . . are part of the price which the English speaking race has paid for being world conquerors. [V]ictories . . . are the manifestation and evidence of a spirit, which is all important. [T]his great democracy is moving onward to its great destiny. Woe to the men or nations that bar its imperial march" (qtd. in Gems, *For Pride* 26). Helmets were not required until 1939, so players wore their hair long for padding, but this minimal protection offered little safeguard, as 18 deaths and 159 serious injuries occurred in 1905 alone. In 1909, the death toll was 33, and the rising casualty lists fostered a backlash.

College officials from 68 institutions met in 1905 to organize a governing body. The Intercollegiate Athletic Association of the United States soon became the National Collegiate Athletic Association (NCAA). New rules, such as allowance of forward passes, were instituted to open up the game and decrease the mass plays. Few teams adopted the new strategy, however, because defenders tended to attack pass receivers and because, by rule, incomplete passes resulted in a turnover until further changes were made. Notre Dame, a small Catholic college in Indiana, did much to

popularize the new technique by employing the strategy in a stunning 35-13 upset of a powerful Army team in 1913.

Football became big business by the dawn of the twentieth century. John D. Rockefeller, benefactor of the University of Chicago, offered a $3 million donation for a win over Wisconsin in 1895, and the team responded with a 22-12 come-from-behind victory. By the 1890s, Yale raised $100,000 through its football program, and in 1904 Harvard had a $50,000 surplus in its football budget; in fact, only tuition produced greater revenue for the institution. In 1903, Harvard built a concrete stadium with forty thousand seats to accommodate the multitudes who paid to watch its team perform. Other schools followed Harvard's lead in stadium construction. In 1906, the $42,000 excess in the University of Chicago's football receipts funded all other sports in its athletic program.

Independent promoters capitalized on the commercialization of football as well. James Wagner, president of the Rose Parade committee in Pasadena, offered the University of Michigan a $3,500 guarantee to meet Stanford in the first Rose Bowl game in 1902. Meant to bolster a burgeoning California tourist industry, the game proved a mismatch. Michigan had scored 501 points that season while holding its opponents scoreless. Its coach,

Fielding Yost, had been dismissed from Stanford and took revenge in a 49-0 rout of the Californians. Stanford's players suffered so many injuries that the game could not continue, and the Rose Parade committee discontinued the spectacle for 14 years.

Yost's star player, Willie Heston, had followed him to Michigan from California, and such moves by "tramp athletes," as well as recruitment of star players by coaches and alumni, had been under way for at least two decades by that time. Yale proved particularly effective at recruiting, with nouveau-riche alumni throughout the country funneling information to football managers. Under Walter Camp, the football program achieved a machinelike precision in a bureaucratic, businesslike organization that produced efficient and effective results. Between 1886 and 1895, Yale won 124 games, losing only 3 and tying 3. Its 1888 contingent scored 698 points while holding opponents scoreless. Other schools sought former Yale players as coaches and introduced the Yale system. William Rainey Harper, a former Yale professor and the newly appointed president of the University of Chicago, hired Amos Alonzo Stagg, a Yale All-American, as the school's first football coach. Harper gave Stagg tenured faculty status and a salary that exceeded that of most professors, providing college coaches with immediate credibility and prestige. Over the previous decade, students had hired temporary professional trainers, who would prepare the team (only during the season) to enhance its chances against intercollegiate rivals.

Stagg's teams soon challenged even his alma mater for national honors. As with Yale, Stagg's recruiting network secured top athletes with substantial inducements, as the coach manipulated an $80,000 scholarship fund for ostensibly needy students. One of Stagg's recruits, who later won All-American honors, warned Midwestern rivals, "You fellows can't get me at Northwestern, and they can't get me at Wisconsin, you haven't got the money. I am going to Chicago" (Jordan 19–20, 23 [qtd. passage from Jordan cited in Gems, *For Pride* 94]). In 1901, Yale recruited 27-year-old James Hogan, who, as team captain in 1904, got free tuition, room, and board; a Caribbean vacation; a share of profits from the sale of baseball programs; and commission on all packages of cigarettes sold in the city of New Haven.

The combination of such incentives with community pride, increased emphasis on winning, and associated gambling led to the overt professionalization of football. Walter "Pudge" Heffelfinger, a Yale All-American and the most acclaimed player of his day, began accepting "expenses" to play for

a Chicago athletic club team in 1892. Later that season, the Allegheny Athletic Association paid him $500 for one heavily wagered game against its archrival in Pittsburgh. Professionalism quickly spread throughout western Pennsylvania and eastern Ohio, as communities imported players for big games. In 1897, even Butte, Montana, bought players for its games against West Coast teams. With money on the line, teams sought any player who might make the winning difference, and even racism was sometimes diminished, as Ohio teams signed African American stars such as Charles Follis and Charles "Doc" Baker to contracts. Football thus offered more opportunities at the highest levels than baseball or the nascent sport of basketball for African American and working-class athletes.

Many professional teams started as company organizations. Among them, the Columbus (Ohio) Panhandles represented the Pennsylvania Railroad starting in 1901. The six Nesser brothers, the sons of German immigrants who worked as boilermakers for the railway company, formed the backbone of the unit and terrorized opponents into the 1920s. The roughness of football meshed naturally with the hard lives of working-class participants and fans. Unlike middle-class adherents, who needed the game to prove their masculinity because of their increasingly sedentary lives, working-class players admired toughness and athletic prowess as a reflection of their own value systems. For the latter, roughness was an inherent part of life.

Football drew mixed reactions from women. Some idolized football heroes, while others agreed with men like President Teddy Roosevelt, who saw football as a necessary antidote to the increasing feminization of culture. As middle-class boys spent more time with their mothers and with female schoolteachers, male leaders feared the potential loss of virility, aggressiveness, and martial spirit that characterized American competitiveness. The Georgia legislature moved to ban the sport when one of its players died in an 1897 game with Virginia—until the player's mother protested the proposal. But when four players died in separate incidents on the same day in 1909, mothers railed against the collegiate emphasis on football, the anti-intellectualism associated with the game, and the ongoing drive for victories and commercial profits, as well as the brutality. In 1907, a millionaire heiress, Anna Jeanes, died and left her estate worth millions in coal and mineral rights to Swarthmore College on the condition that it abolish its athletic program. The gift marked the most prominent effort by a woman to transform the commercialized patriarchal ideology of sport

People & Places

William George "Gilbert" Patten

William George "Gilbert" Patten (1866–1945) published his first short story at the age of 20, setting him on a career as a writer. Employed by *Tip Top Weekly*, a boys' magazine, and adopting the pseudonym of Burt L. Standish, he created a fictional hero, whom he named Frank Merriwell, for a short story in 1896. The character became so famous that Patten continued to portray his idealistic champion as a role model for youth for the next 17 years as a student at Yale, often engaged in last-second heroics on the athletic field, depending on the season of sport. Merriwell not only excelled in sports but also solved ethical dilemmas with equal ease. American youth followed his exploits regularly, with *Tip Top* claiming a circulation of two hundred thousand weekly. Patten would write more than two hundred novels, and the Merriwell character was even featured in two movies.

that had become fixated among boards of trustees and alumni. The Swarthmore president suspended play for a year but finally declined the gift rather than forgo competition. The sanctity of the game as a male bastion—and the projection of its aggressive, militaristic virtues as American cultural characteristics—overrode concerns about brutality and commercialization.

Recreational Spaces

Reformers sought to alleviate the urban ills of pollution, overcrowding, and disease by restructuring the teeming cities and bringing a measure of aid and relief to their inhabitants. Children, who were most at risk, elicited particular concern and were the focus of Progressive assimilation efforts. Whereas children commonly played on their own in streets, alleys, and vacant lots, Progressive plans called for playgrounds, parks, and ball fields with adult supervision. The initiative started modestly when Bostonians provided a sand garden at the Parmenter Street Chapel in 1885. Within two years, the city was offering 11 sandlots to meet the needs of small children, and Philadelphia and New York soon expanded upon the concept to construct small parks. Although some immigrant parents welcomed such safe play spaces in the neighborhood, others opposed the interventions of well-meaning Progressive reformers. Play spaces such as settlement houses, parks, and playgrounds were controlled and supervised by Anglo-American men and women whose influence over children might undermine parental authority. In fact, a number of intended beneficiaries—American Indians, immigrant ethnic groups, women from diverse backgrounds, and members of the working class—did not readily or entirely accept the dominant WASP vision, which generated social tensions and political debate.

Settlement Houses

Settlement house workers, often allied with and supported by socialites and commercial interests, attempted to shape cities in accord with their particular visions of order, efficiency, and morality. As part of the Americanization process, reformers founded settlement houses in the urban immigrant neighborhoods of New York, Boston, Chicago, Detroit, Philadelphia, and other cities. They believed they might fashion a more homogeneous society and bridge the class and social divisions created by the capitalistic industrial process. Reformers situated settlement houses squarely in teeming ethnic neighborhoods to engage residents in their assimilation programs. The settlements provided educational classes and an orientation to American society, and programs included sport and physical training—promoted as alternatives to the immoral and unhealthy amusements available in city life—along with English instruction, civics classes, vocational education, stenography for women, clubs, and other activities that reformers deemed wholesome and appropriate.

Hull House in Chicago is one example of a settlement house aimed at assisting families in an immigrant ghetto. It was founded by Jane Addams, one of the first generation of college-educated women, and she eschewed the traditional roles for women. After touring Europe and observing the social work being done in the slums of London, Addams returned to Chicago in 1889 and, along with Ellen Gates Starr, her college friend, she opened Hull House that year to provide assistance and education to myriad indigent European Americans. Typical of most settlement settings, the Hull

House area housed seventy thousand residents representing 18 nationalities. The average family of five members lived in three (or fewer) rooms and subsisted on a weekly income of $5 (Ely 17–21). Addams used her considerable social contacts to provide funding for her charitable and social programs in an attempt to acculturate members of diverse ethnic minorities, despite opposition by Irish American politicians who controlled the ethnic vote. Her initial attempts to introduce high culture through art classes drew few participants, but the kindergarten provided much-needed childcare. With the support of wealthy patrons who questioned the excesses of the capitalist system or exhibited charitable motives, Hull House expanded its programs and facilities, attracting youth to its play spaces and sponsoring athletic teams for boys and girls.

To escape the steamy Chicago summers, Addams and her staff also took immigrant children and adults on excursions to experience outdoor sports. Bowen Park in Waukegan, Illinois, became the summer retreat for children and adults of Jane Addams' Hull House Association, organized in 1895. In this natural setting away from the density of Chicago, Hull House residents found a wholesome retreat where they engaged in sports and outdoor recreation activities such as tennis, swimming, walking, basketball, and baseball.

Churches, other religious organizations, and social agencies soon copied the Hull House model, founding 68 settlement houses in Chicago alone by 1917. Other municipalities in densely populated urban areas embarked on similar quests that emphasized sport as a means of assimilation and acculturation. As in Chicago, New York social workers such as Stanton Coit, Lillian Wald, and Mary Simkhovitch ran settlement houses in blighted areas. Operating much like Jane Addams, Wald founded the popular Henry Street settlement in 1895 with the aid of philanthropists. Reformers in other cities soon initiated similar ventures, and by 1910 nearly four hundred settlements cared for needy residents in American communities (Fass 762).

Despite their charity, settlement houses displayed a distinctly middle-class, WASP-oriented value system that was not always intelligible to—and was often at odds with—the religious and working-class cultures of ethnic immigrant groups. As a result, Catholics and Jews countered with their own programs. Wealthy German Jews who had assimilated into the American capitalist system but wished to maintain their religious

People & Places

Chicago Hebrew Institute

One example of a prominent Jewish settlement house was the Chicago Hebrew Institute, organized in November 1903 to promote the moral, physical, religious, and civic welfare of Jewish immigrants in America. It served as a key institution in the Americanization of Eastern European immigrants, offering a comprehensive range of classes in citizenship, English, commerce, domestic science, Jewish culture, literature, art, physical culture, drama, and music; it also featured one of the best athletic departments of the early 1900s. Harry Berkman, athletic director from 1908 to 1923, explained the institute's approach in a 1913 newspaper article: "Developing the body as well as the mind is a religion with us. . . . We train the boys and girls to be self-reliant, independent, and on the square in everything" ("'Good, Clean Sport'" n.p.).

The sports programs proved to be one of the primary means for gaining respect and a measure of acceptance in American society, and the Institute produced Jewish champions in several sports. Its extensive athletic fields and splendid facilities attracted males and females of all ages, with more than 113,000 program participants in 1913 alone (*Chicago Hebrew Institute Observer*). Journalist Bertha A. Loeb, writing in the American Jewish paper *The Sentinel* in 1914, asserted that the "undersized, anaemic 'Jewish weakling' will soon be a recollection of by-gone days" (qtd. in Borish, "Athletic Activities" 253). The Chicago Hebrew Institute's wrestling team won the Amateur Athletic Federation championship in 1911 by defeating other athletic clubs and the YMCA. Benjamin Reuben, a five-time Amateur Athletic Union (AAU) wrestling champion, represented the United States, along with a Chicago Hebrew Institute teammate, in the 1920 Olympic Games in Antwerp, Belgium (Gems, "The Rise of Sport" 152–153). Jewish women also excelled at sport. In 1921, the girls' basketball team went 26-0 and won the Central AAU Girls' Basketball Championship. That same year, the girls' swimming team, coached by a Danish Olympian, won the open city swimming championship of Chicago.

faith endeavored to integrate their more orthodox Eastern European brethren into modern American society by founding their own settlement houses in New York, Milwaukee, Boston, Pittsburgh, and Chicago (Borish, "Women").

Playgrounds

Settlement house directors such as Jane Addams and Lillian Wald joined their concerns about health issues with those of physicians Luther Gulick and Henry Curtis in a Washington, D.C., conference that produced the Playground Association of America (PAA) in 1906. The PAA directed national efforts to incorporate supervised play and sport as wholesome ways to achieve the moral and civic education of youth. Curtis (a former student of G. Stanley Hall) and Gulick (who taught at the YMCA training school and organized New York's Public Schools Athletic League) adhered to the psychological theory of play as a scientific rationale for their use of sport and their call for appropriate play spaces. Jane Addams fostered the concept of pragmatic experimentation, invoking John Dewey's belief in learning by doing. Dewey, a philosophy professor at the University of Chicago, became a Hull House trustee in 1897, and support from such an eminent personage provided a great impetus to the playground movement. By 1917, reformers counted 3,940 playgrounds in the United States (Gorn and Goldstein 177), and 504 American cities offered recreational programs, most of them modeled on the Chicago plan (Riess, *Sport* 142).

The Chicago plan included trained park directors and a watchful police officer or assistant to ensure proper play and lessons in Americanization. Women offered summertime kindergarten and craft classes for girls, while a professional coach instructed the boys in sports skills. In 1905, the Chicago Parks Commission optimistically reported that "this feature of the playground work has saved many a young man, by drawing him away from bad companions and the vicious atmosphere of saloons and dance halls" (*A Plea for Playgrounds* 17). The city took further steps to attract boys and girls by constructing field houses in the parks, and by 1904 these large buildings served as community centers, with meeting and craft rooms, separate gyms for boys and girls, playgrounds, and even swimming pools in some cases. The field house concept provided for year-round usage, especially during the winter months, when staff members had previously had fewer opportunities to inculcate Progressive values in the neighborhood children. Many municipalities then copied the Chicago model of year-round usage of facilities under trained adult supervisors.

In New York City, Mayor Abram Hewitt campaigned in 1887 for parks and public baths to serve

Dvorak Park, located on the Lower West Side of Chicago and named after Czech composer Antonin Dvorak (1841–1904), was one of several Chicago playgrounds.

Courtesy of John Graf.

the needs of poor residents. Although he managed a $1 million subsidy from the state government, real park development began with the administration of Mayor William Strong in 1896. Strong also built recreational piers along the waterfront, and the Board of Education required that its schools have playgrounds (some of which were constructed on the schools' fenced rooftops). By 1905, New York schools were home to more than 100 playgrounds, and the city operated 15 municipal baths, but even this proved inadequate (Riess, *City* 136). The playgrounds accommodated less than 10 percent of the children, and youth gangs had their own agenda, using the parks as headquarters for gambling, fighting, and criminal activities, thus thwarting reformers' efforts to socially control recalcitrant youth (Riess, *Sport* 142).

Still, Clarence Rainwater, director of Chicago's playgrounds, believed that such spaces gave the authorities "the opportunity to gain control of 80 percent of the population during the 64 hours per week when even laborers are at leisure" (Hogan 70). E.B. DeGroot, athletic director of the city's South Park District, instructed his staff to "bring about order and esprit de corps, to teach obedience to authority and instant execution of orders" (Halsey 32). In 1908, sociologist Allen T. Burns concluded that the Chicago system had reduced delinquency by more than 28 percent but admitted that prevention did not constitute reformation (Halsey 34). The desire for tight control of unruly juveniles also led Chicago to establish the first juvenile court in the United States in 1900 as a way to address delinquent behavior. The strict supervision of playgrounds and athletic fields by urban playground workers and social workers was meant to prevent youth from getting into trouble or skipping school by instilling WASP-oriented, middle-class standards, but youngsters continued to challenge the tight control of city spaces.

Parks

The adoption of the Chicago model throughout the United States brought some resolution to a contentious debate that had persisted throughout the latter half of the nineteenth century over the proper usage of parks. Early park advocates agreed on the need for open spaces and fresh air in the congested urban environments, but class interests collided in determining the nature and design of recreational spaces. Wealthy park patrons proposed and sponsored amenities and facilities in the parks—such as museums, zoos, libraries, and art galleries—that reflected their own interests in education and high culture. In such environments, in order to maintain the aesthetic ambience and the sense of order and respect, authorities forbade even walking on the grass. The laborers of the working class, on the other hand, wanted to make more active use of park acreage.

By the 1870s, Sunday picnic crowds numbered as high as thirty thousand in Chicago's massive Lincoln Park, and ball players, cyclists, horse racers, and tennis players all defied orders to "Keep Off the Grass." In 1904, the Chicago Parks Commission recorded more than a million users of the city's playgrounds, but not all were deemed desirable, and some failed to learn the prescribed

People & Places

Luther Halsey Gulick

Born to a missionary family in Hawaii, Luther Halsey Gulick (1865–1918) returned to the continental United States for his collegiate education, earning his medical degree from New York University in 1889. By that time he had already established the physical education department at Springfield College, which served as the training school for YMCA instructors. There he instructed James Naismith, who in 1891 was tasked with the assignment of developing a winter game to busy the young men, resulting in the sport of basketball.

By 1900, Gulick moved on to New York, where he became the director of physical training in the public schools and established the Public Schools Athletic League in 1903. He served as the national president of the American Physical Education Association from 1903 to 1906 and as president of the Playground Association of America in 1907. In 1912, he and his wife formed Camp Fire Girls of America as a female correlate to the Boy Scouts organization. Gulick was an instrumental leader in a wide-ranging effort to establish physical education and sport as integral components of the curriculum during the Progressive Era. The Gulick Award, established in 1923, is the highest honor given to members of the American Alliance for Health, Physical Education, Recreation and Dance (now SHAPE America).

lessons of the playground supervisors (*A Plea for Playgrounds* 17). For example, football games had to be discontinued because of the rough tactics employed by older boys. Some middle-class interests gained greater favor, however, and they claimed space for their games. In 1885, Central Park in New York City featured 30 tennis courts, and by 1915 Chicago had 300 just in its South Parks system, one of three separate park administrations in that city. Van Cortland Park in New York opened a public golf site in 1895, and public golf courses arrived in Boston's Franklin Park in 1898. By 1910, only 24 public links existed in the United States. These public golf courses enabled affordable play for middle-class participants and began to diminish the elite status of the game (Riess, *City* 62). As urban parks increasingly accommodated the interests of the middle and working classes, the wealthy sought more exclusive environs for their recreational practices.

Racetracks

Before the advent of country clubs, elites enjoyed their leisure time at opulent racetracks. In Chicago, the horse-racing center of the Midwest, the lavish Washington Park Jockey Club was opened in 1884 with General Philip Sheridan as its president. By 1892, 96 of Chicago's 278 millionaires held membership in the organization, and entry required a unanimous vote of the executive council. Its 500 members were acknowledged to be worth $300 million, and they built a $50,000 clubhouse reserved for the upper echelon of society and a $40,000 grandstand. The private clubhouse included a café, a dozen dining rooms, a wine room, a billiard parlor, sleeping rooms, and servants' quarters in the attic. An expansive veranda and balcony decorated the exterior, and two rooftop observatories afforded sweeping vistas. The club's American Derby proved to be the highlight of the social season, as women displayed their finery and men basked in their ownership of thoroughbreds. Such grand spectacles permitted the wealthy to demonstrate their power, privilege, and status to fellow citizens and to one another. Sociologist Thorstein Veblen labeled such demeanor "conspicuous consumption"—a means to construct social-class lines in a supposedly classless democracy. Members of the sport's plebeian

Members of the upper classes wanted aesthetic parks suitable for repose and reflection. In its heyday, Ellis Park, one of the oldest parks in Chicago, contained fountains, large trees, well-manicured lawns, and pathways for strolling (Graf 59).

Courtesy of John Graf.

following gawked at the elites in their finery, thus reinforcing the class distinctions.

At the elite tracks, expensive thoroughbreds competed for stakes as high as $50,000. Railway lines, trolley cars, and wide boulevards permitted even the lower classes to attend and, more important, wager on the races. The incessant gambling led to corruption at many tracks, and track owners formed a Board of Control in 1891 to address such abuses. In 1894, the sport's leaders formed the Jockey Club to further regulate conduct by codifying rules, licensing jockeys, registering horses, and appointing proper officials. The following year, the New York legislature initiated a racing commission to augment state control. Despite such supervision, problems persisted, and states enacted periodic bans on horse racing throughout the remainder of the Progressive Era. The restrictions, however, merely inconvenienced the wealthy, who transferred their betting interests to golf, tennis, cards, and other activities at their private country clubs.

In the West, horse racing assumed different forms and carried different class connotations. Since wealthy owners lived in the East, near top racing sites, a lack of thoroughbreds in the West forced a reliance on work animals, requiring shorter competitive distances. Quarter horses specialized in short sprints or raced in quarter- or half-mile (0.4- or 0.8-kilometer) events. As early as 1883, cowboys tested their work skills in competitive rodeos in Pecos, Texas, and early contests offered money prizes and accepted wagers on horse races, calf roping, bronco riding, and even dancing. Such work-related skills tested the physicality of participants—a very different approach from that employed by the wealthy thoroughbred owners of the East. By 1888, the rodeo concept appeared as far west as Prescott, Arizona, and 1897 saw the first edition of the annual Cheyenne Frontier Days festival, which by 1900 offered separate competitive horse races for men, women, and American Indians. The Native American participants displayed their lost ferocity in a war dance, and the white settlers enjoyed an evening with an orchestra at a grand ball. Other exhibitions of technology and civilization at the festival included a baseball game and a parachutist who jumped from a hot air balloon. Conducted in conjunction with the local newspaper and the Union Pacific Railway, the celebration drew competitors and spectators (in the thousands) from throughout the West by creating a commercialized civic spectacle that merged work skills with recreation and promoted particular Western sport forms and regional identity.

Country Clubs

In the more congested cities of the East and Midwest, upper-class Americans seeking a place to maintain their elite status also reorganized metropolitan spaces by developing country clubs in outlying areas, making them inaccessible to all but the elites by virtue of both location and steep membership fees, thus further establishing the social stature of participants. As a social and sporting haven for the rich, country clubs upheld their exclusive membership by excluding all but white, Anglo-Saxon, Protestant applicants. Golf and tennis, in particular, appealed to those wishing to maintain elite status.

Because golf required expensive equipment and a large parcel of land, it carried distinct class connotations. Although played in Scotland for centuries, the sport arrived in the United States relatively late. Scotsmen introduced the game in the 1880s and, led by John Reid, founded the St. Andrew's Golf Club in 1888 with a primitive course. Three years later, wealthy New Yorkers built a nine-hole course at Shinnecock Hills on Coney Island. Charles Macdonald, a second-generation Scotsman and an organizer of the Chicago Golf Club in 1893, established himself as a course architect. His Chicago club built the first 18-hole course in the United States. Other Scots served as teaching professionals and equipment manufacturers. Socialites formed country clubs with restrictive membership covenants where boys toted their bags as caddies.

National tournaments appeared in 1894, and five clubs formed the United States Golf Association in 1895 as a governing body. The first U.S. Open was held at the Newport Country Club in October of that year, and a women's tournament followed only a month later at the Meadowbrook Club on Long Island. Since it was an open tournament, amateurs and professionals alike could compete, and among the golfers in the second U.S. Open at Shinnecock Hills were John Shippen, an African American who had learned the game as a caddie, and Oscar Bunn, a Shinnecock Indian, whose tribe had helped build the course. When the white players protested and threatened a walkout, club president Theodore Havemeyer courageously upheld the right of Shippen and Bunn to compete—a bold move that contrasted starkly with the typical social conditions for minorities at that time. The Intercollegiate Golf Association was formed in 1897, and by the end of the century there were enough clubs on the West Coast to form the Southern California Golf Association. Golf course

Golf soon became the sport of choice for American presidents, such as avid golfer William Howard Taft, who wished to portray a vigorous image.

Image courtesy of Library of Congress, LC-USZ62-41721.

development in the warmer Southeastern states allowed the wealthy to pursue their pastime on a year-round basis.

Like golf, tennis required an expanse of land on which to build a court or courts. Adopted from the British, it, too, provided an aristocratic pretense, and it soon became a favorite pastime of upper-class men, and then women, who played on the lawns of country clubs. At the Seabright Lawn Tennis and Cricket Club, organized in Rumson, New Jersey, in 1877, tennis became a major focal point of the sporting scene. One of the earliest clubs in the United States, it hosted well-known American and international tennis players in the Seabright Invitational Tournament starting in 1884 (women's competition was added in 1920). The site consisted of a cricket crease from England and three tennis courts in 1886, and substantial additions brought the total to 22 tennis courts by 1910.

Back-to-Nature Movement

City dwellers' concerns about moral and physical well-being fostered an outdoor recreation movement during the latter half of the nineteenth century. Many perceived the overcrowded cities as dirty slums teeming with infection and overridden by vice and corruption. Moreover, the increasing number of white-collar, middle-class occupations seemed to produce increased stress, as well as the confounding condition known as neurasthenia (nervous breakdown) that affected sedentary workers. The West and outlying areas seemed more attractive and healthier to urban residents beset by grime and pollution in the industrial cities, and those who could afford it built palatial homes in areas away from the city, while others sought relief in the back-to-nature movement that encouraged outdoor pursuits and wilderness excursions. The confrontation with nature and the elements, it was thought, required hardiness and sometimes courage, and thus might restore one's vigor and manhood.

Riflery originally served a utilitarian function for sustenance, but it had little use other than sport in the crowded cities, where what were once outdoor recreations soon became competitive events. The National Rifle Club was organized as early as 1858, and many immigrant and labor groups formed their own militias for drill and marksmanship practice. Target matches for men and women were being held by the 1870s, and in 1888 George Ligowsky invented the first practical clay pigeon, allowing for trapshooting championships. Such competitive simulations of hunting merged modern technology with premodern pastimes to ease the ills of the urbanization process. Others distanced themselves from the cities by hiking, fishing, camping, or attempting to conquer natural impediments through mountaineering.

European immigrants brought their winter pastimes with them to America, but informal ice-skating contests took on greater regulation and standardization with the formation of the American Skating Congress in 1868. Scottish immigrants introduced speedskating contests to the United States, and the first national championship for men was staged in 1889. The International Skating Union, organized in 1892, offered the first world championship that winter in Amsterdam. Competition for female speedskaters did not develop until the twentieth century. The National Amateur Skating Union, which had been organized in 1886, merged with the International Skating Union in 1907 as the governing body for both speedskating and figure skating.

Snowshoeing and skiing served a practical function during the winter months and allowed particular ethnic groups to retain their traditional sports. Scandinavians brought skiing techniques to America as a recreational activity, but during the mid-century California Gold Rush, skiers delivered the winter mail to mining camps. Downhill skiing

The winter sports introduced to the United States by Nordic immigrants produced a reverse cultural flow as they were adopted by Americans in the northern states.
Image courtesy of Library of Congress, LC-USZ62-135333.

competitions for both men and women ensued, and the immigrants who settled in the northern areas of the Midwest began to hold organized competitions by the 1890s. The first tournament of the United States Ski Club took place at Ishpeming, Michigan, in 1891. The next year, the Aurora Club of Red Wing, Minnesota, used the Ishpeming site for a ski jumping exhibition that promoted Scandinavian culture.

Meanwhile, adapting rules from rugby and lacrosse, Canadians had produced a version of ice hockey by the 1870s. Played outdoors on frozen waterways when weather permitted, it became a Canadian favorite. In the United States, Yale and Johns Hopkins universities adopted the game by 1893, and New York teams formed an amateur league in 1896. A Baltimore league appeared a year later, followed by creation of the Intercollegiate Hockey League in 1898 and a professional league in 1903, but the organization of such winter sports further removed them from their rural connotations and favored urban and middle-class standards of practice. By the 1890s, indoor ice rinks in New York City fostered a transition from the rural pastime to an urban game (Kirsch, Harris, and Nolte 231), and the ongoing organization of hockey by

governing bodies created regulations and rules that coincided with and promoted sportification (the competitive organization of previously recreational activities).

Other outdoor sports, such as camping, fishing, boating, and hiking, attracted numerous practitioners to remote areas. For them, fresh air meant health and peaceful solace. Perhaps the most famous of such groups, the Boone and Crockett Club, numbered one hundred members, including Theodore Roosevelt, who engaged in big game hunting and wilderness adventures. Such excursions required adequate leisure time and expendable income, limiting these sport forms to wealthy participants. As president, Roosevelt designated millions of acres as federal reserves and created 18 national monuments to preserve historic sites, natural resources, and areas of particular beauty intended for future generations and all classes. In 1916, President Woodrow Wilson authorized the National Park Service to manage the public lands, but private entrepreneurs and railroad companies had already begun operating tours and hotels in many of the most scenic locations. The lack of sufficient travel funds or vacation time denied such opportunities to most workers, however, restricting the growing tourism industry to middle- and upper-class prospects.

Cities, however, began efforts to conserve nearby natural areas that were somewhat more accessible to laborers. Famed architect Daniel Burnham developed city plans for Washington, D.C., Cleveland, San Francisco, Chicago, and even Manila and Baguio, the capital and summer haven, respectively, of Americans in the (at that time) U.S. colony of the Philippines. In Chicago, Burnham provided an integrated design for parks and playgrounds, with the lakefront safeguarded as public space. Forest preserves ringed the perimeter of the city, and wide boulevards strategically connected its parts via public transport systems. Still, the outer reaches remained inaccessible for most of the urban poor.

Ethnic Groups

Germans were among the first of the large waves of Europeans to migrate to America in the wake of the failed revolution of 1848. Many of them expected to return to their homeland once a republic had been established, but that would not occur for decades and so they remained in the United States, where they gained the freedom and rights unavailable in Germany. Germans began organizing their nationalistic Turner gymnastics clubs shortly after their arrival, and German saloons, unlike their American counterparts that catered to the bachelor subculture, offered entertainment for the whole family. In the Midwestern cities, Germans assumed a prominent role in civic affairs. By 1885 they managed to adopt the German Turner system as the official physical education program in the Chicago public schools, and the German language was taught as part of the curriculum (Riess, "Introduction"; Gems, *Windy*).

Germans were instrumental in the labor movement of the late nineteenth century, and many advocated socialist political views. The workers maintained their own militia units for defense, which posed a threat to employers and nativist authorities. Tens of thousands of workers and their supporters attended labor rallies in the cities. As early as 1878, the socialists elected their candidates to the Illinois legislature, and their mayoral candidate in Chicago won 20 percent of the vote. Milwaukee would elect a socialist as mayor in 1910, and dozens of smaller communities did so by 1913. When authorities in Chicago denied the socialists access to public meeting places, the Turner halls opened their doors. The number of socialist groups

in Chicago alone had grown to 26 by 1886, and the infamous Haymarket Massacre occurred in the city that year when police confronted a group of protestors, who retaliated by throwing a bomb that killed eight and wounded another 66. Three Turners were among the six Germans and two other anarchists arrested and sentenced to death in a decidedly partial trial that made them international martyrs (Riess, "Introduction"; Gems, *Windy*).

By 1890 Chicago counted 34 Turner societies with five thousand members and, a year later, three hundred labor unions with sixty thousand members (Riess, "Introduction"; Gems, *Windy* 30). Although labor discontent lingered for years afterward, sport helped alleviate some tensions. Turner clubs fractured over their support for socialism, and German youth increasingly adopted American sport forms in lieu of gymnastics. Twenty-three German Turner clubs were prominent competitors at the 1904 Olympic Games in St. Louis, and the Buffalo Germans basketball team from Buffalo, New York, composed entirely of German players, won the basketball tournament and then turned professional (Gems, "The Chicago Turners"). Among baseball players, Honus (Johannes) Wagner exemplified the transition to American sport as a top star in the National League for the Pittsburgh Pirates, where he garnered a salary of $10,000 by 1908, more than 10 times the annual earnings of the average American (Baseball's Milestone Contracts).

The American entry into World War I in 1917 sounded the death knell for German culture in the United States. Germans were ostracized and the media depicted them as enemies. They faced persecution and imprisonment if accused of being traitors or disloyal in their allegiance. The German language and the Turner physical education system were eliminated from school curriculums, although some Turner societies continued to conduct meetings in their ancestral tongue into the 1930s. By that time only six Turner clubs remained in Chicago as suppression and repression forced assimilation and sport Americanized the children of former dissidents (Gems, "The Chicago Turners").

Czechs, also known as Bohemians, formed Sokols, nationalistic gymnastics organizations similar to the German Turners, as early as 1862 in Prague and soon established their ethnic clubs in the United States (St. Louis, 1865; Chicago, 1866; and New York, 1867). By 1884 a National Sokol Union was founded in Chicago largely by Czech freethinkers (atheists), known as reds. Catholic Czechs, designated as blues, organized other units. The Sokols supported baseball teams as early as the 1880s, and despite their religious viewpoints, reds and blues competed against each other. The atheist clubs, unlike their paternalistic counterparts, differed in their roles allotted to women. Women formed their own clubs as early as 1870 and served in official capacities, organizing dances, picnics, theatrical productions, and athletic events as fundraisers for socialist causes. Some women campaigned for suffrage rights, and Bohemian feminists in Chicago even published their own newspaper. Women also organized their own gymnastics classes and exhibitions and participated in fencing bouts and cycling clubs (Riess, "Introduction"; Gems, "Sport and the Americanization").

The Sokols, like the German Turners, held national *slets*, or gymnastics festivals, in which groups traveled to the host city to promote their ethnic values and activities. Sokol members also returned to Europe for the national slets held in their homeland every six years, thus retaining and reinforcing ties with the motherland and retarding assimilation efforts of the Progressive reformers in the United States.

During the 1910s, Czechs in America adopted the game of soccer, which had become popular in Europe, and formed clubs to compete against other ethnic teams. By 1917, Chicago Czechs had enough teams to form their own league. Although the second generation of Czech youth, born in the United States, was increasingly attracted to American sport forms, such transatlantic ties "allowed ethnics to selectively participate in the American system while retaining their religious and cultural values (Riess, "Introduction"; Gems, *Windy* 226).

Like the Germans and Czechs, Poles also formed nationalistic gymnastics clubs, known as Falcons, in 1867 and transferred them to America. So many Poles migrated to the United States that Chicago eventually became the second most populous Polish city (after Warsaw). The Poles differed from the Czechs, however, in their strict adherence to Catholicism. In the United States, they formed Polish communities around their parish churches. St. Stanislaus Kostka Church in Chicago would become among the world's largest, with as many as fifty thousand parishioners. Such ethnic parishes were often headed by Old World clergy who reinforced European languages, customs, and values. Although such ethnic leaders fostered provincialism, others advocated assimilation. Poles elected their own alderman, August Kowalski, to the Chicago city council in 1888, and by 1900 Kowalski organized an American football team at the parish to compete with other ethnic teams,

confusing their opponents by calling their signals in Polish. A three-year winning streak reinforced Polish pride as it engaged parishioners in the mainstream American culture.

Reflecting that pride, the local baseball team changed its name to the Kosciuszko Colts in 1906 in reference to the Polish military hero Thaddeus Kosciuszko, who served with the American forces during the Revolutionary War, an indication of the gradual shift in identity. By 1908 the team included Irish, German, and Swedish players as the importance of winning began to surpass ethnic solidarity. By World War I, Poles would become ardent supporters of the American cause and fight for Polish independence from Germany. When the Polish Falcons issued a call to arms in Chicago, 215,000 responded (Gems, "Sport and the Americanization"; Gems, *Windy*).

Jews had faced the lack of a homeland and widespread persecution in Europe for centuries. Although some German Jews had come to the United States as early as the 1840s, vast numbers of eastern European and Russian Jews fled pogroms in the latter decades of the nineteenth century. In America they found religious freedom but a lack of acceptance. Their religion valued scholarly achievement rather than physicality, making Jewish children easy prey for ethnic bullies. By necessity Jews had to fight to defend themselves, spawning a host of professional boxers that dethroned many of the Irish champions. As early as 1901, Harry Harris captured the bantamweight championship, and by 1917 Benny Leonard (Leiner) became a Jewish hero as the lightweight champion, dispelling any notions of Jewish debility.

The German Jews who had preceded their eastern European brethren had earned a great deal of success if not full acceptance by the time the Orthodox members arrived in America. Worried that the latecomers might jeopardize their social and economic status, the German Jews promoted and financially supported settlement houses in the immigrant communities to foster their assimilation, particularly in the large Jewish enclaves of New York and Chicago. The Chicago Hebrew Institute boasted some of the finest athletic facilities in the nation, which were utilized by Jews and gentiles alike. Its teams won numerous championships and concurrent respect from other ethnic minorities; and by 1920 Benjamin Reuben, its champion wrestler, competed for the United States Olympic team, a mark of more rapid assimilation than other ethnic groups.

Italians, among the largest group of immigrants from 1880 to 1920, were slower to assimilate.

Largely illiterate peasants from a recently liberated country, they had no sense of a national identity and little sporting culture. Perceived as nonwhites by American nativists, they were stigmatized and repressed. They did, however, possess the physicality necessary for rural agricultural work, which would find expression in America on construction sites and lend itself to the development of sports skills. Italian parents were recalcitrant in their adherence to child labor laws because of the need for increasing family income and sustenance; but with eventual exposure to athletic competition in the public schools, Italian children took readily to the physical activities.

As early as the 1890s, Ed Abbaticchio, the son of Italian immigrants, became one of the first professional football players in the United States as a fullback and punter for the Latrobe, Pennsylvania, team. In the summers he played professional baseball, where he earned as much as $5,000—evidence of the social mobility possible for top athletes. By the 1910s, Ping Bodie (Francesco Pizzolo) had gained stardom as a slugging outfielder in the American League; but his father

International Perspective
The Hiking Movement—a Youth Initiative

In the wake of industrialization and the social changes taking place in Western countries, new occupations developed and work changed fundamentally. This led to higher demands on the skills of employees, which made a prolongation of education necessary. Thus, a new age group—youth—emerged, a cohort of young adults with specific wishes, needs, and behavior patterns. Among the responses to the growing significance of childhood and youth were organizations and initiatives aimed at supervision and education. One of these initiatives was the Scout Movement, which spread to the United States from its origin in England. With the help of outdoor skills, especially camping and hiking, the movement's aim was to train boy and girl scouts to become good citizens. Scout leaders were invariably adults.

In Europe, by contrast, a youth movement arose with the motto "Youth leads youth," which in Germany grew into a mass movement. The restrictive climate of the German Reich led to generational conflicts, especially in paternalistic and authoritarian middle-class families, and young people reacted with opposition. With a back-to-nature outlook on life, they sought to escape the pressures of bourgeois society, the confines of the cities, and what they perceived as menacing processes of modernization. Hiking, with its promise of freedom and adventure, seemed to offer a way out of a civilization they experienced as oppressive. The hiking movement began in Berlin, the capital of the Reich, at the turn of the century. The hiking craze swiftly spread among the city's bourgeois youth, and in 1901 they formed an association, naming themselves *Wandervögel* (migrating birds). A similar movement emerged in France with a focus in Normandy and Brittany.

In Germany, the Berlin group was the nucleus of a large movement that included a huge number of groups, some more strictly organized and others less so. Nonetheless, the many thousands of *Wandervögel* were bound together by a sense of belonging and pursued similar practices and forms of organization. The leaders were young adults whom the others were willing to follow on account of their personal authority. Their main activity was hiking together in a group for days or even weeks on end, an activity which became a self-defined way of life. It was a frugal way of living; they slept in the open or in barns and cooked on campfires. Instead of stiff shirt-fronts and collars, the *Wandervögel* wore open shirts, and instead of polished boots they wore sandals. They had a longing for a glorified past, which they tried to re-create with their songs and folk dances. Although the majority of the *Wandervögel* were young men, some clubs accepted girls and women or even consisted entirely of girls, who set off into the wilds with a young woman as their leader.

In 1913, shortly before the First World War, three thousand Wandervögel took part in a festival along with other reform-oriented youth groups on a hill called the Hoher Meissner in Hesse. With the prospect of war looming, they felt moved to protest against national chauvinism, and their standpoint was summed up in the declaration: "Free German youth wishes to shape its future in self-determination, bearing its own responsibility and faithful to an inner truth." After the German defeat, the youth movement turned into an assemblage of numerous youth groups, some of which were well organized and harbored nationalist sentiments. In 1933, the youth organization of the National Socialists (Nazis), named the Hitler Youth, pressed their claim to be the sole representatives of all young people. All other groups were prohibited.

Information from Laqueur, Walter. Young Germany: A History of the German Youth Movement. New York: Basic Books, 1962.

disowned him for Anglicizing his name, a dilemma faced by others in the assimilation process. As early as 1899 an Italian blacksmith, Lawrence Brignoli(a), won the Boston Marathon, and Italians in America began to develop a sense of an Italian identity. In 1912 an Italian immigrant, Gaston Strobino, won a bronze medal in the Olympic marathon running for the American team, marking a gradual transition in identity. By World War I Italian fighters, often assuming Irish aliases, would begin to supplant the Irish and Jewish boxers as world champions in a sport that rewarded their strength and endurance (Gems, *Sport*).

Body Culture

The transition in gender norms affected both men and women as they departed from Victorian standards of decorum and strict morality. The body became a source of pleasure and eroticism. Just as feats of prowess glorified the physical, classical Greek sculpture was hailed as exemplifying male morphological ideals. Scientists viewed the body as a machine that might be made more efficient and effective, and sport performance was used to measure human capabilities. Sport—in schools, parks, playgrounds, settlement houses, and even colonial territories—served the purposes of Americanization, leadership training, and character development. As some sought the perfection of the body, others sought the reparation of sickly ones, or simply good health in specialized treatment centers.

The Perfect Body

Eugen Sandow, born Friederich Wilhelm Mueller, in Prussia, symbolized the international ideological transition. He began his career as a circus performer and acrobat before graduating to weight-lifting stunts and exhibitions in vaudeville shows and theatrical tours. Sandow portrayed his physique as a work of art, carefully marketed as the new standard of health and vitality. His chiseled body had an erotic appeal, and he posed nearly nude, wearing only loincloths or simple fig leafs to cover his genitals. At the Chicago World's Fair of 1893, he became an American sensation, and one wealthy socialite paid $300 to feel his muscles in a private exhibition. Sandow made global tours thereafter. He organized the first bodybuilding competition in London in 1901 and opened a chain of physical culture studios to train men in pursuit of the new ideal in body composition. Sandow

expanded his enterprise to include selling health products and exercise devices, and his books promised fitness, vitality, and muscular development through strength training.

Sandow's counterpart in the United States, Bernarr Macfadden, insisted that "weakness was a crime." He advocated physical fitness through exercise, the consumption of natural rather than processed foods, and a lifestyle that included bodybuilding and outdoor activities. The flamboyant Macfadden railed against prudery, and he organized national contests to determine the most perfectly developed man and woman. These activities brought arrests on obscenity charges, but Macfadden persisted. By 1903, his *Physical Culture* magazine was selling more than one hundred thousand copies per month. The publication endured for more than 50 years, and Macfadden created a publishing empire of books, magazines, and films that made him a millionaire (Ernst). Macfadden's emphasis on natural beauty led him

Eugen Sandow: the idealized male body.

Image courtesy of Library of Congress, LC-USZ62-95729.

to oppose corsets, makeup, high-heeled shoes, and constrictive clothing for women. Contestants in his beauty contests posed in formfitting tights, and their photos in his publications undoubtedly titillated viewers. Macfadden established a health resort in New Jersey; schools to train teachers, coaches, and therapists; and a sanitarium in Battle Creek, Michigan.

Battle Creek Sanitarium

The most important health retreat in Battle Creek, however, gained its fame from its founder, Dr. John Harvey Kellogg. The Battle Creek Sanitarium, built in 1903, was designed as a comprehensive facility for health, exercise, and medicine. It provided a healthy diet to treat dyspepsia (digestive trouble) and offered some sports to help patients improve their bodily health. Thus, health became not only a medical issue but a business concern as well.

The Battle Creek Sanitarium gained worldwide recognition, attracting famous patients and visitors who included athletes, politicians, and other public figures. It housed a swimming pool, gymnasium, and solarium. Kellogg developed a program of "biologic living" and promoted new types of treatment and new foods to improve the health of patients and visitors. He advocated a vegetarian diet and urged patients to abstain from alcohol, tobacco, and fad medicines, preferring instead to help them through healthy diet, physical exercise, outdoor excursions, water therapy, physical therapy, and exposure to proper air, heat, and light. In the kitchen, Kellogg invented the first corn flakes in 1894, launching the cereal industry in Battle Creek. In 1902, a huge fire destroyed most of the sanitarium's structures, and the new, larger sanitarium building, five stories high, was constructed in 1903. In this new facility, treatment rooms provided places for men and women to receive therapy, and guests also used indoor gymnasium facilities. The grounds of the Sanitarium included a lovely garden and a lakefront area for outdoor exercise.

President William H. Taft became the hundred-thousandth person to register as a guest in 1911. Other famous people who visited the Sanitarium and used the health and sport facilities in the first decades of the twentieth century included John D. Rockefeller, George Bernard Shaw, Henry Ford, J.C. Penney, Clara Barton, Eleanor Roosevelt, Eddie Cantor, Booker T. Washington, Montgomery Ward, Johnny Weissmuller, Admiral Richard E. Byrd, and William Jennings Bryan. Visitors could participate in indoor or outdoor gymnastics, swimming, biking, boating, horseback riding, hiking, and other athletic activities to achieve vigorous health, and thousands of health-seeking persons came to the institute yearly (Butler).

Sport and Technology

The Progressive Era, with its quest for human and societal improvement, spawned new technologies that affected sporting practices, and this was the beginning of an increasingly close relationship between sport and technology. The Dunlop pneumatic tire, patented in 1881, changed cycling and harness racing. The development of the safety bicycle in 1888 replaced the more dangerous high-wheeler and enabled the setting of numerous speed records. In 1899, Charles Murphy covered a mile (1.6 kilometers) in less than a minute by drafting behind a train. The new bicycle sulkies, with ball-bearing axles, enabled Star Pointer, a pacer, to break the 2-minute barrier for the mile in 1897.

The growing media also served as a primary spur to the growth of sport. Newspapers were increasing in number, circulation, and coverage of sporting events. In addition to the prominence given to boxing in the *National Police Gazette,* the *Spirit of the Times* provided extensive coverage of horse racing and track-and-field competitions. A mechanical typesetting machine became available in 1886, greatly increasing production, and the *Sporting News,* the bible of baseball, appeared that same year. Such publications proved especially popular with the bachelor subculture and gamblers. By the 1890s, the *New York World* newspaper featured a special page devoted to sports, and other papers soon followed suit. By that time, middle-class magazines such as *Harper's Weekly, Outing, Popular Science, Cosmopolitan,* and the *Atlantic Monthly* were among the many that devoted space to sports coverage as sporting practices assumed greater emphasis among the middle class. Ethnic newspapers also reported on baseball games played by German, Czech, Polish, and Jewish teams. Illustrations and photographs enhanced the stories, helping athletes make improvement in technique and performance.

Thomas Edison invented the kinetoscope in 1889, and motion pictures soon followed. Boxing films appeared by 1894 and held great interest for both men and women. Theater owners scheduled matinees to accommodate the large numbers of women attracted to the erotic sight of barely clad young men displaying their physical prowess. The gradual acknowledgment of women's carnal passions, which had long been accepted in and expected of men, moved the mainstream middle-class culture further from Victorian inhibitions of the past.

Thomas Edison's invention of the electric light in 1879 made it possible to provide artificial lighting in sports arenas, and experimentation with night baseball games started as early as 1883. The Chicago World's Fair of 1893 featured electric lighting for evening strolls, and football fans witnessed five night games, all enabled by the new technology. The Olympic Club of New Orleans opened the first modern boxing venue in 1890, and the extensive network of railroads provided for transport from across the country.

In the 1880s, German engineers developed internal combustion engines, which soon led to horseless carriages in the form of automobiles and motorcycles. Frank and Charles Duryea of Springfield, Massachusetts, built the first American model in 1893. In June 1894, the first auto race took place in France (from Paris to Rouen), sponsored by the *Le Petit Journal* newspaper, which offered a $1,000 prize. Larger races from Paris to Bordeaux followed a year later, and the *Chicago Times-Herald* promoted the first American race, with $5,000 in prize money, on November 2, 1895. Only

one vehicle (built and driven by the Duryea brothers) finished the 53-mile (85-kilometer) course.

Motorcycle racing began during the same year, and local promoters built enclosed racecourses in cities such as Atlanta, Daytona Beach, and Indianapolis. Eighty thousand spectators attended the first Indianapolis 500 car race, held in 1911 (Riess, *Sport* 41). Commercial production of cars allowed for a more mobile society and greatly changed the nature of American culture, as the assembly-line production of Henry Ford's Model T and other affordable models made ownership possible for an increasing number of people. A one-cylinder auto producing three horsepower built by Ransom Olds (and called the Oldsmobile) sold for $650. In 1904, Olds sold more than 5,000 vehicles (Foner and Garraty 64–65). Within the decade, human flight was achieved, and air races soon followed.

Modern Olympic Games

Progressive Era idealists tackled substantial issues ranging from body culture to feminism to health reform, but some attempted even grander schemes. In France, a minor nobleman, Pierre de Coubertin, envisioned a more peaceful world and saw

Photography, such as this Muybridge motion photo sequence, greatly enhanced imagery of and research into sport performance.

Image courtesy of Library of Congress, LC-USZ62-103032.

As had been the case with horses, the new horseless carriages were tested on racetracks against competitors.
Image courtesy of Library of Congress, LC-USZ62-100197.

athletics as a means to achieve his goal. Affected by the French loss in the Franco-Prussian War of 1870, he sought a mechanism to restore French vigor and to teach friendship and harmony. He toured both Great Britain and the United States and determined that they derived their strength from their educational systems in general, and their pursuit of athletics in particular. He believed fair competition brought good health, strong values, and improved morality. In 1894, he organized an international athletic conference in Paris and called for a resurrection of the ancient Olympic Games in order to bring individual athletes together in a festival of fellowship and camaraderie.

De Coubertin realized his dream in the first modern Olympics, held at Athens, Greece, in 1896. A chauvinist, he, along with the Greek organizers, refused to let women compete in the scheduled events. Males competed as individuals rather than as representatives of a country, but nationalistic reporters soon began to tally medal counts based on citizenship or political affiliation. Thirteen American athletes answered the initial call, including one swimmer, two marksmen, and ten track-and-field athletes, one of whom quit Harvard in order to make the trip when his request for a leave was denied. This defector, James B. Connolly, won the first event, the triple jump, and the other Americans, from Princeton and the

Boston Athletic Association, nearly monopolized the track-and-field events, but a Greek shepherd, Spiridon Louis, won the marathon. Fellow Greeks showered him with gifts, including free meals, clothes, and haircuts for the rest of his life.

The 1900 Olympics, enveloped within the Paris World's Fair, lost the grandeur and cohesion established in Athens. Many competitors were unaware that they had even participated in anything more than an adjunct to the exposition, which in addition to competitions for men also provided competition for women in tennis, golf, yachting, croquet, hot air ballooning, and equestrian events. Some of the best American male athletes were excluded from the 1900 event finals because they refused to compete on Sundays.

The 1904 Games ran in conjunction with the St. Louis World's Fair, and in the end they amounted to a national competition, as few beyond the American shores made the inland journey. One notable feature of the fair was its Anthropology Days, featuring competitions between various racial and ethnic groups on exhibit in tribal villages.

W.J. McGee, first president of the American Anthropological Association, imported nearly three thousand persons who were deemed less civilized, from various locations around the world, to be displayed in living exhibits. The groups included Native Americans, Alaskan Inuit, Asians, African

International Perspective

Hidden From History—Female Marathon Runners at the Olympic Games in 1896

Baron Pierre de Coubertin, founder of the modern Olympic Games, held the opinion that women should not "sully the Olympic arena with their sweat." The Olympic Games, he thought, should be a men's preserve, a celebration of masculinity. Accordingly, only male athletes were allowed to participate in the first Olympic Games, held in Athens in 1896—at least officially.

Unofficially, two women did participate in the Games and perpetrated further sacrilege by running the marathon, an event especially contrived for the 1896 event. The marathon race was intended to glorify Greek antiquity and enact Greek heroism at a time when Greece had become a small and poor country, still partly occupied by the Turks. It did not matter in the slightest that the "marathon story"—that is, the story of a Greek soldier running from Marathon to Athens in order to proclaim the Greek victory over the Persian army, and of his subsequent death from exhaustion—was a legend based on no historical evidence. For the Greeks, the marathon race was a "place of remembrance," and the victory of native son Spiridon Louis was unquestionably the highlight of the Games.

Whereas Louis became a celebrity, the first female marathon runners remained hidden from history. A young woman who called herself Melpomene wanted to register for the race but was not accepted by the organizing committee. She refused to give up, however, and ran the 26 miles (42 kilometers) from Marathon to Athens in 4 1/2 hours before the official start of the Games. Another woman, Stamatia Rovithi, was so excited about Spiridon Louis' achievement that she decided to follow his example. According to sources, this 35-year-old mother of seven children completed the distance in 5 1/2 hours. She confessed that she could have been faster if she had not done some window shopping along the way. Official textbooks do not mention the two female runners because they participated in the Games without approval. Thus, they do not appear in the official sources and have not become part of the accepted history. Although both runners had proven that women were capable of completing the marathon distance, it took almost 90 years for women to be allowed to participate officially in the event.

Information from Tamini, Noel. "Women Always in the Race." *Olympic Review* (1993): 204–208, 221. www.la84foundation.org/OlympicInformationCenter/OlympicReview/1993/ore308/ORE308a.pdf.

pygmies and Zulu warriors, and South Americans from Patagonia, as well as more than 1,200 Filipinos from the new American colony in the Pacific. In their reconstructed facsimiles of village life, they performed their native dances and produced handicrafts for the amusement of tourists and fairgoers, for whom they appeared to be not only primitive but also exotic.

James E. Sullivan, a founder and secretary of the Amateur Athletic Union, which governed such sporting events in the United States, served as head of the fair's Physical Culture Department. He considered the occasion an opportunity to conduct athletic events among the various peoples, which he and the anthropologists could use to assess their physical abilities and ascertain stages of human evolution. Events consisted of javelin and baseball throws, a shot put, five running races of various distances, both long and high jumps, a 56-pound (25-kilogram) weight throw, a pole climb, a tug-of-war, archery, throwing stones for accuracy,

a bolo throw, and even a mud fight among the pygmies. Other Native Americans who attended American Indian schools—and were considered to be more civilized—demonstrated American team sports such as lacrosse, baseball, track events, and boxing. An American football game resulted in a 38-4 victory for the Carlisle Institute over the Haskell Indian School (Parezo).

Although relatively few of the foreign tribesmen and women agreed to participate, anthropologists took physical measurements and recorded their physical efforts for comparative purposes with the white Olympic athletes. The competitors in the Anthropology Days events were untrained and did not take the competitions seriously, but their marks were recorded as official results. For example, in a sprint event, some competitors stopped before the finish line to wait for slower friends, while others ducked under the tape rather than running through it. Relay races were discarded because runners did not know what to do with the baton. Results were so dismal that a second competition was organized after some practice and money prizes awarded for performance. Most of the events were won by American Indians, who were somewhat more familiar with the activities. Thousands of spectators reportedly witnessed the competitions, and the anthropologists deduced that "primitive men are far inferior to modern Caucasians in both physical and mental development" (Parezo 112).

Western sport forms, unknown to most of the contestants, resulted in hapless, even ludicrous, outcomes that reinforced white beliefs in their own racial superiority (Dyreson, *Making*). George Poage challenged such beliefs, however, as the first African American medal winner, by taking third place in the 200- and 400-meter hurdles. At the same world fair, in the unofficial women's basketball championship, the Native American girls from the Fort Shaw Indian School in Montana overwhelmed all competition, further undercutting the assertion of Anglo-American supremacy.

With Olympic spirit waning, de Coubertin accepted the Greek offer to stage an interim competition in Athens in 1906. This time, President Theodore Roosevelt served as honorary chairman of an Olympic committee that chose an official American team. They did not disappoint, winning 11 of the 19 track-and-field events. France won the overall competition, which included shooting contests, fencing, cycling, rowing, wrestling, tennis, gymnastics, soccer, weightlifting, rowing, and archery. Sport was given increasing nationalistic significance as countries measured themselves against others in international competition.

The quest for athletic and national supremacy reached an acrimonious peak in 1908, when London served as host. The British, with an empire that spanned the globe, considered themselves the preeminent world power, but the Americans, whose economic output had already surpassed that of the British, held notions of republican superiority. In addition, the U.S. team included many Irish Americans who resented the British occupation of their ancestral homeland. One of them, flag bearer Ralph Rose, refused to lower the Stars and Stripes to honor the British king in the opening parade. Rose's teammate Martin Sheridan replied to the outraged English that "this flag dips to no earthly king." Thus, despite de Coubertin's intentions, the Olympic Games had become politicized.

Several international quarrels ensued, but the heated rivalry between the United States and

The Anthropology Days competition proved to be an exercise in racism and an aberration of the Olympic ideal.
Image from George Matthews and Sandra Marshall, St. Louis Olympics 1904 (Images of America Series) (Chicago: Arcadia Publishing, 2003), page 121.

Great Britain engendered the greatest fury. The host nation supplied the officials, and the Americans charged conspiracy when the English judges disqualified both American runners who had apparently beaten the British competitor in the 400-meter run. The Americans refused to rerun the race, and the judges awarded the victory to their countryman by default. The American tug-of-war team also withdrew in protest when the British team was allowed to wear steel-rimmed boots, which provided greater traction, for their match. The marathon, too, produced animosity, when the Italian runner Dorando Pietri (aka Pietri Dorando) reached the stadium in first place but then collapsed on the track before finishing the race. With Irish American Johnny Hayes running a close second, British officials lifted Pietri and assisted him to the finish line. The marathon proved yet another debacle, but the officials eventually returned the victory to Hayes. The United States claimed the track-and-field championship, but Great Britain boasted of the overall victory in myriad other contests that had few if any American entrants. The resulting backlash by both antagonists caused the International Olympic Committee to appoint neutral judges for future competitions.

In a welcome reversal, the 1912 Olympics, held in Stockholm, proved a resounding success. With teams representing 26 countries from Europe, North America, South America, Asia, Africa, and Australia, the well-organized and efficiently staged events received ample media coverage, including headlines in U.S. newspapers. Jim Thorpe, the Native American winner of both the pentathlon and decathlon, won acclaim as the greatest athlete in the world, although a year later it was discovered he had played summer baseball for money, and this violation of Olympic amateur rules resulted in the forfeiture of his Olympic medals. The 1912 Games were the first for female swimmers, as the Swedish organizers included women's aquatic competition without approval from the Olympic committee. The Games also included the first use of electric timing devices for track events, indicating a greater reliance and emphasis on the Progressive values of science, technology, quantification, and rationality.

Throughout the staging of these early Games, women fought to achieve inclusion and gradually made progress toward that goal. At the St. Louis Games in 1904, only six American women (who were archers) represented their country. It was not until 1908, when the Olympic Games were held

British officials assist the fallen Dorando Pietri to a disputed marathon victory at the 1908 Olympic Games in London, which was later reversed.

in England, the birthplace of modern sport, that women's sports achieved a modest upswing, with competition in four disciplines—tennis, sailing, ice skating, and archery—all carrying high social prestige. In 1908 and in 1912, women's gymnastics teams from Denmark, Norway, Sweden, Great Britain (all in 1908), and Finland (1912) demonstrated their physical skills and capabilities. According to the *London Telegraph*, in 1908 "the ladies who took part lent to the exhibition a grace and charm all their own" (qtd. in Daniels and Tedder 43). In 1912, the "feminist" Swedes (the term used in the minutes of the IOC assembly in 1911) allowed women to compete in swimming events (Mitchell 212). The inclusion of such a popular sport in the women's program contributed considerably to the participation of women from other countries, and 11 nations sent female athletes to Stockholm. More than 50 women, representing 2.2 percent of all competitors, took part in these Olympic Games.

More generally, although de Coubertin's idealistic plan for the modern Olympic movement sought to achieve international peace through athletic competition, the nationalistic recriminations of the 1908 Games had exposed the obstacles to achieving such a vision, and the eruption of World War I

International Perspective

The 1900 Olympic Games: Extraordinary Games With Extraordinary Women

The second Olympics took place in Paris, the home city of Baron Pierre de Coubertin, the founder of the modern Olympic Games. However, de Coubertin had no influence over the sporting program of the Games in his hometown. The event was integrated into the program of the World Exposition and organized by the French sport federations and a committee of sports administrators. Although the 1900 Games have often been considered irregular (in particular by Olympic historians), an in-depth analysis of the numerous sources reveals they may be considered innovative and progressive in many ways, in particular with regard to the sports program but also with regard to the gender issue (Drevon).

As these Games were conducted in the context of the Exhibition Universelle, the program stretched over the whole summer, and the events took place on sporting grounds or parks all over the city. Although de Coubertin and his adherents insisted on amateurism as a rule for Olympic participants, at least some professional athletes competed at the Games in Paris. Furthermore, numerous contests that demonstrated the technological progress of the time (e.g., long-distance ballooning and car races) were later not considered as true elements of Olympic Games. Many other events, such as competitions between fire brigades, canoe races between mixed-gender teams, contests in "obstacle swimming" or in fishing, and gymnastics demonstrations of schoolchildren, did not become part of the Olympic program (Drevon).

However, the most important and trailblazing "irregularity" was the participation of women in tennis and golf events; women also took part in numerous mixed-gender competitions. The admission of women to the Olympics was a grave offense of de Coubertin's intention to relegate women to the role of admiring spectators. However, as the events were not specifically announced for men, numerous women participated in many disciplines. Women competed in the fashionable sports of tennis and golf, which were organized as specific women's events. The Americans dominated in golf. Margaret Abbot, who was on a cultural trip in Paris, won the event, and her mother placed seventh. The winner of the tennis competition was Charlotte Cooper, an athlete who had been invited and may have even been paid by the organizers. She was acknowledged as the best female player of the time. Hélène de Pourtalès was the first woman to win an Olympic medal. She did so in the 1-2 ton class sailing regatta, with her husband and another crew member (Lennartz and Teutenburg).

An extraordinary athlete at the Games was Elvira Guerra, an outstanding equestrienne who performed the art of dressage in a sidesaddle wearing a floor-length riding habit. She belonged to a famous family of horse riders and performed at the circus, which was at this time one of the most popular places of entertainment. Haute école riders such as Guerra were the aristocrats of the Big Top; they were admired and accepted even in the upper echelons of society. Many equestriennes married men of the upper classes.

Guerra took part in the event "hacks and hunter combined," a dressage competition that included jumping over small obstacles. In a field of more than 50 riders, most of them cavalry officers, she achieved ninth place (Drevon 56). After 1900, and until 1952, women were again barred and horse riding was a privilege of only male competitors (Hedenborg and Pfister 2012).

in 1914 rocked the globe and signaled the failure of Progressive reformers' attempts to achieve world peace. The conflict forced the cancellation of the 1916 Olympics scheduled for Berlin.

Summary

This chapter has described the Progressive reformers' vision of society and their attempts to restructure cities, alleviate social inequalities, and Americanize diverse immigrant groups based on their own white, Anglo-Saxon, Protestant, middle-class value systems. Sport was given a primary role in the acculturation process. The chapter has also examined the varying reactions to these programs by women seeking greater freedom and by numerous racial, ethnic, religious, and social groups. Some attempted to retain their own sporting cultures, while others both adopted and adapted American games to meet their own needs. The practice of sport proved to be a liberating experience for some, as in the case of white women, and an often-segregating factor for African Americans. For others, such as Native Americans and European ethnic minorities, sport ultimately fostered a more homogeneous culture, as youths were assimilated in the schools, parks, playgrounds, and settlement houses. Baseball prospered as the national sport, while football gained precedence on college campuses as a commercialized business enterprise focused intently on victory. Football games became athletic spectacles displayed in urban centers, and colleges soon built their own stadiums on campus to accommodate the large crowds.

The modern Olympic Games were originated in order to extend brotherhood and fraternity to an international audience as Western sport forms migrated to colonized peoples, but that intention was soon superseded by nationalist rivalries. The 1904 Games in conjunction with the St. Louis World's Fair almost ended the movement with an ill-advised experiment in Social Darwinism known as the Anthropology Days. The dreams of both the Olympics and the Progressive movement were shattered in the flames of World War I, which produced a new homogenized American culture and changed the meaning of being an American, as immigrants selectively adopted and adapted mainstream social values.

DISCUSSION QUESTIONS

1. Explain the process by which various immigrant ethnic groups were acculturated.

2. What role did settlement houses play in the lives of women and ethnic immigrants?

3. How did interscholastic athletic programs become rationalized as part of the educational curriculum?

4. How did progressive reformers reorganize urban spaces to alleviate social and environmental issues?

5. What practical functions did parks and playgrounds play in urban areas?

6. How did the technological advancements of the late nineteenth century change the nature of sport?

Chapter 7

Sport as Symbol: Acculturation and Imperialism
1900–1920

CHAPTER OBJECTIVES

After reading this chapter, you will have learned about the following:

- The uneven response of various ethnic groups to the Progressives' efforts
- The impact of migrant groups on American culture
- The African Americans' quest for acceptance in American society
- Women's use of sport to gain greater independence and challenge gender boundaries
- How the United States spread its culture to disparate groups around the world
- The role of sport in the acculturation process
- The Social Darwinist belief system that subordinated and segregated non-whites
- The role of sport in the imperial process
- The function of sport as a symbol of social class, race, ethnicity, and gender

Federal efforts directed at assimilation began with the first residential school for Native American children in 1879 with the opening of the Carlisle Indian School. Thirty-nine such schools would ensue where American Indian boys and girls had little choice but to effect the trappings of the mainstream white society in their appearance, dress, speech, work habits, and leisure pursuits, including sports and games, under the tutelage of teachers and coaches. Despite the forced assimilation, Native Americans did not gain citizenship rights until 1924, and some states denied suffrage until 1957.

African Americans gained the rights to citizenship by virtue of the Fifteenth Amendment to the Constitution in 1870; but that did not guarantee them acceptance in white society. The Progressive focus on the assimilation of the myriad ethnic immigrant groups largely neglected African Americans. Northern philanthropists funneled some money to the South to build schools for black children, and Booker T. Washington emerged as the leading spokesperson among blacks in the latter half of the nineteenth century. Washington advocated an accommodationist stance with whites, preaching responsible behavior, the development of a strong work ethic, procurement of vocational skills for employment, and patience relative to social acceptance and civil rights. He founded the Tuskegee Institute in Alabama in 1881 to instill such values.

At the turn of the twentieth century W.E.B. DuBois, a free northern black, emerged as a rival to Washington. DuBois had earned a PhD from Harvard, and he assumed a more activist role in obtaining civil rights for blacks. He argued that a "talented tenth" of African Americans (like himself) could compete equally with whites if given an equal chance. In 1909 he became one of the founders of the National Association for the Advancement of Colored People (NAACP). Southern blacks soon began the Great Migration northward in search of better opportunities.

Among the European ethnic groups, the Irish and Germans had been among the first to arrive in the United States in large numbers in the 1840s. While the Irish facility in the English language enabled them to assimilate more quickly into American society and even gain control of some urban political machines, the Germans took longer to fully assimilate. Their republican political philosophies led most Germans to support and even serve the Union cause in the Civil War; but the German Turner societies maintained an emphasis on the German language and lifestyle. The first notable cultural clash occurred in 1855 in Chicago when Mayor Levi Boone attempted to close all saloons in the city on Sundays. German saloons served as the primary gathering place for leisure on the one day available to workers, and Germans marched on the court to support those arrested in what is known as the Lager Beer Riot. Casualties and one death ensued when the mayor called out the militia to support the nativist interests (Gems, *Windy*). Moreover, the German research university system preceded the American version by several decades in the nineteenth century, and Germans believed their learning, culture, and lifestyle to be superior to that of the American Anglos, with no need or desire to change their life in their communities.

Similarly, other European gymnastics organizations such as the Polish Falcons and Czech Sokols emulated the German Turners in their adherence to nationalistic cultures. Poor and oppressed Jews from throughout Europe found a home in America, but they wished to retain their traditional religion in lieu of the American emphasis on Protestant Christianity. Catholic groups, such as the large number of Italians and Poles, faced the same dilemma in their attachment to the religious beliefs of their homeland. Nativists assumed such ethnic and religious differences to be at odds with American nationalism; but a common interest in sport eventually brought the disparate groups closer together.

Sport, Ethnicity, and the Quest for Social Mobility

The perception of sport as a meritocracy, where one might gain a measure of wealth and social mobility based on the cherished physicality of

1900	1901	1902	1903
■ Davis Cup tennis competition begins	■ American League (baseball) debuts	■ First Rose Bowl football game played ■ Young Women's Hebrew Association forms in New York City	■ Chicago Hebrew Institute organized ■ Wright Brothers achieve flight ■ Public Schools Athletic League established in New York City by Dr. Luther Gulick ■ First World Series played

the working class, helped defray the discontent of lower-rank citizens. Immigrant parents, often steadfast in their adherence to a strong work ethic and their European cultures, acquiesced to sport as sons brought home additional income derived from semipro or neighborhood contests. Nonplayers such as the famous gambler Arnold Rothstein might earn even more than the players by organizing athletic competitions.

At the 1893 World's Fair in Chicago, German Turners staged a mass display of their gymnastics prowess intended to convince the American mainstream of its benefits. The skill of ethnic-minority athletic clubs attracted the notice of amateur governing bodies who sought their inclusion. Membership solicitations fostered ethnic pride but also gradually diminished the isolation of such groups by bringing them closer to the mainstream culture. By 1897, the Amateur Athletic Union governed the national championship competitions.

Ethnic minorities managed to retain a measure of their alternative sporting culture in soccer leagues. In the Illinois leagues, Swedes, Danes, Germans, Norwegians, Hungarians, Czechs, Scots, Englishmen, Jews, and Yugoslavs transferred their rivalries to the field. By 1917, the Czechs had enough teams to form their own league, where the Sparta team proudly adopted the Czech national colors. In the Czech contests, even religious differences transferred to the athletic field, as the reds (atheists) battled the blues (Catholics). Such sporting practices enabled ethnic communities to retain a measure of their European traditions and lifestyles, which by World War I was causing some nativists to question their loyalty.

Boxing

For the boys and young men engaged in tough urban street life, boxing proved a popular attraction and even a necessity. For such athletes, sport proved a temporary respite in a hard life. Few achieved more than local fame, yet working-class youth idolized the athletes' displays of physical prowess. In tough urban neighborhoods, one gained social capital with fists more often than with money.

Irish Americans held most of the boxing titles through the 1890s, but by the turn of the century other ethnic groups adored their own idols, although some adopted Irish names in order to win favor with the dominant powers in the boxing world. Among Jewish boxers, Harry Harris won the bantamweight title in 1900, and Abe Attell conquered the featherweights from 1901 to 1912. Attell won the crown at age 17 by defeating the popular black champion, George Dixon. Attell's use of cocaine and his gambling on his own fights diminished his appeal, but Jews took great pride in lightweight champion Benny Leonard. Born Benjamin Leiner to parents who were Russian Jews, he grew up fighting Irish and Italian youths in a tough New York neighborhood. His Orthodox parents disapproved of fighting, so he changed his name as a professional boxer. As a symbol of his Jewish pride, Leonard wore the Star of David on his boxing trunks, and he won the lightweight title in 1917. In one of his possibly apocryphal bouts, he pounded "Irish" Eddie Finnegan until Finnegan clinched and whispered in Leonard's ear in Yiddish to take it easy because he was really Seymour Rosenbaum. The prominence of Jewish ring champions did much to overcome stereotypes of cowardice and debility (Riess, "Tough Jews" 75–76).

The greatest Polish athletic star of the Progressive Era emerged in the boxing ring. Stanislaw Kiecal, known as the "Michigan Assassin," Americanized his name to Stanley Ketchel as a professional boxer. He won the middleweight championship in 1908 after being orphaned as a youth and living a hard life in Western mining camps and lumberyards. A savage fighter, Ketchel courageously battled the much larger Jack Johnson for the heavyweight crown in 1909 and managed to knock down the titleholder before succumbing. Despite the loss and a relatively short career, many considered Ketchel the best middleweight of all time. In 1910, the husband of his lover killed him with a rifle shot in the back, cutting short his flamboyant life at the age of 24.

Italians followed in the parade of champions. Pete Herman, whose real surname was Gulotta, learned to box in his hometown of New Orleans, and in 1916, at the age of 20, he fought a draw for

1904	1905	1906	1908
■ National Ski Association forms	■ Radical labor organization Industrial Workers of the World (IWW) founded ■ National Collegiate Athletic Association founded	■ Playground Association of America founded	■ Production begins on Model T Ford cars ■ African American Jack Johnson defeats Tommy Burns to gain the heavyweight championship

Stanley Ketchel in a boxing pose.

Photo courtesy of Library of Congress, LC-DIG-ggbain-01676.

the bantamweight championship. He earned the crown a year later. Although he suffered only one knockout during his boxing career, the accumulation of blows to his head caused blindness. Such tragedies failed to deter athletic aspirants, who had little hope of reaching greater socioeconomic status without money or an education.

Baseball

As with boxing, baseball provided a measure of social mobility and served as a marker of assimilation. Immigrant youth might aspire to the professional ranks, but even some lesser players earned substantial incomes on neighborhood semipro contingents or on company teams in the industrial leagues.

Italian Ping Bodie, whose real name was Francesco Stefano Pizzolo, fared well as a professional baseball player, enjoying a career that lasted from 1911 through 1921 with the Chicago White Sox and the New York Yankees. Bodie emerged as one of the early players of Southern or Eastern European extraction. Before that time, Irish and German players had dominated the ranks of baseball rosters. Honus Wagner, the best of the Germans, won eight batting championships. Considered the greatest of shortstops, he hit over .300 for 17 straight years in a long career (1897–1917). Polish athlete Oscar Bielaski played professional baseball as early as 1872 and appeared on the Chicago White Stockings team that won the National League championship in 1876. Ed Delahanty, one of numerous Irish stars, began his long pro career in 1887 at the age of 20. During the 1890s, he batted over .400 three times, and he finished with a lifetime average of .345. "Wee Willie" Keeler matched Delahanty's career average in 18 seasons from 1892 through 1910. Although less than 5 feet 5 inches (165 centimeters) and only 140 pounds (64 kilograms), Keeler starred at bat, hitting .432 in 1897 and going more than a hundred games without striking out in 1906. Such performances, along with the comparatively large salaries paid to athletes, endeared them to ethnic-minority and working-class youth and created heroes in urban neighborhoods.

The growth of baseball, particularly the professional and semiprofessional varieties, provided opportunities for the best players (or those with business acumen) to achieve social mobility. Ban Johnson, president of the Western League, renamed it the American League and promoted it as a moral alternative to the gambling and beer-drinking environments of the senior circuit (i.e., the National League) in 1901. When the National League proved unable to run the fledgling organization out of business, it consented to the National Agreement of 1903, which bound both leagues to recognize player contracts and established a three-man commission to govern the sport. The initial World Series between the two league champions was played that year.

By 1914, a third major league aspired to share the profits of the national game. The entry of the

1909	1910		1911
■ National Association for the Advancement of Colored People (NAACP) founded	■ Mann Act passes; prohibits interstate transport of women for immoral activities	■ Jack Johnson–Jim Jeffries (the "Great White Hope") heavyweight championship fight occurs	■ First Indianapolis 500 auto race held; Ray Harroun wins the inaugural race

Ping Bodie in Chicago, 1914.

Photo courtesy of Library of Congress, LC-H261- 4227-A.

new Federal League forced National and American league owners to offer substantial salaries to obtain or retain their star players. With Ty Cobb earning $20,000 for the 1915 season, young boys on sandlot teams aspired to reach fame and fortune in America by developing their physical skills. Cobb's salary dwarfed that of a teacher ($578), and skilled craftsmen earned less than one-tenth ($1,591) of his baseball income. The expansion of the minor leagues from 13 leagues in 1901 to 46 in 1912 provided more opportunities for the realization of such dreams.

While baseball began attracting many second-generation ethnic-minority youth, the Irish still predominated in the ranks of both players and managers. Charles Comiskey progressed from player-manager of the St. Louis Browns in the American Association to owner of the Chicago White Sox in the American League. John McGraw started as a player for the Baltimore Orioles in 1891 but won lasting fame as manager of the New York Giants, leading them to 10 pennants in a managerial career that lasted from 1899 to 1932. In 1915, 11 of the 16 big-league managers were Irish (Riess, *City* 104). Connie Mack (Cornelius McGillicuddy) held the greatest longevity. After starting as a catcher in 1886, he advanced to player-manager in 1894. In the new American League of 1901, as one of the cofounders of the league, he was granted the Philadelphia Athletics franchise, a team he owned and managed in sartorial splendor until 1950.

For such men, sport provided economic mobility. In 1910, baseball salaries averaged $3,000, well above the annual wages of blue-collar workers (Riess, *City* 87). Even college-educated players increasingly signed professional contracts after 1900. Christy Mathewson, educated at Bucknell, starred as a pitcher for the New York Giants from 1900 through 1916. He won 30 games in three different seasons and amassed 20 or more wins in twelve others. Portrayed as an idealistic gentleman, a true Muscular Christian, he brought greater middle-class respectability to the game. Mathewson then managed Cincinnati for two years before joining the American military effort in World War I, and his exposure to a poison gas in Europe would lead to his early death in 1925.

By the turn of the century, even the German, Czech, and Polish gymnastics clubs and Jewish associations fielded baseball teams to retain their young male members. The following accounts (derived from the *Chicago Tribune,* July 7, 1889, p. 12; *Svornost,* June 2, 1890; and the *Dziennik Chicagoski,* August 10, 1896, respectively) show how baseball symbolized assimilation and a degree of inclusion in American society:

THE LITERARY LEAGUE

Six of the Jewish literary societies of Chicago have organized what is known as the Library Base-Ball League. The rivalry existing between the societies has run into the channel of base-ball and the boys are

1912	1913	1914–1918
■ Jim Thorpe wins Olympic gold; is named world's greatest athlete ■ Theodore Roosevelt founds the Progressive Party ■ Woodrow Wilson elected president	■ Sixteenth Amendment ratified (power to levy income tax) ■ Amateur Francis Ouimet wins U.S. Open golf tournament	■ World War I fought (United States enters in 1917)

having it out every Sunday morning on the diamond. The societies are B'nai Abraham, Cremieax Haking, Emerson, Voltaire, Laskav, and Fidelity. The clubs are pretty evenly matched and some good games are witnessed. The standing of the league is as follows:

	Won	Lost	Percent
B'nai Abrahams	2	0	100
Cremieax Hakings	2	0	100
Emersons	1	1	50
Voltaires	1	1	50
Laskava	0	2	50
Fidelitys	0	2	50

The following games will be played today B'nai Abrahams vs. Cremieax Hakings at Athletic Park. Voltaires vs. Emersons at South Side Ball League grounds, and Fidelity vs. Laskavs at South West City League grounds. Games called at 9:00 p.m.

BOHEMIAN BASEBALL GAME

Yesterday morning the "Pilsen Sokols" team played the "Klatovsky Sokols," a game of baseball in the field at 20th and Fisk St. The score ended 28 to 8 in favor of the "Pilsen" team. The "Pilsen" battery was pitcher Kostal, Catcher Turek; for "Klatovsky," pitcher Benes, catcher Kalus.

POLISH SOCIETIES PLAY A BASEBALL GAME

Two Polish Societies from the St. Stanislaus Kostka parish, the St. Casimir's Young Men's Society and the St. Cecilia Society played a baseball game yesterday in Avondale.

The St. Cecilia Society team was captained by its president, Mr. John Czekala, and the St. Casimir Society by its president, Mr. John Nering. On Mr. Czekala's team were the following: M. Schultz, P. Marks, J. Marks, J. Kondziorski, J. Petlak, J. Marks, S. Politowsky, Mroz, and F. Arendt. On Mr. Nering's team were F. Budzban, S.C.P. Myks, J. Budzban, M. Budzban, J. Kanabas, Kimlitz, and J. Bogucki.

The game began at three o'clock in the afternoon on a field near the St. Hyacinth church in Avondale, and was very lively, because both teams were in excellent condition. The heat finally forced the players to quit,

after three hours of playing. The Cecilia team won by a score of thirteen to seven.

qtd. in Gems, *Sports* 118–119

As they became more engaged in American sport forms within the mainstream culture, such organizations increasingly turned away from their radical labor activities, although German Turners helped elect a socialist mayor in Milwaukee. The Germans had even greater influence, however, in the promotion of bowling, a sport closely tied to the saloon culture.

Bowling, Pool, and Saloon Culture

The urban working-class saloon provided the most convenient form of leisure for young men. There, patrons found camaraderie in a club atmosphere that served a free lunch with a 5-cent beer and might even provide showers for bathing. Gambling and sport offered an additional lure. Card games, bookies, and billiards coincided with drinking rituals and customary toasts to friends, acquaintances, and athletic heroes. Some saloons included bowling alleys or adjacent pool halls, and (in the East) even handball courts.

By the 1890s, bowling had become fashionable among middle-class urbanites. The Brunswick Company helped organize the American Bowling Congress in 1895, standardizing rules and equipment, and Germans served as governing officers for many years. By the turn of the century, commercial and industrial bowling leagues proliferated in cities, especially in New York and Chicago. In the latter, merchants, jewelers, bankers, clothiers, and mechanics all had their own leagues, where Anglo-Americans and citizens from various ethnic-minority groups mixed with each other; wagering fixed attention on commercial rivals and enhanced company pride. Some companies formed touring male all-star teams, and bowling tournaments offered significant cash prizes. Women were competing in their own tournaments by 1907, and the Woman's International Bowling Association (later the Women's International Bowling Congress) was founded in 1916. In 1920,

1914	1916	1917	1919
■ Panama Canal opens ■ Federal League (third major baseball league) organized	■ Professional Golf Association (PGA) founded ■ American Tennis Association (for black players) organized	■ National Hockey League established ■ Women's Swimming Association founded (New York City)	■ Red Scare occurs ■ Eighteenth Amendment ratified (Prohibition) ■ Black Sox baseball scandal erupts

People & Places

Successful Native American Baseball Players

Sioux Indian James M. Toy assimilated successfully, at least temporarily, by masquerading as a white baseball player. (His death certificate lists him as white.) The first Native American to reach the major league level, Toy appeared as a catcher and infielder for Cleveland in 1887 and for Brooklyn in 1890 before an injury ended his career. Louis Sockalexis, a Penobscot tribe member from Maine, left a more lasting impression as a Cleveland outfielder from 1897 to 1899. Sockalexis endured a barrage of racial taunts by other players and fans before injury and alcoholism chased him from the game. Even Hall of Fame pitcher Charles Bender endured the seemingly inevitable sobriquet "Chief" during his long career. Bender responded by calling white antagonists "foreigners." A product of the Carlisle Indian School, Bender pitched in five World Series for the Philadelphia Athletics between 1903 and 1914 in a career that lasted until 1927. John Tortes Meyers, of the California Cahuilla tribe, caught for the New York Giants from 1909 to 1915, and in his 14 years as a professional he resisted racist taunts and jeers but still felt treated as an outcast (Powers-Beck 77).

the association offered more than $2,000 in prize money at a national tournament.

By 1909, half of Chicago's taverns featured billiard tables. New York had four thousand pool halls in the 1920s. Detroit's Recreation Room held 142 pool tables, making it the largest establishment of its kind in the United States (Riess, *City* 73–74). Pool games, like beers, cost a nickel, and the Brunswick Company offered both, initially manufacturing the billiard tables and equipment and then branching out to construct bars and bowling alleys.

The best pool players could earn a living as professionals or local hustlers; the latter feigned incompetence, then won wagers against unwily opponents. Professionals competed in tournaments for prize money or engaged in challenge matches for additional wagers in large amphitheaters in front of hundreds of betting fans. Promoters organized pari-mutuel betting operations similar to those at horse-racing tracks, where winners split the proceeds and sponsors drew a commission. In small Western mining towns, competitors played for stakes of $500. In cities, the best players earned enough to open their own businesses.

The largest saloons offered a variety of entertainment, including concerts, vaudeville, and boxing matches. Pictures of boxers and other athletes adorned saloon walls, and many former athletes became owners or proprietors when their playing days had expired, but prizefighters held particular appeal for the laboring classes who earned their pay through physical toil. Boxers were renowned for their power, strength, courage, and endurance. In 1893, Andy Bowen of New Orleans and Jack Burke of Texas fought for 109 rounds in a bout that lasted nearly seven and one-half hours with no clear winner. A year later, Bowen died in the ring, the victim of a knockout but no less a hero to his fans.

Assimilation of Disparate Groups in American Society

As the multitude of largely urban, European ethnic groups wrestled with the assimilation efforts of Progressive reformers, other immigrants faced a variety of responses based on prevailing racial and racist sentiments. Asians, particularly those of Chinese or Japanese origin, faced exclusion by law, as their migration to the United States was forbidden. African Americans were largely ignored or, after the Supreme Court ruling in the *Plessy v. Ferguson* case of 1896, legally segregated from white society in the South. Some politicians even advocated the relocation of blacks to Africa.

1920	1920	
▪ Nineteenth Amendment ratified, granting women's suffrage	▪ U.S. women swimmers compete in the Olympic Games; Ethelda Bleibtrey and others compete	▪ American Professional Football Association forms (later renamed the NFL)
▪ Negro National League founded		

Native Americans, who were conquered but could not be deported, faced forced assimilation in residential boarding schools under white administration.

Native American Acculturation

As with urban ethnic-minority groups, reformers used sport and education in attempts to foster assimilation of Native American tribes. The process of formal acculturation began in 1879, with the opening of the Carlisle Indian School at an abandoned Army barracks in Pennsylvania. Carlisle was the first of many schools across the country designed to convert Native Americans to white notions of civilization. It housed American Indians from 70 different tribes and imposed on them the English language, vocational skills, and WASP values. Forced to cut their hair, don clothing typically worn by whites, and assume WASP standards of decorum, American Indian youth struggled to maintain their own cultural identities.

Although Native Americans adapted well to baseball, the Carlisle football team constituted the most visible success in the forced assimilation process. The team began play in 1890 and within five years embarked on a national schedule. In 1898, its quarterback, Frank Hudson, became the first of many Native American players to win recognition as an All-American.

With no home field, the Carlisle football team traveled across the country, and in 1912 even played in Canada, where it defeated Toronto University 49-1 in a combined game of rugby and football. Carlisle matched its wit and brawn against the best of the collegiate teams, nearly defeating Harvard and Yale in 1896 and beating Penn in 1899. It ranked among the best teams in the country from 1900 to 1914. The 1912 team featured members of 10 tribal groups, including the famed Jim Thorpe. They led the nation in scoring with 504 points, and Jim Thorpe accounted for 25 of the team's 66 touchdowns (Gems, *For Pride* 119).

The Carlisle team became a major attraction in the commercialized world of intercollegiate football, drawing huge crowds in urban stadiums. The University of Michigan provided a $2,000 guarantee for a 1901 game in Detroit, and the University of Chicago paid $1,700 for a 1907 contest. Their success might have provided a rehabilitated image of Native Americans, but they were often portrayed as "noble savages", and their coach, Glenn "Pop" Warner, got most of the credit for their trick plays and innovative formations (e.g., Carlisle nearly beat Harvard by hiding the ball under a player's jersey in 1903). The attribution of this success to Warner's genius only reinforced the Social Darwinist belief in the need for white leadership, and Warner reinforced stereotypes by refusing to number the players' jerseys in the belief that since all American Indians looked alike the identical jerseys would deceive opponents. Of the deceptive plays, he asserted that "[t]he public

A gymnastics class at the Carlisle Indian School.
Image courtesy of Library of Congress, LC-USZ62-120987.

expects the Indians to employ trickery and we try to oblige" (Beale 147).

White sportswriters characterized the Carlisle team as tricksters who won by deceit or by "massacres" if they scored a lot of points. Such media descriptions were meant to reinforce a perception of whites as morally superior, yet American Indians often displayed better sporting behavior than their white opponents. For them, football offered an opportunity to exhibit racial pride and exact a measure of revenge. Their ancestors had suffered at the hands of the American military in its quest for Indian lands, and they took particular joy in defeating the West Point team. The team's historian stated that in confronting Army, the "Redskins play football as if they were possessed" (Steckbeck 95). In the 1912 game, when Jim Thorpe's touchdown run was called back for an alleged infraction, he responded by scoring another on the very next play in a 27-6 victory. For the tribes, such games represented a continuation of the frontier wars.

Football also allowed Native Americans to challenge the Social Darwinists' racial stereotypes by outsmarting their supposedly superior opponents. The 1906 rule changes allowed for forward passes, stipulating only that the ball had to be caught within the boundaries of the playing field. In a 1907 win against the elite University of Chicago team, the Carlisle receiver ran around the opponents' bench and returned to the field to catch a touchdown pass. In 1911, Carlisle defeated mighty Harvard 18-15 when Thorpe scored four field goals and a touchdown. After the game, his teammates mimicked the Bostonians' accents in a parody of their elitist attitudes. After beating Penn, a Carlisle player determined that the white men might be better with cannons and guns, but the Native Americans displayed equal intelligence on the football field (Warner 46).

Football served a number of functions for Native Americans as they both adopted and adapted the game to suit their own needs. Victories over white teams provided a measure of racial pride. The best American Indian players, such as Thorpe and Joe Guyon, were valued performers on professional teams. Thorpe served as the nominal head of the new professional American Football League (soon renamed the NFL) in 1920. In 1922 and 1923, Thorpe and Guyon both played on the Oorang Indians team that featured 12 different tribes on the roster. Although they did not win many games, they enjoyed spending the money of the white owner, who sponsored the team as a marketing tool for his dog breeding business (Gems, "The Construction"; Gems, *For Pride)*.

At least one adaptation exhibited cross-cultural flow between Native Americans and people of Anglo descent, as both Canadians and Americans adopted the traditional American Indian game of lacrosse by the nineteenth century. By the Progressive Era, American Indians were mixing traditional loincloths and moccasins with Anglo team jerseys and athletic shoes. The game became more regulated when a national lacrosse league adopted Canadian rules and held a championship at Newport, Rhode Island, in 1879. An intercollegiate lacrosse association was formed in 1882, and teams from New York and Boston engaged Canadian rivals. All-star teams began making

THE EVOLUTION OF THE INDIAN.

This cartoon, from an 1896 edition of the *World*, is like many that caricatured and stereotyped Native Americans as savages undergoing the processes of civilization.

Image from *World*, Nov. 20, 1896.

barnstorming trips to England and Ireland by 1888. The Amateur Athletic Union (AAU) assumed governance of the sport in 1890 and promoted regional tournaments, but the game retained its greatest popularity among whites in New England and the Atlantic Coast areas thereafter. Native Americans who remained on reservations resisted the sportification process imposed on those who lived at boarding schools, retaining their traditional game of lacrosse with its inherent symbols, rituals, and meanings. By the 1890s, whites deemed them to be professionals and excluded them from mixed competition. White clergy also protested lacrosse play among American Indians because they often chose the game over church attendance (Vennum 277).

Plight of African Americans

Like the newly arrived immigrants, African Americans continued to try to find their place in the mainstream culture of the predominantly white, Protestant United States. The years after the Civil War saw temporary gains by blacks in politics, but that progress ended when Southern Democrats regained control of the region in exchange for delivering the 1876 presidential election to Republican Rutherford Hayes, who lost the popular vote but garnered a one-vote victory in the electoral college (Blum et al. 925). The change meant that freedmen reverted to virtual slavery as sharecroppers under the yoke of white supremacy. By the 1890s, rural Southern blacks had begun their prolonged exodus to Northern cities in search of a better life, and between 1914 and 1919 five hundred thousand blacks traveled to the North in a movement known as the Great Migration (Garraty 606). This shift provided opportunities for black entrepreneurs, as well as chances (albeit limited) for involvement in sport.

People & Places

Jim Thorpe

Selected for the 1912 United States Olympic team, Jim Thorpe captured the gold medal in both the pentathlon and the decathlon. A year later, he ran afoul of the AAU's definition of amateurism when it was discovered that he had played minor league baseball in the summer of 1909 for pay. Forced to return his medals and stripped of his Olympic victory, Thorpe turned to the professional ranks to make a living. He played major league baseball but had a bigger influence as the premier attraction on the nascent pro football circuit, where physical prowess counted more than race or social status. By 1915, town teams paid him as much as $250 per game for his services. In 1920, the fledgling pro league named him its first president in order to capitalize on his national celebrity, and in 1922 and 1923, as player-manager, he guided the Oorang Indians team, composed entirely of Native Americans from 12 different tribes, in the National Football League.

Photo courtesy of Library of Congress. LC-B21- 2729-20[P&P].

Baseball

The growing African American presence in the North supported a number of black baseball teams in the larger cities. In 1895, the all-black Page Fence Company team of Adrian, Michigan, sported a 118-36-2 record. By 1900, Chicago supported two black teams, and the Leland Giants, formed in 1905, competed in the Chicago City League against topflight white competition. In 1906, the Chicago Cubs and Chicago White Sox won their respective league pennants and met in the World Series, but a City League team, the Logan Squares, had beaten both of them that year, an indication of the quality of play. In 1909, Frank Leland's Giants won the City League championship and played the Cubs in a series of postseason games.

The next year, the Giants' star pitcher and manager, Andrew "Rube" Foster, split with the owner and joined John Schorling, a white tavern keeper, in forming the Chicago American Giants in 1911, but a harsh racial climate, exemplified by a resurgent Ku Klux Klan, boded ill for blacks, especially in the South. The increasing number of black migrants who flooded Northern industrial centers in search of employment also faced racism and ostracism as scab laborers who served employers as strikebreakers. Southerners lynched more than 70 African Americans in 1919, and race riots ensued in Washington, D.C., East St. Louis (Illinois), Chicago, and Tulsa, thus negating the best intentions of the Progressive reformers (Blum et al. 616). In 1920, Rube Foster led the formation of the Negro National League, which included teams in Chicago, Detroit, Dayton, Indianapolis, Kansas City, and St. Louis, thereby forming a parallel sporting structure that employed, catered to, and depended on African Americans.

Horse Racing

While black baseball players struggled to gain acceptance, African American jockeys met with greater success, at least on the turf, where they could compete with white opponents. Isaac Murphy won the Kentucky Derby three times (in 1884, 1890, and 1891) and commanded a large salary. Yet his fame and talent could not win a full welcome in the white world. White rivals resented his victories, fame, and salary. His biographer claims he was even poisoned, dying at the age of 35 in 1896 (McDaniels). Willie Sims replaced Murphy as the top jockey, winning the Kentucky Derby in 1896 and 1898, as well as numerous other stakes races. By the time Simms retired in 1901, he had totaled $300,000 in earnings, surpassing even Murphy. Jimmy Winkfield won consecutive Kentucky Derbys in 1901 and 1902, but retaliation by white jockeys forced him to take up residence in Europe, where he enjoyed a long and successful career.

Cycling

African Americans also claimed the best cyclist in the world at the turn of the century in the person of Marshall "Major" Taylor of Indianapolis, who

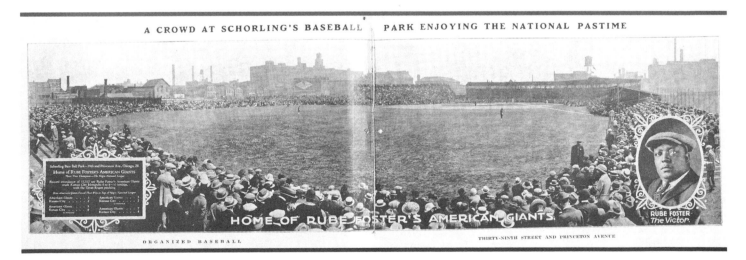

Rube Foster, pioneer of black baseball and founder of the Negro National League.

Schomburg Center for Research in Black Culture, Jean Blackwell Hutson Research and Reference Division, The New York Public Library. A crowd at Schorling's baseball park enjoying the national pastime; Home of Rube Foster's American Giants. New York Public Library Digital Collections. Accessed September 27, 2016. http://digital-collections.nypl.org/items/510d47de-4d69-a3d9-e040-e00a18064a99.

International Perspective

Tour de France

The Tour de France is the most famous cycling race and the ultimate endurance event in sport. It lasts three weeks, during which the cyclists travel at an average speed of 42 kph for four or five hours each day. They traverse the Alps and Pyrenees, covering heights equivalent to climbing Mount Everest three times. The cyclists, called "giants of the road," frequently exceed their physical capacities, often supported by drugs, and a few of them paid for the chance of gaining immortal fame with their lives.

The Tour de France was held for the first time in 1903 at the instigation of Henri Desgrange, the publisher of the newspaper *L'Auto*. Eighty-five years previously, in 1818, Baron von Drais' "riding machine" had been introduced to a wider public in the Parc de Luxembourg, but these heavy and clumsy *draisiennes* did not catch on. It was not until technological advances were made in wheel-making during the 1860s and the invention of the chain-driven "safety bicycle" with two equal-sized wheels in the early 1880s that cycling became truly popular. All over Europe, the years that followed saw a surge of bicycle-related culture. Manufacturing companies were established, clubs and associations were founded, race tracks were built, records were set, and races were organized.

In the 1890s the bicycle became a symbol of progress, rationalism, technology, and dynamism—a hallmark of the new era and its striving for innovation. It held the promise of prestige as well as the experience of new dimensions and physical sensations. It was during this time that the Tour de France was invented, promising a further heightening of excitement and drama because it pushed the limits of what the human body could endure and kept both participants and spectators in suspense for days on end. The Tour de France was clearly staged with an eye on its marketing potential, and this is true for the organizers, the cyclists, and the media alike. All in all, the prize money today amounts to roughly four million dollars.

The Tour de France is a stage race, in which each daily stage is held as a separate race and the times recorded for each cyclist are accumulated. In addition, there are special prizes for victories in such contests as time trials, sprints, and mountain climbs.

In 1903 the Tour consisted of 6 stages covering 2,428 km. As early as 1911, the cyclists had to complete 5,343 km in 15 stages. The greatest challenges of the race are the mountains, especially the Col de Tourmalet, which has a constant uphill gradient of 10 percent.

The Tour de France also has a history of problems and scandals ranging from financial difficulties to fraud and deception, although these did nothing to hinder the growing popularity of the contest. The history of the Tour is also a history of doping, which in the early years was not prohibited. Substances such as alcohol, strychnine, ether, cocaine, and caffeine were used initially to alleviate pain but also to increase performance. In the years that followed, however, the list of performance-enhancing drugs grew longer and longer, with amphetamines, anabolic steroids, glucosteroids, and EPO either replacing or complementing one another. Up to the present day, the antidoping strategies of international sports federations have been unable to take any effective action against doping in professional cycle racing.

The uniqueness of the Tour de France is due both to its backdrop (i.e., the route, which takes the riders around the whole of France) and to its staging, which puts roughly eighteen million spectators and viewers under its spell. The extreme demands on the riders, the dangerous downhill stretches, the great distance covered, the few days of rest, the heat, the rain, the cobblestones—all of these contribute to the drama of the race and provide the yarn which the sports media weaves into an epic narrative of masculine heroism. In times of national self-doubt the Tour de France has always provided the French people with the opportunity to become acquainted with France in its geographic entirety and its history as well as the opportunity to identify with the "grande nation."

Information from www.hickoksports.com/history/tourdefrance.shtml; Fife, Graeme. *Tour De France—The History, the Legend, the Riders*. Edinburgh: Mainstream Publishing Co., 1999.

began his professional career in 1896. In 1898, he set a new mark in the 1-mile (1.6-kilometer) event, and a year later he won the world championship. Taylor held seven world records between 1898 and 1900, despite the actions of jealous white opponents who tried to thwart his efforts by means of blocking and obstruction tactics. Taylor chose to race in Europe and Australia after 1901, winning as much as $10,000 annually.

This kind of success achieved by African American athletes cast doubt on whites' perceptions of their own racial superiority, particularly in individual sports featuring head-to-head competition. Whites rationalized defeats by African Americans in scientific analyses claiming that blacks' primitive natures, akin to animals, gave them innate anatomical advantages. Even in the more liberal atmosphere of France, French scientists X-rayed and measured Taylor's body in search of racial explanations for his victories.

Boxing

Unlike Taylor, black boxers enjoyed the luxury of fighting back. Peter Jackson, a black heavyweight from Australia, fought a 61-round draw with James J. Corbett in 1891, but white champion John L. Sullivan refused to fight Jackson (or any other black boxer), and when Corbett took the crown from Sullivan a year later he upheld the color ban. Similarly, other great black fighters such as Sam Langford, Sam McVey, Joe Jeannette, and Harry Wills never got title fights. Most often they were forced to fight each other, and Langford fought 14 bouts against Jeannette, 15 against McVey, and 23 against Wills (Roberts 45). Several black boxers traveled to Paris, where they perceived the French society to be more liberal and accepting. Bobby Dobbs arrived as early as 1898 and established boxing schools in France and Germany, followed by Aaron Brown, known as "the Dixie Kid." By 1907, Sam McVey also headed to Paris, as did Sam Langford and Joe Jeannette, where Parisians seemed to have a great fascination with the black body. McVey and Jeannette fought a 49-round bout there in 1909 that drew patrons from London and throughout western Europe as African American boxers cultivated the sport in Europe, "where race became an exotic, erotic commodity that could be sold in the boxing arena" (Gems, *Boxing* 35). Historian Theresa Runstedtler termed the black fighters "figures of fear and desire" (Runstedtler 61). Canadian-born George Dixon became the first black world champion when he won the bantamweight title in 1890, and a year later he added the featherweight crown. Joe Gans garnered the lightweight championship in 1912 and held it for six years, but the elusive heavyweight prize symbolized the Social Darwinist triumph, allowing whites to claim physical superiority.

When Jim Jeffries retired as the undefeated heavyweight champ in 1905, the title fell to Canadian Tommy Burns, and Jack Johnson, the flamboyant African American champ, chased Burns around the globe until he secured a title fight in Australia in 1908. Johnson toyed with and pummeled the undersized Burns en route to becoming the first black heavyweight champion. Johnson's victory engendered an immediate and ongoing search for "the Great White Hope" who might restore Anglo-Americans' pride and confidence in their racial superiority. When none could defeat the brash Johnson, whites prevailed upon the never-vanquished Jim Jeffries to come out of retirement. The historic confrontation took place in Reno, Nevada, on July 4, 1910, for a purse exceeding $100,000 and including movie rights. Twenty thousand spectators trekked to the blistering desert to witness the affair, and journalists came from as far away as Europe and Australia. Promoter Tex Rickard served as referee to ensure a fair decision for the enormous wagers, with bettors favoring Jeffries. Rickard had little to fear, as Johnson won decisively, knocking the seemingly invincible white through the ropes and thoroughly crushing the Social Darwinist belief in black inferiority.

African Americans celebrated the victory, and whites retaliated with beatings and lynchings. Race riots killed 11 people across the country, as reported by the *Chicago Daily Tribune*:

RACES CLASH AFTER PRIZE FIGHT

	Dead	Injured
Uvaldia, Ga	3	5
Mounds, Ill	2	0
Little Rock	2	1
Shreveport	2	1
Houston, Tex	1	3
Keystone, W. Va	1	0
New Orleans	0	2
Wilmington, Del	0	12
New York	0	5
Baltimore	0	3
Cincinnati	0	3
St. Joseph	0	1
Roanoke	0	6
Pueblo	0	27
Los Angeles	0	3
Chattanooga	0	2

At least eleven killed and scores of others wounded in race clashes last night in various parts of the United States marked one result of the Jeffries-Johnson fight.

There were battles in the streets of practically every large city in the country. Negroes formed the greater number of those who were victims of the outbreaks. They were set upon by whites and killed or wounded because of cheers for Johnson's victory.

"Eleven Killed in Many Race Riots"

White hopes were crushed with Jack Johnson's historic defeat of the previously unbeaten Jim Jeffries.

Photo courtesy of Nevada Historical Society.

After his loss to Jess Willard, Jack Johnson claimed he was not knocked out but merely shielding his eyes from the sun.

Image courtesy of Library of Congress, LC-USZ62-33753.

People & Places

George Bellows

George Bellows (1882–1925) attended Ohio State University shortly after the turn of the century, where he played on the baseball and basketball teams. Although he was good enough to pursue a professional baseball career, his real interests were in art. He left the university before graduation to seek his muse in New York. There he became a member of the Ash Can School of art, so called for its gritty depiction of working-class urban life. Bellows became one of the leading proponents of the genre, often portraying the dark side of their existence in his paintings. He was most noted for his paintings of boxers. His 1909 oil painting, eventually titled *Both Members of This Club*, showed the struggles of a black and a white fighter engaged in a clandestine bout in a private club, as boxing matches were illegal in New York at that time. The fighters and the patrons each joined the club for one night by paying an admission (membership) fee to avoid the law. Boxing was one of the few sports that did not segregate competitors based on their race.

Photo courtesy of Library of Congress, LC-USZ62-22026.

In Bellows' 1924 painting of the Jack Dempsey and Luis Angel Firpo fight, the artist captured the climax of the bout in which Dempsey, the American champion, was knocked completely out of the ring by Firpo, the Argentinian challenger, only to be pushed back by ringside sportswriters. Dempsey went on to win perhaps the wildest fight in boxing history.

Johnson further infuriated his critics by consorting with and marrying white women (three). The federal government indicted him on Mann Act charges, which forbade the transport of women across state lines for "immoral purposes." Forced to flee the country, Johnson escaped to Europe in 1913. When World War I erupted a year later, he had few opportunities to earn a living. He agreed to a 1915 bout in Havana, Cuba, against the giant Jess Willard, a raw Kansas cowboy. Johnson suffered a mysterious knockout in the 26th round. He later claimed he had a secret deal with the government to return to America after he lost the fight, an unsubstantiated and never-effected agreement. He continued to wander until submitting to a one-year prison sentence upon his return to the United States in 1920. He never got another championship match.

Football

The direct racial confrontations of the boxing ring were somewhat masked on the gridiron, since it was teamwork that brought success in football, but individual black players did win acclaim and some measure of respect in the North and Midwest. George Jewett starred as a running back for the University of Michigan in 1890 but had to endure taunts and threats from opponents and rival fans. In the East, William Tecumseh Sherman Jackson played halfback for Amherst, and William Henry Lewis won All-American honors as a center for Harvard in 1892 and 1893. He later coached the Harvard squad and also distinguished himself beyond the football field, winning election to the city council in Cambridge, Massachusetts, and serving in the state legislature before his appointment as assistant U.S. attorney general for Boston. He served in the national attorney general's office during the administration of President William Howard Taft. Thus, football provided Lewis with fame, and education enabled him to achieve prominence and social mobility as he obtained a measure of social whiteness in the traditionally more liberal environment of New England. W.E.B. DuBois, an African American leader and a Harvard PhD, subsequently asserted that educated blacks could compete with whites on a level playing field.

Black colleges initiated their own intercollegiate rivalries that paralleled those of the elite New England schools. The Lincoln–Howard game became a Thanksgiving spectacle in Washington, D.C., starting in 1894. Tuskegee and Atlanta followed in 1897, and in 1912 Lincoln University of Pennsylvania joined three Southern schools to form the Colored Intercollegiate Athletic Conference. The precedent of the U.S. Supreme Court ruling in the 1896 *Plessy v. Ferguson* case, which legalized segregation, ensured that such associations would remain separate from their white counterparts, and black teams, unable to compete with whites, had to contend for mythical black championships well into the twentieth century.

Nevertheless, after the turn of the century, individual African American football stars became increasingly prominent on high school and college teams. At the University of Minnesota, Bob Marshall gained election to the All-American team in both 1905 and 1906 before mounting a long career as a professional player. Edward Gray was an Amherst All-American in 1906, and Archie Alexander won all-conference honors for Iowa in 1910 despite the refusal of Missouri opponents to play against him. In 1912, Ray Young even fulfilled a leadership role, one of the few accorded to African Americans, as line coach at Northwestern University. By World War I, two outstanding black athletes garnered national media attention. Fritz Pollard, an All-American at Brown in 1916, led his team to the Rose Bowl and then joined the professional circuit, where he became the first black quarterback and first black head coach in the National Football League. Paul Robeson, an All-American end for Rutgers in 1917 and 1918, joined Pollard in the professional ranks before achieving international renown as an actor, singer, and social critic. The successes of these black athletes belied the racial conditions in the United States, as blacks generally faced mounting prejudice, bias, and discrimination in both the South and the North.

Basketball

After the turn of the twentieth century, African Americans increasingly took up the relatively new sport of basketball. With the influx of southern blacks to the north and the increasing educational opportunities available in the burgeoning high schools, more African American youths were exposed to the game. The growing black churches, social clubs, and YMCAs also fielded their own teams and engaged in interracial competition with whites. As more and more blacks migrated from the South to the urban communities in the north,

they gathered in black enclaves that produced a vibrant leisure culture, including cabarets and night clubs known as black and tans that even attracted a white clientele to the music and dancing. In the dance halls, basketball games served as the entertainment during intermission of the dance programs. As individual teams and players gained stature and recognition, they challenged other localities as a measure of civic and communal pride. By the World War I era, a number of black basketball circuits had developed in New York; Washington, D.C.; and Chicago, and not only men's but also women's teams drew attention. National challenges ensued between the top black teams, and by the 1920s, the New York Rens and the Harlem Globetrotters, a Chicago team, emerged from the dance halls to gain national prominence (Gems, "Blocked Shot").

Challenging Gender Boundaries

As with the activities of other subordinate groups, women's increasing involvement in sporting culture over the last two decades of the nineteenth century forged new roles, challenged stereotypes, and frequently exasperated white men. Some women's groups began to bring their feminist perspective to bear more forcefully in arguing for more than suffrage or temperance. Suffrage, first proposed at the Seneca Falls Woman's Rights Convention in New York in 1848, remained an arduous battle for women demanding a measure of citizenship equal to that of men. Between 1870 and 1910, suffrage referenda appeared on 17 occasions, and by 1917 more than two million members had joined the National American Woman Suffrage Association, but women had to wait until 1920 before they could vote in national elections (Coben 94). Women also agitated for jobs, and as more women entered the workforce they gained greater independence—that is, they were less tied to reliance on men.

Activists such as Charlotte Perkins Gilman, Margaret Sanger, and Emma Goldman also called for women to take more control over their lives and bodies. Gilman argued against the exploitation of women and favored socialism. Goldman promoted anarchism, atheism, free speech, and free love, claiming that marriage forced dependency and objectified women as merely sexual beings, and both she and Sanger preached birth control as a means of bettering women's lives.

Women sought greater freedom in their leisure lives as well, and, as they moved from passive to more active leisure practices, sport proved to be a highly visible symbol of cultural change. Gilman promoted athletics for women and helped form a club for that purpose in Providence, Rhode Island. Female practitioners had been accorded usage of some facilities at male clubs when they were not in use by men, and by the 1880s in some New York clubs, women could bowl, play billiards or tennis, swim, and row boats at designated times. By 1901, wealthy women were forming their own clubs and uniting in the Federation of Women's Athletic Clubs. The Chicago Women's Athletic Club featured a gymnasium, a bowling alley, a billiard room, a swimming pool, and facilities for basketball and gymnastics.

Artist Charles Dana Gibson began portraying slim, athletic women in his 1890s illustrations. The "Gibson Girl" symbolized activity, independence, vivaciousness, and a distinct break from the sedate, domestic, and restricted ideal woman of the Victorian Era. These "new women" dismantled many gendered stereotypes and shunned the domesticity of Victorian culture. They represented a new physical vitality and independence. As the Progressive Era moved to a close, women—working-class women, in particular—rapidly joined the

1896   1926
Thirty Years of "Progress"!

Sport helped transform the image and roles of women within one generation.

Image from *Life Magazine*, 1926.

People & Places

Annie Smith Peck

A Smith College scholar and a suffragist, Annie Smith Peck (1850–1935) was also a mountain climber who, when she started mountaineering, was told by a man to "go home where you belong." Instead, she set mountain-climbing records, making most of her ascents without the aid of oxygen. Peck used the sport of mountaineering to further the cause of women, seeking equality in a man's world. A committed campaigner for a constitutional amendment that would grant American women the right to vote, Peck hoped to prove that men and women could achieve equality in all fields, and she decided to set a woman's record for altitude. Peck climbed Mount Coropuna in Peru (21,079 feet, or 6,425 meters) and, upon reaching the peak, hung a banner that read, "Vote for Women."

Photo courtesy of Library of Congress, LC-USZ62-11827.

mass, popular, and public culture that included amusement parks, vaudeville, movies, dance halls, night clubs, and sports.

Educational and Sporting Opportunities for Women

The new women's colleges provided opportunities for recreational play and instruction. Vassar College fielded women's baseball teams as early as 1866, and the women of Mills College in Oakland, California, were playing the game by 1872. Three years later, two women's teams in Springfield, Illinois, competed in a baseball game before paying spectators. Such activities challenged the traditional feminine passivity assigned to women and generated widespread debate that would persist through the next century regarding the propriety of sporting activity by women.

> Danville, Ill, June 9—The "Ladies" base ball club, composed of women from Chicago and Cincinnati, defeated the Danville Browns by a score of 23 to 12 to an attendance of 2,000. Last evening state's attorney Blackburn swore out a warrant for their arrest for unlawfully disturbing the peace and good order of society. Officer Patterson arrested them as they were leaving town in carriages for Covington, Indiana.
>
> *Ottumwa [Iowa] Daily Democrat*, June 11, 1890

Mary Taylor Bissell, a female physician wrote:

> [S]o long as baseball and football and the boat race stand for the national expression of athletics, the experience of girls in any similar department will seem like comparing moonlight unto sunlight, and water unto wine. . . . The spirit for physical recreation has invaded the atmosphere of the girl's life as well as that of the boy, and demands consideration from her standpoint.
>
> qtd. in Gems, *Sports in North America* 9

Educators and physicians fulminated over the advantages and disadvantages of sport and education for women. A writer for *Popular Science Monthly* stated that, since "the average brain weight of women is about five ounces (142 grams) less than that of men . . . we should . . . expect a marked inferiority of intellectual power in the former" (qtd. in Marks 103). A Harvard medical professor claimed that intense study caused women to suffer from neurasthenia (nervous breakdown). G. Stanley Hall, the eminent psychologist, declared that "it was a pity to spoil a good mother to make a grammarian" (qtd. in Townsend 207), and mother-

hood became a prominent issue in considerations of female participation in sport, as the WASP birthrate declined at the end of the nineteenth century and, as some whites saw it, hordes of immigrants overran the country. Thus, it was felt that cultural supremacy was at stake, as doctors worried about possible damage to reproductive organs caused by overexertion, even as others extolled the need for strong bodies to produce healthy WASP children. With the onset of the cycling fad of the 1880s, moralists raised further concerns, with some suggesting that the activity diminished sexual impulses, while others believed that it induced masturbation.

Dudley Sargent, a medical doctor and Harvard professor, began offering physical culture (an early term for physical education) classes to women and opened his own school in 1881, using numerous weight-lifting machines and training teachers. Mary Hemenway's Boston Normal School of Gymnastics (BNSG), opened in 1889 and directed by Amy Morris Homans, also trained a multitude of women as teachers. In 1909, BNSG became a branch of Wellesley College for Women. Many graduates of Sargent's and Homan's programs assumed leadership roles in the women's sports movement over the next half century, including Senda Berenson, who adapted basketball rules for women's play, and Dr. Delphine Hanna, who initiated a physical education program for women and men at Oberlin College in Ohio.

The female graduates of such programs enjoyed a friendship and camaraderie that greatly influenced their sporting ideology. They eschewed the highly competitive and commercialized male model in favor of a less competitive ideal of sport for fun and health; thus, women began to define their own sporting culture. Many became leaders in the Association for the Advancement of Physical Education, established in 1885, and they advocated a nurturing, protective relationship between and among women.

Bryn Mawr, a college for women, was founded in 1885 and offered its students basketball, field hockey, and track-and-field activities by 1901. Indeed, most college women engaged in intramural contests or interscholastic play days, in which two schools merged teams for recreational play to deter rabid spectators, institutional rivalry, and personal enmity. Pre- or postgame festivities might include sharing tea or a picnic, and these sportswomen often claimed that they played for social rather than competitive reasons. However, not all women adhered to the idea of sport as a social rather than a competitive outlet. In 1895,

Chicago high school girls started interscholastic basketball competition, and working-class girls enjoyed the sport on settlement house teams. In 1896, California lost to Stanford, 2-1, in the first basketball game between women's colleges.

Sport as a Challenge to Traditional Domesticity

Some women further challenged the feminine stereotypes of domesticity and debility. In 1885, Annie Oakley (Phoebe Ann Moses) became a celebrity as a trick-shot artist with a rifle in Buffalo Bill Cody's Wild West Show. Her astounding feats included hitting a dime tossed into the air, shooting a cigarette from her husband's lips, and hitting a moving target while perched on a galloping horse. By 1899, women were racing horses in the Wyoming rodeo known as Cheyenne Frontier Days, and they soon took up steer roping and bronco busting as well.

Women challenged the male domain in their demonstration of both physical skills and endurance. Female cyclists engaged in a six-day race in Madison Square Garden in 1896 and other endurance cycling races in New York. Numerous other women completed century runs of 100 miles (161 kilometers) by bicycle, and throughout 1899 a number of female cyclists pushed the endurance tests to 1,000 miles (about 1,610 kilometers) over a five-day period. Elizabeth Cochran Seaman, operating under the pseudonym of Nellie Bly as a reporter for a New York newspaper, traveled around the globe in 72 days. In 1890, Fay Fuller donned bloomers and boys' boots and rode astride a horse like a man rather than in the customary sidesaddle position, as she conquered the 14,410-foot (4,392-meter) peak of Mount Rainier in Washington. Three years later, Helga Estby, wearing a short skirt and accompanied by her daughter Clara, walked the length of the continent from Spokane, Washington, to New York City in a quest for an announced prize of $10,000 to support her family (Hunt). However, the sponsor was unwilling to pay up due to a technicality: Estby had stopped temporarily because her daughter was ill.

Annie Oakley wearing her medals for marksmanship.
Photo courtesy of Library of Congress, LC-DIG-ppmsca-24362.

An 1890 photograph of Nellie Bly.
Photo courtesy of Library of Congress, LC-USZ62-59924.

Women in the New England colleges continued to play baseball, and a few women's teams—notably, the Chicago Stars, the Boston Bloomer Girls, and the St. Louis Stars—barnstormed around the country playing against men's teams after the turn of the century. A number of other barnstorming women's baseball teams gave such enterprises a negative connotation when it was discovered that they were no more than brothels advertising their wares. Several women, however, earned a respectable living as baseball players. Lizzie Arlington, whose real name was Lizzie Stroud, played in a minor league for the Reading, Pennsylvania, men's team during the 1890s. She earned as much as $100 weekly as a pitcher. Alta Weiss earned enough money pitching for an Ohio semipro team from 1907 to 1910 to go to medical school and become a doctor. She continued playing until 1922, and Amanda Clement even umpired men's games throughout the Midwest from 1905 to 1911. Such individual accomplishments signaled a change in women's self-perceptions, indicating a growing sense of independence, confidence, and assertiveness.

Although they maintained their domestic images, both Alice Camp and Stella Stagg served vital functions in assisting their husbands in their football coaching responsibilities. While Walter Camp worked throughout the day at his job at the New Haven Clock Company, it was his wife Alice who attended football practices, carefully taking notes for his evening meetings with team captains, and Mrs. Stagg even charted the plays from the press box at the stadium.

Sport, Fashion, and Liberation

The advent of women's golf and tennis played at country clubs—along with the cycling fad of the latter decades of the nineteenth century—led to a revolution in dress. Bustle skirts, which inhibited

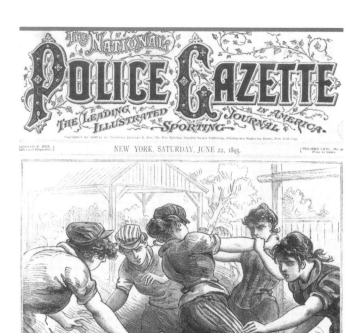

FOOTBALL KICKING MAIDENS.
A LIVELY SCRIMMAGE OCCURS BETWEEN TWO RIVAL TEAMS ON THE WEST TROY, N.Y. GROUND.

The movement of women into the male sphere of athletics fostered great anxieties in some men.

Image from *National Police Gazette*, June 22, 1895.

movement on the court, links, and cycle paths, eventually gave way to shorter skirts, bloomers, and pants. Female cyclists adopted such attire because skirts got caught in the spokes of wheels, causing

People & Places

Eleanora Sears

The wealthy Bostonian Eleanora Sears defied convention in her fashion, lifestyle, and romances. If not for her social standing, she would have been roundly criticized for her behavior. Sears wore pants and challenged men in athletic competitions. She swam and played baseball, golf, and field hockey, but the field in which she excelled was that of racket sports. She won the national doubles title in tennis four times (and the mixed doubles twice) between 1911 and 1917. She rode astride horses as men did, rather than in the customary sidesaddle position expected of women, and in 1912 she became the first woman to play polo. That same year, she walked 108 miles (174 kilometers) in less than 20 hours. Not content with the constricted life ascribed to women, she also raced in cars and airplanes. In 1928, Eleanora Sears won the national squash championship at the age of 44.

accidents. The transition to bloomers or pants did not sit well with men, who felt threatened by women's donning of "masculine" clothing and their involvement in sports that evoked speed or power. Some municipalities banned the wearing of bloomers, while ministers charged that female cyclists were possessed by the devil. Doctors warned that women who cycled faced physical deformities and heart problems. Some even speculated that women's widespread interest in the sport had sexual motivations as the women sought gratification from friction with the bicycle seat (Vertinsky, *Eternally*).

As female tennis players became more competitive, they, too, shed their restrictive clothing, which had included long skirts, long-sleeved blouses, corsets, and hats. Californian May

Blouses and dresses became shorter and less restrictive as women became more competitive, as shown by May Sutton.
Photo courtesy of Library of Congress, LC-B2- 2278-6.

Sutton adopted short-sleeved tops and short skirts, and she used powerful strokes resembling men's play to win the American singles championship in 1904. In the following year, she became the first American woman to win the Wimbledon title. Women initially played tennis in doubles matches that limited the necessity for running or agility, but in 1887 they participated in a national singles championship at the Philadelphia Cricket Club, and a mixed doubles championship was held in 1891.

Women also took up golf but were relegated to using the country clubs when men were not on the links. The Meadowbrook Golf Course on Long Island sponsored the first national championship for women in 1895, and Chicagoan Margaret Abbott became the first American female Olympic champion when she scored a 47 at the 1900 Paris Olympics in the nine-hole golf competition for women. Abbott, who adopted more suitable clothing, bested competitors who showed up in high heels.

Resistance to Social Reform

Although subordinate groups adopted mainstream American sport forms in the schools, parks, and playgrounds of the American cities and colonies,

these activities did not guarantee their acceptance of middle-class WASP values. Just as island residents retained their languages and customs, alternative values persisted in the States as well. Catholic and Jewish groups formed their own settlement houses to attract youth, and the Knights of Columbus, a Catholic fraternal organization, promoted competitive athletic events to counter the Protestant influences of the YMCA. Such groups allowed middle-class and aspiring Americans outside the WASP realm to seek accommodation with the mainstream culture without sacrificing their religious beliefs. The YMCA also found little success in its attempts to convert and instill middle-class morality in either ethnic-minority youths of the working class or the bachelor subculture tied to saloons and pool halls.

For example, Ed Morris, a professional baseball player for the Pittsburgh team, did join the YMCA in 1887. However, he took out a newspaper ad to assure his friends in the sporting fraternity that he had not gotten religious. He joined the YMCA, he maintained, only to have access to the gymnasium. Physicality and the retention of his physical prowess enabled him to retain his identity and status among his blue-collar supporters.

Cycling Pioneers

Throughout history, walking, horseback riding, and using carriages drawn by horses were the only ways of transport on land, which made traveling either slow or expensive. With the invention of the dandy horse, or hobby horse, by German baron Karl Drais in 1817, a new era of locomotion began. The draisine was a machine with two wheels pushed forward by the feet of the riders. However, it took several decades until the first velocipedes with pedals, so-called bone shakers, were constructed, bought, and used by daredevils. In the 1880s, bicycles had a high front wheel, which made cycling faster but also even more dangerous.

With the development of the so-called safety bikes at the end of the nineteenth century, cycling became a mass movement. New bicycles now had pneumatic tires and chains that transferred the drive to the rear wheel. Whereas only few women (and men) had dared to ride the uncomfortable high-wheel machines, the new bikes made cycling easy and popular among both sexes. More and more women used bikes and thus gained a measure of independence. Bicycles also represented a new form of femininity and signaled emancipation. According to the women's rights activist Susan B. Anthony, bicycling "has done more to emancipate women than anything else in the world. It gives women a feeling of freedom and self-reliance. I stand and rejoice every time I see a woman ride by on a wheel . . . the picture of free, untrammeled womanhood" (*Harvard Graduates Magazine* **1896**).

Amalie Rother, a German woman, wrote a long article as one of the first female cyclists in Berlin. Her text, published in 1897, provides excellent insights into the pleasures and problems of female pioneers who dared to participate in an activity considered to be for men only. In 1890, she and Clara Beyer were among the first women to present themselves to a horrified public on the new velocipede. In order not to cause an uproar, their bicycles had to be brought to the outskirts of Berlin, and they rode on isolated forest roads. She writes:

> Later we dared to cycle through the city, but only at dawn. Finally, we set out bravely from the center of Berlin and were immediately surrounded by hundreds of people. A swarm of ragamuffins kept pace with us, chanting remarks of the most charming sort. In short, we ran the gauntlet which caused us to ask ourselves whether the game was worth the candle.

> We met an almost fanatical hatred. Although we referred to and compared ourselves with equestriennes, it was in vain: cycling was considered as a men only affair. . . . However, when we had left the city, we would increase the speed, race under the green crowns of the trees, chest expanded and heart racing, we would reaffirm our eternal loyalty to cycling.

> In September 1893, for the first time a womens' bicycle race was organized and it became a breakthrough as a large and sports-minded audience saw a group of competent cyclists, in becoming clothes, mastering their machines. This sight was very different from the sight of a single female cycler among a shouting mob!

Rother emphasized, based on her experiences, not only the health benefits of cycling but also its great value as a means of transportation, as it made its riders independent of carriages or trains and brought them where they wanted to be and when. Cycling also enforced a new dress code as it did not allow long skirts and tight corsets:

> As women have the same number of legs as men and use them, particularly in bicycling, in the same way, they should clothe them accordingly, giving each leg its own covering rather than placing both into one. . . . The most practical dress for cycling are trousers. Of course, one does not walk around in this dress upon arrival, but wears a skirt (over the trousers) which one has brought along.

Rother was enthusiastic about the surge in women's cycling and associated this positive development with the participation in cycling races. Successful participants gained a measure of fame, such as the Belgian Hélène Dutrieu and Swedish-born American Tillie Anderson. Soon cycling spread to the high society—even the empress Elisabeth of Austria enjoyed this new form of locomotion.

However, the successes of women on the bicycle may have caused resistance, and after the turn of the century, cycling federations forbade the organization of such competitions. For example, by 1902 the United States had banned women from cycling contests, noting that the "weak sex" should not strain its health.

Rother, Amalie. Das Damenfahren. In Paul von Salvisberg (Hg.), *Der Radsport in Bild und Wort, München 1897*. Trans. by Rodelinde Albrecht [Reprint.]. Hildesheim: Olms Presse, 1980. S. 111–127.

Young, mostly working-class males remained mired in the bachelor subculture that the Progressive reformers hoped to rehabilitate. The "sports," as they were known, congregated in saloons, pool halls, bowling alleys, race tracks, boxing arenas, and brothels, where they sought homosocial camaraderie. Sport played a central role in their lifestyle, and athletes served as heroes (see Mike "King" Kelly in chapter 5). Gambling, drinking, and womanizing proved particular affronts to the Progressives' moral sensibilities, and they enacted legal bans on gambling, horse racing, and boxing without great success. In New York, the Horton Law of 1896 legalized boxing temporarily. In 1900, New York banned the sport, but promoters easily circumvented the legal restrictions by arranging bouts in private sports clubs, where attendees paid their "membership dues" upon admittance at the door. In 1911, the Frawley Act allowed for such bouts as long as no decision was rendered as to a winner; but that did not dispel the gambling, as sportswriters simply announced their chosen winners in the next day's newspapers. The Frawley Act did, however, require boxing licenses and some regulation of bouts, and the revenues obtained added to the state's coffers. Although the sport was banned again in 1917, the United States' entry into World War I showed the value of boxing and its similarity to bayonet training for military personnel who might be engaged in personal combat. By 1920, the Walker Act realized the futility of the boxing ban and established the New York State Athletic Commission to regulate the sport, and other states later followed its lead (Gems, *Boxing* 63–64).

In urban parks and playgrounds, reformers often faced a difficult task. Ethnic and racial rivalries arose over the use of these public spaces—as did transgressions into contrary ethnic neighborhoods—which prompted combat as groups sought to protect their own spaces from outside intrusion. Specific ethnic groups claimed particular locations as their own and drove off rivals in violent confrontations. While Jim Crow laws enforced racial segregation in the South, the Northern cities marked boundaries by control of the parks, thus establishing de facto segregation as oppositional groups vied for contested spaces. In a study of Chicago gangs, one researcher noted that "about one-fourth of the membership of the WWW's [a Jewish gang] is composed of professional prize fighters, and more than once this gang has struck terror into the hearts of overaggressive Polish groups" (Thrasher 150). Reformers involved with settlement houses wanted to sublimate such Old World animosities into less sanguinary athletic competitions.

Such problems were exacerbated by the fact that neighborhood gangs adopted sports but used them as a vehicle for gambling. Politicians organized and sponsored some gang activities and even provided headquarters for neighborhood clubs with the expectation of their loyalty—and often their heavy-handed support on election day. Some gangs even took over parks and playgrounds as their center of activity. One of most notorious gangs in Chicago originated as the Morgan Athletic Club. It changed its name to the Ragen's Colts in 1908, when Frank Ragen, a future county commissioner, became club president. With more than two thousand members, the Colts ruled the Sherman Park area, often terrorizing residents. From 1900 to 1913, Chicago newspaper publishers engaged in circulation wars and employed the Colts as intimidators; during that time, 27 newspaper vendors were killed. The Colts also proved largely responsible for the 1919 race riot that rocked Chicago and resulted in 38 deaths. Such political athletic clubs contributed significant support to urban political machines, and some members of "social athletic clubs" (some of which were just gangs and used the letters S.A.C. after their name to provide the perception of greater legitimacy) eventually became mayors of Chicago.

In the 1880s, rowdy laborers in Worcester, Massachusetts, used its parks for drinking parties. Working-class voters in Worcester and other American cities mobilized in a successful effort to gain more active usage of park space, resulting in the construction of ball fields, although Sabbatarian blue laws forbade Sunday games in some locations (Boston, for example, banned Sunday baseball games until 1920).

As schools made efforts to educate and control children, most boys and young men lingered in the workforce in an effort to resist compliance with schooling laws. In 1902, the YMCA organized an industrial recreation branch, and businesses sponsored enough bowling and baseball teams in cities to organize their own industrial leagues. Company teams proved attractive not only to athletes but to their coworkers as well. Despite employers' intentions of providing wholesome recreation for employees, workers realized they might increase their meager wages by gambling on games. A procession of vehicles often followed company teams to away games. In 1914, a crowd of 115,000 witnessed a baseball game in Cleveland between the White Auto Company and the Luxus team of Omaha. Some of the earliest pro football teams developed from early industrial programs. The Columbus Panhandles, made up of blue-collar railroad workers, traveled the Midwest football circuit on weekends, while the Acme Packers represented the small town of Green Bay, Wisconsin. The Staley Starch Company team of Decatur, Illinois, eventually moved to Chicago, where it became the Bears. With players supplementing their paychecks by earning money on the field, fellow workers often attempted to do so by betting, yielding mixed results for employers, as employees simultaneously wagered their earnings (which contradicted the middle-class values that the employers hoped to instill) and developed a loyalty to the company as it competed with commercial rivals. For such workers, then, leisure pursuits revolved around the physicality of the working-class lifestyle, and they adapted employer offerings to fit their own needs.

Even though Progressive Era social reformers did not always meet their goals, many immigrants and other working-class groups did achieve a greater measure of acceptance in the culture of the United States through sport.

Sport and Colonialism

Progressive reformers even invoked sport to inculcate American WASP values in overseas colonies.

Under the guise of the "white man's burden," European powers colonized the globe, rationalizing their occupation of foreign lands as bettering the populations by bringing Christianity and white civilization to them. The British, foremost of the imperial powers in the nineteenth century, counted their worldwide dominions and bragged that the sun never set upon the British Empire. Foreign colonies provided natural resources, cheap labor, and markets for surplus goods in the expanding industrial economies. The United States lagged behind the Europeans in such acquisitions until 1898, but after its victory in the brief Spanish-American War, the young country claimed the previous Spanish colonies of Cuba, Puerto Rico, Guam, and the Philippines. That same year, it annexed Hawaii in the wake of a coup orchestrated by American businessmen who had wrested control of the islands from the Hawaiian monarch in 1893. A quote from Albert J. Beveridge's speech to the U.S. Senate in 1900 highlights part of the reasoning behind such acquisitions:

> God has not been preparing the English-speaking and Teutonic peoples for a thousand years for nothing but vain and idle self-admiration. No. He made us master organizers of the world to establish system where chaos reigned. He has given us the spirit

People & Places

Lottie Dod and Elite Women's Sport

Charlotte "Lottie" Dod (1871–1960) was the last of four children born to a wealthy merchant. She and her siblings, a sister and two brothers, enjoyed private schooling and proved to be versatile athletes. Their father built tennis courts on the family estate, and tennis parties forged networks and gained social capital among upper-class British families at the end of the nineteenth century. Like Lottie Dod, wealthy women in the United States began to indulge in sports and particular sport forms that required leisure time and expense that segregated elites from the lower classes in what sociologist Thorstein Veblen termed "conspicuous consumption." Throughout the 1890s, wealthy Americans congregated at Newport, Rhode Island, for a national tennis tournament, and they joined exclusive country clubs to golf with other members of their social class. Yachting and ownership of racehorses further distinguished the wealthy from those who could not afford such symbols of the luxurious lifestyle.

Dod first distinguished herself by winning the Wimbledon national English tennis championship as a 15-year-old in 1887, a feat she would repeat in 1888, 1891, 1892, and 1893. She partnered with her sister to win the doubles championship. Like other female players of her day, Dod served underhand; but unlike others, she developed a one-hand grip and hit the ball forcefully. By the turn of the century, Dod had taken up field hockey and represented the English national team in 1899 and 1900. Her life of leisure permitted her to travel throughout Europe and America, and in the winters she participated in curling, tobogganing, and ice skating, earning the highest male certification in the latter. With her brother she climbed the highest mountains in Europe.

Dod's interests and skills included archery. In 1908, she won a silver medal at the London Olympic Games, while her brother, Willy, captured a gold medal. With the outbreak of World War I, Dod joined the Red Cross to serve British troops in England. She was later elected to the International Tennis Hall of Fame.

of progress to overwhelm the forces of reaction throughout the earth. He has made us adept in government that we may administer government among savage and senile peoples. Were it not for such a force as this the world would relapse into barbarism and night. And of all our race He has marked the American people as His chosen nation to finally lead in the redemption of the world.

qtd. in Blum et al. 536

American missionaries had been active in the islands long before that time. Arriving in 1820, they won favor by ingratiating themselves with the monarchy over the next generation, and they imposed their own values by banning the Hawaiian sports of surfing, canoe racing, and boxing, as well as gambling and the erotic hula dances. The missionaries introduced residential boarding schools to inculcate their religious beliefs in native children, and their efforts to Americanize Hawaiians also included the introduction of baseball. When Alexander Cartwright, formerly the secretary of the New York Knickerbockers baseball club, moved to Hawaii in 1849, he was surprised to see the game already being played in the islands. By the 1870s, Honolulu featured a four-team league that drew thousands of spectators. In the following decade, polo, tennis, and track-and-field competition were pursued, but the cultural transition remained incomplete and

contested. Native Hawaiians resurrected canoe racing in 1875, and hula dancers entertained the nationalistic King Kalakaua at his birthday party in 1886. The rising sense of Hawaiian nationalism led to a clash with the American minority, and white businessmen imposed a new constitution on the king in 1887, stripping him of his powers. When his successor, Queen Liliuokalani, proved just as fierce in her independence, the whites, aided by an American diplomat and a contingent of U.S. Marines, imprisoned her and elected one of their own, plantation owner Sanford Dole, as president until the U.S. government heeded their request for annexation.

Like their mainland counterparts, the plantation owners used sport as a means of social control, organizing baseball leagues for their polyglot labor force of Filipino, Japanese, Chinese, and Portuguese workers. A Chinese Hawaiian baseball team traveled to the mainland in 1910 and won a majority of its games. By 1913, they had won 54 of 59 games played against American college teams. The Asahi team of Japanese Hawaiians, formed in 1905, won the Hawaiian championship 15 times and traveled to Japan, the Philippines, and the United States on successful baseball tours. As with mainland immigrants, the second generation of Japanese and Chinese immigrants to Hawaii adopted and even excelled in mainstream sport forms, but their successes also reinforced the racial

A 1920 woodcut print of surfers in Honolulu, by artist Charles William Bartlett.
Photo courtesy of Library of Congress, LC-USZC4-2063.

pride denied them in other spheres of life, such as the workplace.

The aquatic sports of the Hawaiians even reversed the cultural flow, as Hawaiian swimmers formed the backbone of the U.S. Olympic team from 1912 through the 1920s. Its most famous member, Duke Kahanamoku, won six Olympic medals from 1912 through 1932 and served as a cultural ambassador for sport, popularizing Hawaiian surfing around the world. His native land served as a cultural crossroads in the Pacific, hosting both American and Japanese teams. Kahanamoku's travels, his fame, and his perceived exoticism generated interest in and tourism to the islands.

Even before the United States began its imperial march, American traders had sought foreign ports. American expatriates brought baseball to China as early as 1863, and teachers, missionaries, and the YMCA promoted American games throughout Asia. By 1877, missionaries had established more than two hundred schools that endeavored to promote Christianity in China. By the 1890s, more than one thousand Americans preached Protestantism and sport as a means to modernization; but physical activity seemed too much like work to upper-class Chinese. Still, the Americans persisted with baseball and track-and-field competitions, and the YMCA introduced basketball in 1896. Foreign impositions of the Americans and the European powers, however, brought resistance and retaliation. The summer of 1900 erupted in the Boxer Rebellion as Chinese nationals killed foreign missionaries as well as their native converts and besieged the compounds of the interlopers until a multinational force, including American soldiers and marines, came to their rescue. The Americans resumed their proselytism and athletic campaign, and by 1910 the YMCA organized national athletic championships over five days that drew forty thousand spectators. In 1915, China hosted the Far East Games, a regional variation of the global Olympics, which had been discontinued while World War I was raging in Europe. Despite the adoption of Western sport forms indignation lingered, and a resurgent nativism in the 1920s and a civil war in 1927 finally chased the foreigners from China. The Chinese would conduct their own political, commercial, and athletic affairs thereafter under communist leadership (Gems, *The Athletic Crusade*).

American Protestant missionaries engaged in similar evangelical efforts in Japan in the 1850s after Commodore Matthew Perry forced the reclusive Japanese to open their ports in 1853. More receptive to modernization than the Chinese, Japan sent students to be educated in American colleges, where they learned to play baseball. Baseball became a favorite of the Japanese, and their elite Ichiko prep school defeated several American teams during the 1890s. In the early twentieth century, baseball became a form of surrogate warfare, as Japan and the United Sates contended for leadership in the Pacific. Japanese university teams barnstormed to Hawaii and the United States, and the universities of Washington and Wisconsin lost to Japanese schools in 1908 and 1909, respectively, on tours characterized as "invasions" of the Asian nation. The University of Chicago redeemed American pride by going undefeated against the Japanese in 1910, then declaring its team the "champions of the Orient."

Although some political tensions played out on the athletic fields, Japan took a more overt stance in expressing its Asian leadership. In 1895 it defeated the Chinese in the Sino-Japanese War and occupied the island of Taiwan, introducing

Duke Kahanamoku bridged cultures as an athlete and racial pioneer.

Image courtesy of Library of Congress, LC-DIG-ggbain-10653.

the inhabitants to baseball. In 1904–1905, Japan proved victorious over Russia in a war to control the Korean peninsula, where the winners also initiated baseball among the populace.

Japanese muscle became more prominent when Tokyo hosted the Far East Olympics in 1917 and Osaka did so in 1923. Japanese baseball teams dominated the University of Chicago in its 1925 and 1930 visits to the islands. Japan further tested Social Darwinian precepts in the global Olympic Games thereafter, making impressive showings throughout the 1930s. In 1931, it invaded Manchuria on the Chinese mainland, further exerting its Asian influence. Japanese baseball teams established a professional league in 1936 and called for a true World Series with their American counterparts (Gems, *The Athletic Crusade*).

A similar spirit arose in the Philippines when Waseda University of Japan played a Filipino team from Cebu in 1905. The Japanese viewed the Filipinos, then under American rule, as lackeys, and the game was described as a bitter rivalry played for blood. When Cebu triumphed 3-1, its players became national heroes. The United States took control of the Philippines after the 1898 war with Spain, but guerrilla warfare and a strong nationalist movement thwarted full domination, and the Filipinos finally gained their independence in 1946. During the time of U.S. control, however, American administrators enacted a program of social reform in the archipelago even more comprehensive than those in the United States. As with efforts to transform stateside ethnic groups, sport proved a primary means of Americanization activity in the Philippines. American soldiers introduced baseball and boxing to Filipinos shortly after arriving in 1898, and General James Franklin Bell, commander of U.S. forces in Manila, claimed that "baseball had done more to 'civilize' Filipinos than anything else" (Seymour 324–325). W. Cameron Forbes, a former Harvard football coach and heir to the Bell Telephone Company with political connections, served as governor-general of the islands. He constructed a polo field and a golf course at the summer capital in Baguio and promoted widespread emphasis on physical education in the schools; boys and girls competed for interscholastic, district, and provincial honors. Schools added sports facilities, including tennis courts and tracks, to instill competitive spirit, discipline, a strong work ethic, and community pride.

Forbes further extended the use of sport in conjunction with the YMCA. Under YMCA direction, the Manila Carnival, initially a commercial fair, became an athletic spectacle that spurred town and

Colonial administrators used basketball in efforts to Americanize subject peoples.

Image from Facts and figures about the Philippines, Manila: Bureau of printing, 1920. Digitized by the University of Michigan Library, Ann Arbor, Michigan.

tribal rivalries, offering national championships in men's and boys' baseball, basketball, volleyball, and track and field, as well as girls' basketball, along with open competition in swimming, tennis, track, golf, polo, soccer, football, and bowling. The baseball tournament included a team from Japan, and under the leadership of Elwood Brown of the YMCA, the Manila Carnival invited other Asian nations and became known as the Far Eastern Olympics.

By the end of Forbes' administration, more than 1,500 uniformed baseball teams competed for trophies and prizes, and 95 percent of public school students participated in sport and games (Beran 74). The YMCA prepared the official recreation manual, trained playground directors, and spread its own games of basketball and volleyball. The Filipinos adopted basketball as their national sport, and Filipino boxers became world champions, as sport became one of the more subtle means of acculturation. Thus, the Americans quelled Filipino discontent and rebellion with a brutal military occupation, then transferred indigenous nationalism into athletic rivalries with Japan, a country perceived as a common rival in the Pacific.

Filipino discontent with American rule, however, could be channeled through the boxing ring, where Francisco Guilledo assumed the alias of Pancho Villa, the Mexican bandit who terrorized the American Southwest during World War I. Villa defeated the champion of the American army in 12 of 13 contests and fought to a draw in the other. He held the world flyweight championship from 1923 to 1925, and Filipinos reveled in his prowess. In the 1930s, Filipino boxers would travel to California to further test their mettle against American counterparts (Gems, *The Athletic Crusade*; Gems, *Boxing*; Gems, *Sport and the American Occupation of the Philippines, 159-160*).

In Caribbean nations, baseball preceded American occupation, as several Cuban students learned the game while studying in the United States and taught it to other islanders upon their return in 1864. Games with American teams began in 1866, and the Cuban professional league started play in 1873. Cubans introduced baseball to Puerto Ricans and Dominicans even before American troops arrived to garrison their new possessions after the Spanish-American War. The arrival of the Americans, however, greatly promoted the sport, and company and school teams were engaging in tournaments by 1900.

Even as American administrators and evangelical missionaries brought sports to the islands, they attempted to eliminate some activities. They banned bullfights, cockfights, and gambling, and the Woman's Christian Temperance Union tried to prohibit alcohol. Protestant missionaries carved up the islands in denominational jurisdictions, trying to convert the already Christian Catholics, and English was made the required language in the reorganized schools. The YMCA opened operations in Cuba in 1904 and in Puerto Rico a few years later, and it introduced a particular WASP brand of morality. Along with racially segregated facilities, the YMCA invoked Sabbatarian restrictions, refusing to allow play on Sundays. Cultural differences became apparent in 1906, when a YMCA director explained to a Cuban athlete that Sunday was the day to think about God. The Cuban replied that he did so six days a week, but Sunday was his only opportunity for fun (Gems, *Athletic* 89).

Cuba endured a brief series of occupations by American troops for a decade after the Spanish-American War, but as an independent nation it soon reverted to its Spanish language and Latin culture. Americans developed a perception of Caribbean life as exotic, and Cuba became a favorite destination as a vacation playground for wealthy Americans in search of gambling and illicit pleasures not readily available on the more inhibited mainland. Professional American baseball teams found the Caribbean climate particularly salubrious and many made annual winter barnstorming trips to the island. Cuban teams often beat the Americans, and the best of the light-skinned Cuban players signed contracts with American major league clubs.

The YMCA sent missionaries to Cuba in 1904 and introduced basketball, volleyball, and track-and-field competition to the island. The Havana Sports Club, the Vedado Tennis Club, and the University of Havana all adopted American football, and the latter played against the YMCA, the

American military, and college teams. The first professional boxing matches in Cuba took place in 1909, and Havana hosted one of the most controversial heavyweight championships in 1915 when Jess Willard defeated Jack Johnson to reclaim the title and pretensions of white racial superiority. Black Cuban boxers would later dispel that notion in the United States.

Although the Cubans introduced baseball to the Dominican Republic, the game was reinforced with the onset of American intervention in the early nineteenth century. In 1905, U.S. Marines occupied the country and took control of the Dominican customs house to pay off debts owed to American financiers, and subsequent intrusions continued throughout the century. Baseball served as a useful means of social control when the United States established a military government to oversee the country until 1924. Already by 1913, the U.S. minister had reported to the Secretary of State that

I deem it worthy of the Department's notice that the American game of base-ball is being played and supported here with great enthusiasm. The remarkable effect of this outlet for the animal spirits of the young men, is that they are leaving the plazas where they were in the habit of congregating and talking revolution and are resorting to the ball fields where they become wildly partizen (sic) each for his favorite team.

qtd. in Gems, *The Athletic Crusade* 117

In later years, Dominicans would gain their independence and supply a cheap labor force for Major League Baseball teams in the United States (Gems, *The Athletic Crusade*).

Puerto Ricans fared less well, as the United States maintained an ongoing presence that eventually resulted in commonwealth status. The YMCA introduced basketball and volleyball, and U.S. government administrators tried to Americanize the islanders through sport and games on playgrounds and at settlement houses. Baseball prospered, but Puerto Ricans clung to their Spanish language and Catholic religion despite the ongoing efforts of the YMCA. The YMCA even permitted boxing as a means to attract members, but with little success. Boxing did, however, produce the first national sport hero in Puerto Rico, when Sixto Escobar won the world bantamweight championship in the 1930s. Puerto Ricans chose a limited assimilation, adopting American sport forms but employing national teams and their own flag in athletic competitions to emphasize their independent cultural identity. Americans soon reflected upon their growing international importance:

The West Indies drift toward us, the Republic of Mexico hardly longer has an independent life, and the city of Mexico is an American town. With the completion of the Panama Canal all Central America will become part of our system. We have expanded into Asia, we have attracted the fragments of the Spanish dominions, and reaching out into China we have checked the advance of Russia and Germany. . . . We are penetrating into Europe, and Great Britain especially is gradually assuming the position of a dependency. . . . The United States will outweigh any single empire, if not all empires combined. The whole world will pay her tribute. Commerce will flow to her from both east and west, and the order which has existed from the dawn of time will be reversed.

qtd. in Blum et al. 537

The expansion of American influence extended to Central America, where American companies had operated in Nicaragua since the late nineteenth century. Nicaraguan students who studied in the United States brought baseball back to their homeland, and by 1911 they had enough teams to organize a league. American troops arrived in the same year to protect American businesses during a local uprising. By 1915, the Nicaraguans established a baseball league, in which a team of U.S. Marines became a member. Throughout the World War I years and thereafter, the native contingents faced off against their American occupiers on the baseball field in less violent confrontations. By 1916, the Nicaraguans had also adopted boxing, and featured matches often preceded the baseball confrontations (Gems, *The Athletic Crusade*).

Americans maintained a greater and longer presence in Panama. After the failure of the French to complete a transoceanic canal through the isthmus, American president Teddy Roosevelt engineered the secession of Panama, a northern province of Colombia, in 1903. When the Colombian government failed to ratify a proposed treaty with the United States, Panamanian politicians— backed by the U.S. Navy and a contingent of Marines—declared their independence, which the United States quickly recognized. The new Panamanian government granted Canal Zone rights to the United States, which it held for the remainder of the century. The Americans built tennis courts, baseball fields, bowling alleys, and gymnasiums for the workforce, and there were enough baseball teams by 1912 to create a league. As in other regions, baseball and boxing assumed greater popularity among the local populace as well, and by the 1920s, Panamanians could take pride in Al Brown as flyweight champion of the world.

Sport During World War I

In the United States, sport became a means to train combatants and produce camaraderie, nationalism, and patriotic spirit. In 1914, General Leonard Wood produced a manual for the physical training of soldiers. Dr. Joseph Raycraft, director of athletics at Princeton, assumed leadership of the Army sports program, and Walter Camp, famed football coach at Yale, did the same for the Navy. Camp compiled a "daily dozen," a series of exercises to produce fitness in sailors, but competitive sport fostered the greatest interest, and baseball, football, basketball, volleyball, and tug-of-war activities were used to encourage aggressiveness and courage. Professional boxers became instructors for bayonet training, where parrying, slashing, and defense reflected the intimate conflicts that occurred in the ring.

Such athletic training was intended to produce pugnacious warriors for trench warfare and furious assaults, but it also addressed moral concerns. Sport was thought to serve the purpose of social control in Europe by keeping soldiers away from prostitutes and alcohol in their leisure hours. Venereal disease felled many American soldiers in France, and the Army eventually organized a baseball league that included more than two million players (Pope, *Patriotic* 148). Bible classes and YMCA activities were held to further deter the doughboys from indulging in illicit pleasures.

In the United States, the Boy Scouts adopted Camp's training regimen, and mayors in major American cities advocated physical education for fitness. More than 80 percent of Army applicants in 1915 and 1916 were rejected because of various deficiencies, and one-third of draftees were deemed unfit, sparking a national concern. After the war, 22 states adopted mandatory physical education laws, and West Point, under the direction of General Douglas MacArthur, initiated a comprehensive athletic program for all trainees (Pope, *Patriotic* 128–129, 197).

During the war, the armed services produced some of the best football teams in the nation. The 1918 Rose Bowl featured the Mare Island Marines from Vallejo, California, against the Camp Lewis Army team from Tacoma, Washington. The Marines won 19-7, and proceeds from the contest benefited the Red Cross. Sport taught self-sacrifice for the good of the whole, and nearly half of the 32 players in the game eventually made the ultimate sacrifice, losing their lives while in military service. The following year, with the war over, Mare Island faced the Great Lakes Naval Training Station team from Illinois. Great Lakes emerged victorious, 17-0, and 10 players in the contest earned recognition as professional football players during the 1920s, including George Halas, founder of the Chicago Bears franchise (Hibner 42, 58).

The Armistice of November 11, 1918, effectively ended hostilities, but many American servicemen awaited ships to carry them home, while others were stationed in the occupied European territories. Sport served as a more wholesome and enjoyable means of training than military drills, and from June 22 to July 6 the joint administrators organized the Inter-Allied Games, similar to the Olympics. Soldiers built Pershing Stadium in Paris, and 16 of the 29 allied countries entered teams in events that included grenade throwing and various athletic competitions. Charles Paddock set a world record in the 200-meter dash (and later won an Olympic championship at 100 meters in the 1920 games at Antwerp, Belgium). French scholar Thierry Terret has ascertained that the Inter-Allied Games were a demonstration of American power and ascendance in Europe (Terret 2006).

American involvement in World War I greatly changed the nation's relationship with the rest of the world, establishing for it a new role as global leader—one which it was unwilling to fully accept. The war and its aftermath caused Americans to examine their own values, their democratic institutions, and what

The Inter-Allied Games, a postwar military Olympics, signaled American ascendance.

Image courtesy of Library of Congress, 262-135332, Lot 7711.

it meant to be an American. Those deemed to be disloyal were arrested, imprisoned, or deported, and immigration was curtailed. The 1920s would bring a homogenization of culture and a solidifi-

People & Places

Robert Tait McKenzie

Robert Tait McKenzie (1867–1938) was born in Canada and earned his medical degree from McGill University in Montreal, where he was a friend, classmate, and coworker of James Naismith, who would later invent the game of basketball. McKenzie became the first professor of physical education at the University of Pennsylvania in 1904, where he espoused his belief in physical activity as preventive medicine and a necessity for good health. He had begun sculpting athletes for use in his classes, but he became well known for his masks and medals that were awarded to victorious competitors. With the outbreak of World War I, McKenzie joined the military service, where he provided his medical services for wounded soldiers and became interested in physical therapy, assuming the post of professor of physical therapy after the war. When the war ended, his skill as a sculptor was in demand, and he created war memorials for nearly the next two decades. The McKenzie Award is the most prestigious of all honors bestowed upon physical educators in Canada and one of the top awards issued by the Society of Health and Physical Educators (SHAPE) in the United States.

cation of cultural identity, greatly prompted by a flourishing popular culture that revolved around movies, radio, and sport, with the media enthralling the populace with stories of celebrities, who became the new American heroes and heroines.

Summary

With the outbreak of hostilities in Europe in 1914, the United States initially took a neutral stance before openly siding with the Allied forces against Germany, the Austrian empire, and Turkey. The United States' entry into the war soon decided the outcome and marked the country as a new world power with its own colonies; but its rejection of the League of Nations signaled an isolationist stance from European issues as the nation concentrated on addressing concerns in American society. By that time, the United States had made great strides in the assimilation of its Native American Indian tribes and the acculturation of the myriad ethnic immigrants who had traveled to America. In the aftermath of the war it banned the manufacture, sale, and transport of liquor (Prohibition) as yet another attempt to enforce conservative WASP values but also allowed for female suffrage as a measure of social change. The nation soon restricted immigration by establishing quotas to further limit outside influences on the American culture; but racial, ethnic, gender, and social-class differences continued to limit the homogenization efforts of the authorities.

DISCUSSION QUESTIONS

1. What dilemma did the influx of new immigrants pose for the Progressive reformers?

2. What role did sport play in the assimilation of disparate groups?

3. How did sport help quell the radical philosophies of some immigrant groups?

4. In what ways did sport represent a contested space?

5. What role did sport play in the global spread of American values?

6. In what ways did sport liberate women?

7. How did African American athletes dispel the theory of Social Darwinism?

8. Was the Progressive Movement successful? Why or why not?

Chapter 8

Sport, Heroic Athletes, and Popular Culture
1920–1950

CHAPTER OBJECTIVES

After reading this chapter, you will have learned about the following:

- Why the United States took an isolationist stance after World War I
- How racial, ethnic, and religious distinctions affected American culture and sport
- Why American society needed heroes in the aftermath of World War I and the Great Depression
- How the Great Depression affected sporting culture, and how entrepreneurs responded
- The media's role in constructing a popular culture
- The government's role in the developing popular sporting culture
- Social ramifications of the desegregation of baseball

Outlined against a blue-gray October sky, the Four Horsemen rode again. In dramatic lore they are known as Famine, Pestilence, Destruction, and Death. These are only aliases. Their real names are Stuhldreher, Miller, Crowley, and Layden. They formed the crest of the South Bend cyclone before which another fighting Army football team was swept over the precipice at the Polo Grounds yesterday afternoon as 55,000 spectators peered down on the bewildering panorama spread over the green plain below.

A cyclone can't be snared. It may be surrounded, but somewhere it breaks through to keep on going. When the cyclone starts from South Bend, where the candle lights still gleam through the Indiana sycamores, those in the way must take to storm cellars at top speed. Yesterday the cyclone struck again, as Notre Dame beat the Army, 13 to 7, with a set of backfield stars that ripped and crashed through a strong Army defense with more speed and power than the warring cadets could meet.

Rice 177

Thus did Grantland Rice describe the Notre Dame juggernaut that won the national football championship after the 1924 season. With such florid prose, Rice and other sportswriters created a bevy of athletic heroes throughout the decade as sport and media transformed American culture. Another prominent sportswriter, Paul Gallico, described athletic stars as "the Golden People," noting that in the years following World War I sport had "its first million-dollar prizefights[,] and the adulation of sports heroes [rose] to the point almost of national hysteria" (13).

When Grantland Rice wrote the account of the Four Horsemen, he penned some of the most famous lines in sportswriting history in lyrical but overstated prose. An astute publicist photographed the stars on horseback, sealing an indelible image.

Photo courtesy of Library of Congress, LC-USZ62-26735.

1920	1920s–1930	1920s–1930s	1921
■ Warren Harding elected president ■ First commercial radio broadcast begins	■ Helen Wills wins U.S. tennis championships	■ Bill Tilden dominates men's tennis championships	■ Dempsey–Carpentier fight staged

As World War I came to a close, however, "the Golden People" were anything but. The horrible devastation of the war and its terrible new weapons had shattered the idealistic notions of the Progressive reformers. And shortly thereafter, the limits of the Progressive moral agenda were again exposed in a sport scandal that shocked the nation, as even the national game of baseball, which had been used to assimilate millions of immigrants, proved corruptible. Gambling had long been a part of baseball, and widespread betting pools served as a poor man's lottery, where bettors might gamble on games, hits, runs, and so on over the course of a week, with newspapers reporting the box scores. Wealthier gamblers staked their bets instead with big bookies, but all relied on the honesty of the game and of its players' performances. As in the nineteenth century, however, sport continued to serve as both a means of community formation and a site of conflict, and the Black Sox scandal of 1919 registered the conflicting pressures and the anomalies in sport.

The Chicago White Sox had defeated the New York Giants in the 1917 World Series, but World War I service had depleted the team roster during the next year. In 1919, however, the Sox fielded one of the best teams in baseball history. Star pitcher Eddie Cicotte won 29 games, and outfielder "Shoeless" Joe Jackson hit .351 (although five points below his lifetime percentage of .356). Despite their sterling performances, Cicotte was denied a bonus, and Jackson had played six years without a raise in his $6,000 salary. In contrast, the best hitter on the Cincinnati team, their 1919 World Series opponents, made $11,000 per season (Frommer 86). Thus, the White Sox players felt underpaid and underappreciated by club owner Charles Comiskey, and, at the behest of a tangled web of gamblers, some of them colluded to throw the series to the underdog Cincinnati team. The gamblers ultimately crossed each other and the players, paying them only a fraction of the promised bribes. Nevertheless, the White Sox dropped the nine-game series. Although suspicions about their faulty play lingered for a year, the 1920 season produced record attendance that

stood for more than a quarter century (it was surpassed in 1946). That year, despite featuring four 20-game winners on the pitching staff and taking a 3 1/2-game lead late in the season, the White Sox finished third. By September of the 1920 season, a Chicago grand jury investigated alleged widespread gambling fraud in baseball, eventually indicting eight of the White Sox players for fixing the 1919 World Series.

The jury trial, held in Chicago, produced evidence that seven of the eight players had received between $5,000 and $10,000 for their participation in the conspiracy. Third baseman George "Buck" Weaver claimed he had been aware of the scheme but had not participated in it. Despite their admissions of guilt, and signed confessions by some, which mysteriously disappeared during the trial, the Chicago jury exonerated the players. The illiterate Joe Jackson's confession resurfaced when he later sued Comiskey for back pay. Despite the players' acquittal, baseball authorities quickly enacted the National Agreement of 1921, which produced a commissioner of baseball. Judge Kenesaw Mountain Landis, a flamboyant and controversial federal magistrate, assumed the role in dictatorial fashion. He immediately banned all eight Chicago players from the game and purged it of any gambling influences. Buck Weaver spent the remainder of his life trying to clear his name of the charges. Weaver's reluctance to implicate his teammates had exemplified ongoing class differences within America. Weaver had sought to maintain his personal and working-class honor by not snitching and by playing his best (he hit .324 and made no errors) during the World Series. Despite the fact that he accepted no bribe money, however, the commissioner judged him to be equally guilty. The differences in perception reflected social-class distinctions that continued to haunt American society, but journalists soon attempted to rectify the divisions by portraying sport as a meritocracy and resurrecting the promise of opportunity and mobility in the United States.

The decade of the 1920s was termed "the Golden Age of Sports," and the media's creation

1922	1923	1924
■ U.S. Field Hockey Association founded	■ Teapot Dome oil scandal exposed	■ Intercollegiate football features Red Grange and the Four Horsemen
■ Glenna Collett wins U.S. Women's Amateur Golf Championship for the first time	■ President Warren Harding dies, and Calvin Coolidge serves as president	■ First Winter Olympics held; Sonja Henie and Gilles Grafstrom compete in ice skating
		■ Immigration Quota Law passed by Congress

of sports heroes during this time provided a stabilizing influence in a rapidly changing American culture. Sports stars were lionized as All-American types who exemplified American cultural values. The Four Horsemen of Notre Dame represented the American ideology of spirit, teamwork, and assimilation of diverse groups within society. Babe Ruth, the most famous of all the athletic heroes, symbolized the American dream, the land of opportunity and meritocracy, where one could succeed despite humble origins. The depiction of such heroes presented a more homogeneous culture and solidified an American cultural identity, but it also masked social tensions inherent in the United States in the aftermath of World War I and during the Great Depression and World War II.

War, Depression, and the Shaping of America

After World War I, the United States declined to join the League of Nations despite the efforts of President Woodrow Wilson in launching the organization intended to achieve world peace. Thus isolated from international affairs, the United States focused on domestic issues. The 1920 census indicated that, for the first time, most Americans lived in cities, and this increasing urbanization brought cultural transitions that produced tensions and conflict. Employment issues and worker discontent resulted in labor unions that continued to question the capitalist economy, with thousands of workers participating in strikes to protest their miserable

International Perspective

The Rise of Asian Athletes

After westerners entered Japan in the mid-nineteenth century, the country embarked on a modernization campaign, industrializing its economy and adopting western education models and sport forms. American teachers introduced Japanese students to baseball and by the 1890s they began to challenge and defeat American teams. Japan defeated China in the Sino-Japanese War of 1894-1895 and then vanquished Russia in 1905. Its military victories challenged Social Darwinian perceptions of Asian inferiority and sports competition provided a means to test such notions in a more peaceful setting.

Japan first entered the Olympic Games in 1912, and Japan entered the Far East Games hosted by the American YMCA in Manila to challenge its Asian competitors thereafter. In the 1928 Olympics, Kinue Hitomi, the top Japanese female athlete, won a silver medal in the 800 meter run, although she had never run that race before the qualifying round. Hitomi, a journalist and a poet, had begun her athletic career as a tennis player, but found her passion as a track and field athlete, setting numerous national and world records in sprints, hurdles, long jump, shot put, and javelin. At the 1926 international women's competition in Gothenberg, Sweden, she had entered six events and won recognition as the top scorer. In 1929 she set a world record in the triathlon (100 meters, high jump, javelin throw), a predecessor to the modern heptathlon. She excelled again, winning three medals at the women's competition in Prague in 1930. She contracted pneumonia and died at the age of 24 in 1931 (Kietlinski 54-65).

At the 1932 Olympics in Los Angeles and again in 1936 at Berlin, Japanese male and female swimmers excelled and male track and field performers gained worldwide recognition in their competition with western athletes. In Japan baseball teams challenged American collegiate teams and troupes of barnstorming professionals and the Japanese called for a true World Series to determine national prowess in the game. Their quest went unheeded and the eruption of World War II soon tested nationalistic spirit in a violent and deadly fashion.

1925	1926	1927	
■ Scopes Trial conducted	■ Gertrude Ederle swims the English Channel	■ Sacco and Vanzetti Trial conducted	■ First talking movie appears (*The Jazz Singer*)
		■ Babe Ruth hits 60 home runs	■ Dempsey–Tunney rematch held (the long-count fight)
		■ Charles Lindbergh makes first solo, nonstop transatlantic flight	■ Harlem Globetrotters begin barnstorming tours

wages and working conditions (Dawley 234). Socialists, communists, and anarchists challenged the government, and, after Bolsheviks toppled the Russian tsar, capitalists feared a similar revolt in the United States, thus prompting the Red Scare. The Department of Justice arrested thousands of suspected radicals on a single night in 1920, deporting many as undesirable aliens. Anti-immigrant paranoia ensued, and for many European immigrants the promises of America went unrealized. Nativists, those persons wanting to uphold the values and power of white, native-born U.S. citizens, reacted to perceived threats to the dominant WASP culture by enacting restrictive immigration laws in 1924 that established quotas for Southern and Eastern Europeans and curtailed Asian immigration in an attempt to safeguard the republic for Anglo-Americans. In 1920, the Nineteenth Amendment granted women the right to vote, further threatening some aspects of male hegemony and the traditional gender order.

Throughout the 1920s, blacks, Jews, and members of other ethnic groups asserted their own forms of expression in popular culture. Blues and jazz evolved out of African American experiences in the South, and during the Great Migration the music moved to the North, where it combined with urban experiences to produce new genres. In the movies, ethnic-minority (especially Jewish) producers drew upon their immigrant pasts in featuring working-class heroes and heroines, and film became a primary means of entertainment and recreation during the decade. Young urban women also challenged dominant middle-class norms by engaging in the risqué "flapper" lifestyle. Eschewing the religious strictures of the past, they smoked cigarettes, frequented speakeasies (where they freely drank prohibited alcohol), and danced to the new music. The dance fads of the era were considered lascivious by traditionalists, and the sexual escapades of celebrities and common flappers shocked even the liberal elements of society.

The Stock Market Crash of 1929, however, created a worldwide economic depression and abruptly halted the sports boom of the 1920s. Unemployment skyrocketed, and American workers increasingly questioned the capitalist system.

By 1932, the unemployed numbered eleven million. In Chicago alone, seven hundred thousand people (accounting for 40 percent of the workforce) were unemployed, and in Boston more than forty thousand families sought relief funds. With the failure of more than 4,300 banks between 1929 and 1931, there was little to be had (Blum et al. 656). Protests ensued, and hunger marches made clear the desperate state of poor people. Millions of homeless people wandered the country in search of work or begged on urban streets. The state of the economy proved especially dire for African Americans. Sixty-nine percent of the black population in Pittsburgh was unemployed, and in Detroit the figure reached 75 percent (Ashby 240).

President Franklin Delano Roosevelt's economic recovery plan, known as the New Deal, entailed a massive recreational program that allotted $1.5 billion to labor and construction costs in a wide variety of federal agencies. The Civilian Conservation Corps (CCC), started in 1933, employed five hundred thousand people within two years in conservation projects and environmental programs in rural areas, improvement of national and state parks, and construction of hiking trails throughout the country. The Civilian Works Administration (1933), the Federal Emergency Relief Administration (1934), the National Youth Administration (1935), and the Works Progress Administration (1935) all employed multitudes in the construction of stadiums, swimming pools, sports fields, playgrounds, parks, gymnasiums, and winter sports facilities. Such programs created jobs, and the fruits of this labor addressed the forced leisure needs of unemployed citizens throughout the 1930s (Foner and Garraty 177, 1168).

The entry of the United States into World War II alleviated any economic concerns. Production boomed in order to supply materials for the war effort, and men were needed to fill the military ranks. Football coaches extolled the values of their game as preparation for battle, and President Franklin Roosevelt maintained that baseball was necessary for the national morale. Previously disparate groups united to confront the fascist threat to democracy, as class consciousness diminished, nationalism triumphed, and capitalists prospered.

1928	1929	1930	1932
■ Amelia Earhart becomes first woman to fly across the Atlantic ■ Herbert Hoover elected president	■ Stock Market Crash signals the Great Depression ■ Carnegie Report on intercollegiate athletics issued	■ Bobby Jones wins Grand Slam in golf ■ Catholic Youth Organization founded	■ Franklin D. Roosevelt elected president for his first term ■ Olympic Games held in Los Angeles; Babe Didrikson, Lillian Copeland, Eleanor Holm, and other U.S. women triumph

Cities were not the only areas affected by the depression. Poor people in rural areas also lived in dilapidated conditions.

Image courtesy of Library of Congress, LC-USF-3301-31322.

Social Change and the Spread of Sport

The United States' concerted efforts against the fascist powers in World War II unified the members of the nation's previously disparate cultures. Second-generation immigrants sought to prove their loyalty and their American identity.

Sport and the Accommodation of Religious Groups

The Protestantism of mainstream America had long held alternative faiths, such as Catholicism or Judaism, at bay. The entry of different religious groups into the sporting culture brought them closer to the mainstream, reduced ignorance about their contrasting beliefs, and fostered a somewhat greater degree of acceptance, although nativists

such as the Ku Klux Klan continued to oppose their citizenship.

Notre Dame and the Acceptance of Catholics

Under famed coach Knute Rockne, Notre Dame, a small Catholic college in South Bend, Indiana, fashioned a national football powerhouse. Rockne eschewed individualism when his tragic but flawed All-American George Gipp (a non-Catholic) died after the 1920 season. A nonconformist who eschewed practice and academic classes, Gipp nevertheless possessed brilliant athletic abilities that brought Notre Dame to national prominence. After his death, however, Rockne opted for an emphasis on team play, and to this day Notre Dame football players do not have their names on the backs of their jerseys. The return to a team-centered approach better suited traditional Catholic com-

1933	1934	1935
■ Twenty-First Amendment ratified (repealing Prohibition) ■ Civilian Conservation Corps established ■ First MLB All-Star Game played	■ First college all-star football game played ■ First Masters Tournament (golf) held	■ National Youth Administration established ■ Works Progress Administration established ■ Social Security Act signed ■ Congress of Industrial Organizations (CIO) forms ■ MLB begins playing night games ■ First Heisman Trophy awarded (to Jay Berwanger)

International Perspective

Sport Stars and Politics: The Price of Dissent

Athletes seem to prove the "quality" of a society and their fame transfers to their nations. Based on the ideological power of sport, nations invest considerable financial resources in their athletes in the hope that they bring fame and glory to their countries.

Athletes have risked their lives in the fight against brutal regimes, such as the National Socialist State in Germany. Werner Seelenbinder (1904–1944), a successful German wrestler with a proletarian background, competed in the light heavyweight class in the Greco-Roman style. A member of the worker's movement from an early age, Seelenbinder won gold medals in the 1925 "Workers' Olympiad," in Frankfurt/Main, and in the 1928 and 1929 *Spartakiades* in Moscow.

In 1933, the Social-Democratic and the Communist parties were banned in Germany and their leaders were persecuted. Many escaped, and others were imprisoned, forcing the dissolution of the worker's sport movement. The political change did not change Seelenbinder's political opinion and his support of communist ideologies and politics. During the award ceremony of the German Wrestling Championship in 1933, he refused to perform the Nazi salute, which resulted in his temporary banishment from training and competition.

Seelenbinder became a member of the resistance movement, the Uhrig group, which spread news and information despite Nazi crackdowns.

In 1936, Seelenbinder competed at the Olympics in Berlin, and he took fourth place. Thus, his plan to embarrass the Nazis by refusing to salute Hitler at the winner's podium failed. In 1942, he was arrested together with other members of the resistance. After more than two years in concentration camps, he was beheaded in October 1944.

munalism, and Rockne's 1924 squad, featuring quickness and teamwork, went undefeated and beat Stanford 27-10 in the Rose Bowl to claim the national championship. Rockne created national rivalries by scheduling contests throughout the country, thus unifying the Catholic constituency. He gained the support of ethnic-minority communities by stocking his polyglot team with Irishmen, Italians, Poles, Germans, assorted Eastern Europeans, and even Protestants and Jews, thus fashioning a team that more closely resembled the makeup of American society. Even here, however, blacks were excluded. Still, Rockne exemplified the American dream of the hard-working immigrant who gained wealth, status, and celebrity by virtue of his abilities.

Notre Dame's football success did much to foster Catholic pride when Catholics felt besieged by the likes of the Ku Klux Klan. The KKK had marched on South Bend before the 1924 season.

Notre Dame students repulsed the KKK, but racists managed to gain control of the state government. Notre Dame stood as a bulwark against such WASP fanaticism. In 1928, Al Smith, the Catholic presidential candidate, was swamped in the national election as the KKK campaigned ardently against him, further indicating a lack of full acceptance of Catholics. Football, however, provided Catholics with a semblance of religious respect, as Notre Dame demolished its foes. In the process, it helped incorporate an ethnically diverse and largely working-class constituency into American mainstream culture, and other Catholic colleges and high schools copied the Rockne system to release social tensions on the gridiron.

Notre Dame established a similar dynasty in the 1940s, when it won four national championships. Under coach Frank Leahy, a Rockne protégé, the Catholic juggernaut built a record of 107-13-9, going undefeated from 1946 through 1949. During

1936	1938	1939
■ Avery Brundage, president of U.S. Olympic Committee, elected to International Olympic Committee	■ National Invitational Tournament (basketball) launches	■ First televised baseball game is shown
■ Berlin Olympics ("Nazi Olympics") held: Jesse Owens triumphs, some Jewish athletes boycott	■ Joe Louis–Max Schmeling boxing rematch staged	■ National Collegiate Athletic Association basketball tournament is launched
		■ New York Rens (all-black team) reign as pro basketball champions
		■ Little League Baseball founded

World War II, Leahy took a coaching respite to join the U.S. Navy, and he urged his players to enlist in the Marines. Football held a close ideological relationship to warfare, not only in its strategy but also in its inculcation of martial spirit, toughness, courage, and leadership ability, and Leahy's admonitions further tied previously marginalized Catholics to a militaristic and nationalistic Americanism during the war. Shortly after the U.S. entry into the war, one-third of the NFL players enlisted, and 638 pros eventually served in the armed forces. By 1950, 80 Navy admirals and 98 Army generals had been football players (Gems, *For Pride* 99–100).

The West Point team proved the biggest challenge for Notre Dame during the war. Featuring Felix "Doc" Blanchard, a bruising fullback, and fleet-footed halfback Glenn Davis, Army rolled over its opponents in 1944 and 1945, averaging more than 50 points per game. Army beat Notre Dame 59-0 and 48-0 in those years, while Leahy and his charges lent their brains and brawn to the military. The Navy cadets at Annapolis fielded the number two team until Leahy returned to restore Notre Dame to the top. Army and Notre Dame played to a scoreless tie in 1946, but the latter notched a 27-7 victory over Army in 1947. Forty-two of the players from that squad went on to the professional football ranks (Littlewood 135). For many Catholics, Notre Dame, like Seabiscuit, the famed thoroughbred of the late Depression era, represented the underdog, the independent, the outsider who forged a path to success despite the odds.

The Catholic Youth Organization (CYO)

The perception of boxing as a sporting meritocracy, coupled with the hardships of working-class lives, attracted many young men to the sport. World War I demonstrated the need for combative skills, and 23 states authorized boxing by 1917. New York lifted its ban in 1920, and Illinois did so in 1926. By 1928, the *Chicago Tribune* and the *New York Daily News* sponsored regional tournaments designated as the Golden Gloves competition, with winners fighting for the national championship. The Chicago tournament, under the direction of Irish Catholic sports editor Arch Ward, had close

ties to the Catholic Youth Organization (CYO), which supplied him with a steady stream of seasoned fighters. By 1933, Golden Gloves champions were competing against international teams, channeling working-class and ethnic skepticism into mainstream American nationalism and patriotism.

That transition proved especially true for Catholics of various ethnic backgrounds who had maintained their traditional lifestyles in communal parishes often directed by Old World priests, who resisted the assimilation efforts of the Irish American hierarchy. In 1930, Bishop Bernard Sheil of Chicago organized the CYO to combat delinquency through sport. The CYO's programs included the largest basketball league in the world, with 120 teams in 1931, and it offered a host of other activities as well, but boxing remained at the root of its popularity and success. Sheil accepted all races and creeds in his boxing tournaments but required a pledge of allegiance to God and country. CYO team members received free medical care, a full suit of clothes, jobs or college scholarships, and all-expenses-paid international trips. Three CYO boxers represented the United States on the 1936 Olympic team, and many others pursued professional careers in the ring. CYO managers assured watchful care, as criminal elements increasingly operated in the pugilistic arena. Although a Catholic enterprise, the CYO followed Sheil's guidelines, which fit nicely with the WASP prescriptions of the Progressive Era, as contesting religious groups found some common ground in sport.

By the end of the decade, Sheil's program had reached nationwide proportions, and he assumed national prominence as a social and labor activist, opposing anti-Semitism and racial discrimination. As an advisor to the president, his influence extended all the way to the White House. His use of sport to bring about the assimilation of disparate Catholic ethnic groups within mainstream American culture further thwarted working-class radical sentiments, as religious faith triumphed over class consciousness under his guidance. By 1948, the partnership of Bishop Sheil and Arch Ward produced a Golden Gloves tournament that featured 120 bouts, with fights conducted simultaneously

1941–1945	1943–1954	1945	1946
■ U.S. involved in World War II	■ All-American Girls Baseball League operates	■ United Nations founded	■ All-American Football Conference founded (including black and white players)

in three rings and featuring participants from 31 states (Littlewood 80). The fusion of Catholicism with nationalistic patriotism in the sporting culture pushed a previously ostracized group into mainstream acceptance.

Boxing and Jewish Americans

As with Catholics, sport provided an entrée into mainstream popular culture for Jewish Americans. Despite anti-Semitic sentiments, Jews reached the pinnacle of boxing success during the 1920s and 1930s. Eighteen Jewish champions rose to prominence during that period, most notably Benny Leonard (aka Benjamin Leiner), the lightweight titleholder. Jackie Fields (Jacob Finkelstein) won

a gold medal as a featherweight in the 1924 Olympics at the age of 16, and five years later he won the professional welterweight championship. Barney Ross (Barnet Rosofsky) wore the Star of David on his trunks en route to winning three world titles in the 1920s. Such boxers changed their names to hide their pugilistic activities from Orthodox parents who disdained fighting. As youths, these fighters had learned their trade on demand in encounters with other ethnic-minority opponents in rough urban ghettos, and Jewish settlement houses even provided boxing lessons. The best became professionals, and their successes, often against other ethnic-minority boxers, helped dispel stereotypes of Jewish frailty and weakness.

Weight check for boxers Barney Ross and Phil Furr.
Photo courtesy of Library of Congress, LC-DIG-hec-33436.

1947	1949
■ Jackie Robinson reintegrates baseball	■ National Basketball League (NBL) and Basketball Association of America (BAA) merge to form National Basketball Association (NBA)
	■ Ladies Professional Golf Association (LPGA) founded

Jewish athletes also starred as basketball players. The South Philadelphia Hebrew All-Stars gained a national reputation, and Irish and Polish barnstormers and numerous semipro contingents offered competition in Midwestern cities. So many Jews starred on the basketball court that observers considered it to be "a Jewish sport," for which Jews had a particular affinity and aptitude.

Ascendancy of a Black Sporting Culture

During and after World War I, more than a million blacks left the South for Northern cities in a mass exodus. In the Northern urban centers, a vibrant African American culture revolved around churches, music, sport, and the arts. Black nationalists such as Marcus Garvey and W.E.B. DuBois preached black pride, self-esteem, and economic independence. The black pride movement, centered in the Harlem area of New York City, became known as the Harlem Renaissance. In 1922, Robert Douglas founded the Harlem Renaissance basketball team (aka the Harlem Rens), composed entirely of African Americans. During the 1925–1926 season, the Rens split a six-game series with the white New York Celtics before winning 88 straight games. Among the top basketball clubs of the era, the Celtics established themselves by barnstorming throughout the country, and in 1923 they won 204 of the 211 games they played (Riess, *City* 108). Thus, the Rens' series with the Celtics proved they could compete with the best white teams. In 1939, the Rens won the first national professional championship tournament. At that time, the marginal status of professional basketball followed the developmental pattern of pro baseball and football, with teams accepting black players in order to reach a level of acceptability and greater profit, then dismissing them as unworthy.

Although New York remained the primary center of the black pride movement, Chicago developed a similar hub of activity. More than 100,000 blacks had flocked to Chicago by 1920, and a decade later the city counted nearly 234,000 African American residents. They established a thriving community within the city known as Bronzeville, and basketball games accompanied the dances at the Savoy Ballroom. The local team, known as the Savoy 5, found it increasingly difficult to find fair play when facing white teams, but with the aid of manager (and then owner) Abe Saperstein, a Jewish agent, they persevered to become one of the most famous basketball teams in the world. In 1927, they began barnstorming, and they thrilled crowds with the swift play, crisp passing, and flair that had distinguished black teams for at least a decade. They adopted a new sobriquet, the Harlem Globetrotters, as a measure of their racial pride and aspirations. Initially operating throughout the Midwestern heartland, the Globetrotters purposely kept games close against town teams in order to ensure return engagements. They lost to the Rens in the first pro tournament but captured the national championship a year later, proving their abilities against the best teams in the United States. International tours and the clowning that characterized Globetrotters' games intensified after the National Basketball Association began signing black players at mid-century, which deprived Saperstein of his near monopoly on black talent. For African Americans, basketball became an economic and expressive outlet, and it assumed a growing importance in black urban culture.

Rube Foster, the baseball magnate, also followed Marcus Garvey's lead and founded the Negro National League in 1920 after the race riots of the previous year. Forced to live in urban ghettos and banned from participation in Major League Baseball—the national pastime—African Americans felt particularly excluded from the mainstream culture. Under Foster's leadership, the Negro National League served as a parallel and an alternative to the white major league system. Independence allowed blacks greater control over their own destiny, but factionalism soon led to a second professional black circuit, known as the Eastern Colored League (ECL). In 1923, one of the ECL teams, Hilldale of Philadelphia, defeated white major league teams in six of seven contests. Such victories by black athletes upset whites' belief in their racial superiority, and baseball commissioner Kenesaw Mountain Landis banned unauthorized interracial play (Mangan and Ritchie 106).

Dark-skinned Latin American players suffered the same indignities as black athletes. Denied the chance to perform in the major league system, Cuban stars joined the Negro National League in 1935. The Cuban stars team was operated by influential New York racketeer Alex Pompez; their polyglot roster included African American, Hispanic, and West Indian players. Pompez constructed a $60,000 stadium, complete with lights for night games, in Manhattan. When the stadium was not in use for baseball, he featured Cuban boxers and an African American football team known as the Brown Bombers, in deference to heavyweight boxing champion Joe Louis. In such ways, nonwhite athletes, promoters, and fans fashioned a parallel, commercialized sporting culture of their own (Burgos).

In Pittsburgh, the underground economy merged with sport, as Gus Greenlee, a local African American rackets boss, also owned the dominant black baseball team, the Pittsburgh Crawfords. Greenlee organized the second Negro National League after the death of Rube Foster, and served as its first president. Under his leadership, the league held its first all-star game at Chicago's Comiskey Park in 1933; the nation's largest black newspapers, the *Chicago Defender* and the *Pittsburgh Courier,* promoted the spectacle. The Crawfords, however, played in their own stadium rather than renting a white facility, marking their success as a black enterprise, created by and for African Americans (Wiggins, *African* 129; Lester, "Black").

As football rivalries heated up, the search for top athletes provided more opportunities for exceptional African American stars at Northern schools. Fritz Pollard and Paul Robeson had won All-American honors at Brown and Rutgers, respectively, but much was expected of such stars by their white critics and black fans. They had to succeed not only for themselves but also for those who would follow. Jack Trice, the first black athlete to attend Iowa State, wrote himself a note before the 1923 game with Minnesota: "[T]he honor of my race, family and self is at stake. Everyone is expecting me to do big things. I will." (Gems, *For Pride* 117). He played despite a serious injury and died two days later. Such athletes carried the burden of hope and respectability for generations of African Americans. Fred "Duke" Slater proved a standout lineman for Iowa in the early 1920s, earning All-American recognition and playing professionally for the Chicago Cardinals before pursuing a legal career that won him a judgeship. Six different professional teams hired more than a dozen total African American players, until owners banned black players after the 1933 season.

Similarly, Northern college teams routinely left their African American players at home, rather than offend Southern sensibilities, when traveling to the South for interregional contests. Such "gentleman's agreements" between coaches and institutions continued for decades. In one well-known case in 1937, Syracuse left behind its star player, Wilmeth Sidat-Singh (an African American who had been adopted by a Hindu doctor), when it traveled to Maryland, which won the contest 14-0. The following year, in a rematch played at Syracuse, Sidat-Singh took part and led his team to a 51-0 rout.

In the boxing arena, top black challengers such as Sam Langford and Harry Wills were denied the opportunity to fight for the heavyweight title; as a result, Langford and Wills fought each other 22 times (Wiggins, *African* 408). The problem lay in the fact that after Jess Willard finally wrested the crown from Jack Johnson, he imposed a color ban, which was maintained by successive white champions. African Americans would wait another generation before Joe Louis got his chance.

Social Significance of Baseball

Baseball's wide popularity clearly established it as the national game, a favorite of the Progressive reformers until the Black Sox scandal. The game quickly redeemed itself during the following decade. The heavy drinking and rowdy baseball players and the brewers who owned several teams threatened the stature of the sport with a negative image, resulting in the formation of the rival American League as a "moral alternative" in 1901. Thereafter, baseball adopted a more patriotic and nationalistic stance. During World War I, professional baseball players, who largely avoided the military draft by getting jobs in war-related

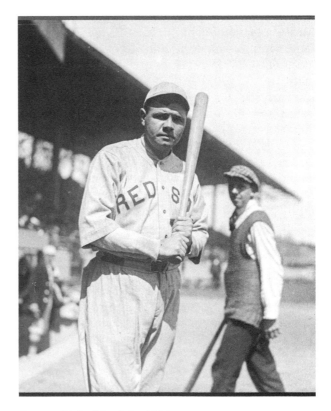

George "Babe" Ruth in 1919.

Photo courtesy of Library of Congress, LC-F8- 4544-A.

industries such as shipbuilding, had faced accusations of being unpatriotic slackers. To counter such charges, baseball team owners began playing the "Star-Spangled Banner" at the 1918 World Series games (although it did not become the official national anthem until 1931).

Baseball authorities also took concerted steps to generate more interest in the game (which would, in turn, help create the Golden Age of Sports during the 1920s) by banning the pitch known as the "spitball" (which deceived batters with its unpredictable trajectory) and by using more lively balls. The result was an offensive barrage, particularly an upsurge in home runs, that prompted a strategic shift from the tactical ("scientific") baseball of the past to a new power-oriented game. Whereas only 384 home runs had been hit in 1915, sluggers produced 1,565 in 1930 (Rader, *American Sports* [1983] 203), and the most prodigious power hitter, George "Babe" Ruth, was crucial in ushering in American sport's Golden Age. Even as a pitcher, Ruth had set a new home run record of 29 in 1919, and when the New York Yankees bought him in 1920 for $125,000, he became an everyday position player and hit 54 home runs that year, more than any other *team,* earning a $52,000 salary. The media attention given to Ruth's prodigious blasts helped assuage the injury of the breaking Black Sox scandal and soon produced a cult of celebrity as newspapers assigned reporters to cover Ruth's daily activities.

Despite the tribulations of baseball in the beginning of the decade, the media continually portrayed sport and athletes in an idealistic manner. They espoused sport as a common good, a prime element in the democratic process that fostered a unified, homogenous culture while building character in individual participants. Babe Ruth served as a typical example. Portrayed as an orphan (which was untrue) and raised by Catholic clergy who taught him to play baseball, he soon demonstrated his great potential to reach the pinnacle of success. Despite his humble origins, Ruth was by the end of the decade requesting a higher annual salary than the president of the United States, and sportswriters regaled readers with accounts of his generosity and concern for sick children. In reality, Ruth had been placed in the St. Mary's Industrial School for Boys near his Baltimore home for theft and incorrigibility. Sportswriters also overlooked his gluttony, drinking, womanizing, and generally rough behavior in order to lionize his physical feats in the construc-

Joe Jackson, a central figure in the Black Sox scandal.
Image courtesy of Library of Congress, LC-USZ62-78070.

tion of an American hero. Fans identified with his flaws and human appetites as they cheered his prodigious baseball feats. Indeed, Ruth brought greater cohesion to baseball fans, as middle-class executives might value his productivity, while members of the working class could identify with his physical prowess. Thus, baseball, as the national game, represented the values of divergent groups within the society.

Baseball also remained a national measuring stick for race relations. For years, African Americans, along with a few liberal white sportswriters and the communist press, had clamored for the integration of baseball as a symbolic gesture of true freedom and democracy within the United States. World War II, supposedly a struggle for freedom against fascism, seemed an exercise in hypocrisy to African Americans. During the war, at the request of President Franklin Roosevelt, Major League Baseball was continued as a morale builder for Americans, but, even though team rosters were depleted by military service, owners still refused to hire black players. In 1945, the Washington Senators even employed Bert Shepard, a one-legged veteran of the war, as a pitcher, and the St. Louis Browns featured one-armed Pete Gray in the outfield. In this context, Branch Rickey, general manager of the Brooklyn Dodgers, devised a plan to desegregate the game.

A devout Methodist who was sympathetic to the plight of African Americans, Rickey also proved a shrewd businessman. In order to integrate baseball, he needed a particular player and a viable scheme. To this end, he organized the United States Baseball League, purportedly another major league for black teams. The league soon ceased operations, but a New York law required that military veterans retain their jobs. Rickey had signed Jackie Robinson to a contract, and Robinson, a four-sport letterman at UCLA, had been an Army lieutenant during World War II. His older brother, Mack, although a 1936 Olympic medalist, found work only as a menial laborer upon his return. Jackie demonstrated leadership qualities and confronted racism when he was court-martialed (but exonerated) for refusing to obey segregationist norms during the war. Rickey admired Robinson's courage and fortitude. After his military discharge, Robinson played baseball for the black Kansas City Monarchs before signing with Rickey's black franchise. When the sham league was abandoned, Rickey assigned Robinson to a minor league affiliate in Montreal, a cosmopolitan Canadian city in the International League, to ease his transition to the white circuit. Robinson led the league in batting average, and the next year Rickey brought him to the parent organization. There he endured segregated spring training, racial taunts, threats of violence, and lurking strikes by teammates and opponents. Despite the overwhelming prohibitions and obstacles, he persevered, with the weight of all African Americans to bear. If Rickey's "Great Experiment," as it was termed, failed, it could have ramifications for race relations and blacks' social mobility for years to come.

Record crowds overflowed baseball stadiums when the Dodgers came to town. African Americans traveled hundreds of miles to cheer their hero, who not only conducted himself with the utmost honor but also won the Rookie of the Year award. In 1949, Robinson won the National League's Most Valuable Player award, and he played with the Dodgers until 1956, leading them to six National League championships and a World Series title. Moreover, his dignified demeanor and performance paved the way for other African Americans,

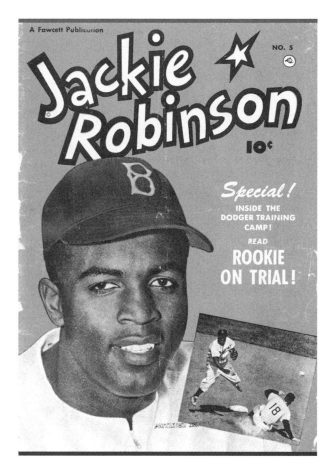

Jackie Robinson: More than an athlete, a racial pioneer.
Photo courtesy of Library of Congress, LC-USZC4-6144.

and, in 1948, Bill Veeck, the flamboyant owner of the Cleveland Indians, hired Larry Doby, the first black player in the American League. In 1959, the Boston Red Sox became the last team to integrate, and by that time black ball players had won 9 of the 13 Most Valuable Player awards in the National League since 1947 (Gorn and Goldstein 217). Many of the black stars played for the Brooklyn Dodgers, emphasizing the visionary acumen of Branch Rickey and the pioneering fortitude of Jackie Robinson.

Robinson's entry to the ranks of Major League Baseball came seven years before the crucial *Brown v. Board of Education* case, in which the Supreme Court struck down segregation. In that sense, Robinson, Rickey, and Brooklyn served as catalysts to social change in the United States. Robinson's exciting play, along with his dignified demeanor, as well as the thousands of African Americans who turned out to witness his games, indicated that a significant transition had already occurred in race relationships.

People & Places

Dan Bankhead

Jackie Robinson is well known as the ball player who desegregated the major leagues in 1947; but few know that during that same season the Brooklyn Dodgers, in dire need of pitching, also signed Dan Bankhead (1920–1976), who appeared later that same season on August 26, 1947. Bankhead and four of his brothers all played in the Negro Leagues. Dan had started with the Birmingham Black Barons in 1940 and played with them and in the Puerto Rican league during the winter, but in 1943 he joined the U.S. Marine Corps for military service during World War II. He joined the Memphis Red Sox of the Negro American League in 1946, leading the league in strikeouts with his blazing fastball. He also led the Puerto Rican League in strikeouts that winter. After a sparkling performance in the Negro Leagues all-star game, Branch Rickey bought his contract and brought him to the Dodgers, where he became Jackie Robinson's roommate and was subjected to the same racist abuse. Unlike Robinson, his play on the field was less than auspicious, as he appeared in only six games, four as a pitcher. He hit a home run in his first at bat, but his first pitch hit the white batter, and he feared racial retribution. His performances with the Dodgers never matched his Negro Leagues prowess. He spent the next two seasons in the minor leagues, before rejoining the Dodgers in 1950. During the 1951 season he developed an arm injury and his contract was sold. He continued to play in the Caribbean leagues, in Canada, and in the Mexican leagues. He continued to play in the latter until 1966, and then tried his hand as a team manager. He ended his days in Houston, delivering food until he succumbed to lung cancer at the age of 55 in 1976.

Information from Rory Costello, Bankhead biography, www.sabr.org.

Attraction of Sport for the Working Class

Inner-city sports attracted large numbers of participants and spectators during the enforced leisure of the Depression. For the best athletes, sports even provided a way to earn a living. Both men and women played softball, which required little equipment and less space than baseball. The American Softball Association offered championships for men and women in 1933, and by 1940 it claimed three million players. Chicago, the birthplace of the game, fielded hundreds of teams in nightly games.

Neighborhood teams played for pride and money. Even boys' teams earned $10 to $20 for their victories, as gamblers and taverns operated local leagues. By 1933, teams could earn $1,500 in prize money per tournament, the equivalent of the annual family income that year. Mario Bruno, one of many Italian players in the city, won $1,650 in one game at a time when the local bank would not offer $100 for a paid-up home. Another legendary Italian player, Rocco "Lewa" Yacilla, pitched for more than 50 years, as softball provided workers with a measure of autonomy and economic mobility. This sport-based black market economy available to the working class during the Depression upheld the faith in capitalism, thus negating the efforts of the radical workers' sport movements, and, unlike developments in Europe, socialist sport movements dissipated in the United States after the Depression.

The Windy City Softball League started play in 1934, and the tournament of the *Chicago Evening American* newspaper consisted of 4,800 games witnessed by more than a million spectators. Women's games proved especially attractive to many fans, as some teams featured players in satin shorts. During the summer months, the women's games drew a greater following than the Chicago White Sox did at their professional baseball games (Gems, *Windy* 190–191).

For many unemployed young men, billiard halls also proved to be a strong attraction during the Depression. With the repeal of Prohibition in 1933, taverns reopened and catered to the bachelor subculture with cheap, coin-operated pool tables. Some taverns also provided alleys for bowling, a sport that surpassed even softball during the 1930s, gaining particular prominence in Midwestern cities such as Detroit, St. Louis, and Chicago. The latter counted nearly five hundred thousand bowlers in more than nine hundred leagues by the end of the decade. Bowling was the most popular sport for women, and during the 1930s in Chicago alone more than fifteen thousand held membership in the Women's International Bowling Congress (WIBC). The 1935 national tournament, held in Chicago, provided more than $15,000 in prizes (Gems, *Windy* 191), and more than ten thousand women registered for one local tournament (Riess, *City* 78). Poles displayed a distinct affinity for the game, and Polish champions became heroes in their ethnic neighborhoods. Some earned enough to forgo working-class occupations in favor of buying their own businesses, while others were elected to political offices. Many working-class youth continued to view sport as a meritocracy where one might gain social mobility based on physical prowess rather than on wealth, lofty social status, or education.

Alternative political parties made feeble attempts to gain greater visibility and resurrect class consciousness among workers. The Communist Party organized a Workers' Olympics in Chicago during the summer of 1932 as a cultural alternative to the IOC events held in Los Angeles, as sport assumed greater political connotations. Another workers' athletic meet took place in New York in 1936 but found little success. The communists urged sport for all instead of emphasizing elite athletic stars. They especially championed the cause of African American athletes, but their efforts made little difference at the polls. For most Americans, sport had become an integral part of the capitalist system, providing an opiate for the disenchanted masses. While those stricken by poverty might question the failed economy, they still maintained hope in sport as a meritocracy that valued their cherished physicality. In the 1932 presidential election, the socialist candidate garnered only nine hundred thousand votes, while the communist entrant gained just one hundred thousand (Pope, *The New* 293).

Sport as a Political Tool

The federal government became increasingly involved in sport after World War I, with the United States Supreme Court ruling in 1922 that baseball was exempt from antitrust laws. Baltimore, one of the defunct teams in the Federal League, a third major circuit that lasted from 1913 to 1915, had sued Major League Baseball in an antitrust suit, but the court reasoned that baseball was not a business and thus could not be held to the same commercial statutes that affected other businesses engaged in interstate commerce. This exemption allowed baseball team owners to operate with impunity in regard to labor relations for most of the twentieth century.

Throughout the 1930s, sport was given more overt political significance, as fascists gained control of government in Italy, Germany, Spain, and Japan. Hitler's doctrine of Aryan supremacy could be challenged within the athletic sphere,

Bowling offered both male and female working-class patrons the opportunity for social mobility.

Image courtesy of Library of Congress, LC-USZ62-122873.

particularly in sports that required individual competition, and a Jewish American boxer, "Slapsie" Maxie Rosenbloom, upheld Jewish dignity by defeating the German light heavyweight champ, Adolf Heuser, in 1933. Thereafter, Hitler refused to allow competition between Germans and Jews. Other sporting events highlighted the ideological differences between democracy and Nazi fascism throughout the remainder of the decade, as illustrated by two boxing bouts between Joe Louis and German heavyweight Max Schmeling.

Louis and Schmeling first battled on June 19, 1936. Although not a Nazi, Schmeling represented the Nazi regime of Adolf Hitler in the eyes of Americans. Hitler had already embarked upon his program of anti-Semitic oppression and European aggression, and by that time the United States had assumed a position of leadership in the world community of democratic, nontotalitarian governments. Thus, the fight represented more than just a boxing match, as conflicting ideologies clashed

WWII military propaganda illustrating heavyweight boxing champion Joe Louis charging with bayoneted rifle. He was not assigned to a combat unit and spent the war as an instructor and giving boxing exhibitions.

Photo courtesy of Library of Congress, LC-USZC4-1334.

in the pugilistic arena. Schmeling shocked America and delighted Hitler with a 12th-round knockout of the seemingly invincible Louis.

Despite Schmeling's stunning victory, Hitler's belief in the construction of an Aryan super race suffered a severe setback in August 1936. Germany hosted the Olympic Games that year, and Hitler and German sport officials used the occasion to glorify the Nazi Reich and its fascist ideology in its efficient organization, neoclassical architectural monuments, and introduction of rituals and symbols in grand spectacles and lavish displays. Nazi administrators ensured that no "pure" Jews represented the German Olympic team, so as not to compromise Hitler's racist doctrine. The Nazi persecution of both Jews and Roma ("Gypsies") raised international concerns. The treatment of the former even prompted an Olympic boycott movement, but Avery Brundage, head of the American Olympic Committee, declined to participate in the protest.

At the competition, African American athletes severely damaged the doctrine of Aryan supremacy by defeating German male athletes in the most prominent track-and-field events. Jesse Owens, the collegiate champion from Ohio State University, won four gold medals, a record that lasted nearly 50 years. The last, in the 400-meter relay, elicited great controversy in the United States, when Coach Lawson Robertson substituted Owens and another African American, Ralph Metcalfe, for Sam Stoller and Marty Glickman, both of whom were Jewish. In the 1600-meter relay, however, the coach failed to use his black stars, one of whom, Archie Williams, was the Olympic champion, and the United States finished second to Great Britain. Both decisions saved Hitler from further international embarrassment as events were not won by those he deemed inferior to Aryans.

Despite Owens' heroics at the Olympics, he returned to a largely racist America. Stripped of his amateur status by the AAU for refusing to participate in a post-Olympic tour of Europe (he wanted to return home and be with his family), he had few prospects in the United States. At a New York reception in his honor, he could not even enter through the front door of the prestigious Waldorf-Astoria Hotel. In addition, the AAU denied him the Sullivan Award, honoring the best amateur athlete, and thereafter Owens earned income by racing against dogs and horses in deplorable exhibitions. Thus, his heroic stature proved tenuous as an African American—and temporary once his usefulness had been expended.

Jesse Owens, star of the 1936 American Olympic track team.
Photo courtesy of Library of Congress, LC-USZ62-27663.

In 1937, Joe Louis knocked out Jim Braddock to become the heavyweight champion, and on June 22, 1938, he met Schmeling in a rematch at Yankee Stadium. Louis avenged his earlier loss with a first-round knockout as an estimated 67 percent of Americans listened by radio (Rader, *American Sports* [1983] 326). Louis held the title for 12 years, but shortly after the attack on Pearl Harbor he entered the Army. Throughout the war, he lifted morale with patriotic speeches, and he donated the proceeds of exhibition matches to the Navy and Army relief funds that benefited war orphans. And, although the military still practiced segregation, he promoted treasury bonds in the black community. After the war, eroded skills caused Louis to retire temporarily, but, despite his loyalty and generosity to the government, he was sued by the Internal Revenue Service for back taxes, leaving him bankrupt. Ezzard Charles, another African American, beat him in a 1950 title fight, and Louis spent his later years as a doorman in Las Vegas (Max Schmeling paid for his funeral), a sad ending symbolic of the treatment of African American heroes whose past exploits were too often forgotten.

Sporting confrontations between the United States and Germany continued for several years before open conflict erupted in World War II. Don Budge, an American who learned to play tennis on public courts in California, lost a Wimbledon match to the German baron, Gottfried von Cramm, in 1935. In their rematch on July 20, 1937, as part of international team play in the Davis Cup tournament, Budge won one of the greatest tennis matches ever played, and he led the Americans to victory over England, providing their first Davis Cup title since 1926. In 1938, Budge won the Australian, French, British, and U.S. Open championships, becoming the first to achieve the Grand Slam in tennis. Still, Budge failed to gain the attention accorded to other sport stars, as Europe moved closer to another devastating war.

As American athletes confronted fascism abroad, other Americans struggled in their quest for acceptance within the American polity. Asian Americans and African Americans still labored in segregated schools and unequal social conditions, and with the outbreak of the war Japanese Americans on the West Coast were sequestered in internment camps, suspected of treachery and collusion with the enemy merely because of their ancestry. In such camps, the Nisei, second-generation Japanese Americans, practiced American sport forms as one means of demonstrating their loyalty and patriotism. At the Gila River Relocation Camp in Arizona, three baseball leagues featured 28 teams, and four to five thousand spectators showed up for the big games (Elias, *Baseball* 127). Nisei men petitioned the government to let them fight for their country, and eventually the Army's 442nd Regimental Combat Team, composed of Nisei soldiers, embarked for Europe, where they became the most decorated unit in the entire Army, dispelling any notions of conflicted national allegiance.

During the war, some African Americans also served (and devotedly), in segregated units, and they became increasingly dissatisfied with their lot. They campaigned for jobs, an end to segregation, and fair housing practices, and they staged sit-ins and protest marches. In 1943, the volatile situation erupted in reactionary race riots, with attacks by whites against Mexican Americans in Los Angeles and against blacks in New York and Detroit. Riots in Detroit resulted in two days of fighting over recreational space in a public park.

Gretel Bergmann—A Jewish Athlete
at the 1936 Olympic Games

When the National Socialists (Nazis) took power in 1933, the 1936 Olympic Games were jeopardized by the Nazis' racial ideology and policies, such as their delusions of superiority. The race politics of the Nazis led to the marginalization of, and finally the attempt to eradicate, races deemed inferior, especially the Jews but also the Roma ("Gypsies"). In many countries, including the United States, some called for a boycott of the Games, but these efforts were unsuccessful, due in part to racist attitudes in many Western countries. Nevertheless, the National Socialists had to accept the participation of Jewish athletes from other countries. At the same time, they made every effort to keep the German team "free of Jews" without arousing the attention of the rest of the world as to their intentions. One victim of their policy was Gretel Bergmann.

Margarethe Bergmann was born in 1914. An enthusiastic athlete from her childhood, she was active in many types of sport, including running, swimming, tennis, and skiing. From the age of 10, she competed successfully in various track-and-field competitions, and in 1933 her jump of 4 feet 9 1/2 inches (1.51 meters) placed her among the best high jumpers in Germany.

With the Nazi ascent to power, Jewish life in Germany underwent rapid and radical change. Among other discriminations, Jews like Gretel Bergmann were excluded from "German" sport organizations. They were allowed, for a time, to become members of Jewish sport groups, which were at first tolerated but then abolished after the Olympic Games in 1936. The Bergmanns soon realized that there was no future for Jews in Germany, and, during a business trip to London. Edwin Bergmann registered his daughter at the London Polytechnic, where she was immediately accepted by the college's sports teams. In June 1934, Gretel Bergmann became the British champion with a high jump of 5 feet (1.55 meters).

In 1934, Bergmann returned to Germany to participate in preparations for the 1936 Olympic Games, since refusing to do so might have had negative results for her family and for Jewish sport organizations. The Third Reich's sports leaders wanted Jewish champions to participate in training for the Olympics in order to counter international charges of racism. In the meantime, however, Germany had begun intense preparations for the Olympics, and while "Aryan" athletes of both sexes received enormous support, Jews had to train in poor conditions. Gretel Bergmann was the only Jew permitted to attend a training camp with other "German" athletes, doing so in the autumn of 1934 and the spring of 1936.

At the Württemberg Championships in 1936, Gretel Bergmann high-jumped 5 feet 2 1/2 inches (1.6 meters), equaling the German record set by Elfriede Kaun. Since this would normally have won her a place on the Olympic team, she was surprised to learn on July 16, 1936—about two weeks before the opening ceremony—that she would not be part of the German team. Only two athletes were nominated for the women's high jump, and she was not one of them. The National Socialists thus gave up a good chance of winning a medal simply to avoid having a Jew on their team.

Since the American team was already en route for the Games at the time of Bergmann's exclusion, no major protest on their part was to be expected. Her German teammates were told that an injury prevented her from participating. In the end, only "half-Jews" were included in the German team: Rudi Ball, one of the most popular of German ice hockey players, and Helene Mayer, a fencer, who was teaching at an American college at the time.

With no hope of any future in Germany, Gretel Bergmann left her home country in May 1937 to settle in the United States, determined never to set foot in Germany again. She married a former Jewish athlete and physician and had two children. She did visit Germany in 1999, when sport facilities in Berlin and her native city were named in her honor.

Information from Bergmann, Gretel. *Ich war die große jüdische Hoffnung.* Ed. Haus der Geschichte Baden-Württemberg. Karlsruhe: 2003; Teichler, Hans Joachim. "Zum Ausschluss der deutschen Juden von den Olympischen Spielen 1936 (on the exclusion of German Jews from the Olympic Games 1936)." *Makkabi Deutschland 1965-1995.* Ed. Makkabi Deutschland. München: Makkabi 1995, 47–62.

Problems of Intercollegiate Sport

After World War II, the GI Bill allowed military veterans to attend college via government subsidy. By 1946, more than two million American veterans enrolled in higher education classes (Spears and Swanson 303). Their introduction to campus life provided a boon to intercollegiate athletics, as the veterans strengthened college teams that played before immense crowds of cheering fans. The high expectations of success intensified recruiting efforts by coaches and boosters, and widespread cheating, dubious inducements, and unethical recruiting practices led the National Collegiate Athletics Association (NCAA) to issue its Sanity Code in 1948 in order to reinforce amateurism, provide limited financial aid to athletes, spur adherence to academic standards, and enable greater institutional control over growing athletic enterprises. In the absence of strong enforcement efforts, however, the athletic wars and transgressions continued, most noticeably in basketball and football.

Basketball, in particular, grew in popularity, and in some rural states, such as Indiana, Kentucky, and parts of the South, basketball became entrenched in the local culture, as local or state teams symbolized civic or state pride. Oklahoma A&M featured a nearly 7-foot (213-centimeter) center, Bob Kurland, whose defensive goaltending forced the NCAA to adopt a new rule making it illegal to swat shots from the basket. Offensively, however, no rule prevented Kurland's dunk shot, and Oklahoma A&M won national championships in 1945 and 1946. In the latter year, Kurland led the nation in scoring.

The popular image of sport suffered a severe shock in 1950, when the United States Military Academy expelled almost the entire varsity football team for cheating on exams. A year later, a bigger scandal erupted when the New York district attorney charged more than 30 college basketball players with point-shaving. Gangsters, gamblers, and racketeers had long been associated with professional boxing, billiards, horse racing, and even baseball, but collegiate sport had enjoyed a relatively pristine image in that regard. Investigations revealed, however, that the point-shaving practice had been in effect since 1945. Under the scheme, oddsmakers bribed players with cash to keep scores within their predicted totals in order to assure their winning bets. By 1951, players at seven different colleges in New York and the Midwest faced conspiracy indictments for fixing games over the previous two seasons. The NBA banned all charged players for life, the NCAA suspended the University of Kentucky for a year, and Long Island University suspended its own basketball program for six years. Critics assailed the crime nexus in New York City, which effectively diminished the previous attraction of games in Madison Square Garden. Consequently, the NCAA basketball tournament assumed greater prominence than the NIT (National Invitational Tournament). As football recruiting scandals and overt subsidization of athletes came to light, the NCAA forfeited its Sanity Code regulations in favor of acknowledged athletic scholarships but enhanced its enforcement capabilities with a corps of investigators.

Fan loyalty and boosterism also generated numerous problems. The overemphasis on winning pushed coaches' salaries beyond those of college presidents, and even average coaches made more money than full professors. Teams vied for the best players to improve their records and status, and schools and municipalities built ever-larger stadiums to hold increasing numbers of fans as commercialization engulfed collegiate football. Notre Dame even left its campus for the biggest "home" games, opting to play at Chicago's mammoth Soldier Field. In 1929, the Carnegie Foundation published a three-year study of intercollegiate sports that confirmed the existence of serious ethical improprieties. Students and other loyal fans bet thousands of dollars on games, and Ohio State University supporters considered their team victories a "financial investment." In addition to the rampant commercialization and materialism associated with college sports, coaches and alumni, as well as interested "boosters," went to great lengths to ensure winning teams, including widespread recruitment and subsidization of star athletes. Although the Carnegie Report raised a red warning flag, it had little influence and no power to effect change, and conflict persisted between the ideal of amateurism, on one hand, and commercialization and emphasis on winning, on the other. Only the University of Chicago eventually discontinued its athletic program (in 1939).

Sport and the Maintenance of Class Status

Although sport brought ethnic-minority, racial, and working-class groups into the mainstream culture, it still allowed for the retention of social differences based on wealth. The expense of some sports largely excluded those who could not afford equipment, lessons, or club membership fees. Moreover, the aristocratic concept of amateurism still held sway among the upper classes.

The Interwar Era saw an increase in the popularity of golf, as illustrated, for example, by the creation of the Walker Cup—a trophy donated in 1922 by George Walker, former president of the United States Golf Association (USGA)—to foster nationalism, as amateur teams from Great Britain and the United States competed for the prize. Five years later, Samuel Ryder, a British businessman, offered a similar award for professional teams. Americans began to take notice when Francis Ouimet, a working-class caddy and amateur player, defeated British professionals in the U.S. Open tournament in 1913. Walter Hagen, an American pro, dominated the game thereafter and spurred reforms of elitist covenants that had restricted clubhouse usage to the wealthy. As the star player, clubs had to relax their standards against professionals to allow Hagen to use their facilities. Gate receipts and prize money spawned professional tours, with Hagen accumulating most of the winnings and product endorsements. His extravagant lifestyle captured public attention and gained him celebrity status.

Only Bobby Jones, one of the last amateur gentlemen, rivaled Walter Hagen in prominence. A lawyer who retained his amateur status throughout his competitive career, Jones won 13 of the 21 tournaments he entered from 1923 through 1930. His most amazing feat occurred in 1930, when he won the American and British amateur titles, as well as the open championships in both countries, which at that time constituted golf's Grand Slam. Jones then retired from active competition at the age of 28 and devoted time to designing the Augusta National golf course in Georgia, which began hosting the Masters Golf Tournament in 1934.

On the men's professional circuit, Sam Snead and Ben Hogan became household names. Both started their careers in the 1930s, but Snead played over six decades. Snead's graceful swing and his development of the innovative straddle technique for putting resulted in 81 victories on the Professional Golfers' Association (PGA) tour. Both Snead and Hogan derived from working-class roots, and both learned to play the game by working as caddies. The intense Hogan rivaled Snead for golfing laurels. He turned professional at the tender age of 17 in 1929 but didn't win a tournament until 1940. Although small in stature at 5 feet 8 inches (173 centimeters) and 135 pounds (61 kilograms), he won 62 more tournaments thereafter. His greatest triumph, however, occurred after a horrific

Bobby Jones became the darling of golf fans. The working class could identify with his temper and competitive zeal, and the upper classes admired his etiquette, sense of fair play, and adherence to the amateur code. He even penalized himself for an infraction.

Image courtesy of Library of Congress, LC-USZ62-98076.

auto accident in 1949. Playing in pain and still in bandages, Hogan persevered to win the 1950 U.S. Open in a playoff. In 1953, he founded a golf equipment manufacturing company that made him a millionaire. At his death in 1997, his estate held a value of $100 million. For many, Hogan represented the American dream. He literally fought his way out of poverty, beating other boys in battles over newspaper sales and caddying opportunities, and a strong work ethic, along with fierce pride and courageous will, allowed him to overcome the odds and achieve great success. Despite such rags to riches stories, however, the cost of golf greatly limited working-class participation.

Tennis, too, maintained a sense of elitism, with access to the sport at country clubs and tennis clubs reserved largely for upper-class white men and women. The 1920s star "Big Bill" Tilden dominated the tennis world. A tall, thin, graceful athlete, Tilden overpowered his opponents, winning six consecutive U.S. championships starting in 1920. Sports journalist Paul Gallico described Tilden this way:

> Of all the colorful champions of that era, this man was far and away the oddest fish. As a player he dominated the decade at a period when there were more stars, national or international, to challenge him than ever before or since. As a box office attraction both amateur and professional, he lifted the gate from peanuts into the million-dollar class. As a person he was as strange, independent, and controversial a figure as ever strutted across the sports scene. . . . He was a colossus! He was a tremendous athlete of unparalleled skill and inexhaustible endurance.
>
> Gallico 120

Tilden was the first American to win the Wimbledon singles crown (doing so in 1920 and repeating the feat in 1921 and 1930), and he dominated American tennis throughout the decade. He authored books and plays thereafter but lost favor because of his homosexuality and even served prison time for pedophilia in the 1940s (Leab 429–431). In the eyes of the working class, tennis retained an effete image well into the twentieth century (Gems, *Windy* 158).

Women's Fight for Inclusion

Although female athletes did not gain the media coverage or accolades accorded to men, they did make substantial gains in sport during the 1920s as part of the larger sweep of social change and of women's activism in pursuit of public roles. One of the major goals of the women's movement in the United States was achieved in 1920, when women won the right to vote. Music, theater, and movies all presented more liberated images of women, and young urban women in particular sought new ways to express themselves.

People & Places

Bob Mathias

Born in Tulare, California, Bob Mathias (1930–2006) suffered from anemia as a child, so his physician father prescribed medication and built a small track and field facility behind the family house to develop his physical abilities. Mathias proved a quick learner, and by June of 1948, at the age of only seventeen, he not only qualified for, but won the Olympic trials. At the London Games of 1948 he astounded the fans by becoming the youngest male Olympian to ever win the gold medal.

Mathias entered Stanford University in 1949, where he starred in both football and track and field, capturing the Amateur Athletic Union national decathlon championship in both 1949 and 1950, setting a world record in the latter year. At the Helsinki Olympic Games of 1952 Mathias overcame an injury to set yet another world record and win a second decathlon gold medal by the age of 21. He also played in the Rose Bowl game that year, the first intercollegiate contest to be broadcast on national television.

In 1967 Californians elected Mathias to Congress, where he served four terms (1967-1975) in the House of Representatives. Thereafter, he directed the Olympic Training Center in Colorado until 1983, and then served as director of the National Fitness Foundation. Undefeated in the decathlon during his competitive days, winner of four national championships, and the first to garner two gold medals in the Olympic decathlon, Mathias was acknowledged as the greatest all-around athlete of his era and inducted into a dozen halls of fame. He died of cancer in 2006 at the age of 75.

Zarnowski, Frank. "Mathias, Robert Bruce 'Bob'." *The Scribner Encyclopedia of American Lives*. Ed. Arnold Markoe. New York: Scribner's, 2002. 128–130.

Prominent female members of the American Physical Education Association favored physical activity and gender-specific sports such as basketball as beneficial to women's health; however, they opposed competition in public spectacles, believing it was damaging to women's physiology, and deemed such competition unhealthy and morally corrupting for women, who they feared might succumb to the problems that marked men's sports. They made a concerted effort to substitute "play days" as an alternative, in which students of one school might invite those of another school to their campus and mix their teams for a recreational game. The match might then be followed by a social gathering with snacks and drinks in a setting of friendly camaraderie. Not all females adhered to such dictates, however. In Iowa, girls' high school basketball teams retained their competitive state tournament, which drew crowds of enthusiastic fans annually (Beran, *From Six-on-Six*). In many other states, girls were confined to intramural activities. Despite such obstacles, U.S. women persevered, and many working-class women competed on athletic club and company

International Perspective

Milliat and the Push for Female Track and Field

Alice Milliat of France was the driving force behind the international women's sport movement, which fought for women's access to and their acknowledgment in various sports (including soccer), with a focus on the premier Olympic sport of track and field. In 1921, she was elected president of the French Association of Women's Sport (founded in 1917). In the same year she initiated an international women's meeting in soccer and track and field and organized a conference where the International Federation for Women's Sport (FSFI) was founded. Under Milliat's presidency, the FSFI organized four very successful "Olympic" Games for women: in Paris in 1922, Gothenburg in 1926, Prague in 1930, and London in 1934. Held in 1922, the first Women's Olympics offered a day-long international track-and-field meet in Pershing Stadium in Paris, where competitors set 18 new records. The record setters included two American schoolgirls: Camille Sabie, who set the mark in the 100-yard hurdles race, and Lucile Godbold, who won the shot put (www.colacoll.edu/edenslibrary/jane/Teammates.htm). Twenty thousand spectators watched the women's efforts, and the festival's success fostered a larger competition at the second women's World Games in Gothenburg, Sweden.

Concerned over the women's appropriation of the Olympic name, and faced with losing control over a growing sphere of athletics, the IOC and the International Amateur Athletic Federation (IAAF) negotiated with the FSFI. One of the most controversial issues was the number of events. The FSFI demanded 10 track and field events for women at the 1928 Olympic Games in Amsterdam, but the IOC and the IAAF ultimately offered only five: high jump, discus throw, 100-meter dash, 4 × 100 meter relay, and 800-meter run. After long debates, the FSFI accepted this offer, and women participated for the first time in Olympic track events. A 16-year-old Chicagoan, Elizabeth Robinson, won the 100-meter race. Nine athletes participated in the 800-meter event, which was won by the German runner Lina Radke-Batschauer in the world-record time of 2:16.8, but the race proved controversial.

After the competition, several runners sat on the ground, exhausted and disappointed. This allegedly unfeminine behavior and unaesthetic sight caused indignation among the officials and journalists who reported on the collapse of fainting and delirious women, sweating and panting with open mouths and distorted faces. John Tunis wrote of "eleven wretched women, five of whom dropped out before the finish, while five collapsed after reaching the tape," and critics protested any inclusion of women in future Olympic events (Guttmann, *Sports: The First Five Millenia* 265). This fatigue struck critics as the ultimate proof that women were not equal to the demands of the middle distances. But Tunis had taken considerable journalistic license. There were only nine competitors, and all finished the race (Guttmann, *Sports: The First Five Millenia* 265). Several officials and physicians pointed out that the female athletes had not been overexerted and that they showed no more signs of fatigue than male athletes after such a run. Two of the allegedly exhausted athletes were Jean Thompson, world-record holder for 800 meters, and Bobbie Rosenfeld, the silver medal winner of the 100-meter run. It made no impression on the IOC or the public when Rosenfeld noted that she was a 100-meter specialist and had not trained for the 800-meter distance—or that none of the runners had experienced health problems. The 800-meter run was removed from the Olympic program for women until 1960.

teams. American women also took note of changes in sport and society beyond American shores, as in France, where Alice Milliat forcefully advocated greater female participation in track-and-field competition.

Although women made gradual progress in American life throughout the 1920s, many onlookers still questioned their abilities, as well as the propriety of female participation in the sporting culture. Women were still expected by many to be passive supporters of male athletes, and even cheerleading roles had remained the province of men because it was assumed that fans would not follow or take orders from a female leader. Women did enter the ranks of cheerleaders during the 1920s, however, and throughout the following decade they continued to challenge the traditional roles assigned to them.

In spite of the myth of being a weaker sex, women entered various sporting contests that were looked upon as male domains. Female pilots, for example, proved they had abilities equal to those of men. In 1932, Amelia Earhart flew solo across the Atlantic Ocean, matching the historic adventure of Charles Lindbergh in 1927. Jacqueline Cochran received her pilot's license in 1932, and by the time she retired she had surpassed all pilots, male or female, in flight records for speed, altitude,

and distance. Although less prominent than those women who conquered natural obstacles, Jackie Mitchell drew national attention as a baseball player. In a 1931 exhibition game, the 17-year-old phenom pitched for the Chattanooga Lookouts in a contest with the New York Yankees and, to the amazement of all, struck out both Babe Ruth and Lou Gehrig. Baseball commissioner Kenesaw Mountain Landis responded by voiding her contract on the dubious grounds that the game was too strenuous for women.

Baseball

In 1943, with many professional baseball players serving in the military, Cubs owner Philip Wrigley initiated the All-American Girls Professional Baseball League (AAGPBL) as a Midwestern alternative. It was originally designed as a softball organization, but the women soon graduated to baseball rules and enjoyed immense popularity. They drew nearly a million patrons in 1948, and the league lasted until 1954. Although such initiatives provided opportunities for women, the players had to adhere to middle-class norms of respectability, which required proper etiquette, makeup, and a skirted uniform. The all-white league also further marginalized long-suffering African American athletes.

AAGPBL player Marge Callaghan sliding into home plate as umpire Norris Ward watches.
Photo courtesy of the State Library and Archives of Florida.

Track and Field

Throughout the 1920s, many women were exposed to track-and-field competition in the industrial recreation programs of large employers, but Lillian Copeland attended the University of Southern California and became an outstanding athlete, winning nine national titles and setting world records in javelin and discus. In the United States, the Amateur Athletic Union (AAU) offered its first track-and-field championship for women in 1924. At the 1932 Los Angeles Olympic Games, Copeland won the gold medal in the discus throw, setting another world record. Her teammate Mildred "Babe" Didrikson had initially gained fame as an All-American basketball star for the Employers Casualty Insurance Company of Dallas, and the company entered her in the national track championship of 1932, where she single-handedly captured the team title by winning six events, setting four world records (Guttmann, *Sports: The First Five Millenia* 127). At the 1932 Olympics, she won gold medals in the javelin and hurdles and won a controversial silver in the high jump despite a world record (judged a faulty jump).

Tidye Pickett, an African American woman, fared considerably worse as a basketball and track star. Both Pickett and Louise Stokes, another African American, qualified for the 1932 Olympic track team, only to be belittled by teammates and snubbed. Neither was chosen to compete. Pickett did run for the 1936 Olympic team; although favored in the hurdles race, she broke her foot in a preliminary and could not compete. Unlike Fritz Pollard, whose son won a bronze medal at the 1936 Games, Pickett faded into obscurity. Women received little fanfare compared with the coverage of men, and in Pickett's case only the African American newspapers cared at all.

Alice Coachman, another African American, replaced Didrikson as the reigning star of the sport. Coachman competed for Tuskegee Institute as a sprinter and high jumper, winning the national championship 10 times in the latter event, and the Tuskegee women's track team won the national AAU championship 11 times between 1937 and 1948 (Cahn, "Cinderellas" 216). African American women from segregated black schools in the South became the backbone of the American Olympic team thereafter. Coachman captured the Olympic high-jump title in 1948, but the white media still took little notice of accomplishments by black women.

Swimming

The physical freedom that women experienced in swimming coincided with the political freedom of suffrage, as in the case of Charlotte Epstein and her reform-minded National Women's Life Saving League teammates. Epstein promoted both bathing suit reform and political progress in her leadership of swimming organizations, and her endorsement of suffrage visibly linked women's swimming and physical mobility with political power. At an outdoor swimming contest in 1915 at New York's Manhattan Beach, 50 women competed in races to highlight the Women's Life Saving League's advocacy of suffrage. The women were both good swimmers and suffragettes. Epstein was also one of the swimmers on the National Women's Life Saving League team that competed in intercity swimming races in Philadelphia, in turn spurring additional competitions (Borish, "The Cradle"). Others, such as Lucy Freeman, excelled at distance swimming, thus challenging the perception that women could not muster the stamina needed for such grueling events.

To advance women's competitive swimming, Charlotte Epstein founded the Women's Swimming Association (WSA) in New York in 1917. Through her own initiative, she rented a hotel pool and secured use of the Young Women's Hebrew Association pool; she also arranged for famed coach Louis deB. Handley to volunteer to teach swimmers the trudgeon-crawl stroke, a trademark of the famous WSA swimmers. Epstein espoused distance swimming for health benefits and publicized its value for women's physical fitness in order to challenge gender barriers. She challenged male Olympic officials to include female swimmers in the 1920 Olympic Games, and she served as U.S. Olympic Women's Swim Team manager as the Americans captured the championship in Antwerp, Belgium. Epstein fulfilled that role for the 1924 Olympics in Paris and the 1932 Olympics in Los Angeles. Stars of the 1920 Games included Ethelda Bleibtrey, who won two events and added a third gold medal as part of a relay team, and 14-year-old Aileen Riggin, who secured the diving title. American women dominated Olympic swimming and diving contests over the next 12 years, producing 51 world records under Epstein's guidance. American and Olympic swimming heroines such as Alice Lord, Helen Wainwright, Helen Meany, Gertrude Ederle, Eleanor Holm, and Doris O'Mara popularized competitive swimming for women in American culture (Borish, "The Cradle").

In addition to Epstein's efforts, other athletic clubs for women offered facilities and training for competition. Bertha Severin founded the Illinois Women's Athletic Club in 1918, recruiting working-class girls and allowing them to train for free as long as they retained amateur standing and displayed ladylike behavior. Chicagoan Sybil Bauer set nine records by 1922 and surpassed even the men's record in the backstroke. The *New York Times* speculated that she would swim against men in the Olympics, but the IOC would not consider such a confrontation (Gems, *Windy* 145). Bauer easily won the women's 100-meter backstroke event in the 1924 Olympics, and she was still undefeated at her untimely death from cancer in 1926.

Female U.S. swimmers again found success at the 1924 Olympics, where one of the most famous female athletes of the twentieth century, Gertrude Ederle, earned gold and bronze medals. Ederle, a German American, recalled that she had learned to swim at Epstein's swimming club, where she had been taught the American crawl stroke. Ederle set 29 American and world records between 1921 and 1925. Perhaps even more impressive, on August 6, 1926, at the age of 19, Ederle became the first woman to swim the English Channel, establishing a new record to boot by covering the arduous 21-mile (34-kilometer) stretch of rough water in 14 hours and 31 minutes, thus smashing the men's record by more than 2 hours. Hailed as "Queen of Swimmers" and "America's Best Girl," Ederle attracted national acclaim. New York City provided an immense ticker-tape parade, with the public cheering her amazing athletic feat. Sports journalist Paul Gallico described the huge outpouring: "Spectators usually lined the sidewalks to watch the procession go by, but for Ederle, the largest crowd ever turned out, spilling from the curbs and jamming the thoroughfares" (Gallico 52). Ederle spent the next two years touring the United States and Europe in swimming exhibitions and vaude-ville shows, hailed by the media, but the intense pressure of the limelight caused a nervous breakdown and a consequent lapse into anonymity.

Tennis

While not as popular as Olympians Ederle and Holm, female tennis stars also won a measure of fame in American life. Suzanne Lenglen won her native French championship at the age of 14 and took the Wimbledon crown after World War I in 1919. She nearly monopolized the latter, racking up six victories by 1926. She cavorted around the courts sporting risqué attire and a surly demeanor, challenging conventional norms and attracting great media attention and a multitude of fans. In 1926, Lenglen met her American rival Helen Wills Moody—winner of six American and eight British titles, as well as singles and doubles titles at the 1924 Olympics—before an overflow crowd at Cannes, France. Lenglen emerged with a narrow victory, then joined the professional ranks, while Wills went on to rule the amateurs, winning every set between 1927 and 1933. *New York Times* reporter Allison Danzig wrote about Wills winning the U.S. national tennis title in 1928: "The most devastating power ever applied to a tennis ball by a woman, the power described as revolutionizing at Wimbledon, carried Miss Helen Wills, twenty-three-year-old Berkeley (Cal) girl to her fifth national championship yesterday, bringing to a close the campaign that has seen her win the premiere laurels of tennis at Auteuil, Wimbledon and Forest Hills without the loss of a set in three months of play" (18).

Tennis also reached the African American community, where, unable to play against whites, blacks formed their own governing organization. In 1924, Ora Washington won the American Tennis

People & Places

Sybil Bauer

After learning to swim at age 15, Sybil Bauer became the first woman athlete to beat a man's world record in swimming. In 1922, at a meet in Bermuda, Bauer lowered the world record time in the 440-yard (402-meter) backstroke by four seconds to beat Stubby Kruger's (male) record. She earned acclaim as an outstanding backstroker, winning the National Amateur Athletic Union (AAU) 100-yard (91-meter) championships consecutively from 1921 through 1926, as well as the national championships for the 100-meter (109-yard), 150-yard (137-meter), and 220-yard (201-meter) backstroke (events in the United States and the United Kingdom are measured in yards, while events in Europe are measured in meters). She was also part of a team that set a world record and won a national championship in the freestyle relay. At age 22, Sybil Bauer held all 23 existing world records for women in the backstroke.

Association singles title, and she held the championship for 12 years. Sports such as tennis and golf upheld middle-class standards of respectability regardless of racial segregation.

Golf

Female golfers appeared on American links by the 1880s, but it was Glenna Collett (in a career lasting from 1922 to 1935) who achieved golf-star status among women, winning six national amateur championships and earning renown for her 200-yard (183-meter) drives off the tee. Collett authored a book on golf in 1928 and participated in the first Curtis Cup match (a women's team competition between the United States and Great Britain) in 1932. Another star was Elaine Rosenthal, a Jewish golfer from the Chicago area, who was runner-up in the U.S. Women's National Amateur Championship in 1914 and won a major victory on March 29, 1917, at the Women's North and South Amateur Championship at Pinehurst (North Carolina) Country Club. In 1915, Rosenthal won the first of her three Western Women's Golf Association championships (Borish, "Women" 84).

Women's golf gained greater media attention in the 1940s with the appearance of Olympic great Babe Didrikson on the women's tour, where her working-class demeanor challenged upper-class standards of the game. In addition to Didrikson's accomplishments on the women's professional circuit, women's golf benefited from the staging of an intercollegiate tournament for women at Ohio State University in 1941. Organized by Gladys Palmer, the women's competition departed from

Glenna Collett dominated women's golf during her long career.

The Miriam and Ira D. Wallach Division of Art, Prints and Photographs: Photography Collection, The New York Public Library. Gienna Collett, New York Public Library Digital Collections. Accessed September 27, 2016. http://digitalcollections.nypl.org/items/510d47d9-bc05-a3d9-e040-e00a18064a99.

the play-day concept still favored by many educators. It marked a long and gradual return to intercollegiate athletics for women over the remainder of the century.

Basketball

Throughout the states, basketball gained great popularity among women as it spread quickly from New England to the Midwest, the South, and the West Coast. Many female physical educators at the time disliked competition, but athletic clubs, YWCAs, Young Women's Hebrew Associations, commercial businesses, and some schools fielded teams. The AAU initiated its first national basketball championship for women's teams in 1924, and within two years the women's tournament adopted men's rules. Iowa's high schools, however, adhered to their distinctive three-court game as (in their view) more suitable for females. The Iowa version of the game preceded the women's national tournament, as its state association sponsored the first state championship tournament, featuring 24 teams, in 1920. By 1926, Iowa high schools sponsored 159 girls' teams. In 1921, Kentucky offered its first state basketball tournament for girls, but it eventually bowed to pressure from female educators in 1932. Kentucky colleges fielded women's teams throughout the 1920s (Hult and Trekell 167–180).

The nature of female sport remained contested, as female educators battled male administrators and governing bodies over rules, playing conditions, and competition (many female leaders believed aggressive competition was masculine and damaging to women's psyches and bodies). Many schools where female educators exerted more influence opted for less competitive play days. Concern over females' sporting practices continued well into the twentieth century, as administrators, educators, and other parties of differing class interests disagreed over the nature of women's physicality. Although some adhered to notions of female debility, others opposed the male emphasis on competition and winning.

Although opportunities dwindled into intramural contests for many girls in high schools and colleges, older and working-class women found options on club teams and company-sponsored squads. In California, the Pasadena Athletic Club hosted the women's national AAU basketball championship in 1926, with the club's own team emerging as the winner, and the California women's leagues adopted men's rules in 1928. Many companies found women's sports teams to be a popular means of advertising their products, and by 1930 newspapers in Dallas, Texas, covered 48 women's teams in that city alone.

The Sunoco Oil Company team from Dallas went undefeated from 1927 through 1929 and won the national AAU championship each year from 1928 through 1930. Their main rivals, the Employers Casualty Insurance Company of Dallas, featured numerous All-American athletes on its basketball and track teams, including the most celebrated of all, Babe Didrikson. Employers and private athletic clubs began recruiting female as well as male athletes to bring greater prominence and publicity to their establishments.

In the more conservative South, both black and white women formed basketball teams, suggesting various perceptions of femininity based on class, race, and gender. White women of the working class and black women who participated in sports were assumed to be and stereotyped as more physical and sexual. The women of Bennett College dominated black intercollegiate play in North Carolina during the 1930s but lost a three-game series in 1934 to the *Philadelphia Tribune* team that featured Ora Washington, the national black women's tennis champion. By 1942, however, intercollegiate contests gave way to the play-day concept favored by mainstream educators (Liberti). The All-American Red Heads, a white team organized in 1936 in Missouri, barnstormed throughout the country playing against male teams. Playing by men's rules,

People & Places

Violette Morris

Without any doubt, Violette Morris (1893–1944) was one of the best female athletes of her time. Her biography is embedded in the political developments and mirrors the opportunities and challenges of women in sport society.

The daughter of a French aristocrat was educated in a convent where she learned and practiced various sports. Violette became an all-round athlete and began to compete at the age of 15, winning numerous championships in disciplines from athletics to swimming and from tennis to horseback riding. She played soccer on the Fémina team from 1917 until 1919, and on the title-winning team of Olympique de Paris from 1920 to 1926 as one of the most valuable players. In 1922 she won the javelin throw and shot put events in the international women's competitions in Paris. "La Morris" also excelled in other men's sports such as water polo, weightlifting, wrestling and even boxing. She claimed to have defeated male opponents.

Violette was contracted by the Benjamin car company and participated in numerous races with cycle car, and in 1922 finished in fourth place in the Bol d'Or, a 24-hour endurance race. In 1928 she underwent a double mastectomy, according to her own words, to fit better in her racing car (Bouzanquet 2009). An American newspaper reported that she had the operation to make her look more like a man (Decatur Evening Herald, March 19, 1929, 19).

Violette left no doubt that she was lesbian, although from 1914 to 1923 she was married to Cyprien Gouraud. Despite her marriage, she wore men's clothing, smoked heavily, loved to swear, and later owned a car parts shop to build her own racing machines.

The French Women's Athletic Federation (FFSF) declined to renew her license to participate in the 1928 Olympic Games, allegedly because of her habit of dressing as a man, accusations referring to her lack of morals, her bad influence on team members, and her radical feminism. Still Violette refused to wear a dress and went to court, but she lost her case (Bouzanquet 2009). American newspapers published the news with titles such as "Woman sues for right to swear and smoke" (e.g., El Paso Evening Post, Feb 26, 1930, 1).

The women's sport organizations had to fight for their survival and tried to comply with the current conservative gender politics and policies. Morris's behavior, however, endangered the image and status of the Fédération des sociétés féminines sportives de France (FSFSF); therefore, she had to be excluded (Michallat 2005). Despite her cross dressing and her unfeminine behavior, she was a popular member of the demi monde society in Paris.

In 1936, she was allegedly invited to the Olympic Games, lured by the Nazi ideology. Several publications refer to her as the "Hyena of the Gestapo", but lack of sources make it difficult to come to a final conclusion about her role during the German occupation of France. She was assassinated while driving in her car in 1944, presumably by members of the French resistance.

Morris' biography raises numerous questions, not only about her involvement in Nazi politics, but also in the price for her transgressions of gender boundaries.

the Red Heads won more than 80 percent of their games over a 50-year span. In 1949, Hazel Walker, a former Red Head, formed a similar venture, the Arkansas Travelers, who won more than 85 percent of their games played against men. The Travelers endured for 16 seasons, as Didrikson's influence left a lasting legacy for women's sports in general.

Church leagues offered yet another venue for female basketball players, particularly African Americans. In Chicago, black social clubs played each other in women's games as early as 1911, and Olivet Baptist Church, reputedly the country's largest with eleven thousand members, was sponsoring both men's and women's teams by 1919. As with teams sponsored by businesses, these squads attracted a large following and even promoted church attendance. The Chicago Roamers, rivals to the Olivet church team, began play in 1921. Managed by Sol Butler, a former Olympic track star, they featured Isadore Channels, the national African American women's tennis champion. The Roamers played against other women and against boys' teams. The latter competitions pushed the established gender boundaries without invading the traditional demarcation of adult male space.

During this time, Chicago accommodated numerous women's basketball teams in city and church leagues, as well as on industrial and independent teams. In a 1926 interracial match, Olivet lost to the white Taylor Trunks, who had claimed the national women's championship. Such teams proved quite democratic, as domestic workers, meat packers, clerks, schoolteachers, and students joined to form egalitarian teams where ability counted more than social rank. During the early 1930s, the Club Store Co-Eds dominated opponents with a center who stood 6 feet 7 1/2 inches (202 centimeters) tall and Olympic track team member Tidye Pickett. Still, the Spencer Coal Company overcame the wealth of local talent to emerge as national women's champs. Such games attracted thousands of spectators and drew coverage in local magazines, and this kind of media attention to women's athletic exploits and abilities further dismantled stereotypes of feminine frailty.

Jewish women also played basketball, against both Jewish and non-Jewish teams. Across the country—at such locales as the Nashville (Tennessee) YWHA, the New York City YWHA, settlement houses such as the Jewish Educational Alliance of Atlanta, and the Jewish Community Center in Washington, D.C.—basketball was a very popular game for young Jewish women and girls during the first decades of the twentieth century (Borish 2012).

Heroes in the Golden Age

Technological advances produced new sport forms and new heroes in the twentieth century. Chicago hosted the first auto race in the United States in 1895. In Indianapolis, a series of automobile races with bigger cars and more powerful engines took place in 1909, and in 1911 the famed 500-mile (805-kilometer) contest in Indianapolis drew fans to the speedway, which was enlarged over the course of the century to accommodate more than 250,000 spectators around its 2.5-mile (4-kilometer) oval. In 1923, the date of the race became fixed on Memorial Day, a holiday commemorating war fatalities, and nearly 150,000 people participated in a festival that increasingly tied sport to nationalism. The introduction of aircraft produced similar events, with air shows and races for speed and endurance for both men and women. The transatlantic feats of Charles Lindbergh and Amelia Earhart were hailed as nationalistic triumphs. But although technological advances held general interest, cars and planes remained out of the reach of many Americans. Other sport forms provided more immediate benefits.

Baseball Heroes

For Americans outside the mainstream, baseball offered a quicker road to cultural assimilation. Second-generation immigrant youth who had learned the game on public playgrounds or in schools emerged as stars in the Interwar Era, perhaps most notably the German Americans Babe Ruth and Lou Gehrig. Jews took great pride in the accomplishments of Hank Greenberg, the son of immigrants. Greenberg refused to play on Yom Kippur, one of the Jewish High Holy Days, during the playoffs, and some opponents taunted him with anti-Semitic slurs. Even so, "Hammerin' Hank," as his fans called him, amassed outstanding statistics as a slugging first baseman for the Detroit Tigers. He hit 58 home runs in 1938 and led the American League four times in home runs and in RBIs (runs batted in). He played in the All-Star Game each year from 1937 through 1940 and earned Most Valuable Player honors in 1935 and 1940, before military service in World War II interrupted his baseball career.

Joe DiMaggio, one of three Italian American brothers to make it to the major leagues, emerged as a star with the New York Yankees. He displayed excellence in all areas of the game—as a hitter, fielder, and dashing runner—in a career that lasted from 1936 until 1951. For Italian American Catholics,

Mildred "Babe" Didrikson

The distinction of best all-around athlete during this period clearly belonged to a woman: Mildred "Babe" Didrikson. Born into a Norwegian working-class family in Beaumont, Texas, Babe gained her nickname for her baseball-hitting abilities, but she won fame as a brash, multitalented athlete. Her prowess as a high school basketball player earned her a nominal job with the Employers Casualty Company in Dallas, where she was employed as a stenographer; her real value to the company, however, lay in her stellar play for the company basketball team, where she gained All-American recognition from 1930 through 1932 and led the team to the national AAU championship in 1931. In 1932, competing as an individual, she won the national track team championship single-handedly by winning six events. At the 1932 Olympics in Los Angeles, she was limited to three events and won gold medals in the 80-meter hurdles and the javelin throw with world-record performances. A *Los Angeles Times* journalist described her performance: "Mildred (Babe) Didrikson, 128 pounds [58 kilograms] of feminine dynamite, came through yesterday when all competitors of the so-called stronger sex failed in the world record-wrecking attempts. . . . More than 50,000 spectators joined in a wild cheer as the doughty Didrikson dame rifled the javelin 143 ft. 4 in. [43.7 meters] on her very first effort, a mighty heave which erased the

The multitalented Babe Didrikson at track practice before the Olympic Games.
© AP Photo

former world mark of 133 ft. [41 meters]" (Dyer, "Babe" 9). She would have won the high jump as well, but officials claimed her diving style to be an illegal jump and awarded her the silver rather than the gold medal.

Although Didrikson had a bowling average of 170 and could reputedly punt a football 75 yards (68.6 meters) and swim at record pace, she made a living as a barnstorming baseball player and professional basketball player after the Olympics. She then turned to golf and won the West Texas Open in 1935, but the social set did not appreciate her working-class roots or crude manners. A braggart, supremely confident in her abilities, she once asked in the ladies' locker room, "All you girls showed up just to see who would come in second?"

In 1938, she married ex-wrestler George Zaharias, mitigating her "tomboy" image but not curtailing her self-promotion. Her social skills gained some refinement with age, but she never became the darling of the golfing community. Nevertheless, Didrikson's startling success drew attention to the women's golf tour. She won 34 tournaments, including 17 in a row at one point (1946–1947). In 1948, she became one of the pioneers who organized the Ladies Professional Golf Association (LPGA). Despite suffering colon cancer at the relatively young age of 41, she returned to golf, winning Comeback Player of the Year in 1953 as awarded by sportswriters. She died in 1956, leaving an incredible athletic legacy. The Associated Press honored her as Female Athlete of the Year six times and named her the top female athlete of the half-century in 1950. The example set by Didrikson inspired numerous women to challenge prescribed gender and social roles, and her performances brought considerable media attention not only to women's growing participation in sport but to their considerable abilities as well.

DiMaggio sparked a sense of pride, esteem, and long-sought acceptance in American society. He began patrolling centerfield for the New York Yankees during his rookie season, and in his 13 seasons with the team they won 10 league championships and 9 World Series. DiMaggio gained his greatest acclaim in 1941, when he shattered the major league record for consecutive games with a hit. For 56 straight games that summer, baseball fans briefly forgot the European war as they were mesmerized by the feats of the Yankee Clipper.

Although the incredible streak ended on July 17, the 1941 season still held great interest, as Ted Williams, an outfielder for the Boston Red Sox, attempted to become the first player since 1930 to achieve a .400 batting average. On the last day of the season, Williams' average rested at .39955, a figure that would have been rounded off to an even .400, but he chose to play in a doubleheader, thus jeopardizing the amazing achievement. In the course of the two games, he batted eight times, getting six hits and finishing at .406. No one has achieved the .400 mark since, and few have even come close.

The attack on Pearl Harbor on December 7, 1941, shattered the jubilation of the baseball season. Both Williams and DiMaggio entered the military after the 1942 season, forfeiting three seasons of their careers. Williams also served as a marine combat pilot during the Korean War, then continued a Hall of Fame baseball career until his retirement in 1960. (He still hit .388 in 1958.) DiMaggio retired after the 1951 World Series, and in 1954 he married movie star and sex symbol Marilyn Monroe. Although the marriage lasted only briefly, it symbolized the acceptance of immigrant Italians into mainstream American society. Athletes such as DiMaggio could take much credit for the transition in the Italian image from that of gangsters to one of wholesome American citizens, a distinction that proved particularly important as Italy, under the fascist dictator Benito Mussolini, joined the Axis powers aligned against the Allies in World War II. In choosing to join the military service, DiMaggio put to rest any concerns about Italian American loyalty.

Stan Musial became a hero of Polish Americans. He started his long career with the St. Louis Cardinals in 1938 but rose to prominence as the top hitter in the National League in 1943. He continued to play for another 20 years, amassing numerous records. He won the batting championship 7 times, won the Most Valuable Player award 3 times, and played in the All-Star Game 24 times. As ethnic-minority players such as Musial achieved respectability in the national pastime, their transplanted countrymen gained acceptance, "whiteness," and greater social capital in the mainstream culture.

In Joe DiMaggio, an Italian American hero became an American hero.
© AP Photo

Although overshadowed by Babe Ruth, teammate and fellow German American Lou Gehrig quietly but distinctively forged a remarkable career with the New York Yankees from 1923 to 1939. Known as the "Iron Horse," Gehrig set a record for consecutive games played at 2,130 and established another mark with 23 grand-slam home runs. He also earned the Most Valuable Player award four times, before affliction with amyotrophic lateral sclerosis, now known as Lou Gehrig's disease, ended his career and his life.

Italians proudly claimed Tony Lazzeri, yet another New York Yankee (1926–1937). Lazzeri finished his major league career elsewhere in 1939, but as the Yankees' second baseman he overcame epilepsy to establish league records, including two grand-slam home runs in a single game and 11 runs batted in during one contest. The composition of the Yankees team mirrored the polyglot population of New York, and its successes indicated the possibilities of multiethnic cooperation in a democracy. Sport thus fostered the inclusion of various ethnic and religious groups within mainstream American culture.

The 1930s produced numerous athletic heroes, some of them memorialized in baseball's Hall of Fame, which opened in Cooperstown, New York, in 1939. Little League Baseball, which began play that same year, provided a chance for young boys, who emulated their baseball idols, to pursue their own dreams of greatness.

Boxing Heroes

As World War I placed a new emphasis on combative sport and boxing gained a new respectability, the working class found a new hero in heavyweight champion Jack Dempsey. The United States government, however, considered Dempsey a "slacker." Born poor in the small mining town of Manassa, Colorado, Dempsey grew up tough but failed to join the war effort. A brawling slugger known as the "Manassa Mauler," Dempsey knocked down then-champion Jess Willard, who had beaten Jack Johnson, five times in the first round en route to winning the title in 1919. Thereafter, Dempsey's manager, Doc Kearns, and sports promoter Tex Rickard skillfully built Dempsey into a boxing sensation.

Rickard arranged a 1921 battle against Georges Carpentier, the European light heavyweight champion. The bout assumed nationalistic and social-class dimensions when Rickard touted the Frenchman as a sophisticated war hero in a struggle against the rugged and raw American. Rickard built a stadium in Jersey City, and more than eighty thousand fans paid a total of nearly $2 million to see the fight, which Dempsey won easily. In 1923, Rickard reaped another windfall by publicizing a giant, awkward Argentinean, Luis Firpo, as "the Wild Bull of the Pampas." Dempsey met Firpo at the New York Polo Grounds in one of the wildest fights in boxing history. It lasted only two rounds but produced plenty of excitement for the onlookers. After being dropped to the canvas at the start of the fight, Dempsey floored Firpo seven times in the first round before the Argentinean knocked the champion through the ropes and out of the ring. The ringside patrons pushed Dempsey back into the slugfest, and he felled Firpo three more times in round two before the South American challenger succumbed to a knockout (Rader, *American Sports* [1983] 190).

Rickard followed that brawl with a 1926 match pitting Dempsey against Gene Tunney, billed as an erudite Marine war hero and favorite of the social set (i.e., the "upper crust"). More than 120,000 attended, and millions listened by radio to the Philadelphia bout, which, surprisingly, Tunney won by a decision. He used his "scientific" style to score points while avoiding the punitive charges of the less refined Dempsey. The outcome begged for a rematch, and more than 104,000 fans filled Chicago's Soldier Field in 1927, paying a record $2,658,660. Among them, a host of celebrities, the richest Americans, and over a hundred politicians contributed to the proceeds. Seventy-three radio stations affiliated with NBC broadcast the controversial encounter to an estimated fifty million listeners, including 75 percent of all American men (Rader, *American Sports* [1983] 192; Evensen 100, 110, 117–118). In the seventh round, Dempsey seemingly knocked out Tunney, but new rules required him to await the count in a neutral corner. As the referee directed Dempsey to the proper location, Tunney gained valuable time and recovered at the count of nine over what was actually a 14-second interval. Tunney finished the fight with a victory by decision, resulting in a massive but unsuccessful petition by Dempsey fans to overturn the verdict. The ruling seemed to symbolize the fate of working-class Americans, who felt overwhelmed and cheated by the corporate interests that dominated urban life. Sport here symbolized the class and cultural tensions within the evolving American society (Gorn, "The Manassa" 27–47).

Jews, Italians, and African Americans also found heroes in the ring. Barney Ross (aka Barnet Rosofsky), a former employee of Al Capone, wore the Star of David on his trunks to proclaim his Judaism. His loyal followers marched to his bouts and thrilled at his successes. Ross won the amateur Golden Gloves featherweight title in 1929, and as a professional he garnered the lightweight, junior welterweight, and welterweight titles. He earned $500,000 in the ring and donated much of it to Jewish charities. With the eruption of World War II, Ross joined the Marine Corps and proved heroic in the Battle of Guadalcanal. His wounds led to morphine addiction, yet another opponent he eventually conquered. Hollywood producers made two biographical movies about his life, which, along with his autobiography, reinforced the idealistic notion of assimilation and progress through sport.

Joe Louis (Barrow), the eighth child of black Alabama sharecroppers, also got his boxing start in Golden Gloves bouts. His family had moved to Detroit when he was 12, although his father, a patient at an insane asylum, had stayed behind. When his mother remarried, his stepfather brought another eight children to the family. Louis had to go to work in an auto plant for $5 a day but found a refuge from his bleak life in boxing. He lost only two bouts as an amateur, but in the professional ranks, white heavyweights refused to offer championship matches to black fighters after the provocative reign of African American Jack Johnson a generation earlier. Louis' manager and trainer insisted on a carefully crafted plan to assure white America that Louis was not another Jack Johnson. He was never to be photographed with a white woman nor gloat over a fallen white opponent, and he had to appear modest and deferential in his demeanor. The strategy won favor with fans and promoters, and by 1936 Louis emerged as a top heavyweight, as well as a role model for youth in his life as a devoted son, outstanding athlete, and patriotic American. The paragon of African American heroes during his boxing career, his later life was mired in neglect and disregard.

Henry Armstrong (Henry Jackson), another African American boxer, took Barney Ross' welterweight title in 1938 despite a 14-pound (6.4-kilogram) weight disadvantage. Armstrong had already won the featherweight championship against Pete

The Tunney-Dempsey fight of 1927.

The Miriam and Ira D. Wallach Division of Art, Prints and Photographs: Photography Collection, The New York Public Library. "Fight Between Dempsey (left) and Tunney, at Chicago, July 1927." New York Public Library Digital Collections. Accessed September 15, 2016.

Sarron in 1937, a year in which Armstrong had knocked out 22 opponents with a relentless attacking style. Between the Sarron and Ross bouts, Armstrong amassed another 14 wins. He then beat Lou Ambers for the lightweight crown in August 1938, thus holding all three championships. In 1940, Armstrong fought Filipino Ceferino Garcia for the middleweight laurels, but that fight ended in a draw.

Sugar Ray Robinson (Walker Smith) won Golden Gloves titles in 1937 and 1940 before entering the professional ranks. His pro career lasted 24 years and two hundred bouts. A quintessential boxer, he recorded knockout victories in most of them by mixing speed, power, agility, grace, and showmanship. He held the welterweight championship between 1946 and 1951 and won the middleweight crown five times from 1951 to 1960 en route to becoming an international celebrity. His flamboyant style in the ring was matched by his public life, with European tours accompanied by a large retinue that included a valet, a barber, a trainer, and a person with dwarfism who served as a mascot. In the United States he traveled in a pink Cadillac, and his boxing earnings enabled him to engage in several entrepreneurial ventures, including a Harlem nightclub, at a time when economic opportunities for African Americans were generally rather limited.

The sporting successes and business ventures of black athletes served to stimulate African American aspirations, and the larger black population called into question the continuing socioeconomic inequalities in American society, leading the NAACP to challenge segregation policies in the *Brown v. Board of Education* case (1954). Thurgood Marshall won the case and later became the first African American to serve on the U.S. Supreme Court.

As African Americans slowly moved toward fuller acceptance, Italian Americans also gained greater recognition through sport. In addition to Joe DiMaggio in baseball, Italian boxers reached the pinnacle of success. Jake LaMotta, a brawler known as "the Raging Bull," defeated Sugar Ray Robinson in 1943, the only man to do so between 1939 and

1951. Robinson prevailed in five rematches, but LaMotta won the middleweight crown in 1949. He lost it to Robinson two years later. Unlike some other athletes, boxers such as LaMotta retained their working-class lifestyle even after securing sizable incomes, and his (and others') adherence to class habits encouraged fans to form a continuing identification with their heroes.

Rocky Graziano (Thomas Rocco Barbella), a contemporary of LaMotta, displayed a similar style in the middleweight ranks. In 1945, he won Boxer of the Year honors from sportswriters. In three brutal championship bouts with Tony Zale (Zaleski), Graziano displayed the indomitable courage that made him a fan favorite. The 1948 bout, held at Chicago Stadium, close to Zale's Polish base of support, drew a record crowd. In 1952, Graziano lost to Sugar Ray Robinson in another title fight, but in contrast with LaMotta his post-boxing career included pursuits as an artist, actor, and writer. Like LaMotta's, his life, became the subject of a popular movie, but the two exemplified the pitfalls and promises, respectively, of athletic glory. LaMotta went through six marriages and endured

a stint in prison, while Graziano's marriage lasted 47 years as his fame translated into roles in the burgeoning entertainment industry (Hauser and Brunt 107, 135).

The greatest of the Italian champions and the undefeated king of the heavyweights, Rocky Marciano (Marchegiano), had hoped to become a baseball player. A high school dropout, he learned to box as a soldier in World War II and won the heavyweight title by knocking out Jersey Joe Walcott in 1952. Although only 5 feet 11 inches (180 centimeters) and 185 pounds (84 kilograms), Marciano was a devastating puncher who knocked out 43 of his 49 opponents before he retired in 1955. He died a premature death in a 1969 plane crash, still idolized by boxing fans, many of whom considered him to be the greatest boxer in modern history.

Emergence of Black Stars

Joe Louis proved to be the greatest African American athletic hero during the era, but he certainly was not the only one. Eddie Tolan and Ralph Metcalfe earned fame as sprinters at the 1932

People & Places

George "Tex" Rickard

Tex Rickard led an adventurous life as a cowboy, sheriff, Alaskan gold miner, and gambler, but he gained fame as a boxing promoter, invoking nationalist spirit in staging Jack Dempsey's fight against French and Argentinean challengers. In 1920, Rickard assumed a 10-year lease on Madison Square Garden in New York City and turned it into the main indoor sports venue in America. He not only staged lucrative prizefights but also turned his attention to ice hockey, and the Boston Bruins joined the National Hockey League as the first major United States entry in 1924. Chicago, Detroit, and New York entered the league in 1926, and Rickard drew upon his past (raised in Texas) to promote the New York contingent as Tex's Rangers. He changed the names of the Canadian players on the team to reflect New York's ethnic composition. Jews and Italians came to the games expecting to see their countrymen perform and built a fan base for the new sport. Rickard then brought horse and dog racing to Florida, before succumbing to appendicitis in 1929. Fifteen thousand viewed his casket in Madison Square Garden, and nine thousand attended his funeral, confirming his own celebrity status (Rader, *American Sports* [1983] 187–193).

Photo courtesy of Library of Congress, LC-B2-5461-13.

Olympics, and Negro League baseball enjoyed a heyday. Josh Gibson, known as "the black Babe Ruth," surpassed even the legendary feats of his white counterpart. As a catcher for the Homestead Grays and the Pittsburgh Crawfords from 1931 through 1934, Gibson hit more than 60 home runs each season. In another season, he hit as many as 89 (the statistics are a bit sketchy, as the records are incomplete). He batted over .400 several times, including one season of hitting .464 and another of hitting .457, yet the white major leagues never came calling during his stellar 18-year career. He died at age 35 from alcoholism and a brain hemorrhage.

Some of Gibson's teammates on the Pittsburgh teams of the 1930s and 1940s displayed similar outstanding abilities. James "Cool Papa" Bell played the outfield for several contingents. A switch-hitting speedster, Bell had already established his credentials as the fastest man in baseball during the 1920s. He had circled the bases in 13.1 seconds on a wet field and reputedly covered the distance in 12 seconds on a dry one.

One of the Negro Leaguers who eventually did make a belated entry into major league baseball, Leroy "Satchel" Paige, enjoyed international repute as the greatest pitcher of all time. His career included playing appearances in five different decades (from the 1920s to the 1960s) as an active player, and he thrilled crowds with his phenomenal abilities, humor, and flamboyance. Although records of his achievements are incomplete, Paige reportedly pitched 55 no-hit games, as well as hurling 29 games in a single month and recording over 100 wins in a single season (MacCambridge 121). Paige made his major league debut with the Cleveland Indians in 1948, and more than 78,000 fans showed up to watch the 42-year-old (at least) pitcher perform. In 1952, at the age of 46, he still made the American League All-Star Team, and at the age of 59 in 1965 he made yet another appearance, for the Kansas City Athletics.

Other groups besides African Americans also found heroes in sports. Johnny Weissmuller, the son of an Austrian immigrant, became a swimming sensation during the 1920s, capturing all the freestyle world records from 100 yards (91.4 meters) to a half-mile (0.8 kilometer). Weissmuller was the first to swim 100 meters in less than a minute, and he won five total gold medals in the 1924 and 1928 Olympic Games. In the former, he added a bronze medal as a member of the water polo team. After touring Europe and Japan in swimming exhibitions, Weissmuller starred in Hollywood movies over the next two decades, showing his athletic physique as Tarzan.

Satchel Paige mixed speed with guile and tricksterism as perhaps the greatest pitcher of all time.

Image courtesy of the National Baseball Hall of Fame Library.

Horse Racing

Not all heroes or champions were human. Seabiscuit, a small western horse—not part of the elite racing circle—captivated millions of Americans in an improbable run to glory in 1938. In a remarkable upset, underdog Seabiscuit defeated the 1937 Triple Crown winner, War Admiral, in a match race and went on to become the all-time champion in terms of prize money. He seemed a fitting symbol for hard-pressed Americans emerging from the poverty of the Depression.

Eddie Arcaro, the son of a fruit peddler, had a long career as one of the world's greatest jockeys. Arcaro won the first of his five Kentucky Derby victories in 1938. He also triumphed in the Belmont Stakes five times and the Preakness six times, and he emerged as the leading money winner in six different racing seasons. During the 1940s, he won the Triple Crown twice—in 1941 with Whirlaway and in 1948 aboard Citation. The latter horse won 19 out of 20 races entered that year en route to Horse of the Year honors. Arcaro ended a 30-year career in 1962, then founded the Jockeys' Guild, a benevolent organization that provided benefits to his colleagues. The 1940s proved an exciting decade for horse-racing fans. In addition to Arcaro's feats, Count Fleet also won the Triple Crown in 1943, as did Assault in 1946.

Fleeting and Limited Fame

Bowling enjoyed considerable popularity in the 1940s, especially in the Midwest, and the best bowlers earned substantial sums. For most, however, success proved more modest. The American Bowling Congress memorialized its stars by opening its Hall of Fame in 1941, and the National Hockey League promoted its best players in its first All-Star game in 1947. Neither of these sports offered the rewards enjoyed by the top baseball players or boxers, and overall most professional athletes still worked in off-season occupations. Even the vast majority of those who did reach the pinnacle enjoyed only temporary acclaim, as professional sporting careers were generally short-lived. Education still proved to be the best route to social mobility and financial reward for most Americans.

Media and the Commercialization of Sport

The new communication medium of radio became commonplace in the 1920s and contributed to the publicizing of athletic heroes as announcers dramatized and sensationalized sports events for remote audiences. While radio broadcasts catered to a wide variety of popular and ethnically specific tastes in drama and music, sports programming focused on American games, and broadcasts of events such as baseball games, the Kentucky Derby, the Indy 500, and the Rose Bowl tied listeners to American traditions. At first, sports team owners feared radio as a threat to live attendance, but commercial stations bought rights to game broadcasts by selling advertising time. During the 1920s, seven different radio stations broadcast the Chicago Cubs' baseball games, yet the team drew more than fourteen million spectators during the decade (Noverr and Ziewacz 76). In 1926, the National Broadcasting Company (NBC) launched a network of stations, and the Columbia Broadcasting System (CBS) followed a year later. These consolidated networks, often owned by newspapers, created media conglomerates that focused power in the hands of a few.

College football broadcasts rivaled baseball coverage with transmission of the Texas–Texas A&M game on Thanksgiving Day in 1920. The *Chicago Tribune* newspaper forged a media corporation with its WGN (short for "World's Greatest Newspaper") radio station. Its broadcast of the 1924 Illinois–Michigan contest solidified the popularity of Harold "Red" Grange, already a famous football player. Before more than 67,000 fans in the stadium, along with countless radio listeners, Grange returned the opening kickoff 95 yards for a touchdown. He followed that with touchdown runs of 67 yards, 56 yards, and 44 yards in the first 12 minutes of the game. He then rested until the second half, when he scored on an 11-yard run, then passed for an 18-yard touchdown, thus accounting for more than 400 yards of offense during the game.

People & Places

John Tunis

John Tunis (1889–1975) began his career as a freelance writer and sports broadcaster in the 1920s, but he found greater success as an author of young adult fiction. Like the juvenile books of earlier writers, his sports stories portrayed idealistic characters, but unlike his predecessors, Tunis challenged them with adult issues, such as racism and anti-Semitism. A critic of professional sports and the commercialization of collegiate athletics, Tunis promoted the fun inherent in playing the game without an overemphasis on winning. His many works not only attracted American youth, but also influenced fellow writers in following years.

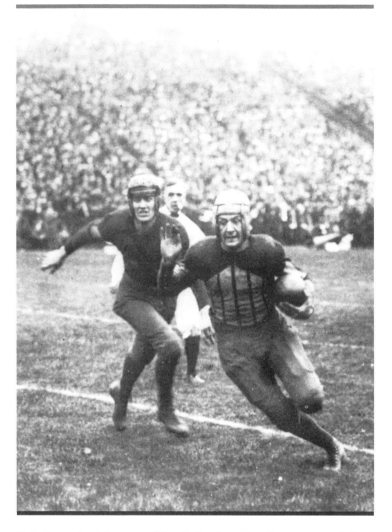

Red Grange's nickname—"the Galloping Ghost"—was one of the colorful monikers that endeared athletes to fans in the 1920s.

Image courtesy of Library of Congress, LC-USZ62-49414.

Sportswriters extolled Grange's shy modesty and plebian background. His mother died five years after his birth, and his father, a policeman, returned to his hometown of Wheaton, Illinois, a Chicago suburb, with four children. There, as a teenager, Red earned money doing farm chores and hauling blocks of ice, earning the sobriquet "the Wheaton Iceman." Writers fashioned an image of a rural innocent who succeeded by virtue of a strong work ethic and abstemious habits. They later dubbed him "the Galloping Ghost" for his on-field exploits and elusive running style, and when Grange left college after the 1925 season to join the professional Chicago Bears team, he was the most acclaimed football player in America (Carroll).

Some of the male sportswriters who made athletes famous became celebrities in their own right. Journalists such as Paul Gallico, Grantland Rice,

Damon Runyon, Allison Danzig, Arch Ward, Westbrook Pegler, Ring Lardner, and Heywood Brown popularized and idealized athletes as heroes and role models for youth. Grantland Rice, considered the dean of the sportswriters, dramatized athletic contests rather liberally, enhancing accounts to the point of exaggeration to create interest among readers.

Another, Nat Fleischer, began his career in sports journalism in 1912 and served as sports editor for several New York newspapers. In 1922, he cofounded *The Ring*, a magazine considered the bible of boxing, and he remained an influential voice in the promotion of boxing for more than 50 years. He wrote numerous books on the sport and its practitioners, served as a referee for championship bouts, provided boxer rankings in each weight class, and conferred championship belts. As a reformer, he campaigned for medical examinations of fighters and the creation of state boxing commissions to regulate the sport (Kirsch et al. 158). Indeed, his scrutiny of the sport made him the most reliable commentator on boxing during the twentieth century.

Among the many others who helped popularize sport, Graham McNamee emerged as a famous radio announcer. Colleges began broadcasts of their football games in 1920, and professional baseball teams and boxing promoters followed suit in 1921. Quickly assuaging owners' fears about radio broadcasts, McNamee used his dramatic style, emotional involvement, and insightful commentary to generate even greater interest, and he became the preferred announcer for major sporting events of the 1920s. His rendition of the 1925 World Series elicited fifty thousand letters from baseball fans (Rader, *American Sports* [1983] 198).

Marketing of Athletes and Coaches

Professional baseball and college football players were held in such high esteem that manufacturers paid them hefty sums to advertise their products. Babe Ruth endorsed not only sports equipment but also men's clothing, candy, cigarettes, cars, milk, appliances, gum, cereal, and a host of other goods; he also appeared in movies and published ghostwritten newspaper articles. His myriad ventures eventually required the services of a sports agent, Christy Walsh, who served as a business manager (Creamer 271–276). Although many products advertised by athletes had little or no relationship to sport, advertisers linked them to more abstract concepts—such as quality, luxury, or performance—that promised material and physical comforts as part of the American dream, which was supposed to be attainable by means of a strong work ethic. Red Grange, the football sensation of the 1920s, hired an agent, Charles C. "Cash and Carry" Pyle, during the fall of his senior year in 1925. Pyle negotiated Grange's contract with the Chicago Bears and arranged endorsements for clothing, dolls, candy, and soft drinks, as well as a movie contract.

In 1916, Fritz Pollard became the first African American running back selected for the All-American football team and the first black to play in the Rose Bowl. He then achieved stardom as the first black quarterback and the first African American head coach in the National Football League. Although paid handsomely for his skills, Pollard faced racist taunts, physical violence, and social ostracism during his athletic career, and, rather than enjoying the sweeping financial rewards that came to white stars such as Grange, he found his numerous business ventures largely limited to the African American community. In addition to his athletic occupations as player and coach, he became a sports promoter, banker, real estate agent, newspaper publisher, theatrical and musical booking agent, movie producer, and tax consultant. Thus, although he was denied the endorsement deals of his white counterparts, Pollard's athletic exploits did gain him social contacts that benefited his varied entrepreneurial enterprises and established him as a hero within the African American community (Carroll 186–206, 224–226).

Some coaches also assumed star status. Knute Rockne of Notre Dame joined Christy Walsh's publishing agency, profited from coaching schools and summer camps, guided tourists on sports-related trips, gave paid lectures, and endorsed products ranging from sporting goods to shaving cream to automobiles. The Studebaker Auto Company even named one of its models (the Rockne) after him, and by 1929 his annual earnings approximated $75,000. He turned down a $50,000 offer for a vaudeville tour in 1930 but agreed to a $30,000 radio contract to cover football games (Sperber 238–239). Rockne's humor and motivational skill also made him a highly sought speaker for corporate groups and social gatherings.

Forging a Commercialized Sporting Culture

The Tunney–Dempsey fights had been fought in the civic stadiums of Philadelphia and Chicago, both capable of accommodating crowds in excess of 100,000, and such spectacles attested to the popularity of sport and its potential as a vehicle for both cultural cohesion and commercial exploitation. The widespread and growing interest in sports, ardently promoted by the media, combined with the economic boom of the 1920s to produce a flurry of stadium construction. Colleges built concrete structures to accommodate larger crowds and reap bigger profits. Ohio State University opened its football stadium in 1922 at a cost of $1.3 million, but even its 66,000 seats proved insufficient for the 71,138 fans who showed up for the rivalry game with Michigan. In turn, Michigan inaugurated a 72,000-seat stadium in 1927 and later enlarged it to accommodate more than 100,000. In 1923 in New York, after renting the Polo Grounds from 1913 through 1922, the New York Yankees opened Yankee Stadium, which was quickly dubbed "the House That Ruth Built" because of the patronage drawn by the New York slugger. The Yankee owners paid $600,000 for the Bronx lot in 1921

Babe Ruth, the biggest celebrity in the Golden Age of Sports, helped foster the commercialization of sport.

Photo courtesy of Library of Congress, LC-DIG-ppmsca-38379.

and spent $2.5 million to construct the edifice, which seated 63,000. That same year, New York's West Side Tennis Club built a 14,000-seat facility to host the U.S. Open (Creamer 276; Riess, *City* 221). The Rose Bowl, in Pasadena, California, had been built a year earlier at a cost of only $325,000, with a seating capacity of more than 52,000, and it was later enlarged to hold 100,000.

Other grandiose municipal stadiums soon followed, and World War I spawned a number of memorial stadiums to commemorate the war dead. Los Angeles Memorial Coliseum was opened in 1923, and its seating capacity was increased to 105,000 to host the 1932 Olympics. Baltimore's Municipal Stadium was opened in 1924, with accommodations for 88,000, at a cost of $500,000, and Cleveland's Municipal Stadium held 78,000 upon its 1931 debut. The largest of the municipal and memorial stadiums was Soldier Field, opened in Chicago in 1924. At its completion in 1929, it held more than 120,000, hosting some of the biggest athletic events of the decade. More than 100,000 saw the 1926 national championship football game between Army and Navy that ended in a 21-21 tie, and in 1927 more than 100,000 fans watched the championship rematch between boxers Jack Dempsey and Gene Tunney. That same year, approximately 117,000 showed up for the Notre Dame football game against the University of Southern California, and a decade later the Chicago high school football championship game drew more than 120,000—at that time the most fans ever to witness a game in U.S. history (Riess, *City* 144, 239). The size, cost, and commemorative value of such edifices displayed not only technological advancement but also the emergence of certain American cultural values in the boom times preceding the Stock Market Crash, as lavish amounts of money and vast spaces were devoted to sites for athletic and commercial spectacles that occurred only infrequently.

The spectacular growth of sport during the Golden Age of the 1920s made it a big business. Baseball's World Series, which had drawn 150,000 fans and earned $326,000 in 1913, attracted 500,000 spectators and generated $1.8 million in 1928. Similarly, whereas the 1921 Dempsey–Carpentier boxing match brought in $1.8 million and 80,000 fans, the 1926 Dempsey–Tunney fight took in $2 million and drew 120,000 spectators, and the 1927 rematch was even bigger, pulling in more than $2.6 million and drawing an estimated 50 million listeners by radio. In 1922, the U.S. Golf Association registered 522 golfing clubs, but by 1930 that figure had risen to 1,195. Indianapolis 500 crowds surged

from 110,000 in 1920 to 160,000 a decade later, and in horse racing the number of races and horses, as well as the amount of prize money, nearly doubled over the decade. Man-o-War, the premier horse in 1920, won 20 of 21 races and earned $8,000 for a victory in the Belmont Stakes. Total prize money amounted to $7.8 million that year, whereas in 1930 purses totaled $13.7 million, and Gallant Fox, the 1930 Belmont winner, earned $66,000. The nascent National Hockey League grew to 10 teams in two divisions by 1927, and the National Football League expanded to 22 franchises in 1926. Between 1921 and 1932, the NFL awarded 36 different memberships before gaining some stability in the 1930s. Previously, the NFL had enjoyed little status, and one commentator had referred to it as "a dirty little business run by rogues and bargain-basement entrepreneurs" (Carroll 102).

When the Depression hit, it left most Americans with little or no expendable income, which of course took a toll on commercial sport. Sporting goods sales, which had reached $88 million in 1929, fell to $38 million by 1933. Similarly, game attendance and profits both dwindled. In 1933, the St. Louis Browns baseball team of the American League averaged only 1,159 fans per game (MacCambridge 126). Professional team owners limited their rosters and offered lower salaries to those they did employ, and sports promoters developed innovative strategies to regain lost patronage during the Depression. Major league teams began offering doubleheaders, giving fans two games for the price of one. In Cincinnati, general manager Larry MacPhail introduced night baseball on May 24, 1935, in order to attract men who were still employed (his Reds beat the Philadelphia Phillies 2-1). In the seven night games that year, the Reds averaged 17,713 spectators, compared with only 4,699 for day games. By 1938, the Dodgers were drawing 30,000 for their evening contests (Spirou and Bennett 112–113). Innovative black teams had played night baseball games years earlier with portable lights, thus giving a lesson to white proprietors. Arch Ward, a *Chicago Tribune* sportswriter, employed a novel strategy that allowed fans to see their favorites all at the same time. He assembled the best players from both leagues for an "all-star" game at Chicago's Comiskey Park in July 1933. Comiskey Park quickly sold out for the affair, with fans coming from 46 states to witness the grand gathering of baseball talent. Fittingly, Babe Ruth hit a home run that gave the American League a 4-2 victory, and an annual midsummer tradition had begun (Littlewood 66–76).

On August 31, 1934, Ward initiated the College All-Star Football Game, a preseason exhibition that pitted the top college players against the defending NFL champs, the Chicago Bears, at Soldier Field. Fans and sportswriters had speculated for years about the quality of play at the two levels, and although the game resolved no arguments (ending in a 0-0 tie) it drew nearly eighty thousand spectators. By the end of the decade, interest in pro games was generating average crowds of twenty thousand (Rader, *American Sports* [1983] 253). The NFL had already adopted new rules to increase scoring and created two divisions, as well as a postseason playoff, in 1933; in 1936, it conducted its first draft of college players, a strategy that gave weaker teams the first choices in the interest of promoting a measure of parity. It also saved team owners money by preventing bidding wars for the best talent.

The Rose Bowl game had long drawn attention to Southern California, and during the 1930s sports promoters in other areas began to use football as a means to pursue civic recognition, tourism, and profit in their own areas. In 1933, Miami hosted the first Palm Bowl, which was renamed the Orange Bowl on New Year's Day of 1935, the same day New Orleans initiated its Sugar Bowl. Dallas followed in 1937 with the Cotton Bowl. Such festivals mixed sport with entertainment and expressions of civic or regional pride that drew tourists to the host cities.

The first Heisman Trophy, awarded by the New York Athletic Club to the best college football player, went to Jay Berwanger of the University of Chicago in 1936. That same year, the Associated Press developed its weekly poll to determine college football rankings, generating interest and angst among loyal followers and alumni across the country. Such awards, along with a mythical but conferred national championship, sparked fans' interests and speculations throughout the season, and these promotional strategies increased newspaper and magazine sales and attracted radio listeners.

Basketball, too, revised its rules and initiated new tournaments to build fans' interest in the game. The 3-second rule appeared in 1935 to keep offensive players from monopolizing the free-throw lane around the basket, and two years later the center jump after each basket was eliminated in order to speed up the game. In 1938, the National Invitational Tournament (NIT), staged in New York City, served as the national championship, and it greatly overshadowed the NCAA tournament that started in 1939. The NIT continued as the premier collegiate basketball event until the 1950s.

Growth of Professional Franchises

Organizers made headway in this regard after the war, as indicated by the organization in 1946 of a second professional football league, known as the All-America Football Conference (AAFC)—yet another entrepreneurial venture by sportswriter Arch Ward. The new league expanded to the South (Miami) and, enabled by the availability of airline service, to the West. Meanwhile, the NFL's Cleveland franchise moved to Los Angeles, and another was formed in San Francisco. The AAFC's Browns replaced the departed team in Cleveland and featured two outstanding African American players, guard Bill Willis and fullback Marion Motley. Two other black players—Kenny Washington and Woody Strode, who starred for UCLA in 1939 and on semipro teams thereafter—signed with the Los Angeles Rams team. The pro football rivalry lasted for four years, until the best AAFC franchises (Baltimore, Cleveland, and San Francisco) merged with the NFL in 1949.

College basketball was still centered in New York City, but professional circuits expanded in the Midwest, and the best of the Eastern and Midwestern pro teams formed the Basketball Association of America (BAA) in 1946. The BAA competed with the American Basketball League, operating in the East since 1934, and the National Basketball League (NBL). Founded in 1937 and based in the Midwest, the NBL featured industrial and small-town teams. In 1949, the BAA and the NBL merged to form the National Basketball Association (NBA). With profits tied to gate receipts at larger arenas, most small towns could not compete with large cities, forcing their teams to drop out of the league or move to bigger urban areas. The merger had produced a 17-team league with three divisions, but by 1954 only eight franchises remained. Big cities and big men began to dominate play, as epitomized by the Minneapolis Lakers and their 6-foot-10-inch (208-centimeter) center, George Mikan. As in the loosely organized days of early professional baseball and football, pro basketball teams sought skilled players regardless of race, and the desegregation of pro football in 1946 and of Major League Baseball in 1947 proved propitious for the new league. The NBA began drafting African American players in 1950, a move that eventually forced the Harlem Globetrotters to seek new sources of profit by extending their barnstorming tours beyond American borders.

People & Places

Jay Berwanger

John Jacob "Jay" Berwanger (1914–2002) was the first player to win the coveted Heisman Trophy in 1935. At that time it was known as the Downtown (New York) Athletic Club Trophy, to be given to the best college football player from a team east of the Mississippi River. It was dedicated to John Heisman, famed college football coach, then athletic director at the Downtown Athletic Club, after his death in 1936. Jay Berwanger was born in Dubuque, Iowa, where he starred as a high school athlete. He attended the University of Chicago, where he excelled in football and track. His school record in the decathlon lasted for more than 70 years, but he gained greater fame as a versatile halfback in football, where he gained more than 4 yards per carry, returned kicks and punts, passed, punted, kicked field goals and extra points, and played linebacker on defense. Though his team won only four games in 1935, Berwanger was elected the winner of the trophy by a wide margin over all other candidates. The Heisman Trophy has since become the most coveted in collegiate sport.

Whittingham, Richard. *Rites of Autumn: The Story of College Football*. New York: The Free Press, 2001; www-news.uchicago.edu/releases/02/020627.berwanger.shtml.

Transition to Televised Sport

Technological advancements provided photo-finish equipment at the Olympic Games during the 1930s, and the Berlin host site also featured some of the earliest television. Leni Riefenstahl's coverage of the 1936 Games in the film *Olympia* even featured slow-motion and underwater photography, and the new technology proved a boon to coaches and athletes questing for improved performance. Telecasts of baseball and football games in the United States began in 1939, but few Americans owned the primitive television sets, which cost as much as $600 (Gems, *For Pride* 188). Even a decade later fewer than a million families owned televisions; by 1955, however, the cost was affordable for even the working class, and 67 percent of American families began to change their recreational habits by owning a TV (Gorn and Goldstein 238).

Summary

With the end of the Progressive Era and the conclusion of World War I, the United States turned inward, taking an isolationist stance toward world affairs and focusing instead on national issues. Intent on homogenizing American culture, Congress enacted immigration quotas, activists used vast and comprehensive sports programs in an effort to acculturate immigrant youth, and idealistic sportswriters portrayed ethnic-minority and working-class sports heroes as role models. The booming 1920s brought increasing commercialization of sporting culture in the form of huge stadiums, sports agents, and the intensifying promotion of athletes as celebrities, but the Great Depression of the 1930s forced entrepreneurs to find innovative means to attract spectators. As fascist regimes assumed power in Europe and Asia, sporting contests were given greater political significance, and when that surrogate warfare erupted into real carnage, sports provided a morale boost in the United States.

The atomic bombs that effectively ended combat cast the world into the nuclear age and the ensuing Cold War, as political alliances were forged along sharp ideological lines. Capitalist and communist forces stood locked in rivalry for the remainder of the century, and sport became a political tool in a global battle. Indeed, capitalism subsumed the American culture, directing work as well as leisure behavior. Within the United States, commercialized sport practices dictated the nature of sports organizations, governance, strategies, and even styles of play. In 1945, the New York Yankees franchise was sold for $2.8 million, even though the federal government did not consider baseball to be a business. Two years later, Major League Baseball televised the World Series, and sponsors paid $65,000 for advertising rights (MacCambridge 150).

Despite such successes in the economy, American society still faced social turmoil. The war for democracy was marked by hypocrisy in American sports until Jackie Robinson achieved the successful desegregation of Major League Baseball. In the process, Robinson joined a host of sports stars who achieved the celebrity status fostered by the broadcast media since the 1920s. The advent of televised sporting events soon spurred a second Golden Age of Sports in the United States. Television exerted an undue influence on sport and society thereafter, shaping economics, power relationships, and perceptions.

DISCUSSION QUESTIONS

1. Why did the United States need heroes during the 1920s?

2. Why was the Black Sox scandal so devastating to the American psyche?

3. How has sports journalism changed since the 1920s?

4. How did government agencies address the forced leisure of the Depression era?

5. How did sports entrepreneurs address the conditions imposed by the Depression?

6. Why did the 1936 Olympics have great political significance?

7. In what ways did World War II affect the practice of sport?

8. What was the social significance of Jackie Robinson's entry into Major League Baseball?

Chapter 9

Sport as TV Spectacle, Big Business, and Political Site

1950–1980

CHAPTER OBJECTIVES

After reading this chapter, you will have learned about the following:

- The role of sport in Cold War politics
- The economic impact of televised sport
- The symbiotic relationship between sport and television
- The ascent of pro football as the national pastime
- The role of sport in the Civil Rights Movement
- The social impact of Muhammad Ali (Cassius Clay)
- The influence of women in challenging gender roles and promoting Title IX and feminism in sport and society

A boxer—subject to so many manly ravages—was unlikely to serve as an Eternal Child, but Clay/Ali fit the bill. He was undeniably playful. Even sitting atop a pile of cash for a *Sports Illustrated* cover, he seemed unfettered by material—or adult—concerns. In his early years his skin was smooth and pretty, his verses elementary and comical. Even after his body had begun to go slack, his demeanor remained boyishly mercurial. As trickster supreme, he was impossible to pin down. He wore at one time or another each of the masks that various historians have identified as those that blacks donned to survive slavery: the deferential "Jack," the submissive "Sambo," the ferocious and threatening "Nat." In scheduling his fights from Manila in the Philippines to the African jungles of Zaire, his restless globetrotting made the world his home.

The myth of the Eternal Child also holds that the trickster in that child represents a "[p]owerfully anar-chic, anti-authoritarian impulse, a drive to revolt, to disrupt or overturn the existing order." In an age that featured a rejection of old authority and a search for new, Ali was most vivid as a figure who recognized little authority other than his own.

Zang 299

Muhammad Ali symbolized the Baby Boomer generation that transformed American society in the years after World War II. They questioned authority, pursued the social ideals expounded by youthful leaders such as John F. Kennedy and Martin Luther King Jr., and carried out their own varied crusades focused on diversity, individual-ism, civil and equal rights, feminism, gay rights, and environmentalism. Their efforts generated a culture war that challenged nationalism, patriotism, sexism, and materialism and produced a more liberal and multicultural America (Steinhorn).

In the years immediately after the war, Amer-ican society presented a facade of homogeneity, stability, and prosperity that masked underlying tensions and anxieties. Youthful questioning of the supposed stability emerged in the mid-1950s, as the exuberance and sensuality of rock 'n' roll music provided a release for the young and chal-lenged mainstream norms and values. Sport, too, became a contentious entity in the culture wars that developed over the course of the next generation.

Muhammad Ali in 1967.
Photo courtesy of Library of Congress, LC-USZ62-115435.

For many, the 1950s represented a second Golden Age of Sports in the United States. New technology, developed during World War II, enabled superior performance; for example, alu-minum, steel, and fiberglass changed the nature of pole vaulting, and aluminum club shafts and vinyl golf balls improved scores on the links. New sports, such as hang gliding, racquetball, and skateboarding, arose to fit into new lifestyles, often symbolizing youth and freedom. The National Hot Rod Association was formed in 1951 to regulate drag racing, as speed fascinated an exploding population. Jet planes reduced air travel times, and rockets even penetrated outer space. It seemed that humans were on the verge of conquering the natural world.

As in the 1920s, the media promoted athletes as heroes and role models for youth, and—much like the scientific advancements of the era—prodigious

1950–1953	1951	1951–1954	1954
■ Korean War fought	■ Major college basketball scandal erupts	■ McCarthyism exerted	■ *Brown v. Board of Education* decision by U.S. Supreme Court begins desegregation of public schools

athletic performances seemed to suggest almost boundless potential. In 1953, New Zealander Edmund Hillary and Tenzing Norgay of Nepal, his Sherpa guide, conquered Mount Everest. In 1954, Roger Bannister, a British medical student, ran the seemingly impossible 4-minute mile (1.6 kilometers) when he finished in 3:59.4 at Oxford, England, and once this physical and psychological barrier had been broken other runners soon followed suit. Australian John Landy lowered the mark to 3:57.9 only a month later, and, in 1958, Herb Elliott, another Australian, ran a mile in 3:54.5. In the 1960s, American high schooler Jim Ryun beat the 4-minute mark, and by the end of the century Moroccan Hicham El Guerrouj had lowered the record to 3:43.13.

The successes of sport symbolized the social progress of some citizens in the United States, as ethnic sport stars mirrored the social mobility of some groups, but masked the unequal situation of many nonwhites. After World War II, the GI Bill enabled many to attend college, and increased socioeconomic mobility (greater than their parents had enjoyed) allowed many second-generation members of ethnic-minority groups to move to the suburbs, achieving their American dream of home ownership away from the bustle and pollution of the big city. Although suburbanization denoted a visible sign of progress for families of Southern and Eastern European descent, the "white flight" from inner cities eventually left Northern manufacturing centers in a state of despair and destitution, resulting in ghettoization over the next generation. The deterioration of urban society and the desperation of inner-city life, combined with constraints on opportunities available to minorities and women, produced campaigns for civil rights and sometimes violent clashes with authorities. The local and national crusades to change American culture coincided with the international threat of expanding communism, and these internal and external tensions besetting the United States in the post–World War II era were played out in sport, which became a highly visible means of protest and cultural transformation as various groups sought their fair share of the American Dream. The perceived threat of the Soviet Union and its growing Communist bloc, however, overrode domestic issues, as the urgency and danger of nuclear war left all else pale in comparison.

Sport in the Cold War

Although the happy days of the 1950s offered the American Dream for some, the era was fraught with the international tension known as the Cold War. The Communist Soviet Union, although allied with the United States against the fascist powers in World War II, emerged from that struggle as an international power espousing a competing political, philosophical, and economic ideology. China and Eastern European nations adopted the communist stance, and capitalist countries battled communism in the Korean War from 1950 to 1953. The Soviet Union achieved nuclear capability by 1951, negating the American atomic advantage that had ended World War II, and the threat of a nuclear holocaust loomed thereafter as the political rivals jockeyed for world domination. In the United States, in a move similar to the Red Scare after World War I, Senator Joe McCarthy led a federal investigation that alleged widespread spying throughout the nation. The Korean War ended in stalemate, with the division of the country into communist and capitalist opponents separated at the 38th parallel, and although McCarthy's witch hunt ended in discredited ignominy, the Red Scare in general persisted.

In 1953, the Kraus-Weber physical fitness tests conducted in Europe and the United States indicated that 60 percent of American youngsters failed, while only 9 percent of Europeans did so. This lack of fitness, an essential factor in any war, disturbed U.S. government officials and physical educators. The nation was apparently becoming one of spectators rather than practitioners, which undercut the tough image that politicians wanted to portray, and, in 1955, President Dwight D. Eisenhower established a presidential physical fitness commission. By 1954, Soviet weightlifters began using steroids to induce better performances, and their U.S. rivals soon followed the

1954–1960s	1955	1956	1959
■ African American Civil Rights Movement challenges segregation	■ AFL–CIO merger takes place ■ Disneyland opens in Anaheim, California	■ Althea Gibson becomes first African American woman to win Wimbledon tennis title	■ American Football League founded; play begins in 1960

practice in their attempts to prove individual and national superiority. The United States seemed to be losing both its physical and scientific prowess, thus jeopardizing its role as a world leader. If war erupted, the nation might not be able to win, and the American sense of confidence and self-assurance was greatly shaken.

In this context, athletes thrilled the masses throughout the 1960s, providing a psychological escape from the ongoing stress of the Cold War and the intensification of the Civil Rights Movement. When the Soviet Union placed ballistic missiles in Cuba, President John F. Kennedy issued an ultimatum that brought the two superpowers to the brink of nuclear war in 1962. The Soviets relented, but a year later JFK was assassinated in Dallas. Only two days later, with the nation deep in mourning, the NFL continued with its regularly scheduled games, as the business of sport had come to supersede even a national tragedy.

When the Soviet Union joined the Olympic movement in 1952, the ideological confrontation of the Cold War extended to sport. Nationalism abounded at the Games in Helsinki, Finland, as Americans took pride in the election of Avery Brundage as president of the International Olympic Committee, but the competition itself revealed the Soviets to be a formidable foe. The communist women clearly outclassed their American counterparts, whereas American men still prevailed in track and field, and both sides claimed overall victory. The Olympics would serve as a surrogate form of warfare thereafter. The Soviet Union demonstrated its might by capturing the overall Olympic championship in 1956. Although a stellar U.S. track-and-field squad captured most of the gold medals, the communist aggregation outscored the Americans in many other areas.

American nationalism again confronted Soviet athletes at the 1960 Olympics, when the United States hosted the Winter Games at Squaw Valley, California, largely thanks to the promotional efforts of Alexander Cushing, a stakeholder in the small ski resort. Few spectators traveled to the remote location, as most opted to watch on television, and the Games resulted in a financial and psycholog-ical loss. Although Americans David Jenkins and Carol Heiss garnered the figure-skating laurels, the Soviet Union clearly outclassed all other nations in the overall standings, overcoming any supposed home-field advantage for the Americans and making clear how quickly the communists had achieved world-class sporting status.

At the Summer Games, held in Rome, the Soviets again fielded a well-rounded team, while the Americans concentrated on swimming and track and field. A trio of African American stars captured the attention of their fellow citizens, and one of them, Wilma Rudolph, a tall sprinter from Tennessee A&I University who had polio as a child, surprised the Russian women by winning three gold medals. The Soviets, however, had concentrated heavily on preparing their female athletes, and despite Rudolph's heroics the communists prevailed in overall competition.

In boxing, the light heavyweight crown went to the fast and flashy (and, at that time, apolitical) Cassius Marcellus Clay, destined of course to become more famous as Muhammad Ali. In the decathlon, African American Rafer Johnson battled his UCLA teammate, Asian American C.K. Yang, who competed for his homeland of Formosa (Taiwan). The two-day affair lasted 26 hours, and, after both had broken the existing record, Johnson emerged as champion by a mere 58 points. Beyond the competition, Yang's participation itself caused a stir, as the Communist government of China, known as the People's Republic of China, protested the inclusion of noncommunist Formosa in the Games and boycotted the competition (and all others thereafter until 1984). Thus, international sporting contests had come to provide a stage for the engagement of political issues (Guttmann, *Sports: The First Five Millennia* 209–210).

The Olympics spawned countervailing forces and interests. Whereas governments used the Games as political vehicles to fight surrogate wars and promote nationalism, individual athletes formed the friendships that Olympics founder Pierre de Coubertin had originally intended. In this sense, sport offered a temporary conciliation during the Cold War and exemplified its poten-

1960	1960s–1970s	1961	1963
■ African American Wilma Rudolph wins three gold medals at Rome Olympics	■ Modern women's rights movement seeks equality in educational institutions, increased sport participation, and equality in overall society	■ Peace Corps established ■ Alan Shepard becomes first American in space	■ Betty Friedan publishes *The Feminine Mystique*, sparks debate about women's rights in the U.S. ■ President John F. Kennedy assassinated

Wilma Rudolph was one of several African American stars who proved equal to Soviet athletes at the 1960 Summer Olympics.

© AP Photo

tial for amicable competition between otherwise ideologically opposed rivals. In 1962, as the United States and the Soviet Union were courting a potential holocaust over the Cuban missile crisis, Payton Jordan, the Stanford track coach, invited the Soviet track-and-field team to compete in California, thus extending a series of meets that had begun a few years before. The largest non-Olympic crowd (153,500) ever to watch a sporting event in America turned out for the two-day affair in Palo Alto and cheered world-record performances by both sides.

The rival athletes bonded on a personal level and concluded the meet with a joint march around the track, arm in arm, as 81,000 rose in acknowledgment. The "magical moment of camaraderie" even produced some lifelong friendships (Cavalli 7).

The quest for athletic supremacy amid larger ideological struggles exacerbated ongoing tensions between the AAU and the NCAA over the control, jurisdiction, and regulation of amateur athletics in the United States. In 1960, the NCAA canceled its agreements with the AAU and stopped recognizing its decisions on athletic eligibility and sanctions. The U.S. government interceded in the dispute in order to field a team for the 1964 Olympics, and in 1968 the American Olympic team produced phenomenal records despite great controversy (discussed later in this chapter).

Throughout the fearful Cold War, then, sport provided a diversion, a psychological escape from the sense of impending doom, and the perception of a strong national spirit. Sport assumed characteristics of ideological warfare; yet that assuaged the ongoing potential for real bloodshed. It also provided cheap programming for television networks in search of an ever-growing fan base.

Evolution of the Sport–Media Relationship

In September 1946, *Sport* magazine published its inaugural issue with the intent "not so much to glorify the athlete but to reveal him in all his dimensions" (Silverman 4). Such an approach, if implemented, would indeed be a distinct departure from the hagiographic sportswriting provided by sports journalists in the first Golden Age of Sports during the 1920s. In a weekly format, *Sport* employed some of the best-known sportswriters of the time, including Grantland Rice, who had been perhaps the most effusive of writers during the earlier golden age. Others, such as Red Smith, occasionally cast a critical eye, but in 1961 *Sport* began producing a series of biographies that celebrated the then-current stars of baseball, football, basketball, and boxing.

1964	1965	1965–1973	1966
■ Muhammad Ali becomes heavyweight boxing champion	■ Malcolm X murdered ■ Houston Astrodome opens	■ Vietnam War fought	■ National Organization for Women (NOW) founded

Diplomats in Tracksuits: Athletes and Sport in East Germany

In the confrontation between the political systems of the East and West, sport played a major role from the 1950s onward. Sport was an instrument of politics, a weapon deployed in the Cold War with huge success, especially by the former German Democratic Republic (East Germany), which, until reunification with West Germany in 1989, was a socialist country and a close ally of the GDR. The GDR was the most successful sporting country in the world, gaining by far the most Olympic medals in relation to its seventeen million inhabitants (winning 514 medals between 1968 and 1988).

From the very beginning, East German officials had aimed not only to undermine West Germany's claim to be the sole representative of the entire German nation but also to end the GDR's isolation and gain diplomatic recognition both inside and beyond the world of sport. In other words, they used sport as a tool in an attempt to demonstrate the superiority of the socialist system. Athletes should not only gain medals but also act as "diplomats in tracksuits." Back at home in the GDR, it was hoped that sporting victories would also help to strengthen people's identification with the system.

As in other rigid socialist countries, sport was shaped by the policies of the state political party, which in East Germany was the SED (the Socialist Unity Party of Germany). The key figures, institutions, and organizations of sport, along with all sport-related practices, were oriented toward the state's political objectives and subordinated to the political will of the SED. Responsibility and control lay in the hands of SED committees and the state apparatus, as well as the umbrella organization of East German sport, the German Gymnastics and Sports Federation. The objectives of competitive sport were laid down by the politburo of the SED's Central Committee. At the administrative level, the body responsible both for sport and for sport science was the State Secretariat for Physical Culture and Sport. Scientific research was harnessed and systematically oriented to the enhancement of performance, and the centralized supervision and management of sport and sport science made a substantial contribution to the GDR's success of top-level sport. Other important factors in the GDR's sporting success were the system of identifying and selecting talent, the systematic and generous backing given to young generations of athletes, and the arrangements made to efficiently combine sport with education or work.

The most effective instruments of selection from 1965 onward were the *Spartakiaden* competitions, in which thousands upon thousands of children competed in many kinds of sport at the school, county, and regional levels, with the very best athletes going on to compete against each other nationally. From 1973 onward, a series of tests was carried out annually in the first and third school years, and twenty-five to thirty thousand children were selected to undergo a course in various sports at a training center over a period of (usually) three years. The most talented of these children, about ten thousand altogether, were sent to attend the children's and youth sport schools, which guaranteed that a sporting career was reconcilable with school education. The highest level of athletic preparation took place in training centers stocked with excellent resources funded and controlled by the state. Of key importance in the training were "planning and control" procedures, that is, precise plans concerning athletes' expected performance (aimed at Olympic success).

Scholars also attribute the GDR's "sports miracle" (*Andreas Michaelis* Die DDR und Olympia, http://www.dhm.de/~jarmer/olympiaheft/olympi10.htm) to the enormous resources of both human power and money that were invested, the system of material and nonmaterial incentives (privileges mostly unattainable for average citizens, e.g., excellent career prospects, travel abroad, use of cars and telephones, and awards), and the systematic use of doping.

Information from Pfister, Gertrud. "Cold War Diplomats in Tracksuits: The Fräuleinwunder of East German Sport." *European Sports History Review* 5 (2003): 223–252.

1967	1968	1969
■ First Super Bowl played	■ Martin Luther King Jr. and Robert F. Kennedy assassinated	■ United States makes moon landing
■ American Basketball Association begins play	■ Two U.S. athletes stage Black Power protest on the medal stand at Mexico City Olympics	
	■ North American Soccer League forms	

A rival, *Sports Illustrated,* appeared in 1954 to challenge *Sport* with a different approach. Published weekly by Time Inc., it aimed for an upscale audience with slick photography and crisp writing. Early issues featured yachting and polo, but the focus was soon expanded to appeal to a wider audience. The magazine's initial swimsuit issue, published in 1964, achieved legendary status and became an annual feature, spawning an eponymous calendar, as well as videos and its own television show. The magazine itself would eventually grow to more than three million subscriptions, with an estimated eighteen million readers weekly in 2016 (*Sports Illustrated,* "Media Kit"). The popularity of such magazines reflected the booming interest in sport and complemented the instant gratification of television coverage with a more reflective and analytical approach that appealed to middle-class, and especially male, consumers.

Television as a Social Element

The televising of sporting events began in the United States in 1939 with coverage of a Columbia–Princeton baseball game (televised sport had appeared in Germany in 1936). The broadcast used relatively primitive apparatus—two cameras, two tables, and a water cooler, which served as the transmitter. By 1948, approximately seven thousand Americans owned television sets, and that figure exploded to four million by 1950, but technological limitations initially restricted coverage to sports with a narrow visual focus, such as boxing, wrestling, and roller derby (Davies 230). In short order, however, college and professional games were being televised on a regular basis, creating instant celebrities and, at least to some degree, assuaging political tensions. Viewers lived vicariously through athletes' exploits, and young boys in particular dreamed of athletic careers. Contests increasingly focused on civic and regional rivalries, and sport became a social opiate, as fans religiously followed their athletic heroes.

Baseball

The first national telecast of baseball games was in 1951, when the American Telephone and Telegraph Company (AT&T) assembled a cable system. The 1951 World Series was scheduled to be the first live event to be broadcast across the entire country, but when an unexpected three-game playoff series became necessary to break a regular-season tie between the National League's Brooklyn Dodgers and New York Giants, the Columbia Broadcasting System (CBS) decided to broadcast the series. The Chesterfield cigarette company sponsored the national transmission of the last two games from the Polo Grounds, the Giants' home field. Chesterfield served as the broadcast sponsor and reaped big dividends, indicating that sports-related advertising had the potential to reach large audiences, and thus setting a pattern for the future. Taverns, too, found that televisions drew patrons. Department stores put televisions in their store

People & Places

Clair Bee

Clair Bee (1896–1983) is known to many as a Hall of Fame basketball coach. Bee had two undefeated seasons at Long Island University in 1936 and 1939. In the latter year and again in 1941 his LIU team won the National Invitational Tournament. He amassed a record of 413-88, an .824 winning percentage; but after three of his players were involved in a point shaving scandal in 1951 he moved on to the NBA. Bee was also an author of more than fifty books. Most were instructional books on basketball, but twenty-four were fictional efforts in the Chip Hilton series, which lasted from 1948 to 1966 and were reissued again in 1999. The wholesome Hilton, a three-sport star, aimed to educate adolescent boys on the value of sport and a clean life. The books sold more than two million copies.

1970

- Women tennis players protest against the USTA for more prize money
- Gladys Heldman founds Virginia Slims Tour (women's professional tennis tour) with Billie Jean King and other women players
- *Monday Night Football* launches

1971

- Association for Intercollegiate Athletics for Women (AIAW) founded

windows, and hotels placed them in their lobbies, as crowds gathered in fascination.

The teams split the first two games, and in the final contest the Dodgers led 4-1 going into the bottom of the ninth inning. The Giants scored a run to make it 4-2 and had two men on base with one out when Bobby Thomson came to bat. A double play would end the game and give the Dodgers a trip to the World Series. Instead, Thomson delivered a home run (sportswriters called it the "shot heard 'round the world") to give the Giants a dramatic victory. Television delivered instant results, and an estimated seventy million watched the ensuing World Series games (Elias, *Baseball* 178–179). Twenty million American households had purchased televisions by 1953, and nearly 90 percent owned one by the end of the decade (Gorn and Goldstein 238).

The lure of the new medium proved irresistible for Americans but worried professional team owners, who feared a decline in paying spectators at their games and thus a reduction in profit. They retaliated by refusing to televise local games, a practice known as "blacking out" games, but, in a series of judicial cases in 1953, courts ruled that blackouts constituted an illegal restraint of free trade. With blackouts halted and no territorial rights standing in their way, television companies began to saturate local markets, and game attendance dropped dramatically, from a total of about forty million fans in 1949 to only fifteen million in 1957 (Rader, *American Sports* [1983] 286).

Many minor league baseball teams went out of business, unable to compete with televised coverage of major league action, and the 51 minor leagues of 1949 shrank to 36 by 1954 (Rader, *American Sports* [1983] 286). Even major league franchises sought new markets in cities where there were no other teams and thus no competition for paying spectators and television viewers. As air travel made transportation easier, some team owners moved clubs westward or into the South. In 1953, after televising their games and seeing attendance drop from almost one and a half million spectators in 1948 to less than three hundred thousand in 1952, the Boston Braves moved to Milwaukee (Rader, *American Sports* [1983] 286–287). The next year, the St. Louis Browns moved east and became the Baltimore Orioles, and, in 1955, the Philadelphia Athletics trans-

New York Yankees announcer Mel Allen, seated, reports the game between the Yankees and Detroit Tigers from the television box behind home plate at Yankee Stadium on May 11, 1956.

© AP Photo/Robert Kradin

1972

- Title IX of the Education Amendments Act ratified
- Swimmer Mark Spitz wins seven Olympic gold medals in Munich

- Israeli athletes killed by Palestinians at Munich Olympic Games
- Curt Flood unsuccessfully takes case for baseball free agency to the U.S. Supreme Court

1972

- The Equal Rights Amendment passes the U.S. Senate and the House of Representatives and is sent to the states for ratification

ferred to Kansas City. By 1958, even the nation's largest city could not support multiple teams, and the New York Giants and Brooklyn Dodgers both left for California. The new host cities, eager to attract professional sports franchises, provided favorable conditions, including publicly financed stadiums, as an inducement.

A host of star players also drew fans to the game, if not to the ballpark. Television allowed for greater intimacy, as fans could now put faces to the imaginary figures of the radio. Young stars such as Mickey Mantle of the Yankees, Willie Mays of the Giants, and Hank Aaron of the Braves excelled in all facets of the sport. Cleveland pitcher Bob Feller proved, by means of comparison with a speeding motorcycle, that he could throw a ball 90 miles (145 kilometers) per hour. In Boston, Ted Williams continued his torrid batting after military service in the Korean War, and Polish fans claimed Stan Musial of the St. Louis Cardinals as a hero. In terms of team play, the New York Yankees dominated professional baseball, winning six World Series during the 1950s, but the greatest individual performance was given by Yankees pitcher Don Larsen, who threw a perfect game in the 1956 championship series against the Brooklyn Dodgers, retiring 27 batters in a row. Television viewers experienced such thrills not only instantaneously, as with radio, but also visually, and therefore more personally.

College Football

Televised games between local or regional rivals generated passionate followings and brought esteem to previously undistinguished populations. In 1946, the president of the University of Oklahoma decided to emphasize the school's football team to counter the image of his state as a "dust bowl" (Ashby 284). The team overpowered its opponents in the 1950s, winning three national championships and building a 47-game winning streak before a 10-7 upset loss to Notre Dame in 1957.

College football had always enjoyed widespread popularity but had lacked strict regulation and organization until the NCAA assumed greater power under the leadership of a new executive director, Walter Byers. Hired in 1951, Byers organized NCAA members in a fashion similar to the economic cartel used by the NFL, used investigative officers and actually enforced rules in order to enhance uniform compliance with regulations, and pursued negotiations with television networks for both football and basketball broadcasting rights that brought a financial bonanza to the NCAA. His long tenure (lasting until 1988) assured the growth and ever-increasing power and wealth of the NCAA.

Pro Football

Under the astute guidance of NFL commissioner Bert Bell, pro football proved to be well suited to the new medium of television. Whereas baseball owners often acted in their own best interests, football owners united behind Bell (former owner and coach of the Philadelphia Eagles) upon his selection to the commissioner's office in 1946, forming an economic cartel, with Bell negotiating television contracts as part of a package that protected each team from territorial incursions. By sharing the television revenue equally among the teams, there was no need to compete against each other for broadcast rights. Revenue sharing allowed teams in smaller cities, such as Green Bay, to survive.

Pro football at this time also benefited from exciting developments on the field. A free substitution rule promoted greater specialization and fan interest. Whereas players previously had to play both offense and defense and also serve as kickers and special teams players, the new rules expanded team personnel and allowed for improved performances. In addition, the 1958 NFL Championship Game ended in a gripping sudden-death overtime, with forty million watching by television as Johnny Unitas quarterbacked the Baltimore Colts to a stunning victory. The popularity of professional football grew enormously, and over the next decade football began to surpass baseball as America's national game.

The tremendous financial potential of sport produced rivalries that altered the bureaucratic structures of sports organizations. In 1959, when

1973	**1974**	**1976**	**1977**
■ Billie Jean King beats Bobby Riggs in "Battle of the Sexes" tennis match	■ President Richard Nixon resigns due to Watergate scandal	■ Women's basketball becomes Olympic sport at the Montreal Summer Games (U.S. team wins the silver)	■ Janet Guthrie becomes first female Indy 500 driver

two Texas millionaires, Lamar Hunt and Bud Adams, were denied franchises in the NFL, they decided to form their own league, and the American Football League began play in 1960, with teams in Boston, Buffalo, Houston, Dallas, New York, Denver, Oakland, and San Diego. In 1963, the Dallas Texans franchise of the AFL moved to Kansas City and became the Chiefs. The NFL, under new commissioner Pete Rozelle, also put teams in Dallas and Minneapolis, and this expansion of pro franchises to the South and West brought greater integration of those areas into the national sporting culture.

The rivalry between the two leagues led to bidding wars and escalating salaries for the best players, and the AFL nearly went bankrupt in the process, losing about $3 million during its first year of operation. The AFL recouped some of its losses by selling television rights to all league games to the American Broadcasting Company (ABC). The NFL packaged all of its games for CBS in 1961. These arrangements were pursued by the leagues, operating as cartels, and the teams shared in the revenue. Such negotiations had been legalized when Congress passed the Sports Broadcasting Act of 1961 (cartels had previously been considered monopolies and restraints of free trade). The resultant television contracts pushed league and team incomes to unimagined levels. CBS paid $4.5 million to the NFL for the right to broadcast its games in 1962 and just two years later had to pay $14 million to outbid its rivals (NBC and ABC). Each of the NFL teams received a million dollars. NBC then outbid ABC for the rights to broadcast AFL games, but it had to pay $42 million over five years to do so, and each AFL team received $850,000. Players' salaries escalated accordingly, and owners in both leagues sought African American players at lower wages (Rader, *American Sports* [1983] 257).

The two leagues ended their rivalry by merging in 1966, eventually forming two separate conferences within the same league—the National Football League (NFL)—with the new championship game, known as the Super Bowl, beginning in 1967. Such an action again constituted a monopoly, but Louisiana congressmen (Senator Russell Long

and Congressman Hale Boggs) promoted successful legislation (the Football Merger Act of 1966) that exempted football owners from such charges, and Louisiana was rewarded with a franchise of its own in New Orleans. The conference arrangement ensued in 1970 with some rearrangement of franchises to equalize the television markets (Rader, *American Sports* [1983] 258).

The growing popularity of professional football became evident on November 17, 1968, when two bitter rivals, the New York Jets and the Oakland Raiders, met in Oakland. The exciting game was broadcast by NBC and featured five lead changes. With 1:05 left to play, the game was going down to the wire, with the Jets leading 32-29, but NBC had scheduled a movie, *Heidi,* to begin promptly at 7 p.m. When the game ran beyond its allotted time, NBC went to a commercial, then switched to the movie. Oakland scored two touchdowns in the last 50 seconds of the game, and irate fans who missed the ending placed so many calls that the telephone switchboard broke down. NBC was forced to issue a public apology, and the *New York Times* provided front-page treatment the next day. Consequently, future television schedules and NFL contracts required that all games be broadcast in their entirety regardless of the score.

Basketball

Basketball faced similar growing pains. Pro basketball, still in its infancy as a national endeavor, laid the foundation for growth and popular appeal in the 1950s, and two of the key developments were the entry of African American players into the league and the stardom of a white player, the Boston Celtics' Bob Cousy. At the start of the decade, Nat "Sweetwater" Clifton, a star for the black team known as the Harlem Globetrotters, joined the New York Knicks, and the Boston Celtics drafted another African American player, Chuck Cooper. As with baseball, the entry of black players enhanced the fan base as the racial comparisons and speculations that had gone on for years were now realized at the highest levels of play.

The National Basketball Association (NBA) established an all-star game in 1951, and Bob Cousy, a white guard for the Celtics, dazzled fans with a style of showmanship that had been evident in black players since the 1920s. Cousy dribbled and passed behind his back, intuitively threw "blind" passes, and scored with both hands. He led the league in assists eight times and once made 28 in a single game.

Under pressure from the NBC television network, the NBA also initiated a new rule in 1954 to

1979	1980
■ ESPN launches	■ U.S. men's hockey team wins Olympic gold in the "Miracle on Ice" ■ United States boycotts Summer Olympics in Moscow

increase scoring and eliminate intentional stalling of the game (Rader, *American Sports* [1983] 296). The change was deemed desirable as a way to spice up low-scoring games such as one in 1950, when, much to the chagrin of fans, the Fort Wayne Pistons had beaten the Minneapolis Lakers by the measly score of 19-18. Under the new rule, each team had to shoot within 24 seconds or lose possession of the ball, thus assuring more aggressive offensive efforts, which were highly appreciated by audiences. Thus, television networks began to influence the nature of the game. Professional basketball's stature, however, grew slowly, in part because of its provincial nature. Many early teams represented small cities, and basketball also had to contend with the established popularity of football and baseball; as a result, basketball owners did not garner large television contracts during this period. NBC decided not to broadcast basketball games in 1962, and ABC offered the relatively small sum of $650,000 for rights to broadcast NBA games on Sundays in 1964.

By 1959, 10 years after its creation by the merger of the NBL and the BAA, the resultant NBA had moved most of it franchises to larger urban centers. The eight teams drew more than two million fans to games in 1959, but such popularity spawned the rival American Basketball League in 1961. It lasted only until 1963, but rivalry rose anew with the organization of the American Basketball Association in 1967. The new league distinguished itself with a red, white, and blue ball, a 30-second shot clock, and a long-range three-point shot—rules that made the game more aggressive and attractive to many fans. As with league rivalry in football, the competition for players increased salaries dramatically until the two competitors merged in 1976.

Boxing

One of the first sports tied to television, boxing fared less well after an initial surge in popularity. The Gillette Razor Company began sponsoring weekly televised bouts as early as 1944, and their popularity led other commercial sponsors to follow suit, but the widespread telecasts proved a bane rather than a boon. Sponsors wanted to assure viewership by promoting only winning boxers and exciting slugfests; as a result, as had happened with minor league baseball, the independent fight clubs lost patrons who opted for the televised bouts. Even more detrimental to the sport, more gangsters assumed management of boxers, inflating their records against weak opponents, fixing fights, and exploiting athletes for their own gain. Bribery, extortion, and violence permeated the sport even outside of the ring, as the International Boxing Club (IBC) controlled 80 percent of championship fights from 1949 to 1953 (Riess, *City* 180). In the latter year, the U.S. government initiated antitrust legal action against the IBC as a monopoly, and Congress conducted investigative hearings that exposed widespread corruption, leading to the termination of the IBC. Boxing virtually disappeared from television screens in the early 1960s.

Glorification of Athletic Heroes

As major sporting organizations came to recognize their historical importance, they began to fete their heroes and preserve associated artifacts in halls of fame. The Baseball Hall of Fame had opened in 1939, but others emerged in the 1960s: the Pro Football Hall of Fame (1963), the International Swimming Hall of Fame (1965), and the Basketball Hall of Fame and United States Hockey Hall of Fame (both in 1968). This trend went hand in hand with the media's glorification of star players in order to promote greater interest among observers and convert some into outright fans.

In hockey, for example, Canadians such as Maurice "Rocket" Richard had drawn American fans to the winter sport, and by the 1960s two other players had firmly established the game in U.S. cities. Gordie Howe led the Detroit Red Wings to four Stanley Cup victories during the 1950s and won the MVP trophy six times. He led the NHL in scoring during six seasons and made the all-star team 21 times before a temporary retirement in 1971. In 1961, Bobby Hull, destined to succeed Howe as a fan favorite, led the Chicago Black Hawks (now known as the Blackhawks) to the only Stanley Cup win of the decade by an American team. Known as "the Golden Jet" for his blond locks and blazing speed, Hull—or, rather, his treatment by the media—illustrated how sportswriters in the 1960s repeated the strategies of colorful nicknaming and dazzling statistical quantification that had been used in the 1920s to promote particular sports and their top stars. Hull possessed a blinding slap shot that traveled well in excess of 100 miles (161 kilometers) per hour, and he led the NHL in scoring during seven seasons. In the 1965–1966 campaign, he registered 54 goals in 65 games, surpassing the record of 50 set by Maurice Richard, a feat equivalent to Roger Maris breaking Babe Ruth's single-season home-run record. Hull became the first NHL player to earn a salary of $100,000 for a single season. In 1972, he opted for the new World Hockey Association, where the Winnipeg Jets offered him in excess of $1.3 million per year.

Gordie Howe plays for the Detroit Red Wings in 1956.
© AP Photo

In the much more genteel environment of the country club, two golfers had surpassed the $100,000 mark by 1962. The phenomenal success of Arnold Palmer and Jack Nicklaus spurred television coverage, fan interest, and larger purses. The Associated Press chose Palmer as its Athlete of the Decade, and his numerous endorsements made him a multimillionaire. Palmer began his string of victories as national amateur champ in 1954 and as winner of the Masters professional tournament four years later, and he made an indelible mark by coming from seven strokes back to win the 1960 U.S. Open. Such comeback "charges" became characteristic of his success, and the relentless, chain-smoking, often disheveled Palmer—perceived as a working-class hero—drew a legion of fans, known collectively as Arnie's Army, who followed him around the course. Palmer's brand of popularity thus countered the notion of golf as an elitist sport, as blue-collar participants began to frequent public courses and golf tournaments became a mainstay of television programming.

Palmer's biggest rival, Jack Nicklaus, eventually won 20 major tournaments (two as an amateur) in his long career. His first big victory over Palmer came in a playoff at the 1962 U.S. Open. Not as charismatic as Palmer, but more consistent, Nicklaus hit long, towering drives that forced golf course developers to restructure their courses. Sportswriters dubbed him the Babe Ruth of golf, and after the most successful career in golf history, Nicklaus turned to designing world-famous courses. The media-generated rivalry between the disparate personalities of Nicklaus and Palmer only strengthened public interest in their confrontations.

ABC and the Transformation of Televised Sport

The youngest of the television networks during the 1950s, ABC seemed excluded from the broadcasting boom. As one strategy for winning a larger audience, its corporate executives decided to increase its sports programming. Under the leadership of Roone Arledge, the network sports division created an extensive schedule of offerings, technological innovations, and controversial coverage that sold sport as entertainment. Producers expanded upon the natural drama of sporting events to create spectacles, using multiple cameras and conducting interviews with competitors in order to provide viewers with new insights. (In 1963, CBS developed instant replay.) Cameramen sought out comely spectators and cheerleaders for "T and A" ("tits and ass") shots to titillate a presumably male audience; in turn, coverage of the fans encouraged attention-getting behaviors, and the crowd became a more active part of the televised scene (Roberts and Olson 270–272).

In 1961, Arledge initiated the Emmy Award–winning *Wide World of Sports*, a weekly program that traveled the globe to cover sometimes-esoteric events. The Gillette Razor Company paid $8.5 million to sponsor the immensely successful program. By the mid-1960s, the show included interviews featuring controversial athletes and the equally controversial announcer Howard Cosell, who became a national celebrity as commentator for *Monday Night Football,* which appeared in 1970. The weeknight scheduling of ABC's football coverage assured the network of a captive audience of football fans (no other games were played on

People & Places

LeRoy Neiman

One of America's most popular artists during his lifetime, LeRoy Neiman (1921–2012) specialized in sporting art. Born to a working class family, his talent became noticeable early as he won a prize in a national art contest while still in elementary school. In high school he began boxing and developed a lifelong interest in the subject. After military service in World War II he began working for *Playboy* magazine, which allowed him to travel and develop his craft and gain a national reputation. His sport themes covered topics from working class subjects to the activities of the wealthy elites, which he depicted in large, colorful representations. By the 1970s he had achieved worldwide fame despite critics' denigration of his work. From 1972 to 1984 he was selected as the official artist for five Olympiads. In the process of composing portraits of athletes and entertainers he became an icon of the popular culture along with his subjects.

© AP Photo/Diane Bondareff

Mondays) and changed the nocturnal and recreational habits of millions of Americans.

This packaging of sport as entertainment drew viewers and revenue to the networks, and some of the programming not only sensationalized but also trivialized the nature of sport. Evil Knievel, a daredevil motorcyclist, became a household name by performing incredible stunts. Jumping over increasingly imposing obstacles and distances, he courted possible death and suffered numerous injuries as astonished viewers tuned in to watch his escapades.

ABC also improved its share of the television market by winning the NCAA college football contract in 1964 at a cost of $3 million per year. That price doubled by the end of the decade, but financial expenditures for football coverage enabled television networks to win concessions from the college and professional administrators, and both schedules and rule modifications were made to suit the needs of the networks. High schools played on Friday nights, college games took place on Saturday, and professionals competed on Sunday. Prime-time schedules assured the maximum audience, and even some

churches eventually changed the times of their Sabbath services, lest they lose members to football coverage. Television producers dictated rule changes that promoted more offense and scoring to maintain viewers' interest, and, in order to allow their sponsors more space for advertisements, they

Howard Cosell ignited ABC's television ratings as the most controversial sports announcer and journalist of the era.
© AP Photo

instituted otherwise unnecessary TV time-outs, as well as football's two-minute warning as a game neared its end. Such innovations changed the structure, rhythm, and flow of games but proved to be a wise business decision. ABC moved from last place to first place in overall viewership during the next decade.

Marriage of Television and Sport

Football team owners flourished thanks to the television contracts negotiated by the league's commissioner. In 1970, the year the NFL–AFL merger took effect, the NFL signed contracts with the three major networks worth $142 million. CBS got rights to the National Football Conference's Sunday games, NBC got the American Football Conference's Sunday contests, and ABC initiated *Monday Night Football,* which involved airing 13 games featuring teams from both conferences. The arrangement offered value to the NFL and the possibility of marketing the sport while forcing the networks to compete with each other. All three networks used play-by-play announcers and analysts to provide viewers with insights, and ABC spruced up *Monday Night Football* telecasts by adding innovative halftime highlights of the Sunday games, whereas the other stations featured marching bands.

Monday Night Football enjoyed phenomenal success and made celebrities of its broadcasting team of Howard Cosell, Don Meredith, and Frank Gifford. Cosell, in particular, displayed an erudite, combative personality that attracted fans devoted to extremes of adoration or hatred. Cosell freely criticized the sports establishment while championing the cause of Muhammad Ali and other black athletes. His ruminations found a welcome reception in liberal areas but generated indignation in the heartland. One Indiana bar procured an old television each week, then raffled off a brick with which the winner could shatter Cosell's image at halftime. Regardless of the game, however, Cosell entertained viewers, and ABC's ratings soared. A Nielsen survey showed that nearly one-third of Americans tuned into the show, and Tuesdays topped Mondays in the rate of absent workers in some businesses (Pope, *New American* 377). In cities scheduled for Monday night games, the event assumed the qualities of a festival, with fans becoming participants in the production by dressing in outlandish garb and performing attention-getting stunts in order to be featured on the telecast, as sport moved even closer to pure entertainment.

The success of *Monday Night Football* spawned a whole series of pseudosport telecasts that became known as "trashsport." On the program *Superstars,* for example, athletes competed against each other in disparate sports other than their own (e.g., weightlifting or running an obstacle course). Networks then followed the same format in pitting actors, actresses, and other nonathletic celebrities against one another for the amusement of viewers. Such programming eventually lost its appeal (only to be resurrected more recently in the form of reality shows).

In 1974, the NFL's package with the three main networks accounted for $200 million in revenue, and CBS began adding pregame and postgame shows to its coverage. The next year, CBS added Phyllis George, a former Miss America, to its coverage team. In 1978, the networks offered the NFL a billion dollars to televise games. For their largesse, the NFL agreed to add two games to the regular-season schedule (increasing the total from 14 to 16) and to allow another team into the postseason (the wild card), thus creating an extra playoff game. While CBS and NBC split the conference coverage, ABC retained Sunday and Monday night games and added a contest on Thursday evening.

Throughout the decade, the NFL enacted new rules to produce more scoring, as desired by many television viewers. Hash marks were moved closer to the center of the field, and goalposts were narrowed, in order to discourage field goals and encourage more tries for touchdowns. Other changes designed to increase offensive production included moving the kickoff position to the 35-yard line from the 40-yard line, which promoted more returns, and reducing penalties for holding. To promote greater emphasis on passing, rules were also instituted by the end of the decade to safeguard quarterbacks and reduce the freedom of defensive backs to interfere with receivers trying to catch a pass. Scoring did increase, games lasted longer, and television networks had more time to sell commercial products.

The riches pouring into the coffers of professional teams flowed into the collegiate ranks as well, and while critics questioned the inherent violence of the game and its link to militaristic and corporate structures, President Richard Nixon, one of football's biggest fans, presented trophies to the top college teams. In 1973, the NCAA reorganized itself into three divisions for intercollegiate sports competition. The Division I football powers garnered the vast bulk of the television revenue, spurring escalating recruitment wars for the best high school athletes. ABC had paid $3 million for broadcast rights to college football games in 1969; the cost rose to $29 million a decade later, and in

1981 ABC and CBS split the collegiate offerings at a rate of a combined $65.7 million per year (Rader, *American Sports* [1983] 271).

Many more colleges played Division I basketball than football, because of the smaller team size, lower costs, and greater possibilities for national recognition (whereas multiple top athletes were necessary for a good football team, just one might vault a basketball quintet to nationwide exposure). The intensity of recruitment may have surpassed even that of football, and the NCAA sanctioned several schools for recruiting violations, but the guilty coaches simply left for another school anxious to become a basketball powerhouse, and the vast amounts of money involved led to widespread abuses and further recruiting violations.

Chasing the Television Market

Television profits also fueled an expansion of Major League Baseball, as new franchises emerged and old ones relocated in search of greater market share. Following the initial moves of the 1950s, other franchises followed suit. In 1961, the Washington Senators left the nation's capital to become the Minnesota Twins. The American League quickly replaced the enterprise in Washington, D.C., and added another in Los Angeles. In 1962, the National League established the Mets in New York. In 1966, the Braves abandoned Milwaukee for a lucrative television deal in Atlanta, where there was no competition for viewers in the Southeast. A year later, the Athletics deserted Kansas City for Oakland, California. Seattle got an American League franchise in 1968; a year later, San Diego joined the National League, and a team known as the Brewers returned to Milwaukee in 1970. Within 15 years, Major League Baseball had expanded from 16 teams to 24 franchises.

Expansion, of course, required a concomitant increase in the player pool, and critics argued that such growth caused a dilution in talent. From 1962 through 1968, the New York Mets lost more than 100 games in five of their six seasons, and in 1963 the loveable losers were a civic phenomenon, as a million fans attended their games to witness their hapless antics. The Mets then startled the baseball world in 1969 by winning the World Series, but the large metropolitan areas inevitably enjoyed an economic advantage; big-market teams had big money. Unlike NFL owners, baseball proprietors refused to share their revenues equally, so teams in the biggest cities or with the best television contracts enjoyed the greatest profits, enabling them to buy the best players.

The New York Yankees used their wealth to buy Roger Maris' services from the Kansas City Athletics, and Maris hit 61 home runs in 1961, breaking the record long held by Babe Ruth. Purists decried the feat, however, because Maris achieved the mark in 162 games, whereas Ruth did so in only 154. The extra eight games had been added to provide greater profit for networks and team owners, but Maris was the one saddled with the role of villain, rather than hero, for his displacement (albeit qualified) of a national icon. Thus, sports was producing story lines not unlike the popular soap operas, with their idols, rogues, and rascals.

The marriage between television and sport became even more evident as ABC paid $25 million to broadcast the 1976 Olympic Games from Montreal, which produced several heroic performances. Bruce Jenner set a new world record in winning the decathlon, and a bevy of American boxers won gold medals: Sugar Ray Leonard, Leon and brother Michael Spinks, Leo Randolph, and Howard Davis Jr. All but Davis would go on to win professional championships, with Sugar Ray Leonard winning recognition as one of the greatest boxers of all time in a Hall of Fame career (Hiestand and Martzke 2003).

Coverage of Alternative Heroes

Sport drew adherents from all sides of the social struggle. It provided a highly visible symbol of racial integration in all major sports by 1950, yet traditionalists continued to esteem the conservative values promoted by coaches and the white power structure. The nature of sport, however, changed greatly during the decade, due largely to the impact of television. Interest in sport expanded exponentially with intensified media coverage, rises in players' salaries, and the increasingly stellar play of athletes. In a period of racial and ethnic tension, athletes symbolized social mobility within the mainstream WASP culture, and various groups found heroes in the athletic world. The marketing of ethnic- or racial-minority heroes fueled greater interest in sport among diverse groups and larger profits for team owners and television networks.

In baseball, Jewish pitcher Sandy Koufax dominated the National League for the Dodgers before injury forced him to retire at the age of 30. A left-hander with a searing fastball and a devastating curve, Koufax struck out more batters than any other pitcher in four different seasons. In 1965, he set a single-season record by striking out 382 batters, and he averaged more than 300 strikeouts per year. He pitched four no-hitters in four years, including a perfect game in 1965, and he won the Cy Young Award, given to the best pitcher in the major leagues, three times. In 1963, he even won the Most Valuable Player trophy (more often awarded to a daily position player), and twice he led the Dodgers to World Series wins over the Yankees. His religion, however, took priority, and during his observance of Yom Kippur, he did not pitch the opening game of the 1965 World Series, but he returned to shut out the Yankees in two other games, winning the series' Most Valuable Player award for the second time. The Baseball Hall of Fame inducted Koufax at the young age of 36. Acknowledgment of his Jewish faith in the media increased awareness and knowledge of a religion that was still seen by many as somewhat alien. Thus, Koufax won not only ball games but also greater acceptance of Judaism in America, and that wholesale approval could not have been obtained, particularly in televised fashion, had he been an accountant or a shoemaker.

Upon Koufax's retirement, Bob Gibson, a right-handed African American pitcher for the St. Louis Cardinals, assumed dominance. He competed with a fixation on winning, and his icy glare and blazing fastball made him a fearsome presence. He became only the second pitcher to record 3,000 career strikeouts, and in 1968 he posted an earned run average of only 1.12 for the season. The next year, MLB lowered the height of the pitcher's mound to give hitters a better chance. Gibson led the Cardinals to World Series wins in 1964 and 1967 and earned two Cy Young Awards. Gibson excelled at a position not usually accorded to blacks; as a pitcher, he held a place of leadership and trust, slowly dismantling yet another stereotype.

In Pittsburgh, the Pirates enjoyed the services of Puerto Rican outfielder Roberto Clemente. Although he was the best all-around player in the game, Clemente rarely received accolades from sportswriters, who lacked an understanding of Latin culture and the Caribbean notion of "beisbol romantico" (the Latin flair for exciting play and love of the game). They often characterized him as sullen and vain, belying his true love for the game and his quest for respect. No one, however, could deny Clemente's impact. He amassed exactly 3,000 hits and batted over .300 in 13 seasons. He won the Most Valuable Player award in 1966, led the league in batting average four times, and made the National League All-Star Team 12 times. He secured the World Series MVP award in 1971 against the Orioles after hitting .414 with 12 hits. On the last day of December in 1972, while traveling to Nicaragua to bring food and supplies to earthquake victims, his plane crashed, killing him. Only months later, baseball writers finally acknowledged his greatness by voting him into the Hall of Fame. Clemente's death confronted stunned readers and viewers with the humanity of athletes, who, of course, had lives beyond the ball field. Many Latin players revered him as a god—the Jackie Robinson of the Caribbean.

Football also produced a bevy of Hall of Famers during the decade, but the one who most symbolized the machismo of the game hailed from Chicago. Dick Butkus, the son of Lithuanian parents with a working-class background, roamed the field as a linebacker for the Bears. Butkus covered the playing area with reckless abandon, relentlessly pursuing ball carriers and anyone else in the way. Fast and fearsome, he terrorized opponents by snarling, allegedly biting, and generally acting nasty. His 245 pounds (111 kilograms) crashed into blockers, runners, and receivers with stunning force. Despite playing on a losing team for most of his nine NFL seasons (1965–1973), he won election to the all-league team seven times. Coaches and opponents considered him to be the prototype of a football player. For many working-class fans, his sheer physicality, prowess, and heedless approach to the game reflected images of their own lives, as they faced the obstacles of life directly and relentlessly. In a time when professional sport reached for a greater bourgeois image, players such as Butkus kept working-class fans captivated by the game of football.

Professional Sport and Labor Relations

Despite the glorification of athletic heroes and immense profits to be had in the sporting world, employers and employees did not share equally in the rewards, and professional athletes and team owners continued to quarrel over salaries, pensions, and rights to free agency. In 1970, the NFL players launched a strike, and Oscar Robertson led NBA team members in a lawsuit against their employers. Although Curt Flood proved unsuccessful in his baseball case, the NBA players won greater freedom from their previously binding contracts, and, in 1972, Baltimore Colts player John Mackey, president of the football players' union, successfully sued the NFL and negated the famed "Rozelle Rule," which allowed commissioner Pete

Pittsburgh Pirate Roberto Clemente robs New York Mets' Cleon Jones of a hit at New York's Shea Stadium, Sept. 21, 1970.

© AP Photo

Rozelle to set the compensation if any player left his assigned team for another. Since the commissioner inevitably sided with team owners, the rule effectively denied players the chance to test their value on an open market. Despite the favorable ruling, NFL team owners showed little interest in free agents, and the average player's salary reached only $69,000 by 1980 (Rader, *American Sports* [1983] 353).

Baseball players had greater success in their pursuit of free agency. Under the guidance of Marvin Miller, executive director of the players' union, pitchers Dave McNally of the Montreal Expos and Andy Messersmith of the Los Angeles Dodgers implemented a different strategy. Having completed the terms of their contracts, they played the 1974 season without signing an agreement with the team owner. Without a contract, they argued

that they were free agents, able to negotiate with any club for their services. An arbitration panel and federal appeals courts agreed, essentially breaking the reserve rule that for nearly a century had bound players to one team. Players' salaries nearly tripled over the next five years, as owners outbid each other to stock their teams with the best players (Rader, *American Sports* [1983] 352). In professional basketball, the bidding wars between the NBA and the rival ABA also resulted in higher salaries for players. When the owners of the two leagues attempted a merger in 1970, the players blocked it with a lawsuit. The ABA ceased operations in 1976, when its Indiana Pacers, Denver Nuggets, San Antonio Spurs, and New York Nets franchises joined the NBA. Lucrative television contracts provided $880,000 to each NBA team in 1980 (Rader, *American Sports* [1983] 298).

Sport for All: A European Sport Concept

Modern sport is based on the principles of competition and performance, engaged by only a small sporting elite. In the United States, for example, sport is generally organized around staging competition for the best athletes rather than encouraging sport for all.

Since the 1970s, various European countries sponsored advertising devoted to the idea of "sport for all" (i.e., recreational sporting activities as well as basic-level competitive sports). The German Sports Federation, for example, propagated the "sport for all" movement with slogans like "Trimm Dich durch Sport" [Fit through Sport]. An increasing number of sporting activities, from aerobics to roller skating, that are oriented toward neither competition nor performance, became popular. This process of "de-sportification" motivated new target groups—women, senior citizens, and disabled persons, among others—to take up sport; transforming sport into an activity that attracts and includes large sections of the population.

The aim of convincing as many people as possible, if not everyone, of the benefits of sport was strongest in those European countries in which the main providers of sport were sports clubs. Sports clubs are nonprofit organizations with charitable status and democratically elected executive boards. They are responsible for sports training and the organizing of competitions as well as for providing recreational sporting activities. Small clubs that offer only one sport exist side by side with huge sports associations that have several thousand members. Members not only take part in the numerous sports provided by their clubs but also make use of the clubs' fitness rooms, swimming baths, restaurants, and other facilities. Germany (around 80 million inhabitants) has 90,000 sports clubs while Denmark (5 million inhabitants) has 14,000, and Netherlands (16.5 million inhabitants) has 29,000.

In countries such as the Netherlands, Belgium, Germany, and the Scandinavian countries, more than 30% of the population are members of a sports club. Sports clubs attract more men than women (who make up around 38% of membership), more young people than older people, and scarcely any immigrants.

Clubs are partly financed by membership fees and entrance fees for events and other activities; this income is supplemented by money from sponsors and public funding in particular. In addition, clubs benefit from the free use of sport facilities, mostly schools' facilities, which they are allowed to use in the evenings and on weekends. In this way clubs can provide a comprehensive and inexpensive range of sports.

Clubs form the base of a pyramid, with regional associations at the next level and national federations at the apex. National federations (like the football or swimming federation) are responsible for a specific sport; they form an umbrella organization which coordinates and oversees sport and physical activities in a country and represents sport in its dealings with the state and the public.

Sports organizations from the club level to the national federation level are based on the principles of democracy and autonomy as well as those of volunteering and reciprocity. The leaders of sports organizations are volunteers, and many of the coaches and instructors are only reimbursed for their expenses or paid a small amount of money in recognition for their work. The principle of reciprocity signifies that the work put in by volunteers is compensated for by the work of others. A club's public relations official, for example, may write reports for the press without getting paid, but he or she is also able to take advantage of the work done free of charge by others (for instance, the trainers).

In most European countries, the state provides the legal as well as parts of the material basis of sports organizations and supports their activities. Funding for sports frequently comes from national lotteries, and grants are given because sports organizations claim to provide work of great value to the society as a whole. The relationship between state and organized sport is characterized by partnership and cooperation.

Information from European Commission. *Eurobarometer—Physical Activity*. 2003 www.eufic.org/upl/1/default/doc/ebs_183_6_en.pdf; Heinemann, Klaus. Ed. *Sport Clubs in Various European Countries*. Hofmann Verlag Schorndorf, 1999.

Sport and the Civil Rights Movement

Adding to political leaders' social concerns, youth of the 1950s began to assume a questioning and rebellious attitude, noticeable in their dress, their hairstyles, and especially their musical tastes. African American singers adapted the laments of the blues to a new genre known as rock 'n' roll, which carried sexual connotations, and Fats Domino, Chuck Berry, and Little Richard attracted fans across racial lines. When the white singer Elvis Presley assumed the black style, rock 'n' roll acquired the status of a national social phenomenon.

Native Americans

Although some Americans prospered in such transitions, others had less faith in the system. Many Native Americans, among the poorest of U.S citizens, languished on desolate reservations or in urban ghettos. In the post–World War II era, American Indians invoked their traditional lifestyles to maintain some semblance of cultural cohesion, but some also used sport as a means to greater recognition and supplemental income by means of participation in rodeos. Both men and women assumed prominent roles in rodeo associations and generated alliances that served political ends, such as protest movements in the 1960s and 1970s. Native American pride was also given a boost with the 1964 Olympic victory of Billy Mills, an orphaned Oglala Sioux. Mills won the 10000-meter race in record time, becoming the first American ever to win that event at the Olympic Games. After his running career, Mills devoted himself to activism, instilling pride in and bringing hope to Native American youth.

Billy Mills winning the 10000-meter race at the 1964 Olympic Games.

From U.S. Marine Corps.

African Americans

Nearly a century after their emancipation, African Americans still faced widespread inequalities. In 1954, they moved to address such disadvantages in the courts by challenging segregated school systems. In the case of *Brown v. Board of Education,* the Supreme Court banned the practice of segregation in all areas—not just education—thus igniting the Civil Rights Movement. But social discrimination cannot be eliminated by law alone, and it continued in many areas, including the labor market, as well as sport.

In 1963, Martin Luther King Jr., the acknowledged leader of the nonviolent Civil Rights Movement of African Americans, led a march in Washington, D.C., which, because of its symbolic meanings (located at the Lincoln Memorial [emancipation] and in Washington, D.C. [the location of federal responsibility and the seat of the national government]), drew enormous attention to the cause.

> When we let freedom ring, when we let it ring from every village and every hamlet, from every state and every city, we will be able to speed up that day when all of God's children, black men and white men, Jews and Gentiles, Protestants and Catholics, will be able to join hands and sing in the words of the old Negro spiritual, "Free at last! Free at last! Thank God Almighty, we are free at last."

Martin Luther King speech, August 28, 1963

At the same time, athletes began increasingly to question the accepted idealism of sport and its function as an integrative force in American society. Congress passed a civil rights bill in 1964, but escalation of the Vietnam War, a military draft (conscription), and widespread poverty led to urban riots and mass protests throughout the decade.

In the world of sports, African American Althea Gibson appeared as an early harbinger of change and generated much-needed interest in tennis. American tennis had languished as top amateur players joined the professional ranks, and the United States managed only three Davis Cup victories between 1950 and 1967. Still, in 1950, Gibson proved a bright spot as the first African American allowed to participate in the United States Lawn Tennis Association's national championship. Aided by the former white champion Alice Marble, Gibson fulfilled an integrative role similar to that of Jackie Robinson in baseball. She won the French Open in 1956, as well as the Wimbledon singles and doubles titles, and she won the U.S. championship the following year. The Associated Press

A promotional shot of tennis champion Althea Gibson.
Photo courtesy of Library of Congress, LC-USZ62-114745.

named her its female Athlete of the Year in 1957, a first for a black woman, and she earned the honor again the next year. She entered the professional ranks in 1959 and turned to professional golf as a member of the LPGA in 1964.

Gibson's success paved the way for her male counterpart, Arthur Ashe Jr. Gibson's discoverer, Dr. Robert Walter Johnson, a black physician who also took an interest in Ashe and provided him with instruction. In 1968, Ashe won both the U.S. amateur championship and the U.S. Open before leading the American team to a Davis Cup win. The next year, he became the first African American on the men's pro tour, and in 1970 he won the Australian Open. In 1973, he became the first black player in a major South African tournament. Because of his success in a "white sport," and because of his political activities, Ashe helped break the bonds of racial segregation in the United States and abroad.

In 1975, Ashe became the first African American to triumph in the men's singles at Wimbledon, and he recaptured the Australian Open in 1977. His life took a decisive turn in 1979, when, after he suffered the first of a series of heart attacks, he contracted AIDS from a contaminated blood transfusion during surgery. Despite his ensuing illness, he founded tennis programs for poor urban youth, became a social activist, and wrote a history of African American athletes. He died in 1993.

Other African American athletes prospered in football and basketball. Jim Brown starred in four sports at Syracuse University before joining the Cleveland Browns football team in 1957. He won the Rookie of the Year award, then dominated the league over the next eight years with a combination of speed and power. During that time, Brown led the league in rushing eight times, averaging more than 5 yards per carry and more than 100 yards per game. In 1965, he won the Most Valuable Player award for the second time and scored 21 of his 126 career touchdowns. He retired at the height of his fame, at only age 30, became an actor, and launched a new movie genre featuring black action heroes. Thus, the way was paved for what would eventually become a stream of athletes making the transition from sport to the entertainment industry. For minorities, however, the road to success had always been littered with more obstacles, and pioneers carried an extra burden. If a black athlete, carrying the hopes of black citizens, failed, it could mean untold years of waiting for another prospect, one acceptable to the establishment, to come along.

African Americans are not usually associated with hockey, but they, too, served as pioneers in the sport. In 1948 Larry Kwong, a Chinese Canadian, appeared in one game for the Montreal Canadiens, momentous only in the sense that it opened the doors for other athletes of color. Arthur Dorrington, a black Canadian, signed a contract with the New York Rangers in 1950 but never progressed beyond the minor leagues. In 1958, Willie O'Ree, another black Canadian, did make it to the NHL with the Boston Bruins for 2 games, and he returned for 43 games in 1961. He declared that the racism he faced in U.S. cities was more virulent than any he experienced in Canada, indicating the difficulties for the first nonwhites who breached the walls of segregation (Burnett).

Sports events provided other highly visible images of social change in America. Increasing numbers of African American players began to appear on college basketball teams in the post–World War II years. The University of San Francisco won two national championships in 1955 and 1956 with three black players who were honored as All-Americans and went on to careers in the NBA: Bill Russell, K.C. Jones, and Mike Farmer. Cincinnati won back-to-back titles in 1961 with three black

Tennis player Arthur Ashe was an activist, entrepreneur, author, and race-relations pioneer.
© AP Photo

sports except hockey. From 1957 through 1969, the Boston Celtics dominated pro basketball, winning 11 NBA championships, largely through the efforts of Bill Russell, the team's African American center and, later, player-coach. Russell had led his University of San Francisco team to two national collegiate titles in 1955 and 1956 before joining Boston in the pro ranks. He played unselfishly, tenaciously grabbing rebounds, blocking shots, and intimidating opponents on defense. With Red Auerbach, the Celtics' cigar-chomping Jewish coach, the team won nine titles. Off the court, Russell refused to accept the role of the acquiescent African American. He spoke out against racism and social inequalities, and, although Boston was one of the most segregated cities in America, the Celtics elected Russell their captain and leader. In 1967, the front office went further and named him head coach, making him the first African American to fulfill that role in the NBA. He consequently directed the team to two more NBA championships, countering the stereotype of blacks' inferior intellectual and leadership abilities.

Other black basketball stars also addressed American racism, although not as forcefully as Russell. On the court, however, their play stood out. Elgin Baylor captivated fans with a combination of power, fluid agility, and leaping ability that would later be characterized as "black style." As a 6-foot-5-inch (196-centimeter) guard for the Minneapolis Lakers in 1960, he scored 71 points in a game, and he averaged more than 27 points per game over his 14-year career in the NBA. His white Lakers teammate, Jerry West, a consummate shooter, also averaged 27 points a game over 14 years. When Baylor's playing career ended in 1971, he overcame another racial stereotype by becoming a coach and executive in the NBA (Raffety 61–62).

Oscar Robertson, another African American, led the nation in scoring for three straight years as a collegian at the University of Cincinnati. Standing 6 feet 5 inches (196 centimeters) as a guard, he was drafted by the NBA's Cincinnati Royals in 1960 and played offense and defense equally well for them. During the 1961–1962 season, he amazingly averaged a triple-double (i.e., double figures [10 or more] in scoring, rebounds, and assists) for the entire season. Such superlative play forced even the white media to take notice of his accomplishments.

The biggest and tallest challenge to Bill Russell was 7-foot-1-inch (216-centimeter) Wilt Chamberlain, the center for the Philadelphia 76ers. After playing at the University of Kansas, then for one year with the Harlem Globetrotters, Chamberlain

players and in 1962 with four African Americans on its team. In 1963, Cincinnati started three black players in the championship game against Loyola of Chicago, which started four, won by Loyola. In 1966, the NCAA's championship basketball game featured Texas Western College (now the University of Texas at El Paso) against favored Kentucky, a perennial collegiate power. Kentucky's starting lineup, consisting of five white players, faced five African American starters for Texas Western, which won 72-65, thus marking a transition in team composition and race relations in America.

African Americans had long been allowed to entertain white audiences as musicians and athletes, and the best could accumulate a measure of wealth and fame, so long as they did not disrupt the prescribed social order of white dominance. By the late 1950s and early 1960s, however, black athletes began to emerge as stars in all major team

joined the NBA in 1959. In his rookie year, he averaged more than 37 points per game, and two years later he averaged a phenomenal 50.4 points per game. Chamberlain also averaged more than 24 rebounds per game in three different seasons, and he set the records of 55 in one game, 27.2 as a per-game average for a season, and 22.9 per game for his career average. In 1962, he scored 100 points in a single game (a feat yet to be matched). Another year, he led the league in assists. His rivalry with Bill Russell produced classic confrontations between the unstoppable offensive force and the immovable defensive bulwark. In the end, teamwork prevailed over individualism, as Chamberlain's 76ers won only one title (in 1967) during Russell's amazing title run with the Celtics. Together, however, the two giants signaled a transition in basketball from a game dominated by white players to a black game rooted on city playgrounds.

On the collegiate level, UCLA, with legendary coach John Wooden at the helm and star centers Lew Alcindor and Bill Walton, dominated the NCAA basketball world, winning 10 titles between 1964 and 1975, including 7 in a row from 1967 through 1973. Alcindor reflected the growing African American discontent of the era by refusing to play for the 1968 Olympic basketball team. He later adopted the Muslim religion as Kareem Abdul Jabbar; his religious change was symbolic of his discontent with the white establishment.

Football as the Harbinger of Social Change in the South

College football coaches developed new high-scoring offensive systems that pleased their rabid fans. Both the United Press International (UPI) coaches poll and the Associated Press (AP) sportswriters poll rated the football teams each week, enhancing fans' interest and enjoyment even as they increased the pressure on coaches and players to win more games—and to do so in decisive fashion. At the University of Alabama, Coach Paul "Bear" Bryant produced three national championships during the 1960s, but his success represented an adherence to traditional Southern values. Since the early part of the century, Southern football teams had employed the sport as a means to uphold the "Lost Cause" of the Confederacy, extolling regionalism and using only white players. Southern schools even refused to let opposing players who were black participate at games on their fields. When Southern teams played Northern teams, football games constituted a sort of surro-

gate reenactment of the Civil War, as bands played "Dixie" and fans waved the Confederate flag. Seven years after the historic *Brown v. Board of Education* court decision, Alabama and Mississippi still had not integrated their public schools.

Bryant had coached at Maryland, Kentucky, and Texas A&M, all Southern schools, before returning to his alma mater in 1958. An autocratic coach, he used brutal practices to instill discipline, toughness, and undying determination in his charges. As Birmingham police attacked civil rights marchers with dogs and fire hoses, Alabama's football team remained emblematic of the South's self-righteous racial attitudes. Its violent play on the field mirrored the treatment meted out to civil rights activists within the region. For his fans, Bryant and his team stood for Southern honor, defiant against the lack of respect with which the rest of the country viewed the region (Doyle).

To maintain its football prestige Alabama accepted invitations to postseason bowl games, where, by the mid-1960s, it encountered black athletes. Not an avowed racist, Bryant responded in pragmatic fashion, placating white boosters until the need for recruiting of black talent became obvious to all. He then kept a low profile on racial matters in order to maintain the benefits of the booster clubs. The turning point was a bowl game pitting Alabama against the University of Southern California (USC) in 1970. USC won 42-21, with Sam Cunningham, its black running back, accounting for four touchdowns. Bryant began recruiting black players, and another big brick fell from the wall of segregation. With integrated teams, Bryant and the University of Alabama won three more national titles in the 1970s, and Bryant counted more victories than any major college coach in history until he was surpassed by Eddie Robinson, the African American coach at historically black Grambling State University (Story, "UK's Northington" 2013; Martin; Schexnayder 2012).

Athletic Revolution

Vince Lombardi, famed coach of the Green Bay Packers, joined that team in 1959. He led them to five NFL championships (including the first two Super Bowls) by insisting on discipline, decorum, and precision. He believed in the traditional patriarchal hierarchy and assumed the roles of field general and paternal critic in his relationships with players. Revered as a hero in Green Bay, he became a national icon of traditionalists, with his small-town team serving as the David who slew the Goliaths of the staid NFL. In stark contrast, Joe

Namath, a white player, represented brash, rebellious, urban youth as quarterback of the New York Jets in the colorful, rambunctious AFL. An untamed, long-haired bachelor, Namath led a fast and hedonistic life that challenged traditional norms. Known as "Broadway Joe," he wore a full-length fur coat, sported a Fu Manchu mustache, and even donned women's panty hose for a television commercial. After the NFL won the first two Super Bowls, he publicly guaranteed that his AFL Jets would win the third, and, like Muhammad Ali, he delivered on his bold promise in a stunning 16-7 upset of the Baltimore Colts in 1969. On display in New York, the media capital of the world, his independence, affluence, and influence as a counterculture figure reverberated throughout the nation.

Black discontent magnified itself in the person of Muhammad Ali. Both loved and reviled, Ali transcended sport and became a focal point of many tensions of the era. With Ali, sport became a stage for the cultural warfare taking place in America, as rebels battled traditionalists in a struggle to define the nature of sport and the larger society. Tradition-alists adhered to an idealistic belief in sport as character building, and Avery Brundage, president of the IOC, steadfastly held to the principle of amateurism despite the many circumventions of the practice. UCLA basketball coach John Wooden maintained his belief in the old-fashioned values of work ethic and respect for authority, and a host of football coaches, most notably Bear Bryant at Alabama, Woody Hayes at Ohio State, and George Allen and Vince Lombardi in the professional ranks, preached discipline and conservative values. Coaches often dictated dress codes, haircut styles, and dating choices for athletes, with interracial matches as a distinct taboo. Their challengers—including both black and white athletes, who were characterized by coaches and much of the media as unwholesome rebels or outlaws—opposed such directives as oppressive, exploitative, and patriarchal. They tested authority with new styles and innovations and provoked radical change in the norms, standards, and mores of mainstream American society. This movement, termed "the Athletic Revolution," found its leader in Muhammad Ali.

Perhaps the most significant athlete of the twentieth century, Muhammad Ali forced America to confront itself.
© AP Photo

After his Olympic victory as Cassius Clay, Ali embarked on a professional career as a heavyweight. He danced, shuffled, and clowned in the ring, entertaining fans while distracting and frustrating opponents. Exceedingly fast for a heavyweight, Clay ducked opponents' punches and threw flurries of his own. He claimed that he could "float like a butterfly and sting like a bee," and he promoted himself and his prowess in poetry, braggadocio, and ranting interviews. Unlike black champions Joe Louis or Floyd Patterson, he extolled his blackness and demanded respect from white fans and the white-controlled media, who generally found his antics somewhat amusing but hard to accept. Despite his quick ascendance, Ali faced another black boxer, heavyweight champion Sonny Liston, as a 7-1 underdog in 1964. Liston, a sullen, scowling, fearsome brute of a man, an ex-convict, and a pawn of underworld gangsters, seemed invincible in the ring. Still, Clay stopped Liston, then announced his name change and conversion to the militant, separatist Black Muslim faith, which many whites viewed as a mysterious, anti-American threat to themselves and the established order.

Ali declared himself "the greatest" and became more vocal in his criticism of U.S. society. With the heavyweight throne as his pulpit, he became more defiant and more influential. He defeated a string of challengers, including former champion Floyd Patterson, who had promised to return the title to Christian America. Ali punished him severely in the ring for his insolence. To many, he seemed the devil incarnate, and for others he represented black retribution (Miller and Wiggins 293). Ali even predicted the specific rounds of his knockout victories, but although he remained undefeated in the ring, the federal government stopped the verbose champ by indicting him for evading the military draft in 1967. Ali refused to join the Army and fight in Vietnam, saying he had no quarrel with the Viet Cong, and he sought conscientious objector status based on his religious beliefs. The government not only denied his request but also levied a five-year prison sentence and a $10,000 fine. Ali appealed his case to the U.S. Supreme Court, but as he awaited the verdict, state boxing associations banned him from the sport. Stripped of his title and unable to pursue his livelihood, he assumed the role of a principled martyr who placed his values above lucre, fame, and glory. His enforced absence only made him more celebrated as the antiwar movement escalated.

Popular lyrics of protest songs exemplified discontent with the Vietnam War and its reliance on poor and working-class soldiers, with blacks providing an inordinate number of draftees. A popular rock song exemplified the sense of working-class fatalism:

And it's one, two, three, what are we fighting for? Don't ask me, I don't give a damn. Next stop, VIETNAM! And it's five, six, seven, open up the pearly gates. Ah, there ain't no time to wonder why. Whoopee! We're all goin' to die!

Country Joe and the Fish

Forced to relinquish his crown by judicial fiat, but undeterred in his mission, Muhammad Ali staged perhaps the most dramatic and prolonged comeback in sports history. Ali engaged deeply in the most serious issues of the nation, including race, religion, and patriotism, but he pursued his fistic encounters with a malevolent sense of play, both clowning and teasing opponents. After wresting the title from Sonny Liston in 1964, he defeated nine straight challengers. Three years later, his conviction on the charge of dodging the draft precluded more fights either at home or abroad, as the State Department revoked his passport. Thus, Ali spent the best physical years of his life in professional limbo.

In 1971, however, the U.S. Supreme Court overturned the 1967 ruling. Meanwhile, Ali had found a way to begin an epic quest to regain his title in 1970 by fighting in Georgia, a state without a boxing commission. After knocking out two white opponents that year, he met then-champion Joe Frazier in Madison Square Garden for the heavyweight crown. Their contrasting styles made for some of the greatest bouts in boxing history. Ali's long absence had diminished his speed and his ability to slip punches, thus forcing him to use more guile. Frazier, a relentless brawler with a devastating left hook and slurred speech, presented a distinct divergence from the loquacious Ali. Frazier emerged victorious in a hard-fought 15-round decision, but Ali earned a 12-round judgment in a return match in 1974. Later that year, Ali met George Foreman in Kinshasa, Zaire, for the heavyweight championship. The younger, bigger, stronger Foreman, a lumbering slugger and patriotic hero of the 1968 Olympics, presented a formidable foe. Ali employed his "rope-a-dope" strategy, letting Foreman hit him with punishing blows as he covered up along the ropes. By the eighth round, Foreman had dissipated his strength and succumbed to a knockout by Ali. In 1975, Ali and Frazier faced each other a third time, in the Philippines, in an epic fight known as "the

Thrilla in Manila." Each man took turns battering the other until both could barely stand, yet they continued to answer the bell. Both demonstrated remarkable courage and a steadfast resolve not to admit defeat. The referee awarded Ali a technical knockout (TKO) in the 14th round, but both fighters exhibited qualities of greatness.

Ali continued to fight well past his prime, but even in retirement he remained a worldwide icon. In 1980, he became a government envoy to Africa, and a decade later he traveled to Iraq to help free 15 American hostages. Later silenced by Parkinson's disease, he continued to demonstrate an unwavering spirit. In 1996, he lit the Olympic torch to open the Atlanta Games. As an athlete, rebel, and social protagonist, he remained a symbol of a defiant generation and of the evolution he helped to spur in American society.

The black athletic revolt coincided with Ali's plight. In 1965, African American players organized a boycott of the AFL All-Star Game and maintained numerous grievances throughout the decade, including lower salaries than their white colleagues, the lack of black coaches, and the practice of "stacking," which assigned African Americans to roles that required athleticism but not leadership or the utmost intelligence, as coaches presumed whites were superior in such areas. Black baseball players, for example, were usually assigned to the outfield, and black football players might be receivers or cornerbacks but never the center or quarterback.

Black discontent occasionally exploded in violence. Malcolm X, the charismatic spokesman of the Nation of Islam, was assassinated by rivals in 1965. That same year, Watts, a black neighborhood in Los Angeles, erupted in a riot that resulted in 35 deaths and $40 million in damage. Two years later, riots ravaged Cleveland, Newark, and Detroit as Black Power advocates called for social, political, and economic potency. Others, such as Stokely Carmichael and H. Rap Brown, leaders of the Student Non-Violent Coordinating Committee (SNCC), extolled racial pride and self-reliance, but extremists such as the Nation of Islam favored a separate black nation, and the militant Black Panther Party engaged in violent confrontations with the white power structure.

After Ali's sentencing, Harry Edwards, a black sociology professor at San Jose State College, organized the Olympic Project for Human Rights (OPHR), an attempt to have black athletes boycott the 1968 Olympic Games. The OPHR listed several demands: restoring Ali to his heavyweight championship; removing the conservative and seemingly racist International Olympic Committee (IOC) president Avery Brundage; excluding countries that practiced segregation from Olympic competition; appointing black coaches to the United States Olympic Committee; and integrating African American athletes into the powerful, all-white New York Athletic Club (NYAC). Black athletes boycotted the NYAC indoor track meet in February 1968, and the IOC did exclude South Africa, an apartheid state, from the Olympics that spring. At the same time, it seemed that American society had been rent asunder, with the assassinations of Martin Luther King and Robert Kennedy. College students and antiwar protesters, battered by Chicago policemen at the Democratic National Convention, mocked the political and judicial system. At least 37 colleges faced athletic boycotts, as well as student demands for black student centers and more black coaches of athletic teams, and the NBA players' association decided to strike.

Edwards' movement lost its cohesion when the student-athletes went on summer break, but athletes maintained their attitudes and their defiance at the Olympic Games, which produced some amazing performances. The most stunning image of the festival appeared after the 200-meter final, in which African American Tommie Smith won the gold medal in world-record time and fellow African American John Carlos took the bronze. On the victory stand, they stood in black socks and raised clenched fists in black gloves to form the Black Power salute as the national anthem played. Thus, a worldwide audience bore witness to America's troubled race relations. The USOC suspended both from the American team and sent them home the next day.

Challenge to Athletic Serfdom

In 1969, the United States took great pride in the *Apollo 11* moon landing, but that success did not allay racial issues in sport, as athletes in general, and African American athletes in particular, sought greater control over their lives. In basketball, the NBA–ABA league rivalry led the Denver Nuggets of the ABA to sign Spencer Haywood, a 20-year-old sophomore from the University of Detroit who had played on the 1968 Olympic team. Haywood had a phenomenal year in the ABA, leading the league in scoring and rebounding and earning recognition not only as Rookie of the Year but also as Most Valuable Player. The next year, he opted for the Seattle SuperSonics of the NBA, but NBA draft rules stated that no player could be signed to a contract until his college class had graduated, a rule intended to keep athletes from leaving school early to join the professional ranks. A federal court decided the issue in Haywood's favor, stating he constituted a hardship case because he provided necessary financial support for his family. The ruling eventually altered the NBA draft system, forcing the league to allow players to enter its draft regardless of their age.

In pro basketball, Julius "Doctor J" Erving created even more excitement for fans. He left the University of Massachusetts after two years to join the Virginia Squires of the ABA in 1971 before playing in the NBA, first for the New York Nets and then for the Philadelphia 76ers. His style of play was electrifying, as his phenomenal jumping ability, combined with expressive flair that later became known as "black style," enabled him to take over a game, shifting the offensive focus from the big center under the basket to the brilliant individualist who was extremely mobile with the ball. Erving ended his career in 1987 as the only noncenter to record thirty thousand points. Such accomplishments raised African Americans to the pinnacle of the sports world and thoroughly demolished any lingering Social Darwinist doubt about the abilities of nonwhites.

In baseball, Curt Flood challenged the reserve clause (standard in players' contracts), which tied them to one team. An all-star centerfielder for the St. Louis Cardinals, he refused to accept a trade to the Philadelphia Phillies in 1969 because he detested being treated like a piece of property. He sat out the 1970 season, then returned to play with a different team, the Washington Senators. The Supreme Court narrowly ruled 5-3 against him (with one justice abstaining), invoking the 1922 trial concept that baseball did not constitute a business and therefore could not be sued as a monopoly. The baseball players' union, established in 1953, assumed real power with the hiring of Marvin Miller as its executive director in 1966. Under Miller, players continually challenged the reserve clause and the owners' ability to bind them to one team and hold down their salaries. In 1969, they boycotted spring training, and three years later they went on strike, forcing the owners to grant better pension plans.

With the changes wrought by the Civil Rights Movement and an increasing acceptance of diversity, African American athletes attained greater exposure in the media, and their athletic presence fostered societal changes. In 1974, Frank Robinson became the first black manager in Major League Baseball when he was named to lead the Cleveland Indians. That year also saw Hank Aaron hit his 715th home run, thus surpassing the seemingly insurmountable record set decades earlier by Babe Ruth—and doing so amid death threats by racists who still subscribed to a false belief in white supremacy. He finished his career with a total of 755 home runs and a .305 batting average and held the career records for most extra base hits, most total bases, and most runs batted in. In track and field, Edwin Moses won the 400-meter hurdles race at the Montreal Olympics in 1976, and a year later he started a 122-race winning streak that lasted nearly 10 years.

NFL players had formed a labor union in 1956, but it lacked impetus until the NFL–AFL merger in 1966. Thereafter, the players demanded better salaries and pension plans, as well as the right to counsel during contract negotiations. Players went on strike before the 1968 season and won some concessions from owners, who raised the minimum salary from $7,000 to $12,000 (Rader, *American Sports* [1983] 350). The owners retaliated, however, by trading or demoting the player representatives who had led the strike.

Although salary, retirement benefits, and respect formed the focus of most professional athletes' concerns, racism fostered other activism in the professional and college ranks. In 1965, African American players refused to play in the AFL All-Star Game in New Orleans after being refused service there, and league officials were forced to move the contest to Houston. The 1969 season brought several player rebellions to collegiate campuses. At Oregon State University, 47 players quit the football team, and player revolts elsewhere protesting harsh treatment of players (e.g., prohibitions on interracial dating, lack of black coaches, and the stacking of athletes) led to the firing of coaches at the universities of Maryland, Wyoming, and Washington (Wiggins, *Glory Bound*).

Sport and Feminism

Adding to the clamor for change, the National Organization for Women fostered a feminist voice in 1966, and female physical educators began advocating for girls and women to have sports opportunities equal to those available to boys and men. Thus, the athletic rebellion spread to women's sport as well. In 1968, Billie Jean King, a top female tennis star, exposed the hypocrisy of the famous Wimbledon tournament, which billed itself as an amateur affair. King boycotted the competition, refusing to play unless she was accorded her true value in the clandestine payments made to male players. Consequently, Wimbledon officials dropped the hypocrisy and declared the matches an open event, admitting professional players, and King went on to win the women's championship.

Women made great gains in securing their own opportunities during the 1970s, and Billie Jean King led the way. In 1970, she and seven other female pros refused to play in a Los Angeles tennis tournament that offered the women only a fraction of the men's purse. Instead, they enrolled in the newly founded Virginia Slims Tour, sponsored by a cigarette company that marketed itself to women, and in 1971 King earned $100,000 by playing tennis, becoming the first female athlete to reach that figure.

She gained much greater fame and social significance, however, for her 1973 match against Bobby Riggs, a former tennis champion, a self-promoter, and an acknowledged chauvinist, then 55 years old, who claimed he could still defeat any woman. He emphasized his point by easily beating Margaret Court, one of the top women, 6-2, 6-1, on Mother's Day in 1973. The loss seemingly checked the growth of women's tennis and to some extent the feminist movement, until Billie Jean King accepted Riggs' challenge. Offered $100,000 to play and double that if she won, King showed up at the Houston Astrodome before more than thirty thousand spectators, the largest crowd to ever witness a tennis match. Satellite television delivered the contest to 36 countries throughout the world. In a lavish, exaggerated spectacle promoted as "the Battle of the Sexes," King destroyed Riggs, 6-4, 6-3, 6-3, to make an emphatic statement about the

Billie Jean King was a champion of women's rights both on and off the court.
© AP Photo

rightful place of women in sport (Rader, *American Sports* [1983] 344). The win also established King as a leader in the feminist movement, and she used her television appearances as an outspoken advocate for the women's rights movement.

People & Places

Gladys Medalie Heldman

Gladys Medalie Heldman started playing tennis only after her two daughters were born, but her contributions were profound. Heldman founded *World Tennis* magazine in 1953, serving as publisher and editor in chief, and she championed the founding of the women's professional tennis tour to provide more equity in prize money for women. In 1970, she spearheaded the movement of the best women's players like Billie Jean King, Rosie Casals, and Nancy Richey to form their own professional tour. Heldman signed these women to $1 contracts with *World Tennis* to play in a pro event in Houston. The Virginia Slims Circuit became the women's professional tour, and this women's professional tour gained popularity, eventually merging with the United States Tennis Association (USTA). Heldman is an inductee of the International Tennis Hall of Fame and the International Jewish Sports Hall of Fame.

Title IX

In 1971, women formed the Association for Intercollegiate Athletics for Women (AIAW) in order to promote more sports opportunities for female college students. Lobbying efforts by female activists in Congress produced a federal law, known as Title IX of the Education Amendments of 1972, which required equal opportunities for both genders in any high school, college, or university that received federal aid. Title IX states:

> No person in the United States shall, on the basis of sex, be excluded from participation in, be denied the benefits of, or be subjected to discrimination under any education program or activity receiving Federal financial assistance.
>
> qtd. in Carpenter and Acosta 3

The law was very often applied to gain equal opportunities in sport, and, although it was challenged by the NCAA, schools, coaches, and individuals, the courts consistently upheld it, thus prompting wholesale changes in the funding and selection of teams in all public school programs (Ware). Girls even won the right to play on Little League baseball teams. Interscholastic girls' teams proliferated, and participants jumped from only 294,000 at the beginning of the decade to almost 2 million at its end (Rader, *American Sports* [1983] 341). At the college level, the AIAW initiated separate championships for women in various sports.

Because female administrators initially intended to forgo the commercialized, overly competitive model of the men's programs, they did not want to offer incentives to the athletes such as scholarships. However, a 1973 court case initiated by a female athlete required athletic scholarships for women similar to those granted to men, and women's basketball, the most popular of female sports, soon had its own version of the recruiting wars that marked men's programs.

The rising popularity of women's sports led the NCAA to offer its own intercollegiate championships for women in 1981 in direct competition with the AIAW. Unable to compete with the overflowing NCAA treasury, which controlled television contracts, the AIAW suffered. Moreover, athletic directors at coed schools were almost universally male, and they tended to opt for membership in the NCAA rather than the AIAW. By 1983, the AIAW had ceased operations and sued the NCAA as a monopoly, a case it lost because the National Association of Intercollegiate Athletics (NAIA), an alternative governing body, provides its own inter-collegiate championships. Despite the promise of Title IX, the demise of the AIAW severely retarded the growth of leadership opportunities for women, as well as any sense of power within the intercollegiate bureaucracy. Male athletic directors tended to hire male coaches, even for women's teams. In 1972, more than 90 percent of women's teams had been led by female coaches, but that number would dwindle to 44 percent by 2004. Similarly, more than 90 percent of women's intercollegiate programs had a female athletic director in 1972, but that figure fell to only 18 percent by 2004 (Acosta and Carpenter, "A Longitudinal Study" 2–3).

Despite such dire trends, women and girls achieved great success in some areas. In 1970, Diane Crump became the first female jockey to ride in the Kentucky Derby, and in 1974 at least 60 women earned their living as jockeys. That same year, Billie Jean King organized World Team Tennis, a new format that provided more opportunities for female professional players. The Ladies Professional Golf Association (LPGA) also continued to grow, providing 33 tournaments and $3 million in prize money for female golfers by 1977. Women also entered the male world of auto racing. Janet Guthrie joined the NASCAR ranks in 1977, and she also competed in the Indy 500. Shirley Muldowney, a drag racer beginning in 1972, garnered three national championships. Such household names established auto racing beyond its rural roots, eventually attracting middle-class Northern suburbanites, both male and female, to its fan base.

While such firsts presented evidence of women's interests, abilities, and accomplishments, one popular female sporting event continued to attract players and fans. The Iowa girls' high school basketball championship surpassed that of the boys in interest. The first state tournament was held in 1920, when six contestants per team played on a divided court that limited players' exertions (the game began a gradual shift to the more conventional full-court game, with five players per team, in 1985). Partly because of their distinctive, traditional style of play, the girls' teams had developed a loyal following, and the girls' tournaments received television coverage as early as 1951. Tournament games were played in the state capital, and tickets and hotel rooms had to be booked months in advance. Tournament week even became a long holiday for some schools, and the festival atmosphere and accompanying rituals of honor bestowed respect upon the players and indicated the value placed on girls' physicality in Iowa. As with boys' sports in other states, winning teams promoted civic pride and local traditions. By the end of the 1970s, a national survey found that Iowa had the nation's highest percentage of female high school athletes (Hult and Trekell 200). Thus, the case of Iowa showed not only that girls could play basketball but also that there were sizable audiences for girls' sport.

Sport, Narcissism, and the Existential Search for Self

The expansion of sport coincided with an ongoing transition in American culture. The Vietnam War dragged on into the 1970s, escalating tensions between protestors and authorities, and in May 1970 the National Guard fired upon protestors at Kent State University in Ohio, killing four students. This overreaction raised questions about the limits of free speech and the authoritarian responses of a police state. The United States suffered additional turmoil in the Watergate scandal of 1972, when reporters for the *Washington Post* revealed that President Richard Nixon had authorized a burglary of the offices of the Democratic Party's national committee. Nixon's lies in attempting to cover up the fiasco led to his impeachment and to even greater concern for the moral and ethical state of the nation.

Because aggressive, martial games were thought to produce or encourage warlike behavior, and because the Cold War brought fears of nuclear annihilation, educators began questioning American cultural values during the 1960s, and some physical educators proposed a New Games Movement consisting of noncompetitive activities, such as Frisbee. Many Americans turned inward, developing an interest in the self, the one thing they might control. Some focused on their appearance or on developing new abilities, while others turned to psychoanalysis to reveal new truths. Many sought refuge or pleasure in new lifestyles, experimenting with Asian religions or unconventional sexual practices. In such a state of inquiry, many people also sought relief in myriad therapies, some of which included experimentation with drugs, especially marijuana. Drugs became commonplace among athletes as well.

Athletes' Fall From Grace

Despite athletic successes—both at the individual level and in the general growth of certain sports—sport lost much of its idealistic connotations. Sportswriters and, in some cases, athletes themselves wrote critical exposés of sport that examined drug use, alcohol abuse, sexual escapades, "wife swapping," and exploitation of players. Jim Bouton's *Ball Four* (1970) became a best seller, and Peter Gent's novel *North Dallas Forty* (1973) further examined the corruption of professional sport and American society. Indeed, the ideology of sport had been transformed by the 1970s. The media no longer uniformly idolized athletes, as investigative reporters delved into their private lives with sensationalized coverage, revealing their all-too-human frailties and failures. In addition, athletes became entertainers and were thus subject to the same stew of adulation, exposure, and criticism that other stars faced. And as their salaries increased, distancing them from the working classes, commoners increasingly lost a sense of identification with their former heroes.

Sport and Physical Activity as an Elixir for Health

The tarnished image of athletes, along with the increasing media portrayal of sport as entertainment, diminished some of its idealistic notions, but physical activity for personal enjoyment or betterment, such as improving one's health, assumed greater importance. While many young people turned to the bright lights and pulsating sounds of disco dancing to relieve their tensions, others found sport. Doctors, philosophers, and psychologists began to extol the virtues of running for health and happiness. Dr. Kenneth Cooper, NASA scientist and later personal physician to President Ronald Reagan, promoted a national campaign for aerobic exercise, which developed into a major activity for women and exerted a large influence on many women's lives. Cardiologist George Sheehan wrote a best-selling book on the existential benefits of running, and theologian Michael Novak equated sport (especially running) with a mystical, religious experience. Approximately twenty million Americans, including President Jimmy Carter, began jogging during the 1970s (Rader, *American Sports* [1983] 359). *The Complete Book of Running*, written by Jim Fixx (who, ironically, died of a heart attack while jogging), sold more than a million copies, and a fitness craze was under way as many Americans sought health and fulfillment in a narcissistic pursuit of human perfection (Plymire).

The exploits of American running stars such as Steve Prefontaine, Frank Shorter, and Mary Decker (Slaney) thrilled onlookers and set many on a path to fitness. Shorter won the Olympic marathon in Munich in 1972, as well as several

Mary Decker Slaney (number 373), America's best runner, never realized her dream of Olympic gold but gave world-record performances in other competitions.

© AP Photo

national championships in distance races. Decker ran a marathon at age 12, and in 1973, at age 14, she defeated Russian women in a dual meet in the 800 meters. A year later, she owned three world records, and she remained America's best throughout the ongoing Cold War, setting numerous records during the 1980s and inspiring many women and young girls to run.

Women Dispel Notions of Physical Debility

Although the modern marathon had been invented for the Olympic Games in 1896, it was only after World War II that new and more realistic opinions about women's endurance capacities began to take hold. Female athletes were allowed to compete in the 800-meter run in the 1960 Olympics and the 1500-meter distance in the 1972 Games. Women's participation in the marathon, however, was still considered unthinkable by those who held the

power in the running world, and attempts by women to run in legendary races such as the Boston Marathon were looked upon as sacrilege.

Nonetheless, in 1966, Roberta Gibb participated without registering. She mixed into the pack shortly after the start and reached the finish line in about 3 1/2 hours without being detected. In 1967, Kathrine Switzer registered as "K.V. Switzer" and got a start number. Soon after the race began, however, she was discovered as a woman, and, although supported by other runners and cheered by the media, she was physically attacked by one of the race's codirectors, who tried to pull her out of the race. Her 235-pound (107-kilogram) boyfriend intervened, hitting the attacker with a cross-body block, and Switzer continued on to finish the race. Not until 1972 could women participate "officially" and without disguise in the Boston Marathon. One year earlier, a female runner had fulfilled the dream of every long-distance runner by participating in the legendary New York City Marathon. In the 1980s, women's long-distance running experienced its breakthrough. The first women's marathon world championship took place in 1983 in Helsinki, and in 1984, for the first time, women could compete for Olympic laurels in the marathon. That year, American Joan Benoit, a former collegiate runner, won the gold medal.

Scientific Advancements and the Growth of Sport

Although football surpassed baseball as America's most popular game in the 1960s, other sports also rose in prominence, as scientific advancements allowed both for the expansion of sport to new locations and for the birth of new kinds of sport.

In 1966, thanks to the building of indoor ice arenas, the National Hockey League expanded its traditional winter sport into the South (Atlanta) and to the West Coast (San Francisco and Los Angeles) in hopes of reaping television profits from such large markets. In 1965, Houston built the Astrodome at a cost of $45 million, launching an era in which such facilities changed the nature of sport, allowing for year-round play, eliminating the effects of weather, and (thanks to artificial turf) increasing the velocity of players and balls in baseball and football, thus placing greater emphasis on speed-based strategies. Leagues staged more night games in order to accommodate daytime workers and to draw additional television viewers

Steve Prefontaine

Upon his early death in a 1975 car accident at age 24, runner Steve Prefontaine (pictured at the front of the pack) held 14 American distance records and had attracted a legion of loyal followers. Brash, outspoken, and confident, like Muhammad Ali, the white Prefontaine expressed a singular devotion to his sport that assumed the characteristics of religious zeal. Prefontaine campaigned against what he considered to be outdated amateur ideals and attacked the bureaucracy for failing to support and develop athletes. His public and verbal war against the AAU attracted disenfranchised youth, who saw him as a hero willing to confront the establishment. Among the first to wear Nike running shoes, Prefontaine provided a major boost to the fledgling company that his University of Oregon coach, Bill Bowerman, had cofounded with Phil Knight, one of Bowerman's former runners. Ironically, Prefontaine's rebellious image was transformed into a corporate icon after his death.

© AP Photo

Kathrine Switzer and friends fighting off Jock Semple, who tried to rip the number off her shirt and remove her from the Boston Marathon on April 19, 1967.

© Paul Connell/The Boston Globe via Getty Images

during prime-time programming. Technology also changed the nature of coaching, as the Dallas Cowboys began using computers to aid analysis and planning in preparing for specific opponents and drafting prospective players.

The effect of new technology was particularly marked in auto racing, as better-designed cars and more powerful engines (along with outstanding drivers) attracted more fans. Popular drivers included A.J. Foyt, who won three Indy 500 races during the 1960s, added a fourth in 1977, and also raced on the United States Auto Club (USAC) circuit, earning five championships, and in the European Grand Prix at Le Mans in 1967. His rival, Italian immigrant Mario Andretti, proved equally popular, winning the 1965 USAC championship, the 1967 Daytona 500 (a NASCAR event), the 1969 Indianapolis 500, and the 1977 European Grand Prix in a sleek Formula One racer. Meanwhile, Richard Petty dominated the NASCAR (stock car) racing circuit, established in 1949 and centered in the South by the 1960s. A North Carolinian, Petty became a superstar by winning two hundred races, seven championships, and seven Daytona 500s. His racing team, composed of family members, developed technological innovations to aid their driver, including a safety roll bar, two-way radios to communicate with the pit crew, and a cooling helmet.

Bowling also benefited from technology. In 1956, the Brunswick Company, a bowling equipment manufacturer, began installing automatic pinspotters in bowling alleys, thus turning a tedious manual job (previously reserved for "pinboys") over to machines that performed the task cheaply, effectively, and efficiently. Bowling alleys began to expand in size, and matinee bowling leagues became a popular attraction for women (Rader, *American Sports* [1983] 337). The Brunswick Company's sales figures rose from $33 million in 1954 to $422 million in 1961, and Brunswick sponsored a championship bowling series on television. Large bowling emporiums appeared in cities and suburbs, with the Edison, New Jersey, establishment featuring 112 lanes (Kogan 172–173). As

with boxing, however, bowling's initial popularity would eventually recede, until bowlers assumed the role of entertainers by amusing spectators not only with their skills but also with antics and emotional displays.

In addition, the confluence of sport and the still-developing modern medium of television continued to pay great dividends for both sides, as regional and previously minor sports became mainstream, providing programming for networks and greater exposure for athletes. Corporate sponsors flocked to support athletic contests, enriching the networks, college teams, professional team owners, and athletes in a symbiotic relationship.

Summary

This chapter has detailed the impact of television on sport, including the innovative broadcasting strategies that generated great popularity, the increased revenue produced by the broadcasting of sporting events, and the labor relations issues created by such wealth. The continual growth of professional football within this process allowed it to surpass baseball as the national sport in the United States.

During the Cold War, sport also became a political tool, with the Olympics being used for nationalistic purposes and highlighting ideological differences between capitalism and communism. Within the United States, minorities and women used sport to address and attack social inequalities and achieve a greater measure of civil rights and women's rights.

Although various sports moved closer to pure entertainment, and the behavior of some athletes caused them to lose their luster, physical activity assumed greater personal importance. The fitness boom fostered a running fad as part of a larger pursuit of health and self-enhancement strategies. The Baby Boomer generation (the one following World War II) produced enormous social change in American society, and sport proved to be an integral part of that process.

International Perspective

Soccer in Europe: From a Men's Sport to a Women's Game

Women's soccer was played at women's colleges in the United States as a recreational activity from the early 1900s onward, viewed as feminine and as a women's game. However, it met with considerable opposition in Europe, where it was seen as one of those sports completely unsuited to a woman's nature, therefore belonging to a male domain that arouses the connotation of masculinity.

Despite all reservations, a women's soccer movement began to develop in a number of European countries at the end of the nineteenth century, especially in England and France. In 1894, the British Ladies' Football Club was inaugurated, and only a year later various women's teams competed against each other, cheered on by thousands of spectators of both sexes. Women's soccer reached a peak of popularity at a time of great national fervor during World War I, when soccer games between women's teams were held in order to raise money for the care of wounded soldiers. After the war, however, the Football Association (FA; the governing body of football in England) called upon its clubs to withdraw their support from women's soccer matches, which it regarded as unworthy of the "fair sex." This development constituted a severe setback to, but not the end of, women's soccer in England.

During the First World War, women's soccer teams were also founded in France, where the first women's soccer championship occurred in 1917, and two cup tournaments were introduced in 1922. During the 1920s, numerous matches were played, not only between French teams but also against women's teams from other European countries. Nonetheless, even though women's sport in France had its own federation, the Fédération des Sociétés Féminines Sportives de France (FSFSF), women's soccer met with increasing resistance, since it allegedly resulted in women players becoming too masculine. In the 1930s, news about women's soccer in France became increasingly scarce. The development of women's soccer in England and France can be explained by specific conditions. In England the purpose of the games for charity compensated for the transgression of femininity by the players. In France, a strong women's sport movement supported the expansion of women's football.

In contrast to the situation in England and France and in some other countries in Europe, there was never any question in Germany that a soccer pitch was no place for women. (On women's soccer in other countries, see, for example, page 18 of issue number 9 of *Sport und Gesundheit* [Sport and Health] from 1938.) Thus, the attempt of a number of women to found a women's soccer club in Frankfurt was doomed to failure.

After the Second World War, interest in soccer was revived among women in various European countries, but soccer associations reacted with either indifference or outright rejection. In 1955, for example, the German soccer association prohibited its clubs from opening women's sections or even making grounds available for women's teams. As evidence to support this stance, the federation cited doctors who warned about the risks to women's health. In several countries, including Denmark and England, women players founded their own associations, but these groups mustered few clubs. In other countries, such as Italy, professional women's teams were formed with the help of private sponsors, but women's soccer continued to play only a marginal role. It was not until the late 1960s that individual initiatives were bundled, pressure on associations was increased, and the ban on women's soccer was lifted in many countries. Women's soccer was then integrated into men's soccer associations, not least because soccer officials did not wish to lose control over the women's soccer movement. In all European countries, cup competitions and leagues were introduced along the lines of those already established in men's soccer.

The growing popularity of women's soccer is also due to the international matches played since 1969. In that year, for example, the privately financed Federation of Independent European Football (FIEFF), based in Italy, organized an official tournament called the Europe Cup with teams from France, Denmark, England and Italy, and one year later an unofficial world championship was organized which enthralled fifty thousand spectators. This was just for women's teams, which were note recognized by FIFA. It was not until 1991 that the first FIFA-organized Women's World Championships were held.

Information from Hong, Fan, and J. A. Mangan, eds. *Soccer, Women, Sexual Liberation: Kicking Off a New Era.* London: Cass, 2003; Pfister, Gertrud. "The future of football is female!? On the past and present of women's football in Germany." Tomlinson, A. and Young, C. *German Football. History, Culture, Society.* London/New York: Routledge, 2006: 93–126.

DISCUSSION QUESTIONS

1. What parallels can be drawn between the 1920s and the 1950s in sport?

2. How did sports journalism change from the 1920s to the 1980s?

3. How did television affect sporting culture?

4. How did the economics of sport change after the introduction of television?

5. In what ways did sport serve a political function during the Cold War?

6. How did the social movements of the 1960s affect sport?

7. Explain the importance of "the Battle of the Sexes" in tennis with regard to challenging gender roles in sport and society.

8. Discuss the various roles of Muhammad Ali as an agent of change in American society.

9. How did Title IX influence the relationships among sport, gender, and American culture?

Chapter 10

Globalized Sport
1980–2000

CHAPTER OBJECTIVES

After reading this chapter, you will have learned about the following:

- The growth of media conglomerates and their relationship to sport
- The role of stadiums in achieving urban status
- The effects of sport on tourism
- Labor negotiations that have structured sport finance
- The ascendance of Michael Jordan as a global icon
- The globalization of sport
- The growing participation of girls and women in sport
- The issues that have marred the images of athletes and sport
- The appearance of new sport forms

The world of sport is expanding and changing rapidly. Some might trace the transformation to 1984, the year Michael Jordan entered the National Basketball Association (NBA):

> Jordan has been called "the new DiMaggio," and "Elvis in high-tops," indications of the Herculean cultural heroism he has come to embody. There is even a religious element to the near worship of Jordan as a cultural icon of invincibility, as he has been called a "savior of sorts," "basketball's high priest," and "more popular than Jesus," except with "better endorsement deals."
>
> Dyson 259

Regarding a 1997 trip by Jordan to Paris, the French media proclaimed, "Michael Jordan is in Paris. . . . That's better than the Pope. It's God in person" (qtd. in Halberstam 4).

When Jordan joined the Chicago Bulls, the franchise was in dire straits, valued at only $18.7 million, with few fans or television viewers. Ten years later, its value had surpassed $190 million (LaFeber 49). Concomitant with the rise and rivalry of Larry Bird and Earvin "Magic" Johnson, the NBA enjoyed a resurgence of interest. By 1996, NBA games were broadcast in 40 languages to more than 175 countries (LaFeber 135). Two years later, *Fortune* magazine credited Jordan with generating $10 billion for the U.S. economy (LaFeber 137). Within a decade of his entry into the NBA, the merger of Jordan, his numerous corporate sponsors, and the media complex dominated the athletic world and achieved prominence in the global communications industry. Jordan's international luster fostered an economic battle by multinational corporations for ever-larger markets, and the NBA, Major League Baseball (MLB), the National Hockey League (NHL), and even the National Football League (NFL) began importing non–North American athletes who might embellish their rosters and, more importantly, attract new viewers inside and outside of North America.

Thus, American sporting culture became a global enterprise, a fact perhaps best seen recently in Yao Ming, the 7-foot-5-inch (226-centimeter) Chinese import who has had the greatest economic impact of any NBA rookie since Michael Jordan. Home attendance for his team, the Houston Rockets, rose 17 percent, and for the first time in years the Rockets were also a draw on the road. The NBA is now aired on six Chinese TV networks (Deitsch et al.).

> Now comes Yao Ming—and all the ill-conceived clichés about those strange Chinese have been shattered like a glass backboard after a monstrous slam dunk. There is no living Chinese in the world today who is as famous as the lantern-jawed National Basketball Association rookie sensation. . . . Ratings for NBA games broadcast on Chinese TV [sic] have never been higher than this year as the nation keeps track of its new favorite team, Yao's Houston Rockets. . . . Across North America, Yao's clean-cut, tattooless visage sells everything from Visa cards . . . [to] Apple computers. . . . Doubtless, marketers see Yao as their entry into the prized Chinese market, but who knew that an oversized hoopster with fragmented English would become the next It Boy for Madison Avenue?
>
> Beech

Yao represents the growing interest in, opportunity for, and expansion of American professional sports organizations in areas outside the United States. Such developments mark a departure from the ethnocentric and insular bias that had previously restricted teams and players to North American locales.

The intercontinental transport of sport forms and players accelerated after 1980, driven by the capitalist search for profitable markets and the growing competition between big media conglomerates. Such expansion had repercussions, however, as American popular culture permeated the world, bringing greater cultural homogeneity at the cost of diversity. In addition to American sports, movies, music, and clothing fashions, the English language also spread inexorably, and American corporations, with their aggressively competitive business practices, intruded upon local cultures. Although some embraced aspects of change, such incursions sometimes prompted volatile responses, as some groups felt threatened with loss of their identity and traditional culture. They feared the overt commercialization, greed,

1984	1986	1990	1990s
■ Eastern Bloc nations boycott Summer Olympics in Los Angeles ■ Joan Benoit wins first women's Olympic marathon	■ *Challenger* space shuttle explodes shortly after takeoff	■ Hubble Space Telescope launches	■ Michael Jordan becomes global icon

Yao Ming represents a new phase in American sport—globalization.

© AP Photo/Ben Margot

plutocracy, violence, and drug abuse they associated with the worst of American culture. More traditional patriarchal cultures feared the changing gender roles and youth culture that they perceived in the United States as a potential source of breakdown in their prescribed social divisions. As the Cold War persisted, both communist governments and some theocracies alike questioned American values, economic practices, and leadership.

In 1979, Iranians seized the United States Embassy in Tehran and held Americans hostage for more than a year. President Jimmy Carter's inability to win their release, along with high inflation and his unpopular boycott of the 1980 Olympics in Moscow, limited his presidency to one term. In the wake of the Iran hostage crisis, the United States elected Ronald Reagan, the California governor and former Hollywood actor, to the presidency. Reagan proved to be the most conservative chief executive in two generations, and his attacks on welfare and social programs hampered the livelihoods of the poverty stricken, who were further endangered by an economic recession in 1982. Moreover, memories of the Vietnam War still racked America with pangs of defeat and guilt. The unveiling of the Vietnam War Memorial in 1982 in Washington, D.C., was intended to soothe tensions, but its controversial and nontraditional design only heightened anxieties and sparked debate on the proper nature of honor, the construction of national memorials, the definition of heroes, and even the nobility of war itself.

Apprehension increased a year later, when the United States invaded the Caribbean nation of Grenada after a military coup installed a Marxist government. With Cuba ensconced in communism, the American government firmly opposed the spread of beliefs antithetical to its ideology. Reagan won a second term and conducted a clandestine war on another Marxist government, this one in Nicaragua.

Meanwhile, as financial wizards amassed fortunes on Wall Street, the number of homeless Americans increased, more people became addicted to drugs (particularly crack cocaine), and AIDS began to devastate the population. Americans were riding a social roller coaster, and the nation as a whole mourned when the U.S. space shuttle *Challenger* exploded shortly after takeoff in 1986, killing all seven crew members. The disaster called into question Americans' faith in their social, economic, and technological superiority even as the Soviet Union began to crumble.

Amid the thriving of corporate culture and corporate values during the Reagan administration, common sport forms and practices were extended, sometimes regulated by unilateral sports governing bodies that increased their reach and influence.

1991	**1994**	**1995**	**1996**
■ Willy T. Ribbs becomes first African American Indy 500 driver ■ U.S. women's soccer team wins the World Cup	■ Major League Baseball strike, World Series cancelled	■ World League of American Football (later NFL Europe) launches	■ U.S. women's soccer team wins Olympic gold

Thus, the governing associations of the sporting culture assumed even greater significance.

Corporate Sporting Culture

Cable television, satellite dishes, and eventually the Internet produced a global explosion of sport in the last two decades of the twentieth century, as promoters fostered particular sport forms and processes of expansion linked to multinational corporate culture. In many cases, this process spread a more homogeneous Western sporting culture throughout the world, although indigenous pastimes and residual sport forms on the national, regional, and local levels resisted the globalization process.

American sports programming, such as ABC's *Wide World of Sports,* occasionally featured sports such as Afghan Buzkashi (an equestrian event with a goat head as the focus) or Japanese sumo wrestling as anomalous or exotic events. The Western sporting process, however, emphasized commercialized, quantified, and male-dominated sport forms, marketed and commodified to sell products, bodies, and ideas within a capitalist market economy. Western European sports associations especially fostered the growth of soccer, and the leaders of North American sports, including football, baseball, basketball, and (to a lesser degree) hockey, sought larger economic markets on a global scale.

The marketing of American popular culture, athletes, and leagues themselves greatly expanded under the shrewd guidance of corporate-minded commissioners. Players, too, hired agents and managers to polish their images, win endorsements, and negotiate even larger salaries laden with incentive clauses in the major team sports. In individual sports, athletes increasingly filled roles as entertainers as well as competitors. Endorsement contracts often depended on visibility, appearance, and lifestyle as much as (or more than) on performance. Free agents continually sought larger markets, larger salaries, and greater endorsement opportunities.

As athletes sought and received more endorsement contracts, agencies were formed to help them manage these new dimensions of their careers. One of the first to cater to athletes in this capacity was Mark McCormack, a Cleveland lawyer who served as manager for golfer Arnold Palmer. McCormack expanded his company in the 1960s, and the resultant International Management Group (IMG) eventually employed more than 2,200 workers in 70 offices in 30 countries, becoming a major player in international sporting enterprises by the end of the century. Its success generated its own television division that produced sports programming for global distribution, spreading the influence of American sports and personalities around the world. As the economy transitioned from its industrial basis to one based on personal consumption in the latter twentieth century, companies relied increasingly on the marketing of goods to convince consumers of their value. The IMG enterprise branched out to include famous entertainers and models as well as athletes among its clients. Similar agencies arose to manage, market, and promote celebrities and their products both on and off the field.

Media Conglomerates

The establishment of the Entertainment and Sports Programming Network (ESPN) gave fans ever-increasing opportunity to saturate their lives with sport. The idea for a sports network originated in 1979 with Bill Rasmussen (public relations director for the New England Whalers), his son Scott, and entrepreneur Ed Eagan. Their modest objectives involved local markets in Bristol, Connecticut, but the enterprise soon exploded into 24-hour-a-day sports programming that met the wishes of "sports junkies" and provided greater exposure to sports previously considered marginal. To fill its schedule, ESPN offered women's basketball, field hockey, soccer, tennis, and golf, as well as men's intercollegiate ice hockey, basketball, tennis, skiing, and motor sports. Even the NFL draft found a host of viewers in a prime-time slot.

ESPN attracted the young male demographic, appealing to its members with a fraternity house atmosphere of raucous sportscasters and commentators. They presented highlights of previous

1997	1998	1999
■ Women's National Basketball Association (WNBA) founded	■ U.S. women's ice hockey team wins Olympic gold	■ U.S. women's soccer team wins World Cup

games with voiceovers by loud, brash, irreverent reporters and analysts who became celebrities in their own right. Eventually, female reporters began to patrol the sidelines of events, sometimes exposing the ignorance or crudeness of some athletes in telling interviews. For example, an obviously drunken and slobbering Joe Namath asked one such reporter for a kiss during a nationally televised football game. A few women earned roles in the studio or even as football broadcasters. ESPN interviews and analyses might make or break athletic heroes. In the process, ESPN changed the way Americans viewed and interpreted sports.

The phenomenal success of ESPN led to greater sports coverage on the major television networks, the creation of local sports channels, and innumerable sports-talk radio shows in imitation. ESPN itself became a media conglomerate, producing numerous spin-offs, such as ESPN HD (i.e., using high-definition broadcasting technology), ESPN2, ESPN2 HD, ESPN Classic, ESPNEWS, ESPN Sports PPV (pay-per-view), ESPN Deportes (Spanish-language), ESPNU (aimed at college students), ESPN360.com (video content player), ESPN Mobile TV, ESPN.com, ESPN Radio, *ESPN The Magazine,* ESPN Zone restaurants, EXPN, and ESPN International, which was broadcast to 180 countries in 21 languages by the turn of the twenty-first century. By that time, the network was valued at $15 billion and had been bought by Disney. With its incorporation into the mainstream media, ESPN lost some of its edge but gained even greater global influence (Freeman). The power of the media to effect cultural change has become evident in the way in which ESPN and its imitators have influenced gambling odds with miniscule bits of information or overwhelming analyses of contests. By 2006, ESPN, always questing for more markets and new viewers, promoted competitions such as poker and paintball as televised sports events with great success. The mass opiate of sports proved highly addictive.

This seemingly overwhelming interest in sports caused an avalanche of ESPN imitators. Professional leagues initiated their own television companies, such as the NFL Network, NBA TV, and NBA Preview, to gain a larger segment of the viewing market. Collegiate athletic conferences followed suit. Other operations focused on particular activities; examples include the Golf Channel, the Outdoor Channel, and the Fox Soccer Channel. Comcast SportsNet offered local and regional programming, as well as an HDTV option, and Nickelodeon Games and Sports focused on the children's market, grooming them for later viewing

as adults. For those still unsatiated by the cornucopia of athletic offerings, numerous other companies provided pay-per-view programming for selected events, and even networks whose primary fare was not sports programming increased their sports coverage. Ted Turner, owner of the Turner Broadcasting System (TBS) and the Atlanta Braves, sold TBS baseball programs to cable stations throughout the United States, and WGN, owned by the *Chicago Tribune* newspaper, which also owned the Chicago Cubs, did likewise. Both teams thus created a national fan base while generating additional profits for the parent company. The NBC network controlled Europe's Super Channel, which served sixty million viewers, and, with nearly 80 percent of European programming originating in the United States, the focus on American offerings produced cultural backlashes in some locations (Maguire, *Global* 150–154).

In 1997, Australian media mogul Rupert Murdoch bought the Los Angeles Dodgers for $311 million. Already owner of Fox Sports Net and 20th Century Fox, as well as worldwide newspapers and cable television units such as Fox College Sports, Murdoch also bought the broadcast rights to Yankees games in New York, then purchased national rights from MLB for $565 million (Elias, *Baseball* 210). He had already secured the rights to broadcast NHL games from 1994 to 1999. As owner of British, Asian, and Japanese satellite systems, Murdoch wielded the power and influence to further Americanize the world. Such financial arrangements proliferated, as the Disney Company owned ABC, ESPN, and portions of European sports channels, as well MLB's Anaheim Angels and the NHL's Anaheim Ducks. The clear benefits led media conglomerate Time Warner Inc. to purchase TBS and the Braves. Such ownership across business genres raised numerous issues, as corporate and large-market teams superseded the ability of small-market or privately owned teams to procure top players. Salaries escalated, as did ticket prices for spectators. The media giants even had the power to manipulate scheduling times to ensure maximum exposure for their teams, resulting in more night games. These interlocking corporations also posed dilemmas for the media wings of the parent companies, as journalistic integrity became suspect when reporting on one's own corporate "family."

Maximizing Profits From Sport

Television networks, league executives, and team officials all worked toward innovations that would increase success both on the field and in terms of attracting fans. Television producers used technological innovations to enhance viewers' interest in broadcasts. In 1986, the widespread use of instant replay (first introduced by CBS in 1963) allowed viewers to become, in a sense, their own referees and thus further enhanced their involvement in the game. Major League Baseball began scheduling more games at night in order to maximize the television audience and added the League Championship Series, a seven-game playoff, as a semifinal round before the World Series (Gorn and Goldstein 239–240).

The NFL introduced its own innovations, as one of its teams, the San Francisco 49ers, directed by cerebral head coach Bill Walsh, attracted new fans with a ball-control passing strategy known as the West Coast Offense. Under the guidance of unflappable quarterback Joe Montana, the 49ers won four Super Bowl titles in the 1980s, and other teams adopted the innovative offense.

The lucrative growth of sport also initiated challenges to established organizations. The United States Football League (USFL), for example, started play in 1983, scheduling its games in the spring to avoid direct competition with the NFL. It lasted three years before switching to the more traditional fall season and suing the NFL as a monopoly that prohibited it from securing a network television contract. The USFL won the case, but the New York jury awarded the league only $1 in damages, rather than the nearly $2 billion it had sought. The jury reasoned that most of the USFL's problems resulted from its own mismanagement, and their decision effectively put the league out of business.

Despite a strike-shortened season of 1981, baseball produced a national phenomenon known as Fernandomania, focused on Fernando Valenzuela, a rotund, 19-year-old, Spanish-speaking Mexican pitcher who arrived in the National League at the end of the 1980 season. Appearing in 10 games as a relief pitcher for the Los Angeles Dodgers, he compiled a flawless 0.00 earned run average and struck out 16 batters in 17 innings. In 1981, manager Tommy Lasorda made Valenzuela the Dodgers' top starting pitcher, much to the pleasure of the large Mexican and Mexican American population of Southern California. Valenzuela did not disappoint, providing timely hitting as well as stellar pitching for the resurgent Dodgers. Record crowds turned out to witness Valenzuela's heroics and inimitable style, and he led National League pitchers in strikeouts and won both the Rookie of the Year Award and the Cy Young Award (for best pitcher). The Dodgers

won the World Series, their first since 1965, and the excitement generated by Fernandomania produced a Hispanic hero that boosted ethnic-minority pride and created a shared interest among mainstream Americans, established Chicanos, and thousands of immigrants and migrant workers.

The latter endured poor working conditions, flimsy housing, and meager wages in servile positions. The burgeoning Chicano nationalism of previous decades had been met with suppression. When Alianza (Alliance), led by Reies López Tijerina, had tried to reclaim the New Mexico lands lost to whites, the U.S. Army had responded and the leader had been imprisoned. Similarly, boxer turned politician Rodolfo "Corky" Gonzales directed the Crusade for Justice movement in search of betterment, but it was Cesar Chavez who had the most success, organizing migrant laborers into the United Farm Workers Union and initiating a national boycott of grapes. Thus, the Hispanic population of the Southwest, previously perceived as docile, began to assert itself. In that context, baseball assuaged some social wounds and unified differing factions in a nonviolent, communal attraction by providing some psychological escape when the parties were not immersed in their own economic problems.

Stadium Construction as a Civic Subsidy

Baseball owners, who did not share their revenue equally (although they did share the $130 million paid by the Arizona Diamondbacks as a new-franchise entry fee in 1995), sought new ways to maximize profits. Small-market teams, in particular, faced distinct disadvantages. Without the broadcasting profits of large-market teams, they had less to offer in acquiring new players. Professional team owners in all sports sought to maximize their income and began to put increasing pressure on municipalities to fund or subsidize construction of revenue-generating venues for sporting events. They held cities hostage as they threatened removal to more advantageous locations. Seven NFL franchises did relocate between 1982 and 1997, and 31 professional teams got new stadiums at public expense between 1989 and 1997 (Guttmann, *Sports: The First Five Millennia* 139; also see the table on stadium construction and renovation). Thus, new ball parks became a primary means by which owners hoped to attract new customers.

Corporate skyboxes, personal seat licenses, and exclusive rights to parking fees, subsidies, and sales of food, drink, and clothing swelled owners' coffers. Teams also sold naming rights to corporate

Stadium Construction and Renovation, 1990–1999

Year	Team and stadium	Cost (in millions) to build or renovate
Baseball stadiums		
1991	Chicago White Sox/U.S. Cellular Field	$150
1992	Baltimore Orioles/Oriole Park at Camden Yards	$235
1994	Cleveland Indians/Progressive Field	$173
	Texas Rangers/Rangers Ballpark in Arlington	$191
1995	Colorado Rockies/Coors Field	$215
1996	Oakland A's/Network Associates Coliseum (shared with Raiders NFL team)	$225 (renovation)
1997	Atlanta Braves/Turner Field	$235
	San Diego Padres/Petco Park (shared with Chargers NFL team)	$78 (renovation)
1998	Arizona Diamondbacks/Chase Field	$355
	Anaheim (Los Angeles) Angels/Edison International Field (later renamed Angel Stadium of Anaheim)	$117 (renovation) $85 (when opened in 1990); $65 (renovation in 1998)
	Tampa Bay Devil Rays/Tropicana Field	$115
1999	Seattle Mariners/Safeco Field	$517
Football stadiums		
1992	Atlanta Falcons/Georgia Dome	$214
1995	Jacksonville Jaguars/Alltel Stadium	$135 (renovation)
	St. Louis Rams/Edward Jones Dome	$300
1996	Carolina Panthers/Bank of America Stadium	$298
	Oakland Raiders/Network Associates Coliseum (shared with A's MLB team)	$225 (renovation)
1997	San Diego Chargers/Qualcomm Stadium (shared with Padres MLB team)	$78 (renovation)
	Washington Redskins/FedEx Field	$251
1998	Baltimore Ravens/M&T Bank Stadium	$229
	Tampa Bay Buccaneers/Raymond James Stadium	$190
1999	Tennessee Titans/The Coliseum	$292
	Buffalo Bills/Ralph Wilson Stadium	$63 (renovation)
	Cleveland Browns/Cleveland Browns Stadium	$309

Data from Slezak, Carol. "What's in a name?" *Chicago Sun-Times*, 2 March 2008: 56A; www.ballparks.com, www.ballparksofbaseball.com, www.leagueoffans.org/mlbstadiums1990.html, www.stadiumsofnfl.com, www.indystar.com/apps/pbcs.dll/section?Category=sports0305-47k-, and www.proplayerstadium.com/content/architecture.aspx.

donors and displayed commercial advertising to increase revenue. For example, in 2000, Pacific Bell paid $54 million to the San Francisco Giants for stadium naming rights lasting 24 years (the company had agreed to the contract even before construction), and Bank One bought naming rights to the Arizona Diamondbacks' ball park at a cost of $66 million for 30 years (Elias, *Baseball* 209). Between 1992 and 2001, NFL teams renovated or constructed 15 stadiums, and, after the great success of the Baltimore Orioles' new venue, baseball teams opened 13 new ball parks between 1995 and 2000 (Spirou and Bennett 188). As stadiums took on the appearance of theme parks, some, like Petco Park in San Diego, even featured a playground for young children, and mascots, not unlike Disney characters, entertained spectators. Politicians rationalized the expenditures as urban development—the redevelopment of downtrodden areas into entertainment districts to attract tourist dollars.

Sport as Tourism

The Chicago White Sox built a new Comiskey Park (later renamed U.S. Cellular Field) in 1991, and in 1992 Baltimore opened the Camden Yards ball park as the new home of the Orioles; nearby locations are home to a separate facility for the NFL's Baltimore Ravens and the Babe Ruth Birthplace Museum. The complex was intended to revitalize the inner-city area by creating or reconstructing historical memories. Babe Ruth's birthplace serves as a general historical link to the city's modern team, which now plays in a new park but one designed with retrospective features to provide the illusion of (and elicit nostalgia for) the stadiums of the past; meanwhile, genuine older venues such as Fenway Park in Boston and Wrigley Field in Chicago continued to attract crowds regardless of their team's fortunes on the field. The smaller playing dimensions of the new parks also allowed for more home runs, always a fan favorite, and the stadiums in Baltimore were linked to the nearby inner harbor area that features restaurants, shops, and other forms of entertainment. Thus, sport and sport complexes became tourist attractions subsidized by cities and therefore requiring somewhat limited team expenditures. The cities often paid for maintenance of the structure, traffic control, and safety measures, and even ensured prescribed attendance levels with subsidies.

Part of that civic restoration involved the organization of sports halls of fame to attract fans. Historians Eric Hobsbawm and Terence Ranger have termed such institutions or events "invented traditions," meant to create significance and identification over time. Some municipalities erected structures to commemorate local history, while others claimed national or even international status as places of remembrance and nostalgia. Such shrines glorified athletic heroes—mostly white, male professionals—in a particular exhibition of masculinity that bordered on a civic religion, and fans made pilgrimages to view the sacred objects of revered stars from baseball, football, basketball, hockey, tennis, golf, boxing, horse racing, soccer, motor sports, swimming, and track and field at various locations throughout the country.

In this vein, the entire city of Indianapolis bills itself as "the Amateur Sports Capital of the World" and has practically become a shrine to sport. *ESPN The Magazine* named it the top professional sports city in 2003, and the city has built its economy largely around sport—and sport tourism. In addition to the historic Indy 500 auto race, it also hosts the Allstate 400 at the Brickyard and a Formula One event. Besides the professional Colts (football) and Pacers (basketball), the city is home to the headquarters of the National Collegiate Athletic Association (NCAA), USA Gymnastics, USA Track and Field, U.S. Diving, U.S. Synchronized Swimming, the American College of Sports Medicine, the Indy Racing League, the Black Coaches Association, the National Federation of State High School Associations, and a host of other organizations. After politicians generated a successful move to a new county governance structure, business interests secured corporate control of the city and outlying areas (Schimmel, Ingham, and Howell 234–237). Between 1977 and 1991, sports-related purchases enriched the local economy by more than $2 billion ("Amateur Sports Capital of the World"). Little of that income trickled down to the poor families displaced by the widespread construction of athletic facilities.

Labor Relations

Although professional sports produced excitement for fans, their enthusiasm was often tempered by labor issues. In 1981, Major League Baseball players went on strike in midseason over free agency issues. They returned, 50 days later, only after owners agreed to recognize the players' rights to negotiate their contracts and salaries. In return, the owners got compensation for departing free agents through draft choices, cash, or the trading of other players.

In 1994, fans were outraged when players went on strike again, forcing cancellation of the World Series for the first time in 90 years. At the time, a Canadian franchise, the Montreal Expos, led the National League; Tony Gwynn of the San Diego Padres was batting nearly .400, a mark no one had (or has) reached since Ted Williams hit .406 in 1941; and Matt Williams of the San Francisco Giants had already hit 43 home runs, giving him a chance to surpass the record of 61, set by Roger Maris in 1961. Moreover, MLB had set an attendance record during the preceding season. Faced with the strike, however, many thoroughly disappointed fans vowed never to return. They blamed both players and owners as greedy. The latter demanded a salary cap, and the former refused. The strike lasted 234 days before a federal judge sided with the players. The 1995 season began under the existing contract, and neither side managed to change the collective bargaining agreement substantially. Before the strike, MLB had been averaging 31,256 attendees per game; a decade later, teams had yet to recover to that level—the 2004 average was 30,290 (*Chicago Sun-Times*).

NFL players followed their MLB counterparts' lead in going on strike shortly after the opening of the 1982 season. They returned 57 days later after negotiations had increased the minimum salary and postseason pay and accorded players new rights that included severance allowances. The owners, however, retained control of television revenues and player transfers. During the 1990s, the NFL quelled labor wars within its ranks under new commissioner Paul Tagliabue, but owners proved less than accommodating in their search for greater profits, and teams left Houston, Cleveland, and Los Angeles. Tagliabue secured new teams for Houston and Cleveland and granted expansion franchises to Charlotte and Jacksonville in 1993. The lack of a team in Los Angeles, however, left a gaping hole in the nation's second-largest market. Despite that shortcoming and its lackluster internationalization efforts, the NFL signed the most lucrative television contract of all professional leagues in 1998. The pact provided more than $17 billion over eight years and guaranteed each team about $75 million per year.

Much of the NBA's prosperity rested upon new commissioner David Stern's considerable business acumen. He brokered the labor agreement between players and owners that gave players 53 percent of gross revenues but gave the latter a salary cap that held down escalating costs. Stern also marketed the league and its players to the youthful demographic, creating presumably lifelong fans by projecting a cooler, more exuberant image that appealed to young consumers, in contrast to the more traditional image of baseball. The NBA All-Star Game expanded to include a slam-dunk contest and a three-point-shooting competition that highlighted individual abilities, and during the ascendancy of Michael Jordan, the NBA marketed individual stars and personalities, covering the spectrum from corporate values to hip-hop culture, thus attracting a following that ranged from business executives to childhood emulators.

That harmony lasted until 1998, when the owners and players could not reach agreement over a salary cap and guaranteed salaries, resulting in a lockout that lasted 204 days. When the two sides finally came to a consensus, they cobbled together an abbreviated season of 50 games. The owners got a salary cap but agreed to raise the minimum salary. The bickering alienated the fans, and both attendance and television ratings dropped.

Commercialization of the Olympics

American athletes thrilled their nationalistic supporters with stunning victories in the 1980 Winter Olympics at Lake Placid, New York. Speedskater Eric Heiden won five gold medals, setting Olympic records in each event he entered, from 500 to 10000 meters. Even more startling, the U.S. hockey team, composed of little-known collegiate players, defeated the mighty Soviet team, regarded as the best in the world. The Americans had lost an exhibition game to the Russians only 13 days earlier by a score of 10-3. After winning their improbable semifinal match by a 4-3 margin amid pandemonium on their home ice, the young Americans then triumphed over Finland, 4-2, by scoring three third-period goals in the gold-medal game. This unlikely march to the top was seen as a triumph for capitalism in its ongoing economic war with the forces of communism. The *New York Times* called the American success "one of the most startling and dramatic upsets in Olympic history" (Eskanazi 1). Immediately after the game with the Soviets, President Jimmy Carter telephoned the team in the dressing room to offer his congratulations, and when a performance at New York's Radio City Music Hall was interrupted to announce the gold-medal triumph, theatergoers paused to sing the American national anthem.

The American celebration temporarily relieved national tension as the new revolutionary Islamic government of Iran held 66 Americans hostage after the overthrow of the Shah. However, the USSR had invaded Afghanistan in December 1979, and U.S. president Jimmy Carter had retaliated by threatening to boycott the Summer Olympics to be hosted in Moscow. The threat became reality when the United States led 36 countries in spurning the competition. Once again, the Olympics had become a pawn in global power struggles.

In the midst of this turmoil, Juan Antonio Samaranch, a Spanish aristocrat, replaced Lord Killanin at the helm of the IOC, but he could not prevent the USSR's retaliation, as 13 nations from the Eastern Bloc refused to participate at the 1984 Summer Games in Los Angeles. In spite of their absence, the American Olympics proved a financial bonanza under the leadership of Peter Ueberroth, who commercialized the Olympics through licensing, merchandising, and marketing. The television contract with ABC guaranteed $225 million, and the festival concluded with a surplus of more than $200 million, an astounding improvement over

The U.S. hockey team after winning against Russia in the 1980 Olympic Games.
© AP Photo

the 1976 Games, which cost Montreal $1.5 billion (Rader, *American Sports* [1983] 310), and transforming the way in which the Olympic Games are bought and sold. Soon the IOC not only accepted commercialism but became an ardent proponent. In 1985, the IOC initiated its own program of corporate sponsors, providing exclusive rights to the Olympic symbols and products for a four-year period and a hefty membership fee of $50 million ("Commercialization").

The successful transformation of the Olympics into a capitalist venture, rather than a drain on the civic treasury, engendered a wholesale competition for future sites and greatly enriched the coffers of the IOC, which ultimately controlled the selection. Thereafter, the IOC imposed its Western values and standards on all solicitors in regulating the Olympic movement.

The 1984 Summer Games saw Carl Lewis begin his long string of Olympic successes by taking four gold medals in track-and-field events. In fact,

Lewis and other African American men accounted for 40 of the 49 golds won by the United States in track and field and 10 of 11 medals won by American boxers (Verney 91). Off the track, Carl Lewis and Juan Antonio Samaranch emerged as two key figures in the gradual decline of Olympic amateurism as it had been treasured by modern Olympics founder Pierre de Coubertin. Some countries partially or fully subsidized their top-level athletes. Athletes of the USSR and other Eastern European countries were employed at public expense, often as members of the military. In the capitalist countries, numerous successful athletes could make money via clandestine endorsements, such as being paid to wear a certain logo or a particular brand of shoes. As early as 1974, the IOC allowed such payments to go to national sports governing bodies, which paid the athletes a salary. Swimmer Mark Spitz, winner of seven gold medals at the 1972 Games, and decathlete Bruce Jenner, the 1976 champion, soon became spokesmen for a host of products (Rader, *American Sports* [1983] 312–313). Carl Lewis and others later managed to maintain their amateur status by placing endorsement revenues in personal financial trusts that disbursed only living expenses. Journalists dubbed such practices "shamateurism," and Samaranch, desirous of seeing the best athletes at the Olympics, gradually conceded. In 1985, the IOC and national sport federations voted to allow professional competitors in tennis, hockey, and soccer; other sports soon followed.

Internationalizing American Sport Forms

Baseball and football also worked to capture a greater share of the international market. To that end, Major League Baseball created an international business division in 1989, and the NFL followed suit in 1996, opening regional offices in Mexico, Canada, and Japan and planning games in China. The NFL had played games in Canada as early as the 1950s and had traveled to Tokyo and Mexico City for exhibitions in the 1970s. An international football league was planned in the 1970s, but the U.S. government, fearing an increase in terrorist activities by radical European groups (e.g., the Red Brigade in Italy, Baader-Meinhof in Germany) that had already staged kidnappings over nationalist and political tensions, intervened and thwarted the scheme.

The following decade featured the American Bowl in London, which drew eighty-six thousand spectators in 1986 (Ford and Foglio; Jozsa 70). Similar games followed in Sweden, Canada, Japan, Germany, Ireland, Spain, and Australia. A 10-team venture known as the World League of American Football initiated play in 1991 but lasted only briefly. In conjunction with the Fox television network, the NFL then established a European league of six teams in 1995, but the American version

of football has failed to supplant the entrenched attraction of soccer. Even Budweiser, the league patron, has not been able to supplant the European beers and had to forsake its name when advertising in Austria, because an Austrian brewery had claimed that name since the seventeenth century. In Mexico, Japan, and the Pacific, American football has had greater success. More than a million children are engaged in flag football programs outside of the United States, and Samoans often graduate to American colleges and even to the NFL, while more than two hundred Japanese colleges field American-style football teams.

Another communist country, Cuba, which had been hindered by an American economic embargo, sold the expertise of its coaches to other developing nations. In fact, Cuba used sport not only as an economic export but also as a political tool, defeating the United States at its own game, first by winning the Olympic gold medal in baseball in 1992 and 1996, and then by challenging the professional Baltimore Orioles and splitting a two-game series in 1999.

Drawing Fans to Baseball

Commissioner Bud Selig introduced another baseball innovation in 1994 by implementing the wild-card system, which allowed one additional team to enter the season-ending playoffs based on compiling the best win-loss record of all the teams that did not win their respective divisions during the regular season. Although rendered moot by the strike in 1994, the change took effect in 1995, and two years later the wild-card Florida Marlins, a 1992 expansion franchise, captured the World Series. Selig initiated yet another change in 1997 by scheduling regular-season interleague play (i.e., games played between teams from MLB's two different leagues), something that previously

People & Places

Karl "Tuffy" Rhodes

From 1990 to 1995, Tuffy Rhodes played for several MLB teams, with a career batting average of .224 and 13 home runs, but he found success in Japan. In 1996, he signed with the Kintetsu Buffaloes in the Pacific League of Nippon Professional Baseball, and through 2007 he had played with two other teams as well. During that time he hit 402 home runs, the most of any foreign player in Japanese baseball history, and he tied the single-season record for any player with 55 in 2001. By 2007, he had surpassed the 3,000-hit mark and recorded 1,089 runs batted in ("Tuffy Rhodes").

had been seen only in the World Series; this shift also allowed MLB to match intercity rivals from the different leagues in large markets including New York, Chicago, Los Angeles, and the San Francisco Bay area. The strategy sustained local interest throughout the season.

The 1998 season provided the greatest impetus to the resurgence of baseball, when the Chicago Cubs' Dominican slugger Sammy Sosa battled the St. Louis Cardinals' Mark McGwire for the home-run championship. Both chased Roger Maris' single-season record of 61, and McGwire broke the record against the Cubs on September 8, only to see Sosa exceed him by hitting 66 home runs. McGwire, however, swatted five homers in his last 11 at-bats to finish at 70. The fans reveled in their heroic feats, but others wondered about the use of a more tightly wrapped (and thus livelier) ball, as well as the possibility that one or both players had used performance-enhancing steroids. McGwire admitted to using androstenedione, a purported ergogenic muscle-building substance. Although the NCAA, the NFL, and the IOC banned the product as a steroid, MLB failed to address the issue, and in 2001, under a similar cloud of suspicion, Barry Bonds broke McGwire's record with 73 blasts. Frenzied fans filled the seats and fought over Bonds' home-run balls despite the looming ethical issues. Bonds' consequent breaking of Hank Aaron's career home-run mark of 755 faced even greater scrutiny, and the significance of such a feat was further questioned when he was indicted for lying about his use of performance-enhancing substances.

It was clear that home runs attracted fans, and Sosa (who, like Bonds, appeared noticeably heavier and thicker than in earlier years) represented a growing market for MLB players and audiences in the Caribbean. The friendly rivalry between Sosa and McGwire had portrayed racial amity and joint happiness in a shared love of the game—a perception that MLB hoped would heal wounds among players, owners, and fans alike. During the home-run barrage, Chicagoans flew Dominican flags alongside American banners, as baseball seemed to transcend both race and nationalism in a unified (if possibly tainted) quest for excellence.

For owners, Latin American players represented a cheaper means of stocking their rosters, and by the turn of the twenty-first century Dominicans accounted for nearly 10 percent of MLB players, while Latin Americans constituted 26 percent. Sosa had been signed by Texas in 1985 for only

With his 715th career home run on May 28, 2006, Barry Bonds surpassed Babe Ruth to sit second in career home runs.
© AP Photo/John Swart

People & Places

Cal Ripken Jr.

Despite the sharp drop in baseball attendance in 1995, even disgruntled fans took interest in the endurance feat achieved by Cal Ripken Jr., who was amassing a huge streak of consecutive games played. Indeed, for five years during the 1980s, he had not missed even a single inning of play, and on September 6, 1995, the Baltimore Orioles' iron man surpassed Lou Gehrig's record by playing in his 2,131st consecutive game. More than 5 million American households tuned in to the nationally televised game. Ripken's longevity, work ethic, and humility, similar to qualities that had been admired in Gehrig, sparked a nostalgic and idealized outpouring of national empathy. Amidst ongoing labor strife and political discord, Ripken represented what Americans wanted to see in themselves—a quiet leader who set the right example. He not only did his job, playing through injuries without complaint, but performed at an all-star level as a power-hitting shortstop, and even his private life, apparently beyond reproach, seemed to symbolize a more traditional and innocent era.

$3,500, and the Dodgers had initially gotten Pedro Martinez, who became a dominating pitcher, for a mere $8,000 in 1988. American baseball academies housed, fed, and tutored young players who were signed to contracts. MLB finally enacted a rule requiring signers to be at least 16 years of age, but independent agents continued to exploit the talents of promising boys as young as 12 (Knisely; Le Batard).

Franchise value increased exponentially during the 1990s, as a globalized labor force helped owners keep costs down even as it promoted larger consumer markets. Before 1980, no MLB team rated $20 million, but during the 1990s teams were sold for more than $100 million, and the New York Yankees franchise was valued at $900 million (Guttmann, *Sports: The First Five Millennia* 363); by 2006, it became the first pro sports team valued at a billion dollars.

Michael Jordan and the Growth of Professional Basketball

Although both baseball and football prospered, basketball fared even better, enjoying explosive growth during the 1980s under the guidance of David Stern, who assumed the commissioner's role in 1984. Stern's astute business sense and the presence of superstars Kareem Abdul Jabbar, Earvin "Magic" Johnson, Larry Bird, and new arrival Michael Jordan did much to popularize the sport. The new focus on individualism within the team concept further marked athletes as entertainers. Johnson, a 6-foot-9-inch (206-centimeter) point guard and a magician with the ball, could play any position and often accomplished the triple-double, a designation of all-around excellence achieved when a player garners at least 10 points, 10 rebounds, and 10 assists during a game. Johnson, along with the 7-foot-2-inch (208-centimeter) Jabbar, also one of the all-time greats, led the Los Angeles Lakers to five NBA titles during the decade. Johnson's rival, Larry Bird, who also stood 6 feet 9 inches, led the Boston Celtics to three championships during the same period. Portrayed as a bumpkin from small-town Indiana, Bird possessed great fundamental basketball skills, particularly as a passer and shooter, and he won the NBA's Most Valuable Player award three times. Sportswriters' portrayal of his whiteness in contrast to Johnson's blackness focused not only on their styles of play but also on geographical and social distinctions in American society. Sport had room for both, and the NBA thrived on the rivalry, promoting its inclusiveness while enjoying contrasts, not unlike the antithetical caricatures portrayed in professional wrestling.

Jordan seemed to define the 1990s as an intensely competitive artist who painted memorable images on the basketball court—a one-man highlight film who reaped the pecuniary benefits of his dazzling artistry. His legend began as a college freshman when he hit the winning shot to give the University of North Carolina the 1982 NCAA title. Two years later, he was deemed the top college player of the year and won the first of two Olympic gold medals as he led the Olympic team in scoring.

Jordan eschewed his senior year in favor of the NBA, where he led the Chicago Bulls to the playoffs. In recognition of his individual accomplishments, he earned an NBA All-Star Game berth and Rookie of the Year honors. Despite a broken

Michael Jordan's fame and that of the NBA reached global proportions.

© AP Photo/Susan Ragan, File

MVP award and was named Defensive Player of the Year. He topped off that season, and the next, by winning the NBA's televised slam-dunk contest, and in 1987–1988 he added the All-Star Game's MVP laurels to his growing list of accomplishments. Despite his individual displays of glory, however, his team failed to win any championships. That shortcoming began to change with the development of teammate Scottie Pippen (who would eventually be voted an all-time top-50 NBA player himself) and the arrival of now-legendary head coach Phil Jackson. In 1991, the Bulls beat the Los Angeles Lakers for their first NBA championship, and Jordan led the league in scoring, capturing MVP honors for both the regular season and the playoffs. He repeated in all three categories the next year, as the Bulls won 67 regular-season games before dismantling the Portland Trail Blazers in the championship.

In the summer of 1992, Jordan led the United States to an easy gold medal at the Barcelona Olympic Games, the first time professional players competed at the Olympics. Joining Jordan on the U.S. "Dream Team" were Scottie Pippen, Magic Johnson, Larry Bird, Charles Barkley, Karl Malone, Clyde Drexler, and collegian Christian Laettner, and this group of the NBA's best overwhelmed their opponents by an average of 44 points per game. Their triumphal tour of Europe produced enormous crowds and swelled the popularity of the sport.

The following season, the Bulls won their third consecutive title, besting the Phoenix Suns, as Jordan averaged 41 points per game in gaining the MVP award once again. Off the court, Nike and Jordan experienced unprecedented success. He appeared omnipresent in ads, and his bald pate became a fashion statement, copied by millions of men. Jordan's exuberance suffered a tragic blow when his father was murdered during the summer of 1993, and for the first time he appeared human, less than invincible, even vulnerable. Criticism of his gambling habits questioned his carefully crafted image, and he decided to retire before the 1993 season. After a two-year hiatus and an unsuccessful flirtation as a minor-league baseball player, Jordan returned to the hardwood at the end of the 1995 season. Although he scored 55 points in a playoff game, the Bulls failed to reach the championship.

With Jordan playing a complete season in 1995–1996, however, and the acquisition of the

foot, Jordan displayed his forceful determination by returning to play at the end of the 1985–1986 season, pouring in 49 and 63 points in playoff contests. By that time, his spectacular dunks attracted a legion of fans and commercial sponsors. In 1985, Nike produced the first of its Air Jordan basketball shoes, which brought the company and the player worldwide exposure. The savvy marketing of the NBA and Jordan made basketball a global phenomenon encroaching on the international popularity of soccer.

Jordan's further exploits only fueled the growth of the game as youth around the world attempted to "Be like Mike," one of the advertising slogans attached to Jordan's lucrative endorsement deals. During the 1986–1987 season, Jordan led the league in scoring, and in the following year he won the

eccentric rebounder and defender Dennis Rodman, Chicago won a record 72 regular-season games and another NBA title. They followed that banner year with consecutive championships in 1997 and 1998, with Jordan leading the NBA in scoring each season. He announced his second retirement in 1999 after winning 10 scoring titles, six league championships, and five NBA MVP awards. ESPN named him the greatest American athlete of the century.

In Jordan's absence, the NBA's television ratings dropped 14 percent in 1999, but the retirement proved brief (Hughes 176). Jordan became part owner of the Washington Wizards franchise in 2000, but his competitive fires still burned, and he renounced his ownership stake in an attempt to rescue his inept team by returning to play through the 2002–2003 season. He still averaged an impressive 20 points per game, but his longevity paled in comparison to his legacy as a cultural phenomenon who globalized the sport of basketball, as well as American consumer goods—and himself—as a paragon of capitalism.

Jordan had earned a salary of more than $33 million for the 1997–1998 season, and much more in endorsement contracts (MacCambridge 284). He became a global icon, deified as "the black Jesus." His 1999 retirement announcement made headlines from Beijing to Bosnia, despite the ongoing war in the latter (Miller and Wiggins 305–306). He had become the most popular person in the world, and the most recognizable since Muhammad Ali. Many African American youth virtually equated Jordan with God as their most admired entities (Miller and Wiggins 312).

The NBA capitalized on such popularity by expanding to Canada with franchises in Toronto and Vancouver in 1995 (the latter returned to the United States, specifically Memphis, in 2001). Between 1988 and 2004, seven new franchises joined the league, and the market value of teams increased significantly. Despite being a small-market team, the Vancouver Grizzlies sold for $160 million in 2000; the Boston Celtics brought $360 million, and the Phoenix Suns commanded $401 million ("Great American" 71). The NBA enjoyed $500 million in revenue through international sales of its products in 1996 but still sought a larger market (Spirou and Bennett 18), and it pursued a greater female audience by initiating and subsidizing the Women's National Basketball Association (WNBA) in 1996. By 2005, the WNBA featured at least 30 players from abroad and televised its games in 193 countries and 31 different languages (Friedman). In the process of commodification, Jordan transcended boundaries of race, social class, and nationality in promoting both basketball and the capitalist value system. By 2000, the NBA was broadcasting its games in 42 languages to more than 750 million people in 205 countries (Miller and Wiggins 308).

Intercollegiate Sport and the NCAA

The NCAA had steadfastly adhered to the amateur ideal, refusing any compensation other than the tuition, room, and board provided by athletic scholarships for college athletes. Many players, however, contended that they were employees of the universities, and, indeed, an NCAA survey in 1988 found that college athletes spent more time in practice than in academic pursuits, averaging 26 hours per week on scholastic matters but 30 hours on sports (Gorn and Goldstein 233). Such protests questioned the entrenched ideology of amateurism and institutional control. Despite the athletes' contentions, the NCAA adhered to its regulations, but in many cases boosters' clandestine efforts continued to lure and subsidize football and basketball stars in particular.

Colleges and universities derived national media exposure from successful athletic teams, and competition for the top players increased. A series of scandals called into question not only the amateur ideal but also the ethical practices of the coaches and alumni found guilty of committing various wrongs—illegal recruiting tactics, grade tampering, under-the-table financial inducements, eligibility violations, transcript fakery, and phantom courses—in order to attract and retain athletes. When coaches guilty of such infractions left or were fired from their posts, they often found new employment quickly with other would-be contenders. The institutions, however, faced probationary penalties from the NCAA. In 1980, for example, five members of the prestigious Pac-10 Conference were placed on probation for such transgressions, making half of the league ineligible for the football championship.

The following year, the NCAA enacted legislation to address the abuses, requiring at least minimal course goals, academic progress, substantial coursework, acceptable grade point averages, and substantiation of eligibility by school administrators. Even so, abuses continued, even as television payouts escalated. NBC paid $7 million for the broadcast rights to the 1983 Rose Bowl football game (Pope, *The New* 376), and the NCAA netted $75 million overall that year (Gorn and Goldstein 235). Major college football programs joined together in the College Football Association (CFA) to challenge the NCAA over the television profits. The big (Division I) schools asserted that because their games produced the most interest and the greatest profits from the television networks, they should receive greater remuneration. The smaller (Division II and III) institutions opposed the CFA, since they wanted to continue sharing in the NCAA distribution of funds from the television packages. The universities of Georgia and Oklahoma, both traditional football powers, sued the NCAA over the matter and won their case, and by 1985 the athletic conferences (and even individual schools) had the right to negotiate their own television contracts.

With such competition for the lucrative payoffs, abuses continued despite new NCAA rules. In 1987, Southern Methodist University, already on probation for numerous NCAA violations, received "the death penalty" for providing illegal payments to its football players. Banned from football competition for the 1987 season and limited to seven away games (and no home games) the following year, and with its team depleted of players who transferred or graduated, the school decided to abandon the sport. The dismissal proved temporary, as school officials submitted to pressure from alumni and boosters and resurrected the football team in 1989.

The top college football conferences began to increase their revenue by entering into their own agreements with the television networks. In 1992, the previously independent bowl selection committees formed an alliance (known as the Bowl Coalition) with the major football conferences in an effort to match top teams in a championship game. The Big Ten and Pac-10 conferences, however, remained contractually obliged to send top teams to the Rose Bowl. In 1995, the Bowl Alliance emerged, wherein the Fiesta, Sugar, and Orange Bowls agreed on a rotating schedule in which each would get the best teams regardless of regional affiliations. Thus, regional teams no longer had guarantees of bowl games, but the Rose Bowl remained committed to its two traditional conferences; as a result, if either the Big Ten or Pac-10 produced a team ranked as number one or number two, the Bowl Alliance could not claim a national championship game. In 1997, the Rose Bowl joined the others after Michigan, a Big Ten team, had to settle for a share of the national title with Nebraska (the teams had each beaten worthy bowl opponents but had not played each other).

In this fashion, the sportswriters' rankings and the coaches' rankings sometimes conflicted, creating never-ending and unwinnable arguments between fans as to which team merited the national title.

Even when all the bowls united in the Bowl Championship Series (BCS), a national title game was still not assured if the two polls lacked agreement, and the issue could be exacerbated if several teams managed to go undefeated throughout the season. The BCS arrived at a computerized mathematical formula to establish a supposedly neutral and objective polling system, but the rankings failed to quell complaints by partisan fans.

Although a handful of top football teams garnered the biggest profits from television, the NCAA devised another prosperous scheme by expanding its basketball tournament from 48 to 64 teams in 1985, thus providing greater regional interest in the quest to find a national champion, and the Final Four semifinal round assumed the stature of a national athletic festival. The next year, the NCAA added the three-point shot, bringing a new dimension to the game. In one 1992 game, Troy State attempted 109 three-pointers (making 51) in a game against DeVry Institute. Other teams also favored the "run-and-gun" style of offense, often a fan favorite, with little pretense of defense. In 1989, the team from U.S. International (in California) scored 150 points against Loyola Marymount and still lost, as the winners tallied 181 points in a game that resembled a track meet. Troy State surpassed even that total, scoring a record 123 points in the first half of the record-breaking game against DeVry. They immediately beat that mark by scoring 135 in the second half en route to a 258-141 win. Such prolific scoring glorified the capitalist emphasis on production, gained national prominence for smaller schools, and intensified fan interest.

During the 1980–1981 academic year, the Association for Intercollegiate Athletics for Women (AIAW), a sports governing body organized by and for women, offered 39 championships, but the NCAA, the predominantly male organization, began direct competition with the AIAW in 1981, effectively running it out of business.

Women and Sport

Despite the entrenched male power structure in sports governing bodies—and the reluctance to grant equal opportunities to women—female athletes continued to destroy myths of physical frailty by setting new standards and overcoming perceived obstacles. Indeed, women registered

Louisiana Tech women's basketball coach Sonja Hogg is carried off the floor following the Lady Techsters' 79-59 win over Tennessee in the AIAW National Basketball Championship on March 29, 1981.
© AP Photo/Harley Soltes

unprecedented successes, many of them at the Olympic Games.

Women as Olympic Heroes

Anita DeFrantz, captain of the women's U.S. Olympic rowing team in 1976, won appointment to the IOC in 1986, becoming both the first American woman and the first African American to gain such stature. DeFrantz became an IOC vice president in 1997. Other Olympic successes included Mary Lou Retton, who became a national hero as the first American to win the women's all-around gymnastics championship at the 1984 Summer Games. Meanwhile, the women's competition grew to include rhythmic gymnastics as well as synchronized swimming. Connie Carpenter-Phinney, an American cyclist, captured the gold medal in the women's road race, and Joan Benoit won the first Olympic women's marathon despite recent knee surgery. Figure skater Debi Thomas, who won national figure skating titles in 1986 and 1988, went on to win Olympic bronze in 1988, becoming the first African American athlete to win a medal at the Winter Games.

In track and field, the flamboyant Florence Griffith-Joyner, known as "Flo Jo" to fans, dominated the 1988 Summer Olympics in Seoul, Korea, by winning four medals (three gold, one silver). Over-coming unproven allegations of steroid use, Flo Jo set an Olympic record at 100 meters and a world record at 200 meters and added another gold as part of the 4 × 100-meter relay team. The versatile Griffith-Joyner even ran a leg of the 4 × 400-meter relay for her silver medal. The United States, France, and the Soviet Union all acknowledged her as Athlete of the Year. Her talents reached well beyond the track, as she popularized avant-garde track attire, designed new uniforms for the NBA's Indiana Pacers, and appeared on-screen in a movie, in television shows, and as a sports commentator. She also wrote children's books and became a spokeswoman for several charities. In 1993, she became the first female to cochair the President's Council on Physical Fitness and Sports. The next year, she established a philanthropic foundation for poor children. Her glamorous life ended in 1998 when she died of an epileptic seizure at the age of 38.

Griffith-Joyner's sister-in-law, Jackie Joyner-Kersee, proved equally versatile, if not as ostentatious. Born into poverty in East St. Louis, Illinois, in 1962, Jackie Joyner earned a basketball scholarship to UCLA, where she became an All-American. (Her brother, Al Joyner, Florence Griffith's husband, took the Olympic gold medal in the 1984 triple jump.) Joyner-Kersee won the seven-event heptathlon and the long jump at Seoul in 1988 despite having asthma. In the process, she broke her own heptathlon world record and set a new Olympic mark in the long jump. In 1992, she repeated her heptathlon triumph at the Barcelona Olympics. Throughout her career, Joyner-Kersee won numerous honors as athlete of the year, and in 2000, *Sports Illustrated for Women* named her the top female athlete of the century. In retirement, she founded a youth center in her hometown.

Bonnie Blair, a speedskating sensation, won five Olympic gold medals and one bronze between 1988 and 1994. No other American woman has accomplished such a feat at the Winter Olympics, and Blair added the Sullivan Award as the top amateur athlete in the United States in 1992. The U.S. Olympic Committee named her Sportswoman of the Year in 1992 and 1994, and in the latter year the Associated Press selected her as Female Athlete of the Year.

Also on the ice, Kristi Yamaguchi won the 1991 Olympic gold medal in figure skating, becoming the first Asian American woman to win a gold

Kristi Yamaguchi skating during her gold medal performance at the 1992 Olympic Games.

© Eric Feferberg/AFP/Getty Images

1975. The following year, she won a silver medal at the Montreal Olympics. She led Old Dominion University (ODU) of Norfolk, Virginia, to two national AIAW titles, and ODU home games drew ten thousand spectators. In 1981, Lieberman played in a men's semipro league until the Dallas Diamonds of the WBL offered her a $100,000 contract. The WABA Dallas franchise then paid her $250,000, and she led them to the league championship. With the demise of the WABA, she then joined a men's pro league, appearing in the United States Basketball League with the Springfield (Massachusetts) Fame. During the 1987–1988 season, she joined the Harlem Globetrotters. She returned to pro basketball with the Phoenix Mercury of the Women's National Basketball Association (WNBA) in 1997 (Berlage 42). Her income far outstripped that of most women but still pointed to ongoing gender inequalities insofar as it was hardly comparable to the money earned by male basketball stars in the NBA.

Like Billie Jean King, Lieberman pioneered opportunities for female athletes. When her playing days ended, she became a television analyst for men's and women's games, authored books, directed basketball camps for girls, and served as president of the Women's Sports Foundation. She assumed administrative duties as head coach and general manager of the Detroit Shock of the WNBA in 1998 and as coach of the Dallas Fury in

medal. On the slopes, Picabo Street won a silver medal at the 1994 Winter Olympics and then, in 1995, became the first American woman to win the World Cup downhill skiing competition. In 1998, the U.S. women's ice hockey team won the Olympic gold medal.

Women's Professional Sports Teams

The popularity of basketball extended to female athletes, who also emerged as stars. The Women's Basketball League (WBL), a professional circuit, initiated play in 1979 but went out of business in 1981. It was succeeded by the Women's American Basketball Association (WABA), which lasted only one season (1984). In each venture, Nancy Lieberman (later Lieberman-Cline) proved to be the top attraction. Raised in a broken home, Lieberman had sought solace and recognition in sports (Berlage 41). While still a high school student, she played on U.S. national basketball teams at the Pan American Games and the world championships in

Nancy Lieberman exemplified the best of early pro basketball for women. Here she coaches Detroit Shock player Astou Ndiaye, August 23, 1999.

© AP Photo/Duane Burleson

2004 in the National Women's Basketball League (NWBL). She had already been inducted into the Basketball Hall of Fame in 1996.

Lieberman proved not to be an anomaly. Cheryl Miller followed with truly exceptional talent, evident in her selection as a high school All-American for four straight years in Riverside, California. In her senior year, she scored 105 points in a single game and averaged more than 32 points and 15 rebounds per game over her four years there. At the University of Southern California, she repeated as a four-time All-American with two NCAA championships, which she bettered by leading the United States to an Olympic gold medal in 1984 and a world championship in 1986. Thereafter she returned to coach her alma mater before becoming both coach and general manager of the Phoenix Mercury in the WNBA from 1997 to 2000. She then assumed a role as a television reporter and basketball analyst before returning to coaching at Langston University in 2014. The Women's Basketball Hall of Fame inducted her in 1999, and the FIBA international basketball Hall of Fame similarly honored her great accomplishments in 2010 (Nelson).

Women also made great strides in soccer during this period. In 1991, the U.S. women's soccer team defeated Norway in the championship match of the World Cup, and Mia Hamm, a prolific scorer, became the role model for aspiring young girls throughout the country. The increasing success of women's sports became most noticeable in 1999, when nearly seventy-nine thousand fans

Brandi Chastain's impromptu celebration and resultant criticism indicated ongoing differences between gender expectations.

© AP Photo/The San Francisco Examiner, Lacy Atkins, File

at the Meadowlands in New Jersey watched the U.S. women's soccer team win a World Cup match against Denmark. The team then captured the world championship in an overtime shootout with China. Exhilaration soon shifted to debate after Brandi Chastain, who scored the winning goal,

People & Places

Mia Hamm

Born in 1972, the same year that Title IX became law, Mariel Margaret "Mia" Hamm would come to symbolize the growing possibilities for female athletes. The daughter of an Air Force colonel and a former ballerina, Hamm grew up in a large family, including two adopted brothers. She began playing soccer in youth leagues, and at age 14 she joined the Olympic Development Team. A year later, she became the youngest member of the women's national soccer team.

Hamm entered the University of North Carolina in 1989 and led its women's soccer team to four NCAA championships before graduating with a political science degree in 1994. She was named to the All-American team three times, and she led the national team to World Cup victories in 1991 and 1999, as well as to Olympic gold medals in 1996 and 2004. During that time, Hamm scored more goals than any other female player in the world, and her stardom and celebrity led to an unprecedented interest in soccer among young girls. Nike signed her to an endorsement contract, and FIFA named her the top player in the world in 2001 and 2002.

Mia Hamm starred as a player for the Washington Freedom team in the short-lived women's professional soccer league (shut down in 2003). She retired in 2004 and was elected to the National Soccer Hall of Fame in 2007. In 1999, she launched the Mia Hamm Foundation to inspire young women through sport and to provide funding for bone marrow research to solve the disease that claimed one of her brothers' lives (Dyer, "Hamm").

ripped off her shirt in celebration, leaving her upper body clothed only in a sports bra. Although male soccer players had cavorted in similar fashion for years, Chastain's action prompted discussion of morality, sexuality, and gender.

Achievements and Social Change

Women during this period also performed several striking endurance feats. Throughout the 1970s, Diana Nyad surpassed men's records for endurance swimming by circling Manhattan Island, as well as covering more than 100 miles (161 kilometers) in the Atlantic Ocean (from the Bahamas to Florida) and covering the distance from Cuba to the United States. In 1983, women organized an all-female triathlon in California that drew more than 600 entrants. Two years later, Libby Riddles won the Iditarod sled-dog race across Alaska against male competitors, and Susan Butcher beat the men in that event four times between 1986 and 1990. In 1987, Lynne Cox swam from Alaska to the Soviet Union across the Bering Strait, a feat no man had ever accomplished. A year later, Stacy Allison climbed Mount Everest, and in 1989 Ann Trason won the Western States 100, an ultra-endurance race that lasted more than 18 hours.

In professional golf, too, female players made great strides. Nancy Lopez earned nearly $4 million on the women's pro golf circuit by 1994 (Jones 247). Women also found opportunities in bowling, where they had greater control over matters through the Women's International Bowling Congress (WIBC). The 1988 WIBC tournament attracted a record 77,735 competitors. When the women's professional bowling tour went out of business in 2003, Liz Johnson, a native of Buffalo, New York, qualified for the men's Professional Bowling Association (PBA) the next year. Johnson had won the national amateur bowling championships in 1993 and 1994. In 1996, she had earned Rookie of the Year honors as a professional, and she won 11 tournaments on the women's tour before becoming the first woman to compete on the men's circuit. Despite her success, however, she aroused little interest among advertising executives, as female athletes continued to struggle to reach equitable levels of exposure and compensation in a male-dominated sports world.

Nonetheless, inspired by female professional athletes in various sports—even racing, as Lyn St. James won 1991 Rookie of the Year honors as the first woman on the Indy car circuit—American girls and women during this period continually increased their rates of sports participation. By

1998, more than a thousand girls' teams played in the National Ice Hockey Association, and nearly two thousand girls joined their high school wrestling teams (although male competitors often forfeited matches rather than face a girl). Thus, throughout the generation that followed the enactment of Title IX, courageous female athletes fought the restrictions of patriarchy to attain excellence, and their efforts brought great social change to the American cultural landscape.

Athletes' lifestyles came under increased, and often intensive, media scrutiny after the Athletic Revolution of the 1960s, and for women, who were displaying more and more athletic prowess—and sometimes sheer power—this scrutiny often involved consideration of gender and sexuality. A case in point was Martina Navratilova, who defected from Communist Czechoslovakia in 1975. A teenage tennis phenom, she proved inconsistent in the United States until she hired basketball great Nancy Lieberman as her trainer in 1981. Proper nutrition and weight training turned her into a power hitter who revolutionized the women's game. She dominated the prestigious Wimbledon tournament from 1982 through 1987, winning a record total of nine singles championships there, and she held the top ranking in the world for seven years. She also received abundant media coverage for her acknowledged lesbianism. In contrast, her consummate rival, Chris Evert, won fame not only for her play but also for her femininity. Her glamour, stylish couture, and style of play differed from that of Navratilova, and the contrast only heightened the interest in women's tennis. Evert won 90 percent of her matches during a long career (1971–1989), but Navratilova enjoyed a 43-37 edge in their 80 head-to-head matches. More lasting than her tennis victories, however, was Navratilova's openness about her sexuality, which forced promoters, sponsors, opponents, and fans to confront their own values and biases.

As early as the 1890s, doctors and social critics had denigrated sports as having a masculinizing effect on women. By 1980, however, Olympian Florence Griffith Joyner was projecting an image of both physical power and alluring femininity that was at odds with the stereotype of the masculine tomboy. She showed that female athletes could be both strong and beautiful, successfully marketing herself as an erotic attraction and paving the way for the current modeling careers of athletic women such as the 1997 beach volleyball champion Gabrielle Reece and the 2004 and 2008 Olympic softball sensation Jennie Finch. This eroticization of the female athletic body has split feminists and fostered controversy over the past two decades, as promoters of women's sports have used aesthetic and sometimes sensual appeal to publicize their events and attract viewers. The LPGA used Jan Stephenson, an attractive pro golfer and 1983 U.S. Women's Open champion, in featured photos in *Sports Illustrated* to publicize the women's tour.

Drug and Body Abuse Among Athletes

Throughout history, athletes have engaged in the blind pursuit of winning at any cost, with some using drugs or abusing alcohol to ease stress and tension and others turning to performance-enhancing drugs that promised greater potential rewards. Endurance athletes, particularly cyclists, had used strychnine to ward off fatigue in the late nineteenth century. By 1935, German scientists had succeeded in isolating the male hormone testosterone, which produced greater muscle mass and strength. During the 1950s, weightlifters injected synthetic forms of testosterone into their bodies to improve their performances. The practice soon spread to track-and-field athletes, swimmers, and American football players. Athletic governing bodies finally banned steroid usage in 1975 and began testing athletes, which led, however, only to various nuanced means of avoiding the tests or masking the results.

Substance Abuse

Allegations of substance abuse clouded athletic hero worship throughout the 1980s and continue to persist. The day after the Boston Celtics drafted Len Bias, an All-American at the University of Maryland, he died of a cocaine overdose. The attempted cover-up cost the coach, Lefty Dreisell, his job and besmirched the university. Eight days later, Don Rogers of the Cleveland Browns died at his own bachelor party, another victim of cocaine. Other stars, including baseball greats Dwight Gooden and Darryl Strawberry, simply lost their jobs and control of their own lives. New York Giants linebacker Lawrence Taylor, who used great strength, blazing speed, and a violent attitude to wreak havoc on opposing quarterbacks during his Hall of Fame career, saw his accomplishments tainted by his drug use. His addiction to cocaine resulted in arrests, suspensions, and, finally, his 1993 retirement, thus damaging his reputation as one of football's greatest players.

In baseball, Donnie Moore, a pitcher for the California Angels, gave up a home run in a 1986 League Championship Game that cost his team the pennant. Beleaguered by fans and the media, and tormented by his own self-doubts and depression over the incident, Moore committed suicide three years later after a bout with heavy drinking and engaging in spousal abuse. Steve Howe joined the Los Angeles Dodgers as a pitcher in 1980, and his cocaine addiction resulted in seven suspensions from Major League Baseball. Despite this repeated abuse, Howe found employment with three other teams eager for his services until commissioner Fay Vincent finally imposed a lifetime ban on the unrepentant hurler in 1992. Even that measure failed, as Howe won a court case that claimed he needed cocaine for attention-deficit disorder. The Yankees did not give up on Howe until his fastball finally deserted him in 1996, but, as a result of such struggles, professional sports teams began investigating players' lifestyles in an attempt to avoid drafting and investing millions of dollars in compromised employees.

Steroid Use

Substance abuse reached a crisis stage at the 1988 Olympics in Seoul, Korea, when Canadian Ben Johnson set a new world record in the 100-meter race, easily defeating the prohibitive favorite, Carl Lewis. Dismay turned to disbelief when Johnson tested positive for a performance-enhancing substance (the anabolic steroid stanozolol). He then asserted such use was widespread among track stars. Worse, the drugs had been supplied by his doctor and encouraged by his coach as a necessary step toward winning. That belief persisted, and drug usage spread to winter sports competitors, baseball players, and even American high school youth desirous of athletic success or just a better body image.

In the quest for wins and self-imposed pressures to succeed, then, some athletes sought any means, even illegal ones, to enhance their performances, and many coaches and administrators looked away when they did not actually condone such methods. In an attempt to deter steroid usage, in 1986 the NCAA instituted mandatory drug testing for athletes involved in football bowl games and championship contests. This attempt at redressing the blemished image of sport and of athletes failed miserably, however, as collegiate players sued, charging that such measures constituted invasions of their privacy. The California Supreme Court sided with the NCAA in 1994, which allowed the governing body to extend its surveillance thereafter (NCAA.org).

Cyclists had long been suspect throughout the century, and that suspicion was confirmed when French police discovered performance-enhancing drugs (PEDs) among the riders in the 1998 Tour de France, which led to an international conference on doping. The IOC conference in 1999 led to the formation of the World Anti-Doping Agency (WADA) to address the issue on a global basis. The IOC provides half of WADA's funding, with the other half coming from national governments, whose contributions are based on size and wealth of the country. By 2004, WADA developed a doping code of banned substances as well as blood and gene doping prohibitions, protocols, testing and analytical procedures, and the random 24-hour surveillance of athletes. The United States initiated its own anti-doping agency (USADA), which began operating in 2000, to coincide with WADA (Teetzel, "Doping").

For female steroid users, very noticeable improvement in performance was accompanied by the growth of masculine physical characteristics, such as wider shoulders, greater muscle mass, facial hair, and a deeper voice. One of the most scandalous examples involved Marion Jones, a world champion track star at the 2000 Olympics who earned multiple gold medals, and later a professional basketball player in the WNBA, whose denials of PED usage were revealed as lies. She eventually spent six months in prison for her criminal activities (Gems and Pfister).

Body Dysmorphia, Abuse, and Injury

The quest for the perfect male body, known as the Adonis complex, sought the mesomorphic ideal and well-defined musculature of Greek sculptures. That particular image of masculinity was reinforced in popular beach movies, muscle magazines, and bodybuilding contests. Teenage boys and young men fell prey to the psychological addiction, turning to steroid usage and extreme bouts of weightlifting, as well as dangerous dehydration that lowered their body fat. High school and college wrestlers, too, sought to "cut" weight in order to gain an advantage over opponents by competing in a lower weight class. Such a practice became

Marco Pantani leading the 1998 Tour De France.
© William Stevens/Gamma-Rapho via Getty Images

so widespread that the NCAA mandated that collegiate wrestlers maintain an acceptable level of body fat and hydration in order to compete.

The denial of nutrients to one's body causes considerable harm, but athletes, especially males, are programmed to play with pain. Such stoicism earns social capital among one's peers, teammates, and fans, although at great cost to one's body. NFL players have a decidedly shorter life span than others; still, most relish their playing days. Jim Otto, a Hall of Fame center for the Oakland Raiders, has undergone 23 surgeries, including five knee replacements. In 1993, a study by the NFL Players Association revealed that more than 40 percent of players left the game because of injuries, and more than 60 percent suffered permanent injuries. Still, Dan Hampton, a Hall of Fame defensive end for the Chicago Bears, asserted that "[t]he true players don't worry about injuries or any of that crap. . . . You can take MRIs, X-rays and all that, and you can stuff it. . . . People accept hazards in all kinds of jobs. My God. Football players ought to be willing to take their panties off, get out there and hit somebody" (Hewitt 17B).

Girls and young women, too, have been greatly affected by the body images portrayed in the media. Conceptions of beauty have changed from the voluptuous figure of Marilyn Monroe in the 1960s to the waiflike image of Twiggy and the slender supermodels of the 1990s. The media emphasis on thin bodies pushed many girls and women to fad diets, weight-loss pills, and even anorexia and bulimia. Cross country runners, in particular, seem susceptible to anorexia or bulimia in attempts to keep their weight at low levels. A high percentage of female runners also develop amenorrhea, the absence of menstruation, because of a lack of body fat. Although the latter seems a temporary condition, the former can be life threatening. Such maladies also have been particularly widespread in gymnastics, where performance standards favor smaller bodies.

Professional athletes are never at a loss for willing sex partners; Wilt Chamberlain claimed to have bedded 20,000 women. Such promiscuity, however, can have dire results. In 1991, Earvin "Magic" Johnson, a heterosexual NBA star, acknowledged that he had been infected with the HIV virus because of his promiscuous lifestyle. The announcement shocked the NBA, spread fear among teammates and opponents, and led to Johnson's retirement. The revelation triggered widespread concern over the lifestyles of athletes, many of whom fathered illegitimate children without supporting them.

Despite Charles Barkley's contention that, as a professional basketball star, he was not a role model, children and youth perceived him and other athletes as such. The ongoing issue of whether athletes are role models called into question athletes' responsibilities to society, as youth quickly copied the fashions, mannerisms, and playing styles of their athletic idols.

Violence in Sport

Among other detrimental side effects of steroid usage, violent temper (sometimes termed *'roid rage*) caused particular concern. Sociologists and psychologists have debated whether the practice of sport alleviates or enhances aggressive tendencies. Noncontact sports (e.g., swimming, gymnastics) seem to be inconsequential in this regard, whereas contact sports (e.g., football, hockey, soccer) can exacerbate animosity (Coakley 173–201), and athletes using steroids may be more prone to such outbursts.

Such issues only increased existing concern over the aggressive nature of some sports, and psychologists disagreed over the value of sport as a means of dissipating violent tendencies. More recent sociological studies, however, showed increased hostility in postgame football viewers, regardless of the outcome. Another study discovered that domestic assaults against women increased after the Super Bowl. Other aggressive sports, such as hockey and wrestling, prompted similar escalations in hostility, whereas no such change was noted in viewers of swimming or gymnastics events (Eitzen and Sage 133). In certain sports, such as hockey, boxing, and football, intensive aggressiveness is even necessary for success. Boxing rules, of course, allow the violent actions required for winning, and hockey violence also serves a sanctioned ritualistic function in the demonstration of masculinity. Hockey teams have even employed "goons" as enforcers to safeguard their star players and intimidate opponents. Uncontrolled aggression, however, has sometimes turned to outright violence.

Hockey has a long history of violent acts, often considered endemic to the game and part of its promotion of tough masculinity. In 1933, Boston Bruins defenseman Eddie Shore slammed the Maple Leafs' Ace Bailey into the ice, fracturing his skull and ending his career. In 1955, Maurice Richard hit an opponent over the head with his stick, then punched a game official. When NHL president Clarence Campbell suspended Richard,

Athletic violence has cast doubt on the character-building qualities of sport. Here the Philadelphia 76ers Julius Erving, left, and Boston Celtics Larry Bird, right, square off during a second-half fight at the Boston Garden, Nov. 9, 1984.

© AP Photo/Ted Gartland

Montreal fans rioted, causing $500,000 in damage. In a 1969 preseason game that did not even count in the championship race, Wayne Maki of St. Louis and Ted Green of Boston engaged in a brawl that ended with Maki clouting Green with his stick. Green's fractured skull left him near death, requiring three operations and a year of recovery.

Violence still riddled the game at the turn of the twenty-first century. Bryan Marchment, an NHL player, equated the violence to a display of masculinity: "Hey, it's a man's game. If you can't play, get out and play tennis" (Coakley 181). The reinforcement of one's masculinity, especially in the presence of other males, is a big factor in winning group acceptance, and that sense of identity has long been an essential socially constructed desire for boys and young men. Professional hockey finally faced forceful restraint in 2000, when Marty McSorley of Boston slashed Donald Brashear of Vancouver across the head. McSorley was charged with assault and suspended by the NHL for a year, effectively causing his retirement.

Such assaults seemed commonplace in hockey, and youth began to emulate their professional idols. In youth sports, even some parents attacked coaches and game officials. In a Chicago hockey game, one player, at the urging of his coach, attacked an opponent after the game as he left the ice, resulting in a spinal cord injury and paralysis (Felsenthal). In Massachusetts, a brawl between

hockey parents resulted in a death during the 2000 season; a game was not even at stake as a father beat the coach into unconsciousness over the nature of a practice session. The offender faced manslaughter charges.

Reports of such violence involving athletes permeated newspapers throughout the latter part of the twentieth century and the start of the twenty-first. In a particularly infamous case, the Oakland Raiders' Jack Tatum, known as "the Assassin," paralyzed the Patriots' Darryl Stingley in an especially brutal hit in 1978. Other incidents included one in which Woody Hayes, famed football coach at Ohio State University, punched a Clemson player in the 1978 Gator Bowl, which cost him his job. College football players faced numerous charges of rape and assault during the 1990s, and NFL player Rae Carruth, found guilty of conspiracy charges in the murder of a pregnant woman who carried their child, received a long prison sentence. Carruth's conviction followed in the wake of the O.J. Simpson debacle, as the NFL was trying to improve its image amid allegations of tolerating or even encouraging violent behavior.

Simpson had enjoyed fame, fortune, and celebrity as a superstar running back for the Buffalo Bills, breaking Jim Brown's single-season rushing record, and upon retirement his celebrity status won him a role on the *Monday Night Football* broadcast team, as well as movie parts and roles in corporate ads on national television, making him the first African American to gain that distinction. After the murders of his white wife and her male friend, however, Simpson led police on a long, televised car chase, and although he was acquitted of murder charges in 1995 after a highly controversial, racially charged criminal trial, he was found liable in a civil suit two years later.

Shortly after Simpson's indictment, star quarterback Warren Moon went to trial on domestic abuse charges, as did Jim Brown in 1999. A year later, Ray Lewis, a popular linebacker for the Baltimore Ravens, faced murder charges. Although convicted only of obstruction of justice for his role in the cover-up, the case did little to repair the NFL's soiled image or to soften the association between football and violence.

While hockey and football engaged in damage control, boxing could claim crisis as a perpetual state, particularly after the arrival of Mike Tyson. In 1986, he gained the World Boxing Council (WBC) heavyweight championship at the age of 20, and he added the World Boxing Association (WBA) crown four months later. A devastating puncher, he amazed fans by knocking out virtually all opponents in amassing a 37-0 record by 1990. In 1992, however, a jury convicted Tyson of raping Desiree Washington, a contestant in an Indianapolis beauty contest. After three years in prison, Tyson returned to the ring and fought a pair of matches against another champion, Evander Holyfield. In their 1997 fight, a frustrated Tyson bit off part of Holyfield's ear. A year earlier, Tyson had earned $75 million in prize money but not a cent in endorsements (MacCambridge 284). He had transgressed even the sanctioned violence of the boxing arena.

Other sports have also been tarred with images of aggression or outright violence. Even the pristine sport of figure skating experienced a scandal when Tonya Harding conspired with thugs to injure and thus eliminate her rival, Nancy Kerrigan, from the 1994 national championships. In baseball, Roberto Alomar spit in the face of umpire John Hirschbeck near the end of the 1996 season. The American League issued a mild suspension, then withdrew it when Alomar's team entered the playoffs. Apparently, winning and television ratings meant more than respect. In 2000, Dodgers players fought with Cubs fans at Wrigley Field, and in 2002 White Sox fans left the stands at Comiskey Park to attack an opposing coach. A year later, another Sox fan attacked an umpire. In 2004, Rangers pitcher Frank Tanana threw a chair at hecklers, breaking a woman's nose.

Basketball also struggled with ongoing issues involving violent behavior. In 1977, Kermit Washington of the Los Angeles Lakers earned a 60-day suspension for punching Rudy Tomjanovich of Houston, leaving him unconscious in a pool of blood with a fractured skull. In 1994, coach John Chaney of Temple University issued a death threat to his opponent, John Calipari of Massachusetts. Eleven years later, the controversial Chaney earned a suspension after directing one of his players to "send a message" to opponents, resulting in a foul that produced a broken arm. During the 1996 NBA season, Dennis Rodman and Nick Van Exel both accosted referees during a game, and in 1997 Latrell Sprewell attacked his coach, P.J. Carlesimo, with a choke hold. The NBA suspended him for a year, but the players' union filed a grievance on his behalf that reduced the penalty to seven months. Jayson Williams of the New Jersey Nets faced manslaughter charges when his shotgun killed his chauffeur in 2002. Although acquitted of that crime, he was convicted of attempting to hide the tragedy by portraying it as a suicide. And one of the game's biggest stars, Kobe Bryant of the Los Angeles Lakers, nearly lost his career after a young woman filed rape charges in 2003. Although the case was dropped, Bryant admitted to adultery and wrongdoing, then settled the civil case out of court, sullying his clean image and hindering the rehabilitation efforts of the NBA. The dust from that affair had hardly settled when, early in the 2004 season, three Indiana Pacers players attacked Detroit fans, resulting in a year's suspension for Ron Artest.

People & Places

Pete Rose

Aggressiveness made Pete Rose a star on the baseball field but also led to the biggest baseball scandal since the Black Sox of 1919. A working-class overachiever, intensely competitive, and driven to succeed, Rose spent 24 years (1963–1986) in the National League with the Cincinnati Reds, Philadelphia Phillies, and Montreal Expos. Known as "Charlie Hustle," he slid headfirst into bases and even ran to first base after receiving a walk. Rose led his teams to six World Series appearances and often led the league in hitting. In 1978, he had a 44-game hitting streak, and in 1985 he surpassed Ty Cobb's seemingly insurmountable record for career hits. Rose finished with a total of 4,256 hits, appearing as a player-manager for Cincinnati after 1984. He continued to manage the Reds until 1988 but as an inveterate gambler he even wagered on his own team. When confronted with the allegations, Rose persistently denied his actions, resulting in a lifetime ban from baseball and ineligibility for the Hall of Fame. His troubles continued in 1990, when the government charged him with tax evasion and imposed a five-month jail sentence. Once again, gambling had stained the reputation of baseball, and critics questioned the value of sport and its relationship to the unsavory behavior that seemed so prevalent during the era.

Discrimination at the End of the Twentieth Century

The Paralympic Games have accommodated disadvantaged athletes for more than a half century. An athletic competition for disabled veterans of World War II first occurred in conjunction with the 1948 Olympic Games; but the first formal Paralympics took place in 1960. The Paralympic Winter Games were added in 1976, and since 1988 the Paralympics have been hosted in the same city as the Olympic Games. The American team gained greater funding after its incorporation into the USOC structure and greater importance for the large number of military veterans who have returned from the hostilities in the Middle East with debilitating injuries (Schultz et al., "Paralympics"; Schultz). Although differently abled athletes saw a rise in opportunities at the end of the century, the United States still struggled with issues of homophobia and racism.

Homophobia

Similar to Chris Evert, diver Greg Louganis enjoyed polished movie-star looks and consummate athletic skill. He won six world championships and four gold medals at the Olympic Games (in 1984 and 1988). Of Samoan heritage and a dyslexic, Louganis also exemplified success for those two groups. After a dramatic double win (springboard and platform diving) at the Seoul Olympics, after which he recovered from a head wound caused by hitting the diving board, Louganis acknowledged not only being gay but also that he had contracted AIDS. In 1994, he competed in the Gay Games, overcoming new social barriers to "coming out" in the process, and he declared, "Being gay and being in sports isn't supposed to mix. I think I proved that wrong" (MacCambridge 258). Thus, gay athletes such as Louganis, Billie Jean King, and Martina Navratilova used sport as a means to challenge dominant notions of gender and sexuality. They won greater, if grudging, acceptance for their achievements, regardless of their sexual preferences. In some sports, at least, ability counted more than lifestyle. In the sports of baseball, football, basketball, and hockey, however, the dominant sense of the requisite machismo pressured male athletes to publicly conform to traditional roles and characteristics throughout the twentieth century. When David Kopay admitted his homosexuality in his 1977 autobiography, five years after his retirement from the NFL, he faced ostracism by former teammates. When John Amaechi, a former NBA player, acknowledged in 2007 (well after retirement) that he was gay, some NBA players ardently disassociated themselves from him and even publicly proclaimed their disgust.

Racism

Nearly a half century after Jackie Robinson's "Great Experiment," the stain of racism endured in American sport. Marge Schott, the bigoted owner of the Cincinnati Reds, further defamed the sport with a series of racist pronouncements. In 1992, she greatly offended Jews by her admiration of Adolf Hitler and her possession of a Nazi armband. That same year, she referred to some of her players as "million-dollar niggers." The league imposed a $25,000 fine and a one-year suspension from team involvement, but when her demeanor failed to improve, a two-year ban followed in 1996, leading to her sale of the team in 1999.

Schott's remarks reflected a lingering racism within the sports world, in spite of advancements made by African American and Hispanic players. Major League Baseball teams increasingly signed Latin American athletes throughout the decade, African American players filled the NBA, and the NFL selected Johnny Grier as its first black referee in 1988. Still, few minorities gained positions as head coaches, team administrators, or owners. On the playing field, the practice of stacking (i.e., assigning white players to the "cerebral" positions such as quarterback and relegating blacks to positions where physical abilities superseded mental qualifications) remained problematic in the midst of a painfully gradual progression toward proper recognition of nonwhites' intellectual capabilities.

Scientists, anthropologists, and sociologists theorized about black dominance in some sports, and the comments of Jimmy "the Greek" Snyder, a football analyst for CBS, created a national controversy in 1988. Snyder professed that black success resulted from breeding practices during slavery, suggesting biological determinism as an explanation. He even claimed African Americans had running advantages because of their larger thighs. CBS fired Snyder the next day, but the heated debate continued. Scientists discovered no genetic superiority for blacks, but sociologists suggested cultural reasons as well as practical opportunities (Pope, *The New* 312–338). The number of African Americans in Major League Baseball has declined considerably to less than 9 percent by 2014, in part because of the lack of urban playing spaces (Solomon 2014).

Eldrick "Tiger" Woods, the successor to Michael Jordan as ubiquitous spokesman for Nike and a host of other commercial products, won the 1997 Masters Golf Tournament at the age of 21, not only setting a new record at 18 strokes under par but also dominating his opponents, the nearest of whom finished 12 strokes behind. The son of a father who was African American, Native American, and Chinese, and a mother who is Thai, Chinese, and European, Woods described himself as a Cablinasian. In any case, he has transcended racial lines and brought new constituencies to the previously white-dominated golf circuit. In 2000, Woods won more than $9 million in prize money and much more in endorsements. His high profile in the white world of golf, along with his replacement of Michael Jordan as a primary spokesman for American commerce, suggests a decline in the level of racism that had previously marked American society.

Woods seemed to live a storybook life. In 2004 he married a Swedish model, Elin Nordegren, and he held the number one ranking from 1999 to 2005; but revelations of his adulterous behavior surfaced in 2009, and the resultant divorce greatly

Tiger Woods was one of the most popular athletes in American sport in the late 1990s. His success on the golf course earned him millions of dollars in prize money and endorsement deals.

© Human Kinetics

tarnished his image, cost him the loss of sponsors and endorsements, and signaled a downward spiral in his performance (Jonsrud, qtd. in Nelson).

The greater acceptance and visibility of people of color in American sport did not extend to all minorities. In 1983, Native Americans formed the Iroquois Nationals lacrosse team, which, like Puerto Rico, competed in international contests as an independent nation with its own national anthem and a distinct flag. Sport provided the most visible avenue to public recognition for the American Indian confederacy. One step in amelioration with Native Americans was taken when the NCAA required its member schools to banish all American Indian mascots for sports events or face the penalty of ostracism by being barred from hosting championship events.

Individuality and Sport Icons

Throughout the latter quarter of the twentieth century, an increasing emphasis on individualism transformed team sports. Athletes sought, and the media provided, individual attention. Incentive-laden contracts and free agency produced astronomical salaries for professional athletes, greatly diminishing any sense of popular identification with heroes, and frequent player trades and departures weakened the former sense of loyalty and communal identity associated with team sports. And, like players who leave their adoring fans, team owners have regularly deserted cities in search of bigger markets and greater profits.

Styles of play changed to emphasize individual brilliance rather than team cohesion, and this transition, most noticeable in basketball, sometimes produced negative results. In the 1988 Olympics, U.S. collegians, usually dominant in the sport, finished a disappointing third. The ascendance of Michael Jordan rectified that aberration in the short term but only exacerbated the rise of individualism. Jordan personified the globalization of American commercial and popular culture at its best and worst. His competitive drive, work ethic, ambition, and success portrayed the possibilities of American life, but criticism of his selfish and domineering control of the team, his promotion of Nike products despite exploitative labor conditions in overseas sweatshops (Coakley 404–405), and his reluctance to use his celebrity to address social conditions indicated the price to be paid in attaining and maintaining his glorified stature.

Despite ongoing negative images generated by some athletes, others upheld the idealistic beliefs treasured by sports fans, strengthening faith in the potentially regenerative quality of athletics. As discussed earlier in the chapter, the various sports halls of fame portrayed such idealistic virtues as the norm, although this was clearly not always the case.

The Edmonton Oilers won four NHL championships during the 1980s, and their success rested largely on the efforts of Wayne Gretzky, who began playing professional hockey in the WHA at the age of 17. Despite a lack of great size or skating speed, Gretzky overshadowed all other players, winning the Hart Trophy, given to the league's MVP, nine times. He led the NHL in scoring 10 times and topped all others in assists for 13 consecutive seasons. In 1988, the Oilers traded him to the Los Angeles Kings, an act considered a sacrilege and a national tragedy in Canada, where Gretzky was idolized as a national hero of virtuous character.

The immense popularity of Gretzky transferred to the United States, allowing hockey to claim status as a major sport, and the NHL expanded to include franchises on the West Coast and in the South, thus introducing a winter sport to warm climates. Gretzky continued his stellar play throughout the 1990s for the St. Louis Blues and the New York Rangers, and upon his retirement after the 1999 season he had set the record for points scored with 2,857. The NHL quickly retired his jersey in deference to his achievements. In 2005, the Phoenix Coyotes made him their head coach, hoping his magic could help resurrect the struggling team.

As Gretzky excited hockey fans, Walter Payton stunned opponents of the Chicago Bears, endearing himself to fans in that city and earning the respect of all others. At only 5 feet 10 inches (178 centimeters) and 205 pounds (93 kilograms), he seemed small for an NFL player when the Bears drafted him from a small college, Jackson State, in 1975. He was, however, possessed of rare athletic gifts, frenetic energy, and a playful spirit, and he transformed a weak team into a Super Bowl champion. A versatile player who excelled in all phases of the game, Payton retired after 13 seasons as the all-time leading rusher in NFL history, having amassed 16,726 yards. He ran for more than 1,000 yards in a season 10 times, and

he won the NFL MVP award twice. Playing for a mediocre team through most of his career, Payton became a Chicago icon before Michael Jordan joined the Bulls. His cheerful attitude in spite of adversity, his indomitable work ethic, his infectious enthusiasm for the game, and the physical way in which he played it led blue-collar fans of the former industrial center to identify with their star player. His charitable works only deepened his bonds of attachment with the inhabitants of Chicago.

In 1985, the Bears assembled a compelling cast of characters under head coach "Iron" Mike Ditka, producing a 15-1 record that culminated in a 46-10 demolition of the New England Patriots in the Super Bowl. Their song and music video, "The Super Bowl Shuffle," clearly exposed the juncture of sport and entertainment as a pop-culture commodity. Payton retired after the 1987 season to engage in entrepreneurial ventures and auto racing, and he owned a CART (Championship Auto Racing Team) car in the Road America series. In 1999, however, he fell victim to a rare liver disease, and, as with the premature demise of baseball great Lou Gehrig, the city and the league mourned his death. In both cases, fans empathized and identified with tragic athletic heroes in whom they saw pieces of themselves or fragments of

Chicago Bears' Walter Payton in the 1986 Super Bowl.
© AP Photos/Red McLendon

who they wanted to be. Such idealizations served functionalist theories (sport as good, beneficial to all, and a character-building endeavor) of the role of sport in society and its need for heroes. Payton assumed near-martyr status in Chicago, his relics housed in his own suburban hall of fame.

Other athletes fulfilled identification roles for other constituencies, although not with the grace and approbation of Gehrig, Gretzky, or Payton. The intimidating Bo Jackson became a media sensation and a pitchman as a multisport athlete, starring in both professional baseball and football. After a hip injury forced Jackson's early retirement, the loquacious "Neon Deion" Sanders assumed the role of self-congratulatory, glamorous, dual-sport superstar. Sanders arrived (by limousine) at his last college game dressed in a top hat and tails. He backed up his flamboyance, arrogance, and boastful swagger by being the only athlete to appear in both the World Series and the Super Bowl. In the era of free agency, he took his talents to a succession of highest bidders, but by 1998 he had renounced his profligate ways and become a born-again Christian, thus reconstructing his image in the manner of celebrities in the movie and music industries.

With the departure of Muhammad Ali from the boxing scene, another fighter, almost as colorful and charismatic, emerged as the consummate showman. Sugar Ray Leonard sported 145 wins in 150 amateur fights before taking the light welterweight gold medal at the 1976 Olympics. He turned professional under the tutelage of Angelo Dundee, the former trainer of Muhammad Ali, and in 1979 he defeated Wilfred Benitez for the WBC welterweight crown. Throughout the 1980s, the flashy, garrulous Leonard became a fan favorite and a media darling as he fought in a series of bouts against other Hall of Fame boxers of the era, including Roberto Duran, Tommy Hearns, and Marvin Hagler. Each of the memorable battles was among the best in ring history. A detached retina in 1982 required surgery and forced Leonard's retirement, although he soon defied medical authorities to return to the ring. From 1984 to 1989, he battled a cocaine habit but managed to accumulate five world titles in five different weight classes before a final retirement in 1997.

Such success stories continued to fuel adolescent dreams, nurture the promise of sport, and deny the deleterious aspects of the sporting culture.

Leonard was idolized by many, including Oscar De La Hoya, a Mexican American who followed in his footsteps. De La Hoya captured an Olympic gold medal at the 1992 Olympics and went on to capture 10 world titles in six different weight classes as a professional. Like many athletes of the newer generation, he became a crossover star as a pop culture entertainer, releasing an album as a singer in 2000. De La Hoya retired in 2009, but unlike so many boxers who had been exploited, he parlayed his wealth into entrepreneurial ventures as a boxing promoter in his Golden Boy Productions and expanding real estate ventures (Gems, *Boxing* 181–182).

Alternative Sports

While women challenged social barriers, young men and women (some still boys and girls) also pushed the boundaries of sport. Individual sports such as in-line skating, mountain biking, windsurfing, cycling, motocross, auto racing, skydiving,

Windsurfing and other alternative sports gained popularity in the 1980s.
© Photodisc/Getty Images

kayaking, and skateboarding grew in appeal. In such endeavors as extreme skiing, rock climbing, and mountain climbing, people challenged themselves, sometimes surpassing their limitations to the point of death. The quest for self-fulfillment and rebellious identification, the search for peak experiences (i.e., adrenaline rush) such as bungee jumping and adventurous treks in isolated or natural settings served as a distinct reaction to urban routines of the era. Such pastimes resonated with restless spirits, renegade mentalities, and outlaw images that served as alternatives to the major corporatized sports and drew youthful, disaffected participants.

International Perspective

Adventure Races

Adventure races (ARs) are mass-media productions which gratify people's craving for heroes, sensation, and intimate glimpses into the lives and suffering of others. Like other dangerous sports, these races give expression to a postmodern outlook on life that drives participants to their limits, to self-discovery and self-reassurance, and even as far as to play with their own lives. The yearning for untamed nature and wilderness, the exaggerated and idealized belief in team spirit, and the sense of belonging to an elite group may be other motives for participants, who, to a large extent, are made up of former long-distance runners and triathletes. A large percentage of participants are management-level corporate agents, and roughly 10 percent are AR professionals.

The origins of adventure races are a matter of debate, but multisport events have been organized since as early as the 1960s. By 1980, the Alpine Ironman race in New Zealand required running, paddling, and skiing. The Alaskan Mountain Wilderness competition in 1982 took six days to complete, and the Raid Gauloises, sponsored by the Gauloises cigarette company and held in New Zealand in 1989, covered more than 400 miles (644 kilometers). The Raid Gauloises inspired TV producer Mark Burnett, who also developed the idea of the *Survivor* reality show, to create the show *Eco-Challenge,* staged for the first time in Utah in 1995. This was the beginning of a symbiotic relationship between AR and TV companies, which own the races and sell them as reality TV shows, thus turning AR into a multimillion-dollar business. *Eco-Challenge* wooed audiences not only with adventure but also with being environmentally friendly—which did not, however, save it from protests by environmentalists, who declared all interference in environmentally sensitive areas to be irresponsible.

ARs are multiday expeditions in remote, often exotic wilderness areas in which only the starting point, certain checkpoints, and the finish point are fixed. These races belong to the category of extreme sports, which in addition to extreme endurance capacities require a variety of skills in order to master disciplines such as orienteering, rappelling, mountain biking, rafting, paddling or kayaking, swimming, spelunking, climbing, and traversing.

AR is a team sport. In some races, teams are accompanied by a support crew, and in others the members have only themselves to rely on. They have to carry equipment, provisions, and water and decide on routes and breaks among themselves. Teams are often made up of four or five members; in many ARs there must be at least one female member, and all team members must finish the race for the team to be included in the scoring. Dropout rates are high. Bad weather, difficult terrain, and, above all, sleep deprivation are frequent causes of injury and illness. Teams are often sponsored by corporations who benefit from the media exposure and the imagery of performance under extreme conditions.

Shorter variations of ARs may last only hours instead of days. Other events accommodate urban teams that combine orienteering skills with the facing of city challenges such as running to the top of skyscrapers, navigating waterways or byways by various means of locomotion, and overcoming diverse obstacles. One of the better-known urban adventure races is the City Chase, created in Canada in 2004 and conducted in nine Canadian cities; it was immediately given enormous media coverage. In the City Chase, teams of two run through a city and have to fulfill numerous physical and mental tasks. The first world championship took place in Chicago in 2006. Adventure races and city chases are clear illustrations of a current trend in which sports and sporting events no longer undergo a slow and lengthy process of development and adaptation at the hands of the players themselves but are, rather, the product of invention and marketing in the hands of the mass media.

Information from Kay, Joanne, and Suzanne Laberge. "The 'New' Corporate Habitus in Adventure Racing." *International Review for the Sociology of Sport* 37.1 (2002): 17–36; and www.citychase.com.

Clothing manufacturers capitalized on such symbolism to produce styles and gear that fostered nonmainstream images. The pervasiveness of such reproductions only drew such practices closer to prevailing norms, hastened by attempts to televise the practices as conventional fare. Corporate-sponsored triathlons and adventure races for prize money, along with snowboarding contests and skateboarding competitions, were soon integrated within standard commercialized programming. Snowboarding, freestyle skiing, tae kwon do, and triathlon were all integrated into the Olympic program, securing their absorption into the corporate mainstream.

As some athletes pursued adventure sports, such as skydiving, surfing, windsurfing, mountain biking, kayaking, whitewater rafting, adventure racing, rock climbing, snowboarding, and extreme skiing, other activities such as in-line skating, skateboarding, and BMX (motocross) bicycling became so prevalent that many communities built half-pipe ramps to accommodate practitioners in their attempts to perform tricks and flips.

Summary

This chapter has explained how the corporate mentality and structure came to pervade sports. Private owners of sports teams pressured municipalities into subsidizing public stadiums with threats of franchise relocation. Politicians promoted such ventures as entertainment zones featuring restaurants, theaters, halls of fame, and assorted amusements to draw tourists to the urban areas. The marketing of sport as entertainment and of athletes as celebrities further transformed the ways in which sport was perceived by viewers and social critics.

The globalization of American sport forms and American business practices escalated with the ascendance of global superstar in Michael Jordan. American cultural values were transmitted to the world, often to the detriment of local cultures. Even the Olympic Games became a commercialized spectacle under the management of Americans in 1984, changing its espoused values thereafter.

The vast amounts of revenue produced by the confluence of sport and various competing television networks led to labor issues between owners and players over the division of the spoils, producing strikes, lockouts, and arbitration. Owners turned to a global labor force to reduce their costs and maximize their profits.

Greater commercialization also affected intercollegiate and interscholastic sports programs, fostering even more abuses in the quest for victories and bigger profits. Cynics decried the greed, violence, homophobia, and lingering racism that seemed all too present in the sporting culture, even as certain athletic heroes and heroines upheld the purported idealistic values of sport. Women, in particular, made great strides in athletic participation after the passage of Title IX in 1972.

Young people ill at ease with the commercialized competitions of the mainstream sporting culture initiated a host of alternative sports, only to be coerced, co-opted, and enticed into the mainstream by television networks and marketing companies. As youth continue to question the values of corporate sport, such alternative sport forms may reappear, but one thing is certain: With forty-one million children involved in sports programs in the United States (Carney 21), sport will remain a major component of American culture.

DISCUSSION QUESTIONS

1. How has ESPN revolutionized sport?

2. How does globalization affect sporting practices?

3. Compare the social and economic influences of Muhammad Ali and Michael Jordan.

4. How has commercialization changed the Olympic Games? Intercollegiate sport? Interscholastic sport?

5. Are subsidized stadiums for professional teams good or bad? Why?

6. How do sports halls of fame create and perpetuate particular value systems?

7. How has women's sport changed since the passage of Title IX in 1972?

Chapter 11

Sport in the Early Twenty-First Century
2000–2015

CHAPTER OBJECTIVES

After reading this chapter, you will have learned about the following:

- The increasing commercialization of sport and franchise values
- The issues relevant to the financing of stadiums
- Labor relations and the increasing role of an international labor force
- The realignment of intercollegiate football conferences in the quest for greater revenue
- The greater inclusion and celebrity of female athletes
- The corruption, scandals, and issues that have marred sport's image

In the wake of the 9/11 (2001) terrorist attacks on the United States, President George W. Bush, adorned in a bulletproof vest, strode to the pitcher's mound in Yankee Stadium on the night of October 30, 2001, to deliver the first pitch in Game 3 of the World Series. The world had greatly changed in the previous month and a half. Sport no longer seemed a safe haven; yet amid overwhelming security, a raucous crowd with nationalistic placards, and chants of "USA, USA," Bush delivered more than a pitch. It was a symbolic show of national unity that reinforced the sense of sport as an escape from stress, tension, and tragedy. Over the next decade and beyond, sports event organizers reinforced the perception of sport as patriotic, nationalistic, and heroic. The NFL especially joined with the U.S. military to appropriate an expression of allegiance to the flag and the American military invasion of the Middle East as a retaliatory measure. When Pat Tillman, an NFL player who eschewed his football career to join the army, died in Afghanistan in 2004, the league memorialized him as a war hero, although he had been mistakenly shot by friendly forces. Still, the NFL promoted him as an exemplar of sport and the American way of life. Football reinforced the martial qualities necessary to protect American interests both at home and abroad.

President George W. Bush waves to the crowd as he poses with Joe Torre and Bob Brenly before game 3 of the World Series at Yankee Stadium in New York, October 3, 2001.

© Doug Pensinger/ALLSPORT/Getty Images

Business of Professional Sports Teams

Commercial television ads for the 2003 Super Bowl cost sponsors $2 million for a 30-second spot (Guttmann, *Sports: The First Five Millennia* 154). That figure reached $5 million by 2016. By 2007, the value of NFL franchises had skyrocketed to the point where even the least valuable (the Minnesota Vikings) was worth $720 million, while the Washington, D.C., franchise was assessed at just over $1.4 billion. The year before, the NFL had received nearly $5.5 billion in television revenue, with 59.5 percent of that earmarked for players' salaries (Bergen). Even the lowest-paid NFL head coach made $1.45 million, and some earned as much as $8 million ("Where's the Love?" 86A).

In the ongoing quest to increase revenue, sports team owners pressured municipalities to build new stadiums with the threat of franchise relocation. Taxpayers often absorbed much of the costs of

2002	2004	2006	2008
■ Salt Lake City Winter Olympics, bribery scandal	■ U.S. women's soccer team wins Olympic gold	■ Japan wins the World Baseball Classic	■ Summer Olympics held in Beijing, China

construction. The Los Angeles Rams football stadium complex, dubbed NFL Disney World, is estimated to have cost $2.6 billion, the most expensive such structure ever built (Ponsford).

Despite the severe economic recession of 2008, professional sport continued to enjoy popularity and profit. Athletic stars such as Serena Williams, Tiger Woods, and LeBron James brought new fans to their respective sports with increasing coverage of their exploits.

Australian media mogul Rupert Murdoch acquired the rights to broadcast NASCAR in 2007. In 2013 he launched Fox Sports 2, another 24-hour cable channel. The Fox network has extended its global reach by buying the rights to both the men's and women's World Cup from 2015 to 2022.

With the absence of Michael Jordan from the ranks of NBA players, a new superman appeared: LeBron James. Hailed as a teenage prodigy and drafted number one in 2003, James bypassed college basketball and went directly to the NBA, where his exploits continued to fuel the international growth of the league and his own fame. James won Rookie of the Year honors in his initial season of 2003–2004 and two Olympic gold medals in 2008 and 2012. In 2010, he left the Cleveland Cavaliers to sign with the Miami Heat, where he won two NBA championships in 2012 and 2013 before returning to Cleveland in 2014. As of 2016 he has been named an NBA All-Star 12 times and is a four-time winner of the NBA's Most Valuable Player Award. He has become one of the most popular athletes in the world (Smith, "LeBron James"; www.bleacherreport.com/articles/1709676-has-lebron-james-become-the-most-popular-athlete-in-the-world).

The wealthiest athlete in the world is boxer Floyd Mayweather Jr. Undefeated as of 2015, Mayweather has amassed 10 world titles across

The Cleveland Cavaliers' LeBron James goes up for a jump ball in the 2016 NBA finals.

© Phil Masturzo/Zuma Press/Icon Sportswire

six different weight classes. Like Oscar De La Hoya, he expanded his performances beyond the boxing ring with television appearances. His fights garnered big purses, being the highest paid matches in 2012, 2013, and 2014, bringing his net worth in the latter year up to $216 million (Gems, *Boxing* 176–177).

Diversifying Rosters for Profit

Major League Baseball also experienced growing pains when its Montreal Expos franchise failed to attract enough fans in French-speaking Quebec. During the 2003 and 2004 seasons, the team played some of its "home" games in Puerto Rico, and before the 2005 season it moved to Washington, D.C., and became the Washington Nationals. By that time, the internationalization of the game had come far enough that foreign athletes made up 28 percent of MLB rosters and nearly $100 million in

2010	2016
▪ South Africa hosts World Cup, first African country to do so	▪ Brazil becomes first South American country to host the Olympics

Stadium Construction and Renovation, 2000–2016

Year	Team and stadium	Cost (in millions) to build or renovate
Baseball stadiums		
2000	Detroit Tigers/Comerica Park	$290
	Houston Astros/Minute Maid Park	$266
	San Francisco Giants/AT&T Park	$306
2001	Milwaukee Brewers/Miller Park	$414
	Pittsburgh Pirates/PNC Park	$233
2003	Cincinnati Reds/Great American Ball Park	$361
2004	Philadelphia Phillies/Citizens Bank Park	$458
	San Diego Padres/Petco Park	$456
2006	St. Louis Cardinals/Busch Stadium	$365
2008	Washington Nationals/Nationals Ballpark	$611
2009	New York Mets/Citi Field	$600
	New York Yankees/Yankee Stadium II	$800
2010	Minnesota Twins/Target Field	$480
2012	Florida Marlins/Marlins Ballpark	$420
2017	Sun Trust Park/Atlanta Braves	$622 (estimate)
Football stadiums		
2000	Cincinnati Bengals/Paul Brown Stadium	$452
2001	Denver Broncos/Invesco Field at Mile High	$360
	Pittsburgh Steelers/Heinz Field	$244
2002	New England Patriots/Gillette Stadium	$395
	Detroit Lions/Ford Field	$300
	Houston Texans/Reliant Stadium	$402
	Seattle Seahawks/Qwest Stadium	$430
2003	Green Bay Packers/Lambeau Field	$295 (renovation)
	Chicago Bears/Soldier Field	$632 (renovation)
	Philadelphia Eagles/Lincoln Financial Field	$520
2006	Phoenix Cardinals/University of Phoenix Stadium	$455
2008	Indianapolis Colts/Lucas Oil Stadium	$675
2009	Dallas Cowboys/AT&T Stadium	$1 billion
2009	Miami Dolphins/Dolphin Stadium	$400 (renovation)
2010	New York Giants and New York Jets (shared)/Met Life Stadium	$1.6 billion
2014	Buffalo Bills Stadium	$130 (renovation)
	San Francisco 49ers/Levi's Stadium	$1.2 billion
2016	Los Angeles Rams Stadium	$2.6 billion
	Minnesota Vikings/U.S. Bank Stadium	$1 billion
	Miami Dolphins/Sun Life Stadium	$400 (renovation)
2017	Atlanta Falcons	$1.5 billion

Data from Slezak, Carol. "What's in a name?" *Chicago Sun-Times*, 2 March 2008: 56A; www.ballparks.com, www.ballparksofbaseball.com, www.leagueoffans.org/mlbstadiums1990.html, www.stadiumsofnfl.com, www.indystar.com/apps/pbcs.dll/section?Category=sports0305-47k-, www.proplayerstadium.com/content/architecture.aspx.

international revenue, an 800 percent increase in revenue from 1989 (Jozsa 8, 17).

Team owners began importing top Japanese stars, as well. Bringing in the best athletes might be expensive, but owners incurred little development cost in training these proven stars. Ichiro Suzuki provided virtually guaranteed value for the Seattle Mariners, and indeed he set the major league record for hits in a season with 262 in 2004. As early as 2001, Seattle had established a foothold in Asia by broadcasting its games to Japan. In 2006, the Boston Red Sox paid more than $51 million just for the rights to negotiate with Japanese pitcher Daisuke Matsuzaka, then signed him to a six-year contract worth much more (Browne).

Major League Baseball teams discovered yet another way to maximize profit and establish greater parity in the league: hiring young general managers steeped in the science of analytics. Their judicious selection of players, reliance on tendencies, and consequent strategies enabled small-market teams to compete with large urban markets and turned perennial losers into winners, as evidenced by the Kansas City Royals' defeat of the New York Mets in 2015. The analytics revolution had become pervasive throughout professional sports during the preceding decade, with a growing influence on football and basketball as well.

As baseball, basketball, and football expanded their domains, the NHL followed with its own strategies for growth. In 1997, the league played a game in Japan, and with the fall of the Iron Curtain it began importing more European and Russian players to its ranks. Alex Ovechkin, the superstar left winger for the Washington Capitals, scored his 400th NHL goal in the 2013–2014 season, while Jaromir Jagr reached the 700-goal mark a year later as a right winger for the New Jersey Devils (www.nhl.com/ice/news.htm?id=697071).

Like baseball, the NBA experienced labor strife, including a strike in 1998, and it, too, turned to international players to partially alleviate costs. The value of such athletes became clear in 2002, as Team USA lost to Yugoslavia, Spain, and Argentina in the world championships, finishing thoroughly embarrassed in sixth place. Two years later, the United States finished in third place at the Athens Olympic Games. NBA clinics throughout the world helped promote the game, as did NBA exhibitions in places such as the Dominican Republic, Puerto Rico, Mexico, Spain, France, Italy, Greece, and Japan. Such locations might provide owners with future players at lower cost, not to mention current income from sales of NBA merchandise, such as caps, jerseys, and jackets. In 2002, the NBA broadcast its regular-season games to 212 countries

The Seattle Mariners' Ichiro Suzuki makes a catch at Yankee Stadium, 2012.

(Jozsa 110) and drafted 17 foreign players, among them 7-foot-5-inch (226-centimeter) Yao Ming of China. The next year, an estimated ten million Chinese families tuned in to NBA broadcasts, opening the world's biggest market to NBA products (Jozsa 17). The nature of Yao Ming's contract, a large part of which devolved to the Chinese government, meant that sports skills had become an exportable commodity in that nation's communist economy.

The number of international players in the NBA continued to grow as the league sought larger markets to promote its product and its personalities. By the 2015–2016 season, the NBA counted 100 players from 37 different countries and territories. As part of its 2013–2014 schedule, the league enacted the NBA Global Games, with nine teams playing exhibition as well as regular-season games in six countries: Brazil, China, Germany, Turkey, Mexico, and England. League games were broadcast to 215 countries as basketball challenged soccer as the world's most popular sport (www.nba.com/global).

Marketing U.S. Sports Abroad

Payroll costs might be offset by merchandising in foreign markets. By 2003, MLB was selling products in 109 countries and broadcasting its games to 215. PepsiCo sponsored an Australian baseball league as American popular culture and American products expanded around the world (Miller, Lawrence, McKay, and Rowe 14–17). In 2007, an MLB promotional delegation traveled to Africa; Ghana had fielded its first national baseball team in 1999, and MLB delegates judged it to be a potentially rich source of baseball talent. Young Ghanaian players might someday even replace the declining number of African American players in the league (9 percent of MLB in 2005) and present yet another market for the game (Rogers 6–7). One baseball scout even conducted a national tryout in India, signing two players to the Pittsburgh Pirates' minor league system (Bernstein).

On the international level, Cuba won the Olympic gold medal in baseball in 2004, again using sport as a surrogate form of political conflict. The political significance of sport was on display yet again when the U.S. government threatened to bar Cuba from competing in the 2006 world championship held in the United States.

Also in 2006, Major League Baseball spent $50 million to organize the World Baseball Classic, inviting 16 countries from five continents to participate in the first edition of what is now a quadrennial event. Much to the dismay of American fans,

Japan and Cuba advanced to the title match, with Japan emerging victorious. (Japan had clamored for a true world series with the United States as early as the 1930s.) The competition, intended to develop new markets and new sources of profit (Rojas), was staged as a spectacle not unlike the Summer Olympic Games. Such programming and scheduling heightens interest, raises expectations, increases nationalistic fervor, and builds an international audience and market for subsequent products (an invented tradition).

Japan succeeded in winning the World Baseball Classic again in 2009. In the 2013 tournament, 16 teams from North and South America, the Caribbean, Europe, Asia, and Australia again contested for the world championship, won by the Dominican Republic (web.worldbaseballclassic.com).

The NFL met with less success, as its ventures in Europe could not displace the popularity of soccer, but by 2014 American football had established a beachhead in China. The NFL streamed five live games per week during the season, and in 2013 an eight-team American Football League of China was established with teams throughout the nation (Astiadi). Although not as well established as baseball, the American version of football is played in 71 countries around the world (IFAF).

The international marketing ventures of the NFL amounted to nearly $100 million in 2002, with $16 million of NFL goods sold in Mexico alone. In Russia, the Super Bowl has attracted ten million viewers (Jozsa 76–98).

Labor Relations

The NBA collective bargaining agreement of 2005 was due to expire in 2011; but by 2010 the two sides were arguing over the issue of salary caps and the players' share of the NBA income, which rose to 57 percent. The owners wanted a bigger share. The negotiations broke down once again, resulting in another lockout by the owners. This time the players pursued opportunities to take their skills elsewhere, and some went to the European teams or China. A federal mediator finally intervened to break the deadlock, and a 10-year agreement was reached; but after 161 days of arbitration, the reclaimed season amounted to only a 66-game schedule (http://hoopspeak. com/2011/09/know-your-nba-lockout-history-1999-lockout-calendar/; www.nba.com/2011/ news/09/09/labor-timeline).

The NFL also faced a lockout in 2011 but managed to save the season when owners and players finally reached agreement. Veteran players received bigger salaries, while rookies lost bigger contracts. All players won a reduction in the number and duration of practices. The owners also won an increase in their income, but they did not get the additional 2 games they wanted to extend the season schedule to 18 contests. In the wildly profitable NFL, the fans found little sympathy for either group as millionaires argued with billionaires over their ever-increasing incomes (Union-Tribune).

The NHL expanded to 30 teams, 24 of them located in the United States. The Canadian winter sport migrated southward to such unlikely places as Georgia, Florida, Texas, California, and Arizona, but support proved only lukewarm in some locations. In the 1999–2000 season, the NHL initiated a four-on-four overtime format to boost fan interest, but owners locked out the players in a labor dispute before the start of the 2004–2005 campaign, relegating the NHL to the status of baseball a decade earlier. When the players' union and the

owners could not agree on a salary cap, they forfeited the entire 2004–2005 season. Hockey, like baseball, tried to recapture fans by generating more offense. In 2005, the league placed greater restrictions on goalies and initiated shootouts to settle overtime deadlocks (Podell 93A). In the 2015–2016 season, the NHL adopted a three-on-three overtime format.

Intercollegiate Sport and Conference Changes

The squabbling over collegiate football superiority continued into the twenty-first century, as college presidents and the NCAA refused to agree to a national playoff system for Division I institutions (such systems were already in place for the smaller schools in Division II and Division III). Administrators maintained that the continuation of the long football season only detracted from student-

International Perspective

Fan Cultures and "Sites of Memory"

Soccer fans form close-knit communities held together by their identification with specific "sites of memories" (i.e., soccer teams). They share personal reminiscences and a common collective memory that is based on a synthesis of perceptions, processes of communication, social constructions, and representations. Collective memory integrates individual memories, selects what is memorable, asserts a group's self-assurance and identity, and ensures solidarity and continuity (Misztal 50ff). Misztal describes the interrelationship between individual and collective memories as follows: "Although we are 'participants' in the events as individuals, our memories remain collective because we always think as members of the group to which we belong, because our ideas originated within it and because our thinking keeps us in contact with that group" (Misztal 53).

For historian Pierre Nora, all the immaterial, material, and conceived "anchors for the memory" are entries in the collective memory, which he imagines not only as a process but also as a storage room, like an archive or a museum. Sites of memory are, then, real or imagined "places," the distinguishing features of a group or society, that are connected with specific associations and, above all, the emotions of its members. According to Misztal, memory is "the essential condition of our cognition and reflexive judgment"; it is based on the past and it evokes emotions, such as nostalgia (Misztal 1). Nora was aware of the role of sport as a product of shared memories and a target of collective emotions. He referred to the Tour de France as a means of identifying with France as the "grand nation" (Nora 86). Soccer, too, provides excellent sites of memories because it unifies the fans in their "basking in reflected glory," which is one of the attractions of fandom.

Besides a love of the game, the community of fans is an important incentive for joining one of the real or virtual fan groups that interact not only in the stadium but also via multiple means of virtual communication, especially blogs, tweets, and other forms of social media. The Internet platforms are the modern meeting places of fans who support both their local clubs and their "dream teams." They provide not only an opportunity for identification but also the content for communication. Attendance at live events and participation in virtual dialogues via the Internet enable fans to create identities and to form imagined communities, social networks that are independent of space and time, but they may also give users a sense of belonging and a feeling of meaningfulness.

How have such ideas and new technologies affected fan cultures in the United States?

athletes' academic responsibilities, and an examination of graduation rates for schools involved in bowl games after the 2004 season confirmed this concern. The NCAA allowed students on athletic scholarships six years to complete the normal four-year course of study. Among all Division I institutions, only 54 percent of players managed to complete their curriculum during that time frame. Among those engaged in bowl games, the rates were considerably worse. Although Boston College, Syracuse, and Notre Dame graduated more than 75 percent of their players within the specified time, most institutions fell below the average, and several graduated fewer than a third of their players (Wieberg and Carey 5B).

College players who feel exploited also want larger stipends for living expenses and compensation for the use of their images on commercial products. The NCAA approved of larger stipends for the athletes competing in the top five conferences in 2014; but such battles will continue to appear as the sports revenues grow continually larger and an employer–employee relationship sets players against owners and administrators.

The ever-growing emphasis on commercialization, revenue, recruitment of top athletes, and winning in intercollegiate sport produced a number of scandals in the early twenty-first century. At the University of Miami (Florida), athletics booster Nevin Shapiro admitted to providing cash payments to football and basketball players from 2002 to 2010 as well as entertaining them at strip clubs, providing prostitutes, and even funding an abortion. Shapiro was convicted of defrauding investors in a Ponzi scheme and sentenced to a 20-year prison term. The NCAA punished the university for a "lack of institutional control" by repealing scholarships and temporary suspension from postseason competition (Litke).

The extent to which some schools would go to field winning athletic teams was further revealed in the case of the University of North Carolina, where administrators, teachers, coaches, academic counselors, a departmental chairperson, and even the head of the faculty conspired to register athletes in a phantom course. The students did not attend the course and had no requirements other than to submit a term paper, which may have been written by someone other than themselves. The papers were graded by a clerical assistant, who forged faculty signatures and gave the athletes high grades they didn't earn in order to stay academically eligible for competition. Further, the supervising professor was paid $12,000 for a class that never met. The fraud continued over a period of 18 years and accommodated more than 3,100 students until the sham class was exposed in 2011. Ironically, the faculty chairperson who steered athletes into the class was a philosophy professor and director of the ethics center on campus (Nocera; Lyall; Thomason, "Key Players"; Thomason, "3 Key Findings"; Stripling).

At the end of the 2013 football season, an agreement was reached to determine a true national champion among Division I football powers. A 13-member committee of experts selects and ranks the top 25 teams each week, with the top 4 teams at the end of the season meeting in a playoff. Bowl games host the semifinal games on a rotating basis, and the host city for the national championship game is decided by a bid, similar to the NFL Super Bowl arrangement. The Dr. Pepper soft drink company paid $35 million to sponsor the championship trophy through 2020, and ESPN paid $7.3 billion to televise all the playoff games through 2025 (Seifried; www.collegefootballplayoff.com/story?id=10328143).

The University of Louisville presents a case study of the role of sport in the marketing of an institution. When John W. Shumaker arrived as the new president of the school in 1995, he embarked on a program to enhance the visibility and reputation of the university. He hired Tom Jurich as the athletic director in 1997, and they partnered with broadcast giant ESPN, offering to "play anyone, anywhere, anytime." ESPN soon filled its fall weeknight schedule with Louisville games on Tuesday and Thursday nights, which achieved the desired exposure. In 2001, the university hired Rick Pitino, a celebrated basketball coach, to raise its fortunes in that sport. As the football and basketball teams gained greater stature, the school left Conference USA for greater profits with the Big East Conference and then the Atlantic Coast Conference. By 2012 it began a $252-million building program that included a new football practice facility, baseball and soccer stadiums, both golf and rowing centers, and a natatorium. The university had arrived in the big time (Chudacoff 125–126).

Wealthy fans, known as athletic boosters, some of whom are alumni, donate large sums to college athletic departments, which they can claim as charitable deductions on their tax returns. T. Boone Pickens has donated $165 million to his beloved Oklahoma State University to augment several athletic programs, including football, baseball, track and field, tennis, women's soccer, and the equestrian team. Likewise, Phil Knight, head of Nike, has bestowed $68 million on the University of Oregon for a Football Performance Center,

Big Ten rivals University of Illinois at Urbana-Champaign and Purdue still face off under the reorganized conference.
© Human Kinetics

which has succeeded in attracting top recruits to the team (Chudacoff 136).

The period between 2009 and 2013 witnessed a wholesale reconfiguration of athletic conferences that had previously been organized on a regional basis. As early as 1990, Penn State joined the Big Ten, which had traditionally been a Midwestern league. Throughout the 1990s, other schools began to seek membership in leagues that would offer larger television markets and bigger payouts. Nebraska left the Big 12 conference in 2011 to join the Big Ten, and a scramble ensued across the country for realignment.

By the end of 2013, five top conferences emerged that enrolled the majority of the football powers. The Southeast Conference, which had been a perennial power over the past decade, included Texas A&M and Missouri, both located outside that region. The Big Ten actually consisted of 14 teams with the addition of Rutgers and Maryland. The first provided the conference with entry into the coveted New York television market, while the second offered the Washington, D.C., area. Colorado and Utah had joined the Pac 12 with the West Coast teams and two state universities in Arizona. The Big 12 consisted of only

10 teams, one of which was West Virginia, which incongruously played against teams in the Midwest, Oklahoma, and Texas. Notre Dame, which claimed a national fan following, joined the Atlantic Coast Conference for most sports but chose to retain its independent status for football. Much to the chagrin of fans, such rearrangements meant the loss of annual games with traditional regional rivals that had been developed over the previous century. History, however, meant little in the quest for ever greater profit. Schools in the Southeast Conference partnered with ESPN to establish a regional cable network to televise its athletic teams, earning $35 million for each school, and another $55 million was obtained from the CBS network for additional football coverage. Some schools, such as the University of Texas, created their own cable networks, while all imagined the possibilities of the Internet for the future. Each member of the Big Ten expected to reap $44 million within a few years (Chudacoff 130; Dosch, 2014; www.usatoday.com/story/sports/college/2014/04/24/ncaa-board-of-directors-meeting-big-conference-autonomy/8108647; www.sbnation.com/college-football/2014/2/13/5404930/college-football-realignment-2014-conference-moves).

Coaches who delivered championship teams were rewarded handsomely. Nick Saban, football coach at the University of Alabama, was paid more than $7 million in salary in 2014; while Mike Krzyzewski, basketball coach at Duke University, garnered almost $10 million annually. Those figures do not include bonuses and amenities such as a car, country club memberships, shoe contracts, radio shows, and so on. While Saban and Krzyzewski are the highest paid coaches in their respective sports, Division I football coaches are generally paid much more than the college presidents (Chudacoff 133).

The quest for national championships and the consequent abuses that often accompanied the unbridled pursuit of victory even infected the high school ranks. Television stations lobbied for additional sports programming, and media outlets such as ESPN touted interscholastic rankings and teenage phenoms. LeBron James, a high school basketball sensation, became a national celebrity even before his entry into the NBA, reportedly amassing more than $100 million in endorsements before his first pro game (Guttmann, *Sports: The First Five Millennia* 321). Some high school football teams boasted million-dollar budgets and private planes, and ESPN featured high school football and basketball teams in nationally televised games, touting their abilities in mythical national rankings.

Title IX and Sport Leadership

Since the enactment of Title IX legislation in 1972, girls and women have gained access to virtually all sports, from Little League baseball to collegiate wrestling. Indeed, the feats of female athletes have been among the most impressive achievements in the generation since the enactment of Title IX. Girls' participation in interscholastic sports has risen continually. In 1971, a total of 294,015 girls played high school sports, but by 2013 that figure had grown to 3 million (Summers), and a 2001 survey found that 48 percent of all girls between the ages of 6 and 17 played on an organized team (Eitzen and Sage 318).

In the high school ranks, girls made up 3,222,723 of the athletes, while boys numbered 4,490, 854 in 2013. Whereas female players accounted for only 16,000 of the intercollegiate athletes in 1972 (15 percent), more than 200,000 competed in 2014. Although females neared parity in participation, women made only incremental advancement in leadership roles (www.acostacarpenter.org 1, 6A).

Despite such remarkable growth, Title IX has proved a mixed blessing. Whereas more than 90 percent of women's collegiate teams were coached by females in 1972, that number dwindled to 43.4 percent by 2014. Similarly, female administrators directed 90 percent of women's intercollegiate athletic programs in 1972 but only 22.3 percent by 2014 (www.acostacarpenter.org 6A). Male athletic directors retained their power when programs merged, and they tended to hire other men as head coaches (Acosta and Carpenter 64).

Under the NCAA, 80 percent of American universities still had not reached compliance with gender equity standards in 2004, more than 30 years after Title IX became law. And although women accounted for 56 percent of all college students in 2003, they received only 36 percent of athletic budget funding and only 32 percent of the money allocated for athletic scholarships (Priest 29; Yiamouyiannis 53). In 2003, men held the vast majority of NCAA leadership roles, including that of president, 15 of the 20 positions on the executive committee, and all of the conference commissioners' offices at the Division I-A level (Lapchick). In 2014, men still continued to hold the vast majority of NCAA leadership roles, including president, although women had gained some positions on the board of directors.

Women have made great strides in executive positions in sports administration at the professional level, yet they remain underrepresented. In the NFL, women held 21 positions at or above the vice-presidential level in 2014, an increase of 5 percent over the previous season. In the NBA, 42 women held such ranks in the 2013–2014 season, and 3 women (Jeanie Buss of the Los Angeles Lakers, Matina Kolokotronis of the Sacramento Kings, and Karen Gail Miller, controlling owner of the Utah Jazz) held ownership. Among the franchises, 58 women held vice-presidential duties, 16.6 percent of the total. In MLB, women filled 30 percent of the jobs in the league office in 2014, but that represented a decrease of 5.6 percent from the previous season. Among senior executives, women accounted for 21.4 percent, a slight drop from 2013. Four teams listed women as partial owners, and 61 women held vice-presidential rank in 24 franchises. Some people have voiced concern over the seeming retrenchment in MLB and the slow pace of change; but the area in which gender inequity is most noticeable is in sports media, where women represent a distinct minority, and almost all sports editors remain white males, who opt to hire other white males. A 2010 study found that "the percentage of sports editors who were women or people of color fell 2.3 percentage points from 11.7 percent in 2008 to 9.42 percent in 2010. White males in particular increased by 3.0 percentage points for sports editors" (Moritz).

Women's Professional Teams and Endorsements

More than 260 women were competing on the LPGA tour by 2002 (Eitzen and Sage 329). They included an international coterie of entrants from Europe and Asia, as well as the United States. Michelle Wie, from Hawaii, qualified for her first LPGA event at the age of 12 in 2002. A year later, she played in a men's PGA tournament. Although women's sports organizations expanded and viewers became more accepting of women on the golf tour, the top female players earned only a fraction of the men's purses, and female golfers deemed pretty, "domestic," or fashionable garnered a greater share of the limited endorsement money than those considered less feminine.

Some female tennis stars have attracted more media coverage for their appearance than for their play on the court. Anna Kournikova reached star status based on her glamorous appeal, although she had never won a major tournament, whereas Venus and Serena Williams combined top-level talent with beauty in their rise to the top echelon, and their combination of power and sexuality heightened interest in women's tennis. By 2002, the number of professional female tennis players had more than tripled from 1977, and the best players earned prize money equivalent to that of some of their male counterparts (Eitzen and Sage 328). Despite the recriminations of some feminists, sex became a primary attraction on the women's tennis circuit.

The Williams sisters dominated professional tennis for more than a decade. They both achieved the number one world ranking and have won multiple Grand Slam events along with four Olympic gold medals each. Like other New Age athletes, their interests and business activities extend well beyond sport. Venus has a clothing and apparel line as well as an interior design business. Serena has been an actress, author, and model, and she sells clothing, jewelry, and purses. Both sisters are part owners of the Miami Dolphins pro football franchise. Despite their success on and off the court, the media often focused on their physicality and derided their entrepreneurial ventures as a lack of focus on their sport (Edmondson; www.biography.com/people/venus-williams-9533011#off-the-court-

pursuits&awesm=~oIemQJJS8FOEgq). Despite Serena's dominance on the court over several years, lower-ranked Maria Sharapova's endorsement deals doubled that of Serena Williams in 2015, evidence of continuing bias (Bunn).

The Women's Sports Foundation, an ardent supporter and promoter of female athletic endeavors and equality, has objected to the use of sexual displays as a marketing device. The Olympic Games, however, have harbored no such qualms, even requiring beach volleyball players to wear skimpy and revealing bikinis to attract television viewers, though these dress regulations were relaxed in 2012. A similar approach accompanied the growth of women's boxing at the 2010 world championships when the International Boxing Association tried to force combatants to wear skirts instead of shorts. Most women refused to submit, and a female reporter explained that "they're

Serena Williams at the Mutua Madrid Open Tennis Tournament, May 2015.

© Oscar Gonzalez/WENN.com/age fotostock

punching the crap out of each other and they're trying to make them look sexy. . . . Let's be honest, it's all about television and selling females. It's all about marketing" (Gems, *Boxing* 234). With the advent of women's boxing at the 2012 Olympics, the organizers accorded only 3 weight classes for the women, but men got 10. A 17-year-old American, Claressa Shields, won the gold medal in the middleweight class.

Female boxers challenged the traditional gender roles and social boundaries; but other athletes continued to promote their bodies rather than their skills as a means to greater acceptance. Three years after her Olympic victory, Claressa Shields still had no endorsements. Conversely, swimmer Jenny Thompson, winner of seven Olympic gold medals (from 1992 to 2004), posed wearing only shorts for *Sports Illustrated* magazine in 2000, and the U.S. Olympic women's swimming team shunned its suits altogether as they draped an American flag around their naked bodies for a publicity shot. Eros thus became a more overt factor in sports marketing despite the concerns of both moralists and feminists.

The women's national soccer team has experienced similar woes. After hosting and winning the 1999 World Cup in a dramatic double overtime, the women's team created "soccer fever" among American fans. The frenzy, however, proved short-lived. Brandi Chastain, the heroine in the victory, got greater attention for her postgame celebration in which she ripped her jersey off after scoring the winning goal and later for posing nude in *Gear magazine* and in *ESPN The Magazine*'s body issue. Multiple attempts to maintain a women's professional soccer league have ended in failure, despite the success of the women's team greatly exceeding that of the national men's team. By 2016, the women had garnered four Olympic championships and three World Cup titles yet were paid only about 25 percent of what the male players earned. The women's team sued U.S. Soccer in 2016 for more equitable pay ("U.S. Women's Team").

Modern Olympic Challenges and Stars

With national pride and global recognition at stake, the bidding for both the Summer and Winter Games became intense, resulting in a major scandal involving the 2002 Games, hosted by Salt Lake

U.S. soccer players after winning the 2015 FIFA Women's World Cup.
© Franck Fife/AFP/Getty Images

City. Allegations of widespread improprieties surfaced, leading to charges of bribery by the bid committee that included not only cash payments, lavish gifts, and donations but also tuition payments for IOC members' relatives to American universities, medical treatments, and "excessive hospitality" for the visiting dignitaries. An IOC member admitted that such largesse had been commonplace since at least 1990. The debacle tarnished the image and the integrity of the IOC and resulted in the expulsion of 10 members and the sanctioning of 10 more (McLaughlin).

The IOC established new rules for bids and limited the number of its visitors to future sites. The profits to be made only increased with the selection of host cities in new markets such as Australia, China, Russia, and Brazil. NBC bid $3.5 billion for the rights to the 2002 to 2008 Games, a figure that reached $4.4 billion for the 2014 to 2020 Games. The Olympic gold mine guaranteed greater exposure for the Games, the host cities, and the corporate sponsors in a capitalistic frenzy of excess that showed no signs of abatement until continual cost overruns and security issues deterred potential suitors by 2016 (Flyvberg and Stewart; "Commercialization").

Americans have generally fared well in the Winter Games, amassing the second most medals behind Norway. Asian American figure skater Michelle Kwan retired in 2006 after winning nine national championships, five world championships, and two Olympic medals. Tara Lipinski captured the gold medal in figure skating in 1998, followed by Sarah Hughes in 2002, while Evan Lysacek won Olympic gold in 2010. Meryl Davis and Charlie White partnered to win the Olympic ice dancing crown in 2014. Apolo Anton Ohno has been the most successful American speedskater since 2002, winning eight Olympic medals and the world championship in 2008.

Among the skiers, Bode Miller has won several Olympic medals including a gold in 2010, and Ted Ligety won gold in both 2006 and 2014. The American women have been equally successful, with Julia Mancuso, Lindsey Vonn, and Mikaela Shiffrin each winning an Olympic championship between 2006 and 2016. American snowboarders have been dominant on the slopes since the sport was introduced to the Winter Games in 1998. Ross Powers won three gold medals, one each in 2002, 2006, and 2010, while Shaun White thrilled fans with wins in 2006 and 2010. Sage Kotsenburg followed with another gold medal in 2014. Female snowboarders also fared well, with Kelly Clark winning a gold medal in 2002, followed by gold medalists Hannah Teter in 2006 and Kaitlyn Farrington and Jamie Anderson at the 2014 Games.

Aquatic sports rarely gain notice among the array of athletic possibilities in America; but Michael Phelps has made the biggest splash since Mark Spitz won seven gold medals at the 1972 Olympic Games. Phelps first swam in Olympic competition in 2000 at the age of 15. Four years later he won eight medals (six gold, two silver) and followed that performance with eight golds and seven world records in 2008. He returned yet again in 2012 to claim six more medals (five gold). In his final Olympic Games in 2016, Phelps added five more gold medals and a silver to his collection. His 28 Olympic medals (23 gold) far surpass any other modern Olympian (Teetzel, "Michael Phelps").

Sporting Crises

Although sports in general have a huge following and enjoy popular support, seeming feats of athletic excellence are often called into question as some of the greatest performers seek even further

Michael Phelps during the medal ceremony for the men's 4 x 100-meter medley relay final at the 2016 Summer Olympics.

© AP Photo/Rebecca Blackwell

enhancement of their abilities through illegal and unethical means.

Doping

In 2004, Jason Giambi, a power hitter for the New York Yankees, admitted to steroid use and implicated Barry Bonds and others associated with the Bay Area Lab Cooperative (BALCO). Victor Conte, the lab owner, claimed he had supplied the drugs to top football players and world-class track stars as well. Marion Jones finally admitted her guilt in 2007 after years of denial. She was forced to surrender the five Olympic medals won in 2000 and sentenced to a six-month prison term for check fraud and lying while under oath. Public and journalistic outcries, along with a government inquiry, finally forced baseball authorities to address the issue, but commissioner Bud Selig responded with a weak testing and enforcement policy until a congressional investigation forced more stringent measures including a 50-game suspension for first-time offenders.

Selig asked George Mitchell, a former U.S. senator, to conduct an investigation into the use of steroids by baseball players. The Mitchell Report was released in 2007 and found rampant use, naming several big stars among the 100 positive tests. Top players such as Roger Clemens, seven-time Cy Young Award winner as the best pitcher in baseball, and Barry Bonds, who became the all-time home run leader, were suspected and eventually indicted. Clemens was found not guilty and Bonds found guilty of perjury; but suspicions remained so entrenched that neither was voted into the Hall of Fame despite their long, record-breaking careers (Balfour and Odenheimer).

Despite the best efforts of the World Anti-Doping Agency (WADA) and the United States Anti-Doping Agency (USADA), athletes persisted in trying to outwit detection by the governing bodies, and performance-enhancing drugs seemed particularly rampant on the European cycling tour. In 1986, Greg LeMond became the first American to win the prestigious Tour De France, succeeding despite a hunting accident that nearly claimed his life, and he repeated his victory in 1989 and 1990. Next up was Lance Armstrong, who succeeded LeMond as America's greatest cyclist. Armstrong overcame a bout of testicular cancer to claim seven consecutive Tour de France wins from 1999 through 2005, despite repeated but unproven allegations of performance-enhancing drug use. Thirteen riders were banned from the 2006 cycling circuit for blood doping, but Americans paid little attention until

Floyd Landis, winner of the Tour de France, failed drug tests for testosterone usage and forfeited his crown (*Mercury Sport* 24).

The USADA charged Armstrong with the use of PEDs in 2012. After constant denials, Armstrong finally made a public televised confession of his guilt in 2013. He was stripped of his Tour de France titles, and the International Cycling Union imposed a lifetime ban.

Violence in Sport

In 2007, Michael Vick, the star quarterback of the Atlanta Falcons, pleaded guilty to animal cruelty charges for running illegal dogfights. Vick had been drafted first overall in 2001; and his 2007 contract with the Falcons made him the highest paid athlete at $130 million over 10 years, with a $37 million signing bonus. But his involvement with the dogfights both tarnished his image and sent him to prison, where he languished for 18 months. The Falcons dismissed him from the team, and he was forced into bankruptcy, until the Philadelphia Eagles and a repentant media campaign offered him redemption. Vick moved to the New York Jets in 2014, where his behavior would be thoroughly analyzed in the media center of the world (Elovaara).

Ben Roethlisberger, the star quarterback of the Pittsburgh Steelers, incurred great media scrutiny when he was accused of rape in 2008 and another sexual assault in 2010. Although he escaped formal charges, commissioner Roger Goodell suspended him for four games for violations of the NFL's personal conduct policy and disparaging the league's integrity and reputation (Bellisle; http://sports.espn.go.com/nfl/news/story?id=5527564).

The endemic nature of football violence became obvious in 2012 with the discovery that the New Orleans Saints conducted a bounty system during the 2009 to 2011 seasons, offering defensive players bonuses as incentives to purposely injure opponents. The apparent perpetrator, defensive coordinator Gregg Williams, had engaged in similar affairs with three previous teams he had coached. Other team officials condoned the practice. The NFL commissioner, Roger Goodell, imposed an indefinite suspension on Williams, a one-year suspension on head coach Sean Payton, an eight-game suspension on general manager Mickey Loomis, and a six-game suspension on assistant coach Joe Vitt, plus a $500,000 fine and the loss of draft picks. Players received suspensions ranging from one game to a full year. The negative publicity surrounding the case only reinforced the violent mentality fostered within the game (Maske; http://espn.go.com/nfl/topics/_/page/new-orleans-saints-bounty-scandal).

Even more damning than the Saints' on-field carnage and Vick's association with off-field violence, Aaron Hernandez, a star tight end for the New England Patriots, was indicted for the 2013 murder of a friend. In 2014, Hernandez faced double murder charges for an unrelated incident that had happened in 2012.

Football scandals involving off-field violence exploded in 2014 when Ray Rice, a star running back for the Baltimore Ravens, was caught on videotape as he punched and knocked out his girlfriend during a dispute in a hotel elevator then dragged her out into the hallway. Commissioner Roger Goodell issued only a two-game suspension, which raised the ire of numerous fans and women's rights organizations. A social media campaign ensued that called for the ouster of the commissioner, who relented by banning Rice indefinitely from the NFL. Although the Rice affair garnered the headlines, more than 30 other NFL players were under investigation or charged with domestic abuse at the time, and Jerry Angelo, former general manager of the Chicago Bears, who had spent 30 years in the NFL, admitted that teams had covered up hundreds of such cases during that time in order to keep players on the field. NFL troubles only increased when one of its premier running backs, Adrian Peterson of the Minnesota Vikings, was indicted for beating his four-year-old son with a tree branch, for which he was also suspended from competition. Such incidents raised questions about social-class differences in the manner of disciplining one's children and, more important, whether aggressive sports such as football promote violence on and off the field (Telander, "Switching" 73; Morrissey).

Gambling

Baseball wasn't the only sport that had image issues. In 2007 Tim Donaghy, an NBA referee, was caught betting on games in which he officiated and passing confidential information to mobsters as well. An investigation found widespread gambling among referees, and Donaghy charged that referees were in collusion with the NBA to prolong playoff series and that certain players received favored treatment, while others were unliked and became the victims of phantom calls or no calls when fouled. Donaghy went to prison, and the NBA revised gambling rules for the referees (Tuohy; www.cbsnews.com/news/ex-nba-ref-tim-donaghys-personal-foul).

Homophobia

Greater acceptance of an individual's sexuality seemed to have made some progress when a trio of well-known athletes announced their homosexuality. After the 2012–2013 season, Jason Collins, a 12-year veteran of the NBA, announced that he was gay, the first active player to do so. Although generally praised and supported for his openness, he garnered no interest as a free agent in the off-season. Collins eventually signed a contract with the Brooklyn Nets in February 2014 and finished out the 2013–2014 season. A measure of acceptance could also be seen in his hiring by a number of major corporations as a spokesman for their products in their attempt to broaden their market among the gay community. Female basketball sensation Brittney Griner, who led Baylor to an undefeated season and a national championship in 2012 before joining the Phoenix Mercury of the WNBA, made her homosexuality public in 2013 as well. Although Baylor, a Christian school, asked her not to publicize her sexuality while at the institution, the WNBA more fully embraces its large lesbian fan base. On the football field, Michael Sam, an All-American at the University of Missouri and the Southeastern Conference Defensive Player of the Year in 2013, openly stated his sexuality and was drafted as a defensive end by the St. Louis Rams, becoming the first openly gay player on an NFL roster (Telander, "Gay Pitchmen"). Sam was later cut by both the Rams and the Dallas Cowboys, then he briefly sought employment with the Montreal Alouettes of the Canadian Football League without success.

The Gay Games, similar to the Olympics, have been conducted every four years since 1982 when they were organized by Tom Waddell, a former U.S. Olympic decathlete. Unlike the Olympics, there are no qualifying standards, and anyone may enter the competitions. Intended to support the lesbian, gay, bisexual, and transgender (LGBT) communities, the Gay Games now attract as many participants as the traditional Olympics, and international bid cities reflect their global reach (www.gg9cle.com).

Female athletes also faced disparaging inquiries relative to their gender. Although not an American, South African Caster Semenya, world champion runner at 800 meters in 2009, was subjected to gender testing after doubts and allegations about her sex. The resultant examination and public discourse cost her a year of competition and international embarrassment before she was reinstated. The finding that she had an elevated level of testosterone and her winning the 800-meter gold medal at the 2016 Rio Olympics only reignited the controversy.

Similarly the case of Bruce Jenner, the 1976 Olympic decathlon champion whoss very public transition to Caitlyn Jenner in 2015 brought worldwide attention to issues of gender and identity. Such issues have since filtered down to interscholastic levels as transgendered youth opt to play on athletic teams of their choosing, forcing school boards and state athletic associations to rule on eligibility issues, with mixed results.

Draft pick Michael Sam during a press conference at Rams Park on May 13, 2014 in Earth City, Missouri.

© Dilip Vishwanat/Getty Images

Sexual Predators

In 1997, Canadians suffered the trauma of sexual deviancy in their beloved game of hockey when Gordon Stuckless, a former teacher and coach and later the equipment manager at Maple Leaf Gardens in Toronto, was convicted of molesting 24 boys on more than 300 occasions. He got a relatively light sentence of four years. Then Theo Fleury, an NHL player, revealed that his coach at the junior level had also abused him. Graham James, the coach, admitted to abusing other players as well and was sentenced to five years in 2011. The horror repeated itself when Stuckless was paroled in 2001 and sexually assaulted another 17 children. The perception of coaches as role models suffers serious doubt under such circumstances.

That question extended to coaches and administrators in the United States as well when one of the biggest scandals in intercollegiate sport history exploded in 2011. Jerry Sandusky, a former assistant football coach at Penn State, was convicted of sexually molesting numerous boys over several years. Although Sandusky was no longer employed by the school when this was discovered, he had access to the institution and its facilities, to which he lured children with gifts and favors through his foundation, allegedly established to help underprivileged children. The university president and athletic director were implicated in a cover-up of the scandal, and famed coach Joe Paterno was also punished. Sandusky received a minimum of 30 years in

prison; the university president resigned and was indicted, as was the athletic director, who was fired. Paterno lost not only his job but also the honor of holding the most wins in NCAA history after the NCAA revoked all his football victories from 1998 to 2011 (eventually reinstated). Paterno died of cancer only two months after his expulsion, while further punishment lingered for the institution. The NCAA levied a four-year ban on postseason play and a $60 million fine, to which the Big Ten Conference added another $13 million. By 2013 the university paid out nearly $60 million in settlements to victims, but the court cases would continue for years, and no amount of money could reclaim the damage done to those molested (Smith, *Wounded Lions*; www.cnn.com/SPECIALS/us/penn-state-scandal).

The NFL, beset with domestic and child abuse scandals in 2014, suffered similar reproach when its players proved promiscuous as well. It was reported that star running back Adrian Peterson fathered six children with as many women. Receiver Santonio Holmes produced three children out of wedlock, while revered linebacker Ray Lewis and running back Marshall Faulk each fathered six, and Hall of Famer Derrick Thomas was responsible for seven. As if such licentiousness were a badge of one's masculinity and potency, such totals paled in comparison to running back Travis Henry, who sired eleven children (Telander, "Switching" 73).

People & Places

Casey Martin

One athlete, whose physical limitations affected his performance, successfully sued the Professional Golf Association. Despite a medical condition that made it difficult to walk, Casey Martin had been a successful collegiate golfer because the NCAA granted him permission to ride in a golf cart during competitions. When the PGA refused such a compensation, Martin's case reached the United States Supreme Court in 2001, which ruled that even professional athletic associations must adhere to the accommodations required by the Americans with Disabilities Act of 1990 (Schultz et al., "Casey Martin").

Racism

In an effort to increase minorities in the ranks of NFL head coaches, the league adopted the Rooney Rule in 2003. Before that time, the NFL compared poorly with the number of minority coaches in MLB and the NBA. Dan Rooney, owner of the Pittsburgh Steelers franchise, headed the committee that established the NFL policy. The rule dictated that when a vacancy for a head coaching position occurred, the team must interview at least one minority coach for that job. The policy has produced uneven results. There were only two minority head coaches in 2002 but eight by 2011. That figure slipped to four by 2014 (Thiel and Bukstein).

Ownership reflects a similar lack of diversity. Of the 122 major professional sport franchises (32 in the NFL, 30 each in the NBA, the NHL, and MLB), Michael Jordan holds a majority share of the Carolina Hornets in the NBA, and Vivek Ranadivé, born in India, owns the Sacramento Kings. Arte Moreno, a Hispanic, is the owner of the Anaheim Angels team in MLB, and Shahid Khan, born in Pakistan, owns the Jacksonville Jaguars of the NFL. Charles Wang, born in Shanghai, China, is the only nonwhite owner in the NHL as head of the New York Islanders (Chalabi; www.diversityinc.com/news/major-league-white-pro-spotsarent-what-they-seem).

The white ownership ranks were reduced by one when Donald Sterling, owner of the Los Angeles Clippers of the NBA since 1981, made racist comments on the Internet that drew immediate criticism from players, fans, and the media during the 2014 playoffs. Players considered a labor strike, and the NBA's new commissioner, Adam Silver, moved quickly to force Sterling to sell the team. Silver also imposed a lifetime ban on any association with the league (Chalabi). The Clippers were sold to Steve Ballmer, the former CEO of Microsoft, for the astronomical sum of $2 billion, restoring white ownership to the franchise.

The Sterling debacle forced other leagues to consider racial issues; the NFL pressured the Washington Redskins to adopt a new name, but owner Daniel Snyder refused. Many fans and other owners consider the name in poor taste and insulting to Native Americans. Some owners are concerned that it hurts marketing opportunities and league revenue as pressure continues for both ethical and commercial reasons. Similar concerns continue to confront the owners of the Cleveland Indians and the Atlanta Braves, indicating that despite claims to the contrary, the United States has not yet achieved a postracial society.

Traumatic Brain Injury

Perhaps the most imminent threat to sport comes from the very nature of some sport forms. Contact sports such as football, soccer, and hockey produce bigger collisions when played by bigger, stronger, faster bodies. When those collisions involve the head, concussions are too often the result. The large number of former athletes who experience dementia and suicidal depression have resulted in class action suits against the NFL and the NHL as well as unionization efforts by college athletes for compensation and better insurance. A growing number of studies have shown that youth, especially girls, may be more susceptible to head trauma as their brains are still growing and that repeated blows to the head, even relatively minor ones, can produce long-lasting effects. Consequently U.S. Soccer has banned heading of the ball for youth aged 10 and under; and Pop Warner football has discontinued the kickoff in football games to avoid collisions. At the professional level, more than 4,500 former NFL players have sued the league, which agreed to a $765 million settlement in 2013. (www.nytimes.com/2014/04/20/sports/hockey/hockey-players-concussion-suits-follow-path-charted-in-nfl-cases.html; Greenstein).

X Games and Alternative Sports

The inherent risk, the rebellious image, and the opportunity for self-expression attracted multitudes to new sport forms in a counterculture set apart from the competitive capitalist model (Beal). Snowboarding grew from 1.6 million participants in 1992 to 3.6 million in 1999, and skateboarders numbered more than 11.5 million by the turn of the century (Barcett; Dean). By 2005, females composed at least one-third of the snowboarders and surfers and more than one-quarter of the skateboarders (Thorpe 219). By the last decade of the twentieth century, however, sport promoters and clothing designers had succeeded in co-opting the activities and fashions for mainstream structures. Surfing, snowboarding, and skateboarding accounted for $9.9 billion a year by 2006, with nearly 80 percent of the expenditure on clothing, shoes, and accessories (Thorpe 219). ESPN featured the X Games competition beginning in 1999, and even the Olympics adopted snowboarding in 1998. Within a few years, skateboarder Tony Hawk and motocross rider Jeremy McGrath ranked among the most recognized athletes among American youth. Marketed and managed by sports agencies, Hawk and surfing champ Kelly Slater became multimillionaires, and even lower-level competitors earned $250,000 per year, equivalent to the minimum salaries of NFL rookies. The incorporation of such rebel sports into the corporate media complex became clear by 2006, when Kevin Monahan, vice president of NBC Sports, announced that the lack of paying spectators at live events was inconsequential. "The tour's about providing programming for the network and Universal, USA, NBC wireless, Internet broadband, Universal DVD, and Telemundo. All those channels can replay parts of the tour, edit highlight shows, or sell DVDs of the gnarliest [best] tricks" (qtd. in Dean 55).

One of the X Games stars, snowboarder Shaun White, fashioned some of those tricks. White became a professional snowboarder at the early age of 13 and soon had his own equipment and clothing lines. He became a professional skateboarder as well in 2003. He won gold medals at the 2006 and 2010 Winter Olympics and has branched out into other entertainment ventures with his own video game and movies and as a member of a rock band. White has been ranked as high as the second most powerful athlete in the world, and one of his sponsors, Red Bull, even built him a private training facility with a 500-foot (150-meter)

Shaun White is one of many athletes to popularize alternative sports, with his skills on the halfpipe drawing crowds and media attention to snowboarding. He is shown here at the 2014 Winter Olympics in Sochi, where the audience remained despite a fourth-place finish.
© Cameron Spencer/Getty Images

superpipe so he might invent new snowboarding tricks, bringing greater interest to the sport and profit to his corporate sponsors (Poniatowski).

The previously regional activity of stock car racing produced national heroes as it mushroomed from its Southern origins to become the fastest-growing sport. By 2000, only football drew a larger percentage of television viewers than NASCAR (*Sports Illustrated* 121), whose events typically drew nine million television viewers by 2003, and the sport claimed thirty-five million fans a year later (Cobb, *Away* 324). Departing from its rural and male roots, stock car racing attracted urbanites, and nearly half its fan base consisted of women. Shawna Robinson, a female driver, became one of the attractions when she entered the Winston Cup series of races in 2001.

NASCAR achieved explosive growth by merging technology, corporate sponsorship, and a nostalgic sense of rugged individualism attributed to those who push the limits. In 1998, racing fans purchased $950 million in NASCAR paraphernalia (MacCambridge 284). In 1999, television rights to Winston Cup races sold for $6 billion over six years. Dale Earnhardt's aggressive driving style earned him the nickname "the Intimidator" and the love of hard-core fans. Drivers accumulated points based on their order of finish in a series of races, and Earnhardt dominated the standings during the 1990s, earning more than $3 million a year and eventually capturing the elusive Daytona 500 in 1998. By 2001, he had reached $41 million in prize money before dying in a fiery crash on the last lap of the Daytona 500. NASCAR fans mourned the loss of the auto racing dignitary for years afterward but transferred their loyalty to his son and successor, Dale Earnhardt Jr.

Both NASCAR drivers and the drag racers of the National Hot Rod Association (NHRA) belied the lower-class images of their initial years as the costs of participation increased. Many teams on the former circuit required corporate sponsors, and even NHRA participants had to sustain the maintenance and replacement of parts for cars that exceeded 250 miles (400 kilometers) per hour. For drag racers, a $1,000 set of tires lasted about 10 trials, and a crankshaft could cost $2,500. Cars themselves cost as much as $150,000. Competitive racing at higher levels was no longer a poor man's sport. Nor was it exclusively male, as an increasing number of females piloted the four-wheeled missiles. One female competitor at the 2003 Darlington Nationals in Hartsville, South Carolina, stated, "I like going fast, but I like winning more than anything. . . . [Y]ou earn a lot of respect by winning" (Warren 116). By 2005, the diminutive Danica Patrick had emerged as a rising star on the Indy Racing League circuit. Sport served such women as a vehicle for dismantling traditional gender roles.

Sports Across the Populace

Such courage continued to reinforce the heroic qualities of sport for some, while it held different meanings for diverse ethnic, racial, religious, gender, social, political, economic, and age groups; sport is not heroic for all but rather a means to a livelihood, leisure, identity, and so on. The elderly continually push physical boundaries in masters' competition. The ever-increasing salaries offered to professional athletes enticed several prodigies, such as Michelle Wie in golf, to embark on early sports careers. Freddy Adu entered the ranks of Major League Soccer with DC United as a 14-year-old in 2004. Venus and Serena Williams joined the

Danica Patrick and Dale Earnhardt Jr. before the 2014 NASCAR Sprint Cup Series.
© AP Photo/Matt Slocum, File

professional tennis tour at the same age. In 1998, Kevin Garnett entered the NBA as a 19-year-old, and during the 2003–2004 season 18-year-old basketball phenom LeBron James won Rookie of the Year honors with the Cleveland Cavaliers. Such success fueled unrealistic dreams for millions of other young Americans and spawned an ever-growing industry of youth travel teams, with parental expectations of winning collegiate athletic scholarships for their offspring.

Both urban and suburban communities throughout the United States offer a plethora of recreational activities for residents. For the more competitive older athletes, masters' championships are offered at the state, regional, national, and international level. Youth soccer, baseball, football, basketball, tennis, volleyball, and hockey programs are ubiquitous at local levels. During the winter months, skiing and ice skating are enjoyable recreation options. Participation in golf and bowling has declined, and although many people engage in fitness activities, few do so regularly, resulting in higher levels of obesity, heart disease, diabetes, and other ailments that beset the American health care system (www.whitehutchinson.com/leisure/articles/whats-happening-to-bowling.shtml). CrossFit training is one activity, however, that has enjoyed explosive growth over the past two decades to become an international enterprise. The CrossFit Games, an international event sponsored by Reebok, are regularly televised on ESPN.

Rise of the Runner

One activity that has prospered is running. The jogging craze of the 1970s has spawned a cultural lifestyle that transcends race, social class, gender, and age as people run daily for exercise and its concomitant health benefits. Each year millions participate in fun runs and charity events at a

International Perspective

Urban Spaces: Challenges and Changes

In the wake of the rediscovery of "the world around us" and a new focus on health, the environment is seen as an important aspect in personality development of children and as an asset with regard to health and the quality of life of adults. Theoretical approaches to socialization provide insights into the way people learn about the world and how they mentally and physically acquire and use the environment. Physicality and physical activity play a major role in the formation of identity and the development of competencies as well as in the acquirement and maintenance of social networks and resources. Depending on needs and wishes, spaces can be appropriated and redefined: A park can be used as a soccer ground, and stairs can be obstacles for skateboarders.

Most American cities do not provide many opportunities for discovery and appropriation of the environment, not the least because of the fragmentation and isolation of spheres—homes, work places, shops, schools, and places for leisure are in different zones that may be reached only by car. In addition, neither suburbs nor cities provide a large number of opportunities for informal play and for recreational physical activities for adults. However, some cities, particularly in northern and central Europe, have re-created the urban environment to provide spaces that invite various groups and encourage multiple uses.

The Danish capital, Copenhagen, is an excellent example of a city with high aspirations for a clean environment and for a physically active population. Striving to be the first carbon-neutral city, the government encourages cycling on designated street lanes and restricts driving (e.g., via high taxes). Copenhagen is surrounded by water, and the inner city harbor and the canals were sanitized to invite swimming and other water sports. Many places in the city have been redesigned, offering fitness equipment, skateboard parks, basketball courts, swings, and even a boxing ring to encourage various games and physical activities. Such places are very popular among people of every age; they even attract migrant girls and women, who find spaces in such areas conducive to socializing.

Throughout the city, buildings are refashioned to accommodate the interests of the inhabitants of both genders and all age groups, with numerous parkways, jogging and cycling trails, and neighborhood sports clubs for more competitive activities. Many ideas for a "sportification" of the city have been developed or supported by a state-funded agency, which encourages new ideas for making Denmark a physically active and healthier society.

Marathons and organized fun runs are now common events across the United States.

© Human Kinetics

variety of distances: 5K, 10K, half marathons, marathons, and ultraendurance events such as the Western States 100 mile race. An international circuit of marathons attracts more affluent sport tourists. The Boston Marathon, oldest of the American events, is an iconic race that requires qualifying times. Some athletes combine swimming and cycling with running in triathlon competitions, most notably the annual Ironman competition in Hawaii. American colleges now offer triathlon teams.

The endurance running boom and triathlon events that emerged in the latter decades of the twentieth century have morphed into mud runs and obstacle course races of varying distances, for both individuals and teams, that have gained local television coverage. Other local events in foreign countries have gained popularity in the United States courtesy of the Internet. Dragon boat racing, which has been commonplace in China for thou-

sands of years, can now be seen on some college campuses and at community events in America.

The Future of Sport

The transitions in sport and new sport forms will continue to fuel dreams well into the future. Whereas boxing offered hope for many impoverished youth during the first decades of the twentieth century, by the turn of the twenty-first century new forms of violent sport, such as mixed martial arts (MMA) and the Ultimate Fighting Championship (UFC) had surpassed interest in boxing in the United States. The MMA format combines boxing with wrestling and jiu-jitsu. The sport originated in Brazil and made its first appearance in the United States in 1993. The violent nature of the bouts met with Congressional opposition, and they were banned in New York. MMA found a home on

International Perspective

Ultimate Running

Running is a central human capacity. To quickly cover long distances enabled human beings to survive in various times and environments. Running served numerous purposes such as traveling, transporting goods, and relaying messages to religious rituals.

Running contests were and still are important events in sport competitions. Since the emergence of modern sport in the nineteenth century, an increasing number of runs over various distances have been organized in numerous places and contexts. One of the most prestigious disciplines and once seemingly the ultimate test of human endurance is the marathon, a race of 26 miles (42 kilometers). However, an increasing number of runners began to master this distance. Athletes who wanted to distinguish themselves had to find new challenges such as ultraendurance events requiring performance exceeding 6 hours. Currently, 6-, 12-, 24-, and 48-hour events over distances from a marathon to more than 124 miles (200 kilometers) are organized all over the world.

The increasing number of such events indicates the popularity of extreme running. Examples include the Spartathlon, a race of 153 miles (246 kilometers) from Athens to Sparta, and the Badwater, run over a distance of 135 miles (217 kilometers) in Death Valley in California. In the Badwater, participants have to master nearly 2.5 miles (4 kilometers) of cumulative ascent and 0.87 mile (1.4 kilometers) of cumulative descent in temperatures between 104 and 122 degrees Fahrenheit (40 and 50 degrees Celsius).

The world's highest marathon is the Everest Marathon, inaugurated in 1985 and conducted every two years since 1987. In 2003, the Tenzing Hillary Everest Marathon was inaugurated in commemoration of the first successful Everest ascent by Edmund Hillary and Tenzing Norgay in 1953.

Who are the runners who dedicate not only their time but also their lives to extreme running? Their number is increasing, but here only three can be highlighted. Astrid Benöhr, born in 1957, is a German professional runner who is still active. She holds the women's world records in the triple, quintuple, and quadruple Ironman (set in the 1990s). American Dean Karnazes, born in 1962, has excelled in long-distance running and swimming. Among his outstanding achievements are a 348-mile (560-kilometer) run in 80 hours and 44 minutes in 2005. In 2006, he ran marathons on 50 consecutive days in each of the American states. Kilian Jornet Burgada, a Catalan mountaineer and ultrarunner, born in 1987, excelled in mountain running and ski mountaineering. Currently he is engaged in the most ambitious endurance endeavor yet, the Summits of My Life project, in which he tries to climb the highest mountains in the world in record time. He already has set several speed-climbing records (e.g., at Mont Blanc in Europe and Aconcagua in South America). His final summit attempt will be running up Mount Everest on a direct route.

Although the ultimate runners seem to be "super humans," their performances may encourage us to try hard and to reach our own limits wherever they may be.

pay-per-view cable stations and gained popularity as it formalized rules; adopted weight classes, rounds, and gloves; and outlawed head butts. Early stars, such as Chuck Liddell and Randy Couture, gained a large fan following, and by 2011 UFC signed a seven-year contract with the Fox network for $100 million per year, an indication of its crossover into mainstream sport programming (Masucci).

The growing regard for men's and women's soccer teams, as seen by the support and enthusiasm for their play in the World Cup, indicate that the sport will continue to grow. The globalization of sport and popular culture will inevitably foster international sports leagues, and the increasing

capabilities of technology, science, and medicine will ensure record-breaking performances. Teachers and coaches already have the technological tools to film and analyze skills previously deemed to be imperceptible.

Social media has transformed fan culture as players tweet with their followers in a seemingly more personal relationship and team officials try to regulate such communication. Professional and college teams monitor blogs to ascertain fans' sentiments and adopt marketing strategies accordingly.

Computer-based game systems, such as the Wii, have already changed the nature in which children and adults participate in sport without leaving their

Ronda Rousey and Holly Holm fight during their 2015 UFC title bout.
© AP Photo/Andy Brownbill, File

homes. On this console, players compete against avatars by simulating physical activity or assume the persona of a star athlete in a test of skill. Other players can live out their dreams on the computer by joining fantasy leagues in which they become the imaginary owner of a team. Early baseball board games of the 1980s provided the impetus for more sophisticated versions made possible by computers. Both male and female "owners" join a baseball, football, or basketball league or leagues. Team members are drafted before meeting opponents in virtual games. Players' performances are rated according to their statistical records, and they can be traded as in the real world. Cash prizes are often awarded based on the league standings at the close of the season (Hutchins and Rowe; Nelson, *American Sports)*.

In 2000, the Samsung Company sponsored the World Cyber Games in Korea, patterned after the Olympic Games, in which professional players competed for cash prizes. Such annual tournaments draw hundreds of players to international destinations, with prize money surpassing $16 million in 2015. Such games and the cyber athletes who play them change not only the nature of sport but even its definition (Hutchins and Rowe; www.telesurtv.net/english/news/World-Cyber-Games-2015-Has-Begun-20150323-0029.html).

Sport has long been utilized as a political tool, a form of soft power (as opposed to the hard power of military force) to achieve national goals. That will only continue in the future as wealthier nations (or wealthier teams) procure their talent from an international labor force. The small nation of Qatar in the Middle East has built world-class facilities to attract foreign youth to its national teams and won the right to host the 2022 World Cup to bolster its economy through sport tourism. Dubai has imported American high school basketball teams and televises their games to advertise its presence on a global scale. It is inevitable that, like the tragedy of the terrorist attack at the 2013 Boston Marathon, some people with alternative political beliefs will target the large assembly of fans at sports events to draw attention to their cause. No longer can sports be considered just fun and games. They should be fun, but they have also become a very serious business (Henricksen).

Summary

Sports have undergone rapid changes as both collegiate and professional teams seek greater success and greater profits. Despite massive stadiums and television revenue, the vast majority of college teams lose money each year, which must be offset by subsidies and raising students' fees. Despite such conditions the athletic arms race continues. Although some professional team owners claim losses, there are none willing to sell their franchises, and many are now valued at more than a billion dollars. In the quest to succeed and reduce costs, professional teams have increasingly turned to the conscription of international players and relied on analytics to acquire niche athletes who can make a small but significant difference.

Title IX legislation increasingly affords more opportunities for females on athletic teams; but it has actually had a negative effect on women in leadership roles, as males still predominate in coaching, executive, and ownership roles. Minorities, too, still struggle to gain such positions, although the NBA and NFL fare much better than MLB or the NHL in that respect.

Civic pride, community or school rivalries, and American competitiveness continue to fuel a "win at all costs" attitude that fosters illegal recruiting, cheating, use of performance-enhancing drugs, and other nefarious means to achieve goals. For example, Tom Brady, famed quarterback of the New England Patriots, faced a four-game suspension for tampering with the game balls in the 2015 AFC Championship Game. Despite such negative aspects, sport retains immense popularity and continues to serve as a harbinger of American cultural values.

DISCUSSION QUESTIONS

1. How has the increased commercialization of sport affected team owners, players, and fans?

2. What are the positive and negative aspects of the globalization of sport?

3. How might women gain greater access to leadership roles in sport?

4. In what ways is sport politicized?

5. Are coaches' and players' salaries justified?

6. Should collegiate athletes be paid?

Afterword

The role of sport in American society today demonstrates the ongoing influence of earlier trends explored throughout time periods presented in *Sports in American History.* The increasing numbers of participants and spectators at all levels of sport suggest that the importance of sport in America remains consistent. Yet some major elements in the sporting culture, such as the values attributed to sport from some of the early advocates in the nineteenth century—good health, character building, preparation for men's and women's gender roles, the Americanization of immigrants—may not follow the traditions and patterns of the past. New technologies, the use of different types of performance-enhancing substances, conflicts and debates about professionalism and amateurism, payment for college athletes, the issues of fair play, and injuries, particularly concussions, are just a few of the factors that could affect the role of sport. The meanings of sport change as people's experiences and events in American culture change. However, the influence sport has on diverse groups of people across the United States certainly persists, and sport will continue to be a major force in American society.

After the Progressive Era, American sporting culture experienced cycles of creation, incorporation, and resistance to a uniform, hegemonic structure. Throughout U.S. history, ethnic minorities had used sport as a means both to assimilate into the mainstream culture and to retain traditional leisure forms. For racial groups, often excluded from mainstream sporting activities, sport had frequently been marked by creation of parallel organizations, struggles for recognition and acceptance, and development of culturally expressive styles of play.

Religious factions have, at various times, both condemned sport as immoral and condoned it as a tool for achieving physical and spiritual health. For institutions such as the Young Men's Christian Association and the Young Women's Christian Association, sport became a means of Protestant proselytism and a vehicle to teach appropriate behaviors. For Catholics and Jews, it brought greater unity between divisive internal factions, as ethnic Catholic parishes gradually accepted the leadership of an Irish American hierarchy. In the growth of reform Judaism in the later decades of the nineteenth century, reformed middle- and upper-class German Jews strived to acculturate the more orthodox and lower-class Eastern European Jews journeying to America by organizing sport and physical health programs for men and women in settlement houses, while more Orthodox factions formed their own leagues.

Women have confronted sex discrimination in their struggle for sporting opportunities and for the choices to participate actively and, for some, professionally in sport. In sport and society, American women have agitated for a change in the culturally prescribed gender roles. Other groups of people have also been underrepresented, such as gay, lesbian, bisexual, and transsexual athletes, although there have been significant breakthroughs in the NBA, WNBA, NFL, and in collegiate sport. Title IX continues to be implemented unevenly at various institutions. Compliance with Title IX remains a challenge; some athletic programs, because of their emphasis on big-time collegiate sports for men, resist the growth of gender equity in sports. A consequence of Title IX in coming years might be to improve the condition of collegiate athletics: "Because the financial resources of modern educational institutions are increasingly stretched, some believe Title IX has the potential to reform and reshape collegiate athletics by causing a halt to the 'arms race' that has caused athletic budgets to escalate in an unending quest for national prominence" (Ware 26).

The impact of Title IX on the non-revenue-producing sports (i.e., minor sports) in collegiate athletics still garners the scrutiny of athletic and college administrators to determine what seems fair for male and female student-athletes on campus. Gains in women's sports from Title IX, often linked to the success of female athletes in the Olympics at the end of the twentieth century, will be scrutinized as some women's sports are cut from the Olympic roster. In the coming years, sport program administrators will need to explore how this will affect women's sport in the United States. Supporters wanting to preserve Title IX within the male-dominated culture of collegiate sport find that the battle continues in governmental and educational institutions.

Despite a bulk of evidence to the contrary, sport retains associations with social mobility for the American underclass. Interscholastic athletes adhere to faith in an American meritocracy, a strong work ethic, and character development, although heroic role models have become rare. The lessons of sport sometimes contradict the professed values of American society, as schools teach individuality, inquiry, and freedom of expression as a basic right, yet athletes are expected to follow the dictates of coaches and officials unquestioningly.

Sport has served political groups in a variety of ways. In different historical eras, many people have viewed sport as a vehicle for propaganda, for promotion of nationalism, and for socialization and Americanization; it has also been used as a means of retaliation and protest and as a cultural expression of these varied political agendas. The Olympics have become as much a political event as they are a global athletic spectacle. Athletic events are generally preceded by patriotic expressions of nationalism, such as the national anthem, while baseball games are interrupted during the seventh inning to invoke a religious blessing. The NFL alliance with the American military is portrayed at football games throughout the season.

Economic ties to sport are equally extensive, and this relationship is likely to continue. The competitive impulses and values of organized sport reinforce a capitalist economy that dominates world trade. On the national level, public subsidization of teams and stadiums even affects nonfans. The considerable costs and expenditures of training national teams and elite athletes might be more wisely spent on sport-for-all programs that address national health concerns of the general public. The business of professional sport has far-reaching global dimensions and employs an international labor force. Bodies are for sale, as African runners sell their abilities to richer Olympic teams, Latin Americans and Asians leave their homelands for employment on American baseball teams, and professional basketball and hockey teams feature international rosters. In a reversal of the global labor flow, American basketball players stock European teams.

Although sports may bring nations together in common pursuits for peaceful purposes, they are also used to promote national or commercial interests. Multinational business firms have transcended the controls of individual governments, promoting their particular ideologies, images, and symbols around the world. Such companies promote the capitalist model of competition, individualism, commodification, and consumption to a global audience. Reacting to such globalization, local cultures try to retain their separate identities through resistance and persistence in their traditional pastimes. The cross-cultural flow, largely spawned by new forms of social media, continues to bring new activities and new ideas to the United States.

In some cases, non-Western nations have risen to prominence in sport, as with Kenya's long-distance runners or the spread of Asian martial arts to the global arena. Other groups have organized festivals, such as the Gay Games and the Paralympic Games, to meet their own needs, allowing participants of these groups to show their athletic capabilities. But the ongoing spread of a monolithic sport system endangers local, regional, and national communities. Cultural imperialism—in the form of the English language, global trade, power relationships (e.g., World Bank policies, multinational corporations' employment practices), and uniform capitalistic sporting practices—has dire consequences at local levels, disrupting economies and causing unemployment as companies cut costs and seek greater profits. With enforced idleness, recreation and leisure practices assume even greater importance.

The recreational patterns and choices of the U.S. population differ by age and interest. Youth sport programs permeate the country, serving as surrogate parenting for some. Despite such proliferation, the emphasis on elite or professional sport tends to relegate most Americans to the role of spectators. As heart disease and obesity climb toward epidemic proportions, health and fitness programs take on greater importance, and older adults search for lifelong activities. Americans spent more than $81.4 billion on sports equipment between 2008 and 2013 (www.statista.com/statistics/240946/sports-products-industry-wholesale-sales-in-the-us). At the same time, the aerobic activities of the health-conscious have been incorporated within the dominant capitalist business structure in the form of fitness studios, health clubs, and personal trainers. Even jogging for health reasons has been eclipsed by the media emphasis on marathons, triathlons, Ironman contests, mud runs, and obstacle courses.

Technology has greatly improved sports equipment, facilities, and skill development, but it has also generated new sedentary pastimes in the form of video games. Sedentary "athletes" no longer need to leave the couch in order to compete; instead, they can take part in fantasy games and simulated experiences and even compete in global tournaments for cash prizes. Should this trend continue, the history of American sport may take a dramatic turn away from the social interactions that have characterized it in past centuries, perhaps in the process greatly changing the nature of American culture. The desire to play sport, evident in the lives of Americans in the past and the present, might then shape new forms of sport and meaningful experiences for future Americans.

Bibliography

Entries marked with an asterisk are primary sources.

Acosta, R. Vivian, and Linda Jean Carpenter. "Women in Intercollegiate Sport." *Women in Sport and Physical Activity Journal* 13.1 (Spring 2004): 62–89.

Acosta, Vivian, and Linda Jean Carpenter. "Women in Intercollegiate Sport." Available: http:webpages.charter.net/womeninsport.

Adams, David Wallace. *Education for Extinction: American Indians and the Boarding School Experience, 1875–1928*. Lawrence: University Press of Kansas. 1995.

*Adams, John. Letter from John Adams to Abigail Adams, Philadelphia, July 3, 1776. *Constructing the American Past: A Source Book of a People's History*. Vol. 1. 3rd ed. Eds. Elliott J. Gorn, Randy Roberts, and Terry D. Bilhartz. New York: Addison-Wesley Longman, 1999. 115.

Adelman, Melvin L. "The First Modern Sport in America: Harness Racing in New York City, 1825–1870." *Journal of Sport History* 8.1 (Spring 1981): 5–32.

Adelman, Melvin L. *A Sporting Time: New York City and the Rise of Modern Athletics*. Champaign: University of Illinois Press, 1986.

"Al Reach." www.baseballlibrary.com/ballplayers/player.php?name=Al_Reach_1840.

*Altherr, Thomas L., ed. *Sports in North America: A Documentary History, Volume I, Part I: Sports in the Colonial Era, 1618–1783*. Gulf Stream, FL: Academic International Press, 1997.

*Altherr, Thomas L., ed. *Sports in North America: A Documentary History, Volume I, Part II: Sports in the New Republic, 1784–1820*. Gulf Stream, FL: Academic International Press, 1997.

"Amateur Sports Capital of the World." Available: www.indychamber.com/sportsRec.asp.

Andrews, David L., ed. *Michael Jordan, Inc.: Corporate Sport, Media Culture, and Late Modern America*. Albany: State University of New York Press, 2001.

Anonymous. "The Health Fact: Spending on Sports," Chicago Sun-Times, August 13, 2006, 6A.

Arnesen, Eric. "Whiteness and the Historian's Imagination." *International Labor and Working Class History* 60 (Fall 2001): 3–32.

Ashby, LeRoy. *With Amusement for All: A History of Popular Culture Since 1830*. Lexington: University Press of Kentucky, 2006.

Astiadi, Sasha. "Chongqing Dockers American Football Champions of China." *The World of Chinese*. 14 January 2014. Available: www.the world of Chinese.com/2014/01/Chongqing-dockers-american-football-champions-of-china.

Avrich, Paul. *Sacco and Vanzetti: The Anarchist Background*. Princeton, NJ: Princeton University Press, 1991.

Baker, William J. *Playing With God: Religion and Modern Sport*. Cambridge: Harvard University Press, 2007.

Baker, William J. *Sports in the Western World*. Rev. ed. Champaign: University of Illinois Press, 1988.

Balfour, Kelly, and Ellie Odenheimer. "Mitchell Report." *American Sports: A History of Icons, Idols, and Ideas*. Ed. Murry R. Nelson. Santa Barbara: Greenwood, 2013. 823–825.

Barcett, Bruce. "American Flyers." *Outside* (February 2006): 58–69.

Barney, Robert Knight. "Knights of Cause and Exercise: German Forty-Eighters and Turnvereine in the United States During the Antebellum Period." *Canadian Journal of History and Sport* 13 (1982): 62–79.

*"Base Ball." *Wilke's Spirit of the Times* 25 August 1860: 389.

*"Base-Ball Match for the Championship." *Frank Leslie's Illustrated Newspaper* 26 August 1865: 356.

"Baseball's Milestone Contracts." SI.com. Available: www.si.com/mlb/photos/2011/02/16baseballs-milestone-contracts.

Beale, Morris A. *A History of Football at Harvard, 1874–1948*. Washington, DC: Columbia, 1948.

Beech, Hannah. "Asian Heroes: Yao Ming." *Time* 24 April 2003. Available: www.time.com/time/asia/magazine/article/0,13673,501030428-446202,00.html.

*Beecher, Catharine E. *Calisthenic Exercises for Schools, Families, and Health Establishments.* New York: Harper & Brothers, 1856.

*Beecher, Catharine E. *Letters to the People on Health and Happiness.* New York: Harper & Brothers, 1855. Rpt. New York: Arno Press, 1972.

*Beecher, Catharine E. *Physiology and Calisthenics for Schools and Families.* New York: Harper & Brothers, 1856.

Bellisle, Martha. "Ben Roethlisberger Settles Lawsuit Alleging 2008 Rape." *Reno Gazette-Journal* 20 January 2012. Available: usatoday30.usatoday.com/sports/football/nfl/steelers/story/2012-01-20/ben-roethlisberger-settles-lawsuit/52702798/1.

Ben-Porat, Guy, and Amir Ben-Porat. "Unbounded Soccer: Globalization and Localization of the Games in Israel." *International Review of Sport Sociology* 39.4 (Dec. 2004): 421–436.

Beran, Janice A. "Americans in the Philippines: Imperialism or Progress Through Sports?" *The International Journal of the History of Sport* 6 (May 1989): 62–87.

Beran, Janice A. *From Six-on-Six to Full Court Press: A Century of Iowa Girls' Basketball.* Ames: Iowa State University Press, 1993.

Bergmann, Gretel. "Ich war die große jüdische Hoffnung." Karlsruhe: Haus der Geschichte Baden-Württemberg, 2003.

Berlage, Gai Ingham. "Lieberman-Kline, Nancy." *The Scribner Encyclopedia of American Lives.* Ed. Arnold Markoe. New York: Scribner's, 2002. Vol. 2: 41–43.

Bernstein, J.B. *Million Dollar Arm: Sometimes to Win, You Have to Change the Game.* New York: Gallery Books, 2014.

Berryman, Jack W. "The Tenuous Attempt of Americans to 'Catch-Up With John Bull': Specialty Magazines and Sporting Journalism, 1800–1835." *Canadian Journal of History of Sport and Physical Education* 10 (1979): 43–61.

Betts, John Rickards. "Public Recreation, Public Parks, and Public Health Before the Civil War." *History of Physical Education and Sport.* Ed. Bruce L. Bennett. Chicago: Athletic Institute, 1972. 33–52.

*Bissell, Mary Taylor. "Athletics for City Girls." *Popular Science Monthly* December, 1894: 145–153.

Blum, John M., Edmund S. Morgan, Willie Lee Rose, Arthur M. Schlesinger, Jr., Kenneth M. Stampp, and C. Vann Woodward. *The National Experience: A History of the United States.* New York: Harcourt Brace Jovanovich, 1981.

Borish, Linda J. "'Athletic Activities of Various Kinds': Physical Health and Sport Programs for Jewish American Women." *Journal of Sport History* 26 (Summer 1999): 240–270.

Borish, Linda J. "'The Cradle of American Champions, Women Champions . . . Swim Champions': Charlotte Epstein, Gender and Jewish Identity, and the Physical Emancipation of Women in Aquatic Sports." *The International Journal of the History of Sport* 21 (March 2004): 197–235.

Borish, Linda J. "'A Fair, Without the Fair, Is No Fair at All': Women at the New England Agricultural Fair in the Mid-Nineteenth Century." *Journal of Sport History* 24.2 (Summer 1997): 155–176.

Borish, Linda J. "'An Interest in Physical Well-Being Among the Feminine Membership': Sporting Activities for Women at Young Men's and Young Women's Hebrew Associations." *American Jewish History* 87 (March 1999): 61–93.

*Borish, Linda J. "Interview With Olympian Aileen Riggin Soule About Charlotte Epstein." Phone Communication. June 1995. Western Michigan University, Department of History, Kalamazoo, MI.

Borish, Linda J. "Jewish American Women, Jewish Organizations and Sports, 1880–1940." *Sports and the American Jew.* Ed. Steven A. Riess. Syracuse: Syracuse University Press, 1998. 105–131.

Borish, Linda J. "Jewish Women in the American Gym: Basketball, Ethnicity and Gender in the Early Twentieth Century." *Jews in the Gym: Judaism, Sports, and Athletics.* Ed. Leonard Greenspoon. Vol. 23. Studies in Jewish Civilization. West Lafayette, IN: Purdue University Press, 2012. 213–237.

Borish, Linda J. "The Robust Woman and the Muscular Christian: Catharine Beecher, Thomas Higginson, and Their Vision of American Society, Health, and Physical Activities." *The International Journal of the History of Sport* 4 (September 1987): 139–154.

Borish, Linda J. "Rural Women and the Pursuit of Physical Recreation and Sporting Activities in Health Reform in Antebellum New England." *The International Journal of the History of Sport* 22 (November 2005): 946–973.

Borish, Linda J. "'Was Woman's Constitution Less Robust . . . ?': Farm Women and Physical Health in the Agricultural Press, 1820–1870." *Canadian Journal of History of Sport* 25 (May 1994): 1–18.

Borish, Linda J. "Women, Sport, and American Jewish Identity in the Late Nineteenth and Early Twentieth Centuries." *With God on Their Side: Sport in the Service of Religion.* Eds. Tara Magdalinski and

Timothy L. Chandler. London: Routledge, 2002. 71–98.

Borish, Linda J. "Young Men's Hebrew Association." *Boyhood in America*. Vol. 2. Eds. Priscilla Ferguson Clement and Jacqueline S. Reinier. Santa Barbara, CA: ABC-CLIO, 2001. 764–767.

boxrec.com/media/index.php/USA:_New_York_Laws.

*Bradford, William. *Of Plymouth Plantation, 1620–1647*. Ed. Harvey Wish. New York: Capricorn Books, 1962.

Breen, Timothy H. "The Cultural Significance of Gambling Among the Gentry of Virginia." *Major Problems in American Sport History: Documents and Essays*. Ed. Steven A. Riess. Boston: Houghton Mifflin, 1997. 31–38.

Brodkin, Karen. *How Jews Became White Folks: And What That Says About Race in America*. New Brunswick, NJ: Rutgers University Press, 1998.

Bronner, Simon J., ed. *Manly Traditions: The Folk Roots of American Masculinities*. Bloomington: Indiana University Press, 2005.

Browne, Ian. "Sox Unveil Matsuzaka." 14 December 2006. Available: http://boston.redsox.mlb.com/news/print.jsp?ymd=20061214&content_id=1761085&vkey=news_bos&fext=.jsp&c_id=bos.

Brulia, Tim. "A Chronology of Pro Football on Television." *Coffin Corner* 26.4 (2004): 18–20.

Building Character for 75 Years: Published on the Occasion of the 75th Anniversary of the Young Men's & Young Women's Hebrew Association. New York: 75th Anniversary Committee, Young Men's & Young Women's Hebrew Association, 1969.

Bunn, Curtis. "Why Does Maria Sharapova Make More in Endorsements Than Serena Williams." *Atlanta Black Star*. Available: atlantablackstar.com/2015/06/09/serena-williams-success-does-not-match-her-tennis-endorsements.

Burnett, Thane. "Willie O'Ree: The First Black NHL Player." *Sun Media* 14 December 2007. Available: http://slam.canoe.com/Slam/Hockey/News/2007/12/07/4713520-sun.html.

Bushman, Richard L. *The Refinement of America: Persons, Houses, Cities*. New York: Vintage Books, 1993.

Butler, Mary, Garth Stoltz, and Frances Thornton. *The Battle Creek Idea: Dr. John Harvey Kellogg and the Battle Creek Sanitarium*. Battle Creek, MI: Heritage, 1994.

Butterfield, Kenyon L. "Farmers' Social Organizations." *Cyclopedia of American Agriculture, Volume 4: Farm and Community*. Ed. Liberty Bailey. New York: MacMillan, 1909. 289–297.

Cahn, Susan. "Cinderellas of Sport: Black Women in Track and Field." *Sport and the Color Line*. Eds. Patrick B. Miller and David K. Wiggins. New York: Routledge, 2004. 211–232.

Cahn, Susan. *Coming on Strong: Gender and Sexuality in Twentieth Century Women's Sport*. New York: Free Press, 1994.

Carney, Steve. "Youth Sports Participation." UpdatePlus (September/October 2006): 21.

Carpenter, Linda Jean, and R. Vivian Acosta. *Women in Intercollegiate Sport: A Longitudinal Study*. Available: webpages.charter.net/womeninsport.

Carroll, John M. *Red Grange and the Rise of Modern Football*. Champaign: University of Illinois Press, 2004.

Carson, Jane. *Colonial Virginians at Play*. Williamsburg, VA: Colonial Williamsburg, 1965. Rpt. Charlottesville: University of Virginia Press, 1989.

Carson, Mina. *Settlement Folk: Social Thought and the American Settlement Movement, 1885–1930*. Chicago: University of Chicago Press, 1990.

*Catlin, George. "George Catlin Describes a Choctaw Lacrosse Match, c. 1830." *Major Problems in American Sport History: Documents and Essays*. Ed. Steven A. Riess. Boston: Houghton Mifflin, 1997: 27-31.

*"Cattle Shows." *New England Farmer* (New Series) 9 (January 1857): 14–15.

Cavalli, Gary. "Cold War: Warm Welcome." *Stanford Magazine* (May/June 2005): 729. Available: www.stanfordalumni.org/news/magazine/2005/mayjun/features/track.html.

Cavallo, Dominick. *Muscles and Morals: Organized Playgrounds and Urban Reform, 1880–1920*. Philadelphia: University of Pennsylvania Press, 1981.

Cayleff, Susan E. *Wash and Be Healed: The Water-Cure Movement and Women's Health*. Philadelphia: Temple University Press, 1987.

Chalabi, Mona. "Three Leagues, 92 Teams and One Principal Black Owner." *Five Thirty Eight* 28 April 2014. Available: fivethirtyeight.com/datalab/diversity-in-the-nba-the-nfl-and-mlb.

City Gazette 26 February 1816.

Chicago Hebrew Institute Observer December 1913.

Chicago Sun-Times 1 August 2004: 84A.

Chicago Tribune 16 March 1887: 9.

Chisholm, Ann. "Incarnations and Practices of Feminine Rectitude: Nineteenth-Century Gymnastics for U.S. Women." *Journal of Social History* 38.3 (Spring 2005): 737–763.

Chudacoff, Howard P. *Changing the Playbook: How Power, Profit, and Politics Transformed College Sports.* Urbana: University of Illinois Press, 2015.

Clement, Priscilla Ferguson, and Jacqueline S. Reiner, eds. *Boyhood in America.* Santa Barbara, CA: ABC-CLIO, 2001.

*Clift, William. *The Tim Bunker Papers, or Yankee Farming.* 1868. Rpt. Freeport, NY: Books for Libraries Press, 1970.

Coakley, Jay. *Sports in Society: Issues and Controversies.* New York: McGraw-Hill, 2001.

Cobb, James C. *Away Down South: A History of Southern Identity.* New York: Oxford University Press, 2005.

*Cobb, Sylvanus, Jr. "An Unexpected Race." *Provincial Freeman* 26 May 1855.

Coben, Stanley. *Rebellion Against Victorianism: The Impetus for Cultural Change in 1920s America.* New York: Oxford University Press, 1990.

Collier, Brian S. "Running." *Native Americans in Sport.* Ed. C. Richard King. Armonk, NY: Sharpe, 2004. 262–266.

"Commercialization." Available: modern-content.usatoday.com/communities/gameon/post/2011/06/olympic-tv-decision-between-nbc-espn-and-fox-could-come-down-today/1#.U6XkdbGGeZE.

Cooper, Helen A., ed. *Thomas Eakins: The Rowing Pictures.* New Haven: Yale University Press, 1998.

Costa, D. Margaret, and Sharon R. Guthrie, eds. *Women and Sport: Interdisciplinary Perspectives.* Champaign, IL: Human Kinetics, 1994.

*Country Joe and the Fish. "I Feel Like I'm Fixin' to Die Rag." 1968.

*"Country Sport." Domestic News. *Hampden Federalist* 23 January 1817: 3.

Creamer, Robert W. *Babe: The Legend Comes to Life.* New York: Simon & Schuster, 1974.

Crepeau, Richard. "There Seems to Be No End in Sight." *Journal of Sport History* 27.3 (Fall 2000): 525–527.

*"A Croquet Problem." *Harper's Weekly* 14 September 1867: 583.

*Crowther, Samuel, Jr., and Arthur Ruhl. *Rowing and Track Athletics.* New York: Macmillan, 1905.

*"Cruelty to Animals." *New England Weekly Journal* 25 September 1732: 1.

*"Cruelty to Animals—'Which Are the Brutes?'" Illustration. *Harper's Weekly* 23 February 1867: 121.

Crunden, Robert M. *Ministers of Reform: The Progressive Achievement in American Civilization, 1889–1920.* New York: Basic Books, 1982.

Daniels, Bruce C. *New England Puritans at Play: Leisure and Recreation in Colonial America.* New York: St. Martin's Griffin, 1995.

Daniels, Roger. *Coming to America: A History of Immigration and Ethnicity in American Life.* New York: Harper & Row Perennial Library, 1991.

*Danzig, Allison. "National Tennis Title Won by Miss Wills." *New York Times* 28 August 1928: 18.

Davies, Richard O. *Sport in American Life: A History.* Malden, Ma: Blackwell, 2007.

Dawley, Alan. *Struggles for Justice: Social Responsibility and the Liberal State.* Cambridge, MA: Belknap Press, 1991.

Dawson, Kevin. "Enslaved Swimmers and Divers in the Atlantic World." *Journal of American History* 92.4 (March 2006): 1327–1355.

Dean, Josh. "Cool Millions." *Outside* (February 2006): 51–55.

Deitsch, Richard, Andrea Woo, Gene Menez, and Elizabeth Newman. "New World Order." *Sports Illustrated* 5 May 2003. Available: www.si.com/vault/2003/05/05/342403/new-world-order-after-years-of-battling-for-fair-opportunities-people-of-color-are-finally-running-the-show-in-some-places-and-driving-the-economics-in-sports.

Demaree, Albert Lowther. *The American Agricultural Press, 1819–1860.* 1941. Rpt. Philadelphia: Porcupine Press, 1974.

de Wilde, Ari. "Lance Armstrong." *American Sports: A History of Icons, Idols, and Ideas.* Ed. Murry R. Nelson. Santa Barbara: Greenwood, 2013. 58–64.

Dosch, Kristi. "College Football Revenue: Running the Numbers." September 24, 2014. Available: http://smartycents.com/articles/college-football-revenue/.

Doyle, Andrew. "Bear Bryant: Symbol for an Embattled South." *Colby Quarterly* 32.1 (March 1996): 72–86.

Drevon, André. 2000. *Les Jeux olympiques oubliés: Paris 1900.* Paris: CNRS.

*Du Bois, W.E.B. *The Souls of Black Folk.* 1903. Rpt. New York: Penguin Books, 1989.

*du Ru, Father Paul. "Excerpts From the Journal of Father Paul du Ru," 1700. *Sports in North America: A Documentary History, Volume I, Part I: Sports in the Colonial Era, 1618–1783.* Ed. Thomas L. Altherr. Gulf Stream, FL: Academic International Press, 1997. 455.

Duis, Perry R. *The Saloon: Public Drinking in Chicago and Boston, 1880–1920.* Champaign: University of Illinois Press, 1983.

Dulles, Foster Rhea. *A History of Recreation: America Learns to Play.* New York: Appleton-Century-Crofts, 1965.

*Dyer, Braven. "Babe Didrikson Cracks World Javelin Record." *Los Angeles Times* 1 August 1932: 9.

Dyer, Leigh. "Hamm, Mariel Margaret ('Mia')." *Scribner's Encyclopedia of American Lives.* Ed. Arnold Markoe. New York: Scribner's, 2002. 384–385.

Dyreson, Jodella K. "Sporting Activities in the American-Mexican Colonies of Texas, 1821-1835." Journal of Sport History 24:3 (Fall 1997): 269-284.

Dyreson, Mark. Making the American Team: Sport, Culture, and the Olympic Experience. Champaign: University of Illinois Press, 1998.

Dyreson, Mark. "Media Nationalism and the 'War' Over Olympic Pictures in Sport's 'Golden Age.'" *The International Journal of the History of Sport* 22 (November 2005): 938–989.

Dyson, Michael Eric. "Be Like Mike? Michael Jordan and the Pedagogy of Desire." *Michael Jordan, Inc.* Ed. David L. Andrews. Albany: State University of New York Press, 2001. 259–268.

Dyson, Rick. "Hoop and Pole." *Native Americans in Sport.* Ed. C. Richard King. Armonk, NY: Sharpe, 2004. 148–149.

Edmondson, Jacqueline. "Serena Williams." *American Sports: A History of Icons, Idols, and Ideas.* Ed. Murry R. Nelson. Santa Barbara: Greenwood, 2013. 1457–1461.

Eisen, George. "Early European Attitudes Toward Native American Sports and Pastimes." *Ethnicity and Sport in North American History and Culture.* Eds. George Eisen and David K. Wiggins. Westport, CT: Praeger, 1994. 1–18.

Eisen, George, and David K. Wiggins, eds. *Ethnicity and Sport in North American History and Culture.* Westport, CT: Praeger, 1994.

Eitzen, D. Stanley, and George H. Sage. *Sociology of North American Sport.* New York: McGraw-Hill, 2003.

Elias, Norbert. *The Civilizing Process: The History of Manners.* Trans. from German by Edmund Jephcott. Vol. 1. New York: Urizen Books, 1978.

Elias, Norbert. *The Civilizing Process: Power and Civility.* Trans. from German by Edmund Jephcott. Vol. 2. New York: Pantheon Books, 1982.

Elias, Norbert. "The Genesis of Sport as a Sociological Problem." *The Sociology of Sport: A Selection of Readings.* Ed. Eric Dunning. London: Cass, 1971. 88–115.

Elias, Norbert, and Eric Dunning. *Quest for Excitement: Sport and Leisure in the Civilizing Process.* Oxford: Blackwell, 1986.

Elias, Robert, ed. *Baseball and the American Dream.* Armonk, NY: Sharpe, 2001.

Elovaara, Mika T. "Michael Vick." *American Sports: A History of Icons, Idols, and Ideas.* Ed. Murry R. Nelson. Santa Barbara: Greenwood, 2013. 1413–1416.

*Ely, Richard T., ed. *Hull House Maps and Papers.* Boston: Crowell, 1895. Rpt. New York: Arno Press, 1970.

*E.M.C. "Farmers' Wives." *American Agriculturist* 4 (September 1845): 287–288.

*Epstein, Charlotte. "Swimming." *Amateur Athlete* (July 1934): 7, 9.

Ernst, Robert. *Weakness Is a Crime: The Life of Bernarr Macfadden.* Syracuse: Syracuse University Press, 1991.

*Eskanazi, Gerald. "U.S. Defeats Soviet Squad in Olympic Hockey by 4-3." *New York Times* 23 February 1980: 1.

Evensen, Bruce J. *When Dempsey Fought Tunney: Heroes, Hokum, and Storytelling in the Jazz Age.* Knoxville: University of Tennessee Press, 1996.

Fagan, Major Louis Estell. "Samuel Nicholas: First Officer of American Marines." *The Marine Corps Gazette* 18.3 (November 1933): 1–20. Available: www.ussnicholas.org/first_officer.html.

*"The Farmer's Daughter." *Massachusetts Ploughman* 27 (February 15, 1868): n. pag.

Fass, Paula S. *Encyclopedia of Children and Childhood in History and Society.* New York: Macmillan, 2004.

Felsenthal, Carol. "Shattered." *Chicago* 49.5 (May, 2000): 94–97, 137–145.

*"Female Jockeys." *The Homestead* 1 (November 15, 1855): 142.

Fielding, Lawrence W. "War and Trifles: Sport in the Shadows of Civil War Army Life." *Journal of Sport History* 4 (1977): 151–168.

Florida, Richard. "The Never-Ending Stadium Boondoggle." *City Lab* 10 September 2015. Available: www.citylab.com/politics/2015/09/the-never-ending-stadium-boondoggle/403666.

Flyvberg, Bent, and Allison Stewart. "Olympic Proportions: Cost and Cost Overrun at the Olympic Games 1960–2012." Oxford University: Said Business School working papers, 2012.

Folsom, Franklin. *Impatient Armies of the Poor: The Story of Collective Action of the Unemployed, 1808–1942.* Niwot: University Press of Colorado, 1991.

Foner, Eric, and John A Garraty, eds. *The Reader's Companion to American History.* Boston: Houghton Mifflin, 1991.

Ford, Mark L., and Massimo Foglio. "The First 'NFL Europe.'" *Coffin Corner* 27.6 (2005): 3–7.

*"Fortieth Anniversary of American Independence." *New Hampshire Patriot* 16 July 1816: 2.

*Franklin, Benjamin. *The Autobiography and Other Writings, 1779.* Ed. Kenneth Silverman. New York: Penguin Books, 1986.

Freeman, Michael. *ESPN: The Uncensored History.* Dallas: Taylor, 2000.

Friedman, Michael Jay. "President Bush Praises U.S. Athletes." Available: usinfo.state.gov/scv/Archive/2006/May/17-645638.html.

Frommer, Harvey. *Shoeless Joe and Ragtime Baseball.* Dallas: Taylor, 1992.

*Gallico, Paul. *The Golden People.* Garden City, NY: Doubleday, 1965.

Garraty, John A. *The American Nation: A History of the United States.* New York: Harper & Row, 1983.

Gems, Gerald R. *The Athletic Crusade: Sport and American Cultural Imperialism.* Lincoln: University of Nebraska Press, 2006.

Gems, Gerald R. "Blocked Shot: The Development of Basketball in the African-American Community of Chicago." *Journal of Sport History* 22.2 (Summer 1995): 135–148.

Gems, Gerald R. *Boxing: A Concise History of the Sweet Science.* Lanham, MD: Rowman & Littlefield, 2014.

Gems, Gerald R. "The Chicago Turners: Sports and the Demise of a Radical Past." *Adolf Cluss und die Turnbewegung.* Eds. Lothar Wieser and Peter Wanner. Stadtarchiv Heilbronn, 2007. 85–95.

Gems, Gerald R. "The Construction, Negotiation, and Transformation of Racial Identity in American Football," *American Indian Culture and Research Journal* 22.2 (July 1998): 131–150.

Gems, Gerald R. *For Pride, Profit, and Patriarchy: Football and the Incorporation of American Cultural Values.* Lanham, MD: Scarecrow Press, 2000.

Gems, Gerald R. "Sport and the Americanization of Ethnic Women in Chicago." *Ethnicity and Sport in North American History and Culture.* Eds. George Eisen and David K. Wiggins. Westport, CT: Greenwood Press, 1994. 177–200.

Gems, Gerald R. "Sport and the Forging of Jewish-American Culture: The Chicago Hebrew Institute." *American Jewish History* 83.1 (March 1995): 15–26.

Gems, Gerald R. *Sport and the Shaping of Italian-American Identity.* Syracuse, NY: Syracuse University Press, 2013.

*Gems, Gerald R. *Sports in North America: A Documentary History, Volume 5: Sports Organized, 1880–1900.* Gulf Breeze, FL: Academic International Press, 1996.

Gems, Gerald R. *Windy City Wars: Labor, Leisure, and Sport in the Making of Chicago.* Lanham, MD: Scarecrow Press, 1997. 131–150.

Gems, Gerald R., and Gertrud Pfister. "Fairy Tales? Marion Jones, C.J. Hunter and the Framing of Doping in American Newspapers." *Sport in Society* 18.2 (March 2013): 136–154.

Gems, Gerald R., and Linda J. Borish. "Sports, Colonial Era to 1920." *Boyhood in America.* Vol. 2. Eds. Priscilla Ferguson Clement and Jacqueline S. Reinier. Santa Barbara, CA: ABC-CLIO, 2001. 637–643.

Gems, Gerald R., and Linda J. Borish. "Sports, 1921 to Present." *Boyhood in America.* Vol. 2. Eds. Priscilla Ferguson Clement and Jacqueline S. Reinier. Santa Barbara, CA: ABC-CLIO, 2001. 643–647.

Gildea, Dennis. *Hoop Crazy: The Lives of Clair Bee and Chip Hilton.* Fayetteville: University of Arkansas Press, 2013.

Gilfoyle, Timothy. *A Pickpocket's Tale: The Underworld of Nineteenth-Century New York.* New York: Norton, 2006.

Gillmeister, Heiner. *Tennis: A Cultural History.* New York: New York University Press, 1998.

Goodman, Cary. *Choosing Sides: Playground and Street Life on the Lower East Side.* New York: Schocken Books, 1979.

Goodyear, Frank H., III. "'Nature's Most Beautiful Models': George Catlin's Choctaw Ball-Playing Paintings and the Politics of Indian Removal." *The International Journal of the History of Sport* 23 (March 2006): 138–153.

Gorn, Elliott J. "'Gouge and Bite, Pull Hair and Scratch': The Social Significance of Gouging in the Southern Backcountry." *Sport in America: From Wicked Amusements to National Obsession.* Ed. David K. Wiggins. Champaign, IL: Human Kinetics, 1995. 35–50.

Gorn, Elliott J. "The Manassa Mauler and the Fighting Marine: An Interpretation of the Dempsey-Tunney Fights." *Journal of American Studies* 19 (1985): 27–47.

Gorn, Elliott. *The Manly Art: Bare-Knuckle Prize Fighting in America.* Ithaca, NY: Cornell University Press, 1986.

Gorn, Elliott J., and Warren Goldstein. *A Brief History of American Sports.* New York: Hill and Wang, 1993.

Gould, Stephen Jay. *The Mismeasure of Man.* New York: Norton, 1996.

Graf, John C. *Chicago's Parks: A Photographic History.* Chicago, IL: Arcadia Publishing, 2000.

"The Great American Sports Atlas." Year-End Double Issue. *Sports Illustrated* 27 December 2004–3 January 2005.

"The Great Foot Race of 1835." American Turf Register and Sporting Magazine (June 1835): 518–520.

Green, Harvey. *Fit for America: Health, Fitness, Sport, and American Society.* Rochester, NY: Margaret Woodbury Strong Museum, 1986.

Greenstein, Teddy. "A Union in College Football?" *Chicago Tribune* 29 January 2014: 1, 11.

Guarneri, Carl. *America in the World: United States History in Global Context.* New York: McGraw-Hill, 2007.

Guterl, Matthew Pratt. *The Color of Race in America, 1900–1940.* Cambridge: Harvard University Press, 2001.

Guttmann, Allen. *From Ritual to Record: The Nature of Modern Sports.* New York: Columbia University Press, 1978.

Guttmann, Allen. *Games and Empires.* New York: Columbia University Press, 1994.

Guttmann, Allen. *Sports: The First Five Millennia.* Amherst: University of Massachusetts Press, 2004.

Guttmann, Allen. *Sports Spectators.* New York: Columbia University Press, 1986.

Guttmann, Allen. *Women's Sports: A History.* New York: Columbia University Press, 1991.

"Gymnastics 5. 19th-Century European Gymnastics." Available: www.hickoksports.com/history/gymnastics05.shtml.

Halberstam, David. *Playing for Keeps: Michael Jordan and the World He Made.* New York: Random House, 1999.

*Halsey, Elizabeth. *The Development of Public Recreation in Metropolitan Chicago.* Chicago: Recreation Commission, 1940.

Hardy, Stephen. "Adopted by All the Leading Clubs: Sporting Goods and the Shaping of Leisure." *Sport in America: From Wicked Amusements to National Obsession.* Ed. David K. Wiggins. Champaign, IL: Human Kinetics, 1995. 133–150.

Hardy, Stephen. *How Boston Played: Sport, Recreation, and Community, 1865–1915.* Boston: Northeastern University Press, 1982.

*Hartwell, Edward M. "President's Address—The Condition and Prospects of Physical Education in the United States." *Proceedings of the American Association for the Advancement of Physical Education, at the Seventh Annual Meeting Held in Philadelphia, PA, 1892.* Springfield, MA: Press of Springfield Print and Binding, 1893. 13–40.

Harvard Advocate 24.5 (November 16, 1877): 49.

Harvard Graduates Magazine 5.17 (September, 1896): 66–68.

Hauser, Thomas, and Stephen Brunt. *The Italian Stallions: Heroes of Boxing's Glory Days.* Toronto: Sport Media Publishing, 2003.

Hedenborg, Susanna, and G. Gertrud Pfister. "Écuyères and 'Doing Gender': Presenting Femininity in a Male Domain." *Scandinavian Sport Studies Forum* 3.1 (2012): S25–47.

Henricksen, Joe. "Like Nothing They'd Seen Before." *Chicago Sun-Times* 29 June 2014: 48.

Hewitt, Brian. "A Game of Pain." *Chicago Sun-Times* 19 September 1993: 17B–19B.

Hibner, Charles. *The Rose Bowl, 1902–1929.* Jefferson, NC: McFarland, 1993.

Hiestand, Michael and Rudy Martzke. "Bidding for the Olympics on TV." USA Today, April 22, 2003 at http://usatoday30.usatoday.com/sports/olympics/2003-04-21-tv-rights_x.htm#fees.

*Higginson, Thomas W. "A Letter to a Dyspeptic." *Atlantic Monthly* 3 (April 1859): 465–474.

*Higginson, Thomas W. "Saints, and Their Bodies." *Atlantic Monthly* 1 (March 1858): 583– 590.

A History of the Schuylkill Fishing Company of the State in Schuylkill, 1732–1888. Philadelphia: Members of the State in Schuylkill (Schuylkill Fishing Company), 1889.

Hofmann, Annette R. "Lady Turners in the United States: German American Identity, Gender Concerns, and Turnerism." *Journal of Sport History* 27 (Fall 2000): 389–390.

Hogan, David J. *Class and Reform: School and Society in Chicago, 1880–1930.* Philadelphia: University of Pennsylvania Press, 1985.

Holland, Barbara. *Gentlemen's Blood: A History of Dueling from Swords at Dawn to Pistols at Dusk.* New York: Bloomsbury, 2003.

Hong, Fan, and J.A. Mangan, eds. *Soccer, Women, Sexual Liberation: Kicking Off a New Era.* London: Cass, 2003.

Horsman, Reginald. *Race and Manifest Destiny: The Origins of American Racial Anglo-Saxonism.* Cambridge: Harvard University Press, 1981.

Hoxie, Frederick E. *A Final Promise: The Campaign to Assimilate the Indians, 1880–1920.* New York: Cambridge University Press, 1989.

http://espn.go.com/nfl/topics/_/page/new-orleans-saints-bounty-scandal.

http://hoopspeak.com/2011/09/know-your-nba-lockout-history-1999-lockout-calendar.

http://sports.espn.go.com/mlb/news/story?id=1856626.

http://sports.espn.go.com/nfl/news/story?id=5527564.

Hughes, Glyn. "Managing Black Guys: Representation, Corporate Culture, and the NBA." *Sociology of Sport Journal* 21.2 (2004): 163–184.

Hult, Joan, and Marianna Trekell, eds. *A Century of Women's Basketball: From Frailty to Final Four.* Reston, VA: American Alliance for Health, Physical Education, Recreation and Dance, 1991.

Hunt, Linda Lawrence. *Bold Spirit: Helga Estby's Forgotten Walk Across Victorian America.* New York: Anchor Books, 2006.

Hutchins, Brett, and David Rowe. *Sport Beyond Television: The Internet, Digital Media and the Rise of Networked Media Sport.* New York: Routledge, 2012.

IFAF (International Federation of American Football). Available: ifaf.org/articles/view/1633.

Ignatiev, Noel. *How the Irish Became White.* New York: Routledge, 1995.

Isaac, Rhys. *The Transformation of Virginia, 1740–1790.* Chapel Hill: University of North Carolina Press, 1982.

Isenberg, Michael T. *John L. Sullivan and His America.* Urbana: University of Illinois Press. 1988.

Jable, J. Thomas. "Pennsylvania's Blue Laws: A Quaker Experiment in the Suppression of Sport and Amusements." *Journal of Sport History* 1 (1974): 107–121.

Jable, J. Thomas. "Social Class and the Sport of Cricket in Philadelphia, 1850–1880." *Journal of Sport History* 18.2 (Summer 1991): 205–223.

Jacobson, Matthew Frye. *Barbarian Virtues: The United States Encounters Foreign Peoples at Home and Abroad, 1876–1917.* New York: Hill and Wang, 2000.

Jacobson, Matthew Frye. *Whiteness of a Different Color: European Immigrants and the Alchemy of Race.* Cambridge: Harvard University Press, 1998.

Jennings, Peter, and Todd Brewster. *The Century.* New York: Doubleday, 1998.

Johns, Maxine James, and Jane Farrell-Beck. "'Cut Out the Sleeves': Nineteenth-Century U.S. Women Swimmers and Their Attire." *Dress* 28 (2001): 53–63.

Johnson, Elmer L. *The History of YMCA Physical Education.* Chicago: Association Press, 1979.

Johnson, Janis A. "Equestrian Competitions." *Native Americans in Sport.* Ed. C. Richard King. Armonk, NY: Sharpe, 2004. 105–107.

*Johnson, Laurence, J. "Half Century of American Swimming." *Amateur Athlete* (December 1938): 9, 51, 55.

Jones, Constance. *1001 Things Everyone Should Know About Women's History* (New York: Broadway Books, 2003).

Jonsrud, Jarrod. "Tiger Woods." *American Sports: A History of Icons, Idols, and Ideas.* Ed. Murry R. Nelson. Santa Barbara: Greenwood, 2013. 1485–1491.

*Jordan, Edward S. "Buying Football Victories." *Collier's* 11 November 1905: 19–20, 23.

*"Joshua Ward. The Champion Sculler of America." *Frank Leslie's Illustrated Newspaper* 8 August 1863: 315.

Jozsa, Frank P., Jr. *Sports Capitalism: The Foreign Business of American Professional Leagues.* Burlington, VT: Ashgate, 2004.

Kay, Joanne, and Suzanne Laberge. "The 'New' Corporate Habitus in Adventure Racing." *International Review for the Sociology of Sport* 37.1 (2002): 17–36

Keith, Susan. "Double Ball." *Native Americans in Sport*. Ed. C. Richard King. Armonk, NY: Sharpe, 2004. 101–102.

Kennedy, John H. *A Course of Their Own: A History of African American Golfers*. Lincoln: University of Nebraska Press, 2000.

Kerber, Linda K. *No Constitutional Right to Be Ladies: Women and the Obligations of Citizenship*. New York: Hill and Wang, 1998.

Kietlinski, Robin. *Japanese Women and Sport: Beyond Baseball and Sumo*. New York: Bloomsbury, 2014.

King, Richard C., ed. *Native Americans in Sport*. Armonk, NY: Sharpe, 2004.

Kingsdale, Jon M. "The Poor Man's Club: Social Functions of the Urban Working Class Saloon." *American Quarterly* 25 (October, 1973): 472–489.

Kirsch, George B. "Baseball Spectators, 1855–1870." *Major Problems in American Sport History: Documents and Essays*. Ed. Steven A. Riess. Boston: Houghton Mifflin, 1997. 103–110.

*Kirsch, George B., ed. *Sports in North America: A Documentary History, Volume 3: The Rise of Modern Sports, 1840–1860*. Gulf Stream, FL: Academic International Press, 1992.

*Kirsch, George B., ed. *Sports in North America: A Documentary History, Volume 4: Sports in War, Revival and Expansion, 1860–1880*. Gulf Stream, FL: Academic International Press, 1995.

Kirsch, George B. "Young Men's Hebrew Association." *Encyclopedia of Ethnicity and Sports in the United States*. Ed. George B. Kirsch, Othello Harris, and Claire E. Nolte. Westport, CT: Greenwood Press, 2000. 501–502.

Kirsch, George B., Othello Harris, and Claire E. Nolte, eds. *Encyclopedia of Ethnicity and Sports in the United States*. Westport, CT: Greenwood Press, 2000.

Knisely, Michael. "Everybody Has the Dream—Baseball Scouting and Players' Hopes of Success in Dominican Republic." *Sporting News* 19 February 2001. Available: findarticles.com/p/articles/mi_m1208/is_8_225/ai_70926950.

Kogan, Rick. *Brunswick: The Story of an American Company from 1845 to 1985*. Skokie, IL: Brunswick Corp., 1985.

Koppedrayer, Kay. "Archery." *Native Americans in Sport*. Ed. C. Richard King. Armonk, NY: Sharpe, 2004. 19–23.

Kozar, Andrew J. *R. Tait McKenzie: The Sculptor of Athletes*. Knoxville: University of Tennessee Press, 1975.

Kreitzer, Matthew E. "Diamonds, Ovals, and Rings: Northwestern Shoshone Sports at the Washakie Colony of Northern Utah, 1903–1929." *The International Journal of the History of Sport* 23.2 (March 2006): 232–246.

LaFeber, Walter. *Michael Jordan and the New Global Capitalism*. New York: Norton, 1999.

Lapchick, Richard. "Lack of Diversity Among Campus, Conference Leaders at Division IA Schools May Contribute to Lack of Diversity in Head Football Coaching Positions." *The Buck Stops Here: Assessing Diversity among Campus and Conference Leaders for Division IA Schools.* November 17, 2004. Orlando, FL: Institute for Diversity and Ethics in Sport at the University of Central Florida. Available: www.bus.ucf.edu/sport/public/downloads/Release%20Lapchick%20Study%20in%20Diversity%20in%20Leaders.

Larkin, Jack. *The Reshaping of Everyday Life in America, 1790–1840*. New York: Harper & Row, 1988.

Laqueur, Walter. *Young Germany: A History of the German Youth Movement*. New York: Basic Books, 1962.

*"A Law, Relative to the Park, Battery and Bowling Green." *New York Courier* 27 March 1816: 3.

Leab, Daniel J. "Tilden, William Tatem, Jr. ('Bill')." *The Scribner Encyclopedia of American Lives*. Ed. Arnold Markoe. New York: Scribner's, 2002. Vol. 2: 429–431.

Le Batard, Dan. "Next Detour." *ESPN The Magazine* 24 December 2001: 105–111.

Ledbetter, Bonnie S. "Sports and Games of the American Revolution." *Journal of Sport History* 6 (1979): 29–40.

Lennartz, Karl, and Walter Teutenberg. *II. Olympische spiele 1900 in Paris*. Kassel, Germany: Agon Sportverlag, 1995.

Lennartz, K. and Teutenberg, W. "The Countess de Pourtales—After All the First Modern Female Starter." *Citius, Altius, Fortius (wurde 1997 zum Journal of Olympic History)*, 4.2 (1996): 30-32.

Lester, Larry. "Black Baseball's National Showcase: The East–West Classic." 8th Annual Jerry Malloy Negro League Conference. Chicago, IL, 2005. 61–66.

Lester, Robin. *Stagg's University: The Rise, Decline, and Fall of Big-Time Football at Chicago*. Champaign: University of Illinois Press, 1995.

Levine, Peter. *A.G. Spalding and the Rise of Baseball: The Promise of American Sport*. New York: Oxford University Press, 1985.

*Levine, Peter. *American Sport: A Documentary History*. Englewood Cliffs, NJ: Prentice Hall, 1989.

Levine, Peter. *Ellis Island to Ebbets Field: Sport and the American Jewish Experience*. New York: Oxford University Press, 1992.

*Lewis, Diocletian. *New Gymnastics for Men, Women, and Children*. Boston: Ticknor and Fields, 1862.

Lewis, R.M. "American Croquet in the 1860s: Playing the Game and Winning." *Journal of Sport History* 18.3 (Winter 1991): 365–386.

Liberti, Rita. "'We Were Ladies, We Just Played Like Boys': African-American Womanhood and Competitive Basketball at Bennett College, 1928–1942." *Sport and the Color Line: Black Athletes and Race Relations in Twentieth-Century America*. Eds. Patrick B. Miller and David K. Wiggins. New York: Routledge, 2004. 83–99.

Lieser, Ethen. "Time for APAs to Embrace Yao Ming." *AsianWeek* (July 19–July 25, 2002) 30 December 2007. Available: http://asianweek.com/2002_07_19/sports_yao.html.

Litke, Jim. "NCAA Knows 'Lack of Institutional Control.'" Available: www.huffingtonpost.com/2013/02/20/ncaa-lack-of-institutional-control.

Littlewood, Thomas B. *Arch: A Promoter, Not a Poet*. Ames: Iowa State University Press, 1990.

lol.gamepedia.com/2013_World_Cyber_Games/Main_Tournament.

Lucas, John A. "A Prelude to the Rise of Sport: Ante-Bellum America, 1850–1860." *Quest* 11 (December 1968): 50–57.

Lucas, John A., and Ronald A. Smith. *Saga of American Sport*. Philadelphia: Lee & Febiger, 1978.

Lyall, Sarah. "A's for Athletes, but Charges of Fraud at North Carolina." 2 January 2014. Available: www.nytimes.com/2014/01/01/sports/as-for-athletes-but-charges-of-tar-heel-fraud.html.

*Lyde, Byfield. *Boston Weekly Newsletter* 5 August 1736: 2.

MacCambridge, Michael, ed. *ESPN: Sports Century*. New York: Hyperion, 1999.

MacGregor, Alan Leander. "Tammany: The Indian as Rhetorical Surrogate." *American Quarterly* 35.4 (Autumn 1983): 391–407.

Maguire, Joseph. "Body Cultures: Diversity, Sustainability, Globalisation." *Games of the Past—Sports for the Future?* Ed. Gertrud Pfister. Sankt Augustin, Germany: Academia Verlag, 2004.

Maguire, Joseph. *Global Sport: Identities, Societies, Civilizations*. Cambridge: Polity Press, 1999.

Majumdar, Boria, and Sean Brown. "Why Baseball, Why Cricket? Differing Nationalisms, Differing Challenges." *The International Journal of the History of Sport* 24.2 (February 2007): 139–156.

Mangan, J.A. *Athleticism in the Victorian and Edwardian Public School: The Emergence and Consolidation of an Educational Ideology*. New York: Cambridge University Press, 1981.

Mangan, James A., and Andrew Ritchie, eds. *Ethnicity, Sport, Identity: Struggles for Status*. London: Cass, 2004.

Mangan, James A., and Roberta J. Parks, eds. *From "Fair Sex" to Feminism: Sport and the Socialization of Women in the Industrial and Post-Industrial Eras*. London: Cass, 1987.

Markoe, Arnold, ed. *The Scribner Encyclopedia of American Lives: Sports Figures*. New York: Scribner's, 2002.

Marks, Patricia. *Bicycles, Bangs, and Bloomers: The New Woman in the Popular Press*. Lexington: University Press of Kentucky, 1990.

Martin, Charles H. *Benching Jim Crow: The Rise and Fall of the Color Line in Southern College Sports, 1890–1980*. Champaign: University of Illinois Press, 2010.

Maske, Mark. "Washington Redskins, New Orleans Saints Had Bounty Systems That Paid for Big Hits." *Washington Post* 2 March 2012. Available: www.washingtonpost.com/blogs/football-insider/post/new-orleans-saints-had-bounty-system-that-paid-for-injuring-opponents-nfl-announces/2012/03/02/gIQAPNDDnR_blog.html.

Mason, Daniel S. "Arthur Dorrington." *African Americans in Sports*. Ed. David K. Wiggins. Armonk, NT: Sharpe, 2004. 87.

Masucci, Matthew A. "Ultimate Fighting Championship (UFC) and Mixed Martial Arts (MMA)." *American Sports: A History of Icons, Idols, and Ideas*. Ed. Murry R. Nelson. Santa Barbara: Greenwood, 2013. 1397–1400.

McAleer, Kevin. *Dueling: The Cult of Honor in Fin-de-Siècle Germany*. Princeton, NJ: Princeton University Press, 1994.

McClymer, John, ed. *This High and Holy Moment: The First National Woman's Rights Convention, Worcester, 1850*. San Diego: Harcourt College Publishers, 1999.

McCrossen, Alexis. *Holy Day, Holiday: The American Sunday*. Ithaca and London: Cornell University Press, 2000.

McDaniels, Pellom, III. *The Prince of Jockeys: The Life of Isaac Burns Murphy*. Lexington: University Press of Kentucky, 2013.

McLaughlin, Martin. "Salt Lake City Bribery Scandal: The Buying of the Olympic Games." 31 January 1999. Available: www.wsws.org/en/articles/1999/01/olym-j13.html.

McMurry, Sally. "Who Read the Agricultural Journals? Evidence from Chenango County, New York, 1839–1865." *Agricultural History* 63.4 (Fall 1989): 1–18.

Meneses, Diana. "Kick Stick." *Native Americans in Sport*. Ed. C. Richard King. Armonk, NY: Sharpe, 2004. 168.

Meneses, Diana. "Shuttlecock." *Native Americans in Sport*. Ed. C. Richard King. Armonk, NY: Sharpe, 2004. 280–281.

Menna, Larry K., ed. *Sports in North America: A Documentary History, Volume 2: Origins of Modern Sports, 1820–1840*. Gulf Stream, FL: Academic International Press, 1995.

Mercury Sport. 28 July 2006: 24.

Meyerowitz, Joanne J. *Women Adrift: Independent Wage Earners in Chicago, 1880–1930*. Chicago: University of Chicago Press, 1988.

"Mia Hamm." Answers.com. Available: www.answers.com/topic/mia-hamm.

"Mia Hamm." Spiritus-Temporis.com. Available: www.spiritus-temporis.com/mia-hamm.

*Miller, Elizabeth Smith. "The Bloomer." *This High and Holy Moment: The First National Woman's Rights Convention, Worcester, 1850*. Ed. John F. McClymer. San Diego: Harcourt Brace College Publishers, 1999, 46–48.

Miller, Patrick B., and David K. Wiggins, eds. *Sport and the Color Line: Black Athletes and Race Relations in Twentieth-Century America*. New York: Routledge, 2004.

Miller, Toby, Geoffrey Lawrence, Jim McKay, and David Rowe. *Globalization and Sport: Playing the World*. London: Sage, 2001.

Misztal, Barbara A. Theories of social remembering. Berkshire, England: Open UP, 2003. http://site.ebrary.com/id/10172378.

Mooney, Katherine C. *Race Horse Men: How Slavery and Freedom Were Made at the Racetrack*. Cambridge and London: Harvard University Press, 2014.

Moritz, Amy. "The Glass Ceiling Still Exists." 27 April 2011. Available: http://awsmonline.org/another-failing-grade-for-gender-diversity.

Morrissey, Rick. "NFL Fans Tune In, Tune Out," *Chicago Sun-Times* 12 October 2014: 80.

Mrozek, Donald J. *Sport and American Mentality, 1880–1910*. Knoxville: University of Tennessee Press, 1983.

*Naismith, James. *Basketball: Its Origin and Development*. 1941. Rpt. Lincoln: University of Nebraska Press, 1996.

Narragansett Boat Club. "History of NBC." Available: www.rownbc.org/club-info/history.

Nash, Gary B., Julie Roy Jeffrey, John R. Howe, Peter J. Frederick, Allen F. Davis, and Allan M. Winkler. *The American People: Creating a Nation and a Society*. Brief 3rd ed. New York: Addison-Wesley Longman, 2000.

Nash, Gary B., Julie Roy Jeffrey, John R. Howe, Peter J. Frederick, Allen F. Davis, and Allan M. Winkler. *The American People: Creating a Nation and a Society*. Vol. 1: To 1877. Brief 5th ed. New York: Longman, 2006.

*Nast, Thomas. "Central Park in Winter." Illustration of winter scenes. *Harper's Weekly* 30 January 1864: 72.

Nathan, Daniel A. "Sometimes, ESPN Seems Ubiquitous." *Journal of Sport History* 27.3 (Fall 2000): 528–531.

NCAA.org. "Key Dates in NCAA Drug-Testing History." Available: http://fs.ncaa.org/Docs/NCAANewsArchive/2006/Association-wide/key+dates+in+ncaa+drug-testing+history+-+11-20-06+ncaa+news.html.

Neely, Wayne Caldwell. *The Agricultural Fair*. 1935. Rpt. New York: AMS Press, 1967.

Nelson, David M. *Anatomy of a Game: Football, the Rules, and the Men Who Made the Game*. Newark: University of Delaware Press, 1994.

Nelson, Kelly. "Miller, Cheryl DeAnn." *The Scribner Encyclopedia of American Lives*. Ed. Arnold Markoe. New York: Scribner's, 2002: 144–146.

Nelson, Murry, R., ed. *American Sports: A History of Icons, Idols, and Ideas*. Santa Barbara, CA: Greenwood, 2013.

*"The New York Times Reports on an International Match: The Harvard-Oxford Boat Race, 1869." *Major Problems in American Sport History, Documents and Essays*. Ed. Steven A. Riess. Boston: Houghton Mifflin, 1997. 113–114.

Nocera, Joe. "Academic Counseling Racket." Available: www.nytimes.com/2013/02/05/opinion/nocera-academic-counseling-racket.html?hp&.

Nora, Pierre. Les Lieux de Mémoire, 7 vols. Paris: Gallimard, 1984–1992.

Noverr, Douglas A., and Lawrence E. Ziewacz. *The Games They Played.* Chicago: Nelson-Hall, 1983.

O'Fearghail, Caoimhin. "Ball Race." *Native Americans in Sport.* Ed. C. Richard King. Armonk, NY: Sharpe, 2004. 29–30.

"O'Leary's Tournament." Chicago Tribune *1 September 1880, 3.*

olympic.blogspot.com/2009/10/commercialization. html.

Overman, Steven J. *The Protestant Ethic and the Spirit of Sport: How Calvinism and Capitalism Shaped America's Games.* Macon, GA: Mercer University Press, 2011.

Oxendine, Joseph B. *American Indian Sports Heritage.* Lincoln: University of Nebraska Press, 1988.

Parezo, Nancy J. "A 'Special Olympics:' Testing Racial Strength and Endurance at the 1904 Louisiana Purchase Exposition." *The 1904 Anthropology Days and Olympic Games: Sport, Race, and American Imperialism.* Ed. Susan Brownell. Lincoln: University of Nebraska Press, 2008. 59–126.

Park, Roberta J. "'Embodied Selves': The Rise and Development of Concern for Physical Education, Active Games and Recreation for American Women, 1776–1865." *Sport in America: From Wicked Amusements to National Obsession.* Ed. David K. Wiggins. Champaign, IL: Human Kinetics, 1995. 69–93.

Park, Roberta J. "Physiologists, Physicians, and Physical Educators: Nineteenth-Century Biology and Exercise, Hygienic and Educative." *Journal of Sport History* 14 (1987): 28–61.

Park, Roberta J. "Physiology and Anatomy Are Destiny! Brains, Bodies, and Exercise in Nineteenth-Century American Thought." *Journal of Sport History* 18.1 (Spring 1991): 31–63.

Park, Roberta J. "Sports and Recreation Among Chinese American Communities of the Pacific Coast From Time of Arrival to the 'Quiet Decade' of the 1950s." *Journal of Sport History* 27.3 (Fall 2000): 445–480.

Pearson, Daniel M. *Baseball in 1889: Players vs. Owners.* Bowling Green, OH: Bowling Green University Press, 1993.

Pfister, Gertrud. "Cold War Diplomats in Tracksuits: The Fräuleinwunder of East German Sport." *European Sports History Review* 5 (2003): 223–252.

Pfister, Gertrud. "Cultural Confrontations: German Turnen, Swedish Gymnastics and English Sport—European Diversity in Physical Activities From a Historical Perspective." *Culture, Sport, Society* 6 (2003): 1, 61–91.

Pfister, Gertrud. "Female Leaders in Sports Organizations—Worldwide Trends." *Hat Fuhrung ein Geschlecht? Genderarrangements in Entscheidungsgremien des Deutschen Sports.* Eds. Gudrun Doll-Tepper and Gertrud Pfister. Cologne: Strauss, 2004. 49–63.

Pfister, Gertrud. "'Die außer-ordentlichen' Spiele: methologische Überlegungen zur historischen Forschung über Frauen in der Olympischen Bewung." *Olympia als Bildungsidee; Beiträge zur olympischen Geschichte und Pädagogik.* Eds. Michael Krüger and Annette Hofmann. Wiesbaden: Springer VS, 2013.

Pfister, Gertrud, and Annette R. Hofmann. "Turnen—a Forgotten Movement Culture: Its Beginnings in Germany and Diffusion in the United States." *Turnen and Sport: Transatlantic Transfers.* Ed. Annette R. Hofmann (Hrsg.). Münster: Waxmann, 2004. 11–24.

Pfister, Gertrude. "1848 und die Anfänge des Mädchen-und Frauenturnens." *Deutsches turnen*, 1981. 1, 8-10; 2, 29-30; 3, 47-49.

*"Philadelphia, 13 May." *Federal Gazette* 13 May 1789.

Pierce, Bessie Louise. *A History of Chicago.* Vol. 2. New York: Knopf, 1940.

Pierce, Bessie Louise. *A History of Chicago: The Rise of a Modern City, 1871–1893.* Vol. 3. New York: Knopf, 1957.

A Plea for Playgrounds. Report by the Special Park Commission of Chicago, 1905.

Plymire, Darcy C. "Positive Addiction: Running and Human Potential in the 1970s." *Journal of Sport History* 31.3 (Fall 2004): 297–315.

Podell, Ira. "New-Look NHL Set to Drop Puck on Return Season." *Chicago Sun-Times* 2 October 2005: 93A.

Poniatowski, Kelly. "Shaun White." *American Sports: A History of Icons, Idols, and Ideas.* Ed. Murry R. Nelson. Santa Barbara: Greenwood, 2013. 1449–1451.

Ponsford, Matthew. "Los Angeles to Build World's Most Expensive Stadium Complex." CNN.com Architecture. 19 January 2016. Available: www.cnn.com/2016/01/19/architecture/new-nfl-stadium-los-angeles/index.html.

Pope, Steven W., ed. *The New American Sport History: Recent Approaches and Perspectives.* Champaign: University of Illinois Press, 1997.

Pope, Steven W. *Patriotic Games: Sporting Traditions in the American Imagination, 1876–1926.* New York: Oxford University Press, 1997.

Powers, Madelon. *Faces Along the Bar: Lore and Order in the Workingman's Saloon, 1879–1920.* Chicago: University of Chicago Press, 1998.

Powers-Beck, Jeffrey. *The American Indian Integration of Baseball.* Lincoln: University of Nebraska Press, 2004.

Priest, Laurie. "The Whole IX Yards: The Impact of Title IX: The Good, the Bad, and the Ugly." *Women In Sport and Physical Activity Journal* 12.2 (Fall 2003): 27–43.

Proctor, John Clagget. "Potomac Boat Club Won National Fame." *Sunday Star* 6 April 1930: 8–9.

profootballtalk.nbcsports.com/2011/07/25/winners-losers-from-the-nfl-lockout.

Pruter, Robert. "Chicago High School Football Struggles, the Fight for Faculty Control, and the War Against Secret Societies, 1898–1908." *Journal of Sport History* 30.1 (Spring 2003): 47–72.

Pruter, Robert. "Chicago Lights Up Football World." *College Football Historical Society* 18.2 (Feb. 2005): 7–9.

"Queen of the Green." MSNBC Sports. 6 February 2008. Available: www.msnbc.msn.com/id/5454494.

Rader, Benjamin G. *American Sports: From the Age of Folk Games to the Age of Spectators.* Englewood Cliffs, NJ: Prentice Hall, 1983.

Rader, Benjamin, G. *American Sports: From the Age of Folk Games to the Age of Televised Sports.* Englewood Cliffs, NJ: Prentice Hall, 2004.

Rader, Benjamin, G. *American Ways: A History of American Cultures, 1500–1865.* Vol. 1. 2nd ed. Belmont, CA: Thompson Wadsworth, 2006.

Rader, Benjamin G. "The Quest for Subcommunities and the Rise of American Sport." *American Quarterly* 29 (1977): 355–369.

Raffety, Matthew Taylor. "Elgin Baylor." *The Scribner Encyclopedia of American Lives.* Ed. Arnold Markoe. New York: Scribner's, 2002. Vol. 1: 61–63.

*Ray, Bob. "Eleanor Holm Wins Swim Crown." *Los Angeles Times* 12 August 1932: 9.

*Ray, Bob. "Field Day Held by Swim Stars." *Los Angeles Times* 10 August 1932: 11.

"Record May Prove Man's Stature as First Native American Player in Baseball History." *Bangor Daily News* 26 January 2006. Available: http://historynews-network.org/article/21008.

Redmond, Gerald. *The Caledonian Games in Nineteenth-Century America.* Cranbury, NJ: Associated University Presses, 1971.

Reed, William F. "Culture Shock in Dixieland." 12 August 1991. Available: www.si.com/vault/1991/08/12/124692/the-sec-culture-shock-in-dixieland-blacks-now-dominate-the-once-lily-white-southeastern-conference.

Reel, Guy. *The National Police Gazette and the Making of the Modern American Man, 1879–1906.* New York: Palgrave Macmillan, 2006.

Reisler, Jim. *Walk of Ages: Edward Payson Weston's Extraordinary Trek Across America.* Lincoln: University of Nebraska Press, 2015.

Reisler, Jim. *Walk of Ages: Edward Payson Weston's Extraordinary Trek Across America.* Lincoln, NE: University of Nebraska Press, 2015.

*Rice, Grantland. *The Tumult and the Shouting: My Life in Sport.* New York: Barnes, 1954.

Riess, Steven A. *City Games: The Evolution of American Urban Society and the Rise of Sports.* Champaign: University of Illinois Press, 1991.

Riess, Steven A. "Introduction." *The Chicago Sports Reader.* Eds. Steven A. Riess and Gerald R. Gems. Urbana: University of Illinois Press, 2009. 1–57.

*Riess, Steven A., ed. *Major Problems in American Sport History: Documents and Essays.* Boston: Houghton Mifflin, 1997.

Riess, Steven A. *Sport in Industrial America, 1850–1920.* Wheeling, IL: Harlan Davidson, 1995.

Riess, Steven A., ed. *Sports and the American Jew.* Syracuse: Syracuse University Press, 1998.

Rinehart, Robert E., and Synthia Sydnor, eds. *To the Extreme: Alternative Sports, Inside and Out.* Albany: State University of New York Press, 2003.

Roberts, Randy. *Papa Jack: Jack Johnson and the Era of White Hopes.* New York: Free Press, 1983.

Roediger, David R., ed. *Black on White: Black Writers on What It Means to Be White.* New York: Schocken Books, 1998.

Roediger, David R. *The Wages of Whiteness: Race and the Making of the American Working Class.* London: Verso, 1999.

Rogers, Phil. "Path to the States?" *Chicago Tribune* 11 February 2007, 3: 6–7.

Rojas, Enrique. "Organizers Have Spent $50 Million on Classic." ESPN.com 16 March 2006. Available: http://espn.go.com/mlb/worldclassic2006/news/story?id=2371119.

Rorabaugh, W.J. *The Alcoholic Republic: An American Tradition.* New York: Oxford University Press, 1979.

Rosengarten, Theodore, and Dale Rosengarten, eds. *A Portion of the People: Three Hundred Years of Southern Jewish Life.* Columbia: University of Southern Carolina Press, 2002.

Rosenzweig, Roy. *Eight Hours for What We Will: Workers and Leisure in an Industrial City.* New York: Cambridge University Press, 1983.

Rosenzweig, Roy, and Elizabeth Blackmar. *The Park and the People: A History of Central Park.* Ithaca, NY: Cornell University Press, 1992.

Rother, Amalie. "Das Damenfahren." *Der Radsport in Bild und Wort, München 1897.* Ed. Paul von Salvisberg. Trans. from German by Rodelinde Albrecht [Reprint.]. Hildesheim: Olms Presse, 1980. S. 111–127.

Rotundo, E. Anthony. *American Manhood: Transformations in Masculinity from the Revolution to the Modern Era.* New York: Basic Books, 1994.

Runstedtler, Theresa. "African American Boxers, the New Negro, and the Global Color Line." *Radical History Review* 103 (Winter 2009): 59–81.

Sage, George H. *Power and Ideology in American Sport: A Critical Perspective.* Champaign, IL: Human Kinetics, 1990.

*Sahagún, Fray Bernardino de. "The Florentine Codex: General History of the Things of New Spain, Book 8." ca. 1550–1569. *Sports in North America: A Documentary History, Volume I, Part II: Sports in the Colonial Era, 1618–1783.* Ed. Thomas Altherr. Gulf Stream, FL: Academic International Press, 1997. 449–450.

Scharff, Virginia. *Taking the Wheel: Women and the Coming of the Motor Age.* New York: Free Press, 1991.

Schexnayder, C.J. "The Integration of Football in the Southeastern Conference." 9 May 2012. Available: www.teamspeedkills.com/2012/5/9/3008248/the-integration-of-football-in-the-southeastern-conference.

Schimmel, K.S., A.G. Ingham, and J.W. Howell. *Professional Team Sport and the American City: Urban Politics and Franchise Relocation.* Champaign, IL: Human Kinetics, 1993.

scholar.lib.vt.edu/ejournals/ALAN/v29n1/simmons.html.

Schultz, Jaime. "Paralympic Games." *American Sports: A History of Icons, Idols, and Ideas.* Ed. Murry R. Nelson. Santa Barbara, CA: Greenwood, 2013. 1003–1004.

Schultz, Jaime, and Callie Batts, Perry Cohen, Sarah Olson, Amie Chaudry, Jaime Ryan, and Caitlin Shannon. "Casey Martin Playing Winning Golf with a Disability." *Encyclopedia of Sports in America.* Ed. Murry R. Nelson. Westport, CTCT: Greenwood, 2009. 529.

Schultz, Jaime, and Callie Batts, Perry Cohen, Sarah Olson, Amie Chaudry, Jaime Ryan, and Caitlin Shannon. "Paralympics." *Encyclopedia of Sports in America.* Ed. Murry R. Nelson. Westport, CT: Greenwood, 2009. 521–522.

Seifried, Chad. "Bowl Championship Series." *American Sports: A History of Icons, Idols, and Ideas.* Ed. Murry R. Nelson. Santa Barbara, CA: Greenwood, 2013. 170–175.

Seymour, Harold. *Baseball: The People's Game.* New York: Oxford University Press, 1990.

Silverman, Al, ed. *Best from Sport.* New York: Bartholomew House, 1961.

*"Skating." Article and image. *Harper's Weekly* 12 February 1859: 100–101.

*"Skating on the Ladies' Skating Pond." *Harper's Weekly* 28 January 1860: 56–57.

Sklar, Kathryn Kish. *Catharine Beecher: A Study in American Domesticity.* New York: Norton, 1973.

Smith, Michael. "LeBron James." *American Sports: A History of Icons, Idols, and Ideas.* Ed. Murry R. Nelson. Santa Barbara, CA: Greenwood, 2013. 603–608.

*Smith, Ronald A., ed. *Big-Time Football at Harvard, 1905—The Diary of Coach Bill Reid.* Champaign: University of Illinois Press, 1994.

Smith, Ronald A. *Sports and Freedom: The Rise of Big-Time College Athletics.* New York: Oxford University Press, 1988.

Smith, Ronald A. *Wounded Lions: Joe Paterno, Jerry Sandusky, and the Crises in Penn State Athletics.* Champaign: University of Illinois Press, 2016.

*Smith, Wilfred. "Claudia Eckert Wins Senior Girls' Crown." *Chicago Tribune* 28 July 1930, pt. 2: 21, 23.

*Smith, Wilfred. "J.P.I. Enters 53 in Tribune Swim Events." *Chicago Tribune* 1 July 1930, pt. 2: 2.

Solomon, Jimmie Lee. "Percentage of Major League African-American Players Has Fallen Drastically." May 7, 2014. Available: http://www.huffingtonpost.com/jimmie-lee-solomon/african-american-baseball-players_b_4923689.html.

Spears, Betty, and Richard Swanson. *History of Sport and Physical Education in the United States.* Dubuque, IA: Brown, 1988.

Sperber, Murray. *Shake Down the Thunder: The Creation of Notre Dame Football.* New York: Holt, 1993.

Spirou, Costas, and Larry Bennett. *It's Hardly Sportin': Stadiums, Neighborhoods, and the New Chicago.* DeKalb: Northern Illinois University Press, 2003.

Sports Illustrated 27 December 2004.

"Sports Illustrated Facts." Available: http://sportsillustrated.cnn.com/thenetwork/tour/sifacts.

Sports Illustrated, "Media Kit." 2016. Available: www.simediakit.com/home/magazine/audience.

*"Sports of the Turf." Advertisement. *City Gazette.* February 26, 1816.

*Stagg, Amos Alonzo. Letter to his sister Pauline Stagg, March 10, 1892. Gems, Gerald R. *Sports in North America: A Documentary History, Volume 5: Sports Organized, 1880–1900.* Gulf Breeze, FL: Academic International Press (1996): 143.

Stanard, William G. "Racing in Colonial Virginia." *Virginia Magazine of History and Biography* 2 (1894–1895): 296–301.

Steckbeck, John S. *Fabulous Redmen: The Carlisle Indians and Their Famous Football Teams.* Harrisburg, PA: McFarland, 1951.

Steinberg, David A. "The Workers' Sport Internationals 1920–28." *Journal of Contemporary History* 13.2 (Apr. 1978): 233–251. Available: www. www.jstor.org/stable/260115.

Steinhorn, Leonard. "How Baby Boomers Made America Better." *Chicago Sun-Times* 15 January 2006: 1B, 4B.

*Stempfel, Theodore. *Festschrift, Celebrating the Completion of Das Deutsche Haus in Indianapolis.* 1898. Rpt. German/English Edition. Ed. Giles R. Hoyt, Claudia Grossmann, Elfrieda Lang, and Eberhard Reichmann. Indianapolis: German-American Center and Indiana German Heritage Society, 1991.

Stepp, John Richard. "Interactions Between the Mississippi Choctaw and European Americans Through the Sport of Toli." *The International Journal of the History of Sport* 23.2 (March 2006): 285–293.

Sterngass, Jon. "Cheating, Gender Roles, and the Nineteenth-Century Croquet Craze." *Journal of Sport History* 25.3 (Fall 1998): 398–418.

Story, Mark. "UK's Northington and Page: The Friendship That Changed the Face of SEC Football." 5 October 2013. Available: www.kentucky.com/sports/spt-columns-blogs/mark-story/article44447571.html.

Story, Ronald. "The Country of the Young: The Meaning of Baseball in Early American Culture." *Sport in America: From Wicked Amusements to National Obsession.* Ed. David K. Wiggins. Champaign, IL: Human Kinetics, 1995. 121–132.

Stripling, Jack. "Widespread Nature of Chapel Hill's Academic Fraud Is Laid Bare." *The Chronicle of Higher Education* 23 October 2014. Available: http://chronicle.com/article/Widespread-Nature-of-Chapel/149603.

Struna, Nancy L. "'Good Wives and Gardeners, Spinners and Fearless Riders': Middle- and Upper-Rank Women in the Early American Sporting Culture." *From 'Fair Sex' to Feminism: Sport and the Socialization of Women in the Industrial and Post-Industrial Eras.* Ed. J.A. Mangan and Roberta J. Park. London: Cass, 1987. 235–255.

Struna, Nancy L. *People of Prowess: Sport, Leisure, and Labor in Early Anglo-America.* Champaign: University of Illinois Press, 1996.

Struna, Nancy L. "The Sporting Life in Puritan America." *Major Problems in American Sport History: Documents and Essays.* Ed. Steven A. Riess. Boston: Houghton Mifflin, 1997. 39–48.

Summers, Nick. "It's Too Soon to Tell if Title IX Is Done Yet." *Columbia Spectator.* 21 February 2003. Available: www.columbiaspectator.com/?q=node/11616.

Tamini, Noel. "Women Always in the Race." *Olympic Review* (1993): 204–208, 221. Available: http://library.la84.org/OlympicInformationCenter/OlympicReview/1993/ore307/ORE307m.pdf.

Teetzel, Sarah J. "Doping." *American Sports: A History of Icons, Idols, and Ideas.* Ed. Murry R. Nelson. Santa Barbara: Greenwood, 2013. 1224–1230.

Teetzel, Sarah J. "Michael Phelps." *American Sports: A History of Icons, Idols, and Ideas.* Ed. Murry R. Nelson. Santa Barbara: Greenwood, 2013. 1017–1020.

Telander, Rick. "Gay Pitchmen: An Easier Sell." *Chicago Sun-Times* 29 June 2014: 61.

Telander, Rick. "Right There in the Huddle." *Chicago Sun-Times* 18 May 2014: 73.

Telander, Rick. "Switching to the Past Tense." *Chicago Sun-Times,* 19 October 2014: 73.

Terret, Thierry. "The Military 'Olympics' of 1919: Sport, Diplomacy and Sport Politics in the Aftermath of World War One." *Journal of Olympic History* 14.2 (August 2006): 22–31.

Thiel, Stephen D., and Scott Bukstein. "Rooney Rule." *American Sports: A History of Icons, Idols, and Ideas.* Ed. Murry R. Nelson. Santa Barbara: Greenwood, 2013. 1113–1115.

*Thomas, Robert B. "Farmer's Calendar." *The Old Farmer's Almanac.* May 1851. Boston: Jenks, Palmer, 1850.

Thomason, Andy. "Key Players in Academic Fraud at U. of North Carolina." *The Chronicle of Higher Education.* Available: chronicle.com/article/Key-Players-in-Academic-Fraud/149583.

Thomason, Andy. "3 Key Findings in Chapel Hill's Academic Fraud Investigation." *The Chronicle of Higher Education.* Available: chronicle.com/blogs/ticker/3-key-findings-in-chapel-hills-academic-fraud-investigation.

Thorpe, Holly. "Betties, Babes, and Bad-Asses: A History of Female Surf, Skate and Snow Boarders." Unpublished graduate student essay, University of Waikato, 2005.

*Thrasher, Frederic. *The Gang: A Study of 1,313 Gangs in Chicago.* 1927. Rpt. Chicago: University of Chicago Press, 1963.

"Time-Line of Rowing: 1850–1899." Friends of Rowing History. 30 July 2007. Available: www.rowinghistory.net.

*Title IX of the Education Amendements of 1972, P.L. 92-318,20 U.S.C.S. Section 1681 et seq.

Todd, Jan. "The Classical Ideal and Its Impact on the Search for Suitable Exercise: 1774–1830." *Iron Game History* 2.4: 6–16.

*"To Our Friends and the Friends of Improved Farming." *The Homestead* 1 (September 4, 1856): 787.

Townsend, Kim. *Manhood at Harvard: William James and Others.* New York: Norton, 1996.

"Tuffy Rhodes." Baseball-Reference.com. Available: www.baseball-reference.com/bullpen/Tuffy_Rhodes.

"Tuffy Rhodes Minor and Japanese Leagues Statistics and History." Baseball-Reference.com. Available: www.baseball-reference.com/register/player.cgi?=rhodes001kar.

Tuohy, Brian. "The Real Story of Tim Donaghy & the NBA." Available: www.thefixisin.net/donaghy.html.

Twombly, Wells. *200 Years of Sport in America: A Pageant of a Nation at Play.* New York: McGraw-Hill, 1976.

Tygiel, Jules. Baseball's Great Experiment: Jackie Robinson and His Legacy. New York: Oxford UP. 2008.

Union-Tribune. "The NFL Is Officially Back in Business." 11 March 2011. Available: www.sandiegouniontribune.com/news/2011/mar/11/what-are-issues-nfl-labor-dispute.

"U.S. Women's Team Files Wage Discrimination Action vs. U.S. Soccer." ESPN (April 1, 2016). Available: espn.go.com/espnw/sports/article/15102506/women-national-team-files-wage-discrimination-action-vs-us-soccer-federation.

Vennum, Thomas, Jr. *American Indian Lacrosse: Little Brother of War.* Washington, DC: Smithsonian Institution Press, 1994.

Verbrugge, Martha H. *Able-Bodied Womanhood: Personal Health and Social Change in Nineteenth-Century Boston.* New York: Oxford University Press, 1988.

Verney, Kevern. *African Americans and US Popular Culture.* New York: Routledge, 2003.

Vertinsky, Patricia. *The Eternally Wounded Woman: Women, Exercise, and Doctors in the Late Nineteenth Century.* Manchester: Manchester University Press, 1990.

Vertinsky, Patricia. "A Militant Madonna: Charlotte Perkins Gilman, Feminism and Physical Culture." *The International Journal of the History of Sport* 18 (2001): 68.

Wakefield, Wanda Ellen. *Playing to Win: Sports and the American Military, 1898–1945.* Albany: State University of New York Press, 1997.

Walters, Ronald G. *American Reformers, 1815–1860.* New York: Hill and Wang, 1978.

Ware, Susan. *Title IX: A Brief History With Documents.* Boston: Bedford/St. Martin's, 2007.

*Warner, Glenn S. "Heap Big Run—Most-Fast." *Collier's.* 24 October 1931: 19, 46.

Warner, Patricia Campbell. When the Girls Came Out to Play: The Birth of American Sportswear. Boston: University of Massachusetts Press, 2006: 182-192.

Warren, Lynne. "Zoom Town." *National Geographic* 206.6 (December 2004): 114–120.

*Watson, John F. *Annals of Philadelphia, and Pennsylvania, in the Olden Time.* 1830. Rpt. Ed. Willis P. Hazard. Vol. 1. Philadelphia: Edwin S. Stuart, 1884.

web.worldbaseballclassic.com.

*"The Weather and the Park—Glorious News for the Boys!" *Harper's Weekly* 28 January 1860: 64.

*The Wheel. *Sporting Life* 28 November 1882: 6.

Wheeler, Robert F. "Organized Sport and Organized Labour: The Workers' Sports Movement." *Journal of Contemporary History* 13.2 (April 1978): 191–210. Available: www.jstor.org/stable/260113.

*"Where Are the *Grahamites*?" *Yankee Farmer* 3 (January 14, 1837): 11.

"Where's the Love?" *Chicago Sun-Times* 25 February 2007: 86A.

*Wilkin, Josephine. Letter to her mother, March 6, 1892. *Sports in North America: A Documentary History, Volume 5.* Ed. Gerald R. Gems. Gulf Breeze, FL: Academic International Press, 1996. 147-148.

The White House Historical Association. *White House Horses: Presidents at the Races.* Available:

Whittingham, Richard. Rites of Autumn: The Story of College Football. New York: The Free Press, 2001.

Whorton, James C. *Crusaders for Fitness.* Princeton, NJ: Princeton University Press, 1982.

Wieberg, Steve, and Jack Carey. "Bowl participants' graduation rates mostly below average." *USA Today* 8 December 2004: 5B.

Wiggins, David K., ed. *African Americans in Sports.* Armonk, NY: Sharpe, 2004.

Wiggins, David K. *Glory Bound: Black Athletes in a White America.* Syracuse: Syracuse University Press, 1997.

Wiggins, David K. "Good Times on the Old Plantation: Popular Recreations of the Black Slave in Antebellum South, 1810–1860." *Journal of Sport History* 4 (1977): 260–284.

Wiggins, David K. "Sport and Popular Pastimes: Shadow of the Slavequarter." *Canadian Journal of History of Sport* 11 (May 1980): 61–88.

Wiggins, David K., ed. *Sport in America: From Wicked Amusements to National Obsession.* Champaign, IL: Human Kinetics, 1995.

*Wood, William. *The Law of Athletics, Showing How to Preserve and Improve Health and Beauty, and to Correct Personal Defects Caused by Want of Physical Exercise.* New York: Dick & Fitzgerald, 1880.

*Wood, William. *Manual of Physical Exercises, Comprising Gymnastics, Calisthenics, Rowing, Sailing, Skating, Swimming, Fencing, Sparring, Cricket, Base Ball, Together With Rules for Training and Sanitary Suggestions.* Vols. 1 and 2. New York: Harper & Brothers, 1867.

*Wood, William. "New Englands Prospects: A True, Lively and Experimental Defcription of that Part of America, Commonly Called Nevv England,"1634. *Sports in North America: A Documentary History, Volume I, Part I: Sports in the Colonial Era, 1618–1783.* Ed. Thomas L. Altherr. Gulf Stream, FL: Academic International Press, 1997. 160-161.

www.acostacarpenter.org.

www.archives.upenn.edu/faids/upt/upt50/mckenzie_rt.html.

www.biography.com/people/oscar-de-la-hoya-9542428#awesm=~oIe5P1ZpDvNpzW.

www.biography.com/people/venus-williams-9533011.

www.bleacherreport.com/articles/1709676-has-lebron-james-become-the-most-popular-athlete-in-the-world.

www.cbsnews.com/news/ex-nba-ref-tim-donaghys-personal-foul.

www.cnn.com/SPECIALS/us/penn-state-scandal.

www.collegefootballplayoff.com/story?id=10328143.

www.diverstiyinc.com/news/major-league-white-pro-sports-arent-what-they-seem.

www.gg9cle.com/gay-games/faqs.

www.legendsofhockey.net.

www.leroyneiman.com/leroy-neiman-biography.asp.

www.nba.com/global.

www.nhl.com/ice/news.htm?id=697071.

www.nytimes.com/1983/05/21/obituaries/clair-bee-ex-liu-coach-dies-gained-basketball-hall-of-fame.html.

www.nytimes.com/1998/07/19/sports/backtalk-the-return-of-chip-hilton-a-young-athlete-with-character.html.

www.nytimes.com/2014/04/20/sports/hockey/hockey-players-concussion-suits-follow-path-charted-in-nfl-cases.html.

www.nytimes.com/2014/04/20/sports/hockey/hockey-players-concussion-suits-follow-path-charted-in-nfl-cases.htmlwww.aaregistry.org.

www.sbnation.com/college-football/2014/2/13/5404930/college-football-realignment-2014-conference-moves.

www.statista.com/statistics/240946/sports-products-industry-wholesale-sales-in-the-us/.

www.sul.stanford.edu/depts/dp/pennies/1890_meriwell.html.

www.telesurtv.net/english/news/World-Cyber-Games-2015-Has-Begun-20150323-0029.html.

www.therichest.com/celebnetworth/athletes/boxer/floyd-mayweather-jr-net-worth.

www.torontosun.com/2013/07/01/theo-fleury-helped-change-societys-view-of-child-sex-abuse.

www.ulib.niu.edu/badndp/patten_william.html.

www.usatoday.com/story/sports/college/2014/04/24/ncaa-board-of-directors-meeting-big-conference-autonomy/8108647.

www.whitehousehistory.org/02/subs_horses/04.html.

www.whitehutchinson.com/leisure/articles/whats-happening-to-bowling.shtml.

Yiamouyiannis, Athena. "The Future of Title IX: Ensuring Success Through Proactive Approaches." *Women in Sport and Physical Activity Journal* 12.2 (Fall 2003): 45–54.

Zang, David W. "The Greatest: Muhammad Ali's Confounding Character." *Sport and the Color Line: Black Athletes and Race Relations in Twentieth-Century America*. Eds. Patrick B. Miller and David K. Wiggins. New York: Routledge, 2004. 283–303.

Zarnowski, Frank. "Mathias, Robert Bruce 'Bob'." *The Scribner Encyclopedia of American Lives*. Ed. Arnold Markoe. New York: Scribner's, 2002. 128–130.

Index

A

AAFC (All-America Football Conference) 257
Aaron, Hank 286
AAU. *See* Amateur Athletic Union
Abbaticchio, Ed 177
ABC (American Broadcasting Company) 270-271, 272-275, 298, 303
Abdul-Jabbar, Kareem (Lew Alcindor) 282, 307
academic institutions. *See also* intercollegiate sport
  African American 202, 242
  importance of winning in 237
  modern sport development 97, 111-112
  Progressive Era sports 161, 163-167
  stadium construction at 255
  Title IX 288-289, 336-337, 351-352
  women's sports 154-155
acculturation. *See* assimilation efforts
Adams, Abigail 53-54
Adams, John 40-41, 43, 49, 51
Addams, Jane 167-168, 169
adventure races (ARs) 324
advertising. *See also* commercialization
  endorsements 298, 308-309, 321, 336, 337-338
  in the Gilded Age 129, 146, 147
  in newspaper articles 254-255
  in the Olympics 304-305
  in radio broadcasts 253
  stadium naming rights 300-302
  on televised sports 267, 271-272, 287, 308, 321, 328
AFL. *See* American Football League
African Americans. *See also* racism against African Americans; slaves/slavery
  in the Antebellum Era 83-87
  "Athletic Revolution" 282-285
  in baseball 132-133, 197, 228-231, 251-252, 270, 286
  in basketball 202, 228, 246, 257, 270, 280-281, 285-286
  in billiards 133-134
  black pride movement 228-229
  black sporting culture 228-229, 251-252
  in boxing 84, 132-133, 199-201, 229, 250, 262-264, 283-285
  in church leagues 246
  civil rights movement 111-112, 279-286
  in cycling 198-199
  in football 166, 201-202, 255, 280

  in the Gilded Age 132-134
  Great Migration of 196, 228
  in horse racing 84-86, 130, 197
  in ice hockey 280-281
  in the military 234-235
  in the Olympics 234, 264-265, 304
  physical prowess of 20-21, 86
  in the Progressive Era 172, 183
  salaries 270
  social mobility in sport 188, 196-202
  in swimming 86
  in tennis 243-244, 279-281
  in track and field 242
agents, for athletes 254-255, 298
agricultural labor/skills 60, 67-68, 72-77, 130, 150, 172
AIAW (Association of Intercollegiate Athletics for Women) 288, 310
aircraft racing 131, 206, 241, 246
alcohol. *See also* saloons; taverns
  in the Antebellum Era 105, 110
  in the Gilded Age 136
  health reformers on 62, 179
  in the Progressive Era 158, 209, 214, 223
Alcott, William A. 62, 68
Ali, Muhammad (Cassius Clay) 252, 262, 264, 274, 283-285, 289
All-America Football Conference (AAFC) 257
Alomar, Roberto 319
alternative sports 323-325, 344-345
Amaechi, John 320
Amateur Athletic Union (AAU) 156, 196, 234, 242, 244-245, 265, 291
amateurism
  big business and 265, 291
  ethnic minorities and 189, 196, 279-280
  in the Gilded Age 126, 131, 142, 155-156
  in intercollegiate sport 138-139, 163, 237
  in the Olympics 184, 185, 234, 283, 304, 308
  in the Progressive Era 161, 163, 174, 185
  in the rise of modern sport 102, 116
  social class and 237-238
  Turner societies on 88-89
amenorrhea 317
American Football League (AFL) 270, 274, 285-286
Americans with Disabilities Act 343
America's Cup races 80, 100
Anderson, Ada 150

Andretti, Mario 292
androstenedione 206
Anglican Church 11-12
animal sport
  as animal cruelty 24-25, 106-107
  in the Antebellum Era 60, 86, 106-107
  in the colonial period 15-16, 19, 25, 28-29, 38-39
  in the Gilded Age 141
Antebellum Era 57-91
  African Americans in 83-87
  health reformers of 58, 60, 62-68, 99
  immigrants in 66, 87-91
  journalism rise 77-79
  middle and upper classes in 63, 69-72, 79-80
  Muscular Christianity and 63-66
  Native Americans in 87
  overview of period 59-62
  public spaces for 81-83
  rural practices in 67-68, 72-77
  summary timeline 58-65
  women in 58, 60, 66-68, 73-75, 82-83
Anthropology Days 182-184
Arcaro, Eddie 252-253
archery 4-5, 48, 152, 184-185, 210
Arlington, Lizzie (Stroud) 206
Armstrong, Henry (Jackson) 250
Armstrong, Lance 340
ARs (adventure races) 324
Ashe, Arthur, Jr. 280-281
Asian American athletes 91, 235, 280
Asian athletes 212-213, 222
assimilation efforts 187-215
  African Americans 188, 196-202
  colonialism and sport 210-215
  gender boundaries 202-207
  Native Americans 188, 194-196
  in the Progressive Era 160, 167-169, 188
  resistance to 207-210
  summary timeline 188-193
  through sports 188-193, 246
Association of Intercollegiate Athletics for Women (AIAW) 288, 310
athletes with disabilities 320
"Athletic Revolution" 282-285
auto racing 180-181, 245-246, 288, 292, 329, 344-345
Aztec sports 2, 5

B

BAA (Basketball Association of America) 257, 271

bachelor subculture 127, 136, 140-142, 179, 209
back-to-nature movement 173-175
Bacon, Nathaniel 16
Bankhead, Dan 232
Baroque horsemanship 17
baseball
    African Americans in 132-133, 197, 228-231, 251-252, 270, 286
    in the Antebellum Era 73, 82
    in colonialism 211-215
    commercialization of 255-256, 305-306
    cricket versus 118-119
    in the Gilded Age 129, 132, 134-136, 147-149
    intercollegiate 121-122, 137
    internationalizing 305, 329, 331-332
    labor relations 143-144, 150, 277
    as modern sport 94, 100, 114-119
    night games 256, 290, 292
    in other countries 118, 212, 214, 305-306, 332
    popular culture and 229-231, 237, 241, 246, 248-249
    professional teams 142-144, 190-191, 233
    in the Progressive Era 160-161, 175-176, 209-210
    rules for 114-116, 119, 121-122, 142, 149, 244
    scandals in 221, 229, 319
    social mobility through 190-192
    sports journalism and 119, 144
    stadium construction 300-302, 330
    televised games 267-269, 275, 300
    violence in 319
    women in 132, 204, 206, 241, 247
basketball
    African Americans in 202, 228, 246, 257, 270, 280-281, 285-286
    commercialization of 308
    gambling by referees 341
    internationalizing 331-332
    labor relations 275, 276-277, 303, 312, 331-333
    in popular culture 244-246, 321
    professionalization of 257, 307-311
    in the Progressive Era 161-163
    rules for 161-162, 257, 270-271
    televised games 270-271
    violence in 319
    women in 162-163, 244-246, 247, 288-289, 312-313, 336
Basketball Association of America (BAA) 257, 271
Battle Creek Sanitarium 179
Bauer, Sybil 243
Baylor, Elgin 281
beach volleyball 314-315, 337
Beaujeu, J.A. 70
Beck, Charles 87-88
Bee, Clair 267
Beecher, Catharine 63, 66-68, 69, 111, 152
Bell, James "Cool Papa" 252

Bellows, George 201
Bender, Charles 193
Benger, Thomas 50
Bennett, James Gordon, Jr. 130
Bennett, Louis 87
Benöhr, Astrid 348
Bergmann, Margarethe "Gretel" 236
Berwanger, John Jacob "Jay" 258
Bielaski, Oscar 190
Big 12 Conference 335
Big Ten Conference 310, 335, 342
billiards
    in the Antebellum Era 60
    billiard halls 106-107, 232
    in the colonial period 27, 28
    in the Gilded Age 129, 131, 133-134, 141, 149-150
    in the Progressive Era 171, 193
Bird, Larry 307, 318
Black Power movement 285
black pride movement 228
blacks. See African Americans
Black Sox scandal 221, 229
Blair, Bonnie 311
Bloomer, Amelia Jenks 72
"bloomers" 71-72, 111, 207
"blue laws" 24, 28
Bly, Nellie 205
boating. See also rowing
    in the Antebellum Era 65, 79-80, 99-100
    in England 97
    in the Progressive Era 174, 179
    regattas 101-104, 119-122, 136-137, 155
    steamboat races 79-80
    yachting 80, 99-100, 127, 130
Bodie, Ping (Francesco Pizzolo) 177-178, 190-191
body dysmorphia 316-317
Bonds, Barry 306, 340
bowling
    in the Antebellum Era 77
    in the colonial period 12, 15, 19-20, 26, 28, 30
    in the Gilded Age 131
    in popular culture 232-233, 253
    in the Progressive Era 192-193
    in the Revolutionary Era 50
    technology in 292
boxing
    African Americans in 84, 132-133, 199-201, 229, 250, 262-264, 283-285
    in the Antebellum Era 65, 79, 84, 90-91
    bareknuckle 105-106, 134-135, 140-141
    in the civilization process 46
    in the Cold War 264
    colonialism and 214-215
    commercialization of 255-256
    corruption in 271
    ethnic minorities in 189-190, 226-228, 249-251
    gambling on 84, 199, 209

    in the Gilded Age 132-133, 134-135, 140-141, 151-152
    media in 179, 235, 249, 256, 271
    in military training 215
    as modern sport 97, 105-106
    popular culture and 226-227, 249-251
    in the Progressive Era 176, 189-190, 193, 209
    social mobility through 189-190
    as sporting fraternity 105-106
    televised matches 271
    violence in 319
    women in 151-152, 337-338
Bradford, William 22
Brosius, George 88
Brotherhood League 144
Brown, Jim 280
Brown, Walter 103-104
Bryant, Kobe 319
Bryant, Paul "Bear" 282
Bryn Mawr College 204-205
Budge, Don 235
Bunn, Oscar 172
Bureaud-Riofrey, Antoine 70
Burgada, Kilian Jornet 348
business of sport. See also advertising; capitalism; commercialization
    in the early twenty-first century 328-333
    in the Gilded Age 142-150
    internationalizing 329-332
    in the Progressive Era 165-166
    summary timeline 262-270
Butkus, Dick 276
Byrd, William II 16, 18, 19

C
calisthenics 69-70, 111-112, 127-128
Camp, Walter 138-139, 140, 164, 166, 206, 215
capitalism
    in early twenty-first century 223, 328-333
    entrepreneurism 144, 146-149, 228-229, 238, 250
    in the Gilded Age sport 129, 138-140, 144, 146-149, 150, 255-257
    globalization and 296-297
    intercollegiate sports and 309-310
    modern sport and 110
    Olympics and 303-305
    popular culture sport and 232-233, 307
    in the Progressive Era 160-161, 165-166
    sports media and 270, 274-275, 298-299
    in stadium construction 255-256, 300-302
capriole 17
card playing
    in the Antebellum Era 60
    in the colonial period 15, 20, 25-26, 28, 40
    gambling on 60, 172

in the Revolutionary Era 47
Carlisle football team 194-195
Cartwright, Alexander 114
Catholics
    in the Antebellum Era 60, 61
    assimilation efforts 188-189, 207,
        214
    in the colonial period 10-11, 13
    in the Gilded Age 132
    in popular culture sports 224-227
    in the Progressive Era 165, 168,
        175-176
    as sports heroes 246, 248, 351
Catholic Youth Organization (CYO)
    226-227
Catlin, George 4, 6, 7
Central Park, New York 81-83, 90, 171
Chadwick, Henry 119, 144, 155
Chamberlain, Wilt 281-282, 317
Chastain, Brandi 313-314, 338
cheating 153, 221, 229, 237, 309, 334
Cherokees 4, 7, 8, 48, 87
Chicago, Illinois
    auto racing in 246
    baseball in 197, 213, 221, 253, 302,
        306
    basketball in 296, 307-309
    black sporting culture 228-229, 246
    boxing in 249-251
    country clubs in 172
    ethnic groups in 88, 175-176
    football in 256-257, 276, 322-323,
        341
    in the Gilded Age 132, 134-135,
        140-143, 146-147, 149, 150-152
    in the Progressive Era 158-161, 163-
        164, 165-166, 167-168, 192-193
    public parks and playgrounds in
        82-83, 169-171, 209
    racetracks in 171
    rapid growth of 126
    softball in 232
    stadiums in 256, 302
    women's sports in 203, 205, 246
    Workers' Olympics of 1932 233
    World's Fair of 1893 178, 180, 189
Chicago Hebrew Institute 168, 176
Chicago model 167-170
children
    Native American 3, 4, 7, 48
    New Gymnastics for 111
    in the Progressive Era 159-164, 167,
        169-170, 209-210
    in the Revolutionary Era 42-43,
        47-48, 51
    in slavery 21-22
China, baseball in 212
Christianity and sport
    in the Antebellum Era 60, 62-66
    in the colonial period 10-13, 19-20,
        22-26, 29, 210, 212
    in the Gilded Age 127-128
    Muscular Christianity 63-66, 111-
        113, 127-128
Church of England 11-12
City Chase 324

civil rights movements
    African Americans 279-286
    "Athletic Revolution" 282-285
    Native Americans 279
Civil War 101-102, 109-110, 112, 117,
    120, 122
Clemens, Roger 340
Clemente, Roberto 276-277
Clias, Phokion Heinrich 70
clothing
    for alternative sports 325, 344
    in the Gilded Age 138-139, 152
    for Native Americans 7
    for women 71-72, 152, 203, 206-207,
        208
coaches
    salaries of 336
    as sexual predators 342
    social change and 224-226, 282
    as stars 224-225, 255, 267
    technology for 292
    under Title IX 336
Coachman, Alice 242
cocaine 315
cockfighting 15-16, 19, 25, 28, 38-39
Cold War 263-266
college sports. See intercollegiate sport
Collett, Glenna 244
Collins, Jason 341
colonial America 10-30. See also
    slaves/slavery
    consumerism in 40-42
    cultural diversity in 15-16, 18, 29
    Great Awakening 35-39
    Jamestown settlement 15
    middle colonies 26-30
    New England colonies 10-13, 22-26
    religion and 10-14, 19-20, 22-26, 29
    southern colonies 15-22
    summary timeline 2-8, 34-36
colonialism and sport 210-215
Columbian Exchange 5
commercialization
    in auto racing 344-345
    in baseball 229-230, 305-307
    in basketball 308
    in bowling 292
    of clothing for alternative sports
        325, 344
    in the Gilded Age 128-129, 138-139,
        148-149
    globalization and 296-297
    in intercollegiate sport 334-335
    marketing focus 245, 254-255, 298,
        332
    media and 253-258
    in the Olympics 258, 303-305
    professional franchises 257
    in running 291
    stadium construction for 255-257
    televised sports and 258, 267, 271,
        272, 287, 328
Communist Party 233
competition
    in the Gilded Age 126-127, 136, 144
    in modern sport 96, 97, 113-119

in the Progressive Era 164
    winning as emphasis 137-138, 158,
        237
    in women's sports 240-241, 242, 244
computer-based game systems 348-
    349, 352-353
consumerism 40-42
contests
    in the Antebellum Era 73-75, 84, 86,
        87-91
    in the colonial period 15-16, 20-21,
        26, 28-30
    frontier and backcountry 44-46, 60,
        172
    in the Gilded Age 127, 130-131,
        134-135, 137-139, 141
    in modern sport 96, 98, 101-104,
        106, 109-110, 120-121
    Native American 3-5, 7
    in the Progressive Era 161, 164,
        172-173, 178-179, 183-184, 189
contracts, player
    in auto racing 245
    in baseball 190-191, 214, 231-232,
        241, 275, 302, 307, 331
    in basketball 271, 275, 312, 332
    in college sports 285-286, 310
    endorsement 298, 308-309, 313,
        321, 336-338
    in football 255, 269-270, 273-275,
        332-333
    in tennis 287
    in Ultimate Fighting Championship
        348
Copeland, Lillian 242
corporate sporting culture 298-305.
    See also commercialization
    drawing fans to baseball 305-307
    globalization of 298
    internationalizing sport forms 305
    labor relations 276-277, 302-303
    maximizing profits 299-300
    media conglomerates 298-299
    Olympics commercialization 303-
        305
    sport tourism 302
    stadium construction 300-302
corruption
    in baseball 221, 229, 319
    in boxing 271
    intentional injuries 319, 340-341
    in intercollegiate sport 237, 309-310
    in Olympics management 339
Cosell, Howard 272-274
country clubs 172-173
Cousy, Bob 270
Creighton, James 142
crew. See rowing
cricket 82, 97-98, 117, 118-119, 131
croquet 69, 71, 152-153
CrossFit training 346
Cuban athletes 214, 228, 305, 332
cultural imperialism 352
curling 90
cycling
    drug use in 340

cycling *(continued)*
  in the Gilded Age 132, 146-147, 148, 150-151
  performance-enhancing drugs in 316
  in the Progressive Era 161, 179, 197-199, 208
  Tour de France 198, 340
  women in 205, 208
CYO (Catholic Youth Organization) 226-227
Czech immigrants 132, 175-176, 188-189, 192

D

dancing and music 20, 26, 202, 223
Decker (Slaney), Mary 289-290
De Coubertin, Pierre 180-181, 182-183, 185
DeFrantz, Aita 311
De La Hoya, Oscar 323
Dempsey, Jack 249-250
Dewey, John 160, 169
dice games 26
Didrikson, Mildred "Babe" 242, 244, 247
diet 62-63, 78, 179, 316-317
DiMaggio, Joe 246, 248
diving 20, 21, 34, 242, 320
Dod, Charlotte "Lottie" 210
domestic labor/skills 60, 66-68, 72-78
Dominican Republic 214, 306
Donaghy, Tim 341
doping 198, 266, 306, 315-316, 340
double ball 9
dragon boat racing 347
drag racing 345
drug and body abuse 198, 266, 306, 315-317, 340
Dubai 349
DuBois, W.E.B. 188, 201, 228
dueling 79
du Ru, Father Paul 10

E

Eakins, Thomas 141
Earnhardt, Dale, Jr. 345
East German athletes 266
Eastman, Seth 8
eating disorders 317
Eco-Challenge TV show 324
Ederle, Gertrude 243
Edwards, Harry 285
Edwards, Jonathan 36
Elias, Norbert 46
eligibility rules 137, 139, 155, 161, 163-164, 245
elite. *See also* Southern gentry
  amateurism versus professionalism 155-156
  in the Antebellum Era 75-77, 79-80, 99-105, 109-110, 118-119
  in the Gilded Age 129-131, 136-139, 153-154
  in intercollegiate sport 119-122, 136-139

  in modern sports 97, 99, 101-104, 109-110, 118-122
  physical activity for 66-67
  in popular culture sport 237-239
  in the Progressive Era 171-173, 210
  in the Revolutionary Era 42-43, 50-52
Elizabeth I (queen of England) 11
endorsement contracts 298, 308-309, 321, 336, 337-338
Enlightenment and sport 37, 42-43, 47
entrepreneurism 144, 146-149, 228-229, 238, 250
Epstein, Charlotte 242
Ernst, Mensen 108
Erving, Julius "Doctor J" 286, 318
ESPN 298-299, 334-336, 344, 346
Estby, Helga 205
Evert, Chris 314
extreme running 348

F

fans 237, 305-307, 333, 334-335, 348
Fédération Internationale de Football Association (FIFA) 145, 293
femininity
  in the Antebellum Era 69-70, 73, 89
  eligibility and 245
  in the Gilded Age 205, 208
  popularity and 314
  in the Progressive Era 246
feminism
  in the Antebellum Era 89
  in the athletic rebellion 286-287
  in the Progressive Era 178, 202-203, 239-242, 245
  in the twenty-first century 337
festivals
  in the Antebellum Era 60
  in the colonial period 12, 13
  in the European Middle Ages 9
  in the Golden Age 246, 257
  in the Progressive Era 118, 172, 176, 177
  in the Revolutionary Era 49
field hockey 8, 204, 210, 298
FIFA (Fédération Internationale de Football Association) 145, 293
fighting, in frontier sport 44-46
fishing
  in the Antebellum Era 60, 72, 77, 86-87
  in the Civil War 122
  in the colonial period 19-20, 23-24, 26, 28-30
  by Native Americans 3
  in the Progressive Era 173-174
  in the Revolutionary Era 36, 51-52
  by slaves 20
Fleischer, Nat 254
Flood, Curt 286
Foley, Tom 134
Follen, Charles 88
football. *See also* soccer
  bowl games 253, 255, 256-257, 270, 305, 310

  commercialization of 253, 255-256
  in the Gilded Age 126, 137-139
  high-school 161
  intercollegiate 137-139, 163-167, 253, 269, 282, 335-336
  internationalizing 305, 332
  labor relations 255, 269-270, 273-275, 276-277, 332-333
  military training and 139, 165, 195, 215-216, 226, 274, 352
  origin of 9, 97
  popular culture spread of 224-226, 322-323
  professional franchises 166, 257, 269-270
  in the Progressive Era 161, 163-167, 176, 177-179, 210
  rules for 137-139, 140, 164-165, 257, 269, 272-274
  soccer versus 139
  stadium construction 300-302, 329-330
  televised 269-270, 272-275, 300, 309-310
  violence in 137-139, 165-167, 318, 340-341, 343
foot racing. *See* pedestrianism; running
Foster, Andrew "Rube" 197, 228
Four Horsemen of Notre Dame 220, 222
Fox, Richard Kyle 144, 146
Foyt, A.J. 292
Franklin, Benjamin 34-35, 42
Frazier, Joe 284-285
free agency 276-277, 302, 321, 323
frontier sport 44-46, 60, 172
Fuller, Fay 205

G

gambling
  in the Antebellum Era 60, 62, 75
  on baseball 221, 319
  on basketball 341
  on billiards 106, 193
  on boxing 84, 199, 209
  on card playing 60, 172
  in the colonial period 15-16, 18, 20, 24-25, 28-29, 38
  in the Gilded Age 130-131
  on horse racing 15-16, 18, 75, 130, 142, 172, 193
  modern sport and 106
  by Native Americans 3, 7, 9-10, 48, 87
  on one's own team 319
  in the Progressive Era 172, 192-193, 209
  in the Revolutionary Era 41-42
  by women 9
games
  in the Antebellum Era 69, 71, 89-90
  of Native Americans 3-4, 6-10, 48
  of plantation slaves 21-22
  in the Progressive Era 160-161
  of the sporting fraternity 106-107
gander-pulling 28, 29

Gay Games 341
Gehrig, Lou 246, 249
gender, in physical culture. *See also* femininity; masculinity; women
  in the Antebellum Era 63-68, 72-75, 76
  in the Gilded Age 150-152
  homophobia 320, 341-342
  in modern sport 94, 96, 105
  in popular culture 245
  in the Progressive Era 202-207
  in the Revolutionary Era 47-48
  Title IX and 288-289, 336-337
gender testing 341-342
German immigrants
  assimilation of 188
  in the Progressive Era 175-178
  Sabbatarian laws and 127
  Turners 87-88, 89, 111, 161, 175, 189
Ghana, baseball in 332
Giambi, Jason 340
Gibb, Roberta 290
Gibson, Althea 279-280
Gibson, Bob 276
Gibson, Josh 252
"Gibson Girl" 203
Gilded Age sport 125-156
  business developments in 142-150
  ethnic leisure forms in 131-136
  gender and class in 128-131, 150-155
  intercollegiate 130-131, 136-139
  male sporting culture in 140-142
  regulation of 126-127, 129, 142-144, 155-156
  social stratification and 127-131
  summary timeline 126-131
Gilman, Charlotte Perkins 202-203
globalization of sport 295-325
  alternative sports 323-325
  anxiety in 297-298
  baseball 305-307
  basketball 307-309
  corporate sporting culture 298-305
  discrimination in 320-321
  drug and body abuse in 315-317
  future projections 348
  individuality and 321-323
  intercollegiate sport 309-310
  internationalizing American sport 305
  Jordan, Michael and 296
  Olympics 303-305
  sport tourism 302
  summary timeline 296-298
  violence in 317-320
  women athletes 310-315
Golden Age of Sport 221-222, 230
Golden Gloves tournament 226-227
golf
  in New York colony 28
  physical limitations and 343
  in popular culture 238-239, 244
  in the Progressive Era 171, 172-173, 185, 207

televised games 272
women in 207, 244, 247, 288, 314, 337
grace, athletes' fall from 289
Graham, Sylvester 62
Grange, Harold "Red" 253-254, 255
Graziano, Rocky 251
Great Awakening, First 35-39, 40
Great Awakening, Second 60
Great Depression 223
Greenberg, Hank 246
Greenlee, Gus 229
Gretzky, Wayne 322
Griffith-Joyner, Florence "Flo Jo" 311, 314
Griner, Brittney 341
Guarneri, Carl 11, 40
Guerra, Elvira 185
Gulick, Luther Halsey 170
Guthrie, Janet 288
GutsMuths, Johann Christoph Friedrich 44, 70
gymnastics
  in the Antebellum Era 70, 87-89
  in the Gilded Age 132
  in the Progressive Era 161, 176-177, 185
  as rationalized sport 111-112

H
Hagen, Walter 238
Hall, G. Stanley 160, 204
Hamill, James 103-104
Hamilton, Gustavus 70
Hamm, Mariel Margaret "Mia" 313
handball 28
Harding, Tonya 319
Harlem Globetrotters 228, 257, 270, 312
harness racing 75-77, 81, 109, 130
Hartford Female Seminary 66, 69
Harvard College
  founding of 26
  gymnastics at 111-112
  intercollegiate sports 96, 136-139, 158, 165, 194-195
  physical education at 43, 161
  in the Progressive Era 165
  rowing at 120, 136
Hawaiian sports 210-212
Haywood, Spencer 285-286
health reforms/reformers
  of Antebellum Era 58, 60, 62-68, 78, 87-88, 99
  gymnastics and 87-89, 111-112
  of Progressive Era 160-161, 167-170, 209-210
Heisman Trophy 257, 258
Heldman, Gladys Medalie 287
Herman, Pete 189-190
Hernandez, Aaron 341
heroes, athletic
  alternative 275-276
  baseball 246, 248-249, 269, 300
  boxing 249-251
  football 253-254

in popular culture 220, 230, 246-253
in the Progressive Era 164-165, 176
in televised games 271-272
Hewlett, Aaron Molyneaux 111-112
Higginson, Thomas Wentworth 58, 62-65, 67, 101, 116
high-school sports
  in the Golden Age 256
  in popular culture 225, 244
  in the Progressive Era 161-164, 202, 204-205, 244
  Title IX in 288-289, 336-337
  women's 204-205, 240, 247
Hispanics
  in the Antebellum Era 60
  in baseball 214, 228, 276-277, 300, 305-307, 306
  in popular culture sports 228-229, 276
Hitler, Adolf, opposition to 233-236
Hitomi, Kinue 222
hockey. *See* ice hockey
Hogan, Ben 238-239
Holm, Holly 349
homophobia 320, 341-342
hoop-and-pole contests 3
horse ballet 17
horse carousel 17
horsemanship
  in the Antebellum Era 60, 65, 84-86, 109-110
  Baroque 17
  in the National Era 54
  by Native Americans 5-6
  in the Progressive Era 185
  in the Revolutionary Era 37, 50-51
horse racing
  African Americans and 84-86, 130, 197
  in the Antebellum Era 60, 74-77, 84-86
  in the colonial period 15-20, 24-25, 28, 30, 36
  commercialization of 255-256
  in European Middle Ages 9, 11, 17
  in the Gilded Age 127, 129-130, 132, 142, 256
  harness racing 75-77
  as modern sport 109-110
  by Native Americans 5-6
  in popular culture 252-253
  in the Progressive Era 171-172, 193
  in the Revolutionary Era 38, 49, 50-51
  trotting races 75-77
  women in 288
Howe, Gordie 271-272
Howe, Steve 315
Hughes, Thomas 64
Hulbert, William 142-144
Hull, Bobby 271-272
Hull House, Chicago 167-168
hunting
  in the Antebellum Era 60, 87
  in the colonial period 15, 19-20, 24, 28-30, 36, 39, 45

hunting *(continued)*
in the Gilded Age 130
in the Progressive Era 174
in the Revolutionary Era 39, 50
hydropathy 62-63
Hyer, Tom 90

I

IAAF (International Amateur Athletic Federation) 240
ice hockey
in the colonial period 29
indoor ice arenas 290
internationalization of 332
labor relations 333
in popular culture 251, 255-256, 271-272, 322
in the Progressive Era 174
violence in 317-318
women in 314
ice skating 19, 28-30, 82-83, 173, 319
Iditarod sled-dog race 314
ill health 62, 66-67, 159
immigrants, sporting cultures of. *See also specific immigrant groups*
in the Antebellum Era 59, 66, 87-91, 140
in the Gilded Age 127, 132-136, 140
in modern sporting fraternity 105-110
in popular culture 223
in the Progressive Era 159-160, 167-169, 173, 188-189
social mobility in 188-193, 238-239, 263, 275-276
Indian club exercises 95
individuality 321-323
industrial life, 134, 158-160, 209
Inter-Allied Games 216
Intercollegiate Association of Amateur Athletes of America (IC4A) 136, 155
intercollegiate sport
broadcasts of 253, 273, 309-310, 334-336
corruption in 237, 309-310, 334
in the Gilded Age 130-131, 136-139
in modern sport 96, 98, 119-122
in popular culture 224-225, 229, 237, 257
in the Progressive Era 163-167
southern values and 282
twenty-first century 333-337
women's sports 154-155, 288-289, 336-337
International Amateur Athletic Federation (IAAF) 240
international perspectives
on the 1900 Olympic Games 185
on adventure races 324
on Asian athletes 222
on baseball in Germany 118
on Bergmann at the 1936 Olympics 236
on boxing and the civilization process 46

on cycling pioneers 208
on East German athletes as diplomats 266
on fan cultures and "sites of memory" 333
on female marathon runners 182
on female track and field 240
on hiking 177
on horsemanship 17
on Mensen Ernst's walking 108
on modern sports 46, 97
on physical education 44
on the soccer craze 145
on sport and religion 14
on sport for all concept 278
on sports stars and politics 225
on Tour de France 198
on traditional European games 9
on Turnen 89
on ultimate running 348
on urban spaces 346
on women and men in soccer 293
on women's physical education 70
Irish American immigrants
in the Antebellum Era 90-91, 105
in boxing 134-135
in the Gilded Age 134-136, 144, 146
in the Progressive Era 183-184, 188-189, 191
Italian immigrants 176-178, 189-190, 246, 248-249, 250-251

J

Jabbar, Kareem Abdul (Lew Alcindor) 282, 307
James, Graham 342
James, LeBron 329, 336
Jamestown settlement 15
Japan, sports in 212-213, 222, 305, 331-332
Japanese Americans 235
javelin throwing 182, 222, 245, 247
Jefferson, Thomas 36, 38, 48, 50
Jenner, Bruce/Caitlyn 342
Jewish athletes
in the Antebellum Era 61, 66
in baseball 246, 275-276
in boxing 176, 189, 227-228, 249-250
in the colonial period 18-19, 20, 29
Hitler's oppression and 234, 236
modern sports clubs of 113
in popular culture sports 234
in the Progressive Era 168, 176, 189, 191-192
racism against 320
women 168, 244, 246
jockeys/jockey clubs 75, 84-86, 110, 197, 252-253, 288
jogging 289, 346-347. *See also* pedestrianism; running
John, Rafer 264
Johnson, Ben 315
Johnson, Earvin "Magic" 307, 317
Johnson, Jack 199-201, 250
Johnson, Liz 314

Jones, Bobby 238
Jones, Marion 316, 340
Jordan, Michael 296, 303, 307-309, 321
journalism, influence of
in the Antebellum Era 75-79
in the Gilded Age 144, 146
in modern sport 98-99, 119
in popular culture 195, 220, 240, 254
in the Progressive Era 159, 161, 179, 195, 206
sport–media relationship 265-271
on women in the Olympics 240
Joyner-Kersee, Jackie 311

K

Kahanamoku, Duke 212
Karnazes, Dean 348
Keeler, "Wee Willie" 190
Kellogg, Harvey 179
Kelly, Mike "King" 135-136
kickball races 5
Kiecal, Stanislaw (Stanley Ketchel) 189, 190
King, Billie Jean 286-287, 288, 320
King, Martin Luther, Jr. 279
KKK. *See* Ku Klux Klan (KKK)
Knickerbocker baseball rules 114-116
Knievel, Evil 273
kolf 28
Kopay, David 320
Koufax, Sandy 275-276
Ku Klux Klan (KKK) 197, 224, 225
Kwong, Larry 280

L

labor relations. *See also* contracts, player
in black athletic revolt 286-287
in the Gilded Age 143-144, 149-150
in popular culture sports 233
in professional sports 276-277, 302-303, 332-333
in the Progressive Era 158-159, 175
strikes 302-303
lacrosse
Native Americans in 6-8, 48, 87, 321
in the Progressive Era 164, 182, 195-196
Lahontan, Baron de 7-8
LaMotta, Jake 250-251
lawn tennis 131, 153-154, 173, 279
Lazzeri, Tony 249
Leahy, Frank 225-226
Lenglen, Suzanne 243
Leonard, Benny (Leiner) 176, 189
Leonard, Sugar Ray 323
Leslie, Hattie 151
Lewis, Carl 304-305
Lewis, Diocletian 98, 111
Lewis, William Henry 201
Lieber, Francis 88
Lieberman, Nancy 312-313, 314
Lithuanian athletes 276
Locke, John 42
Lombardi, Vince 282

Louganis, Greg 320
Louis, Joe (Barrow) 234, 235, 250, 251

M

Macfadden, Barnarr 178-179
magazines. *See* journalism, influence of
Major League Baseball (MLB)
    African Americans and 228, 230, 231, 252, 257
    in anti-trust suit 233
    internationalization of 329, 331, 332
    labor relations 302-303
    television and 275, 330
    women in administration of 336
Manifest Destiny 59-61
marathons
    in the Antebellum Era 107
    in the Progressive Era 178, 182, 184
    ultimate 348
    women in 182, 289-291, 311
marbles and shinny 4
Marciano, Rocky 251
Maris, Roger 275
Martin, Casey 343
masculinity
    bachelor subculture 127, 136, 140-142, 179, 209
    boxing and 105-106
    football and 139, 342
    ice hockey and 318
    sporting fraternity 105-110
Mather, Cotton 23
Mathewson, Christy 191
Mathias, Bob 239
Matsuzaka, Daisuke 331
Mayweather, Floyd, Jr. 329
McCormack, Mark 298
McGee, W.J. 181-182
McGwire, Mark 306
McKenzie, Robert Tait 216
McNamee, Graham 254
media communications. *See also* journalism, influence of; radio broadcasts; televised sport
    in the Antebellum Era 75-79
    commercialization of sport and 253-258, 329
    evolution of sport-media relationship 265-276
    media conglomerates 298-299
    modern sport influence of 98-99, 119
    in the Progressive Era 179
    racism in 195
men. *See* masculinity
Mexicans. *See* Hispanics
Meyers, John Tortes 193
Middle Ages, games in 9, 17
middle class
    in the Antebellum Era 62-72, 79-80, 101-104
    in the Gilded Age 146-147, 152-155
    in intercollegiate sport 119-122
    in the Progressive Era 171
    sporting fraternity 105-110

Middle Colonies 26-30
militia/military training
    Civil War and 117, 122
    in colonial America 13, 26
    football and 139, 165, 195, 215-216, 226, 274, 352
    in the Progressive Era 175, 188, 209, 215-217
    in the Revolutionary Era 49-50, 54
    team sports and 117, 122, 139
    in World War I 209, 215-217
    in World War II 223, 231, 234
Miller, Cheryl 313
Miller, Elizabeth Smith 71-72
Milliat, Alice 240-241
Mills, Billy 279
Mitchell, Jackie 241
mixed martial arts (MMA) 347-348
MLB. *See* Major League Baseball (MLB)
modern sport 93-123. *See also under specific sports*
    competition and 96, 97, 113-119
    concept of 95-99
    England as cradle of 97
    evolution of 96-99
    intercollegiate games as 96, 98, 119-122
    media influence on 98-99
    racket sports 104-105
    rational recreation 110-113
    rowing and regattas 101-104
    sporting fraternity of 105-110
    subcommunities and 99-105
    summary timeline 94-96, 98-100
    team sports 113-119
Molineaux, Tom 84
Monday Night Football 272, 274, 318
Moore, Donnie 315
moral health and sport
    in the Antebellum Era 58, 60, 62, 63-66, 73, 81
    assimilation and 195, 207, 214, 221
    athlete's fall from grace 289
    in the colonial period 12-13, 34-39
    in the Gilded Age 140-141, 150
    military training and 215
    modern sport and 99-100, 105, 112-113, 119
    in the Progressive Era 158-161, 167, 168, 169, 173, 181
    in the Revolutionary Era 42-43, 51
    for women 47, 53, 66-68, 240, 338
Morgan horses 50, 85-86
Morris, Ed 208
Morris, Violette 245
Morrissey, John 90-91
Morton, Thomas 22
motherhood, Republican 52-54
motorcycle racing 180, 344
Murdoch, Rupert 299, 329
Murphy, Isaac 197
muscle dysmorphia 316-317
Muscular Christianity 63-66, 111, 112-113, 127-128
Musial, Stan 248, 269
Muslim athletes 14, 282, 284

Muybridge, Eadweard 137, 141, 180
Myers, Lawrence "Lon" 155-156

N

Namath, Joe 283, 299
NASCAR 288, 292, 329, 344-345
National Association of Base Ball Players 142
National Basketball Association (NBA)
    gambling in 341
    gay athletes in 320, 341
    Jordan and 307-309
    labor relations in 276-277, 303, 331-333
    women in 336
National Basketball League (NBL) 257
National Broadcasting Company (NBC)
    alternative sports 344
    commercialization of sports 253, 270-271, 274
    globalized sport 299
    intercollegiate sport 309
    Olympics 339
National Collegiate Athletic Association (NCAA)
    AAU and 265
    conference changes 333-336
    on drug testing 315-316
    football and 269
    formation of 165
    preventing abuses 237, 309-310, 315-316, 317
    televised sports 273, 274-275, 309-310
    women and 288, 336
National Football League (NFL)
    formation and growth of 195, 256-257, 322, 331, 333
    internationalization of 296, 305
    labor relations 276-277, 286, 303
    racial diversity in 343
    television and 269-270, 274, 282-283, 300
National Hockey League (NHL) 251, 253, 256, 296, 299, 317-318
nationalism
    in the Antebellum Era 58, 59
    auto racing and 246
    baseball and 118-119
    in the Cold War 264
    football and 139
    in the Olympics 303
    popular culture and 246, 249
    in the Progressive Era 183-185, 212-213
National Police Gazette 144, 146, 206
Native Americans
    Antebellum Era sports of 87
    in Anthropology Days 182-184
    assimilation efforts 188, 194-196
    in baseball 184, 193
    civil rights movements 279
    in lacrosse 6-8, 48, 87, 321
    in the Progressive Era 172, 182-183, 193

Native Americans *(continued)*
  racism and 60-61, 83, 87, 321
  in the Revolutionary Era 48
  specific tribes 2-10, 15, 48, 87
  sports in native culture 4-10
nativism 90, 177, 188, 223, 225
Navratilova, Martina 314, 320
NBA. *See* National Basketball Association
NBC. *See* National Broadcasting Company
NBL (National Basketball League) 257
NCAA. *See* National Collegiate Athletic Association
Negro National League 197, 228-229
Neiman, LeRoy 273
New Games Movement 289
New Netherlands 28-30
New York
  in the Antebellum Era 73, 75, 80, 81-83, 88, 89-91
  baseball 114-117, 142-144, 149, 230-231, 246-249, 255-256, 275
  basketball 202, 237, 257, 270
  black sporting culture in 202, 228
  Central Park 81-83, 90, 171
  in the colonial period 25, 28-30
  ethnic groups in 134, 175, 176, 186
  in the Gilded Age 140-142, 150-151
  horse racing 109-110, 129, 172
  ice hockey 251, 280
  in the Progressive Era 159, 164, 168-171, 174, 193, 209
  sport clubs in 80, 99-105, 112-113, 129-131, 172, 285
  women's sports 202-203, 205, 242-243
New York Athletic Club (NYAC) 131, 136, 258, 285
NFL. *See* National Football League
NHL (National Hockey League) 251, 253, 256, 296, 299, 317-318
Nicaragua, sports in 215
Nichols, Mary Gove 62-63
Nicklaus, Jack 272
North-South horse race of 1845 109-110
Notre Dame College 165, 220-222, 224-226, 256, 335
NYAC. *See* New York Athletic Club (NYAC)
Nyad, Diana 314

O

Oakley, Annie 205
Olympic games
  in 1936 under Hitler 234-236, 258
  African Americans in 234, 264-265, 304
  amateurism in 184-185, 234, 283, 304, 308
  black athletic revolt and 285
  in the Cold War 264
  commercialization of 303-305
  corruption in 339
  in the Progressive Era 180-186

recent challenges 338-339
  U.S. boycott of 303
  women in 181-182, 184-185, 240, 242-243, 245, 311-312
outdoor sports
  health reformers on 62, 65
  in the Progressive Era 152-154, 168-170, 172-175
  in the Revolutionary Era 48, 51-52
  in rural areas 73
  women in 69, 71, 78
Outerbridge, Mary Ewing 153
Owens, Jesse 234-235
ownership, diversity in 343

P

Paige, Leroy "Satchel" 252
Palmer, Arnold 272, 298
Panama, sports in 215
pankration 46
Paralympic Games 320
parks, public 81-83, 170-171, 209
Paterno, Joe 342
Patrick, Danica 345
Patten, William George "Gilbert" 167
Payton, Walter 322-323
Peck, Annie Smith 203
pedestrianism 100, 107-108, 130, 141-142. *See also* running
Penn, William 26-27, 28
Pennsylvania colony 26-28
Petty, Richard 292
Phelps, Almira 63
Phelps, Michael 339
Philippines, sports in 175, 211, 213
physical activity/exercise
  in the Antebellum Era 58, 60, 62-73, 99
  in the colonial period 12-14, 23-24
  in the Gilded Age 127-128
  in the New Deal 223
  New Games Movement 289
  in the Revolutionary Era 35, 36-38, 42-44
  for women 53-54, 111-112, 162-163, 168, 176, 242
physical culture, worldview and 14
physical education
  in the Antebellum Era 69
  GutsMuths on 44
  in the Progressive Era 161-164
  rationalized sport and 111-113
  in the Revolutionary Era 42-43
  for women 111-112, 127-128, 204-205
physical fitness/health
  in the Antebellum Era 58, 62-73, 111-113, 116
  in the Cold War 263-264
  in the colonial era 34-35
  military readiness and 58, 62-68, 69-72, 73, 215
  in popular culture 242, 289-290
  in the Progressive Era 161-164
  in the Revolutionary Era 50, 51-52, 53, 54

piaffe 17
Pickett, Tidye 242, 246
Pilgrims, Plymouth 22
Players' League 144
playgrounds 169-170, 209
Plymouth Colony 22
Polish immigrants
  in baseball 190, 192, 233, 248
  in bowling 233
  in boxing 189
  in gymnastics 132, 176, 188
  in popular culture sports 233, 248
politics and sport
  athletic revolution 282-286
  civil rights movement and 279-282
  in the Cold War 263-265, 266
  feminism and 89, 202-203, 239-242, 245, 286-287, 337
  political use of sport 225, 233-236
  Title IX 288-289, 314, 336-337, 351-352
Pollard, Fritz 202, 229, 255
polo 130
Pompey (horse trainer) 85-86
Pope, Albert 146
popular culture of sport 219-258
  baseball social significance 229-232
  black sporting culture 228-229
  boxing and Jewish Americans 227-228, 249-251
  class status maintenance in 237-239
  corruption and 221, 229, 271, 309-310, 339, 340-341
  Depression and war impacts 222-223
  female athletes 239-246
  heroes in 220, 225, 230, 246-253
  intercollegiate sport 224-225, 229, 237, 257
  marketing focus 245, 254-255, 298, 332
  media commercialization 253-258
  participation across the populace 345-346
  religious groups and 224-228
  social change impact on 223, 224-246
  summary timeline 220-227
  women athletes in 239-246
  working class in 232-233
Porter, William T. 79
Prefontaine, Steve 291
professionalization of sport. *See also* amateurism
  in the Antebellum Era 89
  in baseball 116, 142-144, 190
  in basketball 307-311
  in England 97
  in football 166
  in the Gilded Age 126-127, 129-130, 142-144, 155-156
  labor relations in 276-277, 302-303, 332-333
  in soccer 145
  in women's teams 337-338

Progressive Era 158-186
    American ideology of 160-161
    back-to-nature movement 173-175
    body culture 178-179
    colonialism and 210-215
    ethnicity and 175-178, 182-184, 188-202
    football 161, 163-167, 176, 177-179, 210
    gender boundaries in 202-207
    Olympics and 180-186
    physical education of youth 161-164
    recreational spaces in 167-173
    social reformers in 158-160
    social reform resistance in 207-210
    summary timeline 158-160
    technology and 179-180
    World War I 215-217
public spaces for recreation
    in the Antebellum Era 81-83
    in the Gilded Age 129-131
    in modern sports 100, 104-105
    in the Progressive Era 167-173
Puerto Rico, sports in 214
Pullman, George 149-150
Puritans 22-26

Q

Qatar 349
Quakers 27-28
quoits 12, 48, 77

R

racetracks
    in the Antebellum Era 84, 91, 109
    in the Gilded Age 110, 129-130
    in the Progressive Era 171-172
    in the Revolutionary Era 51-52
racism. See also racism against African Americans
    in Anthropology Days 182-184
    against Asian Americans 91
    colonialism as 210-215
    against Native Americans 194-196, 279
    in sports ownership 343
    "whiteness" 61, 133-134, 201, 248, 307
racism against African Americans
    in the 1936 Olympics 233-236
    in the Antebellum Era 60-61, 83, 86-87
    biological determinism theories 320
    in boxing 132
    civil rights movements 279-286
    desegregation of sports 230-231
    in the Gilded Age 126, 130, 132-133, 196-202
    in popular culture sports 228-229, 230-231, 234-235, 255
    in the Progressive Era 166, 172, 182-183, 193-194, 196-202, 209
    Rooney Rule 343
    in sports ownership 343
    stacking and 285, 286, 320

in World War II 235
racket sports 104-105. See also tennis
radio broadcasts
    baseball 269
    boxing 235, 249, 256
    commercialization and 253-257, 336
    football 255, 336
    sports talk 299
Raid Gauloises 324
railroads 96, 98, 120, 127, 130
raquette 132
rationalized sport 95-96, 97, 99, 111-113, 127. See also modern sport
Reach, Alfred J. 129
recapitulation theory 160
records
    in the Antebellum Era 78-79
    fans and 237
    in the Gilded Age 127
    in modern sport 96-97, 114
    in the Progressive Era 179
    in virtual sport 349
recreational pastimes
    in the Antebellum Era 60, 69, 71, 72-75, 86
    in the Gilded Age 149-152
    of Native Americans 3-10, 87
    of plantation slaves 20-22
    in the Progressive Era 167-173, 192-193
    in the twenty-first century 345-346
recruitment practices 116, 166, 237, 274-275, 334
regattas 101-104, 119-122, 136-137, 155
regulation of sport
    in the colonial period 28
    in the Gilded Age 126-127, 129, 142-144, 155-156
    intercollegiate 237, 265, 269, 309
    in modern sport 96, 97, 110
    in the Progressive Era 163-165, 173-174
    in the Revolutionary Era 46, 52
Reid, Bill 158
religion, influence of. See also Christianity and sport; Jewish athletes
    in the Antebellum Era 60, 62-66
    in the colonial period 10-14, 19-20, 22-26, 29
    deism 35
    in the Gilded Age sport 127-128, 246
    Great Awakening 35-39, 40, 60
    in modern sport 112-113
    Muslim athletes 14, 282, 284
    in popular culture 224-228
    in the Progressive Era 168
    in the Revolutionary Era 42
reserve clause 143, 286
Revolutionary Era 34-54
    consumerism in 40-42
    Enlightenment in 42-43
    frontier and backcountry sport 44-46
    Great Awakening 35-39, 40

motherhood in 52-54
    Native American sport 48
    sporting practices in 48-52
    use of horses 50-51
    women's recreation in 47-48
Rhodes, Karl "Tuffy" 305
Rice, Ray 341
Richmond, Bill 84
Rickard, George "Tex" 249, 251
Rickey, Branch 231, 232
riflery 173
Riggs, Bobby 287
Ripken, Cal, Jr. 307
Robertson, Oscar 281
Robeson, Paul 202, 229
Robinson, Jackie 231
Robinson, Sugar Ray 250-251
Rockne, Knute 224-225, 255
rodeos 60, 172
Roethlisberger, Ben 340
roller skating 155, 278
Rooney Rule 343
Roosevelt, Theodore 174, 183
Rose, Pete 319
Rosenthal, Elaine 244
Ross, Barney 249-250
Rother, Amalie 208
Round Hill School, Northampton 88
Rousey, Ronda 349
rowing. See also boating; yachting
    in the Antebellum Era 65
    in the Gilded Age 127, 136-137, 141, 150, 155
    intercollegiate 119-121, 136-137, 334
    in modern sport 94, 95, 97, 101-104
    regattas 101-104, 119-122, 136-137, 155
Rudolph, Wilma 264-265
running. See also pedestrianism
    in the Antebellum Era 87
    in the Cold War 263, 264-265
    in the colonial period 20, 43
    in European Middle Ages 9
    extreme 347-348
    in the Gilded Age 155
    by Native Americans 5, 87
    popularity of 289-290, 346-347
    in the Progressive Era 181-184
    by slaves 20
    women in 182, 289-290, 311, 314
running of the bulls, Pamplona, Spain 9
rural life 19-20, 67, 72-75, 150, 172, 224
Rush, Benjamin 37, 43
Russell, Bill 281
Ruth, George "Babe" 230, 246, 254-256, 302

S

Sabbatarianism
    in Antebellum Era 85-86
    in the colonial period 12, 19-20, 23-24, 26-27, 29
    in the Gilded Age 127

Sabbatarianism *(continued)*
  Jewish athletes and 113
  in the Progressive Era 209, 214
  in the Revolutionary Era 36, 41
  televised sports and 273
safety equipment 165
salaries, sport
  in Depression 256
  of ethnic minorities 191, 197, 285
  in the Gilded Age 142, 143-144
  in popular culture 221, 230, 237, 270-271
  professionalization and 276-277, 286, 309
  in the Progressive Era 166, 175, 190-191
  televised sports and 270-271, 277, 299, 302-303, 328-329, 331
saloons 140-141, 192-193, 209. *See also* taverns
Sam, Michael 341
Sanders, "Neon Deion" 323
Sandow, Eugen 178
Sandusky, Jerry 342
Schlagball 118
Schott, Marge 320
Scottish Caledonian clubs 89-90
Scout Movement 177
Seabiscuit 252
Sears, Eleanora 206
Seelenbinder, Werner 225
Semenya, Caster 341-342
settlement houses 159, 167-169, 176, 205
Seward, George 107-108
sex discrimination
  in nineteenth century 47-48, 52-54
  in the Progressive Era 159-160, 181-182, 184-185
  sexual orientation 320, 341-342
  Title IX 288-289, 314, 336-337, 351-352
  in twentieth-century 239-246
sexuality, female. *See also* femininity
  cycling and 204
  in the Gilded Age 153
  in Olympic marketing 337-338
  in popular culture 223
  in professional sports 272, 314-315, 337
  in the Progressive Era 179-180
sexual orientation 320, 341-342
sexual predators 342
shark fighting 21, 86
Sheil, Bernard 226
Shibe, Ben 129
Shields, Claressa 338
shinny 8
Shippen, John 172
shooting 9, 26, 27-28, 47, 173
shuffleboard 26
Shumaker, John W. 334
shuttlecock 4, 43
Sidat-Singh, Wilmeth 229
Simpson, O.J. 318
Sims, Willie 197

sites of memory 333
skateboarding 344
skiing, downhill 60, 173-174
Skinner, John Stuart 77-79
skittles 28
Slater, Fred "Duke" 229
slaves/slavery. *See also* African Americans
  Antebellum Era and 58, 83-86, 101-102
  boxing matches of 46, 84
  horse racing by 84-86
  play activities of 20-22
  socioeconomics of 15-16, 18, 19-22, 36, 83-85
Snead, Sam 238
snowboarding 339, 344
snowshoeing 173
Snyder, Jimmy "the Greek" 320
soccer
  as colonial sport 145
  fan cultures 333, 338
  football versus 139
  in globalized sport 298-299, 305, 308
  international perspectives on 145
  in the Progressive Era 176
  traumatic brain injury 343
  women in 293, 313-314, 338
social activism/change
  colonialism and 210-215
  gender boundary challenges 202-207
  opposition to Hitler 233-236
  in popular culture 223, 224-228, 232-233, 281
  in the Progressive Era 158-160, 175, 176, 177, 207-210
  by women 202-203
social class/stratification. *See also* elite; middle class; slaves; working class
  in the Antebellum Era 61, 64, 66-68, 75-76, 79-80, 81-82
  in the colonial period 15-16, 18-19, 25-28, 38, 47
  in the Gilded Age 127-136, 150-152
  in international soccer 145
  maintenance of 237-239
  modern sport and 96, 97, 99-105, 111-113
  in the Progressive Era 158-160, 167-171, 209-210
  public spaces for activity and 81-83
  in the Revolutionary Era 38-39, 40-42, 47, 52
  sporting fraternity and 105-110, 140-142
Social Darwinism 127, 137, 195, 199, 213, 222
socialists/socialism 158, 175, 176, 177, 232
social media 333, 341, 348, 352
social mobility
  after World War II 263
  in the Progressive Era 160-161, 177

sport and 135-136, 188-193, 201, 233, 238-239
  televised games and 275-276, 352
Society of Friends 27-28
Sockalexis, Louis 193
softball 232, 241, 314
Sokols 132, 175-176, 188, 192
Sosa, Sammy 306
Southern gentry
  in the Antebellum Era 75, 79, 109
  in the colonial period 15-16, 18-19
  in the Revolutionary Era 38, 47
Southern region. *See also* slaves/slavery
  backcountry sport in 44-46
  colonial pastimes and pursuits 15-22
  Great Awakening influence in 36, 38-39
Spalding, Albert G. 147-149, 155
Spanish Riding School, Vienna 17
spectator sports
  advertising for 267, 271-272, 287, 308, 321, 328
  in the colonial period 8, 16, 24-26, 39, 44-45, 47
  in the Gilded Age 129-130, 142
speed shooting (archery) 4
sport equipment
  endorsements for 298, 308-309, 321, 336, 337-338
  entrepreneurs in 129, 147-149
  modern promotion of 128-129
  shoes 291, 308, 344
  for training 137
Sport magazine 265
sports announcers 253-254, 268, 272-274
sports associations/clubs
  for African Americans 132-133
  after the Civil War 122
  in the Antebellum Era 82, 87-91
  for banned sports 209
  in the colonial period 28
  in Europe 278, 346
  in the Gilded Age 128, 131, 146-147, 153
  modern sport growth in 96, 99-105, 110-113
  in the Progressive Era 190-191, 209
sportswriters 195, 209, 220, 230, 254
sport tourism 302
stadiums
  commercialization and 255-256
  cost of 328-329, 330
  enclosed 290, 292
  naming rights 300-302
Stagg, Amos Alonzo 162-163, 166
standardization, in sport 163-164, 192
Stannard, Henry 87, 107
Stanton, Elizabeth Cady 72
statistics 75, 96, 114, 119
steamboat races 79-80
Sterling, Donald 343
steroid use 206, 263-264, 315-316, 317
Stevens, John Cox 99-100, 107, 109

Stewart, Hattie 151
stickball 9-10
stick races 5
stock car racing 344
Stowe, Harriet Beecher 152
strychnine 315
Stuckless, Gordon 342
Stuyvesant, Peter 29
substance abuse 315-316, 317. *See also* alcohol
suicide 315, 343
Sullivan, John L. 134-135
Sunday sports. *See* Sabbatarianism
Super Bowl 270, 300, 332
surfing 211-212, 344
Sutton, May 207
Swarthmore College football 166-167
swimming
    in the Antebellum Era 82, 86
    in colonial Hawaii 212
    in the Gilded Age 141-142
    in the Olympics 304, 311, 338
    in popular culture 242-243, 252, 347
    in the Progressive Era 184-185
    in the Revolutionary Era 34, 37
    in Southern colonies 20-21
Switzer, Kathrine 290-291

T

taverns. *See also* saloons
    in the Antebellum Era 90-91
    in the colonial period 25-26, 28
    in popular culture 232
    in the Revolutionary Era 36, 40-41, 47
    as sporting fraternity 106-107
Taylor, Lawrence 315
Taylor, Marshall "Major" 197-199
team sports. *See also specific sports*
    adventure races as 324
    competition in 96, 97, 113-119
    in the Gilded Age 126, 129, 132, 135-136, 137-139, 147-149
    individuality in 321-323
    in the Progressive Era 160-167, 175-179, 182, 194-196
    women in 312-314
technological advances
    in the 1950s 262
    in auto racing 180-181, 245, 246, 262, 292
    in bowling 292
    computers in analysis 292
    enclosed stadiums 290, 292
    indoor ice arenas 290
    in the Progressive Era 179-180, 184-185, 198
televised sport 265-276
    ABC's transformation of 272-274
    advertising on 267, 271-272, 287, 308, 321, 328
    baseball 267-269, 275, 300
    basketball 270-271
    blackouts 268
    boxing 271
    cheerleaders 272

football 269-270, 272-275, 300, 309-310
    globalization of 298
    golf 272
    hockey 299
    influence on games 270-275, 299-300
    intercollegiate sport 269, 273, 309-310, 334-336
    media conglomerates 298-299
    night games 256, 290, 292
    salaries and 270-271, 277, 299, 302-303, 328-329, 331
    summary timeline 262-270
tennis
    African Americans in 243-244, 279-281
    in the colonial period 20
    English royalty and 11
    in the Gilded Age 152, 153-154
    lawn tennis 131, 153-154, 173, 279
    in popular culture 239, 243-244
    in the Progressive Era 172-173, 185, 207, 210
    women in 153-154, 207, 210, 243-244, 279-280, 283-287, 337
testosterone 315, 340
Thoreau, Henry David 65
Thorpe, Jim 184, 194-195, 196
Tilden, "Big Bill" 239
Tillman, Pat 328
Title IX 288-289, 314, 336-337, 351-352
tlachtli 2
toli 9-10
Toy, James M. 193
track and field events
    in the Gilded Age 130-131, 136-137, 155
    in popular culture 240, 242
    in the Progressive Era 161, 183-184
transportation, influence of
    airplanes 268
    in the Antebellum Era 61
    railroads 96, 98, 120, 127, 130
traumatic brain injury 343
Trice, Jack 229
trotting races 75-77
Trussell, George 142
Tunis, John 253
Turners 87-88, 89, 111, 161, 175, 189
twenty-first century sport, early 328-350
    alternative sports 344-345
    brain injuries in 343
    business of professional teams 328-333
    crises in 339-343
    fan culture and sites of memory 333
    future of sport 347-349
    intercollegiate 333-336
    Olympic challenges and stars 338-339
    participation across the populace 345-347
    Title IX 314, 336-337, 351-352
    women's professional teams 337-338

Tyson, Mike 319

U

Ultimate Fighting Championship (UFC) 347-348, 349
ultimate running 348
United States Football League (USFL) 300
urban life
    in the Antebellum Era 61, 67-68
    in the Gilded Age 128-129
    modern sport growth and 95, 98
    in popular culture 222-223
    in the Progressive Era 158-161, 167-169, 173-175, 209-210
    recreation spaces and 346
    stadium construction 255-256, 290, 292, 300-302, 303

V

Valenzuela, Fernando 300
Vanderbilt, Cornelius 130
Vassar College 154, 204
vaudeville, women boxers in 151
Vick, Michael 340
Vietnam War 284, 289, 297
violence, in sport
    bounties for injuries 340
    domestic assaults 317, 318, 341
    in the Gilded Age 137-139, 142
    mixed martial arts 347-348
    in players' parents 318
    in popular culture 271
    in professional sports 317-319, 340-341
    in the Progressive Era 165-167, 199
    sexual assaults 340, 342
    Ultimate Fighting Championship 347-348
vital force theory 62
Voarino, G.P. 70
volleyball 163-164, 213, 214, 314-315, 337

W

WABA (Women's American Basketball Association) 312
wagering. *See* gambling
Wagner, Honus 190
Walker, Moses Fleetwood 132-133
walking. *See also* pedestrianism
    in the Antebellum Era 65
    in the Gilded Age 141-142, 150
    in modern sports 100, 107-108
    in the Progressive Era 174, 177
Wandervögel 177
Ward, Joshua 102-104
Warder, Ann 54
Warner, Glenn "Pop" 194-195
War of 1812 54
Washington, Booker T. 188
Washington, George 49, 50
Washington, Ora 243-244
WASPs (white Anglo-Saxon Protestants)
    in the Antebellum Era 61, 64, 69
    in the Gilded Age 150-155

WASPs (white Anglo-Saxon Protestants)
(continued)
  growth of modern sport 99
  in the Progressive Era 158, 160,
    167-169, 171-173, 204
  resistance to reforms by 207-210
Watson, Elkanah 38-39
Weaver, George "Buck" 221
weight throwing 90
Weiss, Alta 206
Weissmuller, Johnny 252
Wellesley College 154-155, 204
West, Jerry 281
Weston, Edward Payson 107
Wheeler, Nathaniel 76
White, Shaun 344
Whitefield, George 36
"whiteness" 61, 133-134, 201, 248, 307.
    See also racism
wicket 50
wild-card system 305
Williams, Serena 337
Williams, Ted 248, 269
Williams, Venus 337
Wills, Helen (Helen Wills Moody)
    243
windsurfing 323, 325
Winkfield, Jimmy 197
winning, as emphasis 101, 116, 127,
    137-138, 158, 237
Winthrop, John 22-24
women. *See also* sex discrimination
  African American 132, 242, 246,
    279-280
  in the Antebellum Era 58, 60, 66-75,
    82-83, 89
  in archery 152, 184-185, 210
  in auto racing 245, 288, 314, 344-
    345
  in baseball 132, 204, 206, 241, 247
  in basketball 162-163, 244-246, 247,
    288-289, 312-313, 336
  in beach volleyball 314-315
  in billiards 203
  body abuse by athletes 317
  in bowling 232-233, 314
  in boxing 151-152, 337-338
  clothing for 71-72, 152, 203, 206-
    207, 208
  as coaches and administrators 336
  in the colonial period 16, 21, 27
  competition in sports 240-241, 242,
    244
  in cycling 205, 208
  endorsements by 337-338
  gambling by 9

in the Gilded Age 132, 150-155
in golf 207, 244, 247, 288, 314, 337
in gymnastics 111-112
in high-school sports 204-205, 240,
    247
in horsemanship 111, 185
in horse racing 288
in ice hockey 314
in intercollegiate sport 154-155
international women's sport move-
    ment 240
in javelin throwing 245, 247
Jewish athletes 168, 244, 246
in Native American sports 8-10
in Olympic games 181-182, 184-
    185, 240, 242-243, 245, 290, 311-
    312, 337
physical education for 111-112,
    127-128, 204-205
in popular culture sports 239-246
in professional teams 312-314, 337-
    338
in the Progressive Era 162-163, 168,
    176, 204-205
Republican Motherhood 52-54
in the Revolutionary Era 47-48
in rowing 155, 311
in running 182, 289-290, 311, 314
in snowboarding 339, 344
in soccer 293, 313-314, 338
sport and moral health of 47, 53,
    66-68, 205-206, 240, 338
in sports reporting 299
steroid use by 316
in swimming 185, 242-243, 314
in tennis 153-154, 207, 210, 243-244,
    279-280, 283-287, 337
Title IX 288-289, 314, 336-337, 351-
    352
in track and field events 240, 242
traumatic brain injury in girls 343
women's rights activists 202-203,
    239-241, 242, 286-287
Women's American Basketball Associ-
    ation (WABA) 312
Wood, William 19
Woods, Eldrick "Tiger" 321
Wooley, Charles 4-6
Workers' Olympics of 1932 233
working class
  in the Antebellum Era 67-68, 81-83,
    87-91, 106
  in the Gilded Age 131-136, 149-155
  modern sport and 94, 97, 105-110
  in popular culture 232-233, 243,
    249-250

in the Progressive Era 158-160, 166,
    167-172, 209-210
in the Revolutionary Era 40-42
social mobility through sport 188-
    193
sporting fraternity 105-110
World Cyber Games 349
World Series
  as big business 256, 258
  early 190, 193, 197
  Jackie Robinson in 231
  Japanese teams and 213, 222
  labor relations and 302-303
  radio broadcasts 254
  televised 267-268
  in World War I 221-222, 230
World War I 215-217, 221-222, 230
World War II 223, 230, 234, 258
wrestling 26, 46, 141, 176, 316-317

X

X Games 344

Y

yachting 80, 99-100, 127, 130
Yale University
  football 138-140, 164-167
  in the Progressive Era 165-166
  in the Revolutionary Era 43
  rivalry with Harvard 96, 98, 158
  rowing club 120-121
Yamaguchi, Kristi 311-312
Yao Ming 296-297, 332
Young Men's Christian Association
    (YMCA) 66, 111-113, 127, 132,
    207, 212-213
Young Men's Hebrew Association 66,
    113, 128
Young Women's Christian Association
    (YWCA) 113, 127-128
Young Women's Hebrew Association
    113, 128
youth sport programs
  alternative sports 344
  in the Antebellum Era 64, 66, 81-
    82
  boxing 226-227
  in the colonial period 37
  in the Early National Era 42-44
  Jewish 113
  Native American 48
  in the Progressive Era 160-164, 168,
    169-170, 175-177
  traumatic brain injury and 343
YWCA (Young Women's Christian
    Association) 113, 127-128

About the Authors

Courtesy of North Central College.

Gerald R. Gems, PhD is an international scholar and the author and editor of 19 books and more than 200 publications. He is a professor of Kinesiology at North Central College in Naperville, Illinois. He is a past president of the North American Society for Sport History and the current vice-president of the International Society for the History of Physical Education and Sport. He has been the book reviews editor for the *Journal of Sport History* since 1996. In 2012 he was granted a Fulbright Scholar Award by the U.S. government, and in 2016 he was awarded the Routledge Prize for scholarship.

Courtesy of Linda Borish.

Dr. Linda J. Borish is Associate Professor in the History Department and Gender and Women's Studies Department at Western Michigan University.

Dr. Borish earned her PhD in American Studies from The University of Maryland, College Park.

Borish's publications in sport history, women's and gender history, and American Jewish history include her work as Lead Editor, *The Routledge History of American Sport* (Routledge, 2017), and she has published numerous book chapters including chapters in *Sports in Chicago*; *Sports and the American Jew*; *Jews in the Gym: Judaism, Sports, and Athletics*; *A Companion to American Sport History*, and others. Her scholarly articles have been published in the *Journal of Sport History*, *The International Journal of the History of Sport*, *Rethinking History: The Journal of Theory and Practice*, *American Jewish History*, and others. Borish is Executive Producer and Historian of the "Jewish Women in American Sport: Settlement Houses to the Olympics," documentary film (2007), and she is a Research Associate of The Hadassah-Brandeis Institute, Brandeis University. She has earned various fellowships for her research on women and American sport history. Borish was selected in 2001–2002 as the International Ambassador for the North American Society for Sport History and served on its Executive Council and Publications Board. Borish was the book review coeditor on the *Journal of Sport History* from 1996–2000.

Anette Damgaard, photographer.
Courtesy of Gertrud Pfister.

Gertrud Pfister, PhD, is professor emeritus at the University of Copenhagen in Denmark. She was president of the International Sport Sociology Society from 2001 to 2007. Pfister was also president of the International Society for the History of Sport and Physical Education from 1993 to 2000 and won the association's award for lifelong achievements in the area of sport history in 2005.

Dr. Pfister earned an honorary doctorate from Semmelweis University in Budapest. She is a fellow of the American Academy for Kinesiology and Physical Education and the European College for Sport Science. She earned a PhD in history from the University of Regensburg and in sociology from Ruhr-University Bochum, as well as a second honorary doctorate from Malmo University in Sweden. In 201 she was knighted as a recipient of the Ridder Cross by the queen of Denmark for her scholarship, and in 2016 the president of Germany awarded her the Verdienst Cross for her promotion of women's sport.